Jewish Travel Guide 2006

INTERNATIONAL EDITION

Published in association with
the *Jewish Chronicle*, London

VALLENTINE MITCHELL
LONDON • PORTLAND, OR

First published in 2006 in Great Britain by
VALLENTINE MITCHELL & CO. LTD
Suite 314, Premier House
112-114 Station Road
Edgware, Middlesex HA8 7BJ, UK
Telephone: +44(0)20 8952 9526
Email: jtg@vmbooks.com
Website: www.vmbooks.com

and in the United States of America by
VALLENTINE MITCHELL
c/o ISBS, 920 NE 58th
Avenue, Suite 300
Portland, Oregon 97213 3786

ISBN 0 85303 706 X
ISSN 0075 3750

Printed in Great Britain by
Creative Print and Design (Wales), Ebbw Vale

Contents

Publisher's Note   iv

Tips for Kosher Travellers   v

Kosher Fish in Europe   376

Kosher Fish outside Europe   378

Jewish Calendars for 2006 and 2007   380

Index   381

Index to Advertisers   392

Advertisers Order Form 2007   393

Update form for 2007 edition   394

Publisher's Note

WE NEED YOUR ASSISTANCE TO KEEP
THIS GUIDE UP TO DATE

The Publishers have made every effort to ensure that the guide is as accurate and up to date as possible.

As in previous years, an update form is included at the back of the book for those who become aware of additions they would like considered for inclusion. In addition, of course, we wish to be notified of any errors that may have occurred in the preparation of this book.

Any information may be sent to:

Jewish Travel Guide Updates
Suite 314, Premier House
112-114 Station Road
Edgware, Middlesex
HA8 7BJ, United Kingdom

Tel: +44(0)20 8952 9526
Fax: +44(0)20 8952 9242
Email: jtg@vmbooks.com
Website: www.vmbooks.com

Email contact preferred

Please include a contact email address whenever possible

Potential advertisers, or those who wish to stock and sell copies of the Jewish Travel Guide, may use any of the above means to contact us for details of advertising rates and trade terms

Tips for Kosher Travellers

Travel has never been more popular with many exotic cruising destinations being added each year to the existing 'portfolio' of the Mediterranean and Caribbean.
But unless you travel on an exclusively kosher cruise how easy is it to keep kosher?
Here frequent traveller Rabbi Dr Avraham Abrahami gives his expert advice – and it's easier than you think.
As many cruises involve a flight to your port of departure and, sometimes, an overnight hotel stay on your outward or inward journey, Rabbi Abrahami has covered that aspect of the journey too.

If you wish to keep kosher while you travel without your kosher deli or kosher butcher close by, it will be a challenge, but it can be done. Here is my step-by-step guide.

AIR TRAVEL AND HOTEL STAY

Kosher meal. Ensure you order your kosher meal and verify it was actually ordered and confirm with the airline at least five days before flying.

Contingency. As a precaution, in case your kosher meal does not turn up after all, take with you some kosher food.

Just in case. In case you do not get your kosher meal on the flight and you forgot to bring with you some kosher food, you may eat some fruit, plain yoghurt (if it contains no gelatine), and you may also eat any other product that you are familiar with, which appears on the list of kosher products in your own country.

Kosher products. Unless you stay in a kosher hotel or in case you will be on the go most of the time, check before you leave home the range of products available in the country in which you are staying. You can do so via the Internet, or contact the local Orthodox rabbi at your destination and he should be able to e-mail or fax to you the relevant information about what you can buy in local supermarkets and/or the restaurants available.

Plates and cutlery. Make sure that before you leave home you take with you, or immediately after you land at your destination, you purchase paper or plastic plates and plastic cutlery.

Kosher labels. As a general rule it's much easier and more practical to live on preserved kosher fish, fruit and vegetables, while you travel. However, particularly in the USA, in main cities, you should be able to find a variety of kosher products, including meat, sold in supermarkets. The best-known kosher label is OU, although there are numerous other kosher labels. The following website is an excellent source of information: www.kashrut.com

What to do if ... you do not have plastic plates and cutlery, you may eat breakfast cereals with a fruit juice or non-supervised cow's milk, using the hotel crockery and cutlery but *only for non-cooked, cold food.* If you travel to countries where their cow's milk may contain milk from non-kosher animals, e.g. Spain, you cannot rely on the authorities and therefore you may not drink this milk.

Hot drinks. It is better to drink from plastic or glass cups but if unavailable, glazed china/porcelain cups are acceptable.

SEA TRAVEL AND CRUISE SHIPS

General. The general advice in the previous section concerning air travel and hotel stay applies also in this case; however, it is less challenging to keep kosher on a cruise ship, if you travel five-star.

Kosher food. Although kosher food is available anyway on most luxury liners, make sure you order it at the time of your booking. You may find that the kosher food on board the cruise ship is not what you expected. I found that the highest quality travel kosher food comes from the UK in a pre-packed airline style, to be heated in a microwave oven or served cold.

And if not ... If you are unable to eat the pre-packed kosher meal then you may ask the restaurant staff to cook for you in a double-packed aluminium foil a kosher fish (e.g. haddock, mackerel, cod, salmon, halibut, carp etc.). Although according to Jewish Law, cooking by a non-Jew is not permitted, if there is no other choice, this may be allowed.

Vegetarian food. Eating a vegetarian meal cooked in the ordinary kitchen utensils – even if all the ingredients are kosher - is not permitted, according to Jewish Law, except in exceptional circumstances, ill health etc. I visited high-class cruise ship kitchens and found them spotless, generally well above the cleanliness standards of most hotels and restaurants. Usually, these luxury cruise ships have a separate vegetarian kitchen and their salads are OK, as well as a boiled egg.

Speak to the restaurant manager. Make sure that unless it is a kosher cruise, whereby the kosher food is supervised and cooked fresh on board the ship in a separate kosher kitchen, you introduce yourself on day one to the restaurant manager and explain to him/her your kosher food needs. Also ensure that other managers on other shifts are likewise informed about your needs. I cannot over-emphasise how important this is, do not be embarrassed and do it as soon as you settle into your cabin or stateroom.

For glatt kosher cruising, I highly recommend www.kosherica.com You may not embark or disembark the ship during Shabbat or Yom Tov, except in an emergency

GENERAL COMMENT AND TIPS

Wine without a kosher label may not be drunk, but whisky, vodka, rum and fruit liqueurs (containing no grape product) are acceptable.

If you do not have kosher wine, you can make Kiddush and Havdala on most other alcoholic drinks, including beer, but not on tea, coffee or a soft drink. Any kitchen or food store would have spices for Havdala.

Vegetable and fruit salads are generally alright but it's better to avoid broccoli and ordinary lettuce, which are not easy to clean from bugs. Carefully check any salad dressing. Whole fruit or vegetable may be provided on request.

Most smoked salmon, sardines and tuna are OK but check the label carefully first and if in doubt ask.

If you have no choice and there is no kosher bread to eat, you may eat French bread that is made from flour and water only.

Ryvita and Jacob's crackers are OK but many places outside the UK do not stock them, so you may take them with you.

It's advisable to take with you some Matza and as many *sealed* kosher food items as you can carry to ease off your journey at least until you locate an appropriate kosher food store.

In most countries, including the USA and Israel, fresh fruit and vegetables and meat and fish are *not allowed* to be taken into the country, only sealed snacks (e.g. crisps, biscuits etc.) and possibly some tinned food. *If in doubt check beforehand.*

Most chocolates are OK, but you may not eat cheese unless it has a kosher label or it appears on the list of kosher products (e.g. Philadelphia).

Be particularly careful with biscuits, sweets and ice creams (except Haagen Dazs, Ben & Jerry's etc.).

La Bruite kosher meals (pre-packed) contain a patented, flameless food heater made of magnesium and iron. Web site: www.labriutemeals.com

Hermolis kosher meals (pre-packed). Web site: www.hermolis.com

Remember to pack your Shabbat candles, prayer book, Tzitzit, Tefillin etc.

ALBANIA

There have been Jews living on the territory now known as Albania since Roman times, and there are remains in Dardania, in the north, of an ancient synagogue. The community was re-established by Jews from Iberia escaping the Spanish Inquisition in the fifteenth and early sixteenth centuries.

By 1930, the Jewish population had grown to only 204 but was soon augmented by refugees escaping the Nazis. Most Jews were helped to hide from Italian occupiers and then from the Nazis,

Post-war communism isolated Jews until the regime fell. In 1991, almost the entire community, about 300, was airlifted to Israel. The few Jews who remain in Albania live in the capital, Tirana.

The Albanian-Israel Friendship Society will be happy to provide any further information.

GMT +1 hours
Country calling code: (+55)
Total population: 3,738,000
Jewish population: Under 100
Emergency telephone: (Police–2445) (Fire–23333) (Ambulance–22235)
Electricity voltage: 220

TIRANA
CONTACT INFORMATION
Albanian-Israel Friendship Society
Rruga 'Barrikatave' 226
Telephone: (42) 22611

ALGERIA

Jews first settled in Algeria soon after the start of the Diaspora following the destruction of the Second Temple. A later influx occurred when Jews were escaping from Visigothic Spain.

In the twelfth and thirteenth centuries, Islamic conversion was forced on the Jews. Many Jews, however, crossed the Mediterranean from Spain during the time of the Inquisition, and these included some famous scholars. In 1830 the French occu-

pied the country and, in due course, granted the Jews French citizenship.

Algerian Jews suffered anti-semitism from both the local Muslim population and the wartime Vichy government. After the Allied landings in 1942, the anti-Jewish laws were slowly lifted. In the late 1950s 130,000 Jews lived in Algeria, but after the civil war, which led to independence from France in 1962, most of the community moved to France, with some to Israel, leaving very few behind. The present-day community, centred in Algiers, has a synagogue but no resident rabbi.

GMT +1 hours
Country calling code: (+13)
Total population: 29,050,00
Jewish population: Under 100
Emergency telephone: (Police–24445) (Fire–23333) (Ambulance–2235)
Electricity voltage: 117/220

ALGIERS
COMMUNITY ORGANISATIONS
Association Consistoriale Israélite d'Alger
6 rue Hassena Ahmed
Telephone: (20) 62-85-72

SYNAGOGUE
6 rue Hassena Ahmed
Telephone: (20) 62-85-72

BLIDA
COMMUNITY ORGANISATIONS
Consistoire d'Algerie
29 rue des Martyrs 4120
Telephone: (3) 492657

ANDORRA

Andorra, which is governed by two co-princes - the Bishop of Urgel in Spain and the President of France, does not have a Jewish history. There are currently, however, around 15 Jewish families.

A synagogue was established in 1997 in Escaldes and is the first in Andorras 1,100-year history. While its liturgy leans towards Sephardism, it is also influenced by its Ashkenazi members. There is a community centre in Escaldes.

GMT +1 hours
Country calling code: (+76)
Total population: **66,000**
Jewish population: **Under 100**
Emergency telephone: **(Police–825 225)**
(Fire–118) (Ambulance–118)

CONTACT INFORMATION
Dr David ben-Chayil or Dr David Bezold
Francesco B.P. 244, Andorra la Vella
Telephone: 333 567
Email: bezold@andorra.ad
For visits to the synagogue contact Isaac Benisty
Telephone 860 758

ARGENTINA

The first Jewish arrivals (*Conversos*, or 'secret Jews') came in the sixteenth and seventeenth centuries from Portugal and Spain. They assimilated quickly. A more significant Jewish immigration occurred in the middle of the nineteenth century from western Europe, and at the end of the nineteenth century many Jews arrived from eastern Europe, taking advantage of the 'open-door' policy towards immigrants. The new arrivals set up some Jewish agricultural settlements, under the auspices of the *Alliance Israelita Universelle*, and on the whole mixed with the local population.

The largest Jewish community is in Buenos Aires, with smaller communities in provincial centres. There are also some Jewish families remaining in the Jewish agricultural colonies, with Moiseville, Rivera and General Roca being the three most important.

There are Jewish newspapers, restaurants and other institutions. The Delegation of Argentine Jewish Associations (DAIA) represents all Jewish organisations.

GMT -3 hours
Country calling code: (+54)
Total population: **35,672,000**
Jewish population: **200,00**
Emergency telephone: **(Police–101) (Fire–100)**
(Ambulance–107)
Electricity voltage: **226**

BAHIA BLANCA
CONTACT INFORMATION
Beit Jabad
Chiclana 763 8000
Telephone: (291) 4453-6582
Fax: (291) 4456-5596
For details of Mikvah please phone

BUENOS AIRES
The first recorded Jewish event in Buenos Aires was a wedding in 1860. Around 220,000 Jews live in Buenos Aires. There are fifty or so synagogues in the city and kosher food is widely available. The most interesting synagogues for visitors are in Once although few Jews live there now.

BAKERIES
Confitería Aielet
Aranguren 2911, Flores
Telephone: (11) 4637-5419

Confitería Ganz
Pasco 752, Once
Telephone: (11) 4961-6918

Confitería Helueni
Tucuman 2620, Once
Telephone: (11) (11) 4961 0541

Confitería Mari Jalabe
Bogota 3228, Flores
Telephone: (11) 4612-6991

Panadería Malena
Av. Pueyrredón 880, Once
Telephone: (11) 4962-6290

BOOKSELLERS
Kehot Lubavitch Sudamericana
San Luis 3281 1186
Telephone: (11) 4865 0625
Fax: (11) 4865 0625
Email: kehot@iname.com
Website: www.kehot-lubavitch.com.ar

Liberia Editorial Sigal
Av. Corrientes 2854 C1193AAN
Telephone: (11) 4861-9501; 4865-7208
Fax: (11) 4962-7931; 4865-7208
Email: liberiasigal@runbox.com
Website: www.liberia-sigal.com

COMMUNITY ORGANISATIONS
AMIA (Central Ashkenazi community)
Pasteur 633
Telephone: (11) 4953-9777; 4953-2862
The community centre has now been reopened following the terror bomb attack in 1964.

Asociacion Israelita Sefaradi Argentina (AISA)
Pasco 493
Telephone: (11) 4952-4707

DAIA (Political representative body of Argentine Jewry)
Pasteur 633, 7th Floor
Telephone: (11) 4378-3200
Fax: (11) 4378-3200
Email: daia@daia.org.ar

CONTACT INFORMATION

Asociacion Shuva Israel
Pasco 557, Once
Telephone: (11) 4962-6255

Beit Chabad Belgrano
O'Higgins 2358, Belgrano 1428
Telephone: (11) 4781-3848
Fax: (11) 4783-4573
Email: shlomo@overnet.com.ar

Beit Chabad Villa Crespo
Serrano 69
Telephone: (11) 4855-9822

Beith Chabad West Area
Sarmiento 933 Moron 1708
Telephone: (11) 4627-3563

Chabad Lubavich Argentina
Agüero 1164, Flores 1425
Telephone: (11) 4963-1221

Congregacion Israelita de la Republica
Libertad 785, Centro
Telephone: (11) 4372-2474
Fax: (11) 4372-2474
The total number of synagogues in Buenos Aires where there is minyan at least on Friday night and shabbat morning exceeds fifty. Call any of the above numbers to locate the synagogue nearest you.

'Continuity' Organization for the spreading of Judaism
Camargo 870 Capital Federal C1414HR
Telephone: (11) 4855-6945
Fax: (11) 4855-9377
Email: Continuidad.com.ar
Website: www.shabuatov.com

Sephardic Community of Buenos Aires
Camargo 870 C1414AHR
Telephone: (11) 4855-6945
Fax: (11) 4855-9377
Email: info@acisba.org.ar
Website: www.acisba.org.ar

EMBASSY

Embassy of Israel
Avenida de Mayo 701-10° 1084
Telephone: (11) 4345-6207/08
Fax: (11) 4345-6207
Email: cidipal@israel-embassy.org.ar

GROCERIES

Almacén Behar
Campana 347, Flores
Telephone: (11) 4613-2033

Almacén Shalom
San Luis 2513, Once
Telephone: (11) 4962-3685

Autoservicio Ezra
Ecuador 619, Once
Telephone: (11) 4963-7062

Autoservicio Siman Tov
Helguera 474, Flores
Telephone: (11) 4611-4746

Azulay
Helguera 507, Flores

Battías
Pasco 706, Once

Kahal Jaredim
Argerich 386, Flores
Telephone: (11) 4612-4590

Kaler
San Luis 2810, Once

Kol Bo Brandsen
Brandsen 1389, Barracas

Kol Bo I
Ecuador 855, Once
Telephone: (11) 4961-3838

Kol Bo II
Viamonte 2537, Once
Telephone: (11) 4961-2012

Kosher Delights
La Pampa 2547, Belgrano
Telephone: (11) 4788-3150

La Esquina Casher
Aranguren 2999, Flores
Telephone: (11) 4637-3706

La Quesería
Viamonte 2438, Once
Telephone: (11) 4961-3171

La Tzorja
Ecuador 673, Once
Telephone: (11) 4961-1096

Lidia's Macolet
Ecuador 586, Once
Telephone: (11) 4863-5595
Fax: (11) 4932-4443

Yehuda Kosher Foods
Moldes 2452, Belgrano
Telephone: (11) 4637-1465

KASHRUT INFORMATION

The Central Rabbinate of Vaad Hakehillot
Ecuador 1110, Once
Telephone: (11) 4961-2944
The Orthodox Ashkenazi Chief Rabbi of Argentina is Rabbi Shlomo Benhamu Anidjar

LIBRARIES

Sociedad Hebraica Argentino
Sarmiento 2233
Telephone: (11) 4952-5570
Also has an art gallery

YIVO Library
Pasteur 633, Third floor
Telephone: (11) 445-2474

MEDIA

Newspapers
Comunidades
Die Presse
Kesher Kehilari
Mundo Israelita

MIKVAOT

Mikva
Moldes 2431, Belgrano 1428
Telephone: (11) 4783-2831
Fax: (11) 4786-8046
Email: rab@ajdut.com.ar

MUSEUMS

Museo Judio de Buenos Aires
Libertad 769
Telephone: (11) 4123-0830
Email: kjba@netizen.com.ar
Hours: Tuesday and Thursday 4pm to 7pm.

RESTAURANTS

Confiterie Helueni
Tucuman 2620, Once
Telephone: (11) 4961-0541

RESTAURANTS

Dairy
Soultani Café
San Luis 2601, Once
Telephone: (11) 4961 3913

Meat
Al Galope
Tucuman 2633, Once
Telephone: (11) 4963-6888

Mama Jacinta
Tucuman 2580 C-P 4052
Telephone: (11) 4962-9149
Fax: (11) 4962-7535
Email: mamajacintakosher@hotmail.com
Supervision: Gran Rasibo Josef Chehebar

McDonald's
Shopping Abasto, (Corrientes and Anchorena), Once
Supervision: Rav Oppenheimer - Ajdut Israel
There are two MacDonalds only one is kosher

Sucath David
Tucuman 2349
Telephone: (11) 4952 8878
Fax: (11) 4953 9656
Email: sucathdavid@sinectis.com.ar

SYNAGOGUES

Ashkenazi
Baron Hirsh
Billinghurst 664
Telephone: (11) 4862-2624

Beit Chabad Once 'LITVISHE SHUL'
Jose Evaristo Uriburu 348
Telephone: (11) 4952-7968
Fax: (11) 4952-7968
Email: aharon@radar.com.ar

Bet Rajel
Ecuador 522
Telephone: (11) 4862-2701

Brit Abraham
Antezana 145
Telephone: (11) 4855-6567

Etz Jaim
Julian Alvarez 745
Telephone: (11) 4772-5324

Torah Vaaboda
Julian Alvarez 667
Telephone: (11) 4854-0462

Zijron le David
Azcuenaga 736
Telephone: (11) 4953-0200

Conservative
Beit Hilel
Araoz 2854, Palermo
Telephone: (11) 4804-2286

Benei Tikva
Vidal 2049
Telephone: (11) 4781-9392; 4786-9374
Fax: (11) 4781-9392; 4786-9374

Colegio Wolfson, Comunidad Or-El
Amenabar 2972
Telephone: (11) 4544-5461

Comunidad Bet El
Sucre 3338
Telephone: (11) 4552-2365

Dor Jadash
Murillo 649, Villa Crespo
Telephone: (11) 4854-4467

Nueva Comunidad Israelita
Arcos 2319
Telephone: (11) 4781-0281

Or Jadash
Varela 850, Flores
Telephone: (11) 4612-1171

German Orthodox and Sephardic

Ajdut Yisroel
Moides 2449 1428
Telephone: (11) 4783-2831
Fax: (11) 4781-6725
Email: rab@ajdut.com.ar
Website: www.ajdut.com.ar, www.kosher.org.ar

Reform

Templo Emanu-El
Tronador 1455
Telephone: (11) 4552-4343
Fax: (11) 4555-4004
Email: kol_emanuel@name.com

Sephardi

Centro Comunitario Chalom
Olleros 2876
Telephone: (11) 4552-2720
Fax: (11) 4552-6730
Email: secretaria@chalom.org.ar
Website: www. chalom.org.ar

Sephardi Orthodox

Aderet Eliahu
Ruy Diaz Guzman 647
Telephone: (11) 4303-1320
Fax: (11) 4303-1320

Agudat Dodim
Avellaneda 2874
Telephone: (11) 4611-0056

Asociacion Comunidad Israelita Sefaradi de Buenos Aires
Camargo 870
Telephone: (11) 4855-6945
Fax: (11) 4855-9377
Email: acisba@continuidad.com.ar

Bajurim Tiferet Israeil
Helguera 611
Telephone: (11) 4611-3376

Etz Jaim
Carlos Calvo 1164
Telephone: (11) 4302-6290

Jaike Grimberg
Campana 460
Telephone: (11) 4672-2347

Kehal Jaredim
Helguera 270, Once
Telephone: (11) 4612-0410

Od Yosef Jai
Tucuman 3326
Telephone: (11) 4963-2349

Or Misraj
Ciudad de la Paz 2555
Telephone: (11) 4784-5945

Shaare Sion
Helguera 453
Telephone: (11) 4637-5897
Fax: (11) 4637-1301
Email: editorial@shaaresion.org.ar
Website: www,shaaresion.org.ar

Shaare Tefila
Paso 733
Telephone: (11) 4962-2865

Shuba Israel
Ecuador 627
Telephone: (11) 4862-0562

Sinagoga Rabino Zeev Grinberg
Felipe Vallese 3047, Ciudad Autonoma de Buenos Aires
Telephone: (11) 4611-3366

Sucath David
Tucuman 2750
Telephone: (11) 4962-1091
Fax: (11) 4962-1264
Email: contacto@judaicasite.com
Website: www.judaicasite.com

Templo la Paz (Chalom)
Olleros 2876
Telephone: (11) 4552-6730

Yeshurun
Republica de la India 3035
Telephone: (11) 4802-9310

Yesod Hadat
Lavalle 2449
Telephone: (11) 4961-1615

CORDOBA

CONTACT INFORMATION

Jabad Lubavitch Cordoba
Sucre 1380, Barrio Cofico 5000
Telephone: (351) 4471 0223
Fax: (351) 4411 9721

GROCERIES

Almacén
Sucre 1378, Barrio Cofico 5000
Telephone: (351) 4471 0223

ROSARIO

CONTACT INFORMATION

Beit Jabad Rosario
S. Lorenzo 1882 P.A. 2000
Telephone: (341) 425 2899

GROCERIES

La Granja Kasher
Montevideo 1833
Telephone: (341) 449 6210

TUCUMAN
CONTACT INFORMATION
Beit Jabad Tucuman
Lamadrid 752 4000
Telephone: (381) 424 8892
Fax: (381) 424 8893
Email: jabadtucuman@amet.com.ar

GROCERIES
Almacén y Carnicería
9 de Julio 625
Telephone: (381) 431 0227

Bet Jabad Tucuman
Lamadrid 752 4000
Telephone: (381) 424 8892
Fax: (381) 424 8893
Email: jabadtucuman@amet.com.ar

ARMENIA

Jews have lived in Armenia for many hundreds of years. Nowadays, nearly all Armenian Jews live in Yerevan, with only a few families living in Vanadzor (Kirokavan) and Gjumri (Leninakan). A handful are scattered throughout other small towns and villages.

Country calling code: (+3741)
Jewish population: 500

YEREVAN
SYNAGOGUES
Yerevan
Nar-Dosa Str. 23, Yerevan, Armenia 375018
Telephone: 57-16-77
Fax: 55-41-32

AUSTRALIA

The first Jews in Australia arrived with the first convict ships from the United Kingdom in 1788, and regular, organised worship started in the 1820s. The first free Jewish settler arrived with her husband, a deported convict, in 1816. The community grew in the nineteenth century, with the first synagogue being established in the mid-1840s. Events such as the gold rush and pogroms in eastern Europe were catalysts for more Jewish immigration.

The Jewish contribution to Australian life has been prominent, with the commander of the ANZAC forces in the First World War being a practising Jew, Sir John Monash. The twentieth century saw some 7,000 Jewish refugees from Nazi Europe settling in Australia, and the community contains the largest percentage of Holocaust survivors in the world. They are a major influence on the present community, which is expanding and predominately religious. There have also been two Jewish Governors-General; one being Sir Issac Issacs, who was the first Australian-born to hold that position.

The community is led by the Executive Council of Australian Jewry. 75 per cent of primary and 55 per cent of secondary Jewish school children attend Jewish schools, and there is a low level of intermarriage. Melbourne has the largest community, (42,000), with 35,000 in Sydney. There are Jewish newspapers, radio programmes of Jewish interest and museums on Jewish themes.

GMT +7 to +10 hours
Country calling code: (+61)
Total population: 19,105,000
Jewish population: 100,000
Emergency telephone: (Police–000) (Fire–000) (Ambulance–000)
Electricity voltage: 240/250

Australian Capital Territory

CANBERRA
EMBASSY
Embassy of Israel
6 Turrana Street, Yarralumla 2600
Telephone: (262) 73-1309
Fax: (262) 73-4279
Email: israelembassy@israemb.org

SYNAGOGUE
The A.C.T. Jewish Community Synagogue
National Jewish Memorial Centre, cnr Canberra Avenue & National Circuit, Forrest 2603
Telephone: (262) 951-052
Fax: (262) 958-608
Website: www.actjewish.org.au
Postal address: POB 3105, Manuka 2603

New South Wales

NEWCASTLE
SYNAGOGUES
Newcastle Synagogue

122 Tyrrell Street 2300
Telephone: (49) 26-2820
Contact: Dr L.E. Fredman, 123 Dawson St, Cooks Hill 2300
N.S.W.

SYDNEY
The first Jewish convict settlers were generally illiterate in both English and Hebrew, and there was no Jewish organisation until a Chevrah Kadishe was formed in 1817 and services were held under the leadership of a former convict Joseph Marcus.
Most of Sydney's Jews are now settled outside the city centre in two suburban areas: the eastern suburbs, including Bondi, and the North Shore.

BAKERIES
Carmel Cake Shop
14 O'Brien Street, Bondi
Supervision: NSW Kashrut Authority

BOOKSELLERS
Gold s World of Judaica
9 O'Brien Street, Bondi 2026
Telephone: (2) 9300-0495
Fax: (2) 9389-7345
Email: sydney@golds.com.au

BUTCHERS
Eilat
173 Bondi Road, Bondi
Telephone: (2) 9387-881
Supervision: NSW Kashrut Authority

Hadassa
17 O'Brien Street, Bondi
Telephone: (2) 9365-4904
Fax: (2) 9130-4760
Supervision: NSW Kashrut Authority

COMMUNITY ORGANISATIONS
Executive Council of Australian Jewry
146 Darlinghurst Road, second floor, Darlinghurst 2010
Telephone: (2) 9360-5415
Fax: (2) 9360-5416
Email: ecaj@.com.ar

EMBASSY
Embassy of Israel
6 Turrana Street, Yarralumla 2600
Telephone: (2) 2 6273 1309
Fax: (2) 2 6273 4273
Email: consular@canberra.mfa.gov.il
Website: www.canberra.mfa.gov.il

HOSPITAL
Wolper Jewish Hospital
8 Trelawney Street, Woollahra
Telephone: (2) 9328-6077
Fax: (2) 9327-5973

Email: info@wolper.com.au
Website: www.wolper.com.au

KASHRUT INFORMATION
Kosher Consumer Association
Telephone: (2) 9337-6657
Fax: (2) 9371-0348

NSW Kashrut Authority
4/58 Hall St, Bondi Beach 2026
Telephone: (2) 9365-2933
Fax: (2) 9365-0933
Email: rabbig@ka.org.au
Website: www.ka.org.au

MEDIA
Newspapers
Australian Jewish News
Level 1,10-14 Waterloo Street, Surry Hills 2010
Telephone: (2) 8218-1600
Fax: (2) 8218-1655
Email: dgoldberg@jewishnews.net.au
Website: www.ajn.net.au

MUSEUMS
Sydney Jewish Museum
148 Darlinghurst Road, Darlinghurst 2010
Telephone: (2) 9360-7999
Fax: (2) 9331-4245
Email: admin@sjm.com.au
Website:www.sydneyjewishmuseum.com.au
Has won many awards for its work documenting Australian Jewish history and the Holocaust, and has a kosher (dairy) cafe.

RELIGIOUS ORGANISATIONS
Sydney Beth Din
166 Castlereagh Street 2000
Telephone: (2) 9267-2477
Fax: (2) 9264-8871
Email: rabbi@greatsynagogue.org.au

RESTAURANTS
Dairy
Red Tomato Café
50 Mitchell St, N Bondi 2026
Telephone: (2) 9300-0707
Fax: (2) 9130-4477

Toovya the Milkman
379 Old South Head Road, North Bondi 2026
Telephone: (2) 9130-4016
Supervision: NSW Kashrut Authority
Not Cholov Yisrael. Vegetarian and vegan food. Delivery to eastern suburbs, including to hotel room. Hours: Sunday to Thursday, 5pm to 10pm; Saturday, after Shabbat to midnight.

Meat

Beaches Kosher Restaurant
11 O'Brien Street 2026
Telephone: (2) 9365-5544
Fax: (2) 9365-5577
Supervision: NSW Kasrut Authority
Lunch is only Pareve. Delivery to all Sydney addresses.

Katzy's Food Factory
Shop 2, 113-115 Hall Street, Bondi Beach
Telephone: (2) 9130-6743
Fax: (2) 9130-6742
Supervision: NSW Kashrut Authority
Also take-away.

Lewis' Continental Kitchen
2 Curlewis Street, Bondi 2026
Telephone: (2) 2 9365-5421
Fax: (2) 2 9300-0037
Email: judith@lewiskosher.com
Website: www.lewiskosher.com
Supervision: NSW Kashrut Authority
Glatt Kosher. Specialise in assisting tourists with their meals in Australia.

The Museum Café
Corner Darlinghurst and Burton Street,
Darlinghurst, Darlinghurst 2010
Telephone: (2) 9360-7999
Fax: (2) 9331-4245
Email: ceo@sjm.com.au
Website:www.sydneyjewishmuseum.com.au
Kosher café situated in the Sydney Jewish Museum

Tibby's Kosher Restaurant at Jaffa
61-67 Hall Street, Bondi Beach 2026
Telephone: (+61) 9130-5051
Supervision: NSW Kashrut Authority
Open Saturday to Thursday for dinner. Continental, Chinese, Sephardi and Israeli food. Glatt kosher.

SYNAGOGUES

Adath Yisroel
243 old south Head Road, Bondi
Telephone: (2) 9300-9447

Bondi Mizrachi Synagogue
101/60 Blair Street, North Bondi 2026
Telephone: (2) 02-9365-3838
Fax: (2) 02-9365-3838
Email: mizrachisydney@bigpond.com
Website: www.mizrachi.org.au
Synagogue location is 339 Old South Head Road, Bondi 2026

Coogee Synagogue
121 Brook Street, Coogee
Telephone: (2) 9315-8291

Cremorne & District
12a Yeo Street, Neutral Bay
Telephone: (2) 9908-1853
Fax: (2) 9908-1852

Illawarra Synagogue
502 Railway Parade, Allawah
Telephone: (2) 9587-5643
Email: geogrefoster@compuserve.com

Paramatta Synagogue
116 Victoria road, Paramatta
Telephone: (2) 9683-5381

Sephardi Synagogue
40-44 Fletcher Street, Bondi Junction 2022
Telephone: (2) 9389-3982
Fax: (2) 9369-2143
Email: mail@sephardi.org.au

Shearit Yisrael
146 Darlinghurst Road, Darlinghurst 2010
Telephone: (2) 9365-8770

South Head & District Synagogue
666 Old South Head Road, Rose Bay 2029
Telephone: (2) 9371-7300
Fax: (2) 9371-7416
Email: admin@southhead.org
Website: www.southhead.org

Strathfield & District Synagogue
19 Florence Street, Strathfield 2015
Telephone: (2) 9642-3550
Fax: (2) 9642-4803

Conservative

Temple Emanuel
7 Ocean Street, Woollahra 2025
Telephone: (2) 9328-7833
Fax: (2) 9327-8715
Email: info@emanuel.org.au
Website: www.emanuel.org.au
Look forward to welcoming visitors from abroad

Orthodox

Great Synagogue
166 Castlereagh Street
Telephone: (2) 9267-2477
Fax: (2) 9264-8871
Email: admin@greatsynagogue.org.au
Website: www.greatsynagogue.org.au
Houses the Rabbi L.A. Falk Memorial Library and the A.M. Rosenblum Jewish Museum. (Entrance for services: 187 Elizabeth Street.) There are synagogue tours on Tuesdays and Thursdays.

Kehillat Masada
9-15 Link road, St Ives 2075
Telephone: (2) 9988-4417
Fax: (2) 9449-3897
Email: k_masada@wm.au

Maroubra Synagogue (K.M.H.C.)
635 Anzac Parade, Maroubra 2035
Telephone: (2) 9344-6095
Fax: (2) 9344-4298
Email: maroubrasyna@bigpond.com

Newtown Synagogue
20 Georgina Street, Newtown 2042
Telephone: (2) 2 9550 1192
Fax: (2) 2 9550 1192
Mobile Phone: 417 462 870
Email: newtownsynagogue@yahoo.com
Website: www.newtown.shul.org.au
Sydney's second oldest synagogue.

North Shore Synagogue
15 Treatts Road, Lindfield
Telephone: (2) 9416-3710
Fax: (2) 9416-7659
Email: nss@bigpond.com

The Central Synagogue
15 Bon Accord Avenue, Bondi Junction
Telephone: (2) 9389-5622
Fax: (2) 9389-5418
Email: central@centralsynagogue.com.au
Website: www.centralsynagogue.com.au

Yeshiva
36 Flood Street, Bondi 2026
Telephone: (2) 9387-3822
Fax: (2) 9389-7652
Email: info@yeshiva.org.au

SYNAGOGUES
Progressive
North Shore Temple Emanuel
28 Chatswood Avenue, Chatswood 2067
Telephone: (2) 919-7011
Fax: (2) 9413-1474
Email: nste@nste.org.au
Website: www.nste.org.au

Sefardim
Beth Yosef
Ground Floor, 243 Old South Head Road, Bondi

TOURS
Jewish Sydney Tours
Telephone: (2) 9328-7604
For information about tours of Jewish Sydney, contact the Great Synagogue on (2) 9267-2477 or Karl Maehrischel at this number.

Queensland
BRISBANE
COMMUNITY ORGANISATIONS
Jewish Communal Centre
2 Moxom Road, Burbank 4156
Telephone: (7) 33-49-9749

MIKVAOT
Queensland Mikvah
46 Bunya Street, Greenslopes 4120
Telephone: (7) 3848-5886

RELIGIOUS ORGANISATIONS
Chabad House of Queensland
43 Cedar Street, Greenslopes 4120
Telephone: (7) 3848-5886
Fax: (7) 3848-5886
Email: kthomas@onenet.au

SYNAGOGUES
Brisbane Hebrew Congregation
98 Margaret Street 4000
Telephone: (7) 3229-3412

Givat Zion
43 Bunya Street, Greenslopes 4000
Telephone: (7) 3397-9025
Fax: (7) 3397-9025

South Brisbane Hebrew Congregation
46 Bunya Street, Greenslopes 4120
Telephone: (7) 3397-9025
Fax: (7) 3397-9025
Email: slatwall@ozemail.com.au

Progressive
Beit Knesset Shalom
13 Koolatah Street, Camp Hill 4152
Telephone: (7) 3398-8843/3391-2579
Fax: (7) 3391-2579
Email: bks@hotmail.com

GOLD COAST
BAKERIES
Goldsteins Bakery
509 Olsen Avenue Ashmore City 4214
Telephone: (7) 5539-3133
Fax: (7) 5597-1064
Supervision: Rabbi Gurevitch, Gold Coast Hebrew Congregation
Under the umbrella of the NSW Kashrut Authority. Challah and kosher breads available at fourteen stores along the Gold Coast, including Surfers Paradise shop. (Tel) 5531-5808

COMMUNITY ORGANISATIONS
Association of Jewish Organisations
31 Ranock Avenue, Benown Waters 4217
Telephone: (7) 5597-2222

SYNAGOGUES
Surfers Central Synagogue
4 Rivers Terrace, Surfers Paradise 4217

Temple Shalom
25 Via Roma Drive, Isle of Capri 4217
Telephone: (7) 5570-1716

Orthodox
Gold Coast Hebrew Congregation
34 Hamilton Avenue,Surfers Paradise 4215
Telephone: (7) 5570-1851
Fax: (7) 5570-1851
Email: gchebrewcong@ausinfo.com.au

South Australia

ADELAIDE

BAKERIES
Bakers Delight
Frewville Shopping Centre, Glen Osmond Road

GROCERIES
Kosher Imports
c/o Hebrew Congregation, 13 Flemington Street, Glenside 5065
Telephone: (8) 8338-2922
Fax: (8) 8379-0142
Email: jewish@ozmail.com
Website: www.adelaidejewish.com
Kosher and Judaica products available

SYNAGOGUES
Orthodox
Adelaide Hebrew Congregation
13 Flemington Street, Glenside 5065
Telephone: (8) 8338-2922
Fax: (8) 8379-0142
Email: jewish@ozmail.com.au
Website: www.adelaidejewish.com
Mikva on premises. Mailing address: PO Box 320, Glenside 5065.

Progressive
Beit Shalom
41 Hackney Road, Hackney 5000
Telephone: (8) 8362-8281
Fax: (8) 8362-4406
Email: bshalom@bshalomadel.com.au
Website: www.bshalomadel.com
Mailing address PO Box 47, Stepney 5069

Tasmania
Established as a penal colony in 1803. Jewish names first appeared in 1819, one being Ikey Solomons, a famous Jewish covict who was said to be the model for Dickens' Fagin in Oliver Twist. The community remained small. The Launcerlin synagogue was closed in 1871 and not reopened until 1939.

HOBART

CONTACT INFORMATION
Jewish Centre
Chadbad House, 93 Lord Street, Bay 7005
Telephone: (3) 6223-7116
Fax: (3) 6223-7116
Email: jwc@southcom.com.au
Contact in advance for Shabbat meals and mikvah.

SYNAGOGUES
Progressive and Orthodox Services
GPO Box 128 7001
Telephone: (3) 03-6234-4720
Email: shule@ hobart.org

Progressive
Orthodox
Hobart Hebrew Congregation
PO Box 128, Hobart , 59 Argle Street 7000
Telephone: (3) 6234-4720
Mobile Phone: 0418 129 233
Email: shule@hobart.org
Website: www.hobartsynagogue.org
Supervision: Executive Council of Australian Jewry
The oldest continuously functioning synagogue in Australia, having been consecrated in July 1845. Orthodox Shabbat services every Saturday (10.30am); for Progressive services please visit our website.

LAUNCESTON

CONTACT INFORMATION
Chadbad House of Tasmania
5 Brisbane Street Launceston 7250
Telephone: (3) 6334-0705
Fax: (3) 6344-9960
Email: ghgoldsteen@netspace.au
For all enquiries please call or fax the Hon. Manager Mr Gershon Goldsteen at (3) 6344-9960 or email him as above.

SYNAGOGUES
Jewish Synagogue
St. John Street 7250
Telephone: (3) 6343-1143
The synagogue in St John Street is the second oldest in Australia, founded in 1846. It is shared by Reform and Orthodox congregations and still has the original convict benches.

Victoria

BALLARAT
Synagogue
211 Drumond Street North 3350
Telephone: (353) 32-6330

MELBOURNE
With 42,000 Jews, Melbourne has the largest Jewish community in the country, and the largest Jewish school in the world (the Mount Scopus).

BAKERIES
Big K Kosher Bakery
316 Carlisle Street, Balaclava 3183
Telephone: (3) 9527-4582
Supervision: Rabbi A.Z. Beck, Adass Israel

Glicks Cakes and Bagels
330a Carlisle Street, Balaclava 3183
Telephone: (3) 9527-2198
Supervision: Melbourne Kashrut

Greenfield Cakes
7 Willow Street, Elsternwick
Telephone: (3) 9528-4261

Supervision: Rabbi A.Z. Beck, Adass Israel.
At same location is King David Kosher Meals on Wheels (Refuah), hospital meals, airline and TV dinners.

Haymishe Bakery
320 Carlisle Steet, Shop 4 3183
Telephone: (3) 9527-7116
Supervision: Rabbi A.Z. Beck, Adass Israel

Kosher Delight Bakery
75 Glen Eira Road, Ripponlea
Telephone: (3) 9532-9994
Supervision: Rabbi A.Z. Beck, Adass Israel

Lowy's Cakes & Catering
59 Gordon Street, Elsternwick
Telephone: (3) 9530-0246
Supervision: Rabbi A.Z. Beck, Adass Israel

Meal-Mart
251 Inkerman Street, St Kilda 3182
Telephone: (3) 9525-5077
Fax: (3) 9525-4230
Supervision: Rabbi A.Z. Beck, Adass Israel
Pies, salads, pre-cooked and frozen foods.

BOOKSELLERS
Judaica Store
Golds World of Judaica
3-13 William Street, Balaclava 3183
Telephone: (3) 9527-8775
Fax: (3) 9527-6434
Email: info@golds.com.au
Website: www.golds.com.au
Trading Hours: Sunday 10.00 - 4.00, Monday - Thursday 9.00 - 5.30, Friday 9.00 - 3.00

BUTCHERS
Continental Kosher Butchers
155 Glenferrie Road, Malvern 3144
Telephone: (3) 9509-9822
Fax: (3) 9509-9099
Email: ckb@bigpond.net.au
Supervision: Rabbi J.S. Cohen and Rabbi M. Gutnick, Melbourne Kashrut.

Melbourne Kosher Butchers
251 Inkerman Street, East St Kilda
Telephone: (3) 9525-5077
Fax: (3) 9525-4230
Supervision: Rabbi A.Z. Beck, Adass Israel.
Sells other kosher products as well. Hours: 10 am to 5.30 pm; Tuesday to Thursday, 7 am to 5.30 pm; Friday 7 am to 3 pm. Winter 2 pm.

Solomon Kosher Butchers
140b-144 Glen Eira Road, Elsternwick 3185
Telephone: (3) 9532-885
Fax: (3) 9532-8896
Supervision: Rabbi Y.D. Groner, Agudas Chabad Kashrut Committee.
Hours: Monday to Thursday , 7 am to 5.30 pm; Friday 7 am to 3 pm.

Yumi's Kosher Seafoods
29 Glen Eira Road, Ripponlea 3183
Telephone: (3) 9523-6444
Fax: (3) 9532-8189
Email: yumis@bigpond.com
Supervision: Rabbi A.Z. Beck, Adass Israel
Also suppliers of kosher fresh fish.

CHOCOLATE SHOPS
Kosher
Alpha Kosher Chocolates
17 William Street, Balaclava
Telephone: (3) 9527-2453
Australias only kosher chocolate factory. Handmade chocolates. Visitors welcome. Open Sunday mornings

COMMUNITY ORGANISATIONS
Jewish Community Council of Victoria Inc.
306 Hawthorn Road, South Caulfield 3162
Telephone: (3) 9272-5566
Fax: (3) 9272-5560
Email: community@jccv.org.au
Website: www.jccv.org.au
Head body of Melbourne Jewish community

CONTACT INFORMATION
Mizrachi Hospitality Committee
81 Balaclava Road, Caulfield 3161
Telephone: (3) 9525-9833
Fax: (3) 9527-5665
Email: mizrachi@iprimus.com.au
Mailing address: PO Box 2247, Caulfield Junction, VIC 3161.

DELICATESSEN
E.S. Delicatessen
74 Kooyong Road, Caufield 3161
Telephone: (3) 9576-0804
Supervision: Melbourne Kashrut

Eshel Take-Away Foods & Catering
59 Glen Eira Road, Ripponlea 3161
Telephone: (3) 9532-8309
Fax: (3) 9532-8089
Supervision: Rabbi A.Z. Beck, Adass Israel

GROCERIES
Dainty Foods (Kravsz)
62 Glen Eira Road, Ripponlea 3183
Telephone: (3) 9523-8463
Grocers/importers.

Milecki's Balaclava Health Food
277 Carlisle Street, Balaclava 3183
Telephone: (3) 9527-3350
Open every day except Shabbat and all Jewish holidays. Hours: 9.00 am to 9.00 pm.

Rishon Foods Party Ltd.
23 William Stree,t, Balaclava 3183
Telephone: (3) 9527-5142

Tempo Kosher Supermarket
5/320 Carlisle Street, St. Kilda 3182
Telephone: (03) 9527-5021
Manufacturers of a range of kosher foods, including cheese, butter and juice drinks.

Liquor
Gefen Liquor Store
328 Carlisle Street, Balaclava 3183
Telephone: (3) 9531-5032
Fax: (3) 9525-7388
Hours: Monday to Thursday, 9 am to 5 pm; Friday, 9 am to 3.30pm. Stocking a wide range of Kosher wines and spirits produced locally and many from around the world.

HOTELS
Quest Kimberley Caulfield
441 Inkerman Street, Balaclava 3183
Telephone: (3) 9526-3888
Fax: (3) 9525-8479
Strictly Glatt kosher

JUDAICA
The Antique Silver Co.
253 Carlisle Street, Balaclava 3183
Telephone: (3) 9525-8480
Fax: (3) 9525-8479
Large selection of Judaica and ritual objects.

KASHRUT INFORMATION
Melbourne Kashrut
81 Balaclava Road, Caulfield 3161
Telephone: (3) 9525-9895
Fax: (3) 9527-5665
Email: melbkash@iprimus.com.au
Mailing address: PO Box 2247 Caulfield Junction, Victoria 3161.

LIBRARIES
Kadimah Jewish Cultural Centre & National Library
7 Selwyn Street, Elsternwick 3185
Telephone: (3) 9523-9817
Hours: 9.30 am to 2.30 pm

Makor Jewish Community Library
306 Hawthorn Road, South Cantfield 3162
Telephone: (3) 9272-5611
Fax: (3) 9272-5629
Email: jlibrary@vicnet.net.au
Website: www.vicnet.net.au/~jlibrary

MEDIA
Newspapers
Jewish News
PO Box 1000, South Cantfield
Publishes weekly newspaper

Yiddishe Gesheften The Jewish Community Advertiser
PO Box 1031 Elsternwick, Victoria 3185
Telephone: (3) 8504-0060
Fax: (3) 9523-0106
Published quarterly

MIKVAOT
Caulfield Mikva
9 Furneaux Grove, East St Kilda 3183
Telephone: (3) 9528-1116/9525-8585
Contact: Mrs C. Sofer

Lubavitch Mikva
38 Empress Road, East St. Kilda 3183
Telephone: (3) 9527-7555
Fax: (3) 9525-8838
Email: ktrubin@wavenet.net.au

MUSEUMS
Jewish Holocaust Centre
15 Selwyn Street, Elsternwick 3185
Telephone: (3) 9528-1985
Fax: (3) 9528-3758
Email: admin@holocaustcentreaustralia.org.au
Website: www.jhc.org.au
Hours: Monday and Wednesday 10.00 am to 4.00 pm, Tuesday, Thursday and Friday 10.00 am to 2.00 pm, Sunday 12.00 to 4.00 pm.

Jewish Museum of Australia
26 Alma Road, St Kilda 3182
Telephone: (3) 9534-0083
Fax: (3) 9534-0844
Email: info@jewishmuseum.com.au
Website: www.jewishmuseum.com.au

RELIGIOUS ORGANISATIONS
Council of Orthodox Synagogues of Victoria
C/- Level 10, 5 Queens Road 3004
Telephone: (3) 9864-4622
Fax: (3) 9864-4666
Email: yaron@jewishnews.net.au

Melbourne Beth Din
Synagogue Chambers, 572 Inkerman Road,, North Caulfield 3161
Telephone: (3) 9527-8337
Fax: (3) 9527-8072

Rabbinical Council of Victoria
c/o Honorary Secretary, Rabbi Mordechai Gutnick, 7 Meadow St., East St Kilda 3183
Telephone: (3) 9525-9542
Fax: (3) 9525-9546

RELIGIOUS ORGANISATIONS
Progressive
Victorian Union for Progressive Judaism
78 Alma Road, St Kilda 3182
Telephone: (3) 9510-1488
Fax: (3) 9521-1229
Email: vupj@tbi.org.au

RESTAURANTS

Dairy

Sheli's Coffee Shop
306 Hawthorn Road, South Caufield
Telephone: (3) 9272-5607

Meat

Delishes Restaurant
8-10 Glen Eira Ave., Ripponlea
Telephone: (3) 9523-1801

Klein's Kosher Gourmet
19 Glen Eira Road, Ripponlea
Telephone: (3) 9528-1200
Fax: (3) 9528-1300
Email: kleinsgourmetfoods@hotmail.com
Website: www.kleinsgourmetfoods.com

Kosher Express
263-265 Carlisle St., Balaclava
Telephone: (3) 9527-9911
Fax: (3) 9527-9922

Lamzini's
219 Carlisle Street, St Kilda
Telephone: (3) 9527-1283
Supervision: Melbourne Kashrut

SYNAGOGUES

Independent

Bet Hatikva Synagogue
233 Nepan Highway, Gardenvale 3185
Telephone: (3) 9576-9755

Liberal

Bentleigh Progressive Synagogue
549 Centre Road 3204
Telephone: (3) 9563-9208
Fax: (3) 9557-9880
Email: bpsadmin@bigpond.com.au
Website: www.bps.org.au

Temple Beth Israel
PO Box 128, St Kilda 3182
Telephone: (3) 9510-1488
Fax: (3) 9521-1229
Email: info@tbi.org.au
Website: www.tbi.org.au

Orthodox

Brighton Hebrew Congregation
132-136 Marriage Road, East Brighton 3187
Telephone: (3) 9592-9179
Fax: (3) 9593-1682
Email: brightonshule@iprimus.com.au
Office hours: Monday to Friday 9 am-1 pm.
PO Box 202 Bentleigh 3204. Visitors welcome.

Burwood Hebrew Congregation
38 Harrison Avenue 3125
Telephone: (3) 9808-3120

Caulfield Hebrew Congregation
572 Inkerman Road, Caulfield 3161
Telephone: (3) 9525-9492
Fax: (3) 9527-8463
Email: admin@caulfieldshule.com
Website: www.caulfieldshule.com
Notes: Rabbi S. Gutnick

Chabad House Malvern
316 Glenferrie Road, Malvern 3143
Telephone: (3) 9822-4985
Fax: (3) 9822-1093
Email: office@chabad.com.au
Website: www.chabad.com.au

East Melbourne City Synagogue
488 Albert St. East Melbourne 3002
Telephone: (3) 9662-1372
Fax: (3) 9662-1843
Email: office@melbournecitysynagogue.com
Website:www.melbournecitysynagogue.com
The only synagogue in the inner city area. A historically significant synagogue classfied by the National Trust of Victoria. It celebrated its 125 year anniversary in 2002.

Elwood Talmud Torah Congregation
39 Dickens Street, Elwood 3184
Telephone: (3) 9531-1547

Kew Synagogue
53 Walpole Street, Kew 3101
Telephone: (3) 9853-9243
Fax: (3) 9853-1354
Email: kewshul@iprimus.com.au

Kollel Beth Hatalmud-Yehuda Fishman
362a Carlisle Street, East St Kilda 3183
Telephone: (3) 9527-6156
Fax: (3) 9527-8034
Email: kbt@blaze.net.au

Melbourne Hebrew Congregation
Cnr. Toorak & St Kilda Roads, S. Yarra 3141
Telephone: (3) 9866-2255
Fax: (3) 9866-2022
Email: mhc@melbournesynagogue.org.au
Website: www.melbournesynagogue.org.au

Mizrachi
81 Balaclava Road, Caulfield 3161
Telephone: (3) 9525-9833
Fax: (3) 9527-5665
Email: mizrachi@iprimus.com.au
Mailing address: PO Box 2247, Caulfield Junction, VIC 31761

Moorabbin & District Synagogue
960 Nepan Highway, Moorabbin 3189
Telephone: (3) 9553-3845

South Caulfield Synagogue
47 Leopold Street, South Caulfield 3161
Telephone: (3) 9578-5922
Fax: (3) 9578-5299

St Kilda Hebrew Congregation Inc.
12 Charnwood Grove, St Kilda 3182
Telephone: (3) 9537-1433
Fax: (3) 9525-3759
Email: office@stkildashule.org
Website: www.stkildashule.org.au

Yeshiva Shule
92 Hotham Street, St Kilda 3183
Telephone: (3) 9522-8222
Fax: (3) 9522-8266

Progressive
Leo Baeck Centre for Progressive Judaism
31-37 Harp Road, Kew East 3102
Telephone: (3) 9819-7160
Fax: (3) 9859-5417
Email: office@lbc.org.au
Website: www.lbc.org.au
PO Box 430 East Kew 3102

Victorian Union for Progressive Judaism
78 Alma Road, St Kilda 3182
Telephone: (3) 9510-1488
Fax: (3) 9521-1229
Email: vupj@tbi.org.au

Sephardi
The Sassoon Yehuda Sephardi Synagogue
79 Hotham Street , East St Kilda 3183
Telephone: (3) 9527-8863
Email: rylco@optusnet.com.au
Sephardi Kiddush follows Saturday service. Monday,
Thursday and Sunday services followed by breakfast.

TOURIST SITES
North Eastern Jewish War Memorial Centre Inc.
6 High Street, Doncaster 3108
Telephone: (3) 9816-3516
Fax: (3) 9857-4430
Email: nejc@one.au

Western Australia

PERTH
BUTCHERS
W.A. Kosher Butcher & Bakery
4 Bayley St., Dianella
Telephone: (8) 9276-2525

COMMUNITY ORGANISATIONS
Council of Western Australian Jewry
J.P. PO Box 763 6062

KOSHER FOODS
Aviv Catering
The Jewish Centre, 61 Woodrow Avenue, Yokinea 6060
Telephone: (8) 9276-6030
Fax: (8) 9276-6030
Supervision: KAWA
Open10.00 am-2.00 pm

Kosher Food Centre
Perth Synagogue Carpark, Plantation Street,
Menora WA 6050
Telephone: (8) 9271-1133/3311
Fax: (8) 9371-1717
Mobile Phone: 0410558383
Email: info@kosherfoodcentre.com.au
Website: www.kosherfoodcentre.com.au
Supervision: KAWA
Kosher Butchery, Bakery, Patisserie, Deli and grocer.

SYNAGOGUES
Orthodox
Chabad House
396 Alexander Drive, Dianella 6062
Telephone: (8) 9275-4912

Dianella Shule
68 Woodrow Avenue, Yokine 6060
Telephone: (8) 9375-1276

Northern Suburbs Congregation
4 Vernon Street, Noranda 6062
Telephone: (8) 9275-5932

Perth Hebrew Congregation
Freedman Road, Menora 6050
Telephone: (8) 9271-0539
Fax: (8) 9271-9455
Email: phc@theperthshule.asn.au
Website: www.theperthshule.asn.au
Also has a mikvah

Reform
Temple David
34 Clifton Crescent, Mt Lawley 6050
Telephone: (8) 9271-1485
Fax: (8) 9272-2827
Email: terndavid@iinet.net.au
Website: www.templedavid.org.au

AUSTRIA

The arrival of Jews in this area of Europe (probably with the Romans) was more than one thousand years ago. The community was expelled from Austria between 1420 and 1421, but Jews were allowed to return in 1451. The Jews were granted their own quarter of Vienna in 1624, but were expelled again in 1670. The economy declined after the expulsion, and so they were asked to return.

It was not until 1782 that the situation became more stable when Joseph II began lifting the anti-Jewish decrees that his mother, Maria Theresa, had imposed on her Jewish subjects. The Jews received equal rights in 1848 and, in 1867, legal and other prohibitions were lifted.

Anti-semitism did continue, however, and many influential anti-semitic publications were available in Vienna and were keenly read by many people, including the young Adolf Hitler. After the First World War Austria lost its empire (which included Czech lands and Galicia, which had a very large Jewish community), and the Jewish population fell accordingly. At the time of the Nazi take-over in 1938, 200,000 Jews lived in the country. Some 70,000 were killed in the Holocaust, the rest having escaped or hidden.

Today there are several synagogues in Vienna. The city has an active Ultra-Orthodox community and kosher food is available. There are prayer rooms in some provincial cities.

Visitors to Vienna should not miss the new Jewish Museum opened in 2001. It combines Rachel Whitereads memorial, the museum of medieval Jewish life and details of the excavation of a medieval synagogue built around the middle of the thirteenth century.

GMT +1 hours
Country calling code: **(+43)**
Total population: **8,086,000**
Jewish population: **10,000**
Emergency telephone: **(Police–133)** **(Fire–122)** **(Ambulance–144)**
Electricity voltage: **220**

BADEN

CEMETERIES
Jewish Cemetery
Halsriegelstrasse 4
Contains some 3,000 graves. (Keys to be obtained from the Jewish Community.)

SYNAGOGUES
Orthodox
Judische Gemeinde Baden
Grabengasse 14, POB 149A-2500
Telephone: (2252) 210-6767
Fax: (2252) 217-0768
Email: synagogenverein@gmx.at
Website: www.synagogenverein.at
Kosher meals are provided by the Jewish community on Shabbatot and Chagim.

EISENSTADT

CEMETERIES
Old Cemetery
The old cemetery, closed around 1875, contains the grave of Rav Meir Eisenstaat (Maharam Esh), who died in 1744. To this day it is the scene of pilgrimages, particularly on the anniversary of his death. Keys to the cemetery are with the porter of the local hospital, which adjoins the old cemetery.

MUSEUMS
Austrian Jewish Museum
Unterbergstrasse 6
Telephone: (2682) 65145
Fax: (2682) 65145; 65144
Email: info@oejudmus.or.at
The museum now also comprises the restored private synagogue of Samson Wertheimer, Habsburg court Jew and Chief Rabbi of Hungary (1658–1724). The museum is open daily except Monday from 10 am to 5 pm. The Eruv Arch, spanning Unterbergstrasse, is at the end near the Esterhazy Palace. The road chain was used in former times to prevent vehicular traffic on Shabbat and Yom Tov.

GRAZ
Graz is considered one of the oldest Jewish communities in Austria. There has been a self-contained Jewish quarter in Graz since 1142. In November 1938 (Kristallnacht) the synagogue was burnt and the Jewish community was expelled.

The new synagogue, consecrated in November 2000, was partially rebuilt using bricks from the old synagogue.

Graz was designated a European City of Culture for the year 2003.

SYNAGOGUES
Jewish Religious Community Synagogue
David-Herzog-Pltz 1 A-8020
Telephone: (316) 712-468
Fax: (316) 720-433
Email: office@ikg-graz.at
Website: www.ikg-graz.at

HINTERGLEMM

HOTELS
Hotel Knappenhof
Dorfstrasse 140 A574
Telephone: 6541-6497
Fax: 6541-64976

INNSBRUCK

COMMUNITY ORGANISATIONS
Community Centre
Sillgasse 15
Telephone: (512) 586-892

KOBERSDORF

CEMETERIES

Jewish Cemetery
Waldgasse

The keys of the cemetery on the Lampelberg are with Mr Piniel , Waldgasse 25 (one of the two houses to the left of the cemetery) and Mr Grässing, Haydngasse 4.

LINZ

COMMUNITY ORGANISATIONS

Community Centre
Bethlehemstrasse 26
Telephone: (732) 779-805

SALZBURG

The Salzburg community dates back to 803 when Archbishop Arno summoned a Jewish doctor to set up a practice in the town.

Synagogue and Mikva

Lasserstrasse 8 A-5020
Telephone: (662) 872228
Fax: (662) 872228/820175
Email: office@ikg-salzburg.at
Website: www.ikg-salzburg.at
Community synagogue and mikva are to be found at the same address

VIENNA

Vienna was in the past the most important centre for Central European Jews. From 180,000 Jews in the 1930s, there are about 1,000 Jews (mainly elderly) in Vienna today. Professor Freud's clinic is a popular attraction, and the Jewish Museum of Vienna gives much information on the history of the Jews.

BED AND BREAKFAST

Pension Lichtenstein
Grosse Schiffgasse 19 1020
Telephone: (1) 216-8498
Fax: (1) 214-7690
Website: www.pension-lichtenstein.at

The pension consists of suites .Visits should be arranged in advance as there is no front desk reception. The key is kept in the owner's office around the block.

BOOKSELLERS

Chabad-Simcha-Center
Hollandstrasse 10 1020
Telephone: (1) 216-2924

BUTCHERS

B. Ainhorn
Stadtgutgasse 7 1020
Telephone: (1) 214-5621
Supervision: Rabbi David Grunfeld
Also supplies 'fast food'

Rebenwurzel
Grose Mohrengasse 19 1010
Telephone: (1) 216-6640
Supervision: Rabbi Chaim Stern

CEMETERIES

Floridsdorfer Cemetery
Ruthnergasse 28 1210
Those wishing to visit must first obtain a permit from the community centre

Rossauer Cemetery
Seegasse 9 1090
This is the oldest Jewish cemetery in Vienna, dating from the sixteenth century. It has now been restored after being devasted by the Nazis and is open daily from 8 am to 3 pm. Access is via the front entrance of the municipal home for the aged at Seegasse 9–11, but a permit must first be obtained from the community centre.

Vienna Central Cemetery
Simmeringer Haupstr. 244 A-1110
Telephone: (1) 531-04-904
The Jewish section (the only one still in use) is at Gate 4 and there is an older Jewish part at Gate 1.

Whringer Cemetery
Semperstrasse 64a 1180
Those wishing to visit must first obtain a permit from the community centre

CONTACT INFORMATION

Jewish Community Centre
Seitenstettengasse 4
Telephone: (1) 531-04104
Fax: (1) 531-04108
Email: office@ikg-wien.at

Jewish Welcome Service Vienna
Stephansplatz 10 1010
Telephone: (1) 533-2730
Fax: (1) 533-4098
Mobile Phone: 6645034656
Email: jewish.welcome@verkehrsbuero.at
Website: www.jewish-welcome.at
Open Monday to Friday 9.00 am to 5.30 pm

DOCUMENTATION CENTRE

Documentation Centre of Austrian Resistance
Old City Hall, Wipplingerstrasse 8 1010
Telephone: (1) 534-36-90319
Fax: (1) 534-36-90319
Email: office@doew.at
Website: www.doew.at
Hours of opening: Monday to Thursday 9 am to 5 pm.

Documentation Centre of Union of Jewish Victims of the Nazis
Salztorgasse 6 A-1010
Telephone: (1) 533-9131
Fax: (1) 535-0397

EMBASSY
Embassy Israel
Anton-Frankgasse 20 1180
Telephone: (1) 476-460

GROCERIES
Gross-Import-Wien
Nicklegasse 1 A-1020
Telephone: (1) 214-0607
Fax: (1) 214-7690

Koscherland
Kleine Sperlgasse 7
Telephone: (1) 212-8169

Kosher Supermarket & Shatnes Laboratory
Hollandstrasse 7 1020
Telephone: (1) 269-9675
Supervision: Rabbi Abraham Yonah Schwartz

Ohel Moshe Kosher Supermarket
1020 Wien, Hollandstrasse 10 A-1020
Telephone: (1) 216-9675
Fax: (1) 214-8708

Rafael Malkov
Tempelgasse 6, Ferdinandstrasse 2 A-1020
Telephone: (1) 214-8394

HOTELS
Hotel Stefanie
Taborstrasse 12 1020
Telephone: (1) 211-500
Fax: (1) 211-50160
Email: stefanie@schick-hotels.com
Website: www.schick-hotels.com
Central organisation: Schick Hotels
Four star hotel with kosher breakfast on request

MEDIA
Newspapers
Die Gemeinde
Telephone: (1) 531-04-271
Fax: (1) 531-04-279
Monthly.

MIKVAOT
Agudas Yisroel
Tempelgasse 3 (Entrance from Czerningasse 4)
1020
Telephone: (1) 214-9973

MONUMENT
Nameless Library
Judenplatz
Rachel Whiteread's monument, opened in 2001, depicts shelves of 9,000 books with their spines turned to the inside. The names of the concentration camps in which Austrian Jews were killed are engraved around the base. Underneath the memorial one can view the ruins of a synagogue razed in 1421.

MUSEUMS
Jewish Museum Vienna
Dorotheergasse 11 A-1010
Telephone: (1) 535-0341 ext. 112
Fax: (1) 535-0424
Email: susanna.koncar@jmw.at
Website: www.jmw.at
Hours: Sunday to Friday, 10 am to 6 pm; Thursday, 10 am to 8 pm. Cafeteria and bookshop on site. The cafeteria is not supervised.

Museum Judenplatz
Judenplatz 8 A-1010
Telephone: (1) 535-0431
Fax: (1) 535-0424
Email: info@jmw.at
Website: www.jmw.at
A memorial to the Austrian victims of the Holocaust. A place of remembrance was created that is unique in Europe. It combines Rachel Whiereads memorial (Nameless Library, see above) and the excavations of a medieval synagogue with the Museum on Medieval Jewish Life to form a commemorative whole. Opening hours 10am to 6 pm, Friday 10 am to 2 pm. Special guided tours for groups by prior arrangement only.

Sigmund Freud Museum
Berggasse 19 1090
Telephone: (1) 319-1596
Fax: (1) 317-0279
Email: office@freud-museum.at
Website: www.freud-museum.at
Hours: March to June 9 am to 5 pm, July to September 9 am to 6 pm

RESTAURANTS
Dairy
Milk'n'Honey
Kleine Spperlgasse 7 1020
Telephone: (1) 219-6886 / 218 0565
Fax: (1) 012197292
Email: info@kosherland.at
Website: www.kosherland.at
Supervision: R.J Schartz

Meat
Restaurant Alef- Alef
Seitenstettengasse 2 A-1010
Telephone: (1) 535-2530
Fax: (1) 535-2530
Website: www.alef-alef.at

Snack Bar
Berl Ainhorn Koscher Fleisch und Imbiss
Gross Stadtgutgasse 7 1020
Telephone: (1) 214-5621

SITE
Mauthausen Memorial Site
Telephone: (1) 723-82269
Fax: (1) 723-83696

Those wishing to visit the site should contact the Jewish Welcome Service

SYNAGOGUES
Orthodox
Agudas Yisroel
Grûnangergasse 1 1010
Telephone: (1) 512-8331
Tempelgasse 3 1020
Telephone: (1) 216-9973

Machsike Haddas
GroBe Mohreng 19 A-1020
Telephone: (1) 216-0679

Misrachi
Judenplatz 8 1010
Telephone: (1) 532-8301
Fax: (1) 214-8010
Email: office@daleno.at
Website: www.misrachi.at

Ohel Moshe
Lilienbrunngasse 19 1020
Telephone: (1) 216-8864

Rambam
Bauernfeldgasse 4 A-1190
Email: office@maimonides.at

Seitenstettengasse Synagogue
Seitenstettengasse 4 1010
Telephone: (1) 531-040
Fax: (1) 531-04108
Email: office@ikg-wien.at
Website: www.ikg-wien.at
Built in 1824-26 and partly destroyed during the Nazi period, this beautiful synagogue was restored by the community in 1988. For information about guided tours contact the Community Centre offices.

Sephardi Centre
Tempelgasse 7 1020
Telephone: (1) 214-3097

Shomre Haddas
Glasergasse 17 1090

Thora Etz Chayim
Grosse Schiffgasse 8 1020
Telephone: (1) 214-5206
Fax: (1) 216-2032
Email: Samikern@csi.com

Progressive
Or Chadasch
Robertgasse 2 1020
Telephone: (1) 967-1329

AZERBAIJAN

Azerbaijan has a remarkable Jewish history, which can be better explored now that the country is independent from the former Soviet Union. The Tats (mountain Jews) believe that their ancestors arrived in Azerbaijan at the time of Nebuchadnezzar. They lived in several mountain villages and adopted the customs of their non-Jewish neighbours. They spoke a north Iranian language known as Judeo-Tat, to which they added some Hebrew words. The Soviets clamped down on their way of life after 1928, changing the alphabet of their language from Hebrew to Latin, and then in 1938, to Cyrillic. Some of their synagogues were also closed down. Zionist feeling is high, with almost 30,000 emigrating to Israel since 1989.

The other strand in Azerbaijan's Jewish population are the Ashkenasis who arrived in the nineteenth century from Poland and other countries to the west.

The community has some 10–15 organisations in the capital Baku, including Zionist and youth groups. The largest synagogue in Baku is the Tat synagogue, but there are also Ashkenazi and Georgian synagogues. Synagogues are found in other towns.

GMT +5 hours
Country calling code: (+94)
Total population: **7,625,000**
Jewish population: **10,000**

BAKU
EMBASSY
Embassy of Israel
Stroiteley Prospect 1

SYNAGOGUES
Mountain Jews
Dmitrova Street 39 370014
Telephone: (12) 892-232-8867

Ashkenazi
Synagogue
Pervomoskaya Steet 271
Telephone: (12) 892-294-1571

KUBA
SYNAGOGUES
Kuba Synagogue
Kolkhoznaya Street 46

BAHAMAS

Luis de Torres, the official interpreter for Columbus, was the first Jew in the Bahamas, as well as being one of the first Europeans there. He was a *Converso*, a 'secret Jew' who officially had converted to Catholicism, but who practised Judaism in private. The British arrived in 1620 and eventually gained control of the islands. Although there was a Jewish attorney-general and chief justice in the islands in the eighteenth century, few Jews settled there until the twentieth century, coming from eastern Europe and the UK after the First World War, and settling in the capital Nassau,

There are approximately 100 Jewish residents in the Bahamas. However, it is estimated that about 350,000 Jews visit the islands each year as tourists. There are congregations in Nassau and Freeport. Both cities have Jewish cemeteries, that in Nassau being more historic.

GMT -5 hours
Country calling code: (+1242)
Total population: 289,000
Jewish population: 300
Emergency telephone: (Police–919) (Fire–919) (Ambulance–919)
Electricity voltage: 120

FREEPORT
SYNAGOGUES
Freeport Hebrew Congregation
Luis de Torres Synagogue, East Sunrise Highway, PO Box F41761
Telephone: 373-2008 and 373-1041 Telephone: 373-4025 (President: Geoff Hurst)
Fax: 871-5528

NASSAU
SYNAGOGUES
Progressive
Bahamas Jewish Congregation
POB CB-11002
Telephone: 363-2305

BARBADOS

Jewish history in Barbados starts in 1628, a year after the British first settled there. Jewish settlers came from Brazil, Surinam,

England and Germany, and were mainly Sephardi. The first synagogue was established in the capital Bridgetown in 1654. Early settlers were engaged in cultivating sugar and coffee.

The Jewish population was well treated, and in 1831 Barbados was the first British possession in which Jews were granted full political emancipation. Despite a largely favourable climate, the community suffered losses from hurricanes, which destroyed sugar plantations, and the Jewish population fell to 70 by 1848. In 1925 no Jews remained, but a new influx (30 families escaping Nazism) came shortly after.

The synagogue was restored in 1987, and postage stamps were produced which commemorated its restoration. The Jewish population remains small, but it was a group of Barbadian Jews who founded the Caribbean Jewish Congress. The Jewish cemetery, one of the oldest in the Americas, is now back in use.

GMT -4 hours
Country calling code: (+1246)
Total population: 262,000
Jewish population: Under 100
Electricity voltage: 110

BRIDGETOWN
COMMUNITY ORGANISATIONS
Barbados Jewish Community
PO Box 651, Bridgetown
Telephone: 427-0703
Fax: 436-8807

Caribbean Jewish Congress
PO Box 1331, Bridgetown
Telephone: 436-8163
Fax: 437-4992

Synagogue Restoration Project
PO Box 256, Bridgetown
Telephone: 432-0840
Fax: 432-2147
Email: altman@caribsurf.com
Local inquiries to Henry Altman, Little Mallows, Sandy Lane, St. James. Tel: 132-6462.

SYNAGOGUES
Nidhe Israel
Synagogue Lane
Telephone: 427-7611

Services are held Friday evenings at 7 pm at True Blue ,
Rockley New Road , Christ Church, during the summer, and
at the synagogue at 7.30 pm in winter.

Shaare Tzedek
Rockley New Road, Christ Church
Friday 7.30 pm

BELARUS

For the adventurous traveller, who has a keen interest in Jewish history, Belarus (also known as White Russia) makes an interesting and unusual destination. Situated on the western side of the former Soviet Union, this largely flat country borders Poland and Lithuania to the west, Ukraine to the south and Russia to the east. Belarus finally achieved independence in 1991, and within its present borders are many towns and villages of Jewish interest, such as Minsk, Pinsk and Grodno. One of the most famous villages in Belarus is Lubavitch, a hamlet in the far east of the country, near the Russian border, where the world-wide Lubavitch movement had its origins.

The majority of this region's Jews died in the Holocaust and although emigration to Israel is high, the community is slowly rebuilding itself after decades of Soviet control. Americans and Israelis are contributing rabbis to help in this revival, and Jewish schools have been set up. Yiddish is used far more here than in other parts of the former USSR.

GMT +2 hours
Country calling code: (+375)
Total population: 10,179,000
Jewish population: 30,000
Emergency telephone: (Police–03) (Fire–03)
(Ambulance–03)
Electricity voltage: 220

BARANOVICHI
COMMUNITY ORGANISATIONS
Jewish Community of Baranovichi
President, Lubov Lvova, 58-48 Kurova St.,
Baranovitch 285320

BOBRUISK
Jewish Community of Bobruisk
President, Boris Gelfand, 31 Komsomolskaya St.,
Bobruisk 213826

SYNAGOGUES
Bobruisk Synagogue
Engels St.

BORISOV
COMMUNITY ORGANISATIONS
Jewish Community of Borisov
President, Boris Gitlin, 1-37 Stekolnaya S., Borisov
222120

SYNAGOGUES
Borisov Synagogue
Trud St.

BREST
COMMUNITY ORGANISATIONS
Jewish Community of Brest
President, Arkady Blyacher, 29-30 Sovetskoy
Konstitutzi St., Brest 224032

SYNAGOGUES
Brest Synagogue
Narodnaya St.

GOMEL
COMMUNITY ORGANISATIONS
Jewish Community of Gomel
President, Mikhael Shechtman, 21a-27 Pobedi St.,
Gomel 246017

CONTACT INFORMATION
Rosa Sorkina
Telephone: (23) 252-5808

SYNAGOGUES
Gomel Synagogue
13 Sennaya St.

GORKI
COMMUNITY ORGANISATION
Jewish Community of Gorki
President, Vladimir Livshitz
4-41 Sovetskaya St., 213410

GRODNO
COMMUNITY ORGANISATIONS
Jewish Community of Grodno
President, Yuri Boyarski, 59aB. Troyskaya St.,
230023

CONTACT INFORMATION
Mishas Kemerov
Telephone: (15) 2313-798
SYNAGOGUES
Menorah Jewish Community
Blk 43, Flat 37 230009
Telephone: (15) 2313-798
Email: sh10@gru.grodno.by

KALINKOVITCH
COMMUNITY ORGANISATIONS
Jewish Community of Kalinkovitch
President, Yaakov Erenburg, 8-31 Komsomolskaya
St., Kalinkovitch 24771

KORBIN
Jewish Community of Korbin
President, Elenora Sacharuk, 38-4 Trudovaya St.,
Korbin 225860

MINSK
Jewish of Minsk (Chabad Lubavitch Or Avner)
Chief Rabbi of Minsk Yossef Gruzman, 22 Kroptkina
St., Minsk 220002
Telephone: (17) 23-42-273
Fax: (17) 22-36-79

Union of Jewish Communities and
Organisations of Belarus
22 Kroptkinav St., Minsk 220002
Email: beiarus@fjc.ru

EMBASSY
Embassy of Israel
Partizanski Prospekt 6A 220002
Telephone: (17) 2304-444

MEMORIAL
Minsk Jewish Memorial
This memorial devoted to 5,000 Jews killed by the Nazis on
Purim 1942 was erected in 1946 and is the only one in
what was the USSR devoted to the Holocaust which
displays Yiddish writing.

SYNAGOGUES
Minsk Synagogue
22 Kropotkina Street
Telephone: (17) 2558-270
13b Daumana Street

Progressive
Association of Progressive Jewish
Congrations in Belarus
Per K Chyornogo 4, apt 18, Simach 220012
Telephone: (17) 2846-089
Fax: (17) 2662-928
Email: simcha@open.by

MOGHILEV
COMMUNITY ORGANISATIONS
Jewish Community of Mogilev
President, Naum Yoffei, 28-11 30 Let Pobedi St.,
Mogilev 221011
Moghilev Jewish sites need care
SYNAGOGUES
Moghilev Synagogue
1 2nd Krutoy La.

MOZIR
COMMUNITY ORGANISATIONS
Jewish Community of Mozir
President, Grigory Skolnukov, 30-4 Prititzkova St.,
Mozir 247760

ORSHA
Jewish Community of Orsha
President, Ysaak Gurevitsh, 20-20 pr. Tekstilshikov,
Orsha 210030
SYNAGOGUES
Orsha Synagogue.
Nogrin St.

OSIPOVITSHI
COMMUNITY ORGANISATIONS
Jewish Community of Osipovitshi
President, Sarra Utevskaya, 43-2 Tshumakova St.,
Osipovitshi 213760

PINSK
Jewish Community of Pinsk
President, Aleksander Lapidus, 140-22 Parkovaya
St., Pinsk 225710

POLOTOSK
Jewish Community of Polotosk
President, Filip Zavt, 18-32 Gogolya St., Polotosk
211401

RECHITZA
Jewish Community of Retshitza
President, Alla Shkon, 22-113 Naumova St.,
Retshitza 247500
SYNAGOGUES
Rechitza Synagogue
120 Lunacharsky St.

SLOTSK
COMMUNITY ORGANISATIONS
Jewish Community of Slotsk
President, Raisa Titshina, 11-27 Parizhskoy
Kommuni St., Slotsk 223610

VITEBSK
Jewish Community of Vitebsk
President, Arkady Shulman, 4-167 pr. Probedi
Vitebsk 210038

BELGIUM

Jewish settlement in the area now called Belgium dates back to the thirteenth century, and suffered a similar fate to other medieval European Jewish communities, taking the blame for the Black Death and suffering expulsions. The Sephardim were the first to resettle in Belgium, mainly in Antwerp. After independence in 1830, conditions for the Jews improved and more Jews began to settle there. The diamond centre of Antwerp later developed rapidly, attracting many Jews from eastern Europe.

By 1939 the Jewish population had grown to 100,000, a large proportion of whom were refugees hoping to escape to America. Some succeeded, but many became trapped after the German invasion. Some 25,000 Belgian Jews were deported and killed in the Holocaust. A national monument listing the names of the victims stands in Anderlecht in Brussels.

The present Jewish population includes a large Hassidic community in Antwerp, where there are some 30 synagogues. There are also more than ten synagogues in Brussels. There are Jewish schools in Antwerp and Brussels, and Jewish newspapers.

GMT +1 hours
Country calling code: (+32)
Total population: 10,188,000
Jewish population: 33,000
Emergency telephone: (Police–101) (Fire–101) (Ambulance–101)
Electricity voltage: 220

ANTWERP
Seen by some as the last shtetl in Europe, Antwerp is a well-known Hassidic centre. Antwerp's Jewish population (15,000) has one of the highest numbers of Ultra-Orthodox in the Diaspora. Served by 30 synagogues (many of them small shtiebels), there are also kosher restaurants and food shops.

BAKERIES
Gottesfeld
Mercatorstraat 20
Telephone: (3) 230-0003

Kleinblatt
Provinciestraat 206
Telephone: (3) 233-7513; 226-0018
Fax: (3) 232-0920

Steinmetz
Lange Kievitstraat 64
Telephone: (3) 234-0947

BOOKSELLERS
I. Menczer
Simonstraat 40
Telephone: (3) 232-3026

N. Seletsky
Lange Kievitstraat 70
Telephone: (3) 232-6966
Fax: (3) 226-9446

BUTCHERS
Berkowitz
Isabellalei 9
Telephone: (3) 218-5111

Fruchter
Simonstraat 22
Telephone: (3) 233-1811; 1557
Fax: (3) 231-3903

Kosher King
Lange Kievitstraat 40
Telephone: (3) 233-6749
Isabellalei 7
Telephone (3) 239-4189

Mandelovics
Isabellalei 96
Telephone: (3) 218-4779

Moszkowitz
Lange Kievitstraat 47
Telephone: (3) 232-6349
Fax: (3) 226-0471

CONTACT INFORMATION
Machsika Hadass (Israelitische Orthodoxe Gemeente)
Jacob Jacobsstraat 22
Telephone: (3) 233-5567

Shomre Hadass (Israelitische Gemeente)
Terlistraat 35 2018
Telephone: (3) 232-0187
Fax: (3) 226-3123
Email: shomre-hadas@net4all.be
Website: www.members.net4all.be/shomre-hadas

DELICATESSEN
Weingarten
Lange Kievitstraat 124
Telephone: (3) 233-2828

GROCERIES
Col-Bo
Jacob Jacobsstraat 40
Telephone: (3) 234-1212

Grosz-Modern
Terliststraat 28
Telephone: (3) 232-4626

Stark
Mercatorstraat 24
Telephone: (3) 230-2520

Super Discount
Belgielei 104-108
Telephone: (3) 239-0666

Superette Lamoriniere
Lamboriniere Sraat 199
Telephone: (3) 239-3110
Fax: (3) 281-3205

MEDIA
Newspapers
Belgisch Israelitisch Weekblad
Pelikaanstraat 106-108 2018
Telephone: (3) 233-7094
Fax: (3) 233-4810
Email: red@biweekblad.be

MIKVAOT
Machsike Hadass
Steenbokstraat 22
Telephone: (3) 239-7588

MUSEUMS
Plantin-Moretus Museum
Vrijdagmarkt (nr Groenplaats)
Telephone: (3) 233-0688
Open daily (except Monday). Contains examples of early Jewish printing, such as the famous Polyglot Bible.

RESTAURANTS
Dairy
USA Pizza
118a Isabellalei
Telephone: (3) 281-2300
Supervision: Machzikey Hadas
Take away option

Meat
Blue Lagoon
Lange Herentalsetraat 70
Telephone: (3) 226-0114
Supervision: Machsike Hadass
Also sells chocolates.

Hoff'y s
Lange Kievitstraat 52
Telephone: (3) 234-3535
Fax: (3) 226-0282
Email: hoffys@pandora.be

Jacob
Lange Kieitstraat 49
Telephone: (3) 233-1124

Lamalo
Appelmanstraat 21
Telephone: (3) 213-2200

Vegetarian
Time Out
Lange Herentalse Straat 58 2018
Telephone: (3) 32-3-281-2300
Fax: (3) 32-3-281-2300
Email: time-out@pandora.be

SYNAGOGUES
Great Synagogue Romi Goldmuntz
Van Den Nestlei 1
Telephone: (3) 232-0187

Sephardic Synagogue
Hovenierstraat 31
Telephone: (3) 232-5339
Built in 1913 this synagogue is located in the middle of the Diamond district

Orthodox
Machsike Hadass
Jacob Jacobsstraat 22 2018
Telephone: (3) 232-0021: 233-5567
Fax: (3) 233-8797
Email: machsike.hadass@antwerpen.be

Oosten Synagogue
Oostenstraat 43
Telephone: (3) 230-9246

TOURS
Toerisme Antwerpen
Grote Markt 15 2000
Telephone: (3) 232-0103
Fax: (3) 231-1937
Email: visit@antwerpen.be
Website: www.visitantwerpen.be

ARLON
SYNAGOGUES
Arlon Synagogue
Rue St Jean 6700
Telephone: (63) 217-985
Fax: (63) 217-985
Email: jeanclaude.jacob1@skynet.be
Website: www.site.voila.fr/synagogarlon
Established 1863. The secretary, J.C. Jacob, can be reached at 11 rue des Martyrs, 6700 Arlon. A monument has been erected in the new Jewish cemetery to the memory of the Jews of Arlon deported and massacred by the Nazis. The old Jewish cemetry is the oldest in Belgium.

BRUSSELS
The capital of Belgium is less well endowed with kosher facilities than Antwerp, although there are 23,000 Jews living in the city. The headquarters of the European Union of Jewish Students is based there. The Anderlecht area has a monument to the Belgian Holocaust victims and a memorial to Jews who fought in the Belgian Resistance.

BAKERIES
Bornstein
62 rue de Sude, St Gilles
Telephone: (2) 537-1679

BOOKSELLERS
Colbo
121 rue du Brabant
Telephone: (2) 217-2620

Menorah
12 Ave. J. Voldens 1060
Telephone: (2) 537-5073

BUTCHERS
Lanxner
121 rue de Brabant 1030
Telephone: (2) 217-2620
Supervision: Rabbinate of the Jewish Orthodox Community of Brussels
Grocery: Hours: Sun, Mon, Fri 8.30 am to 1.00 pm. Tues 8.30 am to 6.00 pm. Wed–Thurs 8.30 am to 7.30 pm

COMMUNITY ORGANISATIONS
Centre Communautaire Laic Juif
Yitzhak Rabin Center, 52 rue Hotel des Monnaies
1060 Brussels
Telephone: (2) 543-0270
Fax: (2) 543-0271
Email: info@cclj.be
Website: www.cclj.be

EMBASSY
Embassy of Israel
40 Avenue de l'Observatoire 1180
Telephone: (2) 373-5500

GROCERIES
Hod Taim
51 Boulevard Jamar
Telephone: (2) 527-1832

MEDIA
Newspapers
Centrale
91 Av. Henri Jaspar
Telephone: (2) 538-8036
Monthly

Fax de Jerusalem
68 Ave Ducptiaux
Telephone: (2) 538-5673
Fax: (2) 534-0236
Email: alyabelgique@skynet.be
Weekly

Kehilatenou
2 rue Joseph Dupont B-1000
Telephone: (2) 512-4334
Fax: (2) 512-9237
Quarterly

Regards
52 rue Hotel des Monnaies, 1060
Telephone: (2) 543-0281
Fax: (2) 537-5565
Email: Regards@cclj.be
Website: www.cclj.be/Regards
Fortnightly

Radio
Radio Judaica (Jewish Radio) FM 90.2
Jewish interest programs 24-hours a day

MIKVAOT
Machsike Hadass
67a rue de la Clinique
Telephone: (2) 537-1439

MUSEUMS
Jewish Musem
74 Av de Stalingrad, Rue des Minimes 21 1000
Telephone: (2) 512-1963
Fax: (2) 513-4859
Email: info@mjb-jmb.org
Website: www.mjb-jmb.org
Hours: Mon-Thurs 10 00am-5 00pm.
Sunday 10.00 am to 5 pm. Friday 10.00 am-1 pm, Closed Saturday and Jewish holidays.

RELIGIOUS ORGANISATIONS
Communaute Israelite de Bruxelles
2 rue Joseph Dupont B-1000
Telephone: (2) 512-4334
Fax: (2) 512-9237

Machsike Hadass (Communaut Isralite Orthodoxe de Bruxelles)
67a rue la Clinique
Telephone: (2) 524-1486; 521-1289

RESTAURANTS
Chez Gilles
Rue de la Clinique 21 1070
Telephone: (2) 522-1828
Open from 9 am-5 pm.

El Assado
Roosendael 154
Telephone: (2) 346-3487

Restaurant Seven-Seventy
87 Avenue du Roi 1060
Telephone: (2) 537-1158

Meat
Athenee Maimonide
Boulevard Poincarte 67
Telephone: (2) 523-6336

SITE
National Monument to the Jewish Martyrs of Belgium
Corner rue Emile Carpentier and rue Goujons,
Square of the Jewish Martyrs, Anderlecht
This monument commemorates the Jews of Belgium who were deported to concentration camps and killed by the Nazis during the Second World War. The names of all 23,838 are engraved on the monument.

SYNAGOGUES
Brussels Airport
Situated in the transit lounge

Conservative
Communaute Israelite Liberale de Belgique Synagogue Beth Hillel
Rue des Primeurs 80 1190
Telephone: (2) 332-2528
Fax: (2) 376-7219
Email: info@beth-hillel.org
Website: www.beth-hillel.org

Orthodox
Adath Israel
126 rue Rogier 1030
Telephone: (2) 241-1664
Near city center

Ahavat Reim
73 rue de Thy
Telephone: (2) 648-3837

Beth Itshak
115 Ave du Roi 1060
Telephone: (2) 538-3374; 520-1359

Communaute Israelite d'Uccle-Forest
11 Avenue de Messidor 1180
Telephone: (2) 32-2-344-6094
Fax: (2) 32-2-344-6094
Email: info@maale.org
Website: www.maale.org

The Great Synagogue
32 rue de la Regence 1000
Telephone: (2) 512-4334
Fax: (2) 512-9237
The synagogue built in 1878 survived the occupation.

Sephardi
Synagogue Simon and Lina Haim
47 rue du Pavilion 1030
Telephone: (2) 215-0525
Fax: (2) 215-0242
This is a memorial to the Jews deported from Rhodes, Greece

CHARLEROI
COMMUNITY ORGANISATIONS
Community Centre
56 rue Pige-au-Croly

GHENT
CONTACT INFORMATION
Jacques Bloch
Veldstraat 60
Telephone: (9) 225-7085
Email: blochjb@yahoo.com
The treasurer of the community will be happy to meet English-speaking visitors. As the community is very small one, there is no permanent synagogue. Services are held on the High Holy Days.

KNOKKE
SYNAGOGUES
Knokke Synagogue
30 Van Bunnenlaan
Telephone: (50) 61-0372
Also has a mikva

LIÈGE
COMMUNITY ORGANISATIONS
Community Centre
12 Quai Marcellis 4020

MUSEUMS
Musee Serge Kruglanski
19 rue L. Frédéricq 4020
Telephone: (4) 438-043
Fax: (4) 224-4360

SYNAGOGUES
Liège Synagogue
19 rue L. Frédéricq 4020
Telephone: (4) 436-106

MONS
CONTACT INFORMATION
SHAPE
Telephone: (65) 445-808; 444-809
Nearby, at Casteau, the International Chapel of NATO's Supreme Headquarters Allied Powers Europe, includes a small Jewish community, established 1951, that holds regular services. Call for further information.

OSTEND
SYNAGOGUES
Israelitic Community Ostend
Philip Van Maastrichtplein 3
Services during July and August, also Rosh Hashana and Yom Kippour. Inquiries to Mrs Liliane Wulfowicz, Parklaan 21, B-8400, Tel: (59) 802-405 or Mr Armand Benizri 477-277223

WATERLOO
SYNAGOGUES
Traditionalist
Communaute Isralite de Waterloo et du Brabant Sud (CIWABS)
140 Avenue Belle-Vue, 1410
Telephone: (2) 354-6833
Fax: (2) 514-5977
Regular services Shabbat and Festivals; English speaking visitors very welcome; tel 351-3631 (evenings).

BERMUDA

Jews have lived in Bermuda since the seventeenth century, but the first formal congregation was not established until the twentieth century.

The resident Jewish population is very small, but the transient population (of tourists largely from the USA, Britain and Canada) is much greater. There is a Jew's Bay but whether this is merely named to balance a nearby Christian Bay or has some other origin is not known.

GMT -4 hours
Country calling code: (+1441)
Total population: 60,000
Jewish population: Under 100
Emergency telephone: (Police–112) (Fire–113) (Ambulance–115)
Electricity voltage: 110

HAMILTON
COMMUNITY ORGANISATIONS
Jewish Community of Bermuda
PO Box HM 1793 HM05
Telephone: 291-1785
Website: www.jcb.bm

BOLIVIA

The history of the Jews of Bolivia dates back to the Spanish colonial period. *Conversos* (converts to Christianity who practised Judaism in secret) came with the Spaniards in the seventeenth century.

The main influx of Jews occurred in 1905 with immigrants from eastern Europe, but the number entering Bolivia was much smaller than that going to other South American countries. In 1933 there were only some 30 Jewish families. At the end of the decade, however, there was a small increase in Jewish immigration as German and Austrian Jews fled from Europe. Ironically, the Jewish community did not grow very much, even though the government granted every Jew an entry visa.

Many Jews started to leave Bolivia in the 1950s because of political instability and the apparent lack of educational opportunities. The present-day community has a central organisation known as the Circulo Israelita de Bolivia.

GMT -4 hours
Country calling code: (+591)
Total population: 8,140,000
Jewish population: 500
Electricity voltage: 110/220

COCHABAMBA
COMMUNITY ORGANISATIONS
Associaciacion Israelita de Cochabamba
PO Box 349, Calle Valdivieso

SYNAGOGUES
Synagogue
Calle Junin y Calle Colombia, Casilla 349

LA PAZ
CONTACT INFORMATION
Jabad Lubavitch Bolivia
Calle 16 #8, Second Floor, Achumani Telephone: (2) 21-40963

SYNAGOGUES

Circulo Israelita de Bolivia
Obrajes, Calle 1 No 307, PO Box 1545
Telephone: (2) 2785083
Fax: (2) 2785371
Email: cibolp@acelerate.com
Representative body of Bolivian Jewry. All La Paz
organisations are affiliated to it. Service Shabbat morning
only.

Communidad Israelita Synagogue
Calle Canada Stronguest 1846, PO Box 2198
Affiliated to the Circulo Israelita de Bolivia. Friday evening
services are held here.

TOURS

Centro Shalom
Calle Canada Stronguest 1846

SANTA CRUZ

COMMUNITY ORGANISATIONS

Centre Cruceño
Po Box 469

WIZO
Castilla 3409

BOSNIA-HERCEGOVINA

Sephardi Jews were the first to arrive in the area, in the late sixteenth century. They established a Jewish quarter in Sarajevo, and this was home for poorer Jews until the Austrians conquered the land in 1878. It was the Turks, however, who emancipated the Jews in the nineteenth century when Bosnia-Hercegovina was under Ottoman rule.

When Bosnia-Hercegovina became part of the newly formed Yugoslavia after the First World War, the community maintained its Sephardi heritage and joined the all-Yugoslav Federation of Jewish Religious Communities. The Jewish population numbered 14,000 in 1941. This number dropped sharply after the Germans conquered Yugoslavia.

After the war the survivors were joined by many who had decided to return. The Sephardi and Ashkenazi communities became unified. La Benevolencija, founded 100 years ago, is a humanitarian organisation which supported the plight of the community and became well known in the early 1990s at the time of the civil war. After the Yugoslav civil war, many made aliyah to Israel, reducing the community still further.

GMT +1 hours
Total population: **3,784,000**
Jewish population: **400**
Emergency telephone: **(Police–664 211) (Fire–93) (Ambulance–94) (emergency–94)**
Electricity voltage: 220

SARAJEVO

CEMETERIES

Kovacici
This historic Jewish cemetery is in town. Not far from the centre of town, on a hill called Vraca, there is a monument with the names of the 7,000 Jews from the area who fell victim to the Nazis.

COMMUNITY ORGANISATIONS

Sarajevo Jewish Cultural-Educational and Humanitarian Society La Benevolencija
Hamdije Kresevljakovica 59 71000
Telephone: (33) 663-472
Fax: (33) 663-473
Email: la_bene@open.net.ba
Website: www.benevolencija.eu.org

MUSEUMS

Jewish Museum
Mulamustafe Baseskije Street
This historic museum is placed in the oldest synagogue in Sarajevo, with priceless relics dating back to the expulsion from Spain .

SYNAGOGUES

Synagogue and Community Centre
Hamdije Kresevljakovica 59
Telephone: (33) 663-472
Fax: (33) 663-473
Email: la_bene@open.net.ba
Website: www.benevolencija.eu.org

TOURIST SITES

The National Museum of Bosnia and Herzegovina
Zmaja od Bosne 3
Telephone: (33) 668027; 668025
Fax: (33) -668025; 262710
Email: z.muzej@zemaljskimuzej.ba
Website: www.zemaljskimuzej.ba
The world famous Sarajevo Haggadah written around 1314 as a wedding gift to a young couple has now been fully repaired and restored. It is in a secure climate-controlled room.

BRAZIL

The first Jewish settlers in Brazil came with the Portuguese in 1500. They were mainly *Conversos*, escaping persecution in Portugal, and initially worked on the sugar plantations. In due course they played important roles as traders, artisans and plantation owners. The huge area which is called Brazil today was in the process of being conquered by the Dutch and the Portuguese. Two synagogues were opened in Recife during the 1640s when many Jews came from Holland. When the Dutch left Brazil in 1654 one of the terms of surrender allowed the Jews who had been on their side to emigrate. Many fled and some went on to found the first Jewish community in New York, then known as New Amsterdam. A seventeenth-century Mikvah was discovered in 2000 in the basement of the Tsur Israel Synagogue in Recife.

With Brazilian independence in 1822, conditions became more favourable for Jews and many came from North Africa and Europe. The majority of Jews in Brazil today, however, originate from the immigration of east European Jews in the early twentieth century. From about 6,000 Jews in 1914, the community grew to 30,000 in 1930. After 1937 Brazil refused to allow Jewish immigrants into the country, but some limited immigration managed to continue despite the restrictions.

A central organisation was established in 1951 (the CONIB), and this includes 200 various Jewish organisations. Brazilian Jews live in an atmosphere of tolerance and prosperity, and assimilation is prominent.

There are synagogues in all the major cities.

GMT -3 to -5 hours
Country calling code: (+55)
Total population: 159,884,000
Jewish population: 110,000
Emergency telephone: (**Police–147**) (**Fire–193**) (**Ambulance–192**)
Electricity voltage: 220/100

Amazonas

MANAUS

COMMUNITY ORGANISATIONS
Comite Israelita Amazonas
R. Leonardo Malcher, 630
Telephone: (92) 247-7647
Fax: (92) 233-6361

Bahia

SALVADOR

SYNAGOGUES
Sociedade Israelita da Bahia
Rue Alvaro Tiberio 60
Telephone: (71) 3321-4204
Fax: (71) 3321-6412
Email: webmail@sibahia.com.br or
sibdoal@yahoo.com.br
Community centre and Zionist organisation are at the same address

Goiás

BRASILIA

EMBASSY
Embassy of Israel
Av. das Nacoes Sul, Lote 38
Telephone: (61) 244-7675, 244-7875
Fax: (61) 244-6129

SYNAGOGUES
ACIB
Entrequadras Norte 305-306, Lote A
Telephone: (61) 273-855
Fax: (61) 366-3651
Email: goldner@tba.com.br
Community centre is at the same address

Minas Gerais

BELO HORIZONTE

COMMUNITY ORGANISATIONS
Associacao Israelita Brasileira
Rua Rio Grande do Norte 477
Telephone: (31) 3224-2129
Fax: (31) 3224-2129
Email: associacaoisraelita@bol.com.br
Supervision: Henry Katina

Uniao Israelita de Belo Horizonte
Rua Pernambucco 326
Telephone: (31) 224-6013
Email: ihim@pib.com.br

CONTACT INFORMATION
Lojinha do Beit Chabad
Av. Serzedelo Corr a 276
Telephone: (31) 241-2250

MIKVAOT
Mikvaot
Rua Rio Grande do Norte 477
Telephone: (31) 221-0690

SYNAGOGUES
Sinagoga da Av
Av. Leonardo Malchez 630, Centro

Reform
Congregacao Israelita Mineira
Rua Rio Grande Norte 477
Telephone: (31) 3224-2129
Fax: (31) 3224-2129
Email: cim@pib.com.br

Para

BELÉM
COMMUNITY ORGANISATIONS
Community Centre
Travessa Dr. Moraes 37
Telephone: (91) 222-3184
Email: cip@zaz.com.br

SYNAGOGUES
Eshel Avraham
Travessa Campos Sales 733

Shaar Hashamaim
Rua Alcipreste Manoel Theodoro 842

Parana

CURITIBA
COMMUNITY CLUB AND JEWISH FEDERATION
Centro Israelita do Parna
Rua Mateus Leme 1431 80530
Telephone: (41) 338-7575
Fax: (41) 338-7922

SYNAGOGUES
Orthodox
Francisco Frischmann
Rua Cruz Machado 126
Telephone: (41) 224-5218
Fax: (41) 224-8172

Pernambuco

RECIFE
COMMUNITY ORGANISATIONS
Community Centre
Rua da Gloria 215

SYNAGOGUES
Synagogue
Rua Martin Junior 29

Rio de Janeiro

CAMPOS
COMMUNITY ORGANISATIONS
Community Centre
Rua 13 de Maio 52

GREATER RIO DE JANEIRO
The old Jewish area is situated around Rua Alfandega. The country's first Ashkenazi Synagogue (Grande Templo Israelite) is an imposing building which was renovated in 1986.

BUTCHERS
Frigorifico
Rua Ronald Carvalho 265, Copacabana 22021-020
Telephone: (21) 295-7341
Supervision: Rav Stauber

Meat
Kosher House
Rua Anita Garibaldi 37A, Copacabana
Telephone: (21) 255-3891

COMMUNITY ORGANISATIONS
Confederacao Israelita de Brazil (Conib)
Avenida Nilo Pecanha 50
Telephone: (21) 240-0034
Fax: (21) 240-2717

Organizaco Israelita do Eatado do Rio de Janeiro
Rua Tenente Possolo 8

Rabinado do Rio de Janeiro
Rua Pompeu Loureiro 40, Copacabana 22061
Telephone: (21) 2256-3587
Fax: (21) 2256-3587
Email: rabinatorio@aol.com

CULTURAL ORGANISATIONS
ASA–Associacao Scholem Aleichem
Rua Sao Clemente 155, Botafogo 22260
Telephone: (21) 2539-7740
Fax: (21) 2266-1980
Email: asa@asa.org.br
Website: www.asa.org.br
The institution is dedicated to promoting cultural events (seminars, debates, video exhibitions, etc.)

EMBASSY
Consul General of Israel
Av. Copacabana 680
Telephone: (21) 255-5432

GROCERIES
Kosher House
Rua Antia Garibaldi 37 lj.A, Copacabana
Telephone: (21) 255-3891

MIKVAOT
Kehilat Yaakov
Rua Capelao Alvares da Silva 15, Copacabana
22041
Telephone: (21) 2236-3922

MUSEUMS
Museu Judaico do Rio de Janeiro
Rua México 90, sala 110, Cep:20031-141
Telephone: (21) 2524-6451
Fax: (21) 240-1598
Email: museujudaico@uol.com.br
Website: www.museujudaico.org.br

RESTAURANTS
Cafeteria in Rabinate Paladar Judaico
Rua Pompeu Loureiro 40, Copacabana
Telephone: (21) 2256-3587
Hours: 10 am to 5 pm Sunday to Thursday

SYNAGOGUES
Liberal
Associaca Religiosa Israelita
Rua General Severiano 170, Botafogo 22290
Telephone: (21) 2543-6320; 2542-5598
Fax: (21) 2542-6499
Email: ari.adm@arirj.com.br

Orthodox
Aqudat Israel
Rua Nascimento Silva 109, Ipanema 22421-020
Telephone: (21) 2267-5567
Fax: (21) 2267-5567
Email: agudatisrael@veloxmail.com.br

Beith Chabad of Rio de Janeiro
Rua Pompeu Loureiro No 40, Copacabana
Telephone: (21) 2256-3587

Grande Templo Israelita
Rua Tenente Possolo 8, Centro 20230
Telephone: (21) 232-3656

Kehilat Yaakov
Rua Capelao Alvares da Silva, Copacabana 22041

TOURS
Michel Mekler
Av. Graca Aranha 81/608, Centro 20030
Telephone: (21) 220-8817
Website: www.orbita.starmedia.com/via/~caritur

NITEROI
COMMUNITY ORGANISATIONS
Centro Israelita
Rua Visconde do Urugui 255 24030

Sociedade Hebraica
Rua Alveres de Azevedo 185, Icarai 24220

PETROPOLIS
RELIGIOUS ORGANISATIONS
Machane Israel Yeshiva
Rua Duarte de Silveira 1246 25600
Telephone: (242) 45-4952

SYNAGOGUES
Sinagoga Israelita Brasileira
Rua Aureliano Coutinho 48 25600

Rio Grande do Sul
ERECHIM
Erechim Synagogue
Av. Pedro Pinto de Souza 131

PASSO FUNDO
Passo Fundo Synagogue
Rua General Osório 1049

PELOTAS
Pelotas Synagogue
Rua Santos Dumont 303

PORTO ALEGRE
BUTCHERS
Kosher Butcher
Rua Fernandes Viera 518
Telephone: (51) 250-441

CULTURAL ORGANISATIONS
Instituto Cultural Judaico Marc Chagall
Projeto Memoria
Rua Dom Pedro II, 1220/sala 216
Telephone: (51) 343-5748

MIKVAOT
Mikva
Rua Francisco Ferrer 170
Telephone: (51) 3335-1264
Fax: (51) 3335-1264
Mobile Phone: 8119-3727/8119-0349
Email: liberowpoa@hotmail.com
Supervision: Rabbi Mendel Liberow, Chabad Rabbi

MUSEUMS
Museu Judaico
Rua Joao Telles 329
Telephone: (51) 226-0379

RELIGIOUS ORGANISATIONS
City Rabbinate
Rua Henrique Dias 73
Telephone: (51) 219-649

SYNAGOGUES
Liberal
SIBRA
Mariante 772
Telephone: (51) 331-8133
Services on Shabbat only

Orthodox
Beit Chabad
Rua Felipe Camarao 748
Telephone: (51) 3335-1264
Mobile Phone: 8119-0349
Email: liberowpoa@hotmail.com
Daily services

Centro Israelita Porto Alegrense
Rua Henrique Dias 73
Telephone: (51) 228-1935
Daily services.

Linath Ha-Tzedek
Rua Bento Figueredo 55
Telephone: (51) 332-1065
Daily services.

Poilisher Farband
Rua Joao Telles 329
Telephone: (51) 226-0379
Daily services.

Uniao Isralita Porto Algrense
Rua Dr Barros Cassal 750
Telephone: (51) 311-6515
Fax: (51) 311-5886
Daily services.

Sephardi
Centro Hebraico Riograndense
Rua Cel. Machado 1008
Services on Shabbat only

Sao Paulo

CAMPINAS
SYNAGOGUES
Beth Yacob Campinas
Rua Barreto Leme 1203
Telephone: (19) 231-4908

GUARUJA
Beit Yaacov
Av. Leomil 628
Telephone: (13) 387-2033

MOGI DAS CRUZES
COMMUNITY ORGANISATIONS
Jewish Society
Rua Dep. Deodato Wertheiner 421
Telephone: (11) 469-2505

SANTO ANDRE
SYNAGOGUES
Beit Chabad
Rua 11 de Junho 172
Telephone: (11) 449-1568

SANTOS
COMMUNITY ORGANISATIONS
Club
Rua Cons. Neblas 254
Telephone: (132) 32-9016

SYNAGOGUES
Beit Sion
Rua Borges 264
Sinagoga Beit Jacob
Rua Campos Sales 137

SAO CAETANO DO SUL
Sociedade Religiosa S. Caetano do Sul
Rua Para 67
Telephone: (11) 442-3514

SAO JOSE DOS CAMPOS
Beit Chabad
Rua Republica do Ira 91
Telephone: (11) 3064-6322

SAO PAULO
Many Conversos came to Sao Paulo to escape the Inquisition, which was centred in northern Brazil. A number rose to positions of importance.

By 1972 the Jews of Sao Paulo built the Albert Einstein hospital as a contribution to the public health service.

BAKERIES
Buffet Mazal Tov
Rua Peixoto Gomide 1724
Telephone: (11) 883-7614
Fax: (11) 3064-5208

Matok Bakery
Al. Barros 921
Telephone: (11) 66-7514
Supervision: Rabbi I. Dichi

BOOKSELLERS
Livraria Séfer
Alameda Barros, 893 01232-001
Telephone: (11) 3826-1366
Fax: (11) 3826-4508
Email: sefer@sefer.com.br
Website: wwww.sefer.com.br
Bookseller and Judaica.

BUTCHERS
Casa de Carnes Casher
Rua Fortunato 241
Telephone: (11) 221-2240
Supervision: Rabbi Elyahu B. Valt.

Kosher Express
Rua Tupi No 506, Higienopolis 01233-000
Telephone: (11) 3367-0863
Fax: (11) 3825-4986
Email: kosherexpress@uol.br

Mehadrin
Rua S. Vicente de Paulo
Telephone: (11) 67-9090
Rua Prates 689
Telephone: (11) 228-1771
Supervision: Rabbi M.A. Iliovitz

EMBASSY
Consul general of Israel
Rua Luis Coelho 308, 7th Floor
Telephone: (11) 257-2111; 257-2814

GROCERIES
All Kosher
Rua Albuquerque Lins 1170
Telephone: (11) 3825-1131

Casas Menora
Rua Guarani 114
Telephone: (11) 228-6105

Chazak
Rua Afonsa Pena 348a
Telephone: (11) 229-5607
Rua Haddock Lobo 1002
Telephone: (11) 3068-9093

Kosher Mart
Rua Tenente Pena 187, Bom Retiro
Telephone: (11) 221-7299
Website: www.koshermart.com.br

Mazal Tov
Rua Peixoto Gomide 1724 01409-001
Telephone: (11) 3061-0179
Fax: (11) 3061-0358

Sta. Luzia
Al. Lorena 1471
Telephone: (11) 883-5844
Look for kosher section

Zilanna
Rua Itamb 506
Telephone: (11) 257-8671

MEDIA
Newspapers
O Hebreu
Rua Cunha Gago 158 05421-000
Telephone: (11) 3819-1616
Fax: (11) 3819-1616
Email: ohebreu@ohebreu.com.br
Website: www.brasiljudaico.com.br
Monthly

Tribuna Judaico
Rua Tanabi 299 05002-010
Telephone: (11) 3871-3234/3873-3020/3862-9074
Fax: (11) 3871-3234
Email: tjudaica@uol.com.br
Weekly

Periodical
Morasha Magazine
Rua Dr Veiga Filho 547, Higienopolis 05607-000
Telephone: (11) 3825-9784
Fax: (11) 3030-5630
Email: morasha@uol.com.br
Website: www.morasha.com
Central organisation: Instituto Morasha de Cultura

MIKVAOT
Beit Yaacov Synagogue
Rua Dr Veiga Filho 547, Higienopols 01229-000
Telephone: (11) 3662-2154
Fax: (11) 3662-2154
Email: morasha@uol.com.br

Congregacao Meor Haim
Rua Sao Vicente de Paulo 276 01229-010
Telephone: (11) 3662-6238; 3826-7699
Fax: (11) 3666-6960
Email: revista_nascente@hotmail.com
Orthodox

Congregacao Monte Sinai
Rua Piaui 624, Higienopolis 01241-000
Telephone: (11) 3824-9229
Fax: (11) 3824-9229
Email: cmsinai@sanet.com.br

Micre Taharat Menachem - Perdizes
Rua Dr. Manoel Maria Tourinho 261
Telephone: (11) 3865-0615
By appointment only

Mikva
Rua Chabad 60 01417-030
Email: chabad@chabad.org.br

RELIGIOUS ORGANISATIONS
Comunidade Israelita Ortodoxa de Sao Paulo
Rua Haddock Lobo 1091
Telephone: (11) 3062-1562; 3082-1562
Fax: (11) 3064-0302
Email: kehilakashrus@terra.com.br

Rabanut- Rabino Elyahu Baruch Valt
Rua Corre de Melo 84 cj 308
Telephone: (11) 3331-5642
Fax: (11) 3064-9054
Email: ravvalt@hotmail.com
Office hours: 9 am to 1 pm weekdays.

RESTAURANTS
Hebraica Kosher Restaurant and the Buffet Mosico
Rua Hungria 1000
Telephone: (11) 3815-6788/3818-8831
Fax: (11) 3815-6980
Email: kosher@hebraica.org.br
Supervision: Rabbi Elyahu B. Valt
Buffet Mosaico inside the Hebraica Sao Paulo club. Closed Mondays, open Saturday night 90 minutes after Shabbat.

Restaurante Kosher Delight
Rua Baronesa de Ita 436
Telephone: (11) 3661-3106

Meat
Bero
Rua Peixoto Gomide 2020
Telephone: (11) 3086-2808
Fax: (11) 3086-2809
Email: berokosher@osite.com.br

Milk
Cantina Do Bero
Rua Pe. Joao Manoel, 881
Telephone: (11) 3064-9022
Email: berokosher@osite.com.br
Open from Sunday to Thursday, 6.00 pm until 11.30 pm. Also delivers.

Milk and Parve
Jacky Gourmet Café
Rua Rosa e Silva 146, Higienopolis
Telephone: (11) 3823-3537
Fax: (11) 3664-7034
Email: jackycafe@webcable.com.br
Supervision: Kashrut supervision: Ha Rav Y.D. Horowitz Shlita.

SYNAGOGUES
Hasidic
Uniao Ortodoxa Judaica
Rua Mamore 597
Telephone: (11) 3224-8639
Fax: (11) 3224-9029

Hungarian
Adas Yereim
Rua Talmud Tora 86
Telephone: (11) 282-1562; 852-9710

Liberal
Congregacao Israelita Paulista
Rua Antonio Carlos 653
Telephone: (11) 256-7811
Fax: (11) 257-1446
Email: scrtgeral@dialdata.com.br
Website: www.cip.sp.com.br

Orthodox
Beit Chabad Augusta
Rua Augusta 259 01305-000
Telephone: (11) 258-7173

Beit Chabad Central
Rua Chabad 54-60 01417-010
Telephone: (11) 3060-9777
Fax: (11) 3060-9778
Email: chabad@chabad.org.br
Website: www.chabad.org.br

Beit Chabad Perdizes
Rua Man. Maria Tourinho, 261
Telephone: (11) 3865-0615

Beit Yaacov
Rua Dr Veiga Filho 547, Higienopolis 01229-000
Telephone: (11) 3662-2154
Fax: (11) 3662-2154
Email: morasha@uol.com.br

Congregacao Mekor Haim
Rua Sao Vicente de Paulo 276 01229-010
Telephone: (11) 3826-7699
Email: revista_nascente@hotmail.com

Progressive
Comunidade Shalom
Rua Coronel Joaquim Ferreira Lobo 195 04544-150
Telephone: (11) 829-1477
Fax: (11) 828-9177

Sephardi
Templo Israelita Brasileiro Ohel Yaacov
Rua Abolicao 457
Telephone: (11) 606-9982
Fax: (11) 227-6793

TRAVEL AGENCIES
Carmel Tur
Rua Xavier de Toledo 121/10
Telephone: (11) 257-2244

Sharontur
Rua Sergipe 475/607~608 Higienopolis 01243-001
Telephone: (11) 3826-8388
Fax: (11) 3825-3828
Email: sharontur@sharontur.com.br
Website: www.sharontur.com.br
Open: 8.00 am to 6.00 pm. Closed Shabat & Sunday. International & domestic tickets. Car rental, exchange, hotel reservations. Languages spoken: English, Hebrew, Spanish. Contact person: Mr Dov Smaletz

Vertice
Rua Sao Bento 545/10 01011-100
Telephone: (11) 3115-1970
Fax: (11) 3115-1970
Email: verticetur@terra.com.br

SOROCABA
SYNAGOGUES
Community Centre
Rua Dom Pedro II 56
Telephone: (11) 31-3168

BULGARIA

Dating back to the Byzantine conquest, the community in Bulgaria was established by Greek Jews in Serdica (Sofia, the capital). The Jewish community grew when the Bulgarian state was founded in 681. Czar Ivan Alexander (1331-71) had a Jewish wife (who converted to Christianity).

The community has included eminent rabbinic commentators, such as Rabbi Dosa Ajevani and Joseph Caro, the codifier of the Shulchan Aruch, who escaped to Bulgaria after the expulsion from Spain. The various Jewish groups joined to form a unified Sephardi community in the late seventeenth century.

About 50,000 Jews lived in Bulgaria in 1939. Bulgaria joined the war on the side of Germany but, despite much pressure from the Nazis, the government and general population refused to allow Bulgarian Jews to be deported. Only Jews from Macedonia and Thrace, then occupied by Bulgaria, were deported. Despite being saved, most of the community emigrated to Israel after the war. The 10 per cent who remained were then under the control of the communists and had little contact with the outside world.

Since the fall of communism, the community has been reconstituted and now has synagogues in Sofia and Plovdiv. The community is ageing, although 100 children attend a Sunday school run by the Shalom Organisation, the central Jewish organisation for Bulgaria.

GMT +2 hours
Country calling code: (+359)
Total population: **8,306,000**
Jewish population: **3,000**
Emergency telephone: (Police–166) (Fire–160) (Ambulance–159)
Electricity voltage: 220

PLOVDIV
LIBRARIES
Library and House of Culture
Vladimir Zaimov St. 20
Telephone: (32) 761-376

SYNAGOGUES
Sephardi
Zion Synagogue
Tsar Kalojan St. 15
In the courtyard of a large apartment complex

ROUSSE
SYNAGOGUES
Community Centre
Ivan Vazoz Sq. 4
Telephone: (82) 270-540

SOFIA
About half of Bulgarian Jewry lives in Sofia. The Great Synagogue of 1878 ranks among the largest of Sephardi synagogues.

CEMETERIES
Jewish Cemetery
Orlandovtzi suburb
Take a tram (Nos2, 10 or 14) to the last stop for this large Jewish cemetery.

COMMUNITY ORGANISATIONS
Social & Cultural Organisation of Bulgarian Jews
Shalom, Alexander Stambolisky St. 50
Telephone: (2) 870-163
Publishes a periodical Evreiski Vesti and a yearbook. It also maintains a museum devoted to the Rescue of Bulgarian Jews, 1941–1944. At the same address are the offices of El Al, the Joint and the Jewish Agency.

EMBASSY
Embassy of Israel
1 Bulgaria Sq. NDK-Admin. building, 7th Floor
Telephone: (2) 951-50-44
Fax: (2) 952-11-01
Email: info@sofia-mfa.gov.il
Hours of opening: Consular Section Mon to Fri 9.30-12.30

RELIGIOUS ORGANISATIONS
Central Jewish Religious Council
Ekzarh Josef St. 16 1000
Telephone: (2) 983-1273
Fax: (2) 985-5085
Email: sofia.synagogue@mail.orbitel.bg
Website: www.sofiasynagogue.com

SYNAGOGUES
Sofia Central Synagogue
Ekzarh Josef St. 16
Telephone: (2) 983-1273
Fax: (2) 985-5085
Email: sofia_synagogue@mail.orbitel.bg
Website: www.shalom.bg
Adjacent to the synagogue is a museum dedicated to the history of Bulgarian Jewry

CANADA

The Jewish settlement of Canada began with the British expansion into Canada. In 1760, the Shearith Israel synagogue was founded in Montreal and in 1832 Jews received full civil rights. In the 1850s the community began to spread from Montreal to Toronto and Hamilton.

The community grew throughout the early twentieth century, from 16,000 in 1900 to 126,000 in 1921. After the Second World War, Jewish immigration increased and by 1961 the population was 260,000.

The headquarters of the Canadian Jewish Congress is in Montreal. This is the main national organisation for Canadian Jewry, and the community is provided with a full range of services, with Jewish schools, yeshivot, newspapers and the unique (in the Americas) Montreal Jewish Library. There are also several kosher restaurants.

GMT -3 to -8 hours
Country calling code: (+1)
Total population: **30,491,000**
Jewish population: **365,000**
Emergency telephone: (Police–911) (Fire–911) (Ambulance–911)
In remote areas, calls have to be made via the operator.
Electricity voltage: **110**

Alberta
CALGARY
BAKERIES
Barels Bakery & Nosh
131, 2515 - 90th Avenue SW T2V 0L8
Telephone: (403) 238-5300
Fax: (403) 238-3023
Email: barels@telus.net
Supervision: Calgary Kosher & Rabbi Menachem M Matusof, Lubavitch

Hours of operation: Sunday 10 am to 2 pm, Monday to Wednesday 9 am to 6 pm, Thursday 9 am to 7 pm, Friday 8am to 5pm (winter 8 am to 4 pm). Closed Shabbat. We are completely nut free and Parve

COMMUNITY ORGANISATIONS
Calgary Jewish Community Council
1607 90th Av. S.W.
Telephone: (403) 253-8600
Fax: (403) 253-7915
Email: cjcc@cjcc.ca
Website: www.cjcc.ca
The Council issues a booklet Keeping Kosher in Calgary

DELICATESSEN
Izzy's Kosher Meats and Deli
2515 90th Av. S.W. T2V 0L8
Telephone: (403) 251-2552
Fax: (403) 281-3322

RELIGIOUS ORGANISATIONS
Calgary Kosher Council
1607-90 Avenue SW
Telephone: (403) 444-3158
Fax: (403) 253-7915
Email: calgarykosher@cjcc.ca

RESTAURANTS
Karen's Café
Calgary Jewish Centre, 1607 90th Av. S.W.
Telephone: (403) 255-5311
Hours: Monday to Thursday, 10 am to 7 pm; Friday, 10 am to 1 pm. Closed on Sunday.

SYNAGOGUES
Conservative
Beth Tzedec
1325 Glenmore Trail S.W. T2V 4Y8
Telephone: (403) 255-8688
Fax: (403) 252-8319
Email: rabbi@edmontonbethisrael.org
Website: www.edmontonbethisrael.org

Orthodox
Congregation House of Jacob-Mikveh Israel
1623 92nd Av., Jerusalem Rd. SW T2V 5C9
Telephone: (403) 259-3230
Fax: (403) 259-3240
Email: hojmi@telus.net
Website: www.hojmi.org

Orthodox Chabad
Outreach Centre
Chabad Lubavitch of Alberta
28-523 Woodpark blvd T2W 4J3
Telephone: (403) 238-4880
Fax: (403) 281-0338
Email: mmatsusof@chabadalberta.org
Website: www.chabadalberta.org

Reform
Temple Bnai Tikvah
Calgary Jewish Centre, 1607 90th Av. S.W. T2V 5C9
Telephone: (403) 252-1654
Fax: (403) 252-1709
Email: temple@cadvision.com

EDMONTON
COMMUNITY ORGANISATIONS
Edmonton Jewish Federation
7200 156th St. T5R 1X3
Telephone: (780) 487-0585
Fax: (780) 482-1854
Email: edjfed@netcom.ca
Contact Gayle Tailman, Director, for additional information

Shoshana Szlachter
B'nai Brith, Western Region Director, 7200-156
Street T5R 1X3
Telephone: (780) 481-6939
Fax: (780) 481-1854
Email: bnaibrith.westcan@shaw.ca

MEDIA
Newspapers
Edmonton Jewish News
7200 156th Street T5R 1X3
Telephone: (780) 488-7276
Fax: (780) 484-4978
Email: ejlife@shaw.ca

Edmonton Jewish Life
#330, 10036 Jasper Av. T5J 2W2
Telephone: (780) 421-7983
Fax: (780) 424-3951

SYNAGOGUES
Conservative
Beth Shalom
11916 Jasper Av. T5K 0N9
Telephone: (780) 488-6333
Fax: (780) 488-6259
Email: info@e-bethshalom.org
Website: www.bethshalomedmonton.org

Orthodox
Beth Israel
131 Wolf Willow Road T5T 7T7
Telephone: (780) 482-2840
Fax: (780) 482-2470
Email: edbeth@telusplanet.net

Chabad Lubavitch
502 Wolf Willow Rd. Edmonton, Alberta
Telephone: (780) 486-7244
Fax: (780) 486-7243
Email: chabad@shaw.ca

Reform
Temple Beth Ora
7200 156th St. T5R 1X3
Telephone: (780) 487-4817
Fax: (780) 481-1854
Email: tboffice@shaw.ca
Services: the first Friday of the month.

British Columbia

COQUITLAM
SYNAGOGUES
Sha'arei Mizrah
2860 Dewdney Trunk Road V3C 2H9
Telephone: 552-7221
Fax: 552-7201
Email: admin@burquest.org
Website: www.burquest.ofg

KELOWNA
SYNAGOGUES
Traditional
Beth Shalom Sanctuary
OJCC, 102-1 North Glenmore Road V1V 2E2
Telephone: (250) 862-2305
Fax: (250) 862-2365
Email: shalom@ojcc.net
Website: www.ojcc.net

RICHMOND
BAKERIES
Garden City Bakery
#360-9100 Blundell Road
Telephone: (604) 244-7888

SYNAGOGUES
Conservative
Beth Tikvah
9711 Geal Road V7E 1R4
Telephone: (604) 271-6262
Email: bethtikvah@btikvah.ca
Website: www.bitikvah.ca

Hasidic
Chabad of Richmond
200-4775 Blundell Road, Richmond
Telephone: (604) 277-6427
Fax: (604) 263-7934
Email: info@chabadrichmond.com
Website: www.chabadrichmond.com

Orthodox
Eitz Chaim
8080 Fraces Road V6Y 1A4
Telephone: (604) 275-0007
Fax: (604) 277-2225
Email: eitzchaim@telus.net

SURREY

SYNAGOGUES

Chadbad
The Center for Judaism of the Lower Fraser Valley,
2351 128th Street Surrey V4A 3W1
Telephone: (604) 542-5454
Email: centerforjudaism@aol.com
Website: www.centerforjudaism.org

VANCOUVER

The most famous of early Jewish settlers were
the Oppenheimer brothers who settled there the
year the city was founded. David Oppenheimer
was the city's second mayor. The city's first
synagogue was built in 1912, although of
course services had been held much earlier.

BAKERIES

Sabra Bakery
3844 Oak Street
Telephone: (604) 733-4912

CONTACT INFORMATION

Shalom BC
950 West 41st Avenue V5Z 2N7
Telephone: (604) 257-5111 ext. # 238
Fax: (604) 257-5119
Email: info@shalombc.org
Website: www.shalombc.org
Hours: Monday to Thursday 9.00 am to 4.00 pm, Friday
9.00 am to 3.00 pm

RESTAURANTS

Green V Organics
2936 West Fourth Av.
Telephone: (604) 730-1808
Supervision: British Columbia Kosher Council

Pinis Pizza
729 West 16th Avenue
Telephone: (604) 562-7232
Fax: (604) 733-4911

Dairy
Nava Creative Kosher Cuisine
950 West 41st Avenue
Telephone: (604) 676-7579
Fax: (604) 676-7633
Email: NHI@shaw.ca
Supervision: BCK

Meat
Omnitsky Kosher B.C.
5866 Cambie Street
Telephone: (604) 321-1818
Fax: (604) 321-1817
Email: kosher@telus.net
Supervision: BCK
Glatt Kosher delicatessen with a full line of prepared foods
and groceries

Sabra Kosher Restaurant and Bakery
3844 Oak Street V6H 2M5
Telephone: (604) 733-4912
Fax: (604) 733-4911
Website: www.sabrakosherestaurant.com
Takeout, eat in and catering

SYNAGOGUES

Conservative
Beth Israel
4350 Oak Street V6H 2N7
Telephone: (604) 731-4161
Fax: (604) 731-4989
Email: info@bethisrael.ca
Website: www.bethisrael.ca

Congregation Har El
1305 Taylor Way, West Vancouver V7T 2Y7
Telephone: (604) 925-6488
Fax: (604) 922-8245
Email: office@harel.org
Website: www.harel.org
Friday, 7.00 pm; Shabbat, 10 am (Seasonal). Visitors
wecome

Hasidic
Chadbad-Lubavitch
5750 Oak Street, V6M 2V9
Telephone: (604) 266-1313
Fax: (604) 263-7934
Email: information@lubavitchbc.com
Website: www.lubavitchbc.com
Hours: Daily 7.00 am; Shabbat 10.00 am; Sunday 9.00 am.
Wheelchair access.

Jewish Renewal
Or Shalom
710 East 10th Avenue V5T 2A7
Telephone: (604) 872-1614
Fax: (604) 872-4406
Website: www.orshalom.bc.ca
Family Kabbalat Shabbat and potluck dinner monthly;
Shabbat 10.00 am. Wheelchair access.

Orthodox
Louis Brier Home
1055 West 41th Avenue V6M 1W9
Telephone: (604) 261-9376
Fax: (604) 266-8172

Schara Tzedeck
3476 Oak Street V6H 2L8
Telephone: (604) 736-7607
Fax: (604) 730-1621
Email: gabriella@scharatzedeck.com
Website: www.scharatzedeck.com
Hours: Monday and Thursday, 7.00 am; Tuesday,
Wednesday and Friday 7.15 am; weekdays, sunset; Friday,
7.30 pm; Shabbat: 10.30 am followed by Kiddush

Torat Hayim Community
483 Eastcot Road
Telephone: (604) 984-4168
Fax: (604) 984-4168
Email: info@hayim.com
Website: www.hayim.com/sposor
Shabbat: 10.30 am followed by Kiddush

Reform
Temple Shalom
7190 Oak Street V6P 3Z9
Telephone: (604) 266-7190
Fax: (604) 266-7126
Email: templeshalom@telus.net
Website: www.templeshalom.ca
Hours: Monday and Wednesday, 7.15 am; Friday, 8.15 pm; Shabbat, 10.00 am. Also has a gift shop.

Sephardi Orthodox
Beth Hamidrash
3231 Heather Street V5Z 3K4
Telephone: (604) 872-4222
Fax: (604) 872-4222

Traditional
Shaarey Tefilah
785 West 16th Avenue V5Z 158
Telephone: (604) 873-2700
Email: office@shaareytefilah.com
Website: www.shaareytefilah.com
Friday evening, call for time, Shabbat and Sunday, 9.00 am. Wheelchair access.

VICTORIA
COMMUNITY ORGANISATIONS
Victoria Jewish Community Centre
3636 Shelbourne Street
Telephone: (250) 477-7184
Fax: (250) 477-6283

SYNAGOGUES
Conservative
Emanu-El
1461 Blanshard V8W 2J3
Telephone: (250) 382-0615
Fax: (250) 382-0615

Manitoba
WINNIPEG
BAKERIES
City Bread
238 Dufferin Avenue R2W 2X6
Telephone: (204) 949-2480

Gunn's
247 Selkirk Avenue R2W 2L5
Telephone: (204) 582-2364

BUTCHERS
Omiitsky's Kosher Foods
1428 Main Street R2W 3V4
Telephone: (204) 586-8271
Fax: (204) 586-8270
Website: www.omnitsky.com

COMMUNITY ORGANISATIONS
Asper Jewish Community Campus
C300- 123 Doncaster Street R3N 2B2
Telephone: (204) 477-7400
Fax: (204) 477-7405
Email: info@jewishwinnipeg.org
Website: www.jewishwinnipeg.org
Home to Rady Jewish Community Centre, Winnipeg Jewish Theatre, the Jewish Federation of Winnipeg, the, Jewish Heritage Centre, and Schmoozers Cafe

MIKVAOT
Herzlia-Adas Yeshurun
620 Brock R3N 0Z4
Telephone: (204) 489-6262
Fax: (204) 489-5899
Email: cbt@execulink.com

MUSEUMS
Jewish Heritage Centre of Western Canada
C116-123 Doncaster Street, Winnipeg, MB, R3N 2B2
Telephone: (204) 477-7461
Fax: (204) 477-7465
Email: ipenn@jhcwc.org
Website: www.jhcwc.org

RESTAURANTS
Garden Café
146 Magnus Avenue R2W 2B4
Telephone: (204) 586-9781

Dairy
Mariner Neptune
472 Dufferin
Telephone: (204) 589-5341

Schmoozers Café
Located at the Asper Jewish Community Campus, 123 Doncaster Street R3N 2B2
Telephone: (204) 477-7418
Fax: (204) 477-7418

SYNAGOGUES
Egalitarian Conservative
Beth Israel
1007 Sinclair Street R2V 3J5
Telephone: (204) 582-2353

Congregation Shaarey Zedek
561 Wellington Crescent R3M 0A6
Telephone: (204) 452-3711
Fax: (204) 474-1184
Email: administration@shaareyzedek.mb.ca
Website: www.shaareyzedek.mb.ca

Orthodox
Chabad Lubavitch
2095 Sinclair Street R2V 3K2
Telephone: (204) 339-8737
Fax: (204) 586-0487
Email: aaltein@merlin.mb.ca

Chevra Mishnayes
700 Jefferson Avenue R2V 0P6
Telephone: (204) 338-8503

New Brunswick
FREDERICTON
GROCERIES
Scoop & Save
934 Prospect
Telephone: (506) 459-7676

SYNAGOGUES
Orthodox
Sgoolai Israel
Westmorland Street E3B 3L7
Telephone: (506) 454-9698
Fax: (506) 452-8889
Email: sgoolai@nbnet.nb.ca
For information on availability of kosher food, call Rabbi
Yochanan Samuels: (506) 454-2717

MONCTON
Tiferes Israel
56 Steadman Street E1C 8L9
Telephone: (506) 858-0258
Fax: (506) 859-7983
Email: tifisrl@nbnet.nb.ca
Mikva on premises

SAINT JOHN
MUSEUMS
Saint John Jewish Historical Museum
29 Wellington Row E2L 3H4
Telephone: (506) 633-1833
Fax: (506) 642-9926
Email: sjjhm@nbnet.nb.ca
Website: www:personal.ebnet.nb.ca/sjjhm
Mid-May to late October 10.00 am to 4.00 pm Monday to
Friday. Also, during July and August, Sunday 1.00 pm to
4.00 pm or by appointment. This is the only Jewish museum
in the Atlantic Provinces of Canada. There are eight display
areas as well as library and archives. Guided tours
available.

Newfoundland
ST. JOHN'S
SYNAGOGUES
Conservative
**Hebrew Congregation of Newfoundland &
Labrador (Beth El)**
Elizabeth Avenue A1B 1S3

Telephone: (709) 726-0480
Fax: (709) 777-6995
Email: mpaul@mun.ca

Nova Scotia
GLACE BAY
SYNAGOGUES
Orthodox
Sons of Israel
1 Price Street B1A 3C8
Telephone: (902) 849-8605

HALIFAX
COMMUNITY ORGANISATIONS
Atlantic Jewish Council
5670 Spring Garden Road, Suite 508 B3J 1H6
Telephone: (902) 422-7491
Fax: (902) 425-3722
Email: atlanticjewishcouncil@theajc.ns.ca
Website: www.theajc.ns.ca
Covers Jewish communities in Nova Scotia, New
Brunswick, Prince Edward Island, Newfoundland and
Halifax. Also at this address: Canadian Jewish Congress,
Atlantic Region, Canadian Zionist Federation, United
Jewish Appeal, Canadian Young Judea, Hadassah, Jewish
National Fund, JSA (Jewish Student Association for Atlantic
Canada.

GROCERIES
Barrington Meat Super Store
1145 Barrington
Telephone: (902) 492-3240

Sobeys
1120 Queen
Telephone: (902) 422-9884

SYNAGOGUES
Conservative
Shaar Shalom
1981 Oxford Street B3H 4A4
Telephone: (902) 423-5848
Fax: (902) 422-2580
Email: shaar.shalom@ns.sympatico.ca

Orthodox
Beth Israel
1480 Oxford Street B3H 3Y8
Telephone: (902) 422-1301
Fax: (902) 422-7251
Email: thebeth@eastlink.com
Website: www.thebethisrael.com
Mikva on premises

TOURIST SITES
Pier 21 Canada's Immigration Museum
1055 Marginal Road, Pier 21
Telephone: (902) 425-7770
Fax: (902) 423 4045
Email: info@pier21.ca
Website: www.pier21.ca
Non profit society.Known as Canada's Ellis Island, Pier 21 was Canada's front door to over one million immigrants. Visitors are able to re-enact the immigrant experience through various multimedia displays. In addition they can explore their family trees.

SYDNEY
SYNAGOGUES
Conservative
Temple Sons of Israel
P.O. Box 311, Whitney Avenue B1P 6H2
Telephone: (902) 564-4650

YARMOUTH
CONTACT INFORMATION
R & V Indiq
13 Parade Street B5A 3A5
Will be happy to provide details of the local Jewish community

Ontario
BELLEVILLE
SYNAGOGUES
Conservative
Sons of Jacob
211 Victoria Avenue K8N 2C2
Telephone: (613) 962-1433
Email: jmarkus@intranet.ca
Website: www.iks.net/-soj

CHATHAM
SYNAGOGUE
Conservative
Children of Jacob
29 Water Street N7M 3H4
Telephone: (519) 352-3544

HAMILTON
BUTCHERS
Hamilton Kosher Meats
889 King Street West L8S 1K5

COMMUNITY ORGANISATIONS
Hamilton Jewish Federation
1030 Lower Lions Club Road, Ancaster L9G 3N6
Telephone: (905) 648-0605
Fax: (905) 648-8350
Email: gfisheruja@on.aibn.com
Website: www.jewishhamilton.org

DELICATESSEN
Westdale Deli
893 King Street West L8S 1K5
Telephone: (905) 529-2605
Fax: (905) 529-2605

MEDIA
Newspapers
Hamilton Jewish News
P.O. Box 7528, Ancaster L9G 3N6
Telephone: (905) 648-0605
Fax: (905) 648-8388

SYNAGOGUES
Conservative
Beth Jacob
375 Aberdeen Avenue L8P 2R7
Telephone: (905) 522-1351

Orthodox
Adas Israel
125 Cline Avenue S. L85 1X2
Telephone: (905) 528-0039
Fax: (905) 528-7497

Reform
Anshe Sholom
215 Cline Avenue N. L8S 4A1
Telephone: (905) 528-0121
Fax: (905) 528-2994

KINGSTON
COMMUNITY ORGANISATIONS
B'nai B rith Hillel Foundation
26 Barrie Street
Telephone: (613) 542-1120

SYNAGOGUES
Orthodox
Beth Israel
116 Centre Street K7L 4E6
Telephone: (613) 542-5012
Fax: (613) 542-9071
Email: bethisrael@kingston.net

Reform
Temple Iyr Hamelech
331 Union Street West K7L 2R3
Telephone: (613) 789-7022

KITCHENER
SYNAGOGUES
Orthodox
Beth Jacob
161 Stirling Avenue South N2G 3N8
Telephone: (519) 743-8422
Fax: (519) 743-9252
Email: bethjacob@on.albm.com

SYNAGOGUES

Reform

Temple Shalom
543 Beechwood N2T 2S8
Telephone: (519) 746-2234

LONDON

COMMUNITY ORGANISATIONS

London Jewish Federation
536 Huron Street N5Y 4J5
Telephone: (519) 673-3310
Email: admin@ljf.on.ca

SYNAGOGUES

Conservative

Or Shalom
534 Huron Street N5Y 4J5
Telephone: (519) 438-3081
Fax: (519) 439-2994
Email: or.shalom@sympatico.ca
Website: www.london.uscjhost.net

Orthodox

Congregation Beth Tefilah
1210 Adelaide Street North N5Y 4T6
Telephone: (519) 433-7081
Fax: (519) 433-0616
Email: office@bethtefilah.org
Website: www.bethtefilah.org
Mikva on premises

Reform

Temple Israel
605 Windermere Road N5X 2P1
Telephone: (519) 858-4400
Fax: (519) 858-2070
Email: templeisrael@bellnet.ca
Website: www.uahc.org/congs/cd/cdool

MISSISSAUGA

SYNAGOGUES

Reform

Solel Congregation
2399 Folkway Drive L5L 2M6
Telephone: (905) 820-5915
Fax: (905) 820-1956
Email: carollouise@solecongregation.org

NIAGARA FALLS

B'nai Tikvah
5328 Ferry Street L2G 1R7
Telephone: (905).354-3934

NORTH BAY

SYNAGOGUES

Conservative

Sons of Jacob
302 McIntyre Street West P1B 2Z1
Telephone: (705) 497-9288
Fax: (705) 497-9812
Email: martybrown@bellnet.ca
Friday evening services

OAKVILLE

SYNAGOGUES

Reform

Shaarei-Beth El
186 Morrison Road L6J 4J4
Telephone: (905) 849-6000
Fax: (905) 849-1134
Email: sbeofc@idirect.com
Website: www.sbe.ca

OSHAWA

SYNAGOGUES

Orthodox

Beth Zion
144 King Street East L1H 1B6
Telephone: (905) 723-2353

OTTAWA

Ottawa is the capital of Canada and its fourth largest city. The first Jewish settler came in 1858 when Ottawa was still known as Bytown. Ottawa has always been strongly traditional and has a growing community presently numbering around 13,000.

BAKERIES

Rideau Bakery
384 Rideau St., K1N 5Y8
Telephone: (613) 789-1019
Supervision: Ottawa Vaad Hair
Also serves dairy food

COMMUNITY ORGANISATIONS

Canadian Jewish Congress National Office
100 Sparks Street, Suite 650 K1P 5B7
Telephone: (613) 233-8703
Fax: (613) 233-8748
Email: canadianjewishcongress@cjc.ca
Website: www.cjc.ca

Vaad Ha'ir (Jewish Community Council)
21 Nadolny Sachs Private K2A 1R9
Telephone: (613) 798-4696
Fax: (613) 798-4695
Website: www.jewishottawa.org
Vaad Hakashruth located here for all kashrut information

EMBASSY
Embassy of Israel
Suite 1005, 50 O'Connor Street K1P 6L2
Telephone: (613) 567-6450
Fax: (613) 237-8865

MEDIA
Ottawa Jewish Bulletin
Telephone: (613) 798-4646
Fax: (613) 798-4730

RESTAURANTS
Dairy
Coffee Bar Dairy
1666 Bank St
Telephone: (613) 737-3356
Fax: (613) 789-2962
Supervision: Ottawa Vaad Hair

Viva Pizza
Soloway JCC, 21 Nadolny Sachs Private
Telephone: (613) 798-9818

SYNAGOGUES
Conservative
Agu dath Israel Congregation
1400 Coldrey Ave., K17 7PG
Telephone: (613) 728-3501
Fax: (613) 728-4468
Email: terry@agudathisrael.net
Website: www.agudathisrael.net

Conservative – Egalitarian
Adath Shalom Congregation
31 Nadolny Sach Private K2A 1R9
Telephone: (613) 240-4564
Email: copresidents@adath-shalom.ca/
Website: www.adath-shalom.ca/
Central organisation: United Synagogue of Conservative Judaism
A Conservative Egalitarian congregation, an equal role for women and men in all aspects of ritual is recognised. Regular services are member-led and a visiting Rabbi provides Rabbinical leadership at High Holy Day services and special Shabbaton weekends. Newcomers always welcome.

Orthodox
Beth Shalom West
15 Chartwell Avenue K2G 4K3
Telephone: (613) 723-1800
Fax: (613) 723-6567
Email: bsw@bethshalomwest.org
Website: www.bethshalomwest.org

Machzikei Hadas
2301 Virginia Drive K1H 6S2
Telephone: (613) 521-9700
Fax: (613) 521-0067
Email: cmh@cyberus.ca
Website: www.cyberus.ca/~cmh/shul.htm

Reform
Temple Israel
1301 Prince of Wales Drive K2C 1N2
Telephone: (613) 224-1802
Fax: (613) 224-0707
Email: temple@ca.inter.net
Website: www.templeisraelottawa.ca

Orthodox
Ottawa Torah Center Chabad
79 Stradwick Avenue K2J 2Z2
Telephone: (613) 823-0866
Fax: (613) 823-7540
Email: OttawaTC@aol.com

OWEN SOUND
SYNAGOGUES
Conservative
B'nai Ezekiel
313 11th Street East N4K 1V1
Telephone: (519) 376-8774

PETERBOROUGH
Beth Israel
Waller Street
Telephone: (705) 745-8398

RICHMOND HILL
Beth Rayim
9711 Bayview Avenue L4C 9X7
Telephone: (905) 770-7639

ST CATHARINE'S
SYNAGOGUES
Traditional
B'nai Israel
190 Church Street L2R 3E9
Telephone: (416) 685-6767
Fax: (416) 685-3100

SUDBURY
SYNAGOGUES
Shaar Hashomayim
158 John Street P3E 1P4
Telephone: (705) 673-0831

THORNHILL
BOOKSELLERS
Israel's the Judaica Centre
441 Clark Avenue West L47 6W7
Telephone: (905) 881-1010
Fax: (905) 881-1016
Email: israels@israelsjudaica.com
Also sells gifts

Matana Judaica Inc.
248 Steeles Avenue West #6   L4J 1A1
Telephone: (905) 731-6543
Fax: (905) 882-6196

RESTAURANTS
Dairy
My Zaidy's Pizza
441 Clark Avenue West   L4J 6W8
Telephone: (905) 731-3029

THUNDER BAY
SYNAGOGUES
Orthodox
Shaarey Shomayim
627 Grey Street   P7E 2E4
Telephone: (807) 622-4867
Email: phlab@baynet.net

TORONTO
There have been one and a half centuries of
organized Jewish life in Toronto since its start
in 1849. The Jewish population increased
significantly during the 1980s, and now Toronto
is home to almost half of Canada's Jews. There
is a good range of Jewish facilities in the city.

BAKERIES
Carmel Bakery
3856 Bathurst Street
Telephone: (416) 633-5315

Dairy Treats Bakery
3522 Bathurst Street
Telephone: (416) 787-0309
Fax: (416) 787-1935

Richman's Kosher Bakery
4119 Bathurst Street
Telephone: (416) 636-9710
Fax: (416) 636-9614
Email: richmansbakery@on.aibn.com
Website: www.richmansbakery.ca
Supervision: COR Kasruth Council of Canada

BOOKSELLERS
Israel's Judaica Centre
870 Eglinton Avenue West   M6C 2B6
Telephone: (416) 256-1010
Email: israels@israelsjudaica.com
Website: www.israelsjudaica.com

Negev Importing Co Ltd
3509 Bathurst Street   M6A 2C1
Telephone: (416) 781-9356
(Toll free: 1-888-618-9356)
Fax: (416) 905-0071
Email: sales@negevjudaica.com
Website: www.negevjudaica.com

COMMUNITY ORGANISATIONS
Bernard Betel (Seniors' Community Centre)
1003 Steeles Avenue West   M2R 3T6
Telephone: (416) 225-2112
Fax: (416) 225-2097
Email: reception@betelcentre.org
Website: www.betelcentre.org
Centre operates Conservative Synagogue–has two
Sephardi congregations on site–Beth Yosef and Tehillat
Yerushalayim

Kashruth Council of Canada–COR
4600 Bathurst Street, Street 240   M2R 3V2
Telephone: (416) 635-9550
Fax: (416) 635-8760
Website: www.cor.ca
Supervision: Kosher supervisory organisation–largest in
Canada
All enquiries about kashrut here.

UJA Federation of Greater Toronto
4600 Bathurst Street, Toronto   M2R 3V2
Telephone: (416) 635-2883
Fax: (416) 635-9565
Email: offioce@ujafed.org
Website: www.jewishtoronto.net

CONTACT INFORMATION
Jewish Information Service of Greater
Toronto - UJA Federation of Greater Toronto
4588 Bathurst Street, Suite 115   M2R 1W6
Telephone: (416) 635-5600
Fax: (416) 636-5813
Email: jinfo@ujafed.org
Website: www.jewishtoronto.com
Information about the Jewish community in the Greater
Toronto area, Canada including synagogues, kosher
restaurants, sites of interest. Tourist information.

EMBASSY
Consul General of Israel
180 Bloor street West, Suite 700   M5S 2V6
Telephone: (416) 640-8500
Fax: (416) 640-8555
Email: hasbara@idirect.com
Israel Government Tourist Office: (416) 964-3784

GIFT SHOP
Miriam's
3007 Bathurst Street
Telephone: (416) 781-8261
Fax: (416) 781-8261

MEDIA
Newspapers
Jewish Tribune
15 Hove Street, Downsview   M3H 4Y8
Telephone: (416) 633-6224
Fax: (416) 633-6224
Email: jewishtribune@jewishtribune.ca

MEMORIAL
Holocaust Education & Memorial Centre
4600 Bathurst Street, Willowdale M2R 3V2
Telephone: (416) 635-2883

MUSEUMS
Baycrest Heritage Museum
Baycrest Centre for Geriatric Care, 3560 Bathurst
Street M6A 2E1
Telephone: (416) 785-2500 Ext. 2802
Fax: (416) 785-4228
Email: pdickinson@baycrest.org
One of the few Judaica museums in Canada. It has an
active exhibit programme.

RESTAURANTS
Dairy
Dairy Treats Cafe
3522 Bathurst Street M6A 2C6
Telephone: (416) 787-0309
Fax: (416) 787-1935

King David Pizza
3020 Bathurst Street M6B 3B6
Telephone: (416) 781-1326
3774 Bathurst Street M3H 3M6
Telephone: (416) 633-5678
221 Wilmington Avenue M3H 5K1
Telephone: (416) 636-3456

Milk 'n Honey
3457 Bathurst Street, Downsview M6A 2C5
Telephone: (416) 789-7651
Fax: (416) 789-4788

Not just Yogurt
7117 Bathurst Street
Telephone: (416) 764-2525

Tov Li Pizza
5982 Bathurst Street, Willowdale M2R 1Z1
Telephone: (416) 650-9800

Yehudale's Falafel & Pizza
7241 Bathurst Street
Telephone: (416) 889-1400

Meat
Colonel Wong Restaurant
2825 Bathurst Street M6B 3B6
Telephone: (416) 784-9664

Hakerem Restaurant
3030 Bathurst Street M6B 3B6
Telephone: (416) 787-6504

Jerusalem One
3028 Bathurst Street M6B 3B6
Telephone: (416) 631-9602

King Solomon's Table
3705 Chesswood Drive, Downsview M3J 2P6
Telephone: (416) 630-1666
Fax: (416) 975-0987
Website: www.kingsolomonstable.com

Open Monday to Thursday 12.00 noon to 10.00 pm. Sunday
4.00 pm to 10.00 pm. Closed Friday and Sunday. Kashrut:
COR.

Marky's Deli & Restaurant
280 Wilson Avenue M3H 1S8
Telephone: (416) 638-1081

Miami Grill
441 Clark Avenue West
Telephone: (416) 709-0096

The Chicken Nest
3038 Bathurst Street M6B 4K2
Telephone: (416) 787-6378

SYNAGOGUES
Conservative
Beth Tzedec Street
1700 Bathurst Street M5P 3K3
Telephone: (416) 781-3514
Fax: (416) 781-0150
Email: info@beth-tzedec.org
Website: www.beth-tzedec.org

Orthodox
Anshei Minsk
10 St Andrews Street K1N 7Y2
Telephone: (416) 595-5723
Fax: (416) 595-9586
Email: minsk@bellnet.ca
Website: www.theminsk.com

Beth Shalom
151 Chapel Street K1N 7Y2
Telephone: (416) 789-3501
Fax: (416) 789-4438

Kiever Congregation
25 Bellevue Avenue M5T 2N5
Telephone: (416) 593-9956
Shabbat and Holiday services

Shaarei Shomayim
470 Glencairn Avenue M5N 1V8
Telephone: (416) 789-3213
Fax: (416) 789-1728
Email: info@shomayim.org
Website: www.shomayim.org
Supervision: Marilyn Somers

The Village Shul–Aish Hatorah Learning Centre
1072 Eglington Avenue West M6C 2E2
Telephone: (416) 785-1107
Fax: (416) 783-9870
Email: mbookbinder@aish.com
Website: www.aishtoronto.com

Reform
Holy Blossom
1950 Bathurst Street M5P 3K9
Telephone: (416) 789-3291
Fax: (416) 789-9697
Email: templemail@holyblossom.org

WINDSOR

COMMUNITY ORGANISATIONS
Jewish Community Council
1641 Ouellette Avenue N8X 1K9
Telephone: (519) 973-1772

MEDIA
Periodical
Windsor Jewish Community Bulletin
Telephone: (519) 973-1774

SYNAGOGUES
Orthodox
Shaar Hashomayim
115 Giles Blvd East N9A 4C1
Telephone: (519) 256-3123
Fax: (519) 256-3124
Email: shaar@mnsi.net

Shaarey Zedek
610 Giles Blvd East N9A 4E2
Telephone: (519) 252-1594

Reform
Congregation Beth-El
2525 Mark Avenue N9E 2W2
Telephone: (519) 969-2422

Quebec

MONTREAL
1760 saw the arrival of the first Jews in
Montreal as civilians attached to the British
army. In the 1920s and 1930s the Boulevard St-
Laurent was equivalent to London's East End or
New York's Lower East Side. There are now just
over 100,000 Jews in the city. Twenty percent of
them are North African Sephardim.

BAKERIES
Adir Bakery
6795 Darlington
Telephone: (514) 342-1991

Andalos
266 Lebeau
Telephone: (514) 856-0983

Biscuit Adar
5458 Westminister
Telephone: (514) 484-1198

Cheskie
359 Bernard West
Telephone: (514) 271-2253

Cite Cashere
4747 Van Horne
Telephone: (514) 733-2838

Delice Cashere
4655 Van Horne
Telephone: (514) 733-5010

Kosher Quality Bakery
5855 Victoria
Telephone: (514) 731-7883
Fax: (514) 731-0205

Montreal Kosher
7005 Victoria
Telephone: (514) 739-3651
2765 Van Horne, Widerton Shopping Centre
Telephone: (514) 737-0393
Fax: (514) 737-2427
2135 St. Louis , St. Laurent
Telephone: (514) 747-5116
Website: www.montrealkosherbakery.com
Supervision: Vaad Ha'ir

New Homemade Kosher Bakery
6915 Querbes
Telephone: (514) 270-5567
Fax: (514) 270-5041
6685 Victoria
Telephone:(514) 733-4141
5638 Westminister
Telephone: (514) 486-2024
Supervision: Vaad Ha'ir

Patisserie Chez Ma Souer
5095 Queen Mary
Telephone: (514) 737-2272

Renfels Bakery
2800 Bates
Telephone: (514) 733-5538

BOOKSELLERS
Kotol Book & Gift Store
6414 Victoria Avenue H3W 2S6
Telephone: (514) 739-4142
Fax: (514) 739-7330

Rodal's Hebrew Book Store & Gift Shop
4689 Van Horne Avenue H3W 1H8
Telephone: (514) 733-1876
Fax: (514) 733-2373
Email: rodal@ican.net

COMMUNITY ORGANISATIONS
Federation CJA
5151 ch, de la Côte Ste-Catherine H3W 1M6
Telephone: (514) 735-3541
Operates the Jewish Information and Referral Service
(JIRS), Tel: 737-2221

Jewish Community Council of Montreal
6825 Decarie, Suite 1000 H3W 3E4
Telephone: (514) 739-6363
Fax: (514) 739-7024
Email: semanuel@mk.ca
Website: www.mk.ca
Visitors requiring additional information about kosher
establishments should contact the Vaad Ha'ir at the above
numbers. Also apply to them for a list of kosher butchers,
bakeries, caterers and restaurants.

JUDAICA
Victoria Gift Shop
5875 Victoria Avenue H3W 2R6
Telephone: (514) 738-1414
Fax: (514) 737-6518

LIBRARIES
Jewish Public Library
1 Carre Cummings Square H3W 1M6
Telephone: (514) 345-2627
Fax: (514) 345-6477
Email: info@jplmtl.org
Website: www.jewishpubliclibrary.org

MEDIA
Newspapers
Canadian Jewish News
6900 Decarie Blvd, #341 H3W 2T8
Telephone: (514) 735-2612
Fax: (514) 735-9090
Email: montreal@cjnews.com

RESTAURANTS
Dairy
Bistrot Casa Linga
5095 Queen Mary H3W 1X4
Telephone: (514) 737-2272

Foxey's
5987A Victoria Avenue
Telephone: (514) 739-8777
Supervision: Vaad Ha'ir

Pizza Pita
5710 Victoria Avenue
Telephone: (514) 731-7482
Supervision: Vaad Hair
Open 9.30 am–11.30 pm daily, Saturday night until 2.30
am

Tatty's Pizza
6540 Darlington
Telephone: (514) 734-8289
Supervision: Vaad Ha'ir

**Cummings Jewish Centre for Seniors
Cafeteria**
5700 av. Westbury Ave. H3W 3E8
Telephone: (514) 342-1234
Fax: (514) 739-6899
Email: michael@cummingscentre.org
Website: www.cummingscentre.org

Meat
El Morocco II
3450 Drummond Street
Telephone: (514) 844-6888; 844-0203
Fax: (514) 844-1204
Email: elmorocco@spring.ca
Supervision: Vaad Ha'ir
Open for lunch and dinner until 10 pm.
Ernies & Ellie's Place

6900 Decarie Blvd H3X 2T8
Telephone: (514) 344-4444
Fax: (514) 344-0001
Supervision: Vaad Ha'ir

Exodus Restaurants
5395 Queen Mary
Telephone: (514) 483-6610
Fax: (514) 483-6810
Supervision: Vaad Ha'ir

SYNAGOGUES
**Canadian Jewish Congress National
Headquarters**
Samuel Bronfman House, 1590 Docteur Penfield,
Avenue H3G 1C5
Telephone: (514) 931-7531
Fax: (514) 931-0548
Email: mikec@cjc.ca
Contact to find out which of the many synagogues in
Montreal is nearest

QUEBEC CITY
SYNAGOGUES
Orthodox
Beth Israel Ohev Shalom
1251 Place de Merici G1R 1Y2
Telephone: (418) 688-3277

TOURIST SITES
Beth Israel Ohev Shalom
Boulevard Rene Levesque, Saint-Foy
Telephone: (418) 688-3277
This is an official monument and historic site–5 miles from
the old centre

STE. AGATHE DES MONTS
A resort in the Laurentian Mountains known as
the Catskills of Montreal where members of the
Montreal community spend their summer
months

SYNAGOGUES
Orthodox
House of Israel Congregation
31 rue Albert J8C 3A3
Telephone: (819) 326-4320
Fax: (819) 326-8558
Website: www.houseofisrael.org

Saskatchewan
REGINA
Beyh Jacob
4715 McTavish Street S4S 6H2
Telephone: (306) 757-8643
Fax: (306) 353-3499

SYNAGOGUES
Reform
Temple Beth Tikvah
Box 33048, Cathedral Post Office S4T 7X2
Email: templebethtikvah@hotmail.com
Website: www.uahc.org/cd/cd012

SASKATOON
SYNAGOGUES
Shir Chadash
610 Clarence South S7H 2E2
Telephone: (306) 242-3756

Conservative
Agudas Israel
715 McKinnon Avenue S7H 2G2
Telephone: (306) 343-7023
Fax: (306) 343-1244
Email: jewishcommunity@sk.sympatico.ca

CEUTA
Ceuta Kashrut Information
Calle Sargento Coriat 8

SYNAGOGUES
Ceuta Synagogue
Calle Sargento Colat 8

CHILE
The original Jewish settlers in Chile were *Conversos*. Rodrigo de Organos, a *Converso*, was the first European to enter the country in 1535. The Inquisition, however, curtailed the growth of the community.

The first legal Jewish immigration, albeit small, occurred only after Chile's independence in 1810. In 1914 the Jewish community numbered some 500, but this increased in the late 1930s with those refugees from Nazism who were able to avoid the strict immigration laws. Antisemitism, however, also grew, and the *Comite Representativo* was formed to respond to it.

There is an umbrella organisation and a large Zionist body in Chile. Most of the community is not religious, but some keep kosher and there are several synagogues in the capital Santiago and a few kosher shops. There are two Jewish schools and several Jewish newspapers are published.

GMT -4 hours
Country calling code: **(+56)**
Total population: **14,622.000**
Jewish population: **21,000**
Emergency telephone: **(Police–133) (Fire–132) (Ambulance–131)**
Electricity voltage: **220**

ARICA
COMMUNITY ORGANISATIONS
Sociedad Israelita
Dr Herzl, Casilla 501

IQUIQUE
Comunidad Israelita
Playa Ligade 3263, Playa Brava

LA SERENA
Community Centre
Cordovez 652

RANCAGUA
Comunidad Israelita
Casilla 890

SANTIAGO
The majority of Chilean Jews live in Santiago. The city has a couple of notable features in connection with its Jewish community. The Circulo Israelita Synagogue has an interesting stained glass design in its interior, and the Bomba Israel is a fire service manned by volunteers who include a few rabbis. Two of their fire engines carry the Chilean and Israeli flags.

BUTCHERS
Kosher Deli
Av Las Condes 8400
Telephone: (2) 251-3145; 848-6921
Fax: (2) 251-3149
Email: kd1301@123.cl
Supervision: Jabad

COMMUNITY ORGANISATIONS
Communal Headquarters (Comite Representativo de las Entidades Judias de Chile)
Miguel Claro 196
Telephone: (2) 235-8669

DELICATESSEN
Shemtov Kosher Delikatesen
47 La Niebla St
Telephone: (2) 325-4180
Fax: (2) 325-3595
Email: shemtovkosher@yahoo.com
Supervision: Rabbi Mensahe Perman
Delivery 24 hours a day

EMBASSY
Embassy of Israel
San Sebastian 2812, Casilla 1224
Telephone: (2) 246-1570

SYNAGOGUES
Ashkenazi
Communidad Israelita de Santiago
Serrano 214-218

German
Sociedad Cultural Israelita B'nei Jisroel
Mar Jonico No 8860
Telephone: (2) 201-1623
Fax: (2) 201-1623
Email: bneisrael@entelchile.net

Hungarian
Maze
Pedro Bannen 0166
Telephone: (2) 274-2536

Orthodox
Bicur Joilim
Av. Matte 624

Jabad (Chabad) Lubavitch
Los Catus 1575, La Dehesa
Telephone: (2) 228-2240
Email: mperman@vtr.net

Jafets Jayim
Miguel Claro 196

Sephardi
Maguen David
Av. R. Lyon 812

TEMUCO
COMMUNITY ORGANISATIONS
Communidad Israelita
General Cruz 355

VALDIVIA
Community Centre
Arauco 136 E.

CHINA

There is archaeological evidence of a Jewish presence in China in the eighth century, but it is believed that their existance as a community only dates from the twelth century. The largest established community of around 1,000 was in Kaifeng. The first Kaifeng synagogue was built in 1163.

The Treaty of Nanking in 1842 opened Shanghai to trade. In 1845 Elias Sassoon pioneered the Jewish settlement of Shanghai. Many Baghdadi Jews followed and were under the protection of the British government. In due course they were in the forefront of the development of the city. A second community was formed later, mainly by Russians and Poles fleeing religious persecution. The final influx was refugees from Nazi oppression in the period 1933–39. Almost all the community left Shanghai after the Second World War. In 1999 a community was again established.

Also included here is Hong Kong, previously listed as a separate entity but, since July 1997, again a region of China.

GMT +8 hours
Country calling code: **(+86)**
Total population: **1,284,100,000**
Jewish population: **2,100**
Emergency telephone: **(Police–110) (Fire–119)**
Electricity voltage: **220/240**

BEIJING
EMBASSY
Embassy of Israel
1 Jianguo Menwai Da Jia 100004
Telephone: (10) 6505-2970/1/2
Fax: (10) 6505-9561

KOSHER FOODS
Mrs Shanen's Bagels
5 Kaifa Jie, Xibaixin Zhuang Shunyi District
Telephone: (10) 8046-4301
Ask for kosher bagels

SYNAGOGUES
Chabad Lubavitch of Beijing China
Kings Garden Villa, 18 Xiao Yun Road, D-5A, Chao Yang District 100016
Telephone: (10) 6468-1321
Fax: (10) 6468-1322
Email: chabadbeijing@hotmail.com
Website: www.chabadbeijing.com
Shabbat services on Friday night and Shabbat as well as Friday night dinners and Shabbat lunches. All are welcome.

GUANGZHOU
Chabad of Guangzhou
3/F, Flat 02, 861 Jiefang Bei Road
Telephone: (20) 8360-1082
Mobile Phone: 011 86 137 1050 5049
Email: chabadcanton@hotmail.com
Website: www.chabad.org

HONG KONG
Although there were some Jewish merchants trading out of Hong Kong over the centuries,

the first permanent community consisted of Jews who came from Baghdad in the early nineteenth century. The first synagogue was not established until 1901, the early settlers preferring to organise communal events from their homes. The majority of the community were Sephardi, but Nazi persecution led to more Ashkenazi settlers arriving in Hong Kong, via Shanghai. Since the Second World War many Chinese Jews have emigrated through Hong Kong to Australia and the USA, although some have remained in Hong Kong. Following the reversion to Chinese control in mid-1997, the Jewish community is still thriving, and the mood is optimistic.

The Jews have contributed greatly to the building of the infrastructure of Hong Kong and, since the 1960s, many Western Jews, attracted by the success of this major financial centre, have made their homes there. The first communal hall was founded in 1905, but a new, multi-purpose complex (the Jewish Community Centre) has recently been opened, which is one of the most luxurious in the world. This centre includes everything from a library and a strictly kosher restaurant to a swimming pool and sauna.

Dialing code (+ 85)

CEMETERIES
The Jewish Cemetery
Located in Happy Valley
Telephone: (852) 2589-2621
Fax: (852) 2548-4200

COMMUNITY ORGANISATIONS
Hong Kong Jewish Community Centre
One Robinson Place, 70 Robinson Road, Mid-Levels
Telephone: (852) 2801-5440
Fax: (852) 2877-0917
Email: csw@jcc.org.hk
Website: www.jcc.org.hk
Two glatt kosher restaurants under the supervisionof a full-time Mashgiach. Regular Shabbat and festival dinners. Kosher supermarket, full banquet facilities, library, swimming pool and leisure facilities and a full programme of activities and classes. Visitors are welcome. Charge to visitors for admission.

CONSULATE
Consul General of Israel
Room 701 Admiralty Centre, Tower 2, 18 Harcourt Street
Telephone: (852) 2821-7500
Fax: (852) 2865-0220
Email: info@hongkong.mfa.gov.il
Website: www.hongkong.mfa.gov.il

RESTAURANTS
Shalom Grill
2/F Fortune House, 61 Connaught Road, Central
Telephone: (852) 2851-6218; 2851-6300
Fax: (852) 2851-7482
Email: darvick@darvick.com.hk
Glatt kosher restaurants under full-time Mashgiach supervision. Meals on Shabbat after services, take-away and delivery servce available. There is also a kosher supermarket, Sunday to Thursday Lunch 12.30 pm to 2.30pm. Dinner 6.30 pm to 9.30 pm. Friday 12.30pm to 2.30 pm.

SYNAGOGUES
Hong Kong Jewish Community Centre
One Robinson Place, 70 Robinson Road, Mid-Levels
Telephone: (852) 2801-5440
Fax: (852) 2877-0917
Email: info@jcc.org.hk
Website: www.jcc.org.hk

Orthodox
Chabad of Hong Kong
Chabad House, 1/F Hoover Court,
7 Macdonell Road
Telephone: (852) 2523-9770
Fax: (852) 2845-2772
Email: info@chabadhk.org
Website: www.chabadhk.org
Shabbat Minyan & meals in Central District.

Ohel Leah Synagogue
70 Robinson Road, Mid-Levels
Telephone: (852) 2589-2621
Fax: (852) 2548-4200
Email: mail@ohelleah.org
Website: www.ohelleah.org
Built in 1902 and carefully restored in 1998, the Orthodox Ohel Leah Synagogue, known by some as the crown jewel of Asian Jewery stillremains the regions' most vibrant centre of Jewish religious activity. Classes, daily services, a Beth Din, and a mikva operate on the premises. Gourmet catered shabbat meals–Friday eve is by reservation and shabbat community kiddush luncheon is complimentary following services. Book nearby hotels at discounted rates throughthe synagogue office.

Zion Congregation
21 Chatham Road, Kowloon
Telephone: (852) 2366-6364
Corner of Mody Road (opposite to Kowloon Shangri-La Hotel)

Sephardi
Beit Midrash Shuva Israel and Community Centre
2/F Fortune House, 61 Connaught Road, Central
Telephone: (852) 2851-6218; 2851-6300
Fax: (852) 2851-7482
Email: darvick@darvick.com.hk

Daily Shacharil at 7.00 and Mincha-Ma'ariv fifteen minutes before sunset. Shabbat services are followed by Shabbat meals. Full day kollel.

KAIFENG

MUSEUMS

Kaifeng Museum

The Kaifeng museum documents the ancient history of Kaifeng Jewry. The most significant artifact is a 15th century etched stone with inscriptions describing Kaifeng's Jewish history and customs from the times of Abraham.

SHANGHAI

Shanghai was opened to foreign trade in 1843. A flourishing Jewish community built up including Jews of many nationalities. There were three synagogues; one of which, the Ohel Rachel built in 1917, was designated in 2001 as an endangered site. The current community is planning to raise money for its restoration.

RESTAURANTS

Meat

Kosher Café

Shangmira Garden, Villa #2, 1720 HongQuiao Road
Telephone: (21) 6278-0225
Fax: (21) 6278-0223
Email: rabbi@chinajewish.org
Website: www.chinajewish.org
Supervision: Rabbi Shalom Greenberg
Daily 10.00-8.00

SYNAGOGUES

Orthodox

Chabad of Shanghai

Villa #1, Shang-Mira Garden 1720 HongQiao Road
Telephone: (21) 6278-0225
Fax: (21) 6278-0228
Email: rabbi@chinajewish.org
Website: www.chinajewish.org
Services and kosher meals available as well as some kosher products. Contact for reservations and more information.

Shanghai Jewish Center

Shanghai-Mira Garden Villa #2, 1720 HongQiao Road 200336
Telephone: (21) 6278-0225
Fax: (21) 6278-0223
Email: rabbishalom@yahoo.com
Website: www.chinajewish.org
Shabbat meals are available. Kosher restaurant

COLOMBIA

The first Jews in Colombia were *Conversos*, as was common in South America. However, they were soon discovered by the Inquisition when it was established in Colombia.

The next influx of Jews came in the nineteenth century, followed by mass immigration from eastern Europe and the Middle East after 1918. Jews were banned from entering after 1939, but this restriction was eased after 1950.

The present community is a mix of Ashkenazi and Sephardi elements, each having their own communual organisations. There are also youth and Zionist organisations. There is a central organisation for Colombian Jewry in the capital Bogota. There are also Jewish schools and synagogues, and Jewish publications and radio programmes.

GMT -5 hours
Country calling code: (+57)
Total population: **36,612,000**
Jewish population: **5,000**
Emergency telephone: (**Police–112**) (**Fire–119**) (**Ambulance–132**)
Electricity voltage: **110/120**

BARANQUILLA

COMMUNITY ORGANISATIONS

Centro Israelita Filantropico

Carrera 43, 85-95, Apartado Aereo 2537
Telephone: (53) 342-310; 351-197

BOGOTA

EMBASSY

Embassy of Israel

Calle 35, No 7-25,Edificio Caxdax
Telephone: (1) 245-6603; 245-6712

MEDIA

Periodical

Menorah

Apertado Aereo 9081

RELIGIOUS ORGANISATIONS

Union Rabinica Colombiana

Tranversal 29, No 126-31
Telephone: (1) 625-4377
Fax: (1) 274-9069
Email: centrocib@tutopia.com

SYNAGOGUES

Congregacion Adath Israel

Carrera 7a, No 94-20
Telephone: (1) 257-1660; 257-1680
Fax: (1) 623-9069
Mikva on premises

Ashkenazi
Centro Israelita de Bogota
Traversal 29, No 126-31
Telephone: (1) 625-4377
Fax: (1) 274-9069
Email: centrocib@tutopia.com
Kosher meals available by prior arrangement with Rabbi
Goldschmidt, 218-2500

German
Asociacion Israelita Montefiore
Carrera 20, No37-54
Telephone: (1) 245-5264

Orthodox
Comunidad Hebrea Sefaradi
Calle 79, No 9-66
Telephone: (1) 256-2629; 249-0372
Mikva on premises

Jabad House
Calle 92, no 10, Adt. 405
Rabbi's Tel: (1) 257-4920

CALI
SYNAGOGUES
Ashkenazi
Sociedad Hebrea de Socoros
Av. 9a #10-15, Apartado Aereo 011652
Telephone: (2) 668-8518
Fax: (2) 668-8521

German
Union Cultural Israelita
Apartado Aereo 5552
Telephone: (2) 668-9830
Fax: (2) 661-6857

Sephardi
Centro Israelita de Beneficiencia
Calle 44a, Av. 5a Norte Esquina, Apartado Aereo 77
Telephone: (2) 664-1379
Fax: (2) 665-5419

MEDELLIN
COMMUNITY ORGANISATIONS
Union Israelita de Beneficencia
Carrera 43B, No 15-150, Apartado Aereo 4702

COSTA RICA

The first Jews arrived in Costa Rica in the nineteenth century from nearby islands in the Caribbean such as Jamaica. The next wave of immigrants came from eastern Europe in the 1920s. Thereafter Costa Rica did not welcome new Jewish immigrants, and passed laws against foreign merchants and foreign land ownership. However, the Jewish community in Costa Rica established a communual organisation in 1930. There is a monthly newsletter, and a synagogue in San Jose. Most Jewish children attend the Haim Weizmann School, which has both primary and secondary classes.

It is interesting to note that the Costa Rican embassy in Israel is in Jerusalem and not Tel Aviv, where most other embassies are situated.

GMT -6 hours
Country calling code: (+506)
Total population: 3,464,000
Jewish population: 2,500
Emergency telephone: (Police–911) (Fire–911) (Ambulance–911)
Electricity voltage: 110/220

SAN JOSE
CONTACT INFORMATION
Centro Israelia Sionista de Costa Rica
PO Box 1473-1000
Telephone: 233-9222
Fax: 233-9321
Email: cisdcr@racsa.co.cr
Website: www.centroisraelita.com

EMBASSY
Embassy of Israel
Edificio Centro Colon, Piso 11, PO Box 5147-1000
Telephone: 221-6011; 221-6444
Fax: 257-0867
Email: embofisr@sol.racsa.co.cr

GROCERIES
Little Israel Pita Rica
Pavas Rd. 1055-1200
Telephone: 290-2083
Fax: 262-5425
Email: pitarica@hotmail.com
Website: www.kosherfoodcostarica.co
The only kosher bakery and mini-market in Costa Rica.
Delivers to hotels.

HOTELS
Barcelo San Jose Palacio
Apdo 458-1150
Telephone: 220-2034; 220-2035
Fax: 220-2036
Email: Palacio@sol.racsa.co.cr
Hotel has separate kosher kitchen, with the key in the Mashgiach's (Rabbi Levkovitz) hands. The hotel is about a half hour walk to the synagogue.

Camino Real
Prospero Ferandezy, Camino Real Boulevard
Telephone: 289-7000
Fax: 231-5834
Email: caminoreal@yiconet.co.cr
Hotel has separate kosher kitchen, with the key in the Mashgiach's (Rabbi Levkovitz) hands.

Melia Confort Corobici
PO Box 2443-1000
Telephone: 232-8122
Fax: 231-5834
Email: melia.confort.corobici@solmelia.com
There is no separate kosher kitchen, but it is fairly close to the Orthodox synagogue. The hotel has two separate storage rooms for kosher cookware.

RESTAURANTS
Meat
Delight-Sabor Mediterraneo
Costado Sur de Perifericos, San Rafael de Escazu, San Jose
Telephone: 288-2707
Email: varditr@hotmail.com
Cuisine: Israeli - Meat

SYNAGOGUES
Cogregacion B'ni Israel-Judaismo Reformista en Costa Rica
Old Road to Escazu. From the sabana Pops 700ms., West, House in the corner on your left
Telephone: 231-5243
Fax: 257-3308
Email: congbnei@racsa.co.cr
A Liberal Synagogue affiliated with World Union of Progressive Judaism Liberal Congregations of Central America and the Caribbean.

Sinagoga B'nai Israel Oficinas de Torneca
Avenida 10 Frente al Cemetario de Extranjeros
Telephone: 386-1666
Website: www.bnei-israel.org

Orthodox
Shaarei Zion
De la Torre Medica en Paseo Colon
Email: mailto:cisdcr@racsa.co.
Website: www.centroisraelita.com

CROATIA

Jews were in the land now known as Croatia before the Croats themselves. The Croats arrived in the seventh century, the Jews some centuries before with the Romans: there are remains of a third-century Jewish cemetery in Solin (near Split).

The first Jewish communites were involved in trade with Italy across the Adriatic Sea, and also in trade along the River Danube. Their success was brief, however, and they were expelled in 1456, only returning more than 300 years later. The area became part of the newly formed Yugoslavia after the First World War, and the Jewish community became part of the Federation of Jewish Communities in Yugoslavia.

The Croatian Jews suffered greatly under the German occupation in the Second World War when the local *Ustashe* (Croatian Fascists) assisted the Germans. Despite their efforts some Jews survived and even decided to rebuild their community when peace returned.

Today, after the civil war, there are synagogues in towns across the country. There are some Hebrew classes and newsletters are published. There are also many places of historical interest, such as Ulicia Zudioska (Jewish Street) in Dubrovnik.

GMT -1 hours
Country calling code: (+385)
Total population: 4,498,000
Jewish population: 2,000
Emergency telephone: (Police–92) (Fire–93) (Other emergency–94)
Electricity voltage: 220

DUBROVNIK
MUSEUMS
Jewish Museum
Zudioska Street 3
The first Jewish museum in Croatia opened in May 2003. It is located in the Dubrovnik Synagogue and has Torah scrolls dating back to the 13th century.

SYNAGOGUES
Dubrovnik Synagogue
Zudioska Street 3
Zudioska means 'Street of the Jews'. This is the second oldest synagogue in Europe and is located in a very narrow street off the main street–the Stradun or Placa. The Jewish community office is in the same building. Zudioska Street is the third turning on the right from the clock tower. There are about thirty Jews in the city. Tourists help to make up a minyan in the synagogue on Friday night and High Holy Days.

OSIJEK

COMMUNITY ORGANISATIONS
Community Building
Brace Radica Street 13
Telephone: (31) 211-407
Fax: (31) 211-407
The community building contains objects from the synagogue that was destroyed during the Second World War. the community numbers about 150 members and has two cemeteries. No regular services are held. A former building of the pre-war synagogue in Cvjetkova Street is a Pentecostal church today. There is a plaque at the site of the destroyed synagogue in Zupanijska Street.

RIJEKA

SYNAGOGUES
Rijeka Synagogue
Filipovieva ul. 9, PO Box 65 51000
Telephone: (51) 425-156; 336-032
The community numbers about sixty. Services are held in the well-maintained synagogue on Jewish holidays.

SPLIT

COMMUNITY ORGANISATIONS
Jewish Community of Split
Zidovski Prolaz 1 21000
Telephone: (21) 345-672
The synagogue at Split is one of the few in Yugoslavia to have survived the wartime occupation.The Jewish community numbers about 200. There is a Jewish cemetery, established in 1578. More information from the community offices at the above number.

ZAGREB

Jewish Community of Zagreb
Palmoticeva Street 16, PO Box 986
Telephone: (1) 434-619
Fax: (1) 434-638
Email: jcz@public.stce.hr
Before the War Zagreb had 11,000 Jews. There are now only 1,500, but they remain very active in Jewish communal life. Services are held in the community building on Friday evenings and holidays.

MONUMENT
Central Synagogue
Praska Street 7
There is a plaque on the spot of this pre-war synagogue

Mirogoj Cemetery
There is an impressive monument in this cemetery to the Jewish victims of the Second World War

TOURIST SITES
National Museum
Features an ashkenazi prayerbook from the 15th century

CUBA

The first Jew to set foot in Cuba (1492) was Luis de Torres. Although hundreds arrived following the Spanish Inquisition they were prohibited from practising their religion. This changed in 1898 following Cuba's liberation from Spain. With the end of Spanish colonial rule in that year, Jews from nearby areas, such as Jamaica and Florida, and Jewish veterans of the Spanish American War, began to settle in Cuba. A congregation was established in 1904. Later, Turkish Sephardim formed their own synagogue. The community was then augmented by immigrants from eastern Europe who had decided to stay in Cuba, which was being used as a transit camp for those seeking to enter America. A central committee was established for all Jewish groups in the 1930s. Cuba imposed severe restrictions on immigration at that time, and the story of the German ship St Louis (full of Jewish refugees), which was refused entry into Cuba, is well known.

About 12,000 Jews lived on the island in 1952. Havana had by far the largest community, and 75 per cent of the Cuban community was Ashkenazi. Although the Cuban revolution did not target Jews, religious affiliations were initially discouraged and many Jews emigrated (as did many non-Jews). The remaining community has synagogues and a Sunday school. Kosher food and Judaica are imported, mainly from Canada and Panama. Cuba broke off diplomatic relations with Israel in 1973, although in 1998/99 a number of Jews were allowed to emigrate to Israel.

GMT -5 hours
Country calling code: (+53)
Total population: **11,509.000**
Jewish population: **600**
Emergency telephone: (**Police–82 0116**) (**Fire–81 115**) (**Ambulance–404 551**)
Electricity voltage: **110/220**

HAVANA

COMMUNITY ORGANISATIONS
Jewish community in Cuba
Casa de la Communidad Hebrea de Cuba, Calle 1,
#259, Esquina de la Habana 10400
Telephone: (7) 832-8953
Fax: (7) 833-3778
Email: beth_shalom@net.cu or
patron_ort@enet.cu

SYNAGOGUES
Conservative
**Patronado de la Casa de la Comunidad
Hebrea de Cuba**
Calle 13 el, Vedado
Telephone: (7) 832-8953
This is also the location of a modern community centre

Orthodox
**Comunidad Religiosa Hebrea Adath Israel de
Cuba**
Acosta No. 357 Esq., Picota, Habana Vieja,
Telephone: (7) 861-3495
Fax: (7) 860-8242
Email: adath@enet.cu
Dan Heller provides a photo essay and material on Cuba's
Jewish community

Hadath Israel
Calle Picota 52 Habana Vieja
Telephone: (7) 861-3495

SYNAGOGUES
Sephardi
Centro Sefardi (Conservative)
Calle 17 Esquina E Vedado, La Habana 10400
Telephone: (7) 832-6623
Jose Levy Tur President

CURAÇAO

KASHRUT INFORMATION
There is no kosher restaurant in Curaçao. However many
kosher items may be purchsed at the 'food store' of the
Congregation Shaarei Tsedek.

MUSEUMS
Jewish Cultural Historical Museum
Hanchi di Snoa 29, PO Box 322
Telephone: (5999) 461-1633
Fax: (5999) 465-4141
Opening Hours: Monday to Friday 9.00 to 11.45 am and
2.30 to 4.45 pm. If there is a cruise ship in port, then also
on Sundays from 9.00 am to noon. Closed on Shabbats and
Holy Days. On permanent display are a great many ritual,
ceremonial and cultural objects, many of which date back
to the seventeenth and eighteenth centuris and are still in
use by the adjacent congregation Mikve Israel-Emanuel
(founded 1651, oldest in the hemisphere).

SYNAGOGUES
Ashkenazi
Congregation Shaarei Tsedek
Leliweg 1a, PO Box 498
Telephone: (5999) 737-5738
Fax: (5999) 736-9546

Sephardi Reconstructionist
United Congregation Mikve'Israel Emanuel
Hanchi di Snoa 29, PO Box 322
Telephone: (5999) 461-1067
Fax: (5999) 465-4141
Email: info@snoa.com
Sabbath services are Friday at 6.30 pm (second Friday in
the month is a family service), Saturday at 10.00 am. Holy
Day services at the same time.

CYPRUS

During the Roman Empire, Jewish merchants made their home on Cyprus.
However, after a revolt that destroyed the
town of Salamis, they were expelled. In
medieval times small Jewish communities
were established in Nicosia, Limassol and
other towns, but the community was never
large.

It is interesting to note that Cyprus was
seen as a possible 'Jewish Homeland' by
the early Zionists. Agricultural settlements
were established at the end of the nineteenth century, but they were not successful. Herzl himself tried to persuade the
British government to allow Jewish rule
over Cyprus in 1902, but met with failure.

Some German Jews managed to escape to
Cyprus in the early 1930s. After the war,
many Holocaust survivors who had tried
to enter Palestine illegally were deported to
special camps on the island. Some 50,000
European Jews were held there. Since the
establishment of the state of Israel, the
Jewish community on the island has
become small; the Israeli embassy serves
as a centre for community activities.

GMT +2 hours
Country calling code: (+357)
Total population: 766,000
Jewish population: **Under 100**
Emergency telephone: (Police–112) (Fire–112)
(Ambulance–112)
Electricity voltage: 240

LARNACA
COMMUNITY ORGANISATIONS
Chabad Lubavitch of Cyprus
Diogenous 7, 6020 Larnaca Cyprus, PO Box 42461 6534, Larnaca
Telephone: (24) 828770
Fax: (24) 828771
Mobile Phone: (99) 931679
Email: chabadofcyprus@cytanet.com.cy
Website: www.chabadcyprus.com
Kosher meals by arrangement

NICOSIA
Committee of the Jewish Community of Cyprus
Po Box 24784 1303
Telephone: (22) 694-758
Fax: (22) 662-077
Email: amiyes@nicosia.mfa.gov.il
Website: www.nicosia.mfa.gov.il

EMBASSY
Embassy of Israel
4 Grypari Strret
Telephone: (22) 369-500; 369-549
Fax: (22) 666-338
Email: press@nicosia.mfa.gov.il
Website: www.nicosia.mfa.gov.il
Contact Mrs Z. Yeshrun for information

CZECH REPUBLIC

Prague, the capital of this small central European country, has become a major tourist attraction. It is one of the few cities to actively promote its Jewish heritage, which dates from early medieval times. The oldest (still functioning) synagogue in Europe is there (the Altneuschul), as well as other interesting Jewish sites.

After the arrival of the first Jews in the country, in the tenth century, they suffered similar tragedies to those of other medieval Jewish communities; forced baptism by the Crusaders and expulsions, together with some tolerance. Full emancipation was reached in 1867 under the Hapsburgs. The celebrated Jewish writer, Franz Kafka, lived in Prague and did not neglect his Judaism, unlike many other Czech Jews who assimilated and intermarried.

The German occupation led to 85 per cent of the community (80,000 people) perishing in the Holocaust. Further difficulties were faced in the communist period after the war, but since the 1989 'Velvet Revolution', Judaism is being rediscovered. The community (mostly elderly) has several synagogues around the country, a kindergarten and a journal, and there are kosher restaurants in the old Jewish Quarter in Prague.

GMT +1 hours
Country calling code: (+420)
Total population: **10,304,000**
Jewish population: **5,000**
Emergency telephone: (Police–158) (Fire–150) (Ambulance–155)
Electricity voltage: **220**

BOSKOVICE
MUSEUMS
Medieval Ghetto
Telephone: (516) 452-077
Fax: (516) 454-607
Email: museum@boskovice.cz
Website: www.boskovice.cz/muzeum
Seventeenth-century Jewish town, synagogue and cemetery

BRNO
COMMUNITY ORGANISATIONS
Community Centre
tr. Kpt. Jarose 3 60200
Telephone: (5) 4524-4710
Fax: (5) 4521-3803
Email: zob@zob.cz
Website: www.zob.cz
The community president can be reached on (6) 0333-2458

SYNAGOGUES
Brno Synagogue
Skorepka 13

HOLESOV
MUSEUMS
Schach Synagogue
Dating from 1650, this synagogue is now a museum. Open in the mornings. At other times the curator will show visitors around if contacted. The old cemetery is close by.

LIBEREC
SYNAGOGUES
Community Centre
Matousova 21, Reichenberg 46001
Telephone: (48) 510-3340
Each weekday 9.00 am to 11.00 am

MIKULOV
SITE
Cemetery and partly restored Synagogue
Only one synagogue, still being restored, remains of the many which flourished here when the town was the spiritual capital of Moravian Jewry and the seat of the Chief Rabbis of Moravia. The cemetery contains the graves of famous rabbis.

OLOMOUC
SYNAGOGUES
Community Centre
Komenskeho 7
Telephone: (68) 522-3119

PILSEN
The Jewish Community of Pilsen
Smetanovy Sady 5, Pilsen 30137
Telephone: (0042) 03 77235749
Fax: (0042) 03 77235749
Services Friday evenings. The Great Synagogue is now closed.

POLNA
MUSEUMS
Museum
A museum was opened in 2000 in a reconstructed seventeenth century synagogue. It charts the spread of anti-Semitism in Central Europe.

PRAGUE
Most of the Jews in the Czech Republic live in Prague, which has had a thousand-year history of Jewish settlement. The impact of the Jews in Prague has been great, the Golem has entered Prague folklore, and the Altneushul is the oldest functioning synagogue in Europe. The Jewish Quarter in the old town contains many historical sites.

Terezin is some forty miles from Prague and is easily visited. On the way is the town of Lidice, destroyed in June 1942 by the Nazis in retaliation for the assassination of Reinhard Heydrich.

CEMETERIES
Old Jewish Cemetery
U Stare Skoly 1 11000
Telephone: (2) 2171-1511
Fax: (2) 2171-1584
Email: office@jewishmuseum.cz
Website: www.jewishmuseum.cz
The oldest Jewish cemetery in Europe, containing the graves of such famous rabbis & scholars as Avigdor Karo (1439), Yehuda Low ben Bezalel (1609), David Gans (1613) and David Oppenheim (1736). Reservation centre Tel: 2231-7191 Fax: 2231-7181.

CONTACT INFORMATION
Jewish Town Hall
Maislova 18
Houses the federation of Jewish Communities in the Czech Republic. It has the world famous Hebrew clock. Also houses the Shalom Jewish Community restaurant.

EMBASSY
Embassy of Israel
Badeniho 2, Prague 7 17076
Telephone: (2) 3309-7500
Fax: (2) 3309-7529
Email: israelba@bohem-net.cz
Website: www.praque.mfa.gov.il

HOTELS
President Hotel
Namesti Curieovych 100 116-88
Telephone: (2) 614100
Fax: (2) 614110
A few minutes walk from the old Jewish quarter

MUSEUMS
Jewish Museum in Prague
U Stare Skoly 1, 3
Telephone: (2) 2171-1511
Fax: (2) 2171-1584
Email: office@jewishmuseum.cz
Website: www.jewishmuseum.cz
2006: centennial celebration of the existence of the Jewish Museum in Prague and many new short-term exhibitions and the accompanying activities are prepared.

RESTAURANTS
Meat
King Solomon Restaurant
Siroka 8, Prague 1 110 00
Telephone: (2) 2481-8752
Fax: (2) 7486-4664
Email: solomon@kosher.cz
Website: www.kosher.cz

SYNAGOGUES
Orthodox
Altneuschul
Cervena ul. 7 1
Telephone: (2) 231-0909
Dates back to 1275. The synagogue has recently reopened after the devasting floods of 2002.

Chabad Center Prague
3 Parizska Street, Prague 1 11000
Telephone: (2) 2232-0896
Fax: (2) 2232-0200
Email: chabadpraque@mbox.vol.cz
Website: www.chabadpraque.cz

TOURS
Precious Legacy Tours
Kaprova 13, Prague 1, Josefov
Telephone: (2) 232-1951
Fax: (2) 232-1954
Email: luba@legacytours.net
Website: www.legacytours.net
Tours in Prague, Kutna Hora, Kolin, Vienna, Budapest etc.

Wittmann Tours
Manesova 8, 120 00 Prague 2
Telephone: (2) 2225-2472
Fax: (2) 2225-2472
Email: sylvie@wittmann-tours.com
Website: www.wittmann-tours.com

TEPLICE
SYNAGOGUES
Community Centre
Lipova 25, Tepliz-Schönau
Telephone: (417) 26-580

TEREZIN
MUSEUMS
The Terezin Museum
Theresienstadt
There is a new museum in the town dedicated to the Jews who were deported from Theresienstadt to Auschwitz

DENMARK

Jews were allowed to settle in Denmark in 1622, earlier than in any other Scandinavian country. Thereafter the community grew, with immigration largely from Germany. The Danish king allowed the foundation of the unified Jewish community of Copenhagen in 1684, and the Jews were granted full citizenship in 1849.

In the early part of the twentieth century many refugees arrived from eastern Europe, and Denmark welcomed refugees from Nazi Germany. When the Germans conquered Denmark and ordered the Jews to be handed over, the Danish resistance managed to save 7,200 (90 per cent of the community) by arranging boats to take them to neutral Sweden. Some Jews did, however, stay behind and were taken to the transit ghetto of Theresienstadt (Terezin), and many died.

After the war most of the Jews returned, and there is now a central Jewish organisation based in Copenhagen. There are also homes for the elderly, synagogues and a mikvah. Kosher food is available.

GMT +1 hours
Country calling code: (+45)
Total population: **5,284,000**
Jewish population: **8,000**
Emergency telephone: (Police–112) (Fire–112) (Ambulance–112)
Electricity voltage: **220**

COPENHAGEN
With a Jewish population of almost 9,000, the vast majority of Danish Jews live in the capital. The Community Centre contains most of the offices of the Jewish community, and three old-age homes are jointly run with the Copenhagen Municipality. The Great Synagogue and the cemetery dating from 1693 are interesting sites.

BUTCHERS
Kosher Delikatesse
87Lyngbyvej 2100
Telephone: 3918-5777

COMMUNITY ORGANISATIONS
Jewish Community Centre
Ny Kongensgade 6 1472
Telephone: 3312-8868
Fax: 3312-3357
Email: mt@mosaiske.dk

EMBASSY
Embassy of Israel
Lundevangsvej 4, Hellerup 2900
Telephone: 3962-6288
Fax: 3962-1938
Email: israel@pip.dknet.dk

GROCERIES
I. A. Samson
Roerholmsgade 3 1352
Telephone: 3313 0077
Fax: 3314-8277
Kosher grocery provisions and delicatessen. Catering for groups, twenty persons plus.

MIKVAOT
Jewish Community Centre
Ny Kongensgade 6 1472
Telephone: 3312-8868
Fax: 3312-3357
Email: mt@mosaiske.dk

Mikva
12 Krystalgade 1172
Telephone: 3393-7662; 3332-9443

SYNAGOGUES
Copenhagen Synagogue
Granavenget 8
Telephone: 4220-0731
Open from Shavuot to Succot

Orthodox
Great Synagogue of Copenhagen
12 Krystalgade 1172
Telephone: 3929-9520
Fax: 3929-2517
Email: bent_lexner@hotmail.com
Website: www.mosaike.dk
Weekly Shabbat services

Machsike Hadass
Ole suhrsgade 12 1354
Telephone: 4970-0731
Email: ek@get2net.dk
Daily and Shabbat services

TOURIST SITES
Copenhagen Walking Tours
Telephone: 4081-1217
Email: info@copenhagen-walkingtours
Website: www.copenhagen-walkingtours.dn
Walking tours of sites of Jewish interest in the old city

HORNBAEK
A resort and seaside town where many members of the Copenhagen community spend the summer months, or weekends. It is the area of the coast from which the Jewish community escaped in 1943.

Hotel Villa Strand

Hornbæk, Elsinore, Copenhagen and Denmark

Hotel Villa Strand has a unique location right at one of Denmarks most popular beaches - Hornbæk Beach. Only a few minutes walk from the Harbour and a wide selection of shops.

The hotel has a private guest garden with two sun terraces and entrance directly to Sand dunes and the Beach. All the rooms have private toilet and shower. Our kitchen is international and specialised in Glat Kosher (Kosher meals).

Hotel Villa Strand lies in the picturesque harbour town of Hornbæk. Hornbæk has everything to offer, beautiful white beaches, a unique selection of excellent restaurants and a wide choice of shops and boutiques which remain open every day all year round.

Kystvej 12 | DK-3100 Hornbæk | Denmark | Phone: +45 49 700 088 | Fax: +45 49 701 100
Email: hotel@villastrand.dk Internet: www.villastrand.dk

HOTELS
Kosher
Hotel Villa Strand
Kystvej 12 DK-3100
Telephone: (49) 700-088
Fax: (49) 701-100

DOMINICAN REPUBLIC

Jewish settlement in the Dominican Republic was comparatively late. The oldest Jewish grave dates back to 1826. Descended from central European Jews, the community was not religious and many married Christians. President Francisco Henriquez y Carvajal (1916) traced his ancestry back to the early Jewish settlers.

In 1938 the republic decided to accept refugees from Nazism (one of the very few countries of the world that did so freely), and even provided areas where they could settle. As a result, there were 1,000 Jews living there in 1943. This number declined as, once again, the Jewish community assimilated and married the local non-Jewish population. Despite this, many non-Jewish husbands, wives and children take part in Jewish events.

Two synagogues and a rabbi who divides his time between them are features of Jewish life. There is also a Sunday school in Santo Domingo and a bi-monthly magazine is produced. There is a small Jewish museum in Sosua.

GMT -4 hours
Country calling code: **(+1 809)**
Total population: **8,097,000**
Jewish population: 150
Emergency telephone: **(Police–999) (Fire–999) (Ambulance–999)**
Electricity voltage: **220/240**

SANTO DOMINGO
COMMUNITY ORGANISATIONS
Consejo Dominicano de Mujeres Hebreas
PO Box 2189
Telephone: (809) 535-6042
Fax: (809) 688-2058

EMBASSY
Embassy of Israel
Av. Pedro Henriquez Urena 80 1404
Telephone: (809) 542-1635; 542-1548

SYNAGOGUES
Conservative
Centro Israelita de la Republica Dominicana
Av. Sarasota #21, Bella Vista
Telephone: (809) 535-6042
Fax: (809) 533-0168
Email: lalo@verizon.net.do

SOSUA
SYNAGOGUES
Liberal
Sosua Synagogue
Calle Alejo Matinez, El Batey, Next door to Hotel Casa Marina Reef
Telephone: (809) 533-0168
Fax: (809) 533-0168
Services: Monthly, last Friday and Saturday

ECUADOR

As in most Latin American countries, *Conversos* comprised the earliest Jewish settlers in Ecuador. It was not until 1904 that East European Jews began to arrive, and numbers increased further following the Nazi take-over in Germany, as Ecuador granted refuge to more Jews than other neighbouring countries. About 3,000 Jews entered Ecuador in the 1930s. The Jewish population peaked in 1950 at 4,000, but this number declined owing to emigration. In recent years, some Jews have moved to Ecuador from elsewhere in South America.

There are no Jewish schools, but children do have access to Jewish education.
GMT -5 hours
Country calling code: **(+593)**
Total population: **11,937,00**
Jewish population: **1,000**
Emergency telephone: **(Police–101) (Fire–102) (Ambulance–131)**
Electricity voltage: **110/220**

QUITO

COMMUNITY ORGANISATIONS
Communidad Judia del Ecuador
Calle Roberto Andrade, OE3 590 y Jaime, Roldos
Urbanizacion Einstein (Carcelen)
Telephone: (2) 2483-800/927
Fax: (2) 2486-755
Email: aiq@cje-ec.com

EMBASSY
Embassy of Israel
Av. Eloy Alfaro 969, Casilla 2463
Telephone: (2) 547-322; 548-431

EGYPT

For more than 2,000 years there has been a virtually continuous Jewish presence in the vicinity of Cairo, and an even more ancient Jewish presence in Egypt is recounted in the Bible. After the exodus, Jews returned to Egypt during the time of Alexander the Great, and at that time the Ben Ezra synagogue was built. The Bible was translated into Greek during that period. In the first century CE, the Jewish presence declined, but a renaissance occurred with Moses Maimonides's arrival in Egypt in the twelfth century. Most of his books were written in Cairo and his yeshiva still exists in the Jewish quarter. From then on the Jewish community expanded and flourished, especially with the arrival of refugees from pogroms and during the First and Second World Wars.

Before 1948 there were about 70,000 Jews in Egypt. The 1956 Suez War and the 1967 Six Day War encouraged Jewish emigration. At present the community is small ,but the Jewish heritage, mostly synagogues classified as antiquities, represents an inestimable treasure worth visiting, as, for example, the recently restored Ben Ezra synagogue, home of the world-famous Genizah of some 400,000 documents (the majority of which are now in Cambridge, England).

GMT +2 hours
Country calling code: (+20)
Total population: **67,974,000**
Jewish population: **Under 100**
Electricity voltage: 220

ALEXANDRIA

SYNAGOGUES
Eliahu Hanavi
69 Nebi Daniel Street, Ramia Station
Telephone: (3) 492-3974, 597-4438

CAIRO

Cairo has had a long and important Jewish history. The community has however declined in line with the rest of Egyptian Jewry. There are a number of interesting sites such as the recently restored Ben Ezra Synagogue where the Cairo Genizah used to be located.

COMMUNITY ORGANISATIONS
Community Organisations
13 Rue Sabyl El Kazindar, Abbassieh
Telephone: (2) 824-613, 824-885
Website: www.geocities.com

EMBASSY
Embassy of Israel
6 Ibn Malek St., Gizeh
Telephone: (2) 361-0528
Fax: (2) 361-0414
Email: isremcai@mail.rite.com

SYNAGOGUES
Ben-Ezra
6 Harett il-Sitt Barbara, Mari Girges, Old Cairo
Telephone: (2) 847-695
The synagogue was built in 1892 and is the oldest in Egypt. According to legend, under the building is the site where Pharoh's daughter found Moses.

Meir Enaim
55 No. 13 Street, Maadi
Supervision: Jewish Community of Cairo
Can be visited on request

Shaarei Hashamayim
17 Adli Pasha Street, Downtown Cairo
Telephone: (2) 292-9025
Fax: (2) 736-9639
Services are held on holidays. There is an interesting library across from the synagogue which is only accessible with a key. Ask the guards.

EL SALVADOR

The Jewish connection to El Salvador is not a strong one. It is believed that some Portuguese *Conversos* crossed the country a few hundred years ago. After that, some Sephardis from France moved to Chaluchuapa. Other Jews came from Europe, but in smaller numbers than those settling in other Latin American countries. There were only 370 Jews in 1976, a number reduced during the civil war, when many emigrated. Some returned, however, when the war was over.

An official community was set up in 1944 and a synagogue was opened in 1950. El Salvador is one of the few countries to have an embassy in Jerusalem, rather than Tel Aviv.

GMT -6 hours
Country calling code: (+503)
Total population: 5,928,000
Jewish population: 120
Emergency telephone: (Police–123) (Fire–123) (Ambulance–123)
Electricity voltage: 110

SAN SALVADOR

EMBASSY

Embassy of Israel
Alameda Roosevelt y 63 Avenida Sur, Centro, Finaciero Gigante Torre B, 11 o piso
Telephone: 211-3434
Fax: 211-3443
Email: elsalvador@israel.org

SYNAGOGUES

Conservative
Comunidad Israelita de El Salvador
Boulevard del Hipodromo 626 #1, Colonia San Benito, PO Box 06-182
Telephone: 263-8074
Fax: 263-8074
Email: cisraelita@integra.com.sv
Services Friday, Shabbat morning and Holy Days

San Salvador Synagogue
23 Blvd. del Hipodromo 626, Colonia San Benito
Telephone: 237-366
Friday evening services only

ESTONIA

Despite being the only country officially declared 'Judenrein' (free of Jews) at the Wannsee conference in 1942, there is a Jewish community here today. The community has always been small, and is believed to have begun in the fourteenth century. However, most Jews arrived in the nineteenth century, when Czar Alexander II allowed certain groups of Jews into the area.

The first community was established in Tallinn in 1830. By 1939, the community

had grown to 4,500 and was free from restraints. After the Soviet and Nazi occupations in the Second World War the Jews returned, mainly from the Soviet Union. Now that Estonia is independent, the Jewish community is able to practise its religion freely.

GMT +2 hours
Country calling code: (+372)
Total population: 1,454,000
Jewish population: 2,500
Emergency telephone: (Police–002 in Tallinn, 01 elsewhere) (Fire–001 in Tallinn, 02 elsewhere) (Ambulance–003 in Talinn, 03 elsewhere)
Electricity voltage: 220

TALLINN

SYNAGOGUES

Orthodox
Tallinn Synagogue
16A Karu Street, PO Box 3576 10120
Telephone: (6) 623-050
Fax: (6) 623-001
Email: rabbi@jewishestonia.com

ETHIOPIA

The Falashas (*Ge'ez* for 'stranger', applied to the Ethiopian Jews) of Ethiopia became known world-wide in the early 1980s, when many were airlifted to Israel. The origins of the Beta Israel, as they call themselves, are unclear and little is known for certain. Historians have concluded that they may have become Jewish as early as the second or third century.

As the area became known to the West through nineteenth-century explorers, some Western Jews set up schools in the country. The Jewish population was believed to have been about 50,000 in 1934. After the establishment of Israel, more interest was taken in the Ethiopian community and the Ethiopian civil war was the catalyst for Operation Moses, when 10,000 people were airlifted to Israel in 1984–85. A further 15,000 left for Israel in 1991.

GMT +2 hours
Country calling code: (+251)
Total population: 63,495,000
Jewish population: 500

Electricity voltage: **220**

ADDIS ABABA
COMMUNITY ORGANISATIONS
Community
PO Box 50
Telephone: (1) 111-725; 446-471

EMBASSY
Israel Embassy in Ethiopia
PO Box 1266 Higher 16 Kebela 22 House, #283
Telephone: (1) 612-456
Email: addisababa@israel.org

ASMARA
SYNAGOGUES
The Synagogue of Asmara
Via Hailemariam Mammo 34 Asmara
The Synagogue of Asmara was built in 1906. It is a
beautiful, serene building just off the main street. The
wooden cornices and fittings are hand carved and the
scrolls of the Torah are hand written.

FIJI

When Henry Marks, at the age of 20, moved
to Fiji from Australia in 1881, he was the
first recorded Jew on the island. Over the
years, he developed a successful business
across the region, and was later knighted.

Indian and other Jews later moved to Fiji
but did not organise any official community. In recent years the Fiji Jewish
Association has been created. The Israeli
embassy organises an annual Seder.

GMT +12 hours
Country calling code: (+679)
Total population: 772,000
Jewish population: **Under 100**
Emergency telephone: (Police–000) (Fire–000)
(Ambulance–000)
Electricity voltage: **240**

SUVA
COMMUNITY ORGANISATIONS
Fiji Jewish Association
Carpenter Street, PO Box 882, Suva
Telephone: 387-980
Email: contex@is.co.fj

EMBASSY
Embassy of Israel
Joske Street, 69, Parade Building, PO Box 15249,
Suva
Telephone: 303-420
Fax: 300-415

FINLAND

When Finland was occupied by Russia in
the nineteenth century, many Jewish con-
scripts in the Russian army settled in
Finland after their discharge. They were
still subject to several restrictions, but
these ended after Finland's independence
in 1917. In addition to these 'Cantonists',
as they were known, immigrants came to
Finland from eastern Europe. Finland
proved a safe haven, as the government
refused to hand over Finnish Jews to the
Nazis, despite being allied to Germany in
its war with Soviet Russia.

The community is keen to preserve a sense
of Jewish identity among the young generation, who are encouraged to experience
Jewish life in Israel. The community is also
keen to help other Jews in the newly independent Baltic states across the sea to the
south of the country. There is a central
body for Jewish communities, and kosher
food is available. There are also synagogues and a school.

GMT +2 hours
Country calling code: (+358)
Total population: 5,140,000
Jewish population: **1,200**
Emergency telephone: (Police–10022) (Fire–112)
(Ambulance–112)
Electricity voltage: **220**

HELSINKI
Some 1,200 Jews (the majority of the Jewish
population in Finland) live in Helsinki. The
community centre is next to the synagogue.
There is also a Jewish cemetery containing an
area dedicated to the Jews who fought in the
Finnish army in various wars, including the
Russo-Finnish war.

BUTCHERS
Butcher/Deli
Kosher Deli
Malminkatu 24
Telephone: (9) 685-4584
Fax: (9) 694-8916
Email: srk@jchelsinki.fi
Website: www.jchelsinki.fi

COMMUNITY ORGANISATIONS
Community Centre

Malminkatu 26
Telephone: (9) 586-0310
Fax: (9) 694-8916
Email: srk@jchelsinki.fi
Website: www.jchelsinki.fi
Kosher meals by arrangement

EMBASSY
Embassy of Israel
Yrjonkatu 36A 00100
Telephone: (9) 681-2020
Fax: (9) 135-6959
Email: info@helsinki.mfa

MONUMENT
**Memorial to Jewish Refugees – Hands
Begging for Mercy**
Laivasillankatu, Ullanlinna
A Monument was unveiled in 2000 in a park opposite the
harbour where Jewish refugees were deported in 1942 to
Germany.

SYNAGOGUES
Orthodox
Jewish Community Synagogue
Malminkatu 26 00100
Telephone: (9) 586-0130
Fax: (9) 694-8916
Email: srk@jchelsinki.fi
Built in 1906. Preserved in the synagogue is a wreath
presented in 1944 by the then President of Finland in
memory of Jews who died in the Russo-Finnish War.
Services Monday and thursday morning, 7.45 pm
(summer), 5 pm (winter); Shabbat and Sunday mornings,
9.00 am.

TURKU
SYNAGOGUES
Orthodox
Turku Synagogue
Brahenkatu 17
Telephone: (2) 231-2557
Fax: (2) 233-4689
The secretary is always pleased to meet visitors

FRANCE

France now boasts the largest Jewish community in Europe. The Jewish connection
with France is a long one which dates back
over 1,000 years as there is evidence of
Jewish settlement in several towns in the
first few centuries of the Jewish Diaspora.
The community grew in early medieval
times, and contributed to the economy of
the region. Two great Jewish commentators, Rashi and Rabenu Tam, both lived in
France. However, French Jewry suffered
both from the Crusaders and from other
anti-semitic outbursts in the medieval
period.

Napoleon's reign heralded the emancipation of French Jewry and, as his armies
conquered Europe, the emancipation of
other communities began. Despite this,
incidents such as the Dreyfus Affair high-
lighted the fact that anti-semitism was not
yet dead. The worst case of anti-semitism
in France occurred under the German
occupation, when some 70,000 Jews were
deported from the community of 300,000.
After the war France became a centre for
Jewish immigration, beginning with
80,000 from eastern Europe, and then
many thousands from North Africa, which
eventually swelled the Jewish population
to nearly 700,000.

The community is well served with organisations. Paris alone has 380,000 Jews,
more than in the whole of the UK. There
are kosher restaurants and synagogues in
many towns throughout the country, and
newspapers, radio programmes and
schools in several cities. In Carpentras and
Cavaillon there are synagogues which are
considered to be national monuments.

GMT +1 hours
Country calling code: **(+33)**
Total population: **58,607,000**
Jewish population: **600,000**
Emergency telephone: **(Police 015017) (Fire
015018) (Ambulance 015015)**
Electricity voltage: **220**

North East
AMIENS
SYNAGOGUES
Amiens Synagogue
38 rue du Port d'Amont 8000

BAR-LE-DUC
Bar-Le-Duc Synagogue
7 Quai Carnot

BEAUVAIS

Beauvais Synagogue
Rue Jules Isaac 60000
Telephone: 03-44-05-46-90

BELFORT

COMMUNITY ORGANISATIONS
Community Publishers
27 Rue Strolz 90000
Telephone: 03-84-28-55-41
Fax: 03-84-28-55-41
Publishes *Notre Communaute* (quarterly).

SYNAGOGUES
Belfort Synagogue
6 rue de l'As-de-Carreau 90000
Telephone: 03-84-28-55-41
Fax: 03-84-28-55-41

BENFELD

Benfield Synagogue
7a rue de la Dime 67230
Telephone: 03-88-74-47-11

BESANCON

BUTCHERS
M. Croppet
18 rue des Granges 25000
Telephone: 03-81-83-35-93
Thursdays only

COMMUNITY ORGANISATIONS
Community
10 rue Grosjean 25000
Telephone: 03-81-80-82-82

SYNAGOGUES
Besancon Synagogue
23c Quai de Strasbourg 25000

BITCHE

Bitche Synagogue
28 rue de Sarreguemines 57230
Services Rosh Hashana & Yom Kippur

BOULAY

Boulay Synagogue
Rue du Pressoir 57220
Telephone: 03-87-79-28-34

BOULOGNE-SUR-MER

Boulogne-Sur-Mer Synagogue
63 rue Charles Butor 62200

SYNAGOGUES
Orthodox
Boulogne-Sur-Mer Synagogue
43 rue des Abondances, Hauts-de Seine 92100
Telephone: 01-46-03-90-63
Fax: 01-46-03-90-63

BOUXWILLER

With a Jewish population of 16,000, this city, contested by France and Germany throughout history, currently has an important Jewish community with several kosher restaurants, butchers and even a kosher vineyard. The earliest evidence of Jewish life dates from 1188. A 13th century Mikvah was recently discovered.

MUSEUMS
Musee Judeo-Alsacien
62a Grand Rue, (on Freeway to Paris) 67330
Telephone: 03-88-70-97-17
Fax: 03-88-70-97-17
Website: www.sdv.fr/juaisme
Visiting hours: from Easter to mid-September, Tuesday to Friday from 2.00 pm to 5.00 pm. Sunday from 2.00 pm to 6.00 pm. The museum, which is housed in an old synagogue, traces the history and culture of the Jews of Alsace.

English spoken and English guidebook

BOUZONVILLE

SYNAGOGUES
Bouzonville Synagogue
3 rue des Benedictins 57320

CHALON-SUR-SAONE

Chalon-Sur-Saone Synagogue
10 rue Germiny 71100

CHALONS-SUR-MARNE

SYNAGOGUES
Chalons-Sur-Marne Synagogue
21 rue Lochet 51000

CHAMBERY

Chambery Synagogue
44 rue St-Real 73000
Services Friday 7 pm and festivals

COLMAR

COMMUNITY ORGANISATIONS
Community Centre
3 rue de la Cigogne 68000
Telephone: 03-89-41-38-29
Fax: 03-89-41-12-96
Kosher food can be purchased in the community centre on Wednesdays and Thursdays. Kosher restaurant Wednesday noon during the school period.

SYNAGOGUES
Colmar Synagogue
3 rue de la Cigogne 68000
Telephone: 03-89-41-38-29
Fax: 03-89-41-12-96

COMPIEGNE
Compiegne Synagogue
4 rue du Dr.- Charles-Nicolle 60200

DIEUZE
Dieuze Synagogue
Av. Foch 57260

DIJON
BUTCHERS
Albert Levy
25 rue de la Manutention 21000
Telephone: 03-80-30-14-42

SYNAGOGUES
Dijon Synagogue
5 rue de la Synagogue 21000
Telephone: 03-80-66-46-47
Mikva on premises

TOURIST SITES
Archaelogical Museum
Has an important collection of old Jewish tombstones

DUNKIRK
SYNAGOGUES
Dunkirk Synagogue
19 rue Jean-Bart 59140

EPERNAY
Epernay Synagogue
2 rue Placet 51200
Telephone: 03-26-55-24-44
Services Yom Kippur only

EPINAL
Epinal Synagogue
9 rue Charlet 88000
Telephone: 03-29-82-25-23

FAULQUEMONT-CREHANGE
Faulquemont-Crehange Synagogue
Place de l'Hotel de Ville 57380
Services festivals & High Holy Days only

FORBACH
Forbach Synagogue
98 Av. St.-Remy 57600
Telephone: 03-87-85-25-57

GROSBLIEDERSTROFF
Grosbliederstroff Synagogue
6 rue des Fermes 57520

HAGONDANGE
Hagondange Synagogue
Rue Henri-Hoffmann 57300

HAGUENAU
Haguenau Synagogue
3 rue du Grand-Rabbin-Joseph-Bloch 67500
Telephone: 03-88-73-38-30

INGWILLER
Ingwiller Synagogue
Cours du Chateau 67340

INSMING
Insming Synagogue
Rue de la Synagogue 57670

LILLE
GROCERIES
Monoprix
Shopping Centre Euralille, rue du Molinel
Telephone: 03-20-06-81-25

SYNAGOGUES
Lille Synagogue
5 rue Auguste-Angellier 59012 59000
Telephone: 03-20-52-12-52
Fax: 03-20-31-35-46
Mikva on premises, phone 03-20-85-27-37

LUNEVILLE
SYNAGOGUES
Orthodox
Luneville Synagogue
5 rue Castara 54300
Telephone: 03-83-74-08-07
The synagogue built in 1785 has been listed as an historic monument.

MERLEBACH
SYNAGOGUES
Merlebach Synagogue
19 rue St-Nicholas 57800

METZ
BUTCHERS
Claude Sebbag
22 rue Mangin, Moselle 57000
Telephone: 03-87-63-33-50
Supervision: Chief Rabbi of Moselle

GROCERIES
Atac
23 rue de 20e Corps Américain, Moselle 57000

Galaries Lafayette
4 rue Winston Churchill, Moselle 57000
Telephone: 03-87-38-60-60

MIKVAOT
Mikva
30 rue Kellerman
Telephone: 03-87-32-38-04
Mme Rivkah Elalouf,

SYNAGOGUES
Adass Yechouroun
41 rue du Rabbin Elie-Bloch, Moselle 57000

Main Synagogue and Community Centre
39 rue du Rabbin Elie-Bloch, Moselle 57000
Telephone: 03-87-75-04-44

MONTBELIARD
Montbeliard Synagogue
Rue de la Synagogue 25200

MULHOUSE
SYNAGOGUES
Mulhouse Synagogue
2 rue des Rabbins 68100
Telephone: 03-89-66-21-22
Fax: 03-89-56-63-49
Email: hayoun.elie@evhn.net
Mikva on premises the old cemetery is also worth a visit

NANCY
COMMUNITY ORGANISATIONS
Communal Centre
19 blvd Joffre 54000
Telephone: 03-83-32-10-67

MIKVAOT
Mikva
53 rue Hoche
Telephone: 03-83-41-34-48
Mme Myriam Dahan

MUSEUMS
The Musee Historique Lorrain
64 Grand rue 54000
While Jewish buildings were plundered in 1944 an
important Jewish collection in the museum survived

RESTAURANTS
Restaurante Universitaire
19 blvd Joffre 54000
Telephone: 03-83-32-10-67
Open weekdays at noon

SYNAGOGUES
Nancy Synagogue
17 blvd Joffre 54000
Telephone: 03-83-32-10-67

OBERNAI
Obernai Synagogue
Rue de Selestat 67210

TOURIST SITES
Ruins
41 rue du General-Gouraud
Remains of an old synagogue

PHALSBOURG
SYNAGOGUES
Phalsbourg Synagogue
16 rue Alexandre-Weill 57370

REIMS
Reims Synagogue
49 rue Clovis 51100
Telephone: 03-26-47-68-47

SAINT-AVOLD
CEMETERIES
The American Military Cemetery
Contains graves of USA servicemen who fell in WWII

SYNAGOGUES
Saint-Avold Synagogue
Pl. Saint-Nabor 57000
Telephone: 03-87-91-16-16

SAINT-DIE
Saint-Die Synagogue
Rue de l'Eveche 88100
Services, festivals and Holy Days only

SAINT-LOUIS
CEMETERIES
The Hegenheim Cemetery
This cemetery dates from 1673

COMMUNITY ORGANISATIONS
Community Centre
19 rue du Temple 68300
Telephone: 03-89-70-00-48
Kosher products available

SYNAGOGUES
Saint-Louis Synagogue
Rue de la Synagogue 68300

Saint-Louis Orthodox Synagogue
3 rue de General Cassagnou 68300
Telephone: 03-89-69-07-05
Fax: 03-89-70-15-15
Kosher shop tel: 03-89-70-00-48

SAINT-QUENTIN
Synagogue
11 ter blvd Henri-Martin
Telephone: 03-23-08-72

SARREBOURG
Sarrebourg Synagogue
12 rue du Sauvage

SARREGUEMINES
Sarreguemines Synagogue
Rue Georges-V 57200
Telephone: 03-87-98-81-40
Mikva on premises

SEDAN-CHARLEVILLE
Sedan-Charleville Synagogue
6 av. de Verdun 82000

SELESTAT
Selestat Synagogue
4 rue Ste.-Barbe 67600

SENS
Association Culturelle Israelite de Sens et Yonne
14 rue de la Grande-Juiverie 89100
Telephone: 03-86-95-16-65
Fax: 03-86-65-02-11
Email: elie.robert@infonie.fr
Mail address: 5 rue Marcel Ayme, 89100 Sens

STRASBOURG
With a Jewish population of 16,000 this city, contested by France and Germany throughout history, currently has an important Jewish community, with several kosher restaurants, butchers and even a kosher vineyard. The earliest evidence of jewish life dates from 1188. A 13th century Mikvah was recently discovered.

BAKERIES
Crousty Cash
4 rue Sellénick, Bas-Rhin 67000
Telephone: 03-88-35-68-21

BOOKSELLERS
Fraenckel
19 rue du Marechal-Foch 67000
Telephone: 03-88-36-38-39
Fax: 03-88-37-96-60

Judaica old books and antiquities
Librairie du Cedrat
15 rue de Bitche 67000
Telephone: 03-88-37-32-37
Fax: 03-88-35-63-11
Email: librairie.cedrat@wanadoo.fr

BUTCHERS
Buchinger
63 rue du Faubourg de Pierre 67000
Telephone: 03-88-32-85-03
13 rue Wimpheling 67000
Telephone: 03-88-61-06-98
David
20 rue Sellenick 67000
Telephone: 03-88-36-75-01
FB Espace Casher
2-4 Av. Foret Noire 67000
Telephone: 03-90-41-18-68
Fax: 03-90-41-19-69

COFFEE SHOP
Coffee Shop
4 rue Strauss-Durkheim

GROCERIES
Cash Center
22 rue Finkmatt
Telephone: 03-88-35-12-38
Yarden
13 Blvd. de la Marne 67000
Telephone: 03-88-60-10-10/Office 03-88-60-51-96
Fax: 03-88-61-71-11

MEDIA
Newspapers
Echos-Unir
1a rue Grand-Rabbin-Rene-Hirschler 67000
Telephone: 03-88-14-46-50
Fax: 03-88-24-26-69
Monthly publication

MIKVAOT
Mikva
1a rue Grand-Rabbin-Rene-Hirschler 67000
Telephone: 03-88-14-46-68

MUSEUMS
Musee Alsacien
23 quai Saint-Nicolas 67000
Telephone: 03-88-52-50-01
Fax: 03-88-43-64-18
Website: www.musees-strasbourg.org
Has a section on Jewish Art

RELIGIOUS ORGANISATIONS
Consistoire Israelite du Bas-Rhin
23 rue Sellenick 67000
Telephone: 03-88-25-05-75
Fax: 03-88-25-12-75
Email: cibr1@libertysurf.fr

Regional Chief Rabbi, Rene Gutman
5 rue du General-de-Castelnau 67000
Telephone: 03-88-25-05-75
Fax: 03-88-25-12-65
Email: cibri1@libertysurf.fr

RESTAURANTS
Restaurant Universitaire
ORT-Laure Weil, 11 rue Sellenick 67000
Telephone: 03-88-76-74-76
Fax: 03-88-76-74-74
Email: strasbourg@ort.asso.fr
Website: www.strasbourg.ort.asso.fr

Dairy
Autre Part
60 blvd Clemenceau
Telephone: 03-88-37-10-02

Meat
Le King
28 rue Sellenick 67000
Telephone: 03-88-52-17-71
Supplies food early on Friday to take to hotels

SYNAGOGUES
Esplanade
17 rue de Nicosie 67000

Ets Hayim
7 rue Turenne 67000 67000
Telephone: 03-88-24-38-36
Fax: 03-88-24-38-36
Email: etzhaim@free.fr

Synagogue de la Paix
1a rue du Grand-Rabbin-Rene-Hirschler 67000
67000
Telephone: 03-88-14-46-50
Fax: 03-88-24-26-69
Email: cis@media-net.fr
Website: www.cisonline.org

THIONVILLE
Thionville Synagogue
31 av. Clemenceau 57100
Telephone: 03-82-54-47-89
Fax: 03-82-53-03-76

TOUL
Toul Synagogue
Rue de la Halle 54200

TROYES
MEMORIAL
Statue of Rashi
A statue of Rashi stands in Place Jean Moulin

MIKVAOT
Mikvaot
15 rue Brunneval
Telephone: 03-25-73-34-44

SYNAGOGUES
Troyes Synagogue
5 rue Brunneval
The only half-timbered shul in France.

VALENCIENNES
Valenciennes Synagogue
36 rue de l'Intendance 59300
Telephone: 03-27-29-11-07

VERDUN
Verdun Synagogue
Impasse des Jacobins 55100
Telephone: 03-83-41-34-48

VITTEL
Vittel Synagogue
211 rue Croix-Perrot 88800
Telephone: 03-29-08-10-87
Open in July and August only

WASSELONNE
Wasselonne Synagogue
Ruedes Bains 67310

North West
ANGERS
Angers Synagogue
12 rue Valdemaine 49100

BISCHEIM-SCHILTIGHEIM
Bischeim-Schiltigheim Synagogue
9 Place de la Synagogue 67800
Telephone: 02-38-33-02-87

BREST
Brest Synagogue
40 rue de la Republic 29200
Services Friday 7.30 pm

CAEN
BUTCHERS
Boucherie Marcel
26 rue de l'Engannerie 14000
Telephone: 02-31-86-16-25

SYNAGOGUES
Caen Synagogue
46 Av. de la Liberation 14000
Telephone: 02-31-43-60-54

CHATEAROUX
CONTACT INFORMATION
Michel Touati
3 Alleé Emile Zola, Montierchaume, Deols 36310
Telephone: 02-54-26-05-47

DEAUVILLE
SYNAGOGUES
Deauville Synagogue
14 rue Castor 14800
Telephone: 02-31-81-27-06

ELBEUF
Elbeuf Synagogue
29 rue Gremont 76500
Telephone: 02-35-77-09-11

LE HAVRE
GROCERIES
Super U Porte Oceane
Bd Francois 1er
Telephone: 02-35-21-31-35

SYNAGOGUES
Le Havre Synagogue
38 rue Victor-Hugo 76600
Telephone: 02-35-21-14-59

LE MANS
Le Mans Synagogue
4-6 Blvd. Paixhans 72000
Telephone: 02-43-86-00-96

LORIENT
Lorient Synagogue
18 rue de la Patrie 56100
Services Friday nights, festivals and Holy Days only

NANTES
Nantes Synagogue
5 Impasse Copernic 44000
Telephone: 02-41-87-48-10
Fax: 02-41-37-11-79
Mikva on premises

ORLEANS
Orleans Synagogue
14 rue Roert-de-Courtenay (to the left of the cathedral) 45000
Information on services to be had from Marcus Sellem, tel: 02-62-89-18

RENNES
COMMUNITY ORGANISATIONS
Centre Edmond Safra
Rue de la Heronniere, 5 alleé du Mont dol 35000
Telephone: 02-99-63-57-18
Services held, telephone for times

ROUEN
SYNAGOGUES
Rouen Synagogue
55 rue des Bons-Enfants 76100
Telephone: 02-35-7101-44
The Jewish Youth Club can provide board residence for student travellers and holiday makers

TOURIST SITES
Old Jewish Quarter
Excavations in the 1970s uncovered the ruins of what is the only known medieval Jewish structure whose walls have survived. Now called 'The house of the Jews' It is considered to most likely have been a yeshiva but it may in fact have been a synagogue.

TOURS
SYNAGOGUES
Tours Synagogue
37 rue Parmentier 37000
Telephone: 02-47-05-56-95

PARIS
The city of Paris is divided into districts (arrondissements) designated by the last two digits of the postcode. In the categories below, establishments are listed in numerical order according to the postcode (that is, -01, -02, -03 and so on).

The historic centre of Paris Jewish life is found in the Marais area (4th arrondissement), although a synagogue stood on Ile de la Cité before Notre Dame was built, Jews having lived in the city since Roman times. Another more central area is that around rue Richer (9th arrondissement) which, although not historic as such, has many kosher restaurants of varying styles and prices.

An important new site to be visited is the Musee d'art and d'histoire du Judaisme which opened in December 1998.

BAKERIES
Charles Tr. Patissier
10 rue Corentin Cariou 75019
Telephone: (01)-47-97-51-83
Supervision: Beth Din of Paris

Douieb
11 bis rue Geoffroy Marie 75009 75009
Telephone: (01)-47-70-86-09
Supervision: Beth Din of Paris

Golan
10 rue Geffroy Marie 75009 75009
Telephone: (01)-48-00-94-71
Supervision: Beth Din of Paris

Kadoche
2 av. Corentin Cariou 75019 75019
Telephone: (01)-40-37-00-14
Supervision: Beth Din of Paris

Korcarz
25 rue Trévise 75009
Telephone: (01)-42-46-83-33
Supervision: Beth Din of Paris/Chief Rabbi Mordechai
Rottenberg.

Le Relais Sucre
135 rue Manin 75019
Telephone: (01)-42-41-20-98
Supervision: Beth Din of Paris

Les Ailes
34 rue Richer 75009 75009
Telephone: (01)-47-70-62-53
Supervision: Beth Din of Paris

Lilo
20 rue Desnoyer 75020
Telephone: (01)-47-97-63-20
Supervision: Beth Din of Paris

Mat'amim
17 rue de Crimée 75019
Telephone: (01)-42-40-89-11
Supervision: Beth Din of Paris

Medayo
17 rue de Meaux 75019
Telephone: (01)-40-03-04-20
Supervision: Beth Din of Paris

Mendez
3 ter rue de la Présentation 75011
Telephone: (01)-43-57-02-03
Supervision: Beth Din of Paris

Mezel
1 rue Ferdinand Duval 75004
Telephone: (01)-42-78-25-01
Supervision: Beth Din of Paris

Nani
104 blvd de Belleville 75020
Telephone: (01)-47-97-38-05
Supervision: Beth Din of Paris

Nathan de Belleville
67 blvd de Belleville 75011
Telephone: (01)-43-57-24-60
Supervision: Beth Din of Paris

Zazou
20 rue du Faubourg Montmartre 75009
Telephone: (01)-47-70-81-32
Supervision: Beth Din of Paris

BAKERIES AND RESTAURANT

Korcarz
29 rue des Rosiers 75004
Telephone: (01)-42-77-39-47
Fax: (01)-48-58-28-44
Email: a.korcarz@wanadoo.fr
Supervision: Beth Din of Paris/Chief Rabbi Mordechai
Rottenberg

BUTCHERS

Adolphe
14 rue Richer 75009
Telephone: (01)-48-24-86-33

Andre Manin
135 rue Manin 75019
Telephone: (01)-42-38-00-43

Aux Viandes Cacheres
6 av. Corentin Cariou 75019
Telephone: (01)-40-36-02-41

Berbeche
15/17 rue Henri Ribiere 75019
Telephone: (01)-42-08-06-06

Berbeche
39 rue Jouffroy 75017
Telephone: (01)-44-40-07-59

Berbeche
46 rue Richer 75009
Telephone: (01)-47-70-50-58

Berbeche
5 rue Vandrezanne 75013
Telephone: (01)-45-88-86-50
6 rue du Mouliet 75013
Telephone: 01-45-80-89-10

Boucherie Guy
266 rue de Charenton 75012
Telephone: (01)-43-44-60-90

Boucherie Claude
174 rue Lecourbe 75015
Telephone: (01)-48-28-02-00

Boucherie Smadja
90 blvd Belleville 75020

Charlot
33 rue Richer 75009
Telephone: (01)-45-23-10-34

Charly Halak B. Y.
51 rue Richard Lenoir 75011
Telephone: (01)-43-4862-26
6 bis villa d'Al sia 75014
Telephone: (01)-45-40-82-35
Fax: (01)-45-40-72-89

Chez Andre
69 blvd de Belleville 75011
Telephone: (01)-43-57-80-38

Chez Jacques
19 rue Bouchardon 75010
Telephone: (01)-42-06-76-13

Chez Jojo
20 rue Louis Bonnet 75011
Telephone: (01)-43-55-10-29

Emsalem
17 quai de la Gironde 75019
Telephone: (01)-40-36-56-64
18 rue Corentin Cariou 75019
Telephone: (01)-40-36-56-64

Espaces Courses Elles
177 rue de Courcelles 75017
Telephone: (01)-47-63-36-26

Gm Levy
83 rue de Lonchamp 75016
Telephone: (01)-45-53-04-24

Henrino
122 blvd de Belleville 75020
Telephone: (01)-47-97-24-52

J V (Temim)
2 rue de Dr Goujon 75012
Telephone: (01)-43-45-78-77

Kassab
88 blvd Murat 75016
Telephone: (01)-40-71-0734

Krief
104 rue Legendre 75017
Telephone: (01)-46-27-15-57

La Rose Blanche
43 rue Richer 75009
Telephone: (01)-48-24-84-65

Maurice Zirah
91 rue de la Roquette 75011
Telephone: (01)-43-79-62-53

Saada
17 rue des Rosiers 75004
Telephone: (01)-42-77-76-22

Ste Delicatess
209 av. de Versailles 75016
Telephone: (01)-44-40-07-59

EMBASSY
Embassy of Israel
3 rue Rabelais 75008
Telephone: (01)-40-76-55-00
Fax: (01)-40-76-55-55
Email: info@amb-israel.fr

GROCERIES
Chekel
14 av. de Villiers 75017
Telephone: (01)-48-88-94-97

Chochana
54 av. Secretan 75019

Compt Pdts Alimentaires
111 av. de Villiers 75017
Telephone: (01)-42-27-16-91

Doueib
11 bis rue Geoffroy Marie 75009
Telephone: (01)-47-70-86-09

Le Haim
6 rue Paulin Enfert 75013
Telephone: (01)-44-24-53-34

GROCERIES AND DELICATESSEN
Keter David
5 rue Benjamin Franklin 75016
Telephone: (01)-42-24-04-42
Fax: (01)-42-24-04-41

HOTELS
Hotel Aida Opéra
17 rue du Conservatoire 75009
Telephone: (01)-45-23-11-11
Fax: (01)-47-70-38-73
Email: reservation@aida-opera.com
Supervision: Beth Din of Paris
Breakfast / Brunch is open to non-residents

Hotel Touring
21 rue Buffault 75009
Telephone: (01)-48-78-09-16
Fax: (01)-48-78-27-74
Email: infos@hotel-touring.fr
Website: www.hotel-touring.fr

L'Hotel de Mericourt
50 rue de la Folie Mericourt 75011
Telephone: (01)-43-38-73-63
Fax: (01)-43-38-66-13
Email: hoteldemericourt@wanadoo.fr
Situated in an area with many kosher facilities

Pavillon De Paris
7 rue de Parme 75009
Telephone: (01)-55-31-60-00
Fax: (01)-55.31.60.01
Email: mail@pavillondeparis.com
Website: www.pavillondeparis.com

LIBRARIES
Library Judica of the Seminaire Israelite de France
9 rue Vauquelin 75005
Telephone: (01)-47-07-22-94
Visit only by appointment

MIKVAOT
Mayan Hai Source de Vie Haya Mouchka
2-4 rue Tristan Tzara 75018
Telephone: (01)-40-38-18-29; 01-46-36-11-09
1 rue des Annelets 75019
Telephone: 01-42-45-57-87
For men and women. Telephone is an answer-machine, for women only.

Mikvaot
176 rue du Temple 75003
Telephone: (01)-42-71-89-28
16-21 rue Galvani 75017
Telephone: 01-45-74-52-80
The mikvah is located in the centre of Paris, near Place de la République, at the rear of the building. The Staff is English-speaking.

Mikve Haya Moucha
25 rue Riquet 75019
Telephone: (01)-40-36-40-92
Fax: (01)-40-36-88-90
75 rue Julien Lacroix 75020
Telephone: 01-46-36-39-20, 01-46-36-30-10
For men and women

MONUMENT
Shoah Memorial
rue Geoffroy-l'Asnier 17 75004
Telephone: (33) 001 42 77 4472
Fax: (33) 001 53 01 1744
The memorial is a tribute to the Jews who perished in the Holocaust. Erected in 1956 it contains the Archives of the Centre de Documentation Juive Contemporaine. At the centre is an eternal flame.

MUSEUMS
Musée d'Art et d'Histoire du Judaisme
Hotel de Saint-Aignan, 71 rue du Temple 75003
Telephone: (01)-53-01-86-53
Fax: (01)-42-72-97-47
Email: info@mahj.org
Website: www.mahj.org
Open Monday to Friday from 11.00 am to 6.00 pm and Sunday from10.00 am to 6.00 pm

Musee Nissim de Camondo
63, rue de Monceau 75008
Telephone: (01)-53-89-06-50
Fax: (01)-53-89-06-42
Website: www.lesartsdeconatifs.fr
Reconstruction of an eighteenth century aristocratic home. This home and its collection were bequeathed to France in 1935 by Comte Moise de Camondo in memory of his son Nissim, who died in combat in 1917.

RELIGIOUS ORGANISATIONS
Communauté Israélite Orthodox de Paris
10 rue Pav e 75004
Telephone: (01)-42-77-81-51
Fax: (01)-48-87-26-29

RESTAURANTS
Dairy
Bistrot Blanc
52 rue Blanche 75009
Telephone: (01)-42-85-05-30
Supervision: Beth Din of Paris

Casa Rina
18 Faubourg Monmarte 75009
Telephone: (01)-45-23-02-22
Supervision: Beth Din of Paris

Cine Citta Café
7 rue d'Aguesseau 75008
Telephone: (01)-42-68-05-03
Supervision: Beth Din of Paris

Cocktail Café
82 av. Parmetier 75011
Telephone: (01)-43-57-19-94
Supervision: Beth Din of Paris

Contini
42 rue des Rosiers 75004
Telephone: (01)-48-04-78-32
Supervision: Beth Din of Paris

Dizengoff Café
27 rue Richer 75009
Telephone: (01)-47-70-81-97
Email: dizengoff@caramail.com
Supervision: Beth Din of Paris
Open from 12.00 am to 10.30 pm.

Gin Fizz
157 blvd Serruier 75019
Telephone: (01)-42-00-51-28
Supervision: Beth Din of Paris

King Solomon
46 Richer 75009
Telephone: (01)-42-46-31-22
Supervision: Beth Din of Paris

Le New's
56 av. de la République 75011
Telephone: (01)-43-38-63-18
Supervision: Beth Din of Paris

Maestro Pizza
19 rue d'Anjou 75008
Supervision: Beth Din of Paris

Meat
Adolphe
14 rue Richer 75009
Telephone: (01)-47-70-91-25
Supervision: Beth Din of Paris

Berbeche Burger
47 rue Richer 75009
Telephone: (01)-47-70-81-22
Supervision: Beth Din of Paris

Brasserie du Belvedere
109 av. de Villiers 75017
Telephone: (01)-4764-96-55
Supervision: Beth Din of Paris

Cash Food
63 rue des Vinaigriers 75010
Telephone: (01)-42-03-95-75
Supervision: Beth Din of Paris

Centre Edmond Fleg
8 bis, rue de l'Eperon 75006
Telephone: (01)-46-33-43-31
Supervision: Beth Din of Paris

Chez David
11 rue Montyon 75009
Telephone: (01)-44-83-01-24
Supervision: Beth Din of Paris

Chez Rene et Gabin
92 blvd de Belleville 75020
Telephone: (01)-43-58-78-14
Supervision: Beth Din of Paris

Darjeeling
1 bis, rue des Colonels Renard 75017
Telephone: (01)-45-72-09-32
Fax: (01)-45-72-03-27
Website: www.darjeeling-ontable.com
Supervision: Chief Rabbi Mordechai Rottenberg.

Dolly's Food
9 rue cit Riverain 75010
Telephone: (01)-48-03-08-40
Supervision: Beth Din of Paris

Douieb
11 bis rue Geoffroy Marie 75009
Telephone: (01)-47-70-86-09
Supervision: Beth Din of Paris

Elygel
116 blvd de Belleville 75020
Telephone: (01)-47-97-09-73
Supervision: Beth Din of Paris

Fradji
42 rue Poncelet 75017
Telephone: (01)-47-54-91-40
Supervision: Beth Din of Paris

Georges de Tunis
42 rue Richer 75009
Telephone: (01)-47-70-24-64
Supervision: Beth Din of Paris

La Petite Famille
32 rue des Rosiers 75003 75003
Telephone: (01)-42-77-00-50
Supervision: Beth Din of Paris

La Verriere du Marais
23 Rue des Rosiers 75004
Telephone: (01) 42 77 12 75
Glatt Kosher

Le Cabourg
102 blvd Voltaire 75011 75011
Telephone: (01)-47-00-71-43
Supervision: Beth Din of Paris
Hours: 12.00 pm to 2.30 pm and 7.00 pm to 11.00 pm.

Le Chateaubriand
125 rue de Tocqueville 75017 75017
Telephone: (01)-47-63-96-90
Fax: (01)-47-63-42-55
Website: www.le-chateaubriand.com
Supervision: Beth Din of Paris

Le Gros Ventre
7/9 rue Montyon 75009
Telephone: (01)-48-24-25-34
Supervision: Beth Din of Paris

Le Lotus de Nissan
39 rue Amelot 75011
Telephone: (01)-43-55-80-42
Supervision: Beth Din of Paris

Le Manahattan
231 blvd Voltaire 75011
Telephone: (01)-43-56-03-30
Supervision: Beth Din of Paris

Les Ailes
34 rue Richer 75009
Telephone: (01)-47-70-62-53
Supervision: Beth Din of Paris

Les Cantiques
16 rue Beaurepaire 75010
Telephone: (01)-42-4064-21
Supervision: Beth Din of Paris
Will deliver

Lumieres de Belleville
102 blvd de Belleville 75020
Telephone: (01)-47-97-51-83
Supervision: Beth Din of Paris

Mille Delices
52 avenue Secrétan 75019
Telephone: (01)-40-18-32-32
Supervision: Beth Din of Paris

Nini
24 rue Saussier Leroy 75017
Telephone: (01)-46-22-28-93
Supervision: Beth Din of Paris

Synagogue Beth El
4 rue Saulnier 75009
Telephone: (01)-45-23-34-89
Supervision: Beth Din of Paris
Shabbat meals by arrangement.

Yun-Pana
115 Boulevard Voltaire 75011
Telephone: (01)-43-79-20-48
Supervision: Beth Din of Paris

Zazou Burger
19 rue du Faubourg Montmarte 75009
Telephone: (01)-40-22-08-33
Supervision: Beth Din of Paris

SYNAGOGUES

Liberal
Union Liberale Israelite de France
24 rue Copernic 75116
Telephone: (01)-47-04-37-27
Fax: (01)-47-27-81-02
Email: communications@ulif.com
Website: www.ulif.com

Masorti
Communaute Juive Massorti de Paris
8 rue George Bernard Shaw (off rue Dupleix)
75015
Telephone: (01)-45-67-97-96
Fax: (01)-45-56-89-79
Email: RuzielDr@aol.com
Website: ww.jtsa.edu/synagogues/adathsfr/
Services Friday night 6.30 pm, Shabbat morning 10.00 am,
festivals and Rosh Chodesh

Orthodox
15 rue Notre-Dame de Nazareth 75003
Telephone: (01)-42-78-00-30
Fax: (01)-42-78-05-18
Central organisation: A.C.I.P.

Adass Yereim
10 rue Cadet 75009
Telephone: (01)-42-46-36-47, 01-48-74-51-78
Fax: (01)-48-74-35-35

Adath Israel
36 rue Basfroi 75011
Telephone: (01)-43-67-89-20

Adath Yechouroun
25 rue des Rosiers 75004
Telephone: (01)-44-59-82-36

Agoudas Hakehilos
10 rue Pavée 75004
Telephone: (01)-48-87-21-54
Fax: (01)-48-87-26-29
A striking Art Nouveau synagogue designed by Hector
Guimard, the creator of the world famous Metro entrances,
in 1913

Avoth Ouvanim
59 av. d'Ivry 75013
Telephone: (01)-45-82-80-73
Fax: (01)-45-85-94-39
223 rue Vercingétorix 75014
Telephone: 01-45-45-50-51

Beith Chalom
25 villa d'Alésia 75014
Telephone: (01)-45-45-38-71
Fax: (01)-43-37-58-49

Beth Chalom
11-13 rue Curial 75019
Telephone: (01)-40-37-65-16, 01-40-37-12-54

Beth Hamidrach Lamed
67 rue Bayen 75017
Telephone: (01)-45-74-52-80

Beth Loubavitch
53 rue Compans 75019
Telephone: (01)-42-02-20-35

Beth Loubavitch
93 rue des Orteaux 75020
Telephone: (01)-40-24-10-60

Beth Loubavitch
25 rue Riquet 75019
Telephone: (01)-40-36-93-90
Fax: (01)-40-36-60-15

Beth-El
3 bis rue Saulnier 75009
Telephone: (01)-45-23-15-75
Email: bethel@eboom.com

Beth-Israël
4 rue Saulnier 75009
Telephone: (01)-45-23-34-89

Centre Edmond Fleg
8 bis rue de l'Ep ron 75006
Telephone: (01)-46-33-43-31
Houses the Union des Centres Communautaires (UCC),
which can be contacted via the same telephone number.
Their fax number is 01-43-25-86-19. Tikvat Nou, the Jewish
youth movenent of the Consistoire, is also located here, tel:
01-46-33-43-24; fax: 01-43-25-20-59.

Centre Rachi
30 blvd du Port-Royal 75005
Telephone: (01)-43-31-98-20

Centre Rambam
19-21 rue Galvani 75017
Telephone: (01)-45-74-52-80
Fax: (01)-45-74-51-81
Email: centrerambam@free.fr

Chaare Tora
1 rue Henri-Turot 75019
Telephone: (01)-42-06-41-12
Fax: (01)-42-06-95-47

Chivtei Israel
12-14 Cité Moynet 75012
Telephone: (01)-43-43-50-12
Fax: (01)-43-47-36-78
Email: ravatlan@club-internet.fr

Consistorial Synagogue
14 Place des Vosges 75004
Telephone: (01)-48-87-79-45
Fax: (01)-48-87-57-58
Email: templedesvosges@noos.fr
Website: www.synadesvosges.com
Shabbat meals 'Only Seouda Shlichit' the Third meal

E.E.I.F.
27 av. de Ségur 75007
Telephone: (01)-47-83-60-33

Ets Haim
18 rue Basfroi 75011
Telephone: (01)-43-48-82-42

Fondation Roger Fleishmann
18 rue des Ecouffes 75004
Telephone: (01)-48-87-97-86

Grande Synagogue de Paris
44 rue de la Victoire 75009
Telephone: (01)-40-82-26-26 ext. 2773, 01-45-26-95-36
Fax: (01)-45-26-95-36
Email: infos@lavictoire.org
Website: www.lavictoire.org

Groupe Rabbi Yehiel de Paris
25 rue Michel-Leconte 75003
Telephone: (01)-42-78-89-17

H khal Moch
218-220 rue du Faubourg St-Honor 75008
Telephone: (01)-45-61-20-25
Located behind the Golden Tulip Hotel

Kollel Ysmah Moch
36 rue des Annelets 75019
Telephone: (01)-43-63-73-94

Maor Athora
16 rue Ramponeau 75020
Telephone: (01)-47-97-69-42

Merkaz Beth Myriam
19 rue Domrémy 75013
Telephone: (01)-45-86-83-99
Fax: (01)-45-86-83-99

Névé Chalom
29 rue Sibué 75012
Telephone: (01)-43-42-07-70
Fax: (01)-43-48-44-50

Ohaley Yaacov
11 rue Henri-Murger 75019
Telephone: (01)-42-49-25-00

Ohel Avraham
31 rue Montevideo 75016
Telephone: (01)-45-05-66-73
Fax: (01)-40-72-83-76
23 bis rue Dufrénoy 75016
Telephone:01-45-04-94-00, 01-45-04-66-73

Ohel Mordekhai
13 rue Fondary 75015
Telephone: (01)-40-59-96-56

Ohr Chimchon Raphaël
5 passage Dagorno 75020
Telephone: (01)-46-59-39-02
Fax: (01)-46-59-14-99

Ohr Tora - AJJ
15 Rue Riquet 75019
Telephone: (01)-40-38-23-36
Fax: (01)-40-36-42-23
Email: ajj@ajj.fr
Website: www.ajj.fr

Ora Vesimha
37 rue des Trois-Bornes 75011 931001
Telephone: (01)-43-57-49-84

Oratoire Mahzik Adath Mouvement Loubavitch
17 rue de Rosiers 75004

Pah'ad David
11 rue du Plateau 75019
Telephone: (01)-42-46-47-03
Fax: (01)-42-46-47-56

Rav Pealim (Braslav)
49 blvd de la Villette 75010
Telephone: (01)-42-41-55-44

S minaire Isra lite de France
9 rue Vauquelin 75005
Telephone: (01)-47-07-21-22
Fax: (01)-43-37-75-92

Si ge du Beth Loubavitch
8 rue Lamartine 75009
Telephone: (01)-45-26-87-60
Fax: (01)-45-26-24-37

Synagogue Achkenaze & Sephardi
49 rue Pali Kao 75020
Telephone: (01)-46-36-30-10

Synagogue ACIP
42 rue des Saules 75018
Telephone: (01)-46-06-71-39
Fax: (01)-46-06-71-39

Synagogue Berit Chalom
18 rue Saint-Lazare 75009
Telephone: (01)-48-78-45-32; 01-48-78-38-80

Synagogue Bet Yaacov Yossef
5 square des Cardeurs, 43 rue Saint-Blaise 75020
Telephone: (01)-43-56-03-11

Synagogue de Montmartre
13 rue Saint-Isaure 75018
Telephone: (01)-42-64-48-34

Synagogue des Tournelles
21 bis rue des Tourelles 75004
Telephone: (01)-42-74-32-65; 01-42-74-32-80
Fax: (01)-40-29-90-27
Email: david-halim@septodont.fr

Synagogue Don Isaac Abravanel
84-86 rue de la Roquette 75011
Telephone: (01)-47-00-75-95

Synagogue Michkan-Yaacov
118 boulevard de Belleville 75019
Telephone: (01)-43-49-39-59

Synagogue Michkenot Israel
6 rue Jean-Nohain 75019
Telephone: (01)-48-03-25-59
Fax: (01)-42-00-26-87

Synagogue Tephilat Isra'l Frank-Forter
24rue de Bourg-Tibourg 75004
Telephone: (01)-46-24-48-94

Synagogue Torath-Hayim
130 rue du Faubourg Saint-Martin 75010
Telephone: (01)-40-05-98-34

Tiferet Yaacob
71 rue de Dunkerque 75009
Telephone: (01)-42-812-32-17; 01-42-49-65-12
4 rue Martel 75010
Telephone: 01-42-85-12-74

Religious Sephardic
Oratoire de la Fondation Rothschild (Maison de Retraite)
76 rue de Picpus 75012
Telephone: (01)-43-44-72-98
Fax: (01)-43-44-71-39

Paris Region

ANTONY

SYNAGOGUES

Orthodox
Community Centre and Synagogue
1 rue Sdérot, angle 1, rue Barthélémy, Hauts-de-Seine 92160
Telephone: 01-46-66-19-17

ASNIERES

MIKVAOT
Mikvaot
82 rue du R.P. Christian-Gilbert, Hauts-de-Seine 92600
Telephone: 01-47-99-26-59

SYNAGOGUES

Orthodox
Asnieres Synagogue
73 bis rue des Bas, Hauts-de-Seine 92600
Telephone: 01-47-99-32-55

ATHIS-MONS

SYNAGOGUES

Orthodox
Athis-Mons Synagogue
55 rue des Coquelicots, Essonne 91200
Telephone: 01-69-38-14-29

AULNAY-SOUS-BOIS

Aulnay-Sous-Bois Synagogue
80 rue Maximilien Robespierre, Seine-Saint-Denis 93600
Telephone: 01-48-69-66-93

BAGNEUX

BUTCHERS
Isaac
188 av Aristide Briand, Hauts-de-Seine 92220
Telephone: 01-45-47-00-21

BAGNOLET

BAKERIES
Sonesta
27 rue Adélaide Lahaye, Seine-Saint-Denis 93170
Telephone: 01-43-64-92-93
Fax: 01-43-60-51-26
Supervision: Beth Din of Paris

SYNAGOGUES

Orthodox
Bagnolet Synagogue
15-17 rue D. Vienot, Seine-Saint-Denis 93170
Telephone: 01-43-60-39-93

BOBIGNY

RESTAURANTS
Dairy
Cez Daryl
22-24 rue Henri Barbusse, Seine-Saint-Denis 93000
Telephone: 01-43-60-39-93
Supervision: Beth Din of Paris

BONDY

SYNAGOGUES

Orthodox
Maison Communautaire
28 av. de la Villageoise, Seine Saint-Denis 93140
Telephone: 01-48-47-50-79

BOULOGNE SUR SEINE

BAKERIES
Ariel
143 avenue J.B. Clément, Hauts-de-Seine 92100
Telephone: 01-46-04-24-42
Supervision: Beth Din of Paris

GROCERIES
Ednale
28 rue Georges Sorel, Hauts-de-Seine 92100
Telephone: 01-46-03-83-37

CHAMPIGNY

SYNAGOGUES

Orthodox
Synagogue Beth-David
25 av. du Général-de Gaulle, Val-de-Marne 94500
Telephone: 01-48-85-72-29

CHELLES

Chelles Synagogue
14 rue des Anémones, Seine-et-Marne 77500
Telephone: 01-60-20-92-93

CHOISY-LE-ROI

MIKVAOT
Mikvaot
28 av. de Newburn, Val-de-Marne 94600
Telephone: 01-48-53-43-70, 02-48-92-68-68

SYNAGOGUES

Orthodox
Choisy-Le-Roi Synagogue
28 av. de Newburn, Val-de Marne 94600
Telephone: 01-4853-48-27

CLICHY-SUR-SEINE

Clichy-Sur-Seine Synagogue
26 rue Mozart (Espace Clichy), Hauts-de-Seine 92210
Telephone: 01-47-39-02-43

CRÉTEIL

BAKERIES

Caprices et Delices
5 rue Edouard Manet, Val-de-Marne 94000
Telephone: 01-43-39-20-20
Supervision: Beth Din of Paris

La Nougatine
20 Esplanade des Abimes, Val-de Marne 94000
Telephone: 01-49-56-98-56
Supervision: Beth Din of Paris

Les Jasmins de Tunis
C.C. Kenndy, Val-de Marne 94000
Telephone: 01-43-77-50-56
Supervision: Beth Din of Paris

Quick Chaud
26 allée Parmentier, Val-de-Marne 94000
Telephone: 01-48-99-08-30
Supervision: Beth Din of Paris

Tov'Mie
25 rue Dr Paul Casalis, Val-de-Marne 94000
Telephone: 01-48-99-00-39

BUTCHERS

Boucherie Patrick
2 rue Edouard Manet, Val-de-Marne 94000
Telephone: 01-43-39-29-64

La Charolaise Julien
Cte Commercial Kennedy, Loge 13 rue Gabriel Peri,
Val-de Marne 94000
Telephone: 01-43-39-20-43

MIKVAOT

Mikvaot
Rue du 8 MMai 1945, Val-de-Marne 94000 94000
Telephone: 01-43-77-01-70; 01-43-77-19-68

SYNAGOGUES

Orthodox

Consistorial Synagogue
Rue du 8 Mai 1945, Val-de-Marne 94000
Telephone: 01-43-77-01-70; 01-43-39-05-20
Fax: 01-43-99-03-60
Email: templedesvosges@noos.fr
Website: www.synadesvosges.com
Possibilities of Shabbat meals

ENGHIEN

MIKVAOT

Mikvaot
47 rue de Malleville, Val-d'Oise 95880
Telephone: 01-34-17-37-11

SYNAGOGUES

Orthodox

Enghien Synagogue
47 rue de Malleville, Val-d'Oise 95880
Telephone: 01-34-12-42-34

FONTAINEBLEAU

Fontainebleau Synagogue
38 rue Paul Seramy, Seine-et-Marne 77300
Telephone: 01-64-22-68-48

FONTENAY AUX ROSES

Centre Moise Meniane
17 av. Paul-Langevin, Hauts-de Seine 92660
Telephone: 01-64-46-60-75-94

FONTENAY SOUS BOIS

MIKVAOT

Haya Mossia
177 rue des Moulins, Val-de-Marne 94120
Telephone: 01-4877-53-90, 01-48-76-83-84

SYNAGOGUES

Orthodox

Fontenay Sous Bois Synagogue
79 blvd de Verdun, Val-de-Marne 94120
Telephone: 01.4877-38-67

GARGES-LES-GONESSE

BUTCHERS

Boucherie Berbeche
C.C. Pal de la Dame Blanche, Val-d'Oise 95140
Telephone: 01-39-86-42-06

Chez Harry
1 rue J B Corot, Val-d'Oise 95140
Telephone: 01-39-86-53-81

MIKVAOT

Mikvaot
15 rue Corot, Val-d'Oise 95140
Telephone: 01-39-86-75-64

SYNAGOGUES

Orthodox

Maison Communautaire Chaare Ra'hamim
14 rue Corot, Val-d'Oise 95140
Telephone: 01-46-48-34-49

ISSY-LES-MOULINEAUX

Issy-Les-Moulineaux Synagogue
72 blvd Gallieni, Hauts-de-Seine 92130
Telephone: 01-46-48-34-49

LA COURNEUVE

La Courneuve Synagogue
13 rue Saint-Just, Seine-Saint-Denis 93120
Telephone: 01-48-36-75-59

LA GARENNE-COLOMBES
Synagogue and Community Centre of Courbevoie / La Garenne-Colombes
13 rue L.M. Nordmann, Hauts-de-Seine 92250
Telephone: 01-47-69-92-17

LA VARENNE ST-HILAIRE
La Varenne St-Hilaire Synagogue
10 bis avenue du chateau, Val-de-Marne 94210
Telephone: 01-42-83-28-75

LE BLANC MESNIL
Le Blanc Mesnil Synagogue
65 rue Maxime-Gorki, Seine-Saint-Denis 93150
Telephone: 01-48-65-58-98

LE CHESNAY
MIKVAOT
Mikvaot
39 rue de Versailles, Yvelines 78150
Telephone: 01-39-54-05-65, 01-39-07-19-19

LE KREMLIN-BICETRE
SYNAGOGUES
Orthodox
Le Kremlin-Bicetre Synagogue
41-45 rue J. F. Kennedy, Val-de-Marne 94270
Telephone: 01-46-72-73-64

LE PERREUX NOGENT
Synagogue-Nogent/Le Perreux/Bry-Sur-Marne
165 bis av. du Gal-de Gaulle, Val-de Marne 94170
Telephone: 01-48-72-88-65

LE RAINCY
MIKVAOT
Mikve du Raincy
67 blvd du Midi, Seine-Saint-Denis 93340
Telephone: 06-19-30-15-68

SYNAGOGUES
Orthodox
Maison Communautaire
19 allée Chatrian, Seine-Saint-Denis 93340
Telephone: 01-43-02-06-11

LE VESINET
MIKVAOT
Mikvaot
29 rue Henri Cloppet, Yvelines 78110
Telephone: 01-30-53-10-45, 01-30-71-12-26

SYNAGOGUES
Orthodox
Maison Communautaire
29 rue Henri Cloppet, Yvelines 78110
Telephone: 01-30-53-10-45

LES LILAS
BUTCHERS
Boucherie Des Lilas
6 rue de la Republique, Seine-Saint-Denis 93260
Telephone: 01-43-63-89-15

LEVALLOIS PERRET
RESTAURANTS
Meat
Delicates Eden
102 rue Rivay, Hauts-de Seine 92300
Telephone: 01-42-70-97-06
Supervision: Beth Din of Paris

SYNAGOGUES
Orthodox
Jewish School
63 rue Louis Rouquier 92300
Telephone: 01-47-57-11-15
Fax: 01-47-57-39-12
Email: accil@accil.org
Website: www.accil.org
Open hours: 7.00 am to 8.00 pm daily

MAISONS ALFORT
MIKVAOT
Mikvaot
92-94 rue Victor-Hugo, Val-de-Marne 94700
Telephone: 01-43-78-95-69

SYNAGOGUES
Orthodox
Maisons Alfort Synagogue
68 rue Victor Hugo 94700
Telephone: 01-43-78-95-69

MASSY
MIKVAOT
Mikvaot
Allée Marcel-Cerdan 91300
Telephone: 01-42-37-48-24

SYNAGOGUES
Orthodox
Massy Synagogue
2 Allée Marcel-Cerdan 91300
Telephone: 01-69-20-94-21

MEAUX
Meaux Synagogue
11 rue P. Barennes, Seine-et-Marne 77100
Telephone: 01-64-34-76-58

MELUN
SYNAGOGUES
Melun Synagogue
Cnr. rues Branly & Michelet 77003
Telephone: 01-64-52-00-05

MEUDON-LA-FORET
MIKVAOT
Mikvaot
Rue de la Synagogue, Hauts-de-Seine 92360
Telephone: 01-46-32-64-82, 01-46-01-32

SYNAGOGUES
Orthodox
Maison Communautaire
Rue de la Synagogue, Hauts-de-Seine 92360
Telephone: 01-48-53-48-27

MONTREUIL
BAKERIES
Korcarz
134 bis rue de Stalingrad, Seine-Saint-Denis 93100
Telephone: 01-48-58-33-45
Supervision: Beth Din of Paris/Chief Rabbi Mordechai Rottenberg

Le Relais Sucre
62 rue des Roches, Seine-Saint-Denis 93100
Telephone: 01-48-70-22-60
Supervision: Beth Din of Paris

Nat Cacher
21 rue Gabriel Péri, Seine-Saint-Denis 93100
Telephone: 01-41-58-05-25
Supervision: Beth Din of Paris

BUTCHERS
Andre Volailles
62 rue des Roches, Seine-Saint-Denis 93100
Telephone: 01-41-58-58-58

Boucherie Andre
64 rue des Roches, Seine-Saint-Denis 93100
Telephone: 01-41-58-58-58

MONTROUGE
MIKVAOT
Ismah-Israel
90 rue Gabriel-P ri, Hauts-de-Seine 92120
Telephone: 01-42-53-08-54

SYNAGOGUES
Orthodox
Centre Communautaire Regional Malakoff-Montrouge
90 rue Gabriel-P ri, Hauts-de-Seine 92120
Telephone: 01-46-32-64-82
Fax: 01-46-56-20-49

NEUILLY
BUTCHERS
Neuilly Cacher
2/6 rue de Chartres, Hauts-de-Seine 92200
Telephone: 01-47-45-06-06

GROCERIES
King David
14 rue Paul-Chatrousse, Hauts-de-Seine 92200
Telephone: 01-47-45-18-19

RESTAURANTS
Meat
King David
14 rue Paul-Chatrousse, Hauts-de-Seine 92200
Telephone: 01-47-45-18-19
Supervision: Beth Din of Paris
Deliver. Hours: 8.00 am to 10.00 pm.

SYNAGOGUES
Orthodox
Neuilly Synagogue
12 rue Ancelle, Hauts-de-Seine
Telephone: 01-47-47-78-76
Fax: 01-47-47-54-79
Website: www.synaneuilly.com

NOISY LE SEC
SYNAGOGUES
Orthodox
Beth Gabriel
2 rue de la Pierre Feuillère, Seine-Saint-Denis 93
Telephone: 01-48-46-71-79

SYNAGOGUES
Orthodox
Rachi Chull
6 rue Ambroise-Thomas 75009
Telephone: (01)-48-24-86-94

PANTIN
BUTCHERS
Levy Baroukh
5/7 rue Antole France, Seine-Saint-Denis 93500
Telephone: 01-48-91-02-14

RESTAURANTS
Dairy
Chez Jacquy
24 rue Pr -Saint-Gervais, Seine-Saint-Denis 93500
Telephone: 01-48-10-94-24
Supervision: Beth Din of Paris

SYNAGOGUES
Orthodox
Pantin Synagogue
8 rue Gambetta, Seine-Saint-Denis 93500

RIS-ORANGIS
SYNAGOGUES
Orthodox
Ris-Orangis Synagogue
1 rue Jean Moulin, Essone 91130
Telephone: 01-69-43-07-83

ROISSY-EN-BRIE
MIKVAOT
Mikvaot
Rue Paul-C zanne, Centre Commercial Bois
Montmartre, Seine-et-Marne 77680
Telephone: 01-60-28-34-65; 01-60-29-09-44

ROSNY-SOUS-BOIS
SYNAGOGUES
Orthodox
Rosny-Sous-Bois Synagogue
62-64 rue Lavoisier, Seine-Saint-Denis 93110
Telephone: 01-48-54-04-11
Fax: 01-69-43-07-83

SAINT GERMAIN
SYNAGOGUES
Liberal
Kehilat Gesher (Franco-American)
7 rue de Léon Cogniet 75017
Telephone: 01-39-21-97-19
Fax: 01-39-21-97-19
Email: kehilatgesher@wanadoo.fr
Website: www.kehilatgesher.org

SYNAGOGUES
Orthodox
Saint Germain Synagogue
6 Impasse Saint Leger 78103
Telephone: 01-34-51-26-60

SAINT-LEU-LA-FORET
MIKVAOT
Mikvaot
2 rue Jules Vernes, Val-d'Oise 95320
Telephone: 01-39-95-96-90, 01-34-14-24-15

SYNAGOGUES
Orthodox
Saint-Leu-La-Foret Synagogue
2 rue Jules Verne, Val-d'Oise 95320
Telephone: 01-39-95-96-90
Fax: 01-39-95-72-13

SAINT-OUEN-L'AUMÔNE
Maison Communautaire
9 rue de Chenneviéres, Val-d'Oise 95310
Telephone: 01-30-37-71-41

SARCELLES
BAKERIES
Louis D'or
90 av. Paul Valéry, Val-d'Oise 95200
Telephone: 01-39-90-25-45
Supervision: Beth Din of Paris

Natania
34 blvd Albert Camus, Val-d'Oise 95200
Telephone: 01-39-90-11-78
Supervision: Beth Din of Paris

Oh Delices
71 av. Paul Valéry, Val-d'Oise 95200
Telephone: 01-39-92-41-12
Supervision: Beth Din of Paris

Zazou
C.C. les Flanades, Val-d'Oise 95200
Telephone: 01-34-19-08-11
Supervision: Beth Din of Paris

BUTCHERS
Boucherie Du Coin
60 blvd Albert Camus, Val-d'Oise 95200
Telephone: 01-39-90-53-02

Hazout
5 av. Paul Valéry, Val-d'Oise 95200
Telephone: 01-39-90-72-95

MIKVAOT
Mayanot Rachel
14 av. Ch.-Péguy, Val-d'Oise 95200
Telephone: 01-39-90-40-17
Postal address:c/o 1 AC 15 av. de l'Escouvrier 95200

RESTAURANTS
Dairy
Marina
103 av. Paul-Val ry, Val-d'Oise 95200
Telephone: 01-34-19-23-51
Supervision: Beth Din of Paris

Meat
Berbeche Burger
13 av. Edouard-Branly, Val-d'Oise 95200
Telephone: 01-34-19-12-02
Supervision: Beth Din of Paris

SYNAGOGUES
Orthodox
Maison Communautaire
74 av. Paul-Valéry, Val-d'Oise 95200
Telephone: 01-39-90-59-59
Mikva on premises

SARTROUVILLE
Synagogue Rabbi Shimon bar Yohai et Rabbi Meir Baal Hannes
1 rue de Stalingrad, Yvelines 78500
Telephone: 01-39-15-22-57

SAVIGNY SUR ORGE
MIKVAOT
Mikvaot
1 av. de l'Armée-Leclerc, Essonne 91600
Telephone: 01-69-24-48-25, 01-69-96-30-90

SYNAGOGUES
Orthodox
Savigny Sur Orge Synagogue
1 av. de l'Armée Leclerc, Essonne 91600
Telephone: 01-69-96-30-90

SEVRAN
MIKVAOT
Mikvaot
25 bis du Dr Roux, Seine-Saint-Denis 93270
Telephone: 01-43-84-25-40
Mikva Kelim

SYNAGOGUES
Orthodox
Synagogue Mayan-Thora
25 bis rue du Dr Roux, BP. 111, Seine-Saint-Denis 93270
Telephone: 01-43-84-25-40

STAINS
Synagogue
8 rue Lamartine (face n°2), Clos St-Lazare, Seine-Saint-Denis 93240
Telephone: 01-48-21-04-12
Provisional address: 8 av. Louis Bordes (Ancient Conservatoire Municipal)

THIAIS
COMMUNITY ORGANISATIONS
Community Centre Choisy-Orly-Thiais
Voie du Four, 128 av. du Marechal de Lattre de Tassigny, Val-Marne 94320
Telephone: 01-48-92-68-68
Fax: 01-48-92-72-82

TRAPPES
SYNAGOGUES
Orthodox
Trappes Synagogue
7 rue du Port-Royal, Yvelines 78190
Telephone: 01-30-62-40-43

VAL-DE-MARNE
BUTCHERS
Tiness
12 Etienne Dollet, Val-de Marne 94140
Telephone: 01-49-77-95-79

SYNAGOGUES
Orthodox
Val-de-Marne Synagogue
1 rue Blanche 94140
Telephone: 01-43-78-86-43

VERSAILLES
SYNAGOGUES
Samuel Sandler
10 rue Albert-Joly, Yvelines 78000
Telephone: 01-39-07-19-19
Fax: 01-39-50-96-34
Email: aciv1@wanadoo.fr
Mikva on premises

VILLEJUIF
SYNAGOGUES
Orthodox
Villejuif Synagogue
106 av. de Gournay, Val-de-Marne 94800
Telephone: 01-46-78-76-53

VILLENEUVE-LA-GARENNE
MIKVAOT
Mikvaot
42-44 rue du Fond-de-la Noue, Hauts-de-Seine 92390
Telephone: 01-47-94-89-98

SYNAGOGUES
Orthodox
Maison Communautaire
44 rue du Fond-de-la-Noue, Hauts-de-Seine 92390
Telephone: 01-47-94-89-98

VILLIERS SUR MARNE
Villiers Sur Marne Synagogue
30 rue Léon Douer, B.P. 15, Val-de-Marne 94350
Telephone: 01-49-30-01-47
Fax: 01-49-30-85-40

VILLIERS-LE-BEL-GONESSE
MIKVAOT
Mikvaot
1 rue L on Blum, Val-d'Oise 95400
Telephone: 01-39-94-45-51, 01-34-19-64-48

SYNAGOGUES
Orthodox
Villiers-Le-Bel-Gonesse Synagogue
1 rue L on Blum, Val-dÕOise 94500
Telephone: 01-39-94-30-49; 01-39-94-94-89

VINCENNES
BUTCHERS
Boucherie Des Levy
32 rue Raymond du Temple, Val-de-Marne 94300
Telephone: 01-43-74-94-18

Boucherie Hayache
146 av. de Paris, Val-de-Marne 94300
Telephone: 01-43-28-16-04

SYNAGOGUES
Orthodox
Synagogue Achkenaze
30 rue Céline-Robert, Vincennes 94300
Telephone: 01-43-74-38-47
Email: bruno.blum@nexans.com

Synagogue Sepharade
30 rue Céline-Robert, Val-de-Marne 94300
Telephone: 01-47-55-65-07

VITRY-SUR-SEINE
Vitry-Sur-Seine Synagogue
133-135 av. Rouget-de-l'Isle, Val-de Marne 94400
Telephone: 01-46-80-76-54, 01-45-73-06-58
Fax: 01-45-73-94-01

YERRES
MIKVAOT
Beth Rivkah
43/49 rue R. Poincare, Essone 91330
Telephone: 01-69-49-62-74, 01-69-49-62-62
Fax: 01-69-79-27-70
Email: beth-rivkah@wanados.fr

South East

AIX-EN-PROVENCE
BUTCHERS
Zouaghi
7 rue de Sevigne, Bouches du Rhône 13100
Telephone: 04-42-59-93-94
Supervision: Grand Rabbinate of Marseille

SYNAGOGUES
Aix-En-Provence Synagogue
5 rue de Jerusalem 13100
Telephone: 04-42-26-69-39

AIX-LES-BAINS
BUTCHERS
Berdah
29 Av. de Tresserve 73100
Telephone: 04-79-61-44-11

HOTELS
Kosher
Auberge de La Baye
Chemin du Tir-Aux-Pigeons, Savoie 73100
Telephone: 04-79-35-69-42
Strictly kosher

MIKVAOT
Pavillon Salvador
Rue du President Roosevelt 73100
Telephone: 04-79-35-38-08

SYNAGOGUES
Aix-Les-Bains Synagogue
Rue Paul Bonne 73100
Telephone: 04-79-35-28-08
Mikva on premises

ANNECY
Association Culturelle Israelite
18 rue de Narvik 74000
Telephone: 04-50-67-69-37

ANNEMASSE
BUTCHERS
Yarden
59 av. de la Liberation, Gaillard 74100
Telephone: 04-50-92-64-05

SYNAGOGUES
Orthodox
Annemasse Synagogue
8 rue du Docteur Coquart 74100

ANTIBES-JUAN-LES-PINS
BUTCHERS
Berreche
12 av. Courbet 6160
Telephone: 04-93-67-16-77

Le Kineret
25 av. D l'Esteral 6160
Telephone: 04-92-93-16-01
Fax: 04-93-88-14-76

RESTAURANTS
Maxime
6 Blvd de la Pinede 6160
Telephone: 04-92-93-99-40

SYNAGOGUES
Eliaou Hanabi
Villa la Monada, 30 Chemin des Sables , 9 Chemim
des Sabber (In Summer) 06160
Telephone: 04-93-61-59-34
Fax: 04-93-67-03-76

AVIGNON
The first archaeological evidence of a Jewish
presence dates from the fourth century. For
years the Avignon Jewish population flourished
and there were many Jewish scholars and
writers who were born and lived there. The first
printing venture in Hebrew was attempted in
Avignon in 1446 before Gutenberg's success in
1450.

BUTCHERS
Cachere Royale
15 rue Chapeau Rouge 84000
Telephone: 04-90-82-47-50
Supervision: Grand Rabbinate of Marseille

HOTELS
Hotel Danieli
17 rue de Republique, 84000
Telephone: 04-90-86-46-82
Fax: 04-90-27-09-24
Email: hoteldaniel@wanadoo.fr
Website: www.hotel-danieli-avignon.com

MIKVAOT
Mikvaot
Vaucluse
Telephone: 04-90-86-30-30
Mme Cohen Zardi

SYNAGOGUES
Orthodox
Avignon Synagogue
2 Place de Jerusalem 84000
Telephone: 04-90-85-21-24
Fax: 04-90-85-21-24
This circular synagogue was built in 1847 on this site of a
13th-century synagogue

BEZIERS
MIKVAOT
A.C.I.B.
19 Place Pierre-Semard 34500
Telephone: 04 67 28 75 98
Fax: 04 67 28 75 98
Email: eouanounou@hotmail.com
Mme Smolinski Tel: 04-67-28-44-24

SYNAGOGUES
Beziers Synagogue
19 Place Pierre-Semard 34500
Telephone: 04-67-28-75-98
Operates a kosher food store

TOURIST SITES
Ghetto
To visit the old Ghetto (Beziers was known as 'the little
Jerusalem'); contact Mr Benyacar (04-67-31-14-23)

CALUIRE-ET-CUIRE
SYNAGOGUES
Caluire-Et-Cuire Synagogue
107 A. Fleming 69300
Telephone: 04-78-23-12-37

CANNES
BUTCHERS
Cannes Casher
9 rue Marceau 6400
Telephone: 04-93-39-85-08

Chez Sylvie
15 rue Mal. Joffre 6400 6400
Telephone: 04-93-39-57-92

COMMUNITY ORGANISATIONS
Cannes Jewish Community Organizations
20 Boulevard d'Alsace 6400
Telephone: 04-93-38-16-54
Fax: 04-93-68-92-81

GROCERIES
La Emounah
32 rue de Mimont 6400
Near the main synagogue

Monoprix
Rue Marechal Fox
Has a comprehensive kosher section

MIKVAOT
Cannes Mikvaot
20 Boulevard d'Alsace
Telephone: 04-93-99-79-03
Contact: Mme Annie Rebibo

RESTAURANTS
Meat
Le Dany's
18 Rue Marechal Joffre
Telephone: 04-92-59-35-50
Meat, fish couscous, Shabbat meals, catering. meat Glatt
Kosher

Le Tovel
34 rue du Dr Gerard Monod 6400
Telephone: 04-93-39-36-25

Pizza Dick
7 bis rue de Mimont 6400
Telephone: 04-92-59-10-82

SYNAGOGUES
Chabad Lubavitch
22 Rue Commandant Vidal 6400
Telephone: 04-92-98-67-51
Fax: 04-92-98-81-29
Email: canorhabad@aol.com
Website: www.jriviera.com

Sephardi
Cannes Synagogue
20 Boulevard d'Alsace 6400
Telephone: 04-93-38-16-54
Fax: 04-93-68-92-81

CARPENTRAS
Jews first settled in Carpentras in the 12th century. In 1343 permission was granted for the erection of a synagogue in which the women were situated in the basement. A 'rabbi of the women' was employed to guide them through the service; the only direct contact being a small window.

SYNAGOGUES
Carpentras Synagogue
Place de la Maire
Telephone: 04-90-63-39-97
The synagogue originally built in 1367 and the oldest in France was reconstructed in 1741–43 and again in 1959. The French government has declared it a historic site.

TOURIST SITES
Cathedral St Siffrein
The 15th-century door on the south side is where Jews had to go on their way to conversion and is known as 'Porte des Juifs'.

CAVAILLON
The Jews originally lived in Rue Hebraique. The present synagogue, classified as a historical monument, was built in 1772 and incorporates parts of the 16th-century former building.

MUSEUMS
Musee Judeo-Comatdin
Telephone: 04-90-76-00-34
The museum, a part of the synagogue, contains items dating back to the 14th century

SYNAGOGUES
Cavaillon synagogue
Telephone: 04-90-76-00-34
Fax: 04-90-71-47-06

CLERMONT-FERRAND
Clermont-Ferrand Synagogue
6 rue Blatin 63000
Telephone: 04-73-93-36-59

EVIAN
Evian Synagogue
Adjacent to 1 av. des Grottes, 74502
Telephone: 04-50-75-15-63

EZE-VILLAGE
HOTELS
Hotel les Terrases d'Eze
Route de la Turbie 6360
Telephone: 04-92-41-55-55
Fax: 04-92-41-55-10
Supervision: Nice Beth Din

FREJUS
SYNAGOGUES
Orthodox
Rue de Progres, Frejus-Plage 83600
Telephone: 04-94-52-06-87

GRENOBLE
BUTCHERS
C. Cohen
19 rue de Turenne 38000
Telephone: 04-76-46-48-14

GROCERIES
Aux Delices du Soleil
49 rue Thiers 38000
Telephone: 04-76-46-19-60

Ghnassia
15 Place Gustave Rivet 38000
Telephone: 04-76-87-80-90

MEDIA
Radio Kol Hachalom 100 FM
BP 342 Grenoble (38 ls re) 38013
Telephone: 04-76-87-21-22
Fax: 04-76-47-58-31
Email: rkh@rkhfm.com
Website: www.rkhfm.com
24 hours a day broadcasting, news in French and Hebrew

SYNAGOGUES
Rachi
11 rue Maginot, Isère 38000
Telephone: 04-76-87-02-80
Fax: 04-76-87-27-14
Email: rabbin38@aol.com
Mikva at same address

Synagogue and Community Centre
4 rue des Bains, ls re 38000
Telephone: 04-76-46-15-14

HYERES
Hyeres Synagogue
Chemin de la Ritorte 83400
Telephone: 04-94-65-31-97

IZIEU
MUSEUMS
The Izieu Children's Home
Bouches du Rhône 1300
Telephone: 04-79-87-20-08
Fax: 04-79-87-25-01
Email: izieu@alma.fr
Website: www.izieu.alma.fr
The Izieu Children's Memorial Museum is dedicated to the memory of forty-four children and their guardians, taken away on 6 April 1944 by the Gestapo under the command of Klaus Barbie. The Museum's mission is to defend dignity, justice and to contribute to the fight against all forms of intolerance. Two buildings may be visited: the House takes the visitors back to everyday life of the chidren's home, the Barn presents the historical background through permanent and temporary exhibitions. Meetings, conferences and discussions are organized throughout the year.

LA CIOTAT
SYNAGOGUES
La Ciotat Synagogue
1 Square de Verdun 13600
Telephone: 04-42-71-92-56
Services Friday 7.00 pm (Winter), 7.30 pm (Summer), Saturday 9.00 am

LA SEYNE-SUR-MER
BUTCHERS
Elie Benamou
17 rue Batistin-Paul 83500
Telephone: 04-94-94-38-60

SYNAGOGUES
La Seyne-Sur-Mer Synagogue
5 rue Chevalier-de-la Barre 83501
Telephone: 04-94-94-40-28

LYON
BAKERIES
Jo Delice
44 rue Rachais
Telephone: 04-78-69-22-98

Nassy Gourmand
41 rue A Boutin, Villeurbanne 69100
Telephone: 04-78-85-72-88

BUTCHERS
Ittah David
267 av. Berthelot 69008
Telephone: 04-78-00-82-35

William (Mr Dahan)
50 rue Tete d'Or 69006
Telephone: 04-78-24-10-10

COMMUNITY ORGANISATIONS
Consistoire Israelite de Lyon
13 Quai Tilsitt 69002
Telephone: 04-78-37-13-43
Fax: 04-78-38-26-57
Email: acil@free.fr

Consistoire Israelite Sepharade de Lyon
Yaacov Molho Community Centre, 317 Rue Duguesclin 69007
Telephone: 04-78-58-18-74
Fax: 04-78-58-17-49

MEDIA
CIV News
4 rue Malherbe, Villeurbanne 69100
Telephone: 04-78-84-04-32

Hachaar
18 rue St. Mathieu 69008
Telephone: 04-78-00-72-50
Fax: 04-78-75-89-74

La Voix Sepharade
317 rue Duguesclin 69007
Telephone: 04-78-58-18-74

MIKVAOT
Chaare Tsedek (Sepharades)
18 rue St.-Mathieu 69008
Telephone: 04-78-00-72-50
Fax: 04-78-75-89-74

Orah Haim
17 rue Albert-Thomas, St-Fons 69190
Telephone: 04-78-67-39-78

Rav Hida (N. African)
La Sauvegarde, La Duchere 69009
Telephone: 04-78-35-14-44

RELIGIOUS ORGANISATIONS
Beth Din
34 rue d'Armenie, 3e
Telephone: 04-78-62-97-63
Fax: 04-78-95-09-47

RESTAURANTS
Dairy
Le Pinnocchio
5 rue A. Boutin, Villeurbanne 69100
Telephone: 04-78-68-62-95

Lippo
9 rue Michel Servet, Villeurbanne 69100
Telephone: 04-78-84-15-00

Pizza Cach
13 rue d'Inkerman, Villeurbanne 69100
Telephone: 04-72-74-44-98

Prestopizza
61 rue Greuze, Villeurbanne 69100
Telephone: 04-78-68-08-41

Meat

Croq Sandwiches
32 Crs Emile-Zola, Villeurbanne 69100
Telephone: 04-78-84-16-07

La Palmeraie
27 Rue des Charmettes, Villeurbanne 69100
Telephone: 04-78-24-37-03

La Petite Maison
35 rue P. Corneille 69006
Telephone: 04-78-24-99-43

Le Belvedere
14 rue Jean-Jaures, Vileurbanne 69100
Telephone: 04-78-54-72-312

Lippmann Henry
4 rue Tony Tollet, Villeurbanne 69002
Telephone: 04-78-42-49-82

Mac David
28 rue Michel Servet, Villeurbanne 69100
Telephone: 04-78-03-31-62

SYNAGOGUES

Orthodox

Chaare Tsedek
18 rue Saint Mathieu (8e) (T.T.)
Telephone: 04-78-00-72-50
Fax: 04-78-75-89-74

Grande Synagogue
13 Quai Tilsitt
Telephone: 04-78-37-13-43
Fax: 04-78-38-26-57
Email: acil@free.fr

Rav Hida
501 Sauvegarde La Duchere (9e) (T.T.)
Telephone: 04-78-35-14-44
Fax: 04-78-64-95-90

MACON

Macon Synagogue
32 rue des Minimes 71000

MARIGNANE

Marignane Synagogue
9 rue Pilote-Larbonne 13700

MARSEILLES

BAKERIES

Atteia et Fils
19 Place Guillardet, Bouches du Rhône 13013
Telephone: 04-91-66-33-28
Supervision: Grande Rabbinate of Marseille

Avyel Cash
28 rue St Suffren, Bouches du Rhône 13006
Telephone: 04-91-87-95-25
Supervision: Grande Rabbinate of Marseille

Cacher Food
31 blvd Barry, Bouches du Rhône 13013
Telephone: 04-91-70-13-43
Supervision: Grande Rabbinate of Marseille

Erets
205 rue de Rome, Bouches du Rhône 13006
Telephone: 04-91-92-88-73
Supervision: Grande Rabbinate of Marseille

Le Parve
72 av. Alphonse Daudet, Bouches du Rhône 13013
Telephone: 04-91-66-95-16
Supervision: Grande Rabbinate of Marseille

BUTCHERS

Chez David
9 blvd G. Ganay, Bouches du Rhône 13009
Telephone: 04-91-75-04-56
Supervision: Grande Rabbinate of Marseille

Lamap
13 place Mignard Bouches du Rhône 13009
Telephone: 04-91-71-11-70
Supervision: Grande Rabbinate of Marseille

Sebane
59 rue Alphonse Daudet, Bouches du Rhône 13013
Telephone: 04-91-66-98-76
Supervision: Grande Rabbinate of Marseille

Zennou Raphael
20 march Capucin, Bouches du Rhône 13001
Telephone: 04-91-54-02-54
Supervision: Grande Rabbinate of Marseille

EMBASSY

Consul General of Israel
146 rue Paradis, Bouches du Rhône 13006
Telephone: 04-91-53-39-87
Fax: 04-91-53-39-94

GROCERIES

Av bon gout
28 rue St Suffren, Bouches du Rhône 13006
Telephone: 04-91-37-95-25

Delicash
94 blvd Barry, Bouches du Rhône 13013
Telephone: 04-91-06-39-04

Emmanuel
93 avenue Clot Bey, Bouches du Rhône 13008
Telephone: 04-91-77-46-08

King Kasher
25 rue François Mauriac, Bouches du Rhône 13010
Telephone: 04-91-80-00-01

Raphael Cash
299 avenue de Mazargues, Bouches du Rhône 13009
Telephone: 04-91-76-44-13

MEDIA

Radio JM
4 impasse Dragon 13006
Telephone: 04-91-37-78-78

MEMORIAL
Memorial of the Death Camps
Quai de la Tourette 13002
Telephone: 04-91-90-73-15

MIKVAOT
Mikve Esther
47 rue St Suffren 13006
Telephone: 04-91-81-45-15
There are some eight mikvaot in Marseilles. This one is close to the main synagogue. The Consistoire will provide details of others.

RELIGIOUS ORGANISATIONS
Consistoire de Marseille
117 rue de Breteuil, Bouches du Rhône 13006
Telephone: 04-91-37-49-64, 04-91-81-13-57
Fax: 04-91-37-83-90
Email: consistoire.israelile@wanadoo.fr

RESTAURANTS
Dairy
Pizzeria Gan Eden
225, Paul Claudel 13010
Telephone: 04-91-75-12-72

Meat
Erets
205 rue de Rome, Bouches du Rhône 13006
Telephone: 04-91-92-88-73
Supervision: Grande Rabbinate of Marseille

Nathania
17 rue du Village, Bouches du Rhône 13006
Telephone: 04-91-42-05-31
Supervision: Grande Rabbinate of Marseille

SYNAGOGUES
Merlan
La Cerisaie, Batiment G1 13014
Telephone: 04-91-98-53-92

Ohel Yaakov
20 Chemin Ste-Marthe 13014
Telephone: 04-91-62-70-42

SYNAGOGUES
Ashkenazi
8 Impasse Dragon 13006

Reform
Marseilles Reform Synagogue
337 Rue Paradis Marseille 13008
Telephone: 04-91-37-54-31
Fax: 04-91-37-54-31
Email: rabbi.liebermann@voila.fr

Sephardi
Bar Yohai
171 rue Abbe-de-l'Epee 13005
Telephone: 04-91-42-38-19

Beth Simha
13 av. Des Olives 13013
Telephone: 04-91-70-05-45
Main Synagogue
117 rue Breteuil 13006
Telephone: 04-91-37-49-64
Fax: 04-91-37-83-89
Merkaz Netivot Chalom
27 blvd Bonifay 13004
Telephone: 04-91-89-40-62
There are over forty more synagogues in Marseilles. The Consistoire de Marseilles will supply details if required.

MENTON
SYNAGOGUES
Menton Synagogue
Centre Altyner, 106 Cours du Centenaire 6500
Telephone: 04-93-35-28-29

MONTPELLIER
BUTCHERS
Eretz
41 rue de Lunaret 3400
Telephone: 04-67-72-67-94

COMMUNITY ORGANISATIONS
Centre Communautaire et Cultural Juif
500 blvd d'Antigone 3400
Telephone: 04-67-15-08-76

GROCERIES
A.C.P.C.
45 rue Proudhon
Telephone: 04-67-02-10-99

SYNAGOGUES
Ben-Zakai
7 rue General-Laffon 34000
Telephone: 04-67-92-92-07

Mazal Tov
18 rue Ferdinand-Fabre 34000
Telephone: 04-67-79-09-82

NICE
The first reference to Jews in Nice was in 1342. The first cemetery was established in 1408 and the synagogue in 1492.

The main synagogue, built in 1886, is worth a visit. Nice is home to the Chagall Museum which contains a permanent collection of his work, including a number of stained glass mosaics.

BOOKSELLERS
Librairie Tanya
25 rue Pertinax 6000
Telephone: 04-93-80-21-74
Fax: 04-93-13-87-90
Email: librairie.tanya@wanadoo.fr

BUTCHERS
K'Gel
18 rue Dante 6000
Telephone: 04-93-86-33-01

GROCERIES
Mickael
37 Rue Dabray 6000
Telephone: 04-93-88-81-23

Riviera Cacher
11 Avenue Villermont 6000
Telephone: 04-93-92-92-00

KASHRUT INFORMATION
Nice Kashrut
Telephone: 04-93-85-82-06
For lists of kosher butchers and bakers

KOSHER FOODS
Galleries Lafayette
Has a kosher food section

MIKVAOT
Nice Mikvaot
22 rue Michelet 6100
Telephone: 04-93-51-89-80

MUSEUMS
Chagall Museum
Avenue Docteur Menard 6000
Telephone: 04-93-53-87-20
Fax: 04-93-53-87-39
The museum has a permanet exhibition of the largest
existing collection of the works of Marc Chagall

RELIGIOUS ORGANISATIONS
Centre Consistorial
22 rue Michelet 6100
Telephone: 04-93-51-89-80
Publishes an annual calendar and guide to Nice and district

**Regional Chief Rabbinate of Nice, Côte
d'Azur and Corsica**
1 rue Voltaire 6000
Telephone: 04-93-85-82-06

RESTAURANTS
Dairy
Le Leviathan
1 av Georges Clemenceau
Telephone: 04-93-87-22-64

Meat
L'Alliance
13 rue Andrioli 6000
Telephone: 04-93-44-11-94

Le Dauphin Bleu
22 av. Malaussena 6000
Telephone: 04-93-82-98-74

SYNAGOGUES
Main Synagogue
7 rue Gustave-Deloye 6000
Telephone: 04-93-92-11-38

Ashkenazi
Synagogue Achkenaze
1 rue Blacas
Telephone: 04-93-62-38-68

NIMES
COMMUNITY ORGANISATIONS
5 rue d'Angouleme 30000
Telephone: 04-66-26-19-51

SYNAGOGUES
Nimes Synagogue
40 rue Roussy 30000
Telephone: 04-66-29-51-81
Mikva on premises

PERPIGNAN
BUTCHERS
Gilbert Sabbah
3 rue P.-Rameil 66000
Telephone: 04-68-35-41-23
Fax: 04-68-51-09-83

SYNAGOGUES
54 rue François Arago 66000
Telephone: 04-68-34-75-81
Fax: 04-68-51-13-31

ROANNE
ACIR
9 rue Beaulieu 42300
Telephone: 04-77-71-51-56

SAINT-ETIENNE
34 rue d'Arcole 42000
Telephone: 04-77-33-56-31

SAINT-FONS
Saint-Fons Synagogue
17 av. Albert-Thomas 69190
Telephone: 04-78-67-39-78

SAINT-LAURENT-DU-VAR
Saint-Laurent-Du-Var Synagogue
Villa 'Le Petit Clos', 35 av. des Oliviers 6700

TOULON
BUTCHERS
Abecassis
8 rue Vincent Courdouan, Var 83000
Telephone: 04-94-97-39-86
Supervision: Grand Rabbinate of Marseille

Fennech
15 av. Colbert, Var 83000
Telephone: 04-94-92-70-39
Supervision: Grand Rabbinate of Marseille

SYNAGOGUES
184 av. Lazare Carnot 83050
Telephone: 04-94-92-61-05
Mikva on premises

VALENCE
Valence Synagogue
1 place du Colombier 26000
Telephone: 04-75-43-34-43

VENISSIEUX
Venissieux Synagogue
10 av. de la Division-Leclerc 69200
Telephone: 04-78-70-69-85

VICHY
Vichy Synagogue
2 bis rue du Marechal Foch 3200
Telephone: 04-70-59-82-83

South West
AGEN
Agen Synagogue
52 rue Montesquieu 47000
Telephone: 05-53-66-24-20

TOURIST SITES
Rue des Juifs 47000
Site of old ghetto of the 15th century

ARCACHON
SYNAGOGUES

Orthodox
36 av Gambetta
Telephone: 05-56-83-63-40
Fax: 05-56-83-63-40

BAYONNE
SYNAGOGUES
Bayonne Synagogue
35 rue Maubec 64100
Telephone: 05-59-55-03-95

BORDEAUX
BAKERIES
Boucherie Peres
64 rue Bouquiere
Telephone: 05-56-52-88-18

COMMUNITY ORGANISATIONS
Centre Yavneh
11 rue Poquelin Moliere 33000
Telephone: 05-56-52-62-69
Fax: 05-56-51-71-95
Meals are available on Shabbat and other occasions

MIKVAOT
Bordeaux Mikvaot
213 rue Ste. Catherine 33000
Telephone: 05-56-91-79-39

RESTAURANTS
Mazal Tov
137 cours Victor Hugo 33000
Telephone: 05-56-52-37-03

Bordeaux Synagogue
8 rue du Grand-Rabbin-Joseph-Cohen 33000
Telephone: 05-56-91-79-39
Fax: 05-56-94-05-12

LA ROCHELLE
SYNAGOGUES

Orthodox
Centre Communautaire
M.C.I. 40 Cours des Dames 17000
Telephone: 05-56-46-41-17-66

LIBOURNE
SYNAGOGUES
Liborne Synagogue
33 rue Lamothe 33500

LIMOGES
Synagogue
25-27 rue Pierre-Leroux 87000
Telephone: 05-55-77-47-26

MONTAUBAN
Montauban Synagogue
12 rue St-Claire 82000
Telephone: 05-63-03-01-37

PAU
Pau Synagogue
8 rue des Trois-Freres-Bernadac 64000
Telephone: 05-59-62-37-85

PÉRIGVEUX
Périgveux Synagogue
13 rue Paul-Louis-Courrier 24000
Telephone: 05-53-53-22-52

POITIERS
Poitiers Synagogue
1 rue Guynemer 86000

TOULOUSE

BUTCHERS
Cacherout Diffusion
37 blvd Carnot 31000
Telephone: 05-61-23-07-59

Lasry
8 rue Matabiau 31000
Telephone: 05-61-62-65-28

Maalem
7 rue des Chalets 31000
Telephone: 05-61-63-77-39

COMMUNITY ORGANISATIONS
Community Centre
2 Place Riquet 31000
Telephone: 05-61-23-36-54

GROCERIES
Novogel
14 rue Edmund Guyaux 31200
Telephone: 05-61-57-03-19

MIKVAOT
Toulouse Mikvaot
13 rue Francisque Sarcey 31000
Telephone: 05-61-48-89-84

RELIGIOUS ORGANISATIONS
Grand Rabbinat du Toulouse et des Pays de la Garonne – A.C.I.T
2 Place Riquet 31000
Telephone: 05-62-73-46-46
Fax: 05-62-73-46-47

RESTAURANTS
Community Centre
2 place Riquet 31000
Telephone: 05-62-73-56-56

SYNAGOGUES
Chaare Emeth
35 rue Rembrandt 31000
Telephone: 05-61-40-03-88

Ashkenazi - Habad
Adat Yechouroun
3 rue Jules-Chalande 31000
Telephone: 05-61-62-30-19
Fax: 05-61-62-86-79

Orthodox
Hekhal David
2 Place Riquet 31000
Telephone: 05-62-76-46-46

Sephardi
Palaprat
2 rue Palaprat 31000
Telephone: 05-61-21-69-56

CORSICA

CONTACT INFORMATION
Jo Michel Reis
La Grande Corniche, Route des Sanguinaires
Telephone: 9521-5752
There are between ten and fifteen families in the town

GEORGIA

Georgia has had a very long history of Jewish settlement, dating back to two centuries before the destruction of the Second Temple if the archaeological findings are correct. These earliest Jewish communities may have descended from the Babylonian exiles. Like the Jews in the other Caucasus regions (Armenia and Azerbaijan) they are known as 'mountain Jews'.

Synagogues are found in major towns, there is a school in the capital Tbilisi and there are some newsletters. It is worth noting that the non-Jewish population has traditionally been far less anti-semitic than the populations of some other ex-Soviet republics.

GMT +4 hours
Country calling code: (+995)
Total population: **5,434,000**
Jewish population: **9,000**
Emergency telephone: (**Police–02**) (**Fire–01**) (**Ambulance–03**)
Electricity voltage: **220**

AKHALTISIKHE
Akhaltisikhe Synagogue
109 Guramishvili Street

BATUMI
Batumi Synagogue
6 9th March Street

GORI
Gori Synagogue
Chelyuskin Street

KUTAISI
Kutaisi Synagogue
12 Gapanove Street
Near main square

ONNI
Onni Synagogue
Baazova Street

POTI
Poti Synagogue
23 Ninoshivili Tskhakaya Street

SUKHUMI
Sukhumi Synagogue
56 Karl Marx Street

SURAMI
Surami Synagogue
Internatsionalaya Street

TBILISI
COMMUNITY ORGANISATIONS
Jews of Georgia Assoc.
Tsarity Tamari Street 8 380012
Telephone: (32) 234-1057

SYNAGOGUES
Ashkenazi
Synagogue
65 Kozhevenny Lane

Sephardi
Synagogue
45-47 Leselidze Street

TSHKINVALI
Synagogue
Isapov Street

TSKHAKAYA
Synagogue
Mir Strret

VANI
Vani Synagogue
4 Kaikavadze Street

GERMANY

It may be a surprise to many that Germany comes immediately after France and the UK in the population table of Western European Jews. German Jews have contributed much to the culture of European Jews in general since their arrival in what is now Germany in the fourth century. The massive Jewish presence in Poland and other east European states stemmed from German Jews escaping persecution in the late Middle Ages. They took the early Medieval German language with them, which formed Yiddish, the old *lingua franca* of European Jews.

The Jews who stayed behind in Germany contributed much towards Jewish and German culture, with the Reform movement starting in nineteenth-century Germany, and Heine and Mendelssohn contributing to German poetry and music respectively. The Enlightenment and modern Orthodoxy also began in Germany.

The rise of Nazism destroyed the belief that the German Jews were more German than Jewish. Many managed to escape before 1939, but 180,000 were killed in the Holocaust (of the 503,000 who lived in Germany when Hitler came to power). Following the events of 1933–45, it seems incredible that any Jew should want to live in Germany again. However, the community began to re-form, mainly with immigrants from eastern Europe, especially Russia. Now there are again Jewish shops in Berlin, and kosher food is once more available. There are many old synagogues which have been restored, and several concentration camps have been kept as historical monuments. There is also a great interest in Jewish matters among some of the non-Jewish younger generation.

Visitors to Berlin should try to visit the new Jewish Museum (officially opened in September 2001). It covers the history of German Jewry through the Middle Ages and up to the present. It revives the tradition of an earlier museum opened in 1933 before the Nazis came to power.

GMT +1 hours
Country calling code: **(+49)**
Total population: **82,071,000**
Jewish population: **100,000**
Emergency telephone: **(Police–110) (Fire–112) (Ambulance–112)**
Electricity voltage: 220

AACHEN
COMMUNITY ORGANISATIONS
Bundesverband Jüdischer Studenten in Deutschland
Oppenhoffallee 50 52066
Telephone: (241) 75998

ALSENZ
SITE
Historic synagogue
Kirchberg 1 67821
Telephone: (636) 23149
Fax: (636) 23149
Restrored eighteenth-century synagogue

ANDERNACH
TOURIST SITES
Historic Mikva
Rhine Valley
This Rhine Valley town cotains an early fourteenth-century mikva. Key obtainable from the Town Hall.

ANNWEILER
Cemetery
Telephone: (623) 53333
The oldest cemetery in the Palatinate dating from the 16th century

BAD NAUHEIM
SYNAGOGUES
Judische Gemeinde
Karlstr. 34, Postfrach 1651 61231
Telephone: (6032) 5605; 0171-4327519
Fax: (6032) 938956
Email: juedischegemeinde-badnauheim@gmx.de
Synagogue is in the Jewish Community Centre.
Restaurant also in the Jewish Community Centre. Entry is from Friedenstrasse.

BADEN-BADEN
Conservative
Baden-Baden Synagogue
Werderstr. 2 76530
Telephone: (722) 21-39-10-21
Fax: (722) 21-39-10-24
Email: info@ikg-bad-bad.de

BAMBERG
COMMUNITY ORGANISATIONS
Community Centre
Willy-Lessing-Str. 7a 96047
Telephone: (951) 297870
Email: ikg.bamberg@gmx.de

BAYREUTH
Bayreuth Synagogue
Munzgasse 2 95444
Telephone: (921) 65404

BERLIN
Jewish life is beginning to grow again in Berlin, formerly an important centre for German Jewry. There are many sites which testify to the tragedy that befell the community before and during the war, such as the ruined Oranienburgerstrasse Synagogue, which has been turned into a Jewish centre. The site of the Wannsee Conference, to the south west of the city, (where the Holocaust was officially planned), has been turned into a museum.

BAKERIES
Backerei Kadtler
Danzigerstrasse 135 10407
Telephone: (30) 030-423-3233
Kasanien Allee 88 10349
Telephone: (30) 281-31222
Supervision: Rabbi Ehrenberg

BED AND BREAKFAST
Guestrooms
Tucholskystrasse 40 Mitte 10117
Telephone: (30) 281-3135
Fax: (30) 281-3122
Website: www.adassjisroel.de
A synagogue and kosher restaurant is in the house

BOOKSELLERS
Literaturhandlung
Joachimstaler-Str. 13 10719
Telephone: (30) 882-4250
Fax: (30) 885-4713

BUTCHERS
Kosher Butcher
Goethestr. 61 10625
The butcher sells certain groceries. Opening hours: 10.00 am to 5.00 pm (Friday until 2.00 pm only).

CEMETERIES
Adass Jisroel
Wittlicherstrasse 2 Weissensee 13088
Telephone: (30) 925-1724
Established in 1880, this historic cemetery is still in use. Rabbi Esriel Hildesheimer, Rabbi Prof. David Zvi Hoffmann, Rabbi Eliahu Kaplan and many other wise and pious Jews are buried here.

Friedhof Heerstaße
Heerstaße 141 Berlin 14055
Telephone: (30) 304-3234
This cemetery of the Jewish Community was opened in 1956. Some 6,000 souls are resting here. The cemetery is still in use.

Friedhof Schönhauser
Allee 23-25
Berlin 10435
Telephone: (30) 441-9824
This cemetery of the Jewish Community was opened in 1827. It has some 25,000 graves.

Friedhof Weissensee
Herbert-Baum-Strasse 45
Telephone: (30) 925-3330
This cemetery of the Jewish Community was opened in 1882. After the liberation in 1945 a memorial for the murdered Jews was mounted near the entrance. More than 107,000 souls rest here. The cemetery is still in use.

COMMUNITY ORGANISATIONS
Community Centre
Fasanenstr. 79-80 off the Kurfurstendamm 10623
Telephone: (30) 88028-250
Fax: (30) 88028-250
Email: vorstand@g-berlin.org
Website: www.jg-berlin.org
This has been built on the site of a famous synagogue, destroyed by the Nazis.

Judische Gemeinde zu Berlin
Joachimstaler Str 13 10719
Telephone: (30) 88020-0
Fax: (30) 88028-150

Judischer Kulturverein (Jewish Cultural Association)
Oranienburgerstr. 26 Berlin-Mitte 10117
Telephone: (30) 282-6669; 285-98052
Fax: (30) 285-98053
Email: jkv.berlin@t-online.de
Hours: Monday to Thursday 11.00 am to 5.00 pm, Friday 11.00 am to 2.00 pm and 1 hour before evening and Sunday events. Friday for Kiddush 6.00 to 9.00 pm. (Summer 7.00 pm). (Entrance around the corner.)

Leo-Baeck-Haus
Tucholskystrasse 40 Mitte 10117
Telephone: (30) 284-4560
Fax: (30) 284-45613
Here the Zeutralrat der Juden in Deutschland has its administration

Zentralrat der Juden in Deutschland
Tucholskystr. 9 10117
Telephone: (30) 28 44 56 0
Fax: (30) 28 44 56 13
Email: info@zentralratdjuden.de
Website: www.zentralratdjuden.de

EMBASSY
Embassy of Israel
Auguste-Viktoria Strasse 74-76 14193
Telephone: (30) 89045-500
Fax: (30) 89045-555
Email: botschaft@israel.de
Website: www.israel.de

GROCERIES
Kolbo
Auguststrasse 77-78 Mitte 10117
Telephone: (30) 281-3135
In addition to kosher food and wines, sifrei kodesh as well as general literature about Jewish subjects can be obtained here

Platzl
Passauer Str. 4 10789
Telephone: (30) 217-7506

Schalom
Wielandstr. 43 10625
Telephone: (30) 312-1131
Fax: (30) 318-09905
Opening hours: 11.00 am to 5.00 pm (Friday until 3.30 pm)

LIBRARIES
Jewish Community
Fassenstrasse 79 10623

Jewish Library
Oranienburger Str. 28 10117
Telephone: (30) 880-28-427/429

MEDIA
Newspapers
Allgemeine Judische Wochenzeitung
Postfach 04 03 69, Haus jur Berlina Haus
Vogleiplatz 12, Berlin 10117
Telephone: (30) 2844-5650
Fax: (30) 2844-5699
Email: ajw@Juedische-Allgeuche.de,
verlag@Juedische-Allgeuche.de
Fortnightly

Hadshot Adass Jisroel
Tucholsky str. 40 10117
Telephone: (30) 281-3135
Published by Adass Jisroel

Periodical
Judischer Kulturveein Berlin e.v.
Oranienburgerstr. 26, Berlin-Mitte 10117
Telephone: (30) 282-6669; 285-98052
Fax: (30) 285-98053
Email: jkv.berlin@t-online.de
Website:
www.migrationsrat.de/Mitglieder/116Jüdischer
Kultuverein
Monthly

Judisches Berlin
Oranienburger Str. 31 10117
Telephone: (30) 88028-260; 88028-269
Fax: (30) 88028-266
Email: jb@jg-berlin.org
Monthly.

MUSEUMS
Jewish Museum
Lindenstrasse 9-14 10969
Telephone: (30) 2599-3305
Fax: (30) 2599-3409
Email: info@jmberlin.de
Website: www.jmberlin.de

The permanent exhibition is a journey through German–Jewish histiory and culture. In addition there are relevant changing exhibitions. There is a restaurant on the premises. Opening hours: Monday 10.00 am to 10.00 pm Tuesday to Sunday from 10.00 am to 8.00 pm.

Topographic des Terrors
Niederkirchnestr 8 U & S- bahn Potsdamer Platz, Former site of Gestapo headquarters

RESTAURANTS
Meat
Bäckerei Taitles
Dahlmannst 22

Bleiberg's
Nürnbergershst 45a

Jewish Museum Berlin
Lindenstrasse 9-14 10969
Telephone: (30) 25993300
Fax: (30) 25993409
Email: info@jmberlin.de
Website: www.jmberlin.de
The museum was designed by Daniel Libeskind. Exhibition: Two Millennia of German Jewish History. There is a Restaurant Liebermanns on the premises, the cuisine is kosher style.

Noah's Arche Community Centre
Restaurant Arche Noah
Fasanenstr. 79-80 10623
Telephone: (30) 882-6138
Shabbat reservations and payment have to be arranged before beginning of Shabbat. The restaurant is located on the first floor of the community building. Opening hours: Daily 12 noon to 3.30 pm and 6.30 pm to 10.30 pm.

SYNAGOGUES
Conservative
Synagogue
Fraenkelufer 10-16

Liberal
Synagogue
Pestalozzistr. 14 1000 10625
Telephone: (30) 313-8411

Orthodox
Adass Jisroel
Tucholskystrasse 40 Mitte 10117
Telephone: (30) 281-3135
Fax: (30) 281-3122
Website: www.adassjisroel.de
Established 1869. Rabbinate, kashrut supervision and mohel can all be reached at this number. Near the community centre, there is a guest house, a kosher restaurant and a shop which sells kosher products.

Synagogue
Joachimstaler Strasse 13 Mitte 16719
Daily minyan, Jewish bookshop on site

Reform
Synagogue
Synagogue Hüttenweg 46, Berlin 14195
Telephone: (30) 327-9666
Email: info@huettenweg.de
Website: www.huettenweg.de

TOURIST SITES
Jewish Culture Edition
Leo-Baeck-House, Tucholsky Street 9 10117
Telephone: (30) 2844-5659
Fax: (30) 2844-5661
Email: Verlaig@Judaicum.de

TOURS
Tours of Berlin
Contact: Iris Weiss
Email: iris.weiss@snafu.de
Website: www.berlin-judentum.de
22 tours about Jewish history and Jewish life

BONN
Bonn Synagogue
Templestr. 2-4, cnr. Adenauer Allee 53113
Telephone: 213560
Fax: 2618366

BRAUNSCHWEIG
COMMUNITY ORGANISATIONS
Community Centre
Steinstr. 4 38100
Telephone: (531) 45536

MUSEUMS
Braunschweigisches Landesmuseum
Abt. Judisches Museum, Burgplatz 1 D 38100
Telephone: (531) 1215-0
Fax: (531) 1215-2607
Email: derda@landesmuseum-bs.de
Website: www.landesmuseum-bs.de
Founded in 1746, this museum was formerly the oldest Jewish museum in the world. It was re-opened in 1987 under the auspices of the Braunschweigisches Landesmuseum. Hours Tuesday to Sunday: 10 am to 5 pm.

BREMEN
Bremen Synagogue
Schwachauser Heerst. 117 28211
Telephone: (421) 498-5104
Fax: (421) 498-4944

CELLE
Jewish Museum
Im Kreise 24 29221

Formerly a beautiful synagogue, it now houses travelling exhibits on various themes of Jewish history and Jewish life in Celle, where a community started between 1671 and 1691. There are now enough Jews in the town to form a minyan. Opening hours: Tuesday to Thursday 3.00 pm to 5.00 pm, Friday 9.00 am to 11.00 am and Sunday 11.00 am to 1.00 pm. Conducted tours of the synagogue and tours on the history of the Jews of Celle are also available by arrangement. Inquire at the Tourist Office, Celle, telephone (421) 5141-1212.

CHEMNITZ
Community Centre
Stollberger Str. 28 Chemnitz 9119
Telephone: (371) 354-970
Fax: (371) 345-9719
Email: JueolGemeiude_Chemuitz@-t-online.de

COBLENZ (KOBLENZ)
Community Centre
Schlachtof Str. 5
Telephone: (261) 42223

COLOGNE
HOTELS
Leonet
Rubensstr. 33
Telephone: (221) 272-300
Fax: (221) 210-893
Email: leontkoeln@netcologne.de
Website: www.leonet-koeln.de

RESTAURANTS
Meat
Community Centre
Roonstr. 50 50674
Telephone: (221) 240-4440
Fax: (221) 240-4440
Phone in advance. Glatt kosher.

SYNAGOGUES
Liberal
Judissche Liberale Gemeinde
Stammheimer Str 22 50735
Telephone: (221) 287-0424
Fax: (221) 719-5024
Email: jlg.koeln@gmx.de
Website: www.gescherlamassoret.de

Orthodox
Synagogue
Roonstr. 50 Köln 50674
Telephone: (221) 921-5600
Fax: (221) 921-5609
Email: synagogue-koeln@netcologne.de
Website: www.sgk.de

Daily services. There is a youth centre, mikva, glatt-kosher restaurant (meat), Jewish museum and library at the same address. Old age home (Elternheim), kindergarten, primary school, social department and administration are located in: Ottstr. 85 / Eingang Nussbaumer Str. 50923 Köln
Telephone: (221) 71662-0 Fax: (221) 71662-599

DORTMUND
COMMUNITY ORGANISATIONS
Landesverband der Judischen Gemeinden von Westfalen
Prinz-Friedrich-Karl-Str. 12 44135
Telephone: (231) 528495
Fax: (231) 5860372
Email: lvjuedwest@aol.com

SYNAGOGUES
Dortmund Synagogue
Prinz-Friedrich-Karl-Str. 9 44135
Telephone: (231) 528497

DRESDEN
In November 2001 the first new synagogue in what was East Germany was consecrated. It is on the site of the Semper synagogue originally built in 1838 and destroyed one hundred years later on Kristallnacht.

A three foot high Star of David, one of the two that was on the top of the synagogue, was all that remained. It will stand above the new synagogue's gate.

Up to date information may be found on www.Synagogue-dresden.de

COMMUNITY ORGANISATIONS
Landesverband Sachsen der Judischen Gemeinden K.d.o.R.
Bautzner Str 20 1099
Telephone: (351) 804-5491; 802-2739
Fax: (351) 804-1445
A memorial to the six million Jews killed in the Holocaust stands on the site of the Dresden Synagogue, burnt down by the Nazis in November 1938

SYNAGOGUES
Dresden Synagogue
Fiedlerstr. 3 1307
Telephone: (351) 693317

DUSSELDORF
Dusseldorf Synagogue
Zietenstr. 50 40476
Telephone: (211) 469120
Fax: (211) 485156

EMMENDINGEN
Community Centre
Kirchstr. 11 D79312

SYNAGOGUES

Orthodox

Juedische Gemeinde Emmendingen

Synagogue and Youth Centre, Landvogtei 11, Office and Community Centre Kirchstr 11, POB 1423 D-79312

Telephone: (7641) 571-989

Fax: (7641) 571-980

Email: juedgemem@aol.com

Website: www.juedgemen.de

ERFURT

Community Centre

Juri-Gagarin-Ring 16 99084

Telephone: (361) 24964

ESSEN

Essen Community Organizations

Sedanstr. 46 45138

Telephone: (201) 273413

Fax: (201) 287112

ESSINGEN

TOURIST SITES

Cemetery

Largest cemetery in the Palatinate dating from the sixteenth century, where Anne Frank's ancestors are buried. Key at the Mayor's Office.

FRANKFURT AM MAIN

BUTCHERS

Aviv Butchery & Deli

Hanauer Landstrasse 50 60314

Telephone: (69) 433013

Fax: (69) 448064

Email: info@aviv.de

Website: www.aviv.de

Supervision: Frankfurt Rabbinate

COMMUNITY ORGANISATIONS

Community Centre (Jgnatz-Bubis-Gemeindezentrum)

Westendstr. 43 60325

Telephone: (69) 768-0360

Fax: (69) 746874

Email: jg.ffm@t-online.de

This community produces a magazine, 'Judische Gemeinde-Zeitung Frankfurt'

Zentralwohlfahrtsstelle de Juden in Deutschland

Hebelstrasse 6 60318

Telephone: (69) 94-43-71-15

Fax: (69) 49-48-17

Email: zentrale@zwst.org

Website: www.zwst.org

GROCERIES

Koschermarket

36 Bornheimer Landwehr 60385

Telephone: (69) 9441-1238

Fax: (69) 9441-2174

MIKVAOT

Judische Gemeinde

Westendstr 43 D60325

Telephone: (69) 768-0360

Fax: (69) 746-874

MUSEUMS

Jewish Museum

Untermainkai 14-15 60311

Telephone: (69) 212-35000

Fax: (69) 212-30705

Email: info@juedischesmuseum.de

Website: www.juedischesmuseum.de

Central organisation: Stadt Frankfurt am Main-Der

Sunday, Tuesday to Saturday 10.00 am to 5.00 pm, Wednesday 10.00 am to 8.00 pm. Closed Monday.

Museum Judengasse

Kurt-Schumacher-Str 10 60311

Telephone: (69) 297-7419

RESTAURANTS

Sohar's Kosher Restaurant

Savignystrasse 66 60325

Telephone: (69) 752-341

Fax: (69) 741-0116

Email: restaurant@sohars-restaurant.com

Website: www.sohars-restaurant.com

Supervision: Rabbi Menachem Halevi Klein, Frankfurt Rabbinate

Hours: Tuesday to Thursday and Sunday, 12 pm to 8 pm; Friday 12 pm to Shabbat; Shabbat, 1.30 pm to 4 pm; Monday closed. Special arrangements can be made by phone. Friday and Shabbat meals must be ordered in advance. Provides part services, airline catering and delivery to hotels.

SYNAGOGUES

Synagogue

Baumweg 5-7 60316

Telephone: (69) 439-381

Westend Synagogue

Freiherr-vom-Stein-Str. 30 60323

Telephone: (69) 723-263

Email: verwaltung@jg-ffm.de

This is the city's main synagogue

FREIBURG

COMMUNITY ORGANISATIONS

Community Centre

Engels Strasse

Telephone: (761) 383-096

Fax: (761) 382-332

Services: Erev Shabbat in Summer 7.30 pm in Winter 6.30 pm. Shabbat morning 9.30 am. Kosher Kiddush after services.

FRIEDBERG

TOURIST SITES
Historic Mikva
Judengasse 20 61169
A Gothic style mikva built in 1260. The town council has issued a special explanatory leaflet about it. It has been restored and it is now scheduled as a historical monument of medieval architecture.

FURTH

COMMUNITY ORGANISATIONS
Community Centre
Blumenstr. 31 90762
Telephone: (91) 177-0879

TOURIST SITES
Synagogue and Mikva
Julienstr. 2
There is a beautifully restored synagogue as well as a historic mikva

GELSENKIRCHEN
Community Centre
Von-der-Recke-Str. 9 45879
Telephone: (20) 923143 & 206628

HAGEN
Hagen Community Organisation
Pottofstr. 16 58095
Telephone: (2331) 711-3289

HALLE
Halle Community Organisation
Grosse Markerstr, 13 6108
Telephone: (345) 233-110
Fax: (345) 233-1122
Email: jghalle@gmx.net

HAMBURG
Hamburg Community Organisation
Schaferkampsalle 27 20357
Telephone: (40) 440-9440
Fax: (40) 410-8430
Mikvah on premises

SYNAGOGUES
Orthodox
Hamburg Synagogue
Hohe Weide 34 20253
Telephone: (40) 4409-4429
Fax: (40) 410-8430
Email: kieseler@jghh.org; zach@jghh.org

HANOVER

COMMUNITY ORGANISATIONS
Community Centre
Haeckelstr. 10 30173
Telephone: (311) 810-472

SYNAGOGUES
Hanover Synagogue
Haeckelstr. 10 30173
Telephone: (311) 810-472

HEIDELBERG

RESTAURANTS
College Restaurant
Theaterstr. 9 69117
Telephone: (6221) 168-767
Kosher meals are available (by arrangement – it is open all year round) Monday to Friday at the college restaurant, 100 yards from the College of Jewish Studies, situated at Friederichstrasse 9

HERFORD
Community Centre
Komturstraße 21 32052
Telephone: (52) 21924702
Fax: (52) 21924704

HILDESHEIM

SYNAGOGUES
Jewish Community in Hildesheim
Postfach 10 07 07, Lower Saxony D31135
Telephone: (512) 170-4962
Fax: (512) 170-4964
Rabbi Dr Walter Homolka is responsible for all Lower Saxony

HOF
Community Centre
Am Wiesengrund 20 95032
Telephone: (92) 815-3249

ICHENHAUSEN
Museum of Jewish History
Located in the fine baroque synagogue, not far from Ulm.

INGENHEIM

TOURIST SITES
Cemetery
Klingenerstr. 20 76831
Sixteenth century cemetery can be visited. Key obtained from Klingenerstr. 20

KAISERSLAUTERN
Community Centre
Basteigasse 4 67655
Telephone: (63) 169720

KARLSRUHE
Karlsruhe Community Organizations
Knielinger Alle 11 76133
Telephone: (72) 172035

KIEL
Orthodox
Kiel Synagogue
Wikingerstrasse 6 24143
Telephone: (431) 739-9096
Fax: (431) 739-9095

KIPPENHEIM
An extensive restoration of the synagogue built
in 1850-1852 and destroyed on Kristallnacht
was started in 1987. The exterior renovation is
complete and work is now taking place on the
interior. It is classified by the state of Burden-
Wurtenburg as a 'cultural monument of
significance'.

**There are no other specific locations of
interest to travellers.**

KONSTANZ
Community Centre
Sigismundstr. 19 78462
Telephone: (75) 312-3077

KREFELD
Krefeld Community Organisations
Wiedstr. 17b 47799
Telephone: (21) 512-0648

LANDAU
Synagogue
Frank-Loebsches Haus, Kaufhausgasse 9 76829
Telephone: (6341) 86472
Fax: (6341) 13294
Email: sabine.haas.landau.de

LUBECK
Orthodox
Synagogue & Community Centre
St.-Annen-Str 13 23552
Telephone: (451) 798-2182
Fax: (451) 7074-9207
Email: jgh_hl@gmx.de

MAGDEBURG
Community Centre
Groperstr. 1a 39106
Telephone: (391) 52665

MAINZ
Mainz Community Organisations
Forsterstr. 2 55118
Telephone: (6131) 613-990
Fax: (6131) 611-767

TOURIST SITES
Jewish Cemetery
Untere Zahlbacherstr. 11
The key to the twelfth-century Jewish cemetery can be
obtained at the 'new' Jewish cemetery

MARBURG AN DER LAHN
Community Centre
Unterer Eichweg 17 35041
Telephone: (642) 132-881

MICHELSTADT
TOURIST SITES
Michelstadt
The town has an old synagogue which is now a museum of
both Judaism and Jewish history. It is open every day in the
summer except Saturday.

MINDEN
Community Centre
Kampstr. 6 32423
Telephone: (57) 123437

MONCHENGLADBACH
Monchengladbach Synagogue
Albertusstr. 54 41363
Telephone: (216) 23879
Fax: (216) 14639
Email: juedischegemeindemg@t-online.de

MULHEIM
Mulheim Community Organisations
Kampstr. 7 45468
Telephone: 835191

MUNICH
BOOKSELLERS
Literaturhandlung Literatur Zum Judentum
Fürstenstr. 17 80333
Telephone: (89) 2800135
Fax: (89) 281601
Email: literaturhandlung@t-online.de
Programs on Jewish subjects

COMMUNITY ORGANISATIONS
**Israelitische Kultusgemeinde München und
Oberbayern (Community Centre)**
Reichenbachstr. 27 80469
Telephone: (89) 202-4000
Fax: (89) 201-4604
Email: info@ikg-m.de
Website: www.ikg-muenchen.de

GROCERIES
Danel Feinkost
Pilgersheimerstrabe 44 81543
Telephone: (89) 669-888
Fax: (89) 669-820
Viktualien-Markt, Westenrienderstrabe 9 80331

Telephone: (89) 2280-0258
Email: danel@t-online.de
Website: www.koscher.net/danel/
Will deliver to hotels or other addresses, throughout
Germany

MUSEUMS
Judisches Museum Munchen
Reichbach Str. 27 80469
Telephone: (89) 2000-9693
Fax: (89) 2024-4838
Email: juedisches-museum@muenchen.de
Website: www.juedisches-museum.muenchen.de
A very small museum

RESTAURANTS
Carmel Prestige
Reichenbachstr. 27 80469
Telephone: (89) 202-05585
Fax: (89) 202-05586
Email: info@carmel-prestige.de
Website: www.carmel-prestige.de
Run by the community centre. Hours: 12 pm to 2.30 pm;
6.00 pm to 9.00 pm. Shabbat meals must be ordered by
Friday noon. Closed Sundays.

SYNAGOGUES
Schwabing Synagogue (Schaarei Zion)
Georgenstr. 71 80798
Telephone: (89) 202-4000
Friday evenings and Sabbath mornings only

Synagogue
Possartstr. 15 81679
Telephone: (89) 474-440
Reichenbachstr 27 80469
Telephone: (89) 202-4000
Fax: (89) 201-4604
Mikva on premises

Liberal
Beth Shalom
Telephone: (89) 20330385
Fax: (89) 8980-9374
Email: beth.shalom@liberale-judes.de
Website: www.beth-shalom.de
Central organisation: World Union for Progressive Judaism
Please ask for address and timetable

NEUSTADT
Community Centre
Ludwigstr. 20 67433
Telephone: (0) 6321-2652
Fax: (0) 6321-397492
Email: jkg989@aol.com

ODENBACH
TOURIST SITES
Synagogue
Kirchhofstrasse 9
Telephone: (67) 532745
There is a unusually shaped historic synagogue built in
1752 with baroque paintings in this small village.
Arrangements to visit need to be made in advance.

OFFENBACH
ORGANISATIONS
Community Centre
Kaiserstr. 109 63065
Telephone: (69) 820036
Fax: (69) 820026

OSNABRÜCK 2
Osnabrück Community Organization
In der Barlage 41 49078
Telephone: (541) 148420
Fax: (541) 143-4701
Kashrut information for visitors who wish to eat kosher on
Shabbat, please contact Rabbi Marc Sterm at Tel: (541)
48553

SYNAGOGUES
Orthodox
Jewish Congregation Synagogue
In der Barlage 41 49078
Telephone: (541) 48420
Fax: (541) 434701
Email: Rabbistern@t-online.de
Website: www.jiddischkeit.org

TOURIST SITES
The Felix-Nussbaum House
Lotter Str 49078
Telephone: (541) 323-2207
Fax: (541) 323-2739
Email: jaehner@osnabrueck.de
Website: www.osnabrueck.de/fmh
About 20 minutes walk from the synagogue

PADERBORN
Community Centre
Pipinstr. 32 33098
Telephone: (52) 512-2596

REGENSBURG
Regensburg Community Organizations
Am Brixener Hof 2 93047
Telephone: (94) 157093; 21819

SAARBRUCKEN

SYNAGOGUES

Synagogengemeinde Saar
Lortzingstr 8 66111
Telephone: (681) 910-380
Fax: (681) 910-3813
Email: info@synagogengemeindesaar.de
Website: www.synagogengemeinde.de

SCHWERIN

COMMUNITY ORGANISATIONS

Judische Gemeinde Schwerin
Schlachtermarkt 7 19055
Telephone: (38) 5550-7345
Fax: (38) 5593-60989
Email: jgemeinde@gmx.net

SPEYER

TOURIST SITES

11th Century Mikva
Telephone: (62) 353332
This town contains the oldest (eleventh-century) mikva in
Germany, Judenbadgasse. To visit it, obtain the key by
contacting the Tourist Office (Maximilianstrasse 11).
Guided tours are available.

STRAUBING

COMMUNITY ORGANISATIONS

Community Centre
Wittelbacherstr. 2 94315
Telephone: (94) 211387

STUTTGART

RELIGIOUS ORGANISATIONS

Israelitische Religionsgemeinschaft
Hospitalstr. 36 Stuttgart 70174
Telephone: (711) 228360
Fax: (711) 2283636
Email: verwattung@irgw.de

RESTAURANTS

Meat

Schalom Kosher Restaurant
Hospitalstrasse 36 70174
Telephone: (711) 294752
Supervision: Orthodox Rav of the Stuttgart community
Open during morning hours through to about 7.00 pm
except Mondays (when closed). Located on the premises of
the Stuttgart Jewish community centre.

TRIER

COMMUNITY ORGANISATIONS

Judische Kultugemeinde Trier
Kaiserstr. 25 D-54290
Telephone: (0) 651-994-5575
Fax: (0) 651-994-5577

VEITSHOCHHEIM

Located a few miles from Wurzburg is the town
of Veitshoechheim, which reconsecrated a pre-
First World War Synagogue and opened as a
Jewish Museum in March 1994. Originally built
in 1730 the synagogue was the community
centre for local Jews who had lived in the area
for nearly three hundred years, from 1644 to
1942, when the last Jews were deported from
Veitshoechheim to the Nazi concentration
camps.

In 1986 the stone fragments of the original
interior, including the Bima and the Ahron
Hakodesch, were discovered beneath the floor,
where they had been buried in 1940. This find
prompted local officials to transform the
Synagogue back to its original function and
splendour, using photographs from the 1920s as
a guide.

MUSEUMS

Judisches Kulturmuseum Veitshoechheim
Thuengersheimer Strasse 17 97209
Telephone: (931) 9802-764
Fax: (931) 9802-766
Email: museum@veitshoechheim.de
Website: www.veitshoechheim.de

WIESBADEN

COMMUNITY ORGANISATIONS

Judische Gemeinde Wiesbaden
Friedrichstr. 31-33 65185
Telephone: (611) 933-3030
Fax: (611) 933-30319
Email: jg.wi@t-online.de
Services every Friday evening and Saturday morning with
kiddush and Jewish holidays

SYNAGOGUES

Community Centre
Wiesbaden Synagogue
Friedrichstr. 31-33 65085
Telephone: (611) 933-030
Fax: (611) 933-0319
Email: jg.wi@t-online.de

WORMS

The original Rashi Synagogue, built in the 11th
century and the oldest Jewish place of worship
in Europe, was destroyed by the Nazis in 1938.
After the Second World War it was
reconsecrated in 1961. The building also
contains a 12th century mikvahh and a Jewish
Museum. There is also the oldest Jewish
cemetery in Europe.

WUPPERTAL
COMMUNITY ORGANISATIONS
Community Centre
Friedrich-Ebert-Str. 73 42103
Telephone: (202) 300233

WURZBURG
Wurzburg Community Organisations
Valentin-Becker-Str. 11 97072
Telephone: (931) 151190
Fax: (931) 118184
Also guest rooms for tourists; kosher meals available

MIKVAOT
Wurzburg Mikvaot
Valentin-Becker-Str. 11 97072
Telephone: (931) 151190
Fax: (931) 118184
Appointments must be made

SYNAGOGUES
Wurzburg Synagogue
Valentin-Becker-Str. 11 97072
Telephone: (931) 151190
Fax: (931) 118184
Email: mail@juedischegemeindewuerzburg.de
Website: www.juedischegemeindewuerzburg.de

TOURIST SITES
Cemeteries
There are old Jewish cemeteries in Wurzburg, Heidingsfeld and Hochberg

GIBRALTAR

The first Jewish people in Gibraltar were Sephardi, who had crossed over the border from Spain before the Inquisition began in the fourteenth century. Many more followed in the ensuing centuries. When Britain took possession Jews were banned, but later they were allowed in as traders and finally, in 1749, they were granted full permission to live there. The community began to flourish and the Jewish population, which now also included many North African Jews rose to 2,000.

At the end of the Second World War some of the community returned after being evacuated to Britain. There are now fairly good Jewish facilities, namely four synagogues, and newsletters. There are no kosher hotels in Gibraltar.

Gibraltar has an Eruv. Gibraltar has had a Jewish prime minister and a Jewish mayor,

Gibraltar's highest offices.

GMT +1 hours
Country calling code: **(+350)**
Total population: **28,000**
Jewish population: **650**
Emergency telephone: **(Police–999) (Fire–999) (Ambulance–999)**
Electricity voltage: **220/240**

BAKERIES
J. Amar
47 Line Wall Road
Telephone: 73516

BUTCHERS AND DELICATESSEN
A. Edery International Ltd
20 Public Market, PO Box 711
Telephone: 75168
Fax: 42529
Email: edery@gibnet.gi
Website: www.ederykosher.com
Supervision: Dayan Ch. Ehrentreu Head of London Beth Din and Rabbi R Hassid Chief Rabbi of Gibraltar
Glatt Kosher meat, delicatessen lamb and poultry
Specialise in orders to hotels and caterers

COMMUNITY ORGANISATIONS
Managing Board of Jewish Community
10 Bomb House Lane
Telephone: 72606
Fax: 40487
Email: mbjc@gibtelecom.net

CONTACT INFORMATION
Solomon Levy M.B.E. J.P
3 Convent Place, PO Box 190
Telephone: 77789; 428128; 78047 (home)
Fax: 42527
Email: slevy@gibnet.gi
The vice-president of the Jewish community is happy to provide information for Jewish travellers

CULTURAL ORGANISATIONS
Jewish Social & Cultural Club
7 Bomb House Lane
Telephone: 79636
Email: asuissa@gibnet.gi
Mailing address: Aver Suissa, 20 Lime Tree Lodge, Montagu Gardens, Gibraltar

DELICATESSEN
Uncle Sam's Deli
62 Irish Town
Telephone: 51236; 51226
Fax: 42516
Email: dabamick@gibnet.gi.com
Provides kosher groceries and wine. Catering and takeaway service. Full glatt kosher service. Fully licensed.

EMBASSY
Consul General of Israel
Marina View, Glacis Road, PO Box 141
Telephone: 77244

GROCERIES
I&D Abudarham
32 Cornwall's Lane, PO Box 216
Telephone: 78506
Fax: 73249
Email: djabudar@gibnet.gi
Kosher wines, meats & poultry

HOTELS
The Rock Hotel
Telephone: 73000
Fax: 73513
The hotel has kosher facilities (meat and dairy) and can cater for pre-booked groups of 10 or more. Kosher takeaway food can also be delivered to a room.

JUDAICA
A. Cohen
3 Convent Place, PO Box 190
Telephone: 52734
Fax: 42527
Email: sofergib@gibtelecom.net
Supplier of Mezuzot, Tephilim, Sifre Tora, Shaatnez and Kashrus organisation

MIKVAOT
Gibraltar Mikvaot
12 Bomb House Lane
Telephone: 77658 &73090
Fax: 72359

RESTAURANTS
Jewish Club
Open daily from 10 am to 11 pm, except Shabbat, but arrangements can be made with the restaurant owner for Shabbat meals

SYNAGOGUES
Abudarham
20 Parliament Lane 78506
Telephone: 78047
Fax: 42527
Email: slevy@gibnet.gi

Nefusot Yehuda
65 Line Wall Road G1
Telephone: 77674
Fax: 73201
Email: benzaquen@gibtelecom.net
Central organisation: Managing Board Jewish Community

Shaar Hashamayim
19 Engineer Lane 78069
Telephone: 74030
Fax: 74029
Enquiries: Joseph de M. Benyunes PO Box 1474

Orthodox
Etz Hayim
91 Irish Town 75955
Telephone: 75563
Fax: 42939

GREECE

After the Hellenistic occupation of Israel (the Jewish revolt during this occupation is commemorated in the festival of Hanukah), some Jews were led into slavery in Greece, beginning the first recorded Jewish presence in the country. The next significant Jewish immigration occurred after the Inquisition, when many Spanish Jews moved to Salonika, which was a flourishing Jewish centre until the German occupation in the Second World War. In 1832 Jews were granted equal civil rights to all other Greek citizens.

By the early 1940s, the Jewish population had grown to over 70,000, with 45,000 living in Salonika. The country was occupied in July 1941 and split among the Axis (German, Italian and Bulgarian) forces. During the occupation a relatively large number of Jews joined the partisans. Many local Christians did protect their Jewish neighbours in Athens. After the war many of the survivors emigrated to Israel.

Today, there are Sephardi synagogues in Greece and in Athens, a community centre and a Jewish museum. There are Jewish publications and a library in the community centre. In Aegina, Corfu and other Greek islands, ancient synagogues may be visited.

GMT +2 hours
Country calling code: (+30)
Total population: 10,552,000
Jewish population: 4,500
Emergency telephone: (Police–100) (Fire–199) (Ambulance–166)
Electricity voltage: 220

ATHENS
Almost 3,000 Jews live in Athens. The community has access to a centre containing a library, and the opportunity to have a kosher meal. The Jewish museum in the centre of the city details the rise and tragic fall of Greek Jewry.

Kosher meals are served at the Athens Jewish Cultural Centre upon request (contact Mrs Rachel Sasson, Tel. (1) 213 3371. Delivery to hotels in Athens can also be arranged).

COMMUNITY ORGANISATIONS
Central Board of the Jewish Communities of Greece
36 Voulis Street 10557
Telephone: (210) 324-4315-18
Fax: (210) 331-3852
Email: hhkis@hellasnet.gr
Website: www.ris.gr

EMBASSY
Embassy of Israel
Marathonodromou Street 1, Paleo Psychico, POB 65140
Telephone: (210) 671-9530

MUSEUMS
Jewish Museum of Greece
39 Nikis Str. 10557
Telephone: (210) 322-5582
Fax: (210) 3223-1577
Email: jmg@otenet.gr
Website: www.jewishmuseum.gr
Open: Monday to Friday 9.00 am to 2.30 pm, Sunday 10.00 am to 2.00 pm, Saturday closed.

RESTAURANTS
Meat
Kosher restaurant
5 Averof St. 10433
Telephone: (210) 520-2880
Fax: (210) 520-2881
Email: chabad@otenet.gr
Telephone for orders

Vegetarian
Eden
Odos Flessa 3, Plaka

SYNAGOGUES
Sephardi
Beth Shalom
5 Melidoni Street 10553
Telephone: (210) 325-2773; 2823; 2875
Fax: (210) 322-0761
Email: isrkath@hellasnet.gr

TOURIST INFORMATION
Community Office
8 Melidoni Street 10553
Telephone: (210) 325-2875
Fax: (210) 322-0761
Email: isrkath@hellasnet.gr

Meals on Wheels
Glatt Kosher Meals delivered
Telephone: (210) 5202-880

CHALKIS
COMMUNITY ORGANISATIONS
Community Centre
35 Kotsou Street 34100
Telephone: (2221) 80690

KASHRUT INFORMATION
Community Centre
Telephone: (2221) 27297

SYNAGOGUES
Chalkis Synagogue
36 Kotsou Street
This synagogue has been rebuilt and renewed many times on its original foundations. Tombstone inscriptions in the cementery go back more then fifteen centuries. Only open on High Holy Days.

CORFU
COMMUNITY ORGANISATIONS
Community Centre
5 Riz. Voulephton St. 49100
Telephone: (2661) 45650
Fax: (2661) 43791

TOURIST SITES
Corfu Synagogue
Velissariou St.
Telephone: (2661) 38802
There was an ancient synagogue and cemetery here, destroyed by the Nazis

CRETE
Etz-Hayyim Synagogue
Parados Kondyllaki 730 11, Hania, Crete
Telephone: (2821) 086-286
Fax: (2821) 086-286
Website: www.etz-hayyim-hania.org

IOANNINA
COMMUNITY ORGANISATIONS
Ioannina Community Organisations
18 Josef Eliyia St. 45221
Telephone: (2651) 25195
Contact: John Kalef-Ezra on 32390

LARISSA
SYNAGOGUES
Community Centre
29 Kentavron St. 41222
Telephone: (241) 532-965

RHODES
Kahal Shalom Kadosh
Simmiou and Dossiadou Street
Telephone: (22410) 22364-70964
Fax: (22410) 73039
Email: jcrhodes@otenet.gr
Website: www.RhodesJewishMuseum.org
The synagogue belongs to the Jewish Community of
Rhodes which has 38 members. It was built around 1577 in
the old Jewish Quarter. The synagogue is on the World
Monuments Fund list of 100 most endangered sites.
Tourists wishing to visit these sites should contact: Jewish
Community of Rhodes, No. 5 Polydorou St. Old City. Rhodes.
Tel: 22410-22364 or Fax: 22410-73039

THESSALONIKI
For many years around the turn of the 20th
century Jews formed the majority of Salonika's
inhabitants. It was known as the 'Jerusalem of
the Balkans'. The official day off was Saturday.

CULTURAL ORGANISATIONS
The Israelite Fraternity House
24 Vassileos Irakliou St.
Telephone: (231) 221030

Yad le Zikaron
24 Vassileos Irakliou St.
Telephone: (231) 275701

MUSEUMS
Jewish Museum of Thessaloniki
13 Agiou Mina Str. 54624
Telephone: (231) 250-406-7
Fax: (231) 250-406-7
Email: jctmuseo@compulink.gr
Website: www.jmth.gr
Tuesday, Friday & Sunday: 11.00 am to 2.00 pm,
Wednesday & Thursday: 11.00 am to 2.00 pm and 5.00 pm
to 8.00 pm. Guided tours for groups, educational
programmes for youngsters.

SYNAGOGUES
Monastirioton
35 Sygrou Str. 54630
Telephone: (231) 524968

TRIKKALA
Synagogue
15 Athanassiou Diakou St

Yad Lezicaron
24 Vassileos Irakliou Str.
Telephone: (231) 223231

VOLOS
COMMUNITY ORGANISATIONS
Volos Community Organisations
Xenophontos & Moisseos Streets 38333
Telephone: (2421) 25302
Fax: (2421) 25302

KASHRUT INFORMATION
Volos Kashrut Information
20 Parodos Kondulaki

SYNAGOGUES
Volos Synagogue
Xenophontos & Moisseos Streets
Open primarily on High Holy Days

TOURIST SITES
Holocaust Monument
Riga Ferreou Square

GUADELOUPE
SYNAGOGUES
Bas du Fort, Lot 1
Telephone: 90-99-09
The Synagogue, community centre and restaurant/kosher
store are all located here.

GUATEMALA
Conversos were the first recorded Jews in
the country, but a few centuries later the
next Jewish immigration occurred with the
arrival of German Jews in 1848. Later some
east European Jews arrived, but
Guatemala was not keen to accept refugees
from Nazism and, as a result, passed some
laws which, although not mentioning Jews
directly, were aimed against Jewish
refugees.

Even though these laws were in place, in
1939 there were 800 Jews in Guatemala.
An Ashkenazi community centre was built
in 1965, but, despite accepting some
Jewish Cuban refugees, the community is
shrinking owing to assimilation and intermarriage.

Most Jews live in Guatemala City, with
others in Quetzaltenango and San Marcos.
There is a Jewish school and kindergarten.

GMT -6 hours
Country calling code: (+502)
Total population: 10,517,000
Jewish population: 1,000
Emergency telephone: (Police–110) (Fire–110)
(Ambulance–125)
Electricity voltage: 110

GUATEMALA CITY
COMMUNITY ORGANISATIONS
Comunidad Judia Guatemalteca
Apartado Postal 502
Telephone: (2) 360-1509
Fax: (2) 360-1589
Email: comjugua@guaweb.net
Website: www.comunidadjudia.com
Has a kosher grocery

EMBASSY
Embassy of Israel
13 Av. 14-07, Zona 10
Telephone: (2) 371305

SYNAGOGUES
Ashenkenazi
Centro Hebreo, 7a Av. 13-51, Zona 9
Telephone: (2) 367643

SYNAGOGUES
Sephardi
Maguen David
7a Av. 3-80, Zona 2
Telephone: (2) 232-0932

HAITI

Christopher Columbus brought the first Jew to Haiti – his interpreter, Luis de Torres, a *Converso* who had been baptised before the voyage. Thereafter more Jews settled, but the community was destroyed in an anti-European revolt by Toussaint L'Ouverture in 1804. A hundred or so years later, Jews from the Middle East and some refugees from the Nazis settled in Haiti, but many subsequently emigrated to Israel.

The remaining community has benefited from the help of the Israeli embassy, and services are held in the embassy or in private homes. There is no central Jewish organisation, and the community is too small to support other Jewish facilities.

GMT -5 hours
Country calling code: (+509)
Total population: **7,492,000**
Jewish population: **Under 100**
Emergency telephone: (**Police–114**)
(**Ambulance–118**)
Electricity voltage: **110**

PORT AU PRINCE
COMMUNITY ORGANISATIONS
The Jewish Community in Haiti
P.O. Box 687
Telephone: 1-20-638

CONTACT INFORMATION
Tourist Information
Religious services are held at the home of the Honorary Israeli Consul, Mr Gilbert Bigio

HONDURAS

During the Spanish colonial period some *Conversos* did live in Honduras, but it was only in the nineteenth century that any significant Jewish immigration occurred. In the early twentieth century refugees from Nazism followed a handful of immigrants from eastern Europe. Honduras was one of the small number of countries to aid refugees from Nazism, and many Jews owe their lives to the help of Honduran consulates which issued visas in wartime Europe.

The capital Tegucigalpa contains the largest Jewish population, but the only synagogue in the country is in San Pedro Sula (services are held in private homes in Tegucigalpa). There is also a Sunday school and WIZO branch.

GMT -6 hours
Country calling code: (+504)
Total population: **76,338,000**
Jewish population: **Under 100**
Emergency telephone: (**Police–119**) (**Fire–198**)
(**Ambulance–37 8654**)
Electricity voltage: **110/220**

BALATONFURED
GUEST HOUSE
Balatonfured Guest House
Holiday Center Udulo, Liszt Ferecc utca 6
Telephone: 8734-3404
Open May to September. It is also a restaurant and there is a synagogue on the premises.

SAN PEDRO SULA
CONTACT INFORMATION
Tourist Information
Telephone: 530157
Services Friday and Shabbat at synagogue and community centre

TEGUCIGALPA
Tourist Information
Telephone: 315908
Services usually held in private homes. Contact secretary at the above number.

EMBASSY
Embassy of Israel
Palmira Building, 5th Floor
Telephone: 324232; 325176

HUNGARY

Jews have lived in Hungary in Roman times, even before the arrival of the Magyars (ancestors of the present-day Hungarians). The Jews suffered during the Middle Ages when there was some anti-semitism, but conditions improved under Austro-Hungarian rule, and Judaism was recognised as being on a legal par with Christianity in 1896.

Hungary lost a considerable amount of territory after the First World War, and as a result many of its original Jewish communities (such as Szatmar) found themselves within other countries. Anti-semitism reached a peak in March 1944, when, during the German occupation, most Jewish communities began to be transported to Auschwitz. A number of those who were deported survived when Auschwitz was liberated by the Red Army in January 1945.

After the war Hungary had the largest Jewish community in central Europe. Inevitably the community dwindled through emigration (especially after the 1956 uprising) and assimilation. Communism in Hungary was far more lenient than in other Warsaw Pact countries, and synagogues were allowed to operate. Since 1989, religious interest has increased, and the government has recently renovated the Dohany Synagogue, the second biggest synagogue in the world and the largest in Europe. The Jewish population is still the largest in the region, although most are not religious. The Hungarian national tourist office had published 'Shalom', an excellent guide to Jewish Hungary.

GMT +1 hours
Country calling code: **(+36)**
Total population: **10,153,000**
Jewish population: **60,000**
Emergency telephone: **(Police–107) (Fire–105) (Ambulance–104)**
Electricity voltage: **220**

BUDAPEST

Once known in the nineteenth century as 'Judapest', this city contains the majority of Hungarian Jews. At its prewar peak its Jewish population was around 200,000. There are several functioning synagogues, from Orthodox to 'Neolog' (Hungarian reform). The recently restored Dohany synagogue was built to accommodate 3,000 in prayer.

BOOKSELLERS
Biblical World Judaica Gallery
Wesselenyi utca. 13 H-1077
Telephone: (1) 267-8502
Fax: (1) 354-1561
Email: gallery@judaica.hu
Website: www.judaica.hu

COMMUNITY ORGANISATIONS
Central Board of the Federation of Jewish Communities in Hungary
VII, Sip utca 12
Telephone: (1) 342-1355
Fax: (1) 342-1790
Email: bzsh@mail.matav.hu

CULTURAL ORGANISATIONS
Tourism and Cultural Center of the Budapest Jewish Community
Sip u. 12 H-1075
Telephone: (1) 343-0420
Fax: (1) 462 0478
Email: zsikk@axelero.hu
Website: www.jewishfesival.hu

EMBASSY
Embassy of Israel
Fullank utca 8 1026
Telephone: (1) 200-0781

GROCERIES
Kosher Bolt
Dob utca 12, 1072 Budapest
Telephone: (1) 267-5691

The Orthodox Central Synagogue
VII, Kazinczy utca 27
Kosher milk and cheese are available here three mornings a week

HOTELS
Kosher
King's Hotel
Nagydiofa u. 27-29, 1075 Budapest 1074
Telephone: (1) 352-7617
Fax: (1) 352-7675
Strictly kosher hotel with a restaurant

MEDIA
Newspapers
Uj Elet (New Life)
Central Board Hotel

MIKVAOT
Budapest Mikvaot
VII Kazinczy utca 16 1074

MUSEUMS
Hungarian Jewish Museum and Archives
Dohany u. 2 1077
Telephone: (1) 343-6756
Fax: (1) 343-6756
Email: bpjewmus@mail.c3.hu
Website: www.c3.hu/-bpjewmus

RELIGIOUS ORGANISATIONS
The Central Rabbinical Council
VII, Sip utca 12
Telephone: (1) 142-1180
Rabbi Schweitzer is Chief rabbi of Hungary and Director of the Rabbinical Seminary

RESTAURANTS
King's Hotel
Nagydiofa Utca 25-27
Telephone: (1) 352-7675
Supervision: Orthodox Community

Meat
Kinor David Restaurant
H-1075 Budapest Dohany u. 10
Telephone: (1) 413 7304 / 5
Fax: (1) 413-7304 / 5
Mobile Phone: 06305128783
Email: kinordavid@hotmail.com
Website: www.zsido.com/kinor
Supervision: Chug Hatam Szofer Bne-Brak
Opening hours: 11 am to 9.30 pm.

SYNAGOGUES
Dohany Street Synagogue
VII, Dohany Utca 4-6
Telephone: (1) 342-2353
Built in 1859, it is the largest in Europe and the second largest in the world. In its grounds lie buried Hungarian Jewish victims of the Nazis. There is also a commemorative plaque to Hanna Senesh, the Jewish parachutist who was captured and tortured before being shot by the Nazis. A plaque commemorating Theodor Herzi, the founder of Zionism is in the Jewish Museum.

Heroes Synagogue
VII Wesselenyi utca 5
Telephone: (1) 3432-2353

Orthodox
The Orthodox Central Synagogue
Kazinczy 27
Telephone: (1) 351-0526
Fax: (1) 322-7200

TOURIST INFORMATION
Jewish Information Service
Telephone: (1) 166-5165
Fax: (1) 166-5165

TOURS
Chosen Tours
Telephone: (1) 185-9499
Fax: (1) 166-5165
Telephone to arrange tours of Jewish sites

Jewish Heritage in Budapest
Sip utca 12 H-1075
Telephone: (1) 317-2754
Email: aviv@aviv.hu
Website: www.aviv.hu
A walking tour of Jewish Budapest.

TRAVEL AGENTS
AVIV Travel-Trade 2000 Kft.
H-0175 Budapest, Sip u. 12
Telephone: (1) 344-5409
Fax: (1) 462-0478
Email: aviv@aviv.hu
Website: www.aviv.hu

SOPRON
MUSEUMS
The Old Synagogue Museum
utca 22-24 H-9400
Telephone: (99) 311-327
Fax: (99) 311-347
Email: smuzeum@mail.c3.hu
A department of the Sopron Museum. A medieval synagogue, originally private , on the ground floor of a baroque house, restored as a museum in 1976. Open 1 May to 1 October daily between 9 am and 5 pm. Closed Tuesdays.

SYNAGOGUES
Orthodox
Jewish Orthodox
Kiss Janos u. 3 H-9400
Telephone: (99) 313-508

TOURIST SITES
Museum
Utca 11
A second medieval synagogue is undergoing restoration.

The Neologue Cemetery
Dating from the nineteenth-century. There is a memorial wall dedicated to the 1,600 local victims of the Holocaust.

INDIA

The Jewish population of India can be divided into three components: the Cochin Jews, the Bene Israel and the Baghdadi Jews. The Cochin Jews are based in the south of India in Kerala. This community can be further divided into Black (believing themselves to be the original settlers) and White (of European or Middle Eastern origin), and the Paradesi. Most of the community has emigrated, but there is still a synagogue in Cochin that is a major tourist attraction.

The Bene Israel believe they are descended from Jewish survivors of a ship wrecked on its voyage from ancient Israel during the period of King Solomon. No reliable documentary evidence, however, exists to support this claim. More reliable evidence dates settlement to around the tenth century. The Bene Israel follow only certain Jewish practices, such as kosher food and Shabbat, and also adhere to certain Muslim and Hindu beliefs; for example, they abstain from eating beef. In the eighteenth century, they settled in Bombay and now form the largest group of Indian Jews.

Baghdadi Jews, immigrants from Iraq and the other Middle Eastern countries, arrived in India in the late eighteenth century, and followed British Colonial rather than local custom. Many emigrated to Israel in the 1950s and 1960s.

During the Indo-Pakistan war of 1972, the leading Indian military figure was General Samuels. In 1999 Lt-Gen J.F.R. Jacob was appointed Governor of Punjab State.

There is a central Council of Indian Jewry, based in Mumbai, where most of the Indian Jews live. Kosher food is available, and there are three Jewish schools in the city. Relations with Israel have recently improved and it is now a major trade partner.

GMT +5 1/2 hours
Country calling code: (+91)
Total population: 1,013,662,000
Jewish population: 5,000
Electricity voltage: 220

ALIBAG
Magen Aboth Synagogue
Alibag
Established in 1848 the synagogue is in what is known as 'Israel' alley to the south-east of the town

COCHIN
COMMUNITY ORGANISATIONS
Association of Kerala Jews
Thekkumbhagom Synagogue Jews Street
Telephone: 366-247; 362-454
Fax: 363-747

CONTACT INFORMATION
Inquiries
Princess Street, Fort
Telephone: 24228; 24988

SYNAGOGUES
Chennamangalam
Jews Street
Built in 1614 and restored in 1916, this synagogue has been declared a historical monument by the Government of India. A few yards away is a small concrete pillar into which is inset the tombstone of Sara Bat-Israel, dated 5336 (1576)

Paradesi
Jew Town, Mattancherry 2
The only Cochin synagogue that is still functioning. Built in 1568. Closed Friday & Saturday.

ERNAKULAM
TOURIST SITES
Kadavumbagom Synagogue
Built in 1200 and rebuilt in 1690

Thekkumbagon Syngogue
Telephone: (484) 390-187
Email: anithamsamson@yahoo.co.in
Built in 1580 and rebuilt in 1939

KHAMASA
SYNAGOGUES
Magen Abraham
Bukhara Mohalla, opp. Parsi Agiari 380001
Telephone: (79) 535-5224

KOLKATA
COMMUNITY ORGANISATIONS
Jewish Association of Kolkata
1 & 2 Old Court House Corner
Telephone: (33) 224861
General inquiries to this telephone number

SYNAGOGUES
Bethel Synagogue
26/1 Pollack Street

Magen David Synagogue
109a Peplabi Rash, Bihari Bose Road, 1, (formerly Canning Steet)

Neveh Shalome Synagogue
9 Jackson Lane, 1

MUMBAI
EMBASSY
Consul General of Israel
50 Kailash, G. Deshmukh Marg, 26
Telephone: (22) 386-2793

GROCERIES
ORT India
68 Worli Hill Estate, PO Box 6571 400018
Telephone: (22) 496-2350; 8423; 8457
Fax: (22) 496-2350; 491-3203
Email: ortbay@bom5.vsnl.net.in
Website: www.ortindia.com

The Jewish Education Resource Centre provides kosher food from its bakery and kitchen to all travellers. ORT India also arranges conducted tours to places of Jewish interest in Mumbai and to ancient synagogues in the Konkan region of Maharashtra State.

SYNAGOGUES
Beth El Synagogue
Mirchi Galli, Mahatma Gandhi Road , Panvel 410206

Etz Haeem Prayer Hall
2nd Lane, Umerkhadi 400009
Telephone: (22) 377-0193

Gate of Mercy (Shaar Harahamim)
254 Samuel Street, Nr Masjid Railway Station 400003
Telephone: (22) 345-2991

This is the oldest Bene Israel synagogue in use in India, established in 1796 and known as the Samaji Hasaji Synagogue or Juni Masjid until 1896 when its name was changed to Shaar Harahamim

Magen David Synagogue
J.J. Nagpada, Byculla 400008
Telephone: (22) 300-6675

The synagogue, built in 1861 with the assistance of the Sasoon family, has a gothic character

Magen Hassidim Synagogue
8 Mohammaed Shahid Marg, (formerly Moreland Road), Agripada 400011
Telephone: (22) 309-2493

Most marriages and bar mitzvahs are held here, it can seat 1000. Only Bene Israel carpenters were used, and they gave their services free.

Rodef Shalom Synagogue
Sussex Road, Byculla 400027

Shaar HaRahamim Synagogue
Tembi Naka, opp. Civil Hospital, Thane 400601
Telephone: (22) 853-4817

Established in 1796, it is the oldest Bene Israel synagogue in India

Shaare Rason Synagogue
90 Tantanpura Street, 3rd Road , Don Tad , Israel Mohalla, Khadak 400009

Tifereth Israel Synagogue
92 K.K. Marg, Jacob Circle 400011
Telephone: (22) 305-3713

Orthodox
Knesseth Eliahu Synagogue
V.B. Gandhi Road (Forbes Street), Fort 400001
Telephone: (22) 283-1502/2368-2296
Fax: (22) 2363-2445
Email: solo@bom8vsnl.net.in

The synagogue was constructed in 1884. Kiddus is held with a lunch after Shabbath services at the synagogue.

Kurla Bene Israel Prayer Hall
275 S.G. Barve Road (c.S.T. Road), Kurla, West Bombay 400070
Telephone: (22) 511-8795

TOURS
ORT India
68 Worli Hill Estate, PO Box 6571 400018
Telephone: (22) 496-2350; 8423
Fax: (22) 364-7308
Email: jhirad@giasbm01.vsnl.in

The Travel and Tourism Department arranges tours in Bombay & Raighad District

TOV Jewish India Tours
96 Penso Villa, 1st Floor, Mbraut Rd. , Shivaji Park 400028
Telephone: (22) 244-50134
Fax: (22) 244-49391
Email: indoisr@hotmail.com,
xotikvacations@yahoo.com
Supervision: Clement Aaron

NEW DELHI
SYNAGOGUES
Judah Hyam Synagogue
2 Humayun Road 110003
Telephone: (11) 463-5500
A/7 Nirman Vihar, Patparganj 110092
Telephone: (11) 224-3136

The Judah Hyam Annexe houses a library and centre for Jewish and inter-faith studies

PARAVUR
Paravur Synagogue
Built in 1165, the synagogue was rebuilt in 1616 by the local Jewish communiy with the help of David Kastiel, who was not a Paradesi Jews, but a man of local origin. Paradesi Jews were associated with Mattancherry and their synagogue was built in 1568.

PUNE
Succath Shelomo
93 Rasta Peth 411011
Inquiries to Hon. Sec. 24/1 Rasta Peth, Trupti Apt., Pune
411011 or Dr S.B. David 9, Bund Garden Road, Pune 411001

SYNAGOGUES
Orthodox
Ohel David Synagogue
9 Dr Ambedkar Road 411001
Telephone: (20) 613-2048
Email: oheldavid@ip.eth.net
The synagogue was built by David Sasoon in 1867. His
grave is in the synagogue grounds.

TOURS
Tov Jewish India Tours
118 Citadel Palace Orchard, Rdindhari, Green Forest
Telephone: (20) 693-1488

THANE
KASHRUT INFORMATION
Pearl Farm
A/1 Dhobi Alley, Sulabha , Maharashtra 400601
Telephone: (22) 536-0539
Kosher goat meat and fish

IRAN

Iran, formerly known as Persia, has an ancient connection with Jews. The first Jewish communities in Persia date from the time of the First Temple. King Cyrus, the Persian king who conquered Babylon, allowed the Jews to return to Israel from their exile. Not all returned, however, and some settled in Persia. The Persian community grew over time, suffering oppression after the Islamic conversion in 642. Certain segments of the Jewish community also grew in wealth in early medieval times.

In the twentieth century there was a brief period of hope for the Jews in Iran when the country became more western-oriented after 1925. However, the 1979 revolution quashed the hope for a more tolerant Iran, and many thousands of Jews decided to emigrate. Association with Zionism became a capital offence and a number of Jews have been executed since 1979. The Jews are seen as 'dhimmi', (subordinates), to Islam, and as such are allowed some

religious practices, but are so closely watched that maintaining a Jewish life is difficult. The tombs of Esther and Mordechai (from the Purim story) are in Hamadan, south-west of the capital Tehran. Iran currently has the largest Jewish community in the Middle East outside Israel.

Kosher food has become expensive and is difficult to obtain.

GMT +3 1/2 hours
Country calling code: (+98)
Total population: 60,694,000
Jewish population: 18,000
Electricity voltage: 220

ISFAHAN
Isfahan Synagogue
Shah Abass Street

TEHRAN
Haim
Gavamossaltaneh Street

TOURIST SITES
Jewish Quarter of Tehran
Mahalleh, off Sirus Avenue

IRISH REPUBLIC

The first report of Jews in Ireland records that in 1079 'five Jews came over the sea'. The small community was expelled in 1290, along with the Jews from the rest of the British Isles. The community slowly grew again after Jews were allowed to return and a few *conversos* settled in Dublin. There was never a strong community, however, and only in 1822 did a significant influx of Jews occur when immigrants came from England and eastern Europe.

Immigration continued and large numbers arrived from the Russian Empire after 1881. Some settled in Ireland intentionally, but others believed that they had landed in America, deceived by the ships' captains. In 1901 the community was 3,800 strong. The highest figure for the Jewish population of Ireland has been estimated at 8,000.

Robert Briscoe (1894–1969) who played an important role in the struggle for Irish independence, was twice Lord Mayor of Dublin.

Currently most Jews live in Dublin, although the community is now shrinking.

GMT +00353 hours
Total population: **3,626,000**
Jewish population: **1,200**
Emergency telephone: **(Police–999) (Fire–999)**
(Ambulance–999)
Electricity voltage: **220**

CORK
SYNAGOGUES
Orthodox
Cork Synagogue
10 South Terrace
Telephone: (21) 487-0413
Fax: (21) 487-6537
Email: rosehill@iol.ie
Services: For information contact Fred Rosehill

DUBLIN
The centre of Irish Jewry, Dublin's position on the east coast meant that many Jews settled there in the flight from Eastern Europe in the nineteenth century. The Jewish Museum in Dublin, opened by the then President of Israel, Irish-born Chaim Herzog, in 1985 during a state visit to Ireland, gives much information on the town's Jewish history.
Dublin was also the home of possibly the world's most famous fictional Jew, Leopold Bloom of James Joyce's Ulysses.

BAKERIES
Connolly Bakery
Super Valu, 13 Braemore Road, Churchtown, Dublin 14

The Bretzel Bakery
1 Lennox Street, Near Kelly's Corner, S.C. Road, Dublin 8

EMBASSY
Embassy of Israel
Carrisbrook House, 122 Pembroke Road, Ballsbridge 4
Telephone: (1) 668-0303
Fax: (1) 668-0418
Email: info@embisrael.iol.ie

MIKVAOT
Terenure Hebrew Congregation
Rathfarnham Road

MUSEUMS
Irish Jewish Museum
3-4 Walworth Road, Portobella, South circular Road 8
Telephone: (1) 490-1857
Open Tuesday, Thursday and Sunday May to September 11 am to 3.00 pm; October to April 10.30 am to 2.30 pm. Group visits by arrangement

RELIGIOUS ORGANISATIONS
Board of Shechita
1 Zion Road
Telephone: (1) 492-3751
Email: irishcom@iol.ie
Website: www.irishjewishcommunity.com

The Chief Rabbinate of Ireland
Herzog House, 1 Zion Road Rathgar, 6
Telephone: (1) 4923751
Email: familylent@eircom.net
On request a list of some suitable food items in Ireland is available. Shul restaurant open on Sundays only. Contact Ms Hilda Bloom on (1) 4562464 or 086 2788326. See our website www.jewishireland.com for further details. Kosher outlets are under the supervision of the Chief Rabbi of Ireland Dr Yaakov Pearlman.

SYNAGOGUES
Orthodox
Dublin Hebrew Congregation
Rathfarnham Road, Terenure 6
Telephone: (1) 490-5969

Machzekei Hadass
Rathmore Villas, Rear of 77 Terenure Road North 6W
Telephone: (1) 86-246-2777
Email: machzekeihadass@eircom.net

The Jewish Home of Ireland
The Bloomfield Nursing Home, Quaker House, Stocking Lane, Rathfarnham, Dublin
Telephone: (1) 4950021
Email: irishcom@aol.ie
Website: www.jewishireland.com

Services are held Friday evening at start of Sabbath and Sabbath morning. Kosher meals may be had in the home's dining room. For eight hours notice is required. For information contact Mr N Gruson on (1) 4063980.

SYNAGOGUES
Progressive
Dublin Jewish Progressive Congregation
7 Leicester Avenue, Rathgar, PO Box 3059 6
Telephone: (1) 285-6241
Email: djpc@liberaljudaism.org
Friday evening at 8.15 pm, please phone for information re Sabbath and Festival services

ISRAEL

General Information

Israel, the Promised Land of the Bible, is today a modern, thriving, bustling and vibrant country. For centuries the sites of many of the most stirring events in the history of mankind lay dormant beneath shifting sands and crumbling terraces, until the land was reclaimed by the People of Israel returning from exile. In today's Israel, cities, towns and villages, fertile farms and green forests, sophisticated industries and well-developed commercial enterprises have replaced barren hillsides, swamps and desert wilderness.

Climate

Israel enjoys long, warm, dry summers (April–October) and generally mild winters (November–March), with somewhat drier, cooler weather in hilly regions such as Jerusalem and Safed. Rainfall is relatively heavy in the north and centre of the country with much less in the northern Negev and almost negligible amounts in the southern areas. Regional conditions vary considerably, with humid summers and mild winters on the coast; dry summers and moderately cold winters in the hill regions; hot, dry summers and pleasant winters in the Jordan Valley; and year-round semi-desert conditions in the Negev.

Languages

Hebrew, the language of the Bible, and Arabic, are the official languages of Israel. Hebrew, Arabic and English are compulsory subjects at school. French, Spanish, German, Yiddish, Russian, Polish and Hungarian are widely spoken. Local and international newspapers and periodicals in a number of languages are readily available. All street and most commercial signs are in Hebrew and English, and often in Arabic.

Passports and Visas

Every visitor to Israel must hold a valid passport; valid for a minimum of six months beyond the intended date of arrival, stateless persons require a valid travel document with a return visa to the country of issue. Visitors may remain in Israel for up to three months from the date of arrival, subject to the terms of the visa issued. Visitors who intend to work in Israel must apply to the Ministry of the Interior for a special visa (B/1).

Electrical Appliances

The electric current in Israel is 220 volts AC, single phase, 50 Hertz. Most Israeli sockets are of the three-pronged variety but many can accept some European two-pronged plugs as well. Electric shavers, travelling irons and other small appliances may require adapters and/or transformers which can be purchased in Israel.

Health Regulations

There are no vaccination requirements for visitors entering Israel.

Pets

Dogs or cats accompanying visitors must be over four months old, inoculated against rabies and bear a valid official veterinary health certificate from the country of origin.

Accommodation

Kashrut

In Israel, kosher means under official rabbinical supervision. Most hotels (but not all) do adhere. Kosher restaurants, hotels and youth hostels are by law required to display a kashrut certificate.

Hotels

Israel has over 300 hotels offering a wide choice of accommodation to suit all tastes, purposes and budgets, ranging from small, simple facilities to five-star luxury establishments, with prices varying according to grade and season. Hotel rates are generally quoted in US dollars and do not include the 15 per cent service charge.

Kibbutz Hotels

The kibbutz (collective settlement) is an Israeli social experience in which all property is collectively owned and members receive no salaries but are provided with housing, education for their children, medical services, social amenities and all other necessities. Most of the 280 kibbutzim throughout Israel are essentially agricultural settlements, but many are moving to a more industrially orientated economy.

Several kibbutzim, mostly in northern and central Israel, have established hotels on their premises, providing visitors with a close view of this world-renowned lifestyle. They offer guests the opportunity of a relaxed, informal holiday in delightful rural surroundings. Some present special evening programmes about the kibbutz experience.

For further information and a special tour of Israel's kibbutzim and kibbutz hotels, contact any Israel Government Tourist Office (IGTO), or the tourist information offices (TIO) in Israel, or Kibbutz Hotels, 1 Smolinskin St., Tel Aviv. Tel: 03-527 8085. Fax: 03-523 0527.

Youth Hostels

The Israel Youth Hostels Association (IYHA), affiliated with the International Youth Hostels Association, operates some 32 youth hostels throughout the country for guests of all ages. All offer dormitory, usually single sex, accommodation, and most also provide meals and self-service kitchen facilities. Some hostels also provide family accommodation for parents accompanied by at least one child.

Individual reservations should be booked directly at specific hostels and group reservations with the IYHA.

The IYHA also arranges individual 14-, 21- or 28-day package tours, called 'Israel on the Youth Hostel Trail'. These include nights in any of 25 hostels with breakfast and dinner, unlimited bus travel, a half-day guided tour, free admission to National Parks, a map and other informative material.

For further information, contact the Israel Youth Hostels Association, 1 Sazar Street, 91060 Jerusalem, Tel: 02-655 8400, Fax: 02-655 8401.

Currency and Bank Information

The currency of Israel is the New Israeli Sheqel (NIS) (plural sheqalim). Each sheqel is divided into 100 agorot (singular agora). Bank notes circulate in denominations of NIS 20, 50, 100 and 200 sheqels and coins in denominations of 1 sheqel, 5 sheqels, 10 sheqels, and 10 and 50 agorot. One may bring an unlimited amount of local and foreign currency into Israel in cash, travellers' cheques, letters of credit or State of Israel Bonds. Foreign currency may be exchanged at any bank and at many hotels.

Most banks are open from Sunday to Thursday from 08:30 am to 12:00 midday, and from 4:00 pm to 6:00 pm on Sunday, Tuesday and Thursday. On the eve of major Jewish holidays, banks are open from 08:30 am to 12.00 midday. Bank branches in major hotels usually offer convenient additional banking hours.

Shopping

Colourful oriental markets and bazaars may be found in the old city of Jerusalem and in several other towns and villages. Bargaining is often expected. The unique variety of goods available includes handmade items of olive wood, mother-of-pearl, leather and straw, as well as hand-blown glass and exotic clothing. In all cities and towns there are shopping malls which are open from 08:00 am to 10:00 pm. There are duty-free shops at Ben Gurion, Eilat and Ovda International Airports.

Opening Hours:

Most shops are open daily, Sunday to Thursday, from 9:00 am to 7:00 pm, although some close for a mid-day break between 1:00 pm and 4:00 pm. On Fridays and the eve of major Jewish holidays, shops close early in the afternoon. Some Muslim-owned establishments are closed on Fridays and some Christian shops on Sundays

Radio and Television

Radio programmes are broadcast daily in English, Arabic, French, Yiddish, Russian and other languages. There are three daily news programmes in English and French. Many programmes shown on Israeli TV are in English with Hebrew, Arabic and Russian subtitles.

The Israel Broadcasting Authority news in English is screened nightly on Channel 1 at 6.00 pm.

Facilities for the Handicapped

Many hotels and public institutions in Israel (including Ben Gurion International Airport) provide ramps, specially equipped lavatories, telephones and other conveniences for the handicapped.

Milbat, the Advisory Centre for the Disabled at Sheba Medical Center in Tel Aviv (Tel: 03-5303 739), will be pleased to answer visitors' questions.

The Yad Sarah Organisation with branches located throughout Israel provides wheelchairs, crutches and other medical equipment on loan, free of charge (a small deposit is requested). For more specific information, contact the organisation's main office in Jerusalem, Tel: 02-624 4242.

Travellers to Israel, especially those with specific medical/paramedical needs, can turn to Traveller Hotline operated by Ezer Mizion, the Israel Health Support Fund.

This volunteer organisation provides all paramedical information and needs free of charge to the traveller, via the International Office (02-537 8070) and Travellers Hotline (02-500 211). Transport and other arrangements can be organised prior to arrival and special inquiries/needs can be seen to while in Israel.

Organised Tours

Numerous organised tours, mostly in air-conditioned buses or minibuses, are conducted by licensed tour operators. Itineraries and prices are determined in accordance with the Ministry of Tourism guidelines to ensure a full sightseeing programme in maximum comfort. Half-day, full-day and longer tours are available, some combining air with road travel. Tours depart regularly from major cities as well as from popular resort areas during the peak season. All organised tours are accompanied by experienced, licensed multilingual guides identified by an official emblem bearing the words Licensed Tourist Guide.

Smaller groups may hire a licensed driver-guide and a special touring limousine or minibus, identified by the red Ministry of Tourism emblem.

Full details of itineraries, prices and schedules are available at travel agencies, tour companies, IGTOs and TIOs.

Major public institutions and organisations such as WIZO, Hadassah, universities and the Knesset (Parliament) conduct guided tours of their facilities. Walking tours of the larger cities are arranged by the municipalities.

Visitors should be aware that certain tourist sites such as the Tomb of the Patriachs and Jericho are now within the boundaries of the Palestinian Authority. They should consult the local tourist offices in Israel concerning travel to those areas.

When visiting religious sites always dress modestly. If not you may be refused entry.

Buses

Buses are the most popular means of urban and inter-city transport throughout Israel. The Egged Bus Cooperative operates nearly all inter-city bus lines and also provides urban services in most cities and towns. (The greater Tel Aviv area is serviced by the Dan Cooperative and independent bus companies operate in Beer Sheva and Nazareth.) Fares are reasonably priced and service is regular. Most bus lines do not operate on the Sabbath (Friday evening to Saturday evening) and on Jewish holidays. Students are eligible for discount fares on inter-urban bus routes on presentation of an International Student Card. Special monthly tickets are available for Dan and Egged urban bus lines. Overseas visitors can purchase Israbus passes valid on all Egged bus lines for periods of 7,14, 21 and 30 days. Tickets can be obtained at any Egged bus station.

Taxis

These are both shared taxis (sheruts) and normal taxis. Taxis are required to operate a meter.

Traffic Regulations

A valid International Driving Licence is recognised and preferred, although a valid national driving licence is also accepted, provided it has been issued by a country maintaining diplomatic relations with Israel and recognising an Israeli driving licence.

An excellent system of roads connects all towns. Traffic travels on the right and overtakes on the left. It is compulsory for the driver and all passengers to wear seat belts. Drivers coming from the right have priority, unless indicated otherwise on the road signs, which are international. Distances on road signs are always given in kilometres (1 km is equal to 0.621 miles).

The speed limit is 50 km (approx. 31 miles) per hour in built-up areas; 80-90 km (approx. 50-56 miles) per hour on open roads.

Special Programmes For Tourists
Plant a Tree With Your Own Hands

Tree-planting centres have been established by the Jewish National Fund at several locations throughout Israel. For a nominal contribution, visitors may plant trees and receive a certificate and pin to mark the event. For further information, contact the Jewish National Fund, PO Box 283, 91002 Jerusalem, Tel: 02-670 7402, or 96 Hayarkon Street, 63432 Tel Aviv, Tel: 03-523 4367, Fax: 03-5246084.

GMT +2 hours
Country calling code: (**+972**)
Total population: **6,100,000**
Jewish population: **5,000,000**
Emergency telephone: (**Police–100**) (**Fire–102**) (**Ambulance–101**)
Electricity voltage: **220**

AFULA
RESTAURANTS
La Cabania
Ha'atzmaut Square
Telephone: (4) 659-1638

San Remo
4 Ha'atzmaut Square
Telephone: (4) 652-2458

AKKO
HOTELS
Palm Beach
PO Box 2192 24101
Telephone: (4) 987-7777
Fax: (4) 991-0434
Email: palmbeach@netvision.net.il
Website: www.palmbeach.co.il
Hotel, restaurant and convention centre, spa and sports centre

Palm Beach Sport E Spa Hotel
Acre Sea Shore 24101
Telephone: (4) 987-7777
Fax: (4) 991-0434
Email: palmbeach@netvision.net.il
Website: www.palmbeach.co.il

MUSEUMS
Akko Municipal Museum
Old City
Telephone: (4) 991-8251
Fax: (4) 981-6686

RESTAURANTS
Vegetarian
Amirei Hagalil
Akko-Safed Road, nr. Moshav Amirim 20115
Telephone: (4) 698-9815/6

YOUTH HOSTELS
Acre Youth Hostel
Telephone: (4) 991-1982
Fax: (4) 991-1982

ARAD
HOTELS
Arad
6 Hapalmach Street
Telephone: (8) 995-7040
Fax: (8) 995-7272

Maragoa
Mo'av Street, POB 20 89100
Telephone: (8) 995-1222
Fax: (8) 995-7778
Email: margoa@mail.inter.net.il

Nof Arad
Mo'av Street
Telephone: (8) 995-7056
Fax: (8) 995-4053

YOUTH HOSTELS
Blau-Weis
Telephone: (8) 995-7150
This organisation is located in the centre of town

AVIHAIL
MUSEUMS
Beit Hagedudim (History of Jewish Brigade WWI)
Telephone: (9) 882-2212
Fax: (9) 862-1619

B'NEI BERAK
HOTELS
Wiznitz
16 Damesek Elizier Street
Telephone: (3) 777-1413

TOURS
Tour Olam
79A Kahaneman St. Bene-Berak 51544 Israel
Telephone: (3) 579-17190
Fax: (3) 579-1710
Email: tourolam@bezeqint.net
Website: www.tour-olam.com

BEERSHEBA
HOTELS
Desert Inn
Tuviyahu Av.
Telephone: (8) 642-4922
Fax: (8) 641-2722

MUSEUMS
Man in the Desert Museum
Situated five miles north-east of the city

TOURS
Bedouin Market
The market is held every Thursday but it has been affected negatively by tourism and modernization. Permanent Bedouin encampments can be seen south of town.

CAESAREA
HOTELS
Dan Caesarea Golf Hotel
PO Box 1120 30600
Telephone: (4) 626-9111
Fax: (4) 626-9122
Email: caesarea@danhotels.com
Website: www.danhotels.com

RESTAURANTS
Caesarean Self Service
Paz Petrol Station
Telephone: (4) 633-4609

DAN
MUSEUMS
Natural History and Archeaology
Beit Ussishkin, Kibutz Dan, 12245
Telephone: (4) 694-1704
Fax: (4) 690-27550
Email: ussishkin@dan.co.il

DEAD SEA
HOTELS
Crown Plaza
Telephone: (8) 659-1919

Grand Nirvana
Telephone: (8) 668-9444
Fax: (8) 668-9400
Email: info@nirvana.co.il

Hod
Telephone: (8) 658-4644

Hyatt Regency
Telephone: (8) 659-1234

Moriah Gardens
Telephone: (8) 659-1591
Fax: (8) 658-4238

Radisson Moriah Plaza
Telephone: (8) 659-1591

HOTELS

Spa

Caesar Premier
Telephone: (8) 668-9666
Fax: (8) 652-0303
Website: www.caesarhotels.co.il
Contact the Caesar Group sales office in Tel Aviv for
information, Tel: (03) 693-0000

DEGANIA ALEF

MUSEUMS

Beit Gordon
Telephone: (4) 675-0040
Fax: (4) 670-9514

EILAT

HOTELS

Ambassador
Coral Beach, PO Box 390 88103
Telephone: (8) 638-2222
Fax: (8) 638-2200
Email: info@ambassador.co.il
Website: www.ambassador.co.il

Americana Eilat
PO Box 27, North Beach 88000
Telephone: (8) 633-3777
Fax: (8) 633-4174
Email: info@americanahotel.co.il
Website: www.americanahotel.co.il

Caesar
North Beach
Telephone: (8) 680-5555
Fax: (8) 633-3497

Club-In Villa Resort
Rte. 90 (Eilat-Taba Road) , Box 1505 Coral Beach
88000
Telephone: (8) 633-4555
Fax: (8) 633-4519

Dalia
North Beach
Telephone: (8) 633-4004
Fax: (8) 633-4072

Dan Eilat
Promenade, North Beach
Telephone: (8) 636-2222
Fax: (8) 636-2333

Edomit
New Tourist Center
Telephone: (8) 637-9511
Fax: (8) 637-9738

King Solomon's Palace
Promenade, North Beach
Telephone: (8) 633-3444
Fax: (8) 633-4189
Email: cro@isrotel.co.il
Website: www.isrotel.co.il

Marina Club
North Beach
Telephone: (8) 633-4191
Fax: (8) 633-4206

Orchid
Rte. 90 (Eilat-Taba Road), Box 994 88000
Telephone: (8) 636-0360
Fax: (8) 637-5323

Princess
Rte. 90 (Eilat-Taba Road), Box 2323 88000
Telephone: (8) 636-5555
Fax: (8) 637-6333

Radisson Moriah Plaza
Promenade, North Beach
Telephone: (8) 636-1111
Fax: (8) 633-4158

Red Rock
North Beach
Telephone: (8) 637-3171
Fax: (8) 637-1705

Royal Beach
North Beach
Telephone: (8) 636-8888
Fax: (8) 636-8811
Email: cro@isrotel.co.il
Website: www.isrotel.co.il

The Neptune Hotel
North Beach
Telephone: (8) 636-9369
Fax: (8) 633-4389

RESTAURANTS

Café Royal
King Solomon's Palace Hotel, North Beach
Telephone: (8) 667-6111

Chinese Restaurant
Shulamit Gardens Hotel, North Beach
Telephone: (8) 667-7515

Dolphin Baguette
Tourist Centre

Egged
Central Bus Station
Telephone: (8) 667-5161

El Morocco
Tourist Centre

Golden Lagoon
New Lagoona Hotel, North Beach
Telephone: (8) 667-2176

Halleluyah
Building 9, Tourist Centre
Telephone: (8) 667-5752

Dairy
La Trattoria
Radisson Moriah Plaza Hotel, North Beach
Telephone: (8) 636-1111

Meat
El Gaucho
Arrava Road (Rte. 90)
Telephone: (8) 633-1549

Shipudei Habustan
The Dan Eilat Promenade
Telephone: (8) 636-2294

GALILEE
HOTELS
Ayelet Hashahar
Upper Galilee, Katzrin 12200
Telephone: (4) 693-2611
Fax: (4) 693-4777

Hacienda
Ma'alot
Telephone: (4) 957-9000
Fax: (4) 997-4404

Rakefet
Mishgav, Western Galilee
Telephone: (4) 980-0403
Fax: (4) 980-0317

MUSEUMS
Bar-David Museum of Jewish Art
Kibbutz Bar'am, off Route 899
Telephone: (4) 698-8295
Fax: (4) 698-7505
Website: www.galil-elion.org.il

Ghetto Fighters' House, Holocaust & Resistance Museum
M.P. Western Galilee 25220
Telephone: (4) 995-8080
Fax: (4) 995-8007
Email: simstein@gfh.org.il
Website: www.gfh.org.il

Sculpture Gallery for Peace and Coexistence
Kawkab Abu Elhija, Gush Segev, Lower Galilee
Telephone: (4) 852-5251
Fax: (4) 852-9166
Email: bhagefen@netvision.il
Website: www.haifa.gov.il/beit-hagefen/index

Tel Hai Sculpture Garden
Tel Hai, Upper Galilee Region
Telephone: (4) 694-3731
Fax: (4) 695-0697

The Museum of Photography
Tel Hai Industrial Park
Telephone: (4) 695-0769
Fax: (4) 695-0771
Website: www.iscar.com

The Open Museum
Tefen Industrial Park, Migdal Tefen
Telephone: (4) 987-2977
Fax: (4) 987-2861
Website: www.iscar.com

RESTAURANTS
Lev Hagolan
30 Dror. Street, Katzin
Telephone: (4) 961-6643

Orcha
Commercial Centre, Katzin
Telephone: (4) 696-1440

YOUTH HOSTELS
Karei Deshe (Tabgha)
Yoram
Telephone: (4) 672-0601
Fax: (4) 672-4818
Eleven miles north of Tiberias

GOLAN HEIGHTS
LEISURE
Hamat Gader
The Golan Heights rise steeply from the Sea of Galilee to the Mount Avital plateau. The Hamat Gader were thought to be the nicest spa baths in the whole Roman world, according to the Byzantine empress Eudocia. There are impressive ruins including the extensive Roman and Byzantine spa, which served as a grand bathing resort for six centuries, and an ancient synagogue. Four mineral springs and freshwater spring emerge at Hamat Gader and so it is used today as a modern bathhouse. There is also an alligator farm where alligators and crocodiles can be seen.

MUSEUMS
The Golan Archeological Museum
Katzrin
Telephone: (4) 696-9636
Fax: (4) 696-9637

NATURE RESERVE
Gamla Nature Reserve
Telephone: (4) 682-2282
Fax: (4) 682-2285
Fifteen kilometres southeast of Katzrin

RESTAURANTS
Hamat Gader Restaurant
Telephone: (4) 675-1039

GUSH ETZION
Pizzeria Efrat
Te'ena Shopping Center, Efrat
Telephone: (2) 993-1630

RESTAURANTS/SHOP
Judaica Center, Gift Shop, Gallery and Restaurant
Judaica Center, Gush Etzion Junction 90433
Telephone: (2) 993-4370
Fax: (2) 993-4949
Email: judaica@gush-etzion.co.il
Website: www.judaica.org.il
Available for groups and events

TOURS
Gush Etzion Judaica Center
Gush Etzion Junction, 90433
Telephone: (2) 993-4040; Tourism Dept.: (2)993-8388
Fax: (2) 993-4949
Email: judaica@gush-etzion.cot.il
Website: www.judaica.org.il
Display and sales hall that features the items of over 200 items of Israeli Judaica. Can be combined with a visit to Kibbutz Kfar Etzion to see an audio visual show that movingly describes the history of Gush Etzion. Available for groups and events.

HADERA
The Khan Museum
74 Hagiborim Street. POB 3232 38131
Telephone: (4) 632-2330; 632-4562
Fax: (4) 632-2072
Website: www.khan-hadera.org.il
Hours: Sunday to Thursday, 8 am to 1 pm; Friday, 9 am to 12 pm; Sunday and Tuesday, 4 pm to 6 pm

HAIFA
HOTELS
Dan Carmel
85-87 Hanassi Avenue 34642
Telephone: (4) 830-3030
Fax: (4) 830-3040
Email: dancarmel@danhotels.com
Website: www.danhotels.com
This luxury hotel is situated on the slopes of Mount Carmel overlooking Haifa bay. Just 50 metres from the magnificent Bahai Hanging Gardens.

Dan Panorama
107 Hanassi avenue
Telephone: (4) 835-2222
Fax: (4) 835-2235
Email: panorama-haifa@danhotels.com

Dvir
124 Yafe Nof Street
Telephone: (4) 838-9131
Fax: (4) 838-1068

Nof Haifa
101 Hanasi avenue
Telephone: (4) 835-4311
Fax: (4) 838-8810
Email: s1@actcom.co.il
Website: nof-hotels.co.il

Shulamit
15 Kiryat Sefer Street 34676
Telephone: (4) 834-2811
Fax: (4) 825-5206
Email: shulamithotel@012.net.il
Website: www.shulamit.biz

MUSEUMS
Haifa City Museum
11 Ben Gurion Avenue

Haifa
Telephone: (4) 8512030
Email: marketing@haifamuseums.org.il
Israel Edible Oil Industry Museum
Shemen Factory, 2 Tovim Street, POB 136 31000
Telephone: (4) 860-4600
Fax: (4) 862-2555
Israel Railways Museum
Haifa East Railway Station
Telephone: (4) 856-4293
Fax: (4) 856-4310
Email: paulc@rail.org.il
Website: www.israrail.org.il/general information
Notes: Museum is open Sunday, Tuesday, Thursday (Holidays excepted), 8.30 am to 12.00 pm
Mane Katz Museum
89 Yafe-Nof Street 34641
Telephone: (4) 838-3482
Fax: (4) 836-2985
Museum of Clandestine Immigration & Navy Museum
204 Allenby Street 35472
Telephone: (4) 853-6249
Fax: (4) 851-2958
Open: Sunday to Thursday 8.30 am to 4.00 pm
Museum of Haifa
26 Shabbtai Levy Street 33043
Telephone: (4) 852-3255
Fax: (4) 855-2714
Email: haifa4@netvision.net.il
Website: www.haifa.gov.il
Includes Museums of Ancient Art, Modern Art and Music & Ethnology. Hours: Sunday, Monday, Wednesday, Thursday, 10 am to 4 pm; Tuesday, 4 pm to 7 pm; Friday and holidays, 10 am to 1 pm; Saturday, 10 am to 2 pm.
Museum of Pre-History
124 Hatishbi Street, Entrance from Gan Ha'em
Telephone: (4) 837-1833
Fax: (4) 855-2714
Reuben & Edith Hecht Museum
Haifa University 31905
Telephone: (4) 825-7773
Fax: (4) 824-0724
Email: mushecht@research.haifa.ac.il
Website: mushacht.haifa.ac.il
Hours: Sunday, Monday, Wednesday, Thursday, 10 am to 4 pm; Tuesday, 10 am to 7 pm; Friday, 10 am to 1 pm; Saturday, 10 am to 2 pm. Admission free. All restaurants at the University are kosher.
The Israel National Museum of Science, Planning and Technology
The Historic Technion Building, Balfour Street, Hadar Ha Carmel
Telephone: (4) 862-8111
Fax: (4) 867-9103
Email: museum@mustsee.org.il
Website: www.mustsee.org.il

The National Maritime Museum
198 Allenby Road
Telephone: (4) 853-662
Fax: (4) 853-9286
Email: curator@nmm.org.il
Hours: Sunday, Monday, Wednesday, Thursday, 10 am to 4 pm; Tuesday, 4 pm to 7 pm; Friday and holidays, 10 am to 1 pm; Saturday 10 am to 2 pm.

Tikotin Museum of Japanese Art
89 Hanassi Avenue, Mount Carmel 34642
Telephone: (4) 838-3554
Fax: (4) 837-9824
Email: japanmus@netvision.net.il
Website: www.haifameseum.org.il
Hours: Monday, Wednesday, Thursday, 10 am to 5 pm; Tuesday, 10 am to 2 pm and 5 pm to 8 pm; Friday and holiday eves, 10 am to 1 pm; Saturday, 10 am to 2 pm.

University of Haifa Art Collection
University of Haifa, Mount Carmel
Telephone: (4) 824-0660
Fax: (4) 824-0309

MUSEUMS
Zoo
Beit Pinchas Biological Insititute and Haifa Educational Zoo
124 Hatishbi Street
Telephone: (4) 810-0476
Fax: (4) 810-3599
Mobile Phone: 0507 482400
Email: biolinst@netvision.net.il
Supervision: Dr Etty Arafat
Includes nature museum, zoo and botanical garden. Entrance via Gan Ha'em. Hours: Sunday to Friday, Winter, 8 am to 5 pm, July to August, 9 am to 7 pm; Friday and holiday eves, 9am to 2 pm.

RESTAURANTS
Egged
Central Bus Station
Telephone: (4) 851-5221
Self-service

Hamber Burger
61 Herzl Street
Telephone: (4) 866-6739

Rondo
Dan Carmel Hotel, 87 Hanassi Blvd
Telephone: (4) 838-6211

Techion
Neve Shaanan
Telephone: (4) 823-3011
Self-servce, lunch only

The Chinese Restaurant of Nof
Nof Hotel, 101 Hanassi Blvd
Telephone: (4) 838-8731

Dairy
Milky Pinky (Milk Bar)
29 Haneviim Street
Telephone: (4) 866-4166

Meat
Mac David
131 Hanassi Blvd
Telephone: (4) 838-3684

TOURIST INFORMATION
Tourist Office
48 Ben-Gurion Street
Telephone: (4) 853-5606
Fax: (4) 853-5610

What's on in Haifa
Telephone: (4) 864-0840

TOURS
Tour Company
Telephone: (4) 867-4342
Bahai shrine and gardens, Druse villages, Muchraka, the Moslem village of Kabair, the Carmelite monastery and Elijah's cave, Wednesday, 9.30 am. Mt Carmel, Druse villages, Kibbutz Ben Oren and Ein Hod artists' colony: Sundays, Mondays, Tuesdays, Thursdays, Saturdays, 9.30 am.

HANITA
MUSEUMS
Tower & Stockade Museum
Route 8990
Telephone: (4) 985-9677
Fax: (4) 985-9677

HAON
HOLIDAY VILLAGE
Kibbutz Haon
Jordan Valley
Telephone: (4) 675-7555/6

HAZOREA
MUSEUMS
Wilfrid Israel House of Oriental Art
Telephone: (4) 989-9566
Fax: (4) 989-0942

HERZLIYA
HOTELS
Dan Accadia
Herzliya on Sea
Telephone: (9) 959-7070
Fax: (9) 959-7092
Email: danhtls@danhotels.co.il

Tadmor
38 Basel Street
Telephone: (9) 952-5000
Fax: (9) 957-5124
Email: hotel@tadmor.co.il

The Sharon
4 Ramot Yam Street, Herzliya on Sea 46748
Telephone: (9) 952-5777
Fax: (9) 927-3448
Email: sharon@sharon.co.il
Website: www.sharon.co.il

MUSEUMS
Herzliya Museum of Contemporary Art
4 Habanim Street 46379
Telephone: (9) 950-2301
Fax: (9) 950-0043
Email: info@herzliyamuseum.co.il
Website: www.herzliyamuseum.co.il

RESTAURANTS
Tadmor Hotel School
38 Basel Street 46660
Telephone: (9) 952-5050
Fax: (9) 957-5124
Email: hotel@tadmor.co.il

Meat
Steak.com
27 Rehov Maskit, Herzliya Pituah
Telephone: (9) 956-1145

TOURIST INFORMATION
English-Speaking Residents Association
PO Box 3132 46104
Telephone: (9) 950-8371
Fax: (9) 954-3781
Email: esra@trendline.co.il
Website: www.esra.org.il

JAFFA
The Antiquities Museum of Tel Aviv-Yafo (Jaffa Museum)
10 Mifratz Shlomo Street, Old Jaffa 68038
Telephone: (3) 682-5375
Fax: (3) 681-3624
Part of Eretz Israel Museum Tel Aviv, Opening hours: Sunday to Thursday 9 am to 1 pm

JERUSALEM
ACCOMMODATION INFORMATION
Good morning Jerusalem
1 Shlomzion Hamalka Street
Telephone: (2) 623-3459
Fax: (2) 625-9330
Email: gmjer@netvision.net.il
Website: www.accommodation.co.il
Lists rooms and apartments available for tourists

BED AND BREAKFAST
Le Sixteen
16 Midbar Sinai Street, Givat Hamivtar 97805
Telephone: (2) 532-8008
Fax: (2) 581-9159
Email: le16@le16-bhb.co.il
Website: www.le16-bhb.co.il
Member of the Jerusalem Home Accomodation Association. Can provide guest studios with kosher dairy kichenettes.

CONTACT INFORMATION
Jeff Seidel's Jewish Student Information Centre
5 Bet-El, Jewish Quarter, Old City
Telephone: (2) 628-2634
Fax: (2) 628-8338
Email: jseidel@jeffseidel.com
Website: www.jeffseidel.com

Jeff Seidel's Jewish Student Information Centre
14 Lechi
Telephone: (2) 581-2240
Fax: (2) 628-8338
Email: jseidel@jeffseidel.com
Website: www.jeffseidel.com

GUEST HOUSE
Bet Shumuel
6 Shamma Street 94101
Telephone: (2) 620-3473; 620-3465
Fax: (2) 620-3467
Single and family guest rooms with capacity of 240 beds; conference facilities and banquet services; restaurant and coffee shop; international culture and education centre with a central location

HOTELS
Ariel Hotel Jerusalem
31 Hebron Road
Telephone: (2) 568-9999
Fax: (2) 673-4066
Email: info@arieljrm.co.il
Walking distance from Old City

Caesar
208 Jaffa Road
Telephone: (2) 538-4111
Fax: (2) 538-1480

Four Points
4 Vilnai Street 96110
Telephone: (2) 655-8888
Fax: (2) 651-2266
The hotel is located in the hotel area at the enterance to the city and within walking distance of the Israel Museum and the Knesset.

Hyatt Regency Jerusalem
32 Lehi Street
Telephone: (2) 533-1234
Fax: (2) 581-5947
Email: hyattjrs@trendline.co.il
Website: www.hyattjer.co.il

Inbal
Liberty Bell Park, 3 Jabotinsky Street 92145
Telephone: (2) 675-6666
Fax: (2) 675-6777
Email: rsv@inbal-hotel.co.il
Website: www.inbal-hotel.co.il

Jerusalem Hilton
7 King David Street 94101
Telephone: (2) 621-1111
Fax: (2) 621-1000

Jerusalem Tower
23 Hillel Street 94581
Telephone: (2) 620-9209
Fax: (2) 625-2167
Email: towerhotels@012.net.il
Website: www.towerhotels.com

King David
23 King David Street 94101
Telephone: (2) 620-8888
Fax: (2) 620-8882
Email: kingdavid@danhotels.com

King Solomon
32 King David Street
Telephone: (2) 569-5555
Fax: (2) 624-1174
Email: solhotel@netvision.net.il

Lev Yerushalayim
18 King George Street
Telephone: (2) 530-0333
Fax: (2) 623-2432
Email: levhotel@netvision.net.il
Website: www.levjerusalem.co.il

Mount Zion
17 Hebron Road
Telephone: (2) 568-9555
Fax: (2) 673-1425
Email: hotel@mountzion.co.il
Website: www.mountzion.co.il

Palatin
4 Agripas Street
Telephone: (2) 623-1141
Fax: (2) 625-9323
Email: info@hotel-palatin.co.il
Website: www.hotel-palatin.co.il

Radisson Moriah Plaza Jerusalem
39 Keren Hayessod Street 94188
Telephone: (2) 569-5695
Fax: (2) 623-2411

Reich
1 Hagai Street, Bet Hakerem
Telephone: (2) 652-3121
Fax: (2) 652-3120

Renaissance Jerusalem Hotel
Ruppin Bridge, at Herz Blvd 91033
Telephone: (2) 659-9999
Fax: (2) 651-1824
Email: renijhot@netvision.net.il
Contact: Eli Velter

Sheraton Jerusalem Plaza
47 King George Street
Telephone: (2) 629-8666
Fax: (2) 623-1667

The Jerusalem Hostel & Guest House
44 Jaffa Road
Telephone: (2) 613 0102
Fax: (2) 613 6092
Email: reservation@jerusalem-hostel.com
Website: www.jerusalem-hostel

Very centrally located (Zion Square). All rooms have attached shower and W.C. No meals served but a modern clean kitchen is available for use of the guests.

Windmill
3 Mendele Street
Telephone: (2) 566-3111
Fax: (2) 561-0964

MUSEUMS

Ammunition Hill Memorial & Museum, Ramat Eshkol
Levy Eshkol Boulevard 91181
Telephone: (2) 582-8442
Fax: (2) 582-9132

Bible Lands Museum Jerusalem
25 Granot Street, Museum Row, POB 4670 91046
Telephone: (2) 561-1066
Fax: (2) 563-8228
Email: contact@blmj.org
Website: www.blmj.org

The home of one of the most important collections of ancient artifacts displaying rare works of art from the dawn of civilisation to the Byzantine period. Gift shop, special exhibitions, weekly lectures and concerts. Daily guided touts in English. Groups by advance reservation. Open daily except Shabbat and Holidays. Call or email the museum for hours and program details. 'Kosher Cafeteria'.

Herzl Museum
Herzl Blvd, Mount Herzl
Telephone: (2) 651-1108

L.A. Mayer Museum for Islamic Art
2 Hapalmach Street Jerusalem 91040
Telephone: (2) 566-1291/2
Fax: (2) 561-9802
Email: islamart@netvision.net.il
Website: www.islamicart.co.il

Display of art of Islamic countries from the 7th-20th centuries including jewelery, ceramics, metal ware, glass, textiles, manuscripts, miniature paintings, arms and armour and the famed David Salomons collection of antique European watches and clocks.

Museum of Natural History
6 Mohilever Street
Telephone: (2) 563-1116
Fax: (2) 566-0666

Nahon Museum of Italian Jewish Art
27 Hillel Street 94581
Telephone: (2) 624-1610
Fax: (2) 625-3480
Email: jija@netvision.net.il
Website: www.jija.org

Collects and preserves objects pertaining to the life of the Jews in Italy from the Middle Ages to the present day. The main attraction is the ancient synagogue of Conegliano Veneto, a township some 60 km from Venice relocated entirely to Israel. Hours: Sunday, Tuesday, Wednesday, 9.00 am to 5.00 pm, Monday, 9.00 am to 2.00 pm, Thursday, Friday, 9.00 am to 1.00 pm. For guided tours contact the number above.

Old Yishuv Court Museum
6 Or Hayim Stree 91016t
Telephone: (2) 628-4636
Fax: (2) 628-4636

The museum is located in the heart of the Jewish Quarter in the old City of Jerusalem in a sixteenth-century building. It displays the story of the Jewish community from the period under Ottoman rule, through the final days of the British Mandate. Hours Sunday to Thursday, 9.00 am to 2.00 pm.

S.Y. Agnon's House
16 Joseph Klausner Street, Talpiot 93388
Telephone: (2) 671-6498
Fax: (2) 673-8285
Email: agnon-h@zahav.net.il
Hours: Sunday to Thursday, 9.00 am to 1.00 pm

Siebenberg House of Archaeological Museum
7 Hagittit Street, Jewish Quarter
Telephone: (2) 628-2341

The Chagall Windows at the Hadassah University Hospital
Ein Kerem 91120
Telephone: (2) 677-6271
Fax: (2) 643-9203
Email: tourism@hadassah.org.il
Closed on Fridays and Saturdays. There is an entrance fee.

The Israel Museum Jerusalem
Ruppin Blvd
Telephone: (2) 670-8811
Fax: (2) 677-1332
Website: www.imj.org.il

Includes Bezalel National Museum, Samuel Bronfman Biblical & Archaeological Museum, Shrine of the Book & the Rockefeller Museum in East Jerusalem

The Sir Isaac & Lady Edith Wolfson Museum, Hechal Shlomo
4th Floor, 58 King George Street
Telephone: (2) 624-7908
Fax: (2) 623-1810
Email: hechalshlomo@bezeqint.net
Opening hours Sunday to Monday 10.00 am to 2.00 pm

Tourjeman Post Museum
4 Hail Hahandasa Street
Telephone: (2) 628-1278
Fax: (2) 627-7061

Tower of David Museum of the History of Jerusalem
Jaffa Gate
Telephone: (2) 626-5333
Fax: (2) 628-3418
Email: shivuk@tower.org.il
24-hour information line: (2)-626-5310

Yad Vashem, The Holocaust Martyrs' and Heroes' Remembrance Authority
Har Hazikaron, PO Box 3477 91034
Telephone: (2) 644-3400
Fax: (2) 644-3443
Email: general.information@yadvashem.org.il
Website: www.yadvashem.org
Open 9 am to 5 pm Sunday to Thursday, 9.00 am to 2.00 pm Friday and eves of holidays, closed on Saturday and all Jewish holidays.

ORGANISATIONS

Ezer Mizion 'Help for Zion'
25 Yirmiyahu St. 94467
Telephone: (2) 537-8070
Fax: (2) 538-3315
Email: ezerm@netvision.net.il
Website: www.ezer-mizion.org.il
Opening hours are 8.00 am to 8.00 pm. Mailing address (midweek) – POB 41130 Jerusalem 91410

Travlers Aid of Israel
PO Box 2828
Telephone: (2) 582-0126
Fax: (2) 623-2742
Email: wolfilaw@netvision.net.il

Legal counselling, social and human services, accident victims legal assistance, immigrant assistance, interest free-loans, stranded travellers, medical assistance, crime-victim assistance, homelessness, emergency assistance

Yad Sarah Public Relations
Yad Sarah House, 124 Herzl Blvd. 96187
Telephone: (2) 644-4634
Fax: (2) 644-4628
Email: AdenaF@yadsarah.org.il
Website: www.yadsarah.org.il

Yad Sarah home care organization lends, free against a returnable deposit, regular and high-tech medical rehab. equipment. Visitors in wheelchairs can use the Yad Sarah special transportation vans at a low fee. By pre-arrangement you can have the van and driver waiting at Ben Gurion airport. Two weeks notice for this service. Yad Sarah has over 100 branches in Israel. More information for disabled visitors on the website

RELIGIOUS ORGANISATIONS
Israel Council of Young Israel
Heichal Shlomo Building, 58 King George Street
Telephone: (2) 623-1631
Fax: (2) 623-1363
Email: young-il@internet-zahav.net
Mailing address: POB 7306 91072 Jerusalem, Israel. Office hours: Sunday through to Thursday 9.00 am to 3.00 pm.

RESTAURANTS
Clafouti
2 Hasoreg Street
Telephone: (2) 624-4491

Pampa
3 Rehov Yosef Rivlin
Telephone: (2) 623-1455

Ye Olde English Tea Room
68 Jaffa Road
Telephone: (2) 537-6595

Dairy
Besograyim
45 Ussishkin Street
Telephone: (2) 624-5353

Café Rimon
4 Luntz Street (off Midrehov)
Telephone: (2) 624-3712

Chamomille
6 Yoel Solomon Street
Telephone: (2) 625-2750

Dagim Beni
1 Mesilat Yesharim Street
Telephone: (2) 622-2403

Daglicatesse
1 Rachel Imenu
Telephone: (2) 563-2657

Little Italy
38 Keren Hayesod Street
Telephone: (2) 561-7638

Mamma Mia
38 King George Street 94262
Telephone: (2) 624-8080
Fax: (2) 623-3336
Air conditioned. Hours: Sunday to Thursday, 12 pm to midnight, Friday 12 pm to 4pm; Saturday, from the end of Shabbat.

Michael Andrew
12 Emil Bota
Telephone: (2) 624-0090

Of Course!
Zion Confederation House, Emile Botta Street
Telephone: (2) 624-5206

Off The Square
8 Ramban Street

Poire et Pomme
The Khan Theatre, 2 Remez Square
Telephone: (2) 671-9602

Rienzi
10 King David Street
Telephone: (2) 622-2312

Rimon
4 Lunz Street
Telephone: (2) 622-2772

Theatre Lounge
Jerusalem Theatre, 20 Marcus Street
Telephone: (2) 566-9351

Zeze
11 Bezalel Street
Telephone: (2) 623-1761

Meat
El Gaucho
22 Rivilin Street, Israel
Telephone: (2) 624-1227
Fax: (2) 623-2660
Email: gaucho1@netvision.net

El Marrakesh
4 King David street
Telephone: (2) 622-7577

Hanevi'im
54 Hanevi'im Street, Jerusalem
Telephone: (2) 624-7433

Marvad Haksamim
16 King George Street

Marziano & Toledano
15 Rehov Yad Harutzim
Telephone: (2) 672-8672

Norman's Steak 'n' Burger
27 Emek Refaim Street
Telephone: (2) 566-6603
Fax: (2) 673-1768
Email: burger@normans.co.il
Website: www.normans.co.il
American steakhouse. Reservations recommended. Hours: Sunday to Thursday, 12 pm to 11 pm; Friday, closed; Saturday, from Shabbat.

Rungsit
2 Jabotinsky Street
Telephone: (2) 561-1757

Shaul's Shwarma Centre
14 Ben-Yehuda Street
Telephone: (2) 622-5027

Shemesh
21 Ben Yehuda Street
Telephone: (2) 622-2418

Shipodei Hagefen
74 Agrippas Street
Telephone: (2) 622-2367

Vanqueiro
54 Hanevi'im Street
Telephone: (2) 624-7432
Email: vanqueiro@softhome.net

Yemenite Step
12 Yoel Salamon Street
Telephone: (2) 624-0477

Pizzerias
Pizzeria Rimini
15 King George street
Telephone: (2) 622-6505
7 Paran Street, Ramat Eshkol

Pizzeria Trevi
8 Leib Yaffe Street
Telephone: (2) 672-4136

Vegetarian
Belinda Cafe
9a Diskin St.reet,
Telephone: (2) 563-3995
Fax: (2) 561-1176
Email: belindacafe@hotmail.com

Chamomile
6 Yoel Solomon St.
Telephone: (2) 625-2750

Village Green
33 Jaffa Street
Telephone: (2) 625-3065
Fax: (2) 625-3062
Catering, takeaway, function hall

SYNAGOGUES
Great Synagogue
60 King George Street

Yeshurun
44 King George Street
Telephone: (2) 624-3942
Fax: (2) 622-4528
Email: netypjer@netvision.net.il

TOURIST INFORMATION
Ministry of Tourism
24 King George Street
Telephone: (2) 675-4811

Tourism Coordinator with the Palestinian Authority
Israel Ministry of Tourism, PO Box 1018, Jerusalem 91009
Telephone: (2) 675-4903
Fax: (2) 624-0571
Email: zvin@tourism.gov.il

TOURS
American P'eylim Student Union
10 Shoarim Street
Telephone: (2) 653-2131
Free tours of Jewish Quarter and free accommodation in the hostal quarters

Knesset (Parliament)
Telephone: (2) 675-3416
Fax: (2) 561-1201
Sunday & Thursday 8.30 am and 2.30 pm

Society for the Protection of Nature in Israel: Israeli Nature Trails
13 Helen Hamalka Street 950-101
Telephone: (2) 624-4605
Fax: (2) 625-4953
Email: spnijeru@inter.net.il

YOUTH HOSTELS
Bet Bernstein
1 Keren Hayesod Street
Telephone: (2) 625-8286
80 rooms

Davidka
67 Ha Nevi'im Street, PO Box 37110
Telephone: (2) 538-4555
Fax: (2) 538-8790
Seventy-five rooms; 4-6 beds

Ein Karem
Telephone: (2) 641-6282

Israel Youth Hostels Association
Youth Travel Bureau, Jerusalem International Convention Center, POB 6001 91060
Telephone: (2) 655-8442
Fax: (2) 655-8431
Email: iyha@iyha.org.il
Website: www.iyha.org.il
There are thirty-one youth hostels in Israel for students, youth groups and adults, which are supervised by the Israel Youth Hostels Association (a member of the International Youth Hostels Federation). All hostels offer the standard facilities of dormitories, kosher dining rooms etc. Most hostels also have a guest house section, with double and family rooms and private facilities. Most are air-conditioned.

KFAR GILADI
MUSEUMS
Beit Hashomer
Telephone: (4) 694-1565
Fax: (4) 695-1505

KIBBUTZ HARDUF
RESTAURANTS
Vegetarian
Jutka's Restaurant
Telephone: (4) 905-9229
Fax: (4) 986-1106
Email:rest@harduf.org.il
Website:harduf.org.il/rest

KIBBUTZ YOTVATA
LEISURE
Biblical Wildlife Reserve Hai Bar Arava
The reserve is situated thirty-seven miles north of Eilat.
Biologists have settled every breed of animal that is
mentioned in the Bible. Animals include herd of Somalian
wid asses, oryx antelope, ibex, ostriches, desert foxes, lynx,
hyenas and the last desert leopard in the Negev, living out
her days on the reserve. Guided tours start at 9 am and
10.30 am, noon and 1.30 pm.

RESTAURANTS
Dairy
Dairy Restaurant
Telephone: (8) 635-7449

KORAZIM
HOLIDAY VILLAGE
Amnon Bay Recreation Centre
Telephone: (4) 693-4431

Vered Hagalil Guest Farm
Telephone: (4) 693-5785
Fax: (4) 693-4964
Email: vered@veredhagalil.co.il

LOD
MUSEUMS
Museum of Jewish Ethnic Heritage
20 David Ha'melech Boulevard, Lod
Telephone: (8) 924-1160
Fax: (8) 924-9466
Email: zmalachi@post.tau.ac.il
P.O.B 383 Lod, 71101

TOURIST INFORMATION
Ministry of Tourism
Ben Gurion International Airport
Telephone: (8) 971-1485

LOHAMEI HAGETAOT
MUSEUMS
**Ghetto Fighters' House, Holocast &
Resistance Museum**
M.P. (Mobile Post) 25220
Telephone: (4) 995-8080
Fax: (4) 995-8007
Email: simstein@gfh.org.il
Website: www.gfh.org.il

Hours: Sunday to Thursday 9.00 am to 4.00pm Friday: main
museum closed. Yad Layeled open: 9.00 am to 1.00 pm,
Saturdays and holidays: main museum closed. Yad Layeled
open: 10.00 am to 5.00 pm.

MAAGAN
HOLIDAY VILLAGE
Maagan Holiday village
Sea of Galilee 15160
Telephone: (4) 665-4400
Fax: (4) 665-4455
Email: maaganhv@netvision.net.il
Website: www.maagan.com

MAAYAN HAROD
YOUTH HOSTELS
Hankin
Telephone: (4) 658-1660
Seven miles east of Afula

MAHANAYIM
Information Office
Zomet Mahanayim
Telephone: (4) 693-5016

MOSHAV SHORESH
Shoresh Hotel
Harey Yehuda
Telephone: (2) 533-8338
Fax: (2) 534-0262
Email: info@shoresh.co.il
Website: www.shoresh.co.il

NAHARIYA
Carlton
23 Ha'agaaton Blvd
Telephone: (4) 900-5555
Fax: (4) 982-3771
Email: carlto2@netvision.net.il
Website: www.carlton-hotel.co.il

Rosenblatt
59 Weizmann Street
Telephone: (4) 992-0069
Fax: (4) 992-8121

LEISURE
Rosh Hanikra
Telephone: (4) 985-7109
Fax: (4) 985-7107
Email: rosh_hanikra@rahan.org.il
Website: www.rosh-hanikra.com
Rosh Hanikra is situated four miles north of Nahariya, on
the Lebanese border. Rosh Hanikra grottos – one of the
wonders of creation. The site offers a variety of attractions:
ride from the top of the mountain down to sea level via
state-of-the-art cable cars, explore the grottos formed over
millennia by the contact of rock and sea.

MUSEUMS
Nahariya Municipal Museum
19 Hagaaton Blvd
Telephone: (4) 987-9863
Fax: (4) 992-2303

NAZARETH
RESTAURANTS
Iberia
Rassco Centre, Nazareth Elite
Telephone: (4) 655-6314

NEGEV
Bulgarian
112 Keren Kayemet Street, Beersheba
Telephone: (8) 623-8504

YOUTH HOSTELS
Bet Noam
Mitzpeh Ramon
Telephone: (8) 658-8433
Fax: (8) 658-8074

Bet Sara
Ein Gedi
Telephone: (8) 658-4165
1.5 miles north of Kibbutz Ein Gedi on Dead Sea

Hevel Katif: Hadarom
Telephone: (8) 684-7597
Fax: (8) 684-7680

NETANYA
FOOD DELIVERY
Kosher Services Worldwide
Hashaked 16 42214
Telephone: (9) 98-626-422
Fax: (9) 98-847-673
Email: kosherisrael@013.net.il

HOLIDAY VILLAGE
Green Beach Holiday Village
Telephone: (9) 865-6166
Fax: (9) 835-0075

HOTELS
Arches
4 Remez Street 42271
Telephone: (9) 860-9860
Fax: (9) 860-9866
Email: arches-hotel@correy.com

Galei Hasharon
42 Ussishkin Street 42273
Telephone: (9) 834-1946
Fax: (9) 833-8128

Galil
26 Nice Blvd
Telephone: (9) 862-4455
Fax: (9) 862-4456

Ginot Yam
9 David Hamelech Street
Telephone: (9) 834-1007
Fax: (9) 861-5722

Goldar
1 Ussishkin Street
Telephone: (9) 833-8188
Fax: (9) 862-0680
Email: order@goldar.co.il

Grand Yahalom
15 Gad Machnes Street
Telephone: (9) 862-4888
Fax: (9) 862-4890

Green Beach
PO Box 230
Telephone: (9) 865-6166
Fax: (9) 835-0075

Jeremy
11 Gad Machnes Street
Telephone: (9) 862-2651
Fax: (9) 862-2651

King Koresh
6 Harav Kook Street
Telephone: (9) 861-3555
Fax: (9) 861-3444

King Solomon
18 Hamaapilim Street
Telephone: (9) 833-8444
Fax: (9) 861-1397
Email: kingsolomon@inisrael.com
Website: www.inisrael.com/kingsolomon

Margoa
9 Gad Machnes Street
Telephone: (9) 862-4434
Fax: (9) 861-1397

Maxim
8 King David Street
Telephone: (9) 862-1062
Fax: (9) 862-0190

Metropol Grand
17 Gad Machnes Street
Telephone: (9) 862-4777
Fax: (9) 861-1556

Orly
20 Hamaapilim Street
Telephone: (9) 833-3091
Fax: (9) 862-5453

Palace
33 Gad Machnes Street
Telephone: (9) 862-0222
Fax: (9) 862-0224
Email: palacent@012.co.il

Park
7 David Hamelech Street
Telephone: (9) 862-3344
Fax: (9) 862-4029

Residence
18 Gad Machnes Street
Telephone: (9) 862-3777
Fax: (9) 862-3711

The Seasons
1 Nice Blvd
Telephone: (9) 860-1555
Fax: (9) 862-3022
Email: seasons@netmedia.net.il

SYNAGOGUES
Netanya Cultural Center
4 Raziel Street
Telephone: (9) 861-1687
Fax: (9) 861-7555
Email: rina@netanya-cultural.co.il

Orthodox
New Synagogue of Netanya
7 MacDonald Street 42110
Telephone: (9) 861-4591
Email: macshul@netvision.net.il
Website: www.macshul.org
Synagogue and Community Centre. Rabbi: Rabbi Raphael Katz.

Young Israel Congregation of North Netanya
39 Shlomo Hamelech Street
Telephone: (9) 862-8737
Email: ezesilas@013.net
Website: www.yinn.org

TOURIST INFORMATION
Information Office
Ha-Atzma'ut Square
Telephone: (9) 882-7286

PETACH TIKVA
MUSEUMS
Beit Yad Labanim
30 Arlozorov Street
Telephone: (3) 922-3450
Fax: (3) 922-3450

QATZRIN
Golan Archaeological Museum
Telephone: (4) 696-9636
Fax: (4) 696-2412
Email: museum@golan.org.il

RA'ANANA
RESTAURANTS
Ady D
158 Achuza
Telephone: (9) 791-6517

Limosa
5 Eliazar Jaffe
Telephone: (9) 790-3407

Pica Aduma
87 Achuza
Telephone: (9) 791-0508

RAMAT GAN
MUSEUMS
Museum of Israeli Art
146 Abba Hillel Street 52572
Telephone: (3) 752-1876
Fax: (3) 752-7377
Email: meirmusun@mail.inter.net.il

Pierre Gildesgame Maccabi Sports Museum
Kfar Hamaccabiah
Telephone: (3) 671-5729
Fax: (3) 574-6565
Email: lod@netvision.net.il

Yechiel Nahari Museum of Far Eastern Art
18 Hibat Zion Street
Telephone: (3) 578-1216
Fax: (3) 619-5837

RAMAT HANEGEV
Information Office
Zomet Mashabay Sadeh
Telephone: (8) 655-7314

RAMAT YOHANAN
YOUTH HOSTELS
Yehuda Hatzair
Telephone: (4) 844-2976
Fax: (4) 844-2976
Eleven miles north-east of Haifa

REHOVOT
MUSEUMS
Havayeda – Science Through Fun Science Park
5 Yechezkai Habibi Street 76000
Telephone: (8) 945-2949
Fax: (8) 945-2949
Website: www.weizmann.ac.il

Weizmann Institute of Science
Yad Haim Weizmann, Marcus Sieff Blvd 76100
Telephone: (8) 934-4499
Fax: (8) 934-4960
Website: www.weizmann.ac.il

ROSH HANIKRA
YOUTH HOSTELS
Rosh Hanikra
Telephone: (4) 998-2516

ROSH PINA
Hovevei Hateva
Telephone: (4) 693-7086
Sixteen miles north of Tiberias

SAFED
HOTELS
David
Mount Canaan
Telephone: (4) 692-0062

Nof Hagalil
Mount Canaan
Telephone: (4) 692-1595

Rimon Inn
Artist Colony
Telephone: (4) 692-0665/6

Ron
Hativat Yiftah Street
Telephone: (4) 697-2590

MUSEUMS
Beit Hameiri Institute (History & Heritage of safed)
Keren Hayesod Street 13110
Telephone: (4) 697-1307
Fax: (4) 692-1902

Israel Bible Museum
Citadel Hill
Telephone: (4) 699-9972
Fax: (4) 699-9972

Museum of Printing History
Artists' Colony
Telephone: (4) 692-3022

TOURIST INFORMATION
Information Office
50 Jerusalem Street
Telephone: (4) 692-0961/633

YOUTH HOSTELS
Bet Benyamin
Telephone: (4) 692-1086
Fax: (4) 697-3514

TEL AVIV
CONTACT INFORMATION
Jewish Student Information Centre
Tel Aviv University Off-Campus Center, 82/10
Levanon Street, Ramat Aviv
Email: jseidel@netmedia.net.il

HOTELS
Adiv
5 Mendele Street
Telephone: (3) 522-9141

Ambassador
56 Herbert Samuel Street
Telephone: (3) 510-3993
Fax: (3) 517-6308

Armon Hayarkon
268 Hayarkon Street
Telephone: (3) 605-5271
Fax: (3) 605-8485

Avia
Ben Gurion Intl Airport area
Telephone: (3) 539-3333
Fax: (3) 539-3319

Basel
156 Hayarkon Street
Telephone: (3) 520-7711
Fax: (3) 527-0005

Bell
12 Allenby Street
Telephone: (3) 517-7011
Fax: (3) 517-4352

Carlton Tel Aviv
10 Eliezer Peri Street
Telephone: (3) 520-1818
Fax: (3) 527-1043
Email: request@carlton.co.il

City
9 Mapu Street
Telephone: (3) 524-6253
Fax: (3) 524-6250

Dan Panorama
Charles Clore Park
Telephone: (3) 519-0190

Dan Tel Aviv
99 Hayarkon Street
Telephone: (3) 520-2525
Fax: (3) 524-9755
Email: dantelaviv@danhotels.com

Grand Beach
250 Hayarkon Street
Telephone: (3) 543-3333
Fax: (3) 546-6589
Email: reservation@grandbeach.co.il
Website: www.grandbeach.co.il
Synagogue on premises

Howard Johnson – Shalom
216 Hayarkon Street
Telephone: (3) 524-3277
Fax: (3) 523-5895
Email: h_shlom@netvision.net.il

Maxim
86 Hayarkon Street, P.O.B. 3442 63903
Telephone: (3) 517-3721/5
Fax: (3) 517-3726

Metropolitan
11-15 Trumpeldor Street 63803
Telephone: (3) 519-2727
Fax: (3) 517-2626
Email: reserve@metrotlv.co.il
Website: www.hotelmetropolitan.co.il

Ramat aviv
151 Namir Road
Telephone: (3) 699-0777
Fax: (3) 699-0997

Renaissance Tel Aviv
121 Hayarkon Street 63453
Telephone: (3) 521-5555
Fax: (3) 521-5588
Email: reserv@renaissance-tlv.co.il
Website: www.renaissancehotels.com/TLVBR
Central organisation: Marriott International
All rooms with private balcony and sea view. Direct access to the beach.

Sheraton Moriah
155 Hayarkon Street
Telephone: (3) 521-6666
Fax: (3) 527-1065
Email: shermor@inter.net.il

Sheraton Tel Aviv Hotel & Towers
115 Hayarkon Street
Telephone: (3) 521-1111
Fax: (3) 523-3322
Email: shtelviv@netvision.net.il

Tal
287 Hayarkon Street
Telephone: (3) 542-5500
Fax: (3) 542-5501

Tel Aviv Hilton
Independence Park 63405
Telephone: (3) 520-2222
Fax: (3) 527-2711
Email: fom_tel-aviv@hilton.com

Yamit Park Plaza
79 Hayarkon Street
Telephone: (3) 517-7111
Fax: (3) 517-4719
Email: yamit@netvision.net.il

MUSEUMS
Beit Bialik
22 Bialik Street
Telephone: (3) 525-3403
Fax: (3) 525-4530

Ben Gurion House
17 Ben Gurion Bpulevard
Telephone: (3) 522-1010
Fax: (3) 524-7293

Eretz Israel Museum
2 Haim Levanon Street 69975
Telephone: (3) 641-5244
Fax: (3) 641-2408

Hagana Museum
23 Rothschild Blvd. 65122
Telephone: (3) 560-8624
Fax: (3) 566-1208

Helena Rubenstein Pavilion for Contemporary Art
6 Tarsat Street
Telephone: (3) 528-7196

Jabotinsky Museum
38 King George Street 62398
Telephone: (3) 528-7320
Fax: (3) 528-5587
Email: museum@jabotinsky.org
Website: www.jabotnsky.org
Hours: Sunday to Thursday, 8 am to 4 pm. Friday 9 am to 1 pm

Lehi Museum
8 Stern Street 66085
Telephone: (3) 682-0288
Fax: (3) 681-9264

Museum of the Jewish Diaspora (Beth Hatefutsoth)
Klausner Street, Ramat Aviv
Telephone: (3) 640-8000
Fax: (3) 640-5767
Email: bhwebmas@post.tav.ac.il
Website: www.bh.org.il

Tel Aviv Museum of Art
27 Shaul Hamelech Boulevard 61332
Telephone: (3) 607-7000
Fax: (3) 695-8099
Email: janusbai@tamuseum.com
Website: www.tamuseum.com
Hours: Monday to Wednesday 10 am to 4 pm, Tuesday and Thursday 10 am to 10 pm, Friday 10 am to 2 pm and Saturday, 10 am to 4 pm. Public transport: buses 9, 11, 18, 28, 70, 82, 90, 91, 111. Parking facilities.

RESTAURANTS
Dairy
Apropo
Alexander Hotel, 3 Havakuk Street
Telephone: (3) 544-4442

Felafelim Shop
86 Rehov Ibn-Gvirol
Telephone: (3) 524-6781

Hungarian Blintzes
35 Yirmiyahu Street
Telephone: (3) 605-0674

Meat
China Lee
102 Hayarkon Street
Telephone: (3) 524-6119

Olive Leaf
Sheraton Tel Aviv Hotel and Towers , 115 Hayarkon Street
Telephone: (3) 521-9300
Fax: (3) 521-9301
Website: www.sheraton-teaviv.com
Innovative cuisine with Mediterranean flavours

Shaul's Inn
11 Elyashiv Street, Kerem Hatemanim
Telephone: (3) 517-3303
Fax: (3) 517-7619
Oriental and Yemenite food.
Hours: 12 pm to 12 am.

SYNAGOGUES
Bilu
122 Rothchild Blvd.

Ihud Shivat Zion
86 Ben-Yehuda Street
Central European rite

Ashkenazi
Main Synagogue
110 Allenby Road

TOURIST INFORMATION
ISSTA
109 Ben Yehuda Street

The Ministry of Tourism
6 Wilson Street
Telephone: (3) 556-2339
The Ministry of Tourism publishes a guide called 'The Best of Israel' detailing shops participating in the VAT refund scheme and recommended restaurants.

TIBERIAS
HOTELS
Ariston
19 Herzl Blvd
Telephone: (4) 679-0244
Fax: (4) 672-2002

Astoria
13 Ohel Ya'akov Street
Telephone: (4) 672-2351
Fax: (4) 672-5108

Caesar
103 Promenade
Telephone: (4) 672-7272
Fax: (4) 679-1013

Carmel Jordan River
Habanim Street
Telephone: (4) 671-4444
Fax: (4) 679-2111

Gai Beach
Derech Hamerchatzaot
Telephone: (4) 670-0700
Fax: (4) 679-2766

Galei Kinnereth
1 Kaplan Street
Telephone: (4) 672-8888
Fax: (4) 679-0260

Golan
14 Achad Ha'am Street
Telephone: (4) 679-1901
Fax: (4) 672-1905
Email: golanhoteltiberias@yahoo.com
Website: www.tzofit.co.il/sites/malon-golan
Tourist hotel with restaurant

Kinar
N.E. Sea of Galilee
Telephone: (4) 673-8888
Fax: (4) 673-8811
Email: kinarmamag@kinar.co.il

Lavi Kibbutz Hotel
Lower Galilee 15267
Telephone: (4) 679-9450
Fax: (4) 679-9399
Email: hotel@avi.co.il
Website: www.lavi.co.il

Pagoda
Lido Beach, PO Box 253 14102
Telephone: (4) 672-5513
Fax: (4) 672-5518
Email: liz@kinneret.co.il
Open Sunday to Thursday 12.30 to 11.30 pm. Saturday opens for dinner only.

Quiet Beach
Gedud Barak Street
Telephone: (4) 679-0125
Fax: (4) 679-0261

TOURIST INFORMATION
Tourist Office
Ha-banim Street, in the Archaeological Park
Telephone: (4) 672-5666

ZICHRON YA'ACHOV
MUSEUMS
Nili Museum & Aaronson House
40 Hameyasdim Street 30950
Telephone: (2) 639-0120
Fax: (2) 639-0119

RESTAURANTS
Dairy
Habayit Bayekev
Carmel Mizachi Winery, Rehov Hayayin
Telephone: (2) 629-0977
Fax: (2) 629-0957

TOURS
Old City Guesthouse and Youth Centre
9 Shoney Halachot Street , Old City of Jerusalem 97501
Telephone: (2) 628-9313
Fax: (2) 628-9314
Email: olyshapira@yahoo.com
Free accommodation

ITALY

Italy has an ancient connection with the Jews, and was home to one of the earliest Diaspora communities. Before the Roman invasion of ancient Israel, Judah Maccabee had a representative in Rome, and one of the reasons for the invasion was the Romans' desire to access the salt supply from the Dead Sea. There were Jewish communities in Italy after the destruction of the Second Temple, as Italy was the trading hub of the Roman empire. After Christianity became the official religion in 313CE, restrictions began to be placed on the Jewish population, forcing the community to migrate from town to town across the country.

In the medieval period there was a brief flourishing of learning, but the Spanish conquered southern Italy in the fifteenth century, expelling the Jews from Sicily, Sardinia and, eventually, Naples. The first ever ghetto was established in Venice in 1516. Later in the century descendants of those expelled from Spain and Portugal arrived. Conquest by Napoleon led to the emancipation of Italian Jewry, and full equal rights were granted in 1870.

Ironically, the Italian Fascist party contained some Jewish members, as Mussolini was not anti-semitic and, even under pressure from Hitler, did not instigate any major anti-semitic policy. The situation changed after Germany's occupation of the north in 1943. Eventually almost 8,000 Italian Jews were killed in Auschwitz, although the local population hid many of those who survived.

Today there is a central organisation which provides services for Italian Jews. There are kosher restaurants in Rome, Milan and other towns. There are also Jewish schools.

GMT +1 hours
Country calling code: (+39)
Total population: 57,523,000
Jewish population: 30,000
Emergency telephone: (Police–112) (Fire–115)
(Ambulance–116)
Electricity voltage: 220

ANCONA
COMMUNITY ORGANISATIONS
Community Offices
Via Fanti 2 bis
Telephone: (71) 202-638

MIKVAOT
Ancona Mikvaot
Via Astagno

ASTI
MUSEUMS
Asti Jewish Museum
Via Ottolenghi 8, Torino
Telephone: (141) 539-281

SYNAGOGUES
Asti Synagogue
Via Ottolenghi 8, Torino

BOLOGNA
CAFETERIA
Comunita Ebraica Bologna
Via Gombruti 9 40123
Telephone: (51) 232-066
Fax: (51) 229-474
Email: comebrbol@libero.it
Supervision: Rabbi Alberto Sermoneta
Lunch Sunday to Friday; dinner Friday; closed mid-July and August

COMMUNITY ORGANISATIONS
Bolgona Community Organization
Via Gombruti 9 40123
Telephone: (51) 232-066 & 227-931 (office of Rabbi)
Fax: (51) 229-474
Email: comebrbol@libero.it
Website: wwww.menorah.it/ceb/indice.htm

MIKVAOT
Mikveh Chaya Mushkah
Via Oreste Regnoli 17/1
Telephone: (51) 623-0316

MUSEUMS
Museo Ebraico di Bologna
Via Valdonica, 1/5 40126
Telephone: (51) 291-1280
Fax: (51) 235 430
Email: info@museoebraicobo.it
Website: www.museoebraicobo.it
The Jewish Museum of Bologna is located in the area of the former ghetto. It was established as a means of conserving the Jewish cultural heritage that for centuries has been deeply rooted in Bologna and in the Emila Romagna region. It has a bookshop specialising in Jewish matters. Jewish itineraries.

ORGANISATIONS
Jewish Community
Via Etrurian n 6 40139
Telephone: (51) 533-699
Kosher food by arrangement

SYNAGOGUES
Bologna Synagogue
Via Mario Finzi

CASALE MONFERRATO
Community Offices
Vicolo Salomone Olper 44
Telephone: (142) 71807
Fax: (142) 76444
Email: qqcasale@mail.dex-net.com
Website: www.menorah.it/qqcasale/indice.htm
The synagogue was built in 1595 is one of the most interesting in North Italy. It also contains a Jewish museum. Casale Monferrato is on the Turin–Milan road. It is advisable to make advance appointments for visiting either the synagogue or museum. Closed in the months of January, February and August.

CUNEO
TOURIST SITES
Cuneo Synagogue
Via Mondovi
Telephone: (171) 692-007
A beautiful synagogue; parts dating from the fifteenth century. Services are now held on Yom Kippur. In 1799 a special Purim was established after the synagogue was saved from destruction by a shell.

FERRARA
COMMUNITY ORGANISATIONS
Community of Ferrara
Via Mazzini 95 44100
Telephone: (532) 247-004
Fax: (532) 247-004

MIKVAOT
Ferrara Mikvaot
Via Mazzini 95
Telephone: (532) 247-004

MUSEUMS
Jewish Museum of Ferrara
Via Mazzini 95 44100 44100
Telephone: (532) 210-228
Fax: (532) 210-228
Email: museoebraico@comune.fe.it
Website: www.comune.fe.it/museoebraico
Guided tour in English, Sunday to Thursday 10.00 am, 11.00 am, 12.00 pm. Closed on Fridays and Saturdays.

SYNAGOGUES
Ferrara Synagogue
Via Mazzini 95
Telephone: (532) 247-033

FLORENCE
Although there is a belief that Jewish merchants lived in the city during Roman times there is no real evidence to substantiate this.

The known community was established in 1437 when Jewish financiers were invited to the city. The Medici family protected the community. Following the Medici leaving in 1494 the Jews were expelled. In due course they returned and a ghetto was established in 1571. Emancipation was only achieved with the entry of Napoleon in 1799.

BAKERIES
Forno dei Ciompi
Piazza dei Ciompi
Telephone: (55) 241-256

BUTCHERS
Bruno Falsettini
Mercato Coperto di S., Ambrogio
Telephone: (55) 248-0740
8.00 am to 10.00 am. Order in advance specifying kosher.

Gionvannino
Via dei Macci 106
Telephone: (55) 248-0734
7.30 am to 1.00 pm. Order in advance specifying kosher.

COMMUNITY ORGANISATIONS
Community Offices
Via L.C. Farini 4, Firenze 50121
Telephone: (55) 245-252
Fax: (55) 241-811
Email: comebrfi@fol.it
Website: www.firenzebraica.net
Open from Sunday to Friday from 9.30 am to 12.30 pm (Sunday closed in July and August).

HOTELS
Hotel Regency
Piazza Massimo D'Azeglio 3 50121
Telephone: (55) 245-247
Fax: (55) 234-6735
Email: info@regency-hotel.com
Website: www.regency-hotel.com
The Hotel overlooks the Piazza D'azeglio and is close to the city's main tourist attractions and the Synagogue

MIKVAOT
Florence Mikvaot
Via L.C. Farini 4, firenze 50121
Telephone: (55) 245-252
Fax: (55) 241-811
Email: comebrfi@fol.it
Website: www.fol.it/sinagoga

MUSEUMS
Jewish Museum
Via L.C. Farini 4, Firenze 50121
Telephone: (55) 245-252
Fax: (55) 241-811
Email: comebrfi@tin.it
Website: www.firenzebraica.net
There is also a religious and artistic souvenir shop. Open Sunday to Thursday. Groups are kindly requested to book in advance. For further information and booking, please contact the Administration Office. (55) 234-6054.

RESTAURANTS
Vegetarian Kosher
Ruth's
Via Farini 2/A
Telephone: (55) 248-0888
Bookings required for Shabbat meals and groups. Takeaway

SYNAGOGUES
Orthodox
Florence Orthodox Synagogue
Via De Banchi
Telephone: (55) 212-474
After the service there is a public Kiddush. For the timetable of service ask in the Community Office.

Florence Syngagogue
Via L.C. Farini 4 Firenze 50121
Telephone: (55) 245-252
Fax: (55) 241-811
Email: combrfi@fol.it
Website: www.fol.it/sinagoga
Services on Shabbat and holidays, After service there is a public Kiddush. The synagogue is open for tourists from Sunday to Thursday (hours vary). Groups should book in advance.

GENOA
Synagogue and Community Offices
Via Bertora 6 16122
Telephone: (101) 839-1513
Fax: (101) 846-1006
Email: comgenova@tin.it
Service every Friday evening and Shabbat morning

GORIZIA
Gorizia Synagogue
Via Ascoli 19, Gradicia
Telephone: (3831) 532-115

LEGHORN
BUTCHERS
Corucci
Banco 25, Mercato Centrale, Livorno
Telephone: (586) 884-596

MIKVAOT
Community Offices
Piazza Benamozegh 1, Livorno
Telephone: (586) 896-290
Fax: (586) 896-290

MUSEUMS
Jewish Museum
Via Micali 21, Livorno
Telephone: (586) 893-361
Visits only by appointment

SYNAGOGUES
Community Offices
Piazza Benamozegh 1, Livorno
Telephone: (586) 896-290
Fax: (586) 896-290

MANTUA
Mantua Synagogue
Via G. Govi 11, Mantova
Telephone: (379) 321-490

MERANO
MUSEUMS
Jewish Museum
Via Schiller 14
Telephone: (473) 236-127
Fax: (473) 206-210
Email: meranoebraica@hotmail.com
Hours: Tuesday and Wednesday 3 pm to 6 pm, Thursday 9 am to 12 am, Friday 3 pm to 5 pm.

SYNAGOGUES
Community Offices
Via Schiller 14
Telephone: (473) 236-127
Fax: (473) 206-210
Email: meranoebraica@hotmail.com

MILAN
Home to the second largest community in Italy, (10,000). The Ambrosiana Museum (Piazza Pio XI) contains a number of Hebrew books, manuscripts and other Judaica.

CULTURAL ORGANISATIONS
Milan Cultural Organization
Sally Mayer 2
Telephone: (2) 483-02806
Fax: (2) 483-04660

DOCUMENTATION CENTRE
Contemporary Jewish Documentation Centre
Via Eupili 8
Telephone: (2) 316-338
Fax: (2) 336-02728
Email: cdec@cdec.it
Website: www.cdec.it

The Institute promotes the study of the history, culture and life of Jews, particularly with regard to Italy and the present age. Through its activities, the Foundation aims to preserve remembrance of Fascist and Nazi persecutions aginst Jews. It includes: the library with volumes, collections of periodicals, university theses and posters; the historical archives who house a variety of documents dating from 1850, focusing particularly on the period of 1938–1945, the video-library containing videos of feature films, historical documentaries, inquiries and eyewitness accounts of events; the observatory on prejudice and anti-semitism in Italy today collects testimonies and documentation, undertakes research, and supports independent studies on the subject.

MIKVAOT
Central Synagogue
Via Guastalla 19
Telephone: (2) 551-2101
Fax: (2) 5519-2699

Chaya Mushka
35 Carlo Poerio

Persian
Angelo Donati Beth Hamidrash
Via Sally Mayer 4–6

RESTAURANTS
Eschel Israel
Via Benvenuto Cellini 2/A First Floor
Telephone: (2) 545-5076
Supervision: Rav G.H. Garelik
Open weekdays. Situated on 1st floor of synagogue.

Mifgash Jewish Center
Via Montecuccoli 35 20146
Telephone: (2) 415-6199
Fax: (2) 412-91105
Email: sissirattan@libero.it

Dairy
Carmel
Via le San Gimignano 10 20146
Telephone: (2) 416-368
Fax: (2) 416-368
Email: info@carmelbylolita.com
Website: www.carmelbylolita.com
Kasrut supervision: Rav M. Malri
Hours 12.00 noon to 2.30 pm and 6.00 pm to 11.30 pm.

Meat
Glat Kosher Beit Yosf
Via Montecuccoli 35 20146
Telephone: (2) 415-6199
Fax: (2) 415-91105
Email: sissirattan@libero.it

Re Salomone
Via Washington 9
Telephone: (2) 469-4643
Fax: (2) 433-18049
Email: resalomomne@tiscalinet.it
Website: www.resalomone.it

International Meat restaurant with Mediterranean, Italian and Oriental food and takeaway

SYNAGOGUES
Central Synagogue
Via Guastalla 19
Telephone: (2) 551-2101
Fax: (2) 5519-2699

Merkos L'Inyonei Chinuch
Via Carlo Poerio 35 20129
Telephone: (2) 295-31213

New Home for Aged
Via Leone XIII
Telephone: (2) 498-2604
Services on Sabbaths and festivals. Kosher food available upon reservation.

New Synagogue
Via Eupili 8
Service on Sabbaths and festivals

Orthodox
Ohel Yacob
Via Benvenuto Cellini 2
Telephone: (2) 545-5076

Orthodox – Ashkenazi
Beth Shlomo
Galleria Vittorio Emanuele, (Via Ugo Foscolo 3 Scala 8) 20121
Telephone: (2) 8646-6118
Fax: (2) 8646-6118
Email: info@bethshlomo.it
Website: www.bethshlomo.it
Services are held on Friday evening, Shabbat, Rosh Hodesh and Holy Days

Orthodox Sephardi
Milan Sephardi Orthodox Synagogue
Via Guastalla 19
Telephone: (2) 551-2029
Fax: (2) 551-92699
Rabbi Dr Laras is the Chief Rabbi

MODENA
BUTCHERS
Macelleria Duomo
Mercato Coperto (Covered Market), Stand 25
Telephone: (59) 217-269

SYNAGOGUES
Community Offices
Piazza Mazzini 26
Telephone: (59) 223-978

NAPLES
Naples Synagogue
Via Cappella Vecchia 31, Napoli
Telephone: (81) 764-3480
Email: c.l.na@virgilio.it

PADUA

MIKVAOT
Padua Mikvaot
Via S. Martino e Solferino 9, Padova
Telephone: (49) 871-9501

SYNAGOGUES
Community Offices
Via S. Martino e Solferino 9, Padova
Telephone: (49) 875-1106

PARMA
Parma Synagogue
Vicolo Cervi 4

TOURIST SITES
Biblioteca Palatina
Palazzo della Pioltta 1 43100
Telephone: (521) 282-217
Fax: (521) 235-662
The collection of 1,700 Hebrew manuscripts, derived from the collection of Giovanni Bernardo Rossi (1742–1831) the first bibliographer of Hebrew incunabula. It is said to be the greatest collection of Judaica put together by a Christian scholar.

PERUGIA
Perugia Synagogue
P. della Republica 77
Telephone: (75) 21250

PISA
Community Offices
Via Palestro 24
Telephone: (50) 542-580
Services are held on festivals and Holy Days. During the week the resident beadle will be glad to show visitors round the synagogue, which is famed for its beauty.

RICCIONE

HOTELS
Vienna Touring Hotel
Telephone: (54) 160-1245
In the summer kosher food is obtainable. Provides vegetarian food and particularly welcomes Jewish guests.

ROME
About half of Italian Jewry (some 15,000) live in Rome. Due to the long period of Jewish settlement, a Nusach Italki (Italian prayer ritual) developed, which is practised in some synagogues in the city. Kosher restuarants and food are available. Titus' Arch, depicting the destruction of Jerusalem by the Romans, is in Rome, and Jews were forbidden to walk under it. The ghetto of Rome is behind the Great Synagogue. An interesting visit worth is to the ancient Jewish burial sites along the Appian Way. Check about tour arrangements with the Jewish Community offices, Tel: (06)580-3667.

BAKERIES
Limentani Settimio
Via Portico d'Ottavia 1 186
Telephone: (06) 687-8637

Pasticceria Bernassconi
Piazza Benedetto Cairoli 16 00186
Telephone: (06) 6880-6264

BED AND BREAKFAST
Italian Kosher Bed & Breakfast
Via Nazionale 00184
Telephone: (06) 627-6995
Fax: (06) 4893-0253
Email: kosherbedbreakfast@tiscali.it
Situated in the heart of the historic center.

Locanda Carmel
Via Goffredo Mameli 11 00153
Telephone: (06) 580-9921
Fax: (06) 581-8853
Email: reservation@hotelcarmel.it
Website: www.hotelcarmel.it
Supervision: Rav Shalom Bahbout
Pension situated in the old district of Trastevere. Kosher breakfast only.

Simcha Labi
Via Imperia 2, CAP 00161
Telephone: (06) 4423-0332
Supervision: Chabad Rabbi

Soggiorno il Boschetto
Via del Boschetto 13 00184
Telephone: (06) 349-182-0287
Fax: (06) 4890-7215
Email: info@soggiornoilgirasole.com
Website: www.soggiornoilgirasole.com
Kosher pension situated in the old town center. Kosher breakfast. Accommodation for Shabbat dinner and lunch.

BOOKSELLERS
Menorah
Via del Tempio 2 00186
Telephone: (06) 687-9297
Email: menorah@menorah.it
Website: www.menorah.it

BUTCHERS
Babani Ben David
Via Lorenzo il Magnifico 70 00161
Telephone: (06) 4424-3959
Supervision: Chief Rabbinate of Rome

Di Porto
Via Damaso Cerquetti 2 00152
Telephone: (06) 534-6992
Supervision: Chief Rabbinate of Rome

Di Veroli
Via Galla e Sidama 51 00199
Telephone: (06) 8620-7971
Supervision: Chief Rabbinate of Rome

Gepe-Gean
Via Stamira 2/B 00162
Telephone: (06) 4424-4055
Supervision: Chief Rabbinate of Rome

Ouazana
Via S. Gherardi 16 18 00146
Telephone: (06) 556-5231
Via Giacomo Boni 18 00162
Telephone: (6) 4420-2626
Supervision: Chief Rabbinate of Rome

Pascarella
Via Cesare Pascarella 36 00153
Telephone: (06) 588-1698
Supervision: Chief Rabbinate of Rome

Spizzichino
Via del Forte Bravetta 148 00164
Telephone: (06) 6615-7796
Supervision: Chief Rabbinate of Rome

Terracina
Via S. Maria del Pianto 62 00186
Telephone: (06) 6880-1364
Supervision: Chief Rabbinate of Rome

COMMUNITY ORGANISATIONS
Unione delle Comunia Ebraiche Italiane (Union of Italian Jewish Communities)
Lungotevere R. Sanzio 9
Telephone: (06) 580-3667
Fax: (06) 589-9569
Email: info@ucei.it
Website: www.ucei.it
Information on Italian Jewry, its monuments and history may be obtained here

DELICATESSEN
Kosher Bistrot
Terracina Angelo, via Santa Maria del Pianto 68-69
Telephone: (06) 686-4398
Supervision: Chief Rabbinate of Rome

Kosher Point Minimarket
Via Orso Maria Corbino 17 00146
Telephone: (06) 556-5760

Sciunnah
Via A. lo Surdo 27/a 00146
Telephone: (06) 556-5760
Supervision: Chief Rabbinate of Rome
Hand made kosher pasta and ravioli

EMBASSY
Embassy of Israel
Via Michele Mercati 14 00197
Telephone: (06) 322-1541
Fax: (06) 3619-8555
Email: info-coor@roma.mfa.gov.il
Website: www.israel-amb.it

Embassy of Israel to The Holy See
Via Michele Mercati 12 00197
Telephone: (06) 3619-8690
Fax: (06) 3619-8626
Email: ambsec-vat@holysee.mfa.gov.il

MEDIA
Newspapers
Shalom
Lungotevere Cenci 1
Telephone: (06) 687-6816
Fax: (06) 686-8324
Email: shalom.mensile@flashnet.it
Website: www.shalom.it
Monthly

MIKVAOT
Rome Mikvaot
Lungotevere Cenci (Tempio) 9
Telephone: (06) 6840-0651
Ask for Mrs Elena Di Capua

Rome Mikvaot
Via Balbo 33
Telephone: (06) 721-4210

MUSEUMS
Museo Storico della Liberazione
Via Tasso 145 00185
Telephone: (06) 700-3866
Fax: (06) 77203514
Email: viatasso@viatasso.it
The museum was extended in 2001 with new displays dedicated to the fate of Roman Jews between 1938 and 1944

The Jewish Museum
Lungotevere Cenci
Telephone: (06) 6840-0661
Fax: (06) 6840-0684
Email: museo.ebraico@romacer.org
The main synagogue building contains a permanent exhibition covering the 2000 year history of the Italian Jewish community. Another link with this long history is the Rome Ghetto almost adjoining. It is a maze of narrow alleys dating from Imperial Roman times, within which, until 1870, all Roman Jews were confined under curfew. A striking monument has been erected to the memory of 335 Jewish and Christian citizens of Rome who were massacred in 1944 by the Nazis in the Fosse Ardeatine. It lies just outside the Porta San Paolo.

RELIGIOUS ORGANISATIONS
The Italian Rabbinical Council
Headquarters, Lungotevere Sanzio 9
Telephone: (06) 580-3667; 580-3670

RESTAURANTS
Dairy
Ristorante Yotvate
Piazza Cenci 70 186
Telephone: (06) 6813-4481
Supervision: Chief Rabbinate of Rome
Open at noon

Meat
Kasher Pizza
Via Luigi Magrini 12 146
Telephone: (06) 559-0790

Kosher Bistrot
Via S. Maria del Pianto, 6869 186
Telephone: (06) 686-4398
Fax: (06) 6880-1364

La Taverna Del Ghetto
Via Portico D'Ottavia 8
Telephone: (06) 68809771
Website: www.latavernadelghetto.com

Oriental Foods Kosher
Via Livorno, 8-10
Telephone: (06) 440-4840
Fax: (06) 440-4840

YESH
Via Silvestro Gherardi, 51 (zona Marconi), 00146
Telephone: (06) 5561697
Email: info@yesh.it

SYNAGOGUES
Orthodox – Ashkenazi
Agudat Ashkenazim
Via Cesare Balbo 33 00184
Daily services in basement

Beth Habad Synagogue
Via Ruggero Fauro 94 00197
Telephone: (06) 8069-227

Orthodox Nussah Italk
Oratorio Di Castro
Via Ceszie Balbo 33
Daily services

The Great Synagogue
Lungotevere Cenci (Tempio)
Telephone: (06) 6840-0061
Fax: (06) 6840-0655
Email: info@romacer.org
Daily services

Orthodox Sephardi
Tempio Beth-El
Via Padova 92 00161
Telephone: (06) 4424-2857

Tempio Spagnolo
Via Catalana, (behind the great synagogue)
Daily services

TOURS
G. Palombo
Via Maggia 7
Telephone: (06) 810-3716; 993-2074
Guides can be contacted also through the Jewish Museum,
Tel: (06) 6840-0661

Ruben E. Popper
12 Via dei Levii
Telephone: (06) 761-0901
Telephone number is afternoons only

SARDINIA
There is no Jewish Sardinian community today, but the island is of more than passing Jewish interest. In 19 CE, the Emperor Tiberius exiled Jews to Sardinia. There was a synagogue at Cagliari, the island's capital, at least as early as 599, for in that year a convert led a riot against it. Sardinia eventually came under Aragonese rule, and when the edict of expulsion of the Jews from Spain was issued in 1492, the Jews of the island had to leave. Since then there has been no community.

There are no other specific locations of interest to travellers

SENIGALLIA
Senigallia Synagogue
Via dei Commercianti

SICILY
Although there are very few Jews in Sicily today, there is a long and varied history of Jewish Settlement on the island stretching back to at least the sixth century and possibly according to some scholars to the first or second centuries.

By the late Middle Ages, the community numbered 40,000. In 1282, Sicily came under Spanish rule. A century or so later, there was a wave of massacres of Jews, and another in 1474. These culminated in the introduction of the inquisition in 1479 and the expulsion of the Jews in 1492.

There are no other specific locations of interest to travellers.

SIENA
Siena Synagogue
Vicolo delle Scotte 14
Telephone: (577) 284-647
The committee has issued a brochure in English giving the history of the community which dates back to medieval times. The synagogue dates from 1750. Services are held on the Sabbath and High Holy Days. Further information from Burroni Bernardi, Via del Porrione. M. Savini, via Salicotta 23. Tel: 283-140 (close to the synagogue)

SPEZIA
Spezia Synagogue
Via 20 Settembre 165

TRIESTE
COMMUNITY ORGANISATIONS
Community Offices
Via San Francesco d'Assisi 19 34133
Telephone: (40) 371-466
Fax: (40) 371-226
Email: info@triestebraica.it or rav@triestebraica.it
Website: www.triestebraica.it
Chief Rabbi: Rav Dr. Avraham Umberto **SYNAGOGUES**

Trieste Synagogue
Via Donizetti 2
Telephone: (40) 631-898

TOURS
Smile Service
Via Martiri della Liberta' 17 34034
Telephone: (40) 375-5638
Fax: (40) 375-5638
Email: smile@com.area.trieste.it
This service agency organises tours around the Jewish sites of Friuli Venezia-Giulia

TURIN
BOOKSELLERS
Biblioteca 'E. Artom'
P.tta Primo Levi 12, Torino 10125
Telephone: (11) 669-9097
Email: comebrato@libero.it
Website: www.torinoebraica.it

Libreria Claudiana
Via Principe Tommaso 1, Torino 10125
Telephone: (11) 669-2458
Fax: (11) 669-2458
Email: libreria.torino@claudiana.it

COMMUNITY ORGANISATIONS
Community Centre
P.tta Primo Levi 12, Torino 10125
Telephone: (11) 658-585
Fax: (11) 669-1173
Email: comebrato@libero.it

GROCERIES
Panetteria Bertino
Via B. Galliari 14, Torino 10125
Telephone: (11) 669-9527

MIKVAOT
Turin Synagogue
P.tta Primo Levi 12 Torino 10125
Telephone: (11) 658-585
Fax: (11) 669-1173
Email: comebrato@libero.it

RESTAURANTS

Salomon e Augusto Segre – Jewish Rest Home
Via B. Galliari 13, Torino 10125
Telephone: (11) 658-585
Only by reservation

SYNAGOGUES
Turin Synagogue
P.tta Primo Levi 12 10125
Telephone: (11) 658-585
Fax: (11) 669-1173
Email: comebrato@libero.it
Daily 6.50 am and sunset; Shabbat 9.00 am and half an hour before sunset (winter) or 6.30 pm (summer); on Shabbat (winter) between Minchah and Maariv a Seudat Shelishit is held

TOURIST SITES
Mole Atonellianta
Now the National Cinema Museum, it was originally built in the nineteenth century and was meant to be the grandest synagogue in Europe but was never completed.

URBINO
Urbino Synagogue
Via Stretta

VENICE
Jews settled in Venice early in the tenth century and became an important factor in the economic life of the city. In 1516 however, the authorities banished the Jews to the Ghetto Nuovo (new foundry) district, so establishing the first ghetto. The high walls surrounding the area still exist.

The 14th century Jewish cemetery (the second oldest in Europe) has recently been restored and was reopened in 1999 for guided tours (for details call the Jewish Museum).

COMMUNITY ORGANISATIONS
Community Offices
1146 Cannaregio, Ghetto Veochio 30121
Telephone: (41) 715-012
Fax: (41) 524-1862
Email: com.ebra@ve.191.it
Supervision: Ravelia Richetti
Central organisation: Union Of italian Jewish Communities

GIFT SHOP
David's
Campo del Ghetto Nuovo 2880
Telephone: (41) 716-278
Email: dcuriel@iol.it
Jewish articles & religious appurtenances are available

Mordehai Fusetti
Ghetto Nuovo 1219
Telephone: (41) 714-024
Jewish articles & religious appurtenances are available

GUEST HOUSE
Jewish Rest Home
2874 Cannaregio, Ghetto Nuovo 30121
Telephone: (41) 716-002
Fax: (41) 714-394
Kosher meals / accommodation available. Book early.

HOTELS
Buon Pesce
50 S. Nicolo, Lido island
Telephone: (41) 526-8599
Fax: (41) 526-0533
Email: info@hotelbuonpesce.com

Kosher
Locanda del Ghetto
Campo del Ghetto Novo, Cannaregio 2892 30121
Telephone: (41) 1275-9292
Fax: (41) 1275-7987
Email: ghetto@veneziahotels.com
Website: www.veneziahotels.com

LIBRARIES
Jewish Library and Archives 'Renato Maestro'
2899 Cannaregio, Ghetto Nuovo / 30121
Telephone: (41) 718-833
Fax: (41) 524-1862
Email: renatomaestro@libero.it

MIKVAOT
Jewish Rest Home
2874 Cannaregio Ghetto Nuovo
Telephone: (41) 715-118
Fax: (41) 718-474
Email: chiefrabbivenice@virgilio.it
Booking 24 hours in advance

MUSEUMS
Jewish Museum
Canneregio, Ghetto Nuovo 2902/B
Telephone: (41) 715-359
Fax: (41) 723-007
Open Sunday to Friday 10.00 am to 4.30 pm October to
May; 10.00 am to 7.00 pm June to September. Closed on
Saturdays and Jewish holidays. Guided visits to the
synagogue in English start every hour from the Jewish
Museum. Sandwiches and drinks are available.

RESTAURANTS
Meat
Gam-Gam
1122 Cannaregio, Sottoportico di Ghetto Vecchio
Telephone: (41) 715-284
Fax: (41) 715-284
Email: jewishvenice.org
Shabbat arrangements available. Open lunch and dinner.
Glatt kosher.

Jewish Rest Home
2874 Cannaregio, Ghetto Nuovo
Telephone: (41) 716-002
It is necessary to book in the morning

SYNAGOGUES
Orthodox
Chabad of Venice
Cannaregio, Ghetto Nuovo 2915
Telephone: (41) 715-284
Fax: (41) 715-284
Email: guide@jewishvenice.org
Website: www.jewishvenice.org
Shabbat and Holiday hospitality available

Schola Levantina
1228 Cannaregio, Ghetto Vecchio
Telephone: (41) 715-012
Fax: (41) 524-1862
Shabbath services are held during winter, Friday about one
hour before sunset and Saturday at 9.00 am; on Saturday
at 4.00 pm (later in spring and summer). Tefillah Mincha
and Seuda Shelishit.

Schola Spagnola
1149 Cannaregio, Ghetto Vecchio
Telephone: (41) 715-012
Fax: (41) 524-1862
Shabbath services are held during winter, Friday about one
hour before sunset and Saturday at 9.00 am; on Saturday
at 4.00 pm (later in spring and summer). Tefillah Mincha
and Seuda Shelishit.

VERCELLI
COMMUNITY ORGANISATIONS
Community Offices
Via Oldoni 20

SYNAGOGUES
Vercelli Synagogue
Via Foa 70

VERONA
COMMUNITY ORGANISATIONS
Community Centre
Via Portici 3
Telephone: (45) 800-7112
Fax: (45) 804-8295
Email: comebraic@libero.it

SYNAGOGUES
Verona Synagogue
Via Portici 3

VIAREGGIO
CONTACT INFORMATION
Mr Sananes
Via Pacinotti 172/B
Telephone: (0584) 961-025
Fax: (0584) 49871
Email: joe.sananes@tirrenstaer.it
Private office: Tirreno Tour, 26 Viale Carducci, Tel: 30777,
during daytime

JAMAICA

During the time of Spanish colonisation, Jamaica witnessed many *Conversos* arriving from Portugal. After the British took over in 1655 many of these could again practise Judaism openly. Soon other Jews, mainly Sephardim, followed from Brazil and other nearby countries. The community received full equality in 1831 (before a similar step was taken in England).

The Jews played an important role in Jamaican life, and in 1849 the House of Asembly did not meet on Yom Kippur! However, assimilation and intermarriage took their toll and in 1921 the Ashkenazi and Sephardi synagogues combined. There is now only one synagogue on the island, but there are remains of old synagogues in Kingston, Port Royal and other towns.

Community life includes WIZO, B'nai B'rith and a school (the Hillel Academy). The community lost members after the Cuban revolution, because many feared a similar revolution in Jamaica.

GMT -5 hours
Country calling code: (+1 809)
Total population: **2,590,000**
Jewish population: **300**
Emergency telephone: (**Police–119**) (**Fire–110**)
(**Ambulance–110**)
Electricity voltage: **110**

KINGSTON
SYNAGOGUES
Shaare Shalom
Duke Street & Charles Street
Telephone: (9) 927-7948
Fax: (9) 978-6240
Services, Friday, 5.30 pm (all year), Shabbat, 10.00 am; festivals, 9.00 am all year round

JAPAN

After Japan became open to Western ideas and Westerners in the mid-nineteenth century, a trickle of Jewish immigrants from the Russian Empire, the UK and the USA began to make their homes there. The first Jewish communtiy at Yokohama was founded in 1860. Many were escaping anti-

semitism and by 1918 there were several thousand in the country.

Individual Japanese, despite being allied to Nazi Germany, did not adopt the anti-Semitic attitude of the Nazis, and the Japanese consul in Kovno Lithuania even helped the Mir Yeshivah escape from occupied Europe in 1940.

The post-war American occupation of the country brought many Jewish servicemen, and the community was also augmented by Jews escaping unrest in China. In recent years, there have been some Jewish 'gaijin', or (foreign workers).

In Tokyo there is a synagogue which provides meals on Shabbat, a Sunday school, and offices for the Executive Board of the Jewish Community of Japan, which is the central body.

GMT +9 hours
Country calling code: (**+81**)
Total population: **125,638,000**
Jewish population: **1,500**
Emergency telephone: (**Police–110**) (**Fire–119**)
(**Ambulance–119**)
Electricity voltage: **110**

HIROSHIMA
TOURIST SITES
Holocaust Education Centre
866 Nakatsuhara, Miyuki, Fukuyama 720
Telephone: (849) 558-001
Fax: (849) 558-001
Email: hecjpn@urban.ne.jp
Website: www.urba.ne.jp/home/hecjpn/
Open Tuesday, Wednesday, Friday and Saturday, 10.30 am to 4.30 pm

KOBE
SYNAGOGUES
Orthodox Sephardi
Ohel Shelomoh (Jewish Community of Kansai)
4-12-12 Kitano-cho, Cho-ku 650 0002
Telephone: (78) 221-7236
Fax: (78) 242-7254
Email: jiyohay@nava21.ne.jp
Website: www.chabonline.com/kobe
Kabalat Shabbat sunset Friday, Shacharit 10.00 Saturday, each followed by kiddush meal (groups please enquire in advance), Mincha 2.30. Mikveh by prior appointment.

TOKYO

COMMUNITY ORGANISATIONS
Japan Jewish Community Centre
8-8 Hiroo, 3-chome, Shibuya-ku 150
Telephone: (3) 3400-2559
Fax: (3) 3400-1827
Email: jccmanager@gol.com
Website: www.jccjapan.co.jp

EMBASSY
Embassy of Israel
3 Niban-cho, Chiyodaku
Telephone: (3) 3264-0911
Website: www.tokyo.mfa.gov.it

MIKVAOT
Tokyo Mikvaot
Telephone: (3) 5789-2846
Fax: (3) 3409-9443

RESTAURANTS
Japan Jewish Centre
8-8 Hiroo, 3-chome, Shibuya-ku 150
Telephone: (3) 3400-2559
Fax: (3) 3400-1827
Email: jcc@crisscross.com

They sell prepared foods and kosher wine, as well as serve meals on Friday evening and Shabbat. Reservation strongly recommended.

SUPERMARKET
National Azabu
4-5-2 Monami-Azabu
Telephone: (3) 3442-3186
Some kosher items stocked. Telephone for details.

Nissin
2-34-2 Higashi-Azubu
Telephone: (3) 3583-4586
Some kosher items stocked. Telephone for details.

SYNAGOGUES
Beth David Synagogue
8-8 Hiroo, 3-chome, Shibuya-ku 150
Telephone: (3) 3400-2559
Fax: (3) 3400-1827

Services are held Friday evening at 6.30 pm (7.00 pm during summer); Shabbat morning, 9.30 am; and on Holy-days and festivals. Advance notification requested. Mikvah on premises.

Chabad Japan
2-27-23 Ebisu Shibuya-ku 150 0013
Telephone: (3) 5789-2846
Fax: (3) 5789-2847
Website: www.chabadjapan.com
Contact them for details of services and meal reservations

KAZAKHSTAN

Essentially this community began when the Soviets rescued several thousand Jews at the time of the Nazi invasion of the Soviet Union in 1941. Others joined after the war. The community is mainly based in Almaty, the former capital, and also in Chimkent. Some 2,000 Bukharan and Tat Jews also live in the country.

The central organisation is the Mitzvah Association, which heads various Jewish groups. It even has a chair on the All-Peoples Assembly of Kazakhstan. There is a high rate of emigration to Israel.

GMT +6 hours
Country calling code: (+7)
Total population: 16,223,000
Jewish population: 10,000
Emergency telephone: (Police–03) (Fire–03) (Ambulance–03)
Electricity voltage: 220

ALMATY

COMMUNITY ORGANISATIONS
Almaty Community Organization
206 e Raimbek St.
Telephone: (3272) 539-358
Fax: (3272) 507-770
Email: info@chabad.kz
Website: www.chabad.kz
Also has a store, kosher butcher, library and mikvah

The Association of Jewish Communities in Kazakhstan
66/120 Buhar-Zhirau Street, Almaty 480057
Telephone: (3272) 450-043
Fax: (3272) 450-043
Email: kazakhstan@fjc.ru

SYNAGOGUES
Orthodox
Almaty Synagogue
206 e Raimbek St.
Telephone: (3272) 439-358
Fax: (3272) 507-770
Email: synagogues@chabad.kz

ASTANA
SYNAGOGUES
Jewish Center of Astana
11 Respublki Street, #3 473000
Telephone: (3172) 216-913
Email: astana@chabad.kz

CHIMKENT
COMMUNITY ORGANISATIONS
Jewish Community in Chimkent
President, Grigory Tzeytlin, 76 Makarova St.
486012Gp - JP 500

SYNAGOGUES
Sephardi
Chimkent Synagogue
Svobody Street, 47th Lane

KENYA

Kenya could have been the site of the first Jewish state for two thousand yearsas this offer was made to the Zionists in 1903. It was however, rejected in 1905. There were some Jews living in Kenya at the time, and a synagogue was built in 1912. Many more Jews came here after the Second World War as Holocaust survivors, and recently some Israeli's have worked on a short-term basis in the country.

Kenya was an ally to Israel in it's rescue of the Jews from Entebbe in Uganda. Jews have contributed much to the hotel industry and professional life of the country.

Regular services are held every Saturday in the Nairobi Hebrew Congregation, and there is a Community Centre next to the synagogue. The centre, the Vermont Memorial Hall offers educational and social events.

GMT +3 hours
Country calling code: (254)
Total population: 33,144,000
Jewish population: 400
Emergency telephone: (Police–999) (Fire–999)
(Ambulance–999)
Electricity voltage: 220/24

NAIROBI
COMMUNITY ORGANISATIONS
Community Centre
Vermont Memorial Hall
Open Monday, Tuesday

CULTURAL ORGANISATIONS
Community Centre
Vermont Memorial Hall

Open Monday, Tuesday, Friday 9.00 am to 1.00 pm; Wednesday 2.30 pm to 5.30 pm; services Friday evening at 6.30 pm; Saturday morning at 8.00 am. All festivals. Kosher chickens available.

SYNAGOGUES
Nairobi Hebrew Congregation
cnr. University Way & Uhuru Highway PO Box
25233 00603
Telephone: (2) 577-871
Fax: (2) 573-345
Email: azfactor@africaonline.co.ke

KYRGYZSTAN

This central Asian ex-Soviet republic has only a short history of Jewish settlement. The community originated from migrants after the Russian Revolution and evacuees from the German advance into the Soviet Union in the Second World War. As a result, community members are almost all Russian speakers and are assimilated into the Russian minority of the country.

Before the collapse of the Soviet Union there was no organised community. There has been a synagogue in the capital Bishkek since 1991 where there is also a Jewish library and an Aish Ha Torah centre. The main umbrella group is the Menorah Society of Jewish Culture.

GMT +5 hours
Country calling code: (+996)
Total population: 4,856,000
Jewish population: 2,500
Emergency telephone: (Police–03) (Fire–03)
(Ambulance–03)
Electricity voltage: 220

BISHKEK
SYNAGOGUES
Bishkek Synagogue
193 Suymbaeva (Karpinsky) Street
Telephone: (3312) 681-966
Fax: (3312) 681-966
Email: chabad@netmail.kg

LATVIA

The Jews in the medieval principalities of Courland and Livonia represent the earliest Jewish settlement in Latvia. Tombstones from the fourteenth century have been found. After the Russian takeover Jews were only allowed to live in the area if they were considered 'useful', or had lived there before the Russians took control, because the area was outside the 'Pale of Settlement' that the Russian Empire had designated for the Jews.

The Jews contributed much to Latvia's development, but this was never recognised by the government, which tried to restrict their influence in business matters. Religious Jewish life, however, was strong. When the Nazis invaded Latvia, 90 per cent of the 85,000 Jews were systematically murdered by them and their Latvian collaborators.

The bulk of today's community originates from immigration into Latvia after the war, although 3,000 Holocaust survivors did return to Latvia. Before the collapse of communism there was much Jewish dissident activity. There is a Jewish school and a Jewish hospital. There are some Holocaust memorial sites, in the capital Riga, and also in the Bierkernieki Forest, where 46,000 Holocaust victims were shot.

GMT +2 hours
Country calling code: (+371)
Total population: 2,474,000
Jewish population: 10,000
Emergency telephone: (Police–02) (Fire–01)
(Ambulance–03)
Electricity voltage: 220

DAUGAVPILS
COMMUNITY ORGANISATIONS
Jewish Community Organization
Saules Street 47
Fax: (54) 8254-24658

SYNAGOGUES
Daugavpils Synagogue
Gogol Street
Suvorov Street

LIEPAJA
COMMUNITY ORGANISATIONS
Jewish Community
Kungu Street 21
Telephone: (34) 25336

REZHITSA
Rezhitsa Synagogue
Kaleyu Street

RIGA
CULTURAL ORGANISATIONS
Latvian Society for Jewish Culture
Skolas 6 LV1322
Telephone: (2) 289-580
Fax: (2) 821-494

EMBASSY
Embassy of Israel
Elizabetes Street 2a LV1340
Telephone: (2) 732-0980
Fax: (2) 783-0170
Email: press@rig.mfa.gov.il

JEWISH CENTER
Chabad Lubavitch Latvia
141 Lacplesa St., LV1003
Telephone: (2) 720-4022
Fax: (2) 783-0444
Mobile Phone: 371-951-8700
Email: rabbi@delfi.lv
Website: www.jewish.lv/www.chbad.lv
Visitors welcomed for Shabbat and holiday meals. Kosher Cafe L'chaim at Skolas 6 (entrance from Dzirnavu) open 10.00 am to 10.00 pm, takeout available

MUSEUMS
The Jewish Museum of Riga
6 Skolas Street LV1322
The museum is small but has many moving exhibits and photos. A short video is shown depicting the tragedy of the Holocaust in Latvia.

SYNAGOGUES
Orthodox
Riga Central Synagogue
6/8 Peitavas Street, Riga 1050
Telephone: (2) 721-4507
Fax: (2) 721-4507
Email: rerd@inbox.lv
Website: www.jrcr.co
Services 3 times daily. Call or write for schedule.

LITHUANIA

The history of Lithuania Jewry is as old as the state of Lithuania itself. There were Jews in the country in the fourteenth century, when Grand Duke Gedeyminus founded the state. The community eventually grew, and produced many famous yeshivas and great commentators, such as the Vilna Gaon. The community began to emigrate (particularly to South Africa) at the beginning of the nineteenth century; even so, in 1941 there were still 160,000 Jews in the country. Ninety-five per cent of these were murdered in the Holocaust by the local population as well as the Nazis.

The remaining post-war community included some who had hidden or had managed to survive by other means, and some Jews from other parts of the Soviet Union. Interestingly, the Lithuanian Soviet Socialist Republic was more tolerant of Jewish activity than some of the neighbouring republics, such as Latvia. Now that Lithuania is independent, Jewish life is free once again.

The Lubavitch movement is present, and there are synagogues in the capital Vilnius (known to many as Vilna), and Kaunas. There is also a school and it is possible to study Yiddish. There are tours available to show the old Jewish life in Lithuania. The grave of the Vilna Gaon can be visited, as well as Paneriai, otherwise known as Ponary, where thousands of Jews were shot during the Holocaust.

GMT +2 hours
Country calling code: (+370)
Total population: 3,701,000
Jewish population: 5,000
Emergency telephone: (Police–02) (Fire–01) (Ambulance–03)
Electricity voltage: 220

DRUSKININKAI
COMMUNITY ORGANISATIONS
Jewish Community
9/15 Sporto Street
Telephone: 54590

KAUNAS
Kaunas Community Organization
26 B Gedimino Street
Telephone: (7) 203-717
Fax: (7) 201-135
Hours of opening Sunday to Thursday 3.00 pm to 6.00 pm

SYNAGOGUES
Kaunas Synagogue
11 Ozheshkienes Street

KLAIPEDA
COMMUNITY ORGANISATIONS
Jewish Community
3 Ziedu Skersqatvis
Telephone: (6) 93758

PANEVEZYS
Panevezys Community Organization
6/22 Sodu Street 5300
Telephone: (54) 68848

SHIAULIAI
Shiauliai Community Organization
24 Vyshinskio
Telephone: (1) 26795

VILNIUS
Otherwise known as Vilna, this city used to be known as the 'Jerusalem of the North'. Jews started to live in Vilnius during the middle of the sixteenth century. In due course it became a pre-eminent centre for rabbinical studies. The town still has the largest community of Lithuanian Jews, and there are many sites of historical interest, including the Vilna Gaon's grave and the State Jewish Museum.

BAKERIES
Matzah Bakery
39 Pylimo Street
Telephone: (5) 61-2523

COMMUNITY ORGANISATIONS
Jewish Community of Lithuania
Pylimo St. 4 2nd Floor 01117
Telephone: (5) 61-1736, 65-2139
Email: jewishcom@post.5ci.lt
Website: www.litjews.org
Opening hours: Monday to Thursday 10.00 am to 6.00 pm, Friday 10.00 am to 4.00 pm

CULTURAL ORGANISATIONS
The Israel Centre of Cultures and Art in Lithuania
4 Pylimo, 2nd Floor 2001
Telephone: (5) 61-1736 or 65-2139

MUSEUMS
The Vilna Gaon Jewish State Museum
Pylimo 4, LT 01117, Naugarduko 10, LT 01141, Pamenkalnio 12, LT 01114
Telephone: (5) 262-4590
Fax: (5) 22-7083212-7083
Email: jewishmuseum@jmuseum.lt
Website: www.jmuseum.lt
The Tarbut School, Exhibition and seat of Jewish Community. Opening hours Monday to Thursday 9.00 am to 5.00 pm and Friday 9.00 am to 4.00 pm.

SYNAGOGUES
Central synagogue of Vilnius Chabad
12 Saltiniu g. St. 2006
Telephone: (5) 250-387

Main Synagogue (Choral Synagogue)
39 Pylimo Street
Telephone: (5) 61-2523

LUXEMBOURG

The small community in Luxembourg faced massacres and expulsions during medieval times, and Jews only began to resettle here several hundred years later. Napoleon heralded the rebirth of the community when he annexed Luxembourg, and by 1823 a synagogue had been built. The community remained small, although in 1899 another synagogue was built.

Later many refugees from the Nazis arrived in the country, bringing the number of Jews to nearly 4,000. After the Nazi take-over 750 Luxembourg Jews were killed, but many others were saved by the local population.

The present community is generally prosperous and assimilated. The Consistoire Israelite, established by Napoleon, is recognised by the government as the representative of the community, and is also financed by the government. The Orthodox synagogue is situated fairly centrally in Luxembourg City.

GMT +1 hours
Country calling code: (+352)
Total population: 417,000
Jewish population: 600
Emergency telephone: (Police–133) (Fire–112) (Ambulance–112)
Electricity voltage: 220

ESH-SUR-ALZETTE
Esh-Sur-Alzette Synagogue
52 rue de Canal
Services held on Friday evenings

LUXEMBOURG CITY
COMMUNITY ORGANISATIONS
Consistoire Israelite de Luxembourg
45 av. Monterey 2018
Telephone: 452914
Fax: 473772

GROCERIES
Calon
Rue de Reins 3

HONONARY CONSULATE
Hononary Consul General of Israel

KASHRUT INFORMATION
Luxembourg City Kashrut
34 rue Alphonse Munchen 2172
Telephone: 452366

SYNAGOGUES
Luxembourg City Synagogue
45 av. Monterey
Telephone: 452914
Fax: 250430

MACEDONIA

At the southern end of the former Yugoslavia, this new country has an ancient Jewish heritage dating back to Roman times. The Jews took advantage of the area's favourable commercial position, lying between Turkey and Western Europe, and the remains of a synagogue at Stobei dating back to the second and third centuries is evidence of a once thriving Jewish community.

Iberian Jews escaping the Inquisition settled in the area, and brought with them Sephardi customs and the Ladino language (based on Spanish). The fate of the 8,000 Macedonian Jews under Bulgarian occupation during the Second World War is in stark contrast to the fate of the Bulgarian Jews. The Macedonian Jews were deported to their deaths, yet the Bulgarian Jews were saved by the defiance of the king and the people. Only ten per cent of the Macedonian community survived, of whom many have emigrated to Israel.

Today's community is mainly based in the capital Skopje, but there are no synagogues and there is little access to Jewish life. However, the community does have contact with Jews in Serbia and Greece.

GMT +1 hours
Country calling code: (+389)
Total population: 2,190,000
Jewish population: Under 100
Emergency telephone: (Police–92) (Fire–93) (Ambulance–94)
Electricity voltage: 220

SKOPJE
SYNAGOGUES
Community Offices / Beth Yaakov
Borka Talevski Street 24 1000
Telephone: (2) 3237 543
Fax: (2) 3214 880
Email: ezrm@ou.net.mk

MALTA

There is evidence of an ancient Jewish community on Malta, as archaeologists have discovered remains from 2,000 years ago. Malta fell into Arab hands in the early Middle Ages when there were still a few Jews on the island. The island then changed to Sicilian hands and, in 1492, the Jews were expelled.

Between the sixteenth and eighteenth centuries the island was used as a prison for Jewish captives of the Knights of St John. They were held for ransom, but managed to find time to build a synagogue. A synagogue in Spur Stree, Valetta, opened in 1912, but was demolished in 1995 as part of a redevelopment scheme.

GMT +1 hours
Country calling code: (+356)
Total population: **378,000**
Jewish population: **100**
Emergency telephone: (Police–191) (Fire–199)
(Ambulance–196)
Electricity voltage: **24**

BIRKIRKARA
COMMUNITY ORGANISATIONS
Birkirkara Community Organization
P.O. Box 4
Telephone: 445924

TA-XBIEX
SYNAGOGUES
Conservative
Jewish Community of Malta
Flat 1, Florida Mansions, Enrico Mizzi St., MSD 02
Telephone: 212-37-309 & 213-12-666
Spokesperson: 213-86-266
Fax: 676-9260
Email: sabra-@keyworld.net and elyhu@net
Website:
www.angelfire.com/al/AttardBezzinaLawrenc
Synagogue services on the 1st & 3rd Sabbath of the month, and on all High Holidays

MARTINIQUE
SYNAGOGUES
Kenafe Haarets
12 Anse Gouraud, Schoeler 97233
Telephone: 61-71-36
A community centre is also located here, which supplies kosher food, plus a kosher meat restaurant.

MELILLA
KASHRUT INFORMATION
Jewish Community
Akda Duguesa de la Victoria 52004
Telephone: (3495) 267 4057
Fax: (3495) 9 526 74057

SYNAGOGUES
Isaac Benarroch
Calle Marina 7

Jacob Almonznino
Calle Luis de Sotomayor 4

Salama
Calle Alfonso XII 6

Solinquinos
Calle O'Donnell

Yamin Benarroch
Calle Lopez Moreno 8

MEXICO

Conversos were the first Jews in the country, and some achieved high positions in early Spanish colonial Mexico. As the Inquisition was still functioning there some 200 years after the sixteenth century, the number of Jewish immigrants was small. When Mexico became independent, Jews gradually began to enter the country, coming from German and other European communities.

It was during the twentieth century that most Jewish immigrants entered Mexico. There were both Ashkenazis and Sephardis, and they settled throughout the country. The communities grew parallel rather than together, with two languages, Yiddish and Ladino.

The current community is largely middle class, and the various factions come under the Comite Central Israelita. There are many synagogues and kosher restaurants.

The community is well equipped with Jewish schools and yeshivas.

GMT -6 to 8 hours
Country calling code: (+52)
Total population: **96,400,000**
Jewish population: **41,000**
Emergency telephone: **(Police–080)** **(Fire–080)** **(Ambulance–080)**
Electricity voltage: **110**

ACAPULCO
HOTELS
The Hyatt Regency
Costera Miguel Aleman 1 39869
Telephone: (744) 69-1234
Fax: (744) 84-3087
Email: hyatt-reserve@acabtu.co.mx
Website: www.acapulco.regency-hyatt.com
Supervision: Rabbinical

The hotel has a synagogue and a mikva. Kosher restaurant is open from December 15th - February 28th.

RESTAURANTS
Kosher Restaurant
Costera Miguel Aleman 1 39869
Telephone: (744) 69-1234
Fax: (744) 84-3087
Email: hyatta@netmex.com

Open only during the high season (Nov/Dec to March/April)

CUERNAVACA
Cuernavaca Synagogue
Madero 404
Telephone: (777) 186-846

At the old peoples' home.

GUADALAJARA
COMMUNITY ORGANISATIONS
Comunidad Israelita de Guadalajara
Juan Palomar y Arias 651
Telephone: (33) 416-463
Fax: (33) 427-168

Includes kosher restaurant, mikva and two synagogues. Phone in advance.

MEXICO CITY
Despite the fact that the first *auto-da-fé* at which *Conversos* were burnt at the stake took place in Mexico City, it has been said that in 1550 there were more crypto-Jews in Mexico City than Roman Catholics. The vast majority of Mexican Jewry now live in Mexico City. With twenty-three synagogues, kosher restaurants and Jewish schools, the city is well equipped with Jewish facilities. Polanco is a Jewish area in the city with some synagogues. The first synagogue, dating from 1912, is in the downtown area.

BUTCHERS
Butcher
Fuente de Templanza 17, Tecamachalco
Mehadrin

Carniceria Sary
Tecamachalco
Mehadrin

Pollos Mugrabi
Platon 133, Polanco
Mehadrin

COMMUNITY ORGANISATIONS
Comunidad Monte Sinai
Tennyson 134, Polanco
Telephone: (55) 280-6369
Fax: (55) 281-3969

EMBASSY
Embassy of Israel
Sierra Madre 215 11000
Telephone: (55) 201-1500
Fax: (55) 201-1555
Email: israel@prodigy.net,mx

GROCERIES
Casa Amiga
Horacio 1719, Col. Polanco
Telephone: (55) 540-1455

Kurson Kosher
Acuezunco 15, San Miguel
Telephone: (55) 905-589-9823, 9860, 3225
Emilio Castelar, Polanco 204-G 11560
Telephone: (55) 280-3500
Fax: (55) 280-3361
Email: kkurson@aol.com

Will also deliver and ship to any resort in Mexico

MEDIA

Newspapers
CDI
Centro Deportivo, Plaza de Toros of Cuatro Caminos
Telephone: (55) 557-3000
Spanish weekly

Foro de Vida Judia en el Mundo
Aviacion Commercial 16, Col. Polanco 15700
Telephone: (55) 571-1114
Spanish monthly

Kesher
Leibnitz 13-10, Colonia Anzures CP 11590
Telephone: (55) 202-0446
Fax: (55) 203-9084
Email: info@kesher.org.mx
Spanish bi-weekly

La Voz de la Kehila
Acapulco 70, 2nd Floor
Telephone: (55) 211-0501
Spanish monthly.

MIKVAOT
Mexico City Mikvaot
Platon 413
Telephone: (55) 520-9569
Av. de los Bosques 53, Tecamachalco
Telephone: (55) 589-5530
Bernard Shaw 110, Polanco
Telephone: (55) 203-9964

Tevila Cuernavaca
Priv. de Antinea 4, Col. Delicias
Telephone: (55) 150-841, 181-655

MUSEUMS
The Holocaust Museum
Acapulco 70, Col Condesa
Telephone: (55) 211-051

RELIGIOUS ORGANISATIONS
Comite Central
Telephone: (55) 520-9393, 540-7376

Comunidad Maguen David
Email: mdavid@ort.org.mx
Contact for any religious questions

Jerusalem de Mexico
Anatore France 359, Local C. Polanco
Telephone: (55) 531-2269

RESTAURANTS
Meat
Aladinos
Ingenieros Militares 255
Telephone: (55) 395-2959
Fax: (55) 395-9219

O Grill/Kosher House
37 Polanco, Mexico City
Telephone: (55) 280-1638
Fax: (55) 280-1638

Restuarant Pini
Ejercito Nacional 458d
Supervision: Maguen David

SYNAGOGUES
Agudas Achim
Montes de Oca 32, Condesa 6140
Telephone: (55) 553-6430

Bet Midrash Tecamachalco
Fuente de Marcela 23, Col. Tecamachalco
Telephone: (55) 251-8454

Beth Moshe
Tennyson No 134, Col. Polanco 11560
Telephone: (55) 280-6369;6375
Fax: (55) 281-3969
Email: monsinai@ort.org.mx

Beth Yehoshua
Fuente de San Sulpicio No. 16, Col. 53950
Tecamachalco
Telephone: (55) 294-8617

Bircas Shumel
Plinio 311, Polanco
Telephone: (55) 280-2769

Jajam Elfasi
Fuente del Pescador 168, Col. Tecamachalco
Shabbat services only

Kolel Aram Zoba
Sofocles 346, Col. Polanco
Telephone: (55) 280-2669; 4886

Kolel Maor Abraham
Lafontaine 344, Col. Polanco
Telephone: (55) 545-2482

Nidche Israel
Acapulco 70, Condesa
Telephone: (55) 211-0575

Or Damesek
Seneca 343
Telephone: (55) 280-6281

Ramat Shalom
Fuente de Prescador 35, Tecamachalco
Telephone: (55) 251-3854
Fax: (55) 251-4363
Website: www.ramat.org

Shaare Shalom
Av. de Los Bosques 53, Tecamachalco
Telephone: (55) 251-0973

Shuba Israel
Edgar Alan Poe 43, Col. Polanco
Telephone: (55) 280-0136

Conservative
Bet El
Horacio 1722, Polanco los Morales
Telephone: (55) 281-2592
Fax: (55) 281-2467
Email: comunidad.betel@bigfoot.com

Beth Israel
Virreyes 114, Lomas
Telephone: (55) 520-8515
Fax: (55) 520-9559
Email: bethisrael@psi.net.mx

Orthodox
Beth Itzjak de Polanco
Eujenio Sue 20, Polanco
Telephone: (55) 280-9296
Fax: (55) 280-0520
Email: bitzjak@prodigy.net.mx

Eliahu Fasja
Fuente de Templanza 13, Col. Tecamachalco
Telephone: (55) 294-9388

Midrash Latorah
Cerrada de Los Morales 8, Col. Polanco 11510
Telephone: (55) 280-0875
Fax: (55) 281-6801
Rabbi Asher Zrihen, formerly of London, will be happy to welcome and assist visitors

Sephardi
Maguen David
Bernard Shaw 110, Polanco
Telephone: (55) 203-9964

Sephardi Synagogue
Monterey 359
Telephone: (55) 564-1197, 1367

MONTERREY
COMMUNITY ORGANISATIONS
Centro Israelita de Monterrey
Canada 207, Nuevo León
Telephone: (81) 461-128
Includes a synagogue and mikva

TIJUANA
CONTACT INFORMATION
JCC Chabad House
Centro Social Israelita de Baja California, Av. 16
Septiembre, Baja California 3000
Telephone: (664) 862-692; 862-693
Fax: (664) 341-532
Email: chabadtj@telnor.net
Synagogue and mikva on premises

SYNAGOGUES
Tijuanua Hebrew Congregation
Amado Nervo 207, Baja California

MOLDOVA

Moldova used to be a Soviet Republic bordering Romania to the west and the Ukraine to the east. When Jews first entered what is now Moldova, the area was known as Bessarabia, and was on an important trade route between Turkey and Poland. By the time of Russian rule in 1812 there was a permanent Jewish community. The Russians included the area in the 'Pale of Settlement', which held the majority of the Jews of their empire. By the end of the nineteenth century there were over 200,000 Jews in the region. However, the twentieth century started with the infamous progrom in the capital Chisinev where 49 Jews were killed, and much damage was done to Jewish property. Emigration began to increase. The area fell under Romanian control between 1918 and 1940, but the community continued to lead a normal life until the Second World War, when many thousands of the pre-war community of over 250,000 were killed during the German occupation.

After the war some survivors continued to live in Moldova, and Jews from other parts of the Soviet Union joined them. There is an umbrella society for Moldovan Jews, and there are synagogues and schools. The Lubavitch movement is active in building up religious life.

GMT +2 hours
Country calling code: (+373)
Total population: 4,335,000
Jewish population: 15,000
Electricity voltage: 220

CHISINAU
Most of Moldova's Jews live in Chisinau (formerly Kishinev). This city was the scene for two notorious progroms in 1903 and 1905.

RELIGIOUS ORGANISATIONS
Yeshiva of Chisinau
Sciusev 5 277001
Telephone: (2) 274-362
Fax: (2) 274-331
Email: agudath@yeshiva.midnet.com
In addition to Jewish studies, a mikva and kosher food supplies are on premises

SYNAGOGUES
Chisinau Synagogue
Chabad Lubavitch Str. 8, Chisinau, Moldova 270005
Telephone: (2) 541-023
Fax: (2) 541-020
Yakimovsky per. 8 277000
Telephone: (2) 221-215
A mikvah is on the premises and kosher food may be obtained

TELENESHTY
Teleneshty Synagogue
4 28th June Street

TIRASPOL
Tourist Information
Telephone: 336-495
Fax: 332-208
Details of the Jewish Community from Dr Vaisman

MONACO

Some French Jews lived in Monaco before 1939, and the government issued them with false papers during the war, thus saving them from the Nazis. This tiny country has also attracted retired people from France, North Africa and the UK.

There is an official Jewish body, the Association Culturelle Israelite de Monaco, and there is a synagogue, a school and a kosher food shop. Half of the total Jewish population are Ashkenazi and the other half are Sephardi, and 60 per cent of the community is retired.

GMT +1 hours
Country calling code: (+377)
Total population: **32,000**
Jewish population: **800**
Emergency telephone: (**Police–17**) (**Fire–18**) (**Ambulance–18**)
Electricity voltage: **220**

MONTE CARLO
COMMUNITY ORGANISATIONS
Association Culturelle Israelite de Monaco
15 Av. de la Costa
Telephone: (9) 330-1646

GROCERIES
Carrefour

SYNAGOGUES
Monte Carlo Synagogue
15 Av. de la Costa, opp. Balmoral Hotel MC 98000
Telephone: (9) 330-1646
Services Friday evening at 6.30 pm and Saturday morning at 8.45 am and Saturday afternoon at 5.30 pm

MOROCCO

There were Jews in Morocco before it became a Roman province (they first arrived after the destruction of the Temple in 587 BCE). Since the first century, the Jewish population settled in Morocco has increased steadily owing to several waves of immigration from Spain and Portugal following the expulsion of Jews by the Inquisition in 1492.

Under Moslem rule the Jews experienced a general climate of tolerance, although they did suffer some persecution. During the Vichy period in the Second World War, Sultan Mohammed V protected the community. Almost 250,000 Jews have emigrated to Israel, Canada, France, Spain and Latin America, but they maintain strong links with the Kingdom.

Since ancient times the Jewish community has succeeded in cohabiting harmoniously with the Berber and then with the Arab community. Today the present Jewish population an active community, playing a significant role in Moroccan society although they have declined in number.

GMT +212 hours
Total population: **27,310,000**
Jewish population: **6,000**
Emergency telephone: (**Police–19**) (**Fire–15**) (**Ambulance–19**)
Electricity voltage: **110/170**

AGADIR
COMMUNITY ORGANISATIONS
Community Offices
Imm. Arsalane Av. Hassan II
Telephone: (8) 840-091
Fax: (8) 822-268

MIKVAOT
Agadir Mikvaot
Av. Moulay Abdallah, cnr. Rue de la Foire
Telephone: (8) 842-339

SYNAGOGUES
Agadir Synagogue
Av. Moulay Abdallah, cnr. Rue de la Foire
Telephone: (8) 842-339

CASABLANCA
At the beginning of the 19th century around one quarter of the city's population was Jewish. The community thrived until restrictions were imposed by the Vichy government during the Second World War.
In 1948 the Jewish population was 74,000. Since then it has declined and is now around 5,000.

COMMUNITY ORGANISATIONS
Community Offices
Rue Abbou Abdallah al Mahassibi
Telephone: (2) 270-976 ,222-861
Fax: (2) 266-953

MIKVAOT
Casablanca Synagogue
32 Rue Officier de Paix Thomas
Telephone: (2) 276-688

RESTAURANTS
Americano
7 Place d'Aknoul

Aux Bon Delices
261 Blvd Ziraoui, opp. Lycee Lyautey

SYNAGOGUES
Benisty
13 Rue Ferhat Achad

Bennaroche
24 Rue Lusitania

Em Habanim
14 Rue Lusitania

Hazan Synagogue
Rue Roger Farache

Ne'im Zemiroth
29 rue Jean -Jacques Rousseau

Temple Beth El
61 rue Jaber ben Hayane
Telephone: (2) 267-192

ESSAOUIRA (FORMERLY MOGADOR)

COMMUNITY ORGANISATIONS
Community Offices
2 Rue Ziri Ben Atyah

SYNAGOGUES
Essaouira Synagogue
2 Rue Ziri Ben Atyah

FEZ

COMMUNITY ORGANISATIONS
Community Offices
Rue Dominique Bouchery

CONTACT INFORMATION
Mrs Danielle Mamane
La Boutique, Hotel Palais Jamai, Fez
Telephone: (5) 562 2353
Email: boutique.palaisjamai@iam.net.ma
Mrs Mamane will be pleased to assist all Jewish vistitors

MIKVAOT
Talmud Torah
Rue Dominique Bouchery

SYNAGOGUES
Fez Synagogue
Rue de Beyrouth

Sadoun Synagogue
Blvd. Mohammed V.

Talmud Torah
Rue Dominique Bouchery

KENITRA

COMMUNITY ORGANISATIONS
Community Offices
58 rue Sallah Eddine

MIKVAOT
Kenitra Mikvaot
58 rue Sallah Eddine

SYNAGOGUES
Kenitra Synagogue
Rue de Lyon

MARRAKECH

COMMUNITY ORGANISATIONS
Community Offices
PO Box 515
Telephone: (4) 448-754

MIKVAOT
Marrakech Mikvaot
Blvd Zerktouni (Gueliz)
Telephone: (4) 448-754
Fax: (4) 438-676
Contact: Mme Kadoch

RESTAURANTS
Le Sepharade
31 Lotissement Hassania, Gueliz
Telephone: (4) 439-809

Le Viennois Hotel Pulman Mansour Eddahbi
Avenue de France, Marrakech
Telephone: (4) 339-100

SYNAGOGUES
Bittoun
Medina, Rue Arset Laamach, Touareg
In course of renovation

Rabbi Pinhas Ha Cohen
Medina Rue Arset, Laamach
Telephone: (4) 389-798

Salat Laazama
Rue Talmud Torah, Mellah, Hay Essalam
Telephone: (4) 403-798

MEKNES

MIKVAOT
Meknes Mikvaot
5 rue de Ghana
Telephone: (5) 21968 or 22549
Tourists

SYNAGOGUES
Meknes Synagogue
5 rue de Ghana
Telephone: (5) 21968 , 22549

OUJDA

COMMUNITY ORGANISATIONS
Community Offices
Texaco Maroc, 36 blvd Hassan Loukili

RABAT

COMMUNITY ORGANISATIONS
Rabat Community Organization
1 Rue Boussouni

MIKVAOT
Rabat Mikvaot
3 Rue Moulay Ismail

RESTAURANTS
Cerle de l'Alliance
3 Rue Mellila
Telephone: (7) 727-679

The Menora
Villa 5, Rue Er Riyad
Telephone: (7) 260-103

SYNAGOGUES
Rabat Synagogue
3 Rue Moulay Ismail

SAFI
SYNAGOGUES
Mursiand Synagogue
Rue de R'bat

Synagogue Beth El
Rue de R'bat

TANGIER
COMMUNITY ORGANISATIONS
Community Centre
1 Rue de la Liberte
Telephone: (039) 931-633
Fax: (039) 937-609

MIKVAOT
Shaar Raphael
27 Blvd Pasteur
Telephone: (039) 231-304

SYNAGOGUES
Tangier Synagogue
27 Blvd Pasteur
Telephone: (039) 231-304

TOURIST SITES
Historic Synagogues
Rue des Synagogues, off Rue Siaghines
There are a number of synagogues in this street which is in the old part of the town

TETUAN
COMMUNITY ORGANISATIONS
Community Offices
16 rue Moulay Abbas

SYNAGOGUES
Benoualid Synagogue
The Old Mellah

MOZAMBIQUE

The small community in Mozambique originally consisted of South African Jews who were forced out of South Africa by President Kruger for supporting the British at the beginning of the twentieth century. The synagogue was opened in 1926, and there is a cemetery in Alto Maha. The biggest Jewish community is in Maputo.

GMT +2 hours
Country calling code: (+258)
Total population: 16,917,000
Jewish population: **Under 100**
Emergency telephone: (Police–119) (Fire–198) (Ambulance–117)
Electricity voltage: 220

MAPUTO
COMMUNITY ORGANISATIONS
Jewish Community of Mozambique
Av. Tomas Nduda 235, PO Box 235
Telephone: (1) 494-413
Email: xero_servicos@mail.garp.co.mz

MYANMAR

The first Jews came to Myanmar in the early eighteenth century from Iraq and other Middle Eastern countries. A synagogue was built in 1896. In the first years of the twentieth century Rangoon and Bassein both had Jewish mayors. The Jewish population swelled to 2,000 before 1939, but most of these fled to Britain and India before the Japanese invasion in the Second World War. More returned after the war [only a few hundred], and the community began to decline through intermarriage and conversion. The handful of remaining Jews are elderly and services are held only on the High Holy Days when a minyan is made up with help from the Israeli embassy.

There is also a tribe of Jews in the north of the country (the Karens), who have their own prayer houses and who believe that they are descended from the tribe of Menashe.

GMT +6 1/2 hours
Country calling code: (+95)
Total population: 46,402,000
Jewish population: **Under 100**

Emergency telephone: (Police–199) (Fire–191)
Ambulance–192)
In Yangon [Rangoon] only
Electricity voltage: 220/230

YANGON (FORMERLY RANGOON)

EMBASSY
Embassy of Israel
No. 15, Kha Baung Street, Hlaing Township
Telephone: (951) 515115
Fax: (951) 515116
Email: info@yangon.mfa.gov.il
Website: yangon.mfa.gov.il

SYNAGOGUES
Musmeah Yeshua
85 26th Street
Telephone: (951) 252814
Email: samuels@mptmail.net.mm

NAMIBIA

Namibian Jewry began at the time when
the country was a German colony before
the First World War. The cemetery at
Swakopmund dates from that settlement.
Keetmanschoop also had a congregation,
but this no longer exists. The Windhoek
synagogue is still in use, and was founded
in 1924. Services are held on Shabbat and
festivals. South Africa provides some help
for the community, such as a cantor on festivals, and the Cape Board of Jewish
Education assists with Hebrew education.
From approximately 100 Jewish families in
the 1920s and 1930s, the number has
dwindled.

GMT +2 hours
Country calling code: (+264)
Total population: 1,613,000
Jewish population: Under 100
Emergency telephone: (Police–1011)
(Fire–2032270) (Ambulance–2032276)
Electricity voltage: 220/240

WINDHOEK

SYNAGOGUES
Windhoek Synagogue
Cnr. Tal & Post streets, PO Box 563
Telephone: (61) 127-0800
Fax: (61) 291-6328

NEPAL

Nepal has no Jewish history. It is however,
well visited by Israeli and other young
Jewish tourists. Each year a large Seder is
organised by the Lubavitch movement. In
2000 approximately 1,000 attended at the
Radisson Hotel.

GMT +5.45 hours
Country calling code: (+977)
Total population: 22,591,000
Jewish population: Under 100

KATHMANDU

EMBASSY
Embassy of Israel
Bishramalaya House, Lazimpat Street, G.P.O. Box 371
Telephone: (1) 411-811
Fax: (1) 413-920
Email: kathmandu@israel.org

NETHERLANDS

Although some historians believe that the
first Jews in Holland lived there during
Roman times, documentary evidence goes
back only to the twelfth century. The contemporary settlement occurred when
Portuguese *Marranos* found refuge from
the Inquisition in Holland. Religious freedom was advocated in the early seventeenth century and Jews contributed much
to the Netherlands' 'golden age' of prosperity and power.

By the time of Napoleon, the community
had grown to 10,000 (the largest in
Western Europe), mainly by incoming
Jewish traders from eastern Europe. The
Jews were emancipated in 1796, but the
community began to decline slowly during
the nineteenth century. Of the 140,000
Jews (including 30,000 German Jewish
refugees) in Holland in 1939, the Germans
transported 100,000 to various death
camps in Poland, but the local Dutch population tended to behave sympathetically
towards their Jewish neighbours, hiding
many. Anne Frank and her family are the
most famous of the hidden Jews from
Holland. Amsterdam witnessed a strike in
February 1941, called as a protest against
the Jewish deportations.

Today there are three Jewish councils in the Netherlands representing the Ashkenazi, Reform and Orthodox communities. There are many synagogues in Amsterdam, as well as synagogues in other towns. There are kosher restaurants in Amsterdam, which also has many historical sites: Anne Frank House, the Portuguese Synagogue, still lit by candlelight, and the Resistance Museum.

GMT +1 hours
Country calling code: (**+31**)
Total population: **15,604.00**
Jewish population: **28,000**
Emergency telephone: (**Police–112**) (**Fire112**)
(**Ambulance–112**)
Electricity voltage: **220**

AMERSFOORT
Amersfoort Synagogue
PO Box 1039 3800 AB- Amersfoort
Telephone: (33) 475-6722
Email: nig.amersfoort@hetnet.nl

AMSTERDAM
The first Jews were said to have come to the city in 1598 following the Union of Utrecht when the northern provinces proclaimed their independence from Catholic Spain and abolished religious discrimination. It soon became the centre of the Converso Diaspora. The Jewish Historical Museum and the Anne Frank house are essential visits. The Rijksmuseum contains a number of paintings of Jewish interest including 'The Jewish Bride' by Rembrandt.

BAKERIES
Thee Boom
Bolestein 45-47
Telephone: (20) 642-7003
Maastraat 16
Telephone: (20) 662-4827
Supervision: Amsterdam Jewish Community
Hours: Sunday to Friday 9.00 am to 5.00 pm, closed on Tuesday.

BOOKSELLERS
Samech Books
Gunterstein 69
Telephone: (20) 642-1424
Fax: (20) 642-1424
Email: samech@dds.nl
Website: www.joodseboeken.nl

CENTRAL ORGANISATIONS
Nederlandse Vegetariersbond
Larenseweg 26 1221 1221
Telephone: (31) 683-4796
Fax: (31) 683-6152
Email: info@vegetariers.nl
Website: www.vegetariers.nl
Provides information on vegetarian hotels, restaurants and guest houses

DELICATESSEN
Mouwes Koshere Delicatessan
Kastelenstraat 261 1082
Telephone: (20) 661-0180
Email: info@mouwes.nl
Website: www.mouwes.nl

HOTELS
Golden Tulip Amsterdam Centre
Stadhouderskade 7 1054 ES
Telephone: (20) 685-1351
Fax: (20) 685-1611
Email: info@gtacentre.goldentulip.nl

NETHERLANDS

Hotel Doria
Damstraat 3 1012 JL
Telephone: (20) 638-8826
Fax: (20) 638-8726
Email: doria@euronet.nl
Website: www.intris.nl/hoteldoria
Kosher breakfast reception open 24 hours.

Hotel la Richelle
Holbeinstr 41
Telephone: (20) 671-7971
Fax: (20) 671-0541
Kosher breakfast on request

JEWISH LIBRARY
Ets Haim Library - Livraria Montezinos
Mr. Visserplein 3 1011 RD
Telephone: (20) 428-2596
Fax: (20) 428-2597
Email: biblio@etshaim.org
Website: www.etshaim.org
Open for research only Monday to Thursday 10.00 am to 4.00 pm, Friday 10.00 am to 12.30 pm

LIBRARIES
Bibliotheca Rosenthaliana
Singel 425 1012 WP
Telephone: (20) 525-2366
Fax: (20) 525-2311
Email: ros@uba.uva.nl
Website: www.uba.uva.nl/rosenthaliana
The Amsterdam University Library contains an extraordinary collection of Judaic and Hebrew writings given to the city in 1880 by the heirs of Lesser Rosenthal (1794-1868). The German occupation in the Second World War had severe repercussions for the Bibliotheca Rosenthaliana. The books were sent to Germany, where they were found by the Americans, and returned to Amsterdam in 1946. The collection now contains over 100,000 volumes, some dating back to the fifteenth century.

MEDIA
Newspapers
Nieuw Israelietisch Weekblad
Burg. Haspelslaan 23 1181 NB Amstelveen
Telephone: (20) 627-6275
Fax: (20) 624-2519
Email: info@niw.nl
Website: www.niw.nl

MIKVAOT
Mikwe Amsterdam
Heinzstraat 3
Telephone: (20) 662-0178/671-9383

MUSEUMS
Anne Frank House
Prinsengracht 267
Telephone: (20) 556-7105
Fax: (20) 620-7999
Website: www.annefrank.nl

The original hiding place of Anne Frank where she wrote her diary. Open daily from 9.00 am to 7.00 pm (April 1st to September 1st daily from 9.00 am to 9.00 pm. January 1st from 12.00 noon to 7.00pm, May 4th from 9.00am to 7.00 pm; December 21nd from 9.00 am to 5.00 pm; December 25th from 12.00 noon to 5.00 pm and December 31st 9.00 am to 5.00 pm. Closed on Yom Kippur (in 2006 on October 2nd) Last entry thirty minutes before closing time.

Dutch Resistance Museum
Plantage Kerklaan 61 1018 CX
Telephone: (20) 620-2535
Fax: (20) 620-2960
Email: info@verzetsmuseum.org
Website: www.verzetsmuseum.org
Open all year, except January 1st, April 30th and December 25th. Hours: 10.00 am to 5.00 pm, Tuesday to Friday, 12.00 noon to 5.00 pm, Saturday to Monday. Permanent Exhibition. From 10th May 1940 to May 1945, the Netherlands were occupied by Nazi Germany. Almost every Dutch person was affected by the consequences of the occupation. The Plancius Building, in which the museum is located, was built in 1876 as the social club for a Jewish choir.

Jewish Historical Museum
Jonas Daniël Meÿerplein 2-4 1011 RH
Telephone: (20) 626-9945
Fax: (20) 624-1721
Email: info@jhm.nl
Website: www.jhm.nl
Housed in a complex of four former synagogues. Sandwich shop serving kosher food. Open daily from 11.00 am to 5.00 pm. Group visits by arrangement. Next to the permanent collection on the culture and history of the Jews in the Netherlands, there are changing exhibitions and a program of events.

RELIGIOUS ORGANISATIONS
Ashkenazi Community Offices/Community Center
Van der Boechorststr. 26, PO Box 7967 1008 AD
Telephone: (20) 646-0046
Fax: (20) 646-4357
Email: info@nihs.nl
Website: www.nihs.nl

RESTAURANTS
Nasj Viel Restaurant
Jewish Youth Center, De Lairessestraat 13, (near Concertgebouw) 1071
Telephone: (20) 676-7622
Fax: (20) 673-5215
Email: info@nasjviel.nl
Supervision: Amsterdam Rabbinate
Open: Sunday to Thursday, 6.00 pm to 10.00 pm (kitchen closes at 9.00 pm). Groups can be accommodated, reserve in advance.

Sandwichshop Sal. Meijer
Scheldestraat 45 1078 GG
Telephone: (20) 673-1313
Fax: (20) 642-9020
Supervision: Amsterdam Jewish Community

Dairy
Museum Café
Jewish Historical Museum, Jonas Daniel Meijerplein 2-4
Telephone: (20) 626-9945
Fax: (20) 624-1721
Supervision: Amsterdam Jewish Community
Hours 11.00 am to 5.00 pm daily.

Meat
Carmel
Amstelveenseweg 2234 1075 XT
Telephone: (20) 675-7636
Fax: (20) 773-5960
Supervision: Amsterdam Jewish Community
Hours: 12.00 pm to 11.30 pm, Sunday to Thursday. Caters for Shabbat meals for groups if ordered in advance.

King Solomon
Waterlooplein 239 1011 PG
Telephone: (20) 625-5860
Fax: (20) 625-5860
Website: www.kingsolomon.nl
Notes: Opening hours Monday to Thursday 12.00 to 10.00 am, Friday 12.00 to 2.00 am fior Shabbat. Winter Saturday night open

Shabbes - Tisch
Plantage Westermanlaan 9 1018 DK
Telephone: (20) 623-4684
Supervision: Rabbinate of The Netherlands
Five minutes from Portuguese Synagogue. Friday night and Shabbath only. Reservations in advance.

Vegetarian
Bolhoed
Prinsengacht 60-62
Telephone: (20) 626-1803
Hours: 12.00 pm to 10.00 pm daily. Serves organic vegetarian and vegan food.

Restaurant Betty's
Rijnstraat 75 1079 GX
Telephone: (20) 644-5896

SYNAGOGUES
Liberal
Liberaal Joodse Gemeente
Jacob Soetendorpstr. 8 1079 RM
Telephone: (20) 642-3562
Fax: (20) 442-0337
Email: ljgadam@ljg.nl
Website: www.ljg.nl
Also houses the Judith Druk Library and the Centre for Jewish studies

Orthodox
Gerard Doustraat Synagogue
Gerard Doustr. 238
Telephone: (20) 675-0932
Fax: (20) 867-1626
Email: gd_sjoel@joods.nl
Website: www.joods.nl/gd_sjoel
Services: Saturday and Festival mornings

Inter-Provincial Chief Rabbinate
Van der Boechorstraat 26 1081 BT
Telephone: (31) 20 301 8495
Fax: (31) 20 301 8491
Email: ipor@planet.nl
Postal Address: PO Box 7967
1008 AD Amsterdam

Kehilas Ja'Akow (E. Europe)
Gerrit van der Veenstraat 26 1077 XG
Telephone: (20) 676-3602

Sephardi
Portuguese Jews' Congregation
Mr. Visserplein 3 1011 RD
Telephone: (20) 624-5351
Fax: (20) 625-4680
Email: info@esnoga.com
Website: www.esnoga.com
Completely restored. Open Sunday to Friday 10 am to 4 pm. In August 2000 Holland's unique Sephardi Judaism collection was returned from safe keeping at The Hebrew University at Jerusalem. After the expulsion of spanish Jewry in 1492, many families settled in the Netherlands. At the beginning there were three small communities which ultimately merged into one, which became known as the 'Portuguese Community', services are held on Shabbat and festivals. Open for visitors: Sunday to Friday 10am to 4pm.

Portuguese Synagogue & Community Centre
Texlstr. 82
Telephone: (20) 624-5351

TOURIST SITES
Portuguese Jewish Cemetery
Kerkstraat 7, Ouderkerk aan de Amstel 1191
Telephone: (20) 496-3498
Fax: (20) 496-5496
Email: bethaim@wxs.nl
Established 1614. One of the oldest Sephardi cemeteries still in use in Europe. Menasseh ben Israel is buried here, as are the parents of the philosopher Spinoza. Ten kilometres south-east of Amsterdam.

TOURS
Easy Rider Excursions
POB 9086 1180 MB Amstelveen
Telephone: (20) 297 527 444
Mobile Phone: 0611292616
Email: maxmeron@hotmail.com
Website: www.easyriderexcursions.nl
Walk through the Jewish history of Amsterdam. Licensed tour guides. By reservation only, from June 1st till September 30th.

Footstep Tours
Admiralengracht 42-3 1057 EZ
Telephone: (20) 612-5252
Fax: (20) 689-3276
Email: info@footsteptours.nl
Website: ww.footsteptours.nl
Jewish destinations from Amsterdam throughout the
Netherlands, licensed tour guides , walking & museum
tours, city & country tours all year round, reservation only.
6-1443-4530.

ARNHEM
SYNAGOGUES
Arnhem Synagogue
Pastoorstr. 17a
Telephone: (26) 4442-5154

Liberal
Liberaal Joodese Gemeente Arnhem
Veluws Hof 24, Ermelo 3852
Telephone: (26) 557-860
Email: elisjewa@hetnet.nl

BUSSUM
Orthodox
Bussum Synagogue
Kromme Englaan 1a
Telephone: (35) 691-4882
Email: info@nig-bussum.nl

DELFT
CULTURAL ORGANISATIONS
Beth Studentiem
Hillel House, Jewish Students Centre , Technical
University, Koornmarkt 9 2611EA
Telephone: (15) 212-0300
'Kosher Mensa' Mondays to Thursdays, in order to join for
dinner please call before 12.30pm on that day

EINDHOVEN
Eidhoven Synagogue
H. Casimirstr. 23
Telephone: (40) 751-1253

ENSCHEDE
Enschede Synagogue
Prinsestr. 16
Telephone: (53) 432-3479
Fax: (53) 430-9725
Email: jmhartog@vromen.nl

Liberal
Liberal Congregation Inquiries
Haaksbergen
Telephone: (53) 435-1330

GRONINGEN
Groningen Synagogue
Postbus 550 9700
Telephone: (50) 312-3151
Email: NIG_Groningen@hotmail.com

HAARLEM
Haarlem Synagogue
Kenaupark 7
Telephone: (23) 332-6899, 324-2051

LEIDEN
ORGANISATIONS
Jewish Students Centre
Levendaal 8
Telephone: (71) 513-0382

SYNAGOGUES
Jewish Congregation Leiden
Levendaal 14-16 2311 JL
Telephone: (71) 512-5793
Fax: (71) 513-6879
Email: nigleiden@hetnet.nl

MAASTRICHT
Maastricht Synagogue
Capucijnengang 2
The present synagogue was built in 1841. It is believed ho
that there was one in the town in the 14th century.

ROTTERDAM
SYNAGOGUES
Liberal
**Liberaal Joodse Gemeente Rotterdam
(Liberal Jewish Community of Rotterdam)**
Mozartlaan 99 Rotterdam - Hillegersberg 3007
Telephone: (180) 423474
Email: norbird@hetnet.nl
Central organisation: Verbond Van Liberaal - Religieuze
Joden In Nederland
Mailing Address: (Secretary) Rietvink 5, 2986 XD
Ridderkerk

Orthodox
Joodse Gemeente Rotterdam
A B N Davidsplein 2
Telephone: (180) 466-9765
Fax: (180) 467-5713
Email: nig.rotterdam@zonnet.nl
Mikva on premises

THE HAGUE
DELICATESSEN
Jacobs
Haverkamp 220
Telephone: (70) 347-4980
Fax: (70) 347-4980
Email: pmjakob@chello.nl

EMBASSY
Embassy of Israel
Buitenhof 47 2513
Telephone: (70) 376-0500
Fax: (70) 376-0555
Email: info@hague.mfa.gov.il
Website: www.thehague.mfa.gov.il or
www.israel.nl

RESTAURANTS
Vegetarian
Restaurant De Wankele Tafel
Mauritskade 79 2514
Telephone: (70) 364-3267

SYNAGOGUES
Liberal
Liberal Synagogue
Prinsessegracht 26
Telephone: (70) 750-4680
Fax: (70) 750-4681
Email: infi@ljgdenhaag.nl
Website: www.ljgdenhaag.nl

Orthodox
Beis Jisroel
Doorniksestraat 152 2587 2587
Telephone: (70) 358-6363
Fax: (70) 347-9002

The Hague Synagogue
Corn. Houtmanstraat 11, Bezuidenhout 2593
Telephone: (70) 347-0222
Fax: (70) 347-9002
Email: raabinaat-haag@zonnet.nl
Mikva on premises, appointments should be made twenty-
four hours in advance by telephoning 350-7621

TOURIST SITES
Spinoza House
Paviljoensgracht
Spinoza House is of special interest, as is the eighteenth-
century Portuguese synagogue in the Prinsessegracht,
which is now used by the Liberal congregation.

UTRECHT
RESTAURANTS
Eetkafee De Baas
Lijnmarkt 8 3511
Telephone: (30) 231-5185

SYNAGOGUES
Liberal
Liberal Synagogue
Telephone: (30) 644-2619
Email: batja@hetnet.nl
Inquiries to (30) 603-9343

Synagogue LTG Utrecht
Magdalenastraat 1A 3512
Telephone: (30) 254-3492
Email: ljg-utrecht@ljg.nl

Orthodox
Utrecht Synagogue
Springweg 164 3511 VZ
Telephone: (30) 231-4742
Fax: (30) 272-2091
Email: nigutrecht@hotmail.com

ZWOLLE
SYNAGOGUES
Zwolle Synagogue
Samuel Hirschstr. 8 PO Box 1468 8001
Telephone: (38) 211-412

EMBASSY
Consul General of Israel
Blauwduifweg 5, Willemstad
Telephone: (5999) 736-5068
Fax: (5999) 737-0707
Email: midalya@ibm.net

CURAÇAO

KASHRUT INFORMATION
There is no kosher restaurant in Curaçao. However many kosher items may be purchsed at the 'food store' of the Congregation Shaarei Tsedek.

MUSEUMS
Jewish Cultural Historical Museum
Hanchi di Snoa 29, PO Box 322
Telephone: (5999) 461-1633
Fax: (5999) 465-4141
Opening Hours: Monday to Friday 9.00 to 11.45 am and 2.30 to 4.45 pm. If there is a cruise ship in port, then also on Sundays from 9.00 am to noon. Closed on Shabbats and Holy Days. On permanent display are a great many ritual, ceremonial and cultural objects, many of which date back to the seventeenth and eighteenth centuris and are still in use by the adjacent congregation Mikve Israel-Emanuel (founded 1651, oldest in the hemisphere).

SYNAGOGUES
Ashkenazi
Congregation Shaarei Tsedek
Leliweg 1a, PO Box 498
Telephone: (5999) 737-5738
Fax: (5999) 736-9546

SYNAGOGUES
Sephardi Reconstructionist
United Congregation Mikve'Israel Emanuel
Hanchi di Snoa 29, PO Box 322
Telephone: (5999) 461-1067
Fax: (5999) 465-4141
Email: info@snoa.com
Sabbath services are Friday at 6.30 pm (second Friday in the month is a family service), Saturday at 10.00 am. Holy Day services at the same time.

NEW ZEALAND

New Zealand Jewry is almost as old as the European presence in the country. The year 1829 marks the beginning of Jewish settlement, and Jews played a prominent role in the development of the country in the nineteenth century, especially in trading with Australia and Britain.The Auckland Jewish community was founded in 1841, followed by one in Wellington in 1843. There was also a Jewish Prime Minister, Sir Julius Vogel, in the nineteenth century.

British Jews emigrated to New Zealand in the twentieth century, but New Zealand restricted immigration from Nazi Europe.

Today the community has six synagogues, four on the North Island and two on the South Island. Auckland and Wellington have Jewish day schools, and the 'Kosher Kiwi Guide' is published in Auckland. There has been recent Jewish immigration from South Africa.

GMT +12 hours
Country calling code: (+64)
Total population: 3,811,000
Jewish population: 5,000
Emergency telephone: (Police–111) (Fire–111) (Ambulance–111)
Electricity voltage: 230

AUCKLAND
COMMUNITY ORGANISATIONS
Auckland Jewish Council
80 Webb St., Wellington
Telephone: (9) 384-4229
Fax: (9) 384-4229
Has a small shop selling kosher food

SYNAGOGUES
Orthodox
Auckland Hebrew Congregation
108 Greys Avenue
Telephone: (9) 373-2908
Fax: (9) 303-2147
Email: office@ahc.org.nz
Website: www.ahc.org.nz
New Zealands largest selection of kosher goods. Open Tuesday to Friday 8.30 am to 3.30 pm. Sundays 9.00 am to 11.00 am. Mailing address: PO Box 68224 Newton Auckland.

Progressive
Beth Shalom Progressive Synagogue
180 Manukau Road, Epsom 1003
Telephone: (9) 524-4139
Fax: (9) 524-7075
Email: bshalom@ihug.co.nz
Website: www.bethshalom.org.nz

CHRISTCHURCH
COMMUNITY ORGANISATIONS
Christchurch Jewish Council
Telephone: (3) 358-8769

SYNAGOGUES
Christchurch Synagogue
406 Durham Street North Christchurch
Telephone: (3) 365-7412
Fax: (3) 355-7982
Email: coxst@chch.planet.org.nz
Orthodox service 9.30 am Saturday. Progressive servce 6.30 pm first Friday of the month. Mailing address: PO Box 21253, Christchurch.

WELLINGTON
COMMUNITY ORGANISATIONS
Wellington Jewish Community Centre
80 Webb Street
Telephone: (4) 384-5081
Fax: (4) 384-5081
Email: beth@ihug.co.nz

There are no kosher restaurants in Wellington. Visitors who want kosher meals & kosher food should contact the office of the Community Centre or the Kosher Co-Op,

Wellington Regional Jewish Council
54 Central Terrace 5
Telephone: (4) 475-7622
Email: zwartz@actrix.gen.nz

DELICATESSEN
Dixon Street Delicatessen
Telephone: (4) 384-2436
Fax: (4) 384-8692

Not fully kosher but provides kosher challahs and various American & Israeli foods

EMBASSY
Embassy of Israel
Level 13, 111 The Terrace, Equinox House, PO Box 2171
Telephone: (4) 472-2368
Fax: (4) 499-0632
Email: israel-ask@israel.org.nz
Website: www.webnz.co.nz/israel

GROCERIES
Kosher Co-Op
80 Webb Street
Telephone: (4) 384-3136
Fax: (4) 384-5081
Email: bethel@ihug.co.nz
Website: www.go.to/koshernz

Open on Wednesday, Friday and sunday for kosher meats, cheese and imported products. Goods can be sent anywhere in New Zealand.

MEDIA
Newspapers
New Zealand Jewish Chronicle
PO Box 27-156 6001
Telephone: (4) 934-6077
Fax: (4) 934-6079
Email: mike@rifkov.co.nz

Monthly newspaper of local, Israeli and Jewish News

MIKVAOT
Wellington Jewish Community Centre
80 Webb Street
Telephone: (4) 384-5081
Fax: (4) 384-5081
Email: bethel@ihug.co.nz
Website: ww.beth-el.org.nz

SYNAGOGUES
Orthodox
Beth-El Synagogue
80 Webb Street
Telephone: (4) 384-5081
Fax: (4) 384-5081
Email: bethel@ihug.co.nz

Progressive
Temple Sinai
147 Ghuznee Street
Telephone: (4) 385-0720
Fax: (4) 385-0572
Email: office@sinai.org.nz
Website: www.sinai.org.nz

NORTHERN IRELAND
BELFAST
There were Jews living in Belfast in the year 1652, but the present community was founded in 1869.

ORGANISATIONS
Vegetarian & Vegans Northern Ireland
66 Ravenhill Gardens BT6 8GQ
Telephone: (028) 9028-1640

RESTAURANTS
Jewish Community Centre
49 Somerton Road BT15 4DD
Telephone: (028) 9077-7974
Email: bjcinfo@yahoo.co.uk
Website: www.belfastjewishcommunity.org.uk

Open by arrangement only. Please phone ahead. Both meat and dairy.

SYNAGOGUES
Orthodox
Belfast Synagogue
49 Somerton Road BT15 3LH
Telephone: (028) 9077-7974

Services Saturday, Sunday, Monday & Thursday am, Friday pm

NORWAY
The only way Jews could enter Norway before the nineteenth century was with a 'Letter of Protection', as Danish control limited the amount of Jewish entry. The situation changed in 1851 when a Norwegian liberal poet, Henrik Wergeland, argued for the admission of Jews into the country, and the parliament eventually agreed. There were only some 650 Jews in the country after emancipation in 1891, mainly in Oslo and Trondheim. By 1920

the community numbered 1,457, and by the time of the Nazi invasion there were 1,800. Despite attempts by the Norwegian resistance to smuggle Jews to Sweden 767 Jews were transported to Auschwitz, although 930 were able to reach Sweden. The Jewish survivors were joined after the war by Displaced Persons, especially invited by the Norwegian government.

The current situation forbids shechita, but there are no other restrictions on Jewish life. There is a synagogue in Oslo, and a kosher food shop. There is also a Jewish magazine. An old-age home was built in 1988. Trondheim, in the north of the country, has the northernmost synagogue in the world.

GMT +1 hours
Country calling code: (+47)
Total population: **4,445,000**
Jewish population: **1,500**
Emergency telephone: **(Police–112) (Fire–110) (Ambulance–113)**
Electricity voltage: **220**

OSLO

Oslo is the major centre of Norwegian Jewry with 900 Jews living there. The Resistance Museum is of interest, as is the Wergerland Monument in the Var Frisler Cemetery. A monument consisting of 8 empty chairs in remembrance of the Norwegian Jews who were killed during the War is located near the Akershus fortification.

COMMUNITY CENTRE
Oslo Community Centre
Bergstien 13, 0172 Oslo 131
Telephone: (2) 320 5750
Fax: (2) 320 5781
Email: adm@dmt.oslo.no
Website: www.dmt.oslo.no
Kosher groceries available at Marmaris, Ullevalsveien 37, Oslo. Telephone:(2) 246 9921
Kosher catering, Tone Rubin, Telephone: 90649048

EMBASSY
Embassy of Israel
Parkveien 35, P.O. Box 534 Skoyen 0258
Telephone: (2) 101-9500
Fax: (2) 101-9530
Email: israel@oslo.mfa.gov.il
Website: www.oslo.mfa.gov.il

RESTAURANTS
Kosher Food Centre
Corner Bergstien/Waldemar Thranes Gate 171
Telephone: (2) 260-9166
Supervision: Rabbi Michael Melchior
There are no kosher hotels or restaurants in Oslo but there is the Kosher Food Centre. Open 4.00 pm to 6.00 pm Tuesday and Thursday, and 12.00 noon to 2.00 pm on Friday. Closed Shabbat.

SYNAGOGUES
Orthodox
Mosaiske Trossamfund (The Jewish Community)
Bergsien 13 172
Telephone: (2) 320-5750
Fax: (2) 320-5781
Email: kontor@dmt.oslo.no
Website: www.dmt.oslo.no
Postal address: Postboks 2722 St. Hanshaugen, 0131 Oslo, Norway

TOURIST SITES
Ostre Gravlund Cemetery
There is a Jewish war memorial here

TRONDHEIM
Synagogue
Ark. Christiesgt. 1
Telephone: 7352-6568, 4752-2030
Fax: 7353-1108
Email: palkom@online.no
The world's northernmost synagogue. The synagogue also has a museum. Postal address Postboks 2722 St. Hanshaugen, 0131 Oslo, Norway.

PANAMA

Some Jews, most of them pretending to be Christians, came to Panama during colonial times. Panama was an important crossroads for trade and, as a result, many Jews passed through the country on their journeys in the region.

In 1849, immigrant Sephardic Jews in Panama founded the Hebrew Benevolent Society, the first Jewish congregation in the Isthmus. They came from the pious congregation of the Netherlands Antilles (Curaçao) to settle in Panama.

Jews from Saint-Thomas (Virgin Islands) and Curaçao founded the Kol Shearith Israel Synagogue in 1876 in Panama City, and in 1890 the Kahal Hakadosh Yangacob in Colon.

By the end of the First World War a number of Middle Eastern Jews had settled in the country and founded the Israelite Benevolent Society Shevet Ahim. During the Second World War, immigrants from Europe arrived in Panama, establishing Beth-El, the only Ashkenazi community in the country. The majority of Jewish community is Sephardi (around 80 per cent).

There have been two Jewish presidents in Panama, the only country – apart from Israel – where this has happened.

GMT -5 hours
Country calling code: (+507)
Total population: 2,719,000
Jewish population: 7,000
Emergency telephone: (Police–104) (Fire–103)
Electricity voltage: 120

PANAMA CITY

BAKERIES
Pita Pan
Plaza Bal Harbour, Paitilla
Telephone: (2) 642-786

BUTCHERS
Shalom Kosher
Plaza Bal Harbour, Paitilla
Telephone: (2) 644-411

Super Kosher
Calle San Sebastian, Paitilla
Telephone: (2) 635-254
Fax: (2) 632-067
Email: mzakay@skosher.com
Supervision: Shevet Ahim Rabbinate
Mailing address POB 8242 Panama 7. Also Kosher supermarket, bakery and restaurant. Open from 8.30 am to 8.30 pm Sunday to Thursday, Friday until 4.30 pm.

CHOCOLATE SHOPS
Candies Bazaar
Via Argentina, 155 L-2
Telephone: (2) 694-857

La Bonbonniere
Calle Juan XXII, Paitilla
Telephone: (2) 645-704

COMMUNITY ORGANISATIONS
Jewish Centre: Centro Cultural Hebreo de Panama
Calle 50 Final, PO Box 7166 55
Telephone: (2) 260-455
Fax: (2) 260-869
(K) Restaurant open daily for lunch and supper. Closed Saturday.

CULTURAL ORGANISATIONS
Consejo Central Comunitario Hebreo de Panama
PO Box 3309 4
Telephone: (2) 638-411
Fax: (2) 647-936

EMBASSY
Embassy of Israel
Edificio Grobman, Calle Manuel Maria Icaza, 5th Floor
Telephone: (2) 648-257

MIKVAOT
Beneficiencia Israelita Beth El
Calle 58, Urb. Obarrio
Telephone: (2) 233-383

Sociedad Israelita Shevet Ahim
Calle 44-27
Telephone: (2) 255-990
Fax: (2) 271-268

RESTAURANTS
Dairy
Pita Pan
Plaza Bal Harbour, Paitilla
Telephone: (2) 642-786

Meat
Shalom Kosher
Plaza Bal Harbour, Paitilla
Telephone: (2) 644-411

Pizzeria
Pizzeria Italiana
Centro Cultural Hebreo de Beneficiencia, Calle 50 Final
Telephone: (2) 260-455
Fax: (2) 260-869

SYNAGOGUES
Ashkenazi
Beneficiencia Israelita Beth El
Calle 58E, Urb. Obarrio
Telephone: (2) 640-058
Fax: (2) 640-058
Mikva on premises

Singoge Beth El
Calle 58 Obarrio
Telephone: (2) 233-383
Fax: (2) 640-058

Orthodox Sephardi
Ahavat Sion
Calle XXIII, Paitilla
Telephone: (2) 651-891
Daily Services. Mikva for women on premises.

Sociedad Israelia Shevet Ahim
Calle 44-27
Telephone: (2) 255-990
Fax: (2) 271-268
Daily services

Reform
Kol Shearith Israel
Av. Cuba 34-16 5
Telephone: (2) 254-100

PARAGUAY

Jewish settlement in this land-locked country came late for this area of South America. The few who came over from Western Europe at the end of the nineteenth century rapidly assimilated into the general population. The first synagogue was founded early in the twentieth century by Sephardis from Palestine, Turkey and Greece. Ashkenazis arrived in the 1920s and 1930s from eastern Europe,and some 15,000 came to the country to escape Nazism, intending to move on into Argentina. Some of these settled in Paraguay.

Paraguay, in more recent times, has accepted Jews from Argentina who were fleeing from the military regime.

Today there are three synagogues, a Jewish school and a Jewish museum in Asuncion. There is a high rate of intermarriage, but children of mixed marriages may receive a Jewish education.

GMT -5 hours
Country calling code: (+595)
Total population: 5,085,000
Jewish population: 900
Emergency telephone: (Police–00) (Fire–00)
(Ambulance–00)
Electricity voltage: 220

ASUNCION
COMMUNITY ORGANISATIONS
Chad-Lubavitch Center
Paraguari 771, Asuncion
Telephone: (21) 228-669
Fax: (21) 440-598

Consejo Representativo Israelita de Paraguay
General Diaz 657, PO Box 756
Telephone: (21) 441-744
Fax: (21) 448-289

EMBASSY
Embassy of Israel
Calle Yegros No. 437 C/25 de Mayo , Edificio San Rafael, Piso 8, PO Box 1212
Telephone: (21) 495-097; 496-043; 496-044
Fax: (21) 496-355

SYNAGOGUES
Asuncion Synagogue
General Diaz, 657

PERU

The first Jews in Peru arrived with the first Europeans, as many *Conversos* were officers in the Spanish army which invaded the country in 1532. After the Inquisition was set up in 1570,the Jews were persecuted, and many were burned alive. From 1870 groups of Jews came over from Europe, but tended to disappear into the general population. In 1880, a group of North African Jews settled in Iquitos and worked in the rubber industry. More Jewish immigration occurred after the First World War, and later,Nazi refugees entered the country. By the end of the Second World War the Jewish population had reached 6,000, but this subsequently declined.

Almost all of the present Jewish population are Ashkenazi.There are two Jewish newspapers, and most Jewish children go to the Colegio Leon Pinelo school, which is well known for its high standards. There is a cemetery at Iquitos built by the nineteenth-century community. The community is shrinking owing to intermarriage and assimilation.

GMT -5 hours
Country calling code: (+51)
Total population: 25,015,000
Jewish population: 3,000
Emergency telephone: (Police–105) (Fire–116)
(Ambulance–470 5000)
Electricity voltage: 220

LIMA

COMMUNITY ORGANISATIONS

Asociacion Judia de Beneficencia y Culto de 1870
Libertad 375, Miraflores 18
Telephone: (1) 445-1089
Fax: (1) 445-1089
Email: AJBC1870@terra.com.pe

EMBASSY

Embassy of Israel
Natalio Sanchez 125 sexto Piso, Santa Beatriz 1
Telephone: (1) 433-4431
Fax: (1) 433-8925

GROCERIES

Minimarket Kasher
Av. Gral. Juan A. Pezet 1472, San Isidro 27
Telephone: (1) 264-2187
Fax: (1) 264-2187
Email: minimarket@terms.com.pe
Supervision: Rabbinate of the Union Israelita del Peru
Hours of opening: Monday to Thursday 9.00 am to 6.00 pm,
Friday 9.00 am to 3.00 pm.

HOTELS

Hotel Libertador
Los Eucaliptos 550, San Isidro, 27
Telephone: (1) 421-6680
Fax: (1) 442-3011
Website: www.libertador.com.pe
A short walk away from the Union Israelita Synagogue

KASHRUT INFORMATION

Chief Rabbi Abraham Benhamu
Telephone: (1) 442-4505
Fax: (1) 442-8147
Email: absolben@terra.com.pe
Rabbi Benhamu is the Chief Rabbi of Peru

KOSHER FOODS

Salon Majestic
Av. Bolivar 965, Pueblo Libre, 21
Telephone: (1) 463-0031
Fax: (1) 461-8912
Supervision: Chief Rabbi Abraham Benhamu
Catering for special groups and parties by prior
arrangement only

MEDIA

Newspapers
Menora
Jose Quinones 290, Miraflores 18
Telephone: (1) 441-3461
Fax: (1) 422-5796
Email: jta_bnaibrith@terra.com.pe
Daily

Shofar
Jose Bielovucic 1350, Lince 14
Telephone: (1) 440-0853
Fax: (1) 440-0853
Bimonthly

MIKVAOT

Beit Jabad Peru
Av. Salaverry 3075, San Isidro 27
Telephone: (1) 264-6060
Fax: (1) 264-5499
Email: chabadperu@telefonica.net.pe
Website: www.lp.edu.pe/jabad
Mikveh, daily minyan, kosher meals

Union Israelita
Ave. Gral. Juan A. Pezet 1472, San Isidro, 27
Telephone: (1) 264-2187
Sociedad Israelita Sefardi;,beit Jabad

MUSEUMS

Inquisition and Congress Museum
Juin 548 1
Telephone: (1) 311-7801, 311-7777 anexo 2910
Fax: (1) 311-7801
Website: www.congreso.gob.pe/museo.htm
The museum is open from Monday to Sunday, from 9.00
am to 5.00 pm. The services are free and the tour is given in
Spanish, French, Italian, German and Portuguese.

Museum of the Inquistion
Junin 548 1
Telephone: (1) 427-0365
Dungeon and torture chamber of the headquarters of the
Inquisition for all Spanish South America from 1570 to
1820

SYNAGOGUES

Conservative
Asociacion Judia de Beneficiencia y Culto de 1870
Jose Galvez 282, Miraflores 18
Telephone: (1) 445-1089, 445-5148
Fax: (1) 445-1089
Email: AJBC1870@terra.com.pe

Orthodox
Beit Jabad
Av. Salaverry 3095, San Isidro, 27
Telephone: (1) 264-6060
Fax: (1) 274-5499
Email: chabadperu@unired.net.pe
Website: www.lp.edu.pe/jabad
Synagogues (services daily), mikva, kosher food

Sciedad de Beneficiencia Israelita Sefardi
Enrique Villar 581, Santa Beatriz, 1
Telephone: (1) 471-7230
Fax: (1) 422-8147
Email: absolben@terra.com.pe

Union Israelita del Peru
Av. Dos de Mayo 1815, San Isidro 27
Telephone: (1) 421-3688
Fax: (1) 421-3684
Website: www.orbita.starmedia.com/~uiperu
Services are held at the Centro Sharon

TOURIST SITES
Pilatos House
Ancash 390, Lima 1
Telephone: (1) 427-5814
Seventeenth-century private mansion, now used by the
Constitutional Court. On the 2nd floor was the synagogue
of the *Converso* Jews. Located in front of the San Francisco
Monastery.

PHILIPPINES REPUBLIC

Conversos who came with the Spanish in
the sixteenth century were the first Jewish
presence in the region. In the late nineteenth century, western European Jews
came to trade in the area, and after the
Americans occupied the country in 1898,
more Jews arrived from a variety of places,
including the USA and the Middle East. The
first synagogue was built in 1924. The
Philippines accepted refugees from Nazism,
but the Japanese occupied the islands
during the war and the Jewish population
was interned. After the war many of the
community emigrated. However, a new synagogue opened in 1983, and services are
also held in the US Air Force bases around
the country.

GMT +8 hours
Country calling code: (+63)
Total population: **73,527,000**
Jewish population: **100**
Electricity voltage: **220**

MANILA
EMBASSY
Embassy of Israel
Trafalgar Plaza 23rd Foor, 105 H.V. de la Costa
Street, Salalcedo Village, Makkati City 1200
Telephone: (2) 891-5329/30/31/34
Fax: (2) 894-1027
Email: israelembph@netasia.net
Postal address: POB 1697 MCPO, Makati Metro, Manilla
1299

MIKVAOT
**Jewish Association of the Philipines (Beth
Yaacov Synagogue)**
110 H.V. de la Costa Corner Tordesillas West,
Salcedo Village, Makati City, Metro Manila 1227
Telephone: (2) 825-0265
Fax: (2) 840-2566
Email: jap.minila@usa.net
By arrangement.

SYNAGOGUES
Orthodox Sephardi
Beth Yaac Synagogue
110 H.V. de la Costa Corner Tordesillas West,
Salcedo Village, Makati City, Metro Manila 1227
Telephone: (2) 815-0265
Fax: (2) 840-2566
Email: jap.manila@usa.net
Services; Friday at 6.30 pm, Saturday at 9.30 am

POLAND

After just five years of German occupation
in the Second World War the thousand-
year-old Jewish settlement in Poland, one
of the largest Jewish communities in the
world, had been almost totally eradicated.
Jews came to Poland in order to escape
anti-semitism in Germany in the early
Middle Ages. They were initially welcomed
by the rulers, and Jews became greatly
involved in the economy of the country.

Until 1918 most Jews lived in the east and
south of the country, under Russian and
Austrian domination, respectively.

After 1918, Poland became an independent
country once more, with over 3,000,000
Jews (300,000 in Warsaw.) The community
continued to flourish before 1939, with
Yiddish being the main language of the
Jews. The community was destroyed in
stages during the war, as Poland became
the centre for the Nazi's destruction of
European Jewry. After the war, the borders
shifted again, and the 100,000 or so survivors mostly tried to emigrate. The few
who remained endured several programs
even after the events of the Holocaust.

Today the community is comparatively
small and most of the members are elderly,
but there is a functioning synagogue in
Warsaw and many Jewish historical sites
are scattered throughout the country. The

Polish Tourist Board publishes information about the Jewish heritage in Poland.

GMT +1 hours
Country calling code: (+48)
Total population: 38,650,000
Jewish population: 5,000
Emergency telephone: (Police–997) (Fire–998) (Ambulance–999)
Electricity voltage: 220

BIELSKO-BIALA
ORGANISATIONS
Elzbieta Wajs
ul. Mickiewicza 26-43-300
Telephone: (2) 22438

CRACOW
BOOKSELLERS
Jarden
2 Szeroksa Street, Miodowa 41
Telephone: (12) 217-166

COMMUNITY ORGANISATIONS
The Jewish Religion Congregation
2 Skawinska Street
Telephone: (12) 429-5735
Mondays to Thursdays 9.00 am to 2.00 pm, Friday 9.00 am to 12.00pm

CULTURAL FESTIVAL
Jewish Culture Festival
ul. Jozeeta 36 31-056
Telephone: (12) 431-1517, 431-1535
Fax: (12) 431-2427
Email: office@jewishfestival.art.pl
Website: www.jewishfestival.pl
The 15th annual Jewish Festival will be held between July 1st and July 9th 2006 in the restored Jewish quarter of Kasimierz

HOTELS
Kosher
Hotel Eden
ul. Ciemna 15, Cracow 31057
Telephone: (12) 430-6565
Fax: (12) 430-6767
Email: eden@hotelede.pl
Website: www./hoteleden.pl

MUSEUMS
Museum of the History and Culture of the Cracow Jews
The Old Syngogue, 24 Szeroka Street 31-053
Telephone: (12) 422-0962
Fax: (12) 431-0545
Email: starasynagogue@mhk.pl
Website: www.mhk.pl

ORGANISATIONS
Judaica Foundation
ul. Rabina Meiselsa 17
Telephone: (12) 423-5595
Fax: (12) 423-5034
Email: uwrussek@cyf-kr.edu.pl

RESTAURANTS
Meat
Na Kazimierzu
ul Szeroka 39 31-053
Telephone: (12) 229-644
Fax: (12) 219-909
Billed as the 'only kosher restaurant in Cracow and the south of Poland'. Hours: 12.00 pm to 12.00 am everyday. Traditional Shabbat courses are available on Shabbat.

SYNAGOGUES
Isaac Synagogue
18 Kupa Street
Fax: (12) 602-144-262
Email: synagogaizaaka@eranet.pl
Contact Dominik Dybek

Remuh
ul Szeroka 40
Built in 1557 the synagogue is named after Rabbi Moses Isserles the son of its founder, who is buried in the adjacent cemetery. For information; contact 603-860-373 (mobile).

TOURIST SITES
Temple Synagogue
24 Miodowwa Street
Built in 1862 it was used by the Germans during the war as a stable, and is currently being restored

GLIWICE
CONTACT INFORMATION
Gliwice Synagogue
ul Dolnych Walow 9 44100
Telephone: (32) 314-797

KATOWICE
Tourist Information
ul. Mlynska 13 40098
Telephone: (32) 537-742

LEGNICA
Tourist Information
ul. Chojnowska 37 59220
Telephone: (76) 22730

LODZ
COMMUNITY ORGANISATIONS
Jewish Congregation
Zachodinia 78
Telephone: (42) 335-156

RELIGIOUS ORGANISATIONS
Jewish Chabad
Telephone: (42) 331-221, 336-825

LUBLIN
Once a major Jewish town in eastern Europe, Lublin today has fewer than a hundred Jews. Pre-war Lublin was a centre for Torah study, and a large yeshivah was built only a few years before the Second World War, now used as a dental college. Majdanek Concentration Camp lies within the city's boundary. There is a particularly moving memorial in the camp, consisting of the ashes from the camp's crematoria.

CONTACT INFORMATION
Tourist Information
ul. Lubartowska 10 20080
Telephone: (81) 22353

OSWIECIM
MUSEUMS
Auschwitz - Birkenau State Museum
al. Wiezniow Oswiecimie 20 32-620
Telephone: (33) 844-8102
Fax: (33) 843-1934
Email: muzeum@auschwitz.org.pl
Website: www.auschwitz.org.pl

Auschwitz Jewish Center and Chevra Lomdei Mishnayot Synagogue
Pl. Skarbka 5 32-600
Telephone: (33) 844-7002
Fax: (33) 844-7003
Email: info@ajcf.pl
Website: www.ajcf.pl
Hours of opening: April to September: 8.30 am to 8.00 pm; October to March:8.30 am to 6.00 pm; the center is closed on Saturday and Jewish holidays.

RZESZOW
Rzeszow Synagogue
ul Bonicza, edge of Pl. Ofiara Getta

SZCZECIN
Tourist Information
ul. Niemcewicza 2 71553
Telephone: (91) 221-674

WARSAW
Before the war Warsaw had approximately 300,000 Jews. Now there are only a couple of thousand, mostly elderly. There are many sites which can be visited, such as surving fragments of the Ghetto walls and 'A memorial Route to the struggle and Martyrdom of the Jews 1940-1943' known as 'Memory Lane'. The old Jewish cemetery, untouched by the Nazis, is very imposing and is still in use. The Warsaw Ghetto fighters are included in the inscription to Tomb of the Unknown Soldier in the centre of the city. In 2002 the Nozyk synagogue celebrated its centenary.

EMBASSY
Embassy of Israel
ul. Krzywickiego 24 02-078
Telephone: (22) 825-0028
Fax: (22) 825-1607
Website: www.warsaw.mfa.gov.il

MIKVAOT
Nozyk Synagogue
6 Twarda Street
Telephone: (22) 652-2805, 620-4324
Fax: (22) 652-2805, 620-1037
Email: varshe@jewish.org.pl
Website: www.jewish.org.pl; warsaw.jewish.org.pl
Contact: Sharona Kanofsky tel: 652-2150.

MONUMENT
Monument to the Ghetto Heroes
Zamenhofa
Erected in 1948 this monument symbolises the heroic Ghetto defiance of the 1943 uprising

ORGANISATIONS
The Jewish Historical Institute
3/5 Tlomackie Street 90
Telephone: (22) 827-9221
Fax: (22) 827-8372
Email: secretary@jhi.pl
This establishment has a remarkable collection of Judaica. It includes a library of documents on the manuscripts stolen by the Germans from all over Europe.

RESTAURANTS
Menora
Plac Grzybowski 2
Telephone: (22) 203-754

Nove Miasto Ecological Restaurant
Rynek Nowego Miasta 13/15
Telephone: (22) 831-4379
Fax: (22) 831-4379
Website: www.novemiasto.waw.pl

Panorama
Al Witsoa 31
Telephone: (22) 642-0666

Salad Bar
ul. Tamka 37
Telephone: (22) 635-8463

SYNAGOGUES
Nozyk Synagogue, Jewish Community of Warsaw, Union of Jewish Communities in Poland.
6 Twarda Street 00-950
Telephone: (22) 620-4324
Fax: (22) 620-1037
Email: varshe@jewish.org.pl
The synagogue was renovated 1977-83 and is well worth a visit. It is the only pre- war synagogue still standing in Warsaw. Visitors welcomed. Friday night dinner available. Kosher store in the synagogue.

THEATRE
Jewish National Theatre
Plac Grybowski 12/16
Performances are given in Yiddish

TOURS
Shalom Travel Service
Twarda Street 6 00-105
Telephone: (22) 652-2802
Fax: (22) 652-2803
Email: shalom@jewish.org.pl

WROCKLAW
MUSEUMS
Historical Museum
Slezna Street 37
Telephone: (71) 678-236

PORTUGAL

Portuguese Jewry had a parallel history to Spanish Jewry until the twelfth century, when the country emerged from Spain's shadow. Jews worked with the Portuguese kings in developing the country. However, they were heavily taxed and had to live in special areas, although they were free to practise their religion as they pleased. As a result the community flourished.

Persecution began during the period of the Black Death, and the Church was a key instigator of the riots which broke out against the Jews. After the Inquisition in neighbouring Spain many Jews fled to Portugal but were expelled in 1496. Many Jews converted in order to remain in the country and help with the economy. These became the Portuguese *Conversos* and

some of their descendants are converting back to Judaism today.

Over the last century and a half Jews have begun to re-enter the country, and many others used it as an escape route to America during the last war. Most of the community are Sephardi, and there is a Sephardi synagogue in Lisbon. There is also a central Jewish organisation which is a unifying force for Jews in the country.

GMT +0 hours
Country calling code: (+351)
Total population: 9,921,00
Jewish population: 800
Emergency telephone: (Police–115) (Fire–115) (Ambulance–115)
Electricity voltage: 220

ALGARVE
COMMUNITY ORGANISATIONS
Jewish Community of Algarve
Rua Judice Biker 11-5'.; Portimo 8500-701
Telephone: (282) 416-710
Fax: (282) 416-515
Email: Ralf.Pinto@sapo.pt
Website: www.mibdevelopment.com/faro

MUSEUMS
Faro Jewish Cemetery and Isaac Bitton Museum
Telephone: (282) 416-710
Fax: (282) 416-515
Email: Ralf.Pinto@supo.pt
Website: www.mibdevelopment.com/faro
Only remaining vestige of the first post-Inquisition Jewish presence in Algarve. Open weekday mornings from 9.30 am to 12.30 pm. Situated opposite entrance to Faro Hospital. Enquiries to Ralf Pinto, Jewish Community of Algarve

BELMONTE
COMMUNITY ORGANISATIONS
Jewish Community of Belmonte
Apt. 18, Bairo de Santa Maina 6250
Telephone: (275) 912-465
Fax: (275) 912-465

LISBON

Jews settled in Lisbon in the 12th century. Many Jews were prominent in court circles. In 1496 when the Jews were expelled Lisbon was chosen as a point of embarkation.

In the Alfama district, Lisbon's oldest, is the Rua de Judiara and at 8 Beco dos Barretas is the site of what is believed to be an ancient synagogue.

The first official synagogue dates from 1813. The Shaar-7 kuah synagogue, opened in 1904, was constructed inside a garden because legislation at that time did not permit non-Catholic places of worship to be directly on a public highway. It was classified as a 'Building of Public Interest' in 1997.

Communal Offices

Rua do Monte Olivete 16-r/c 1200-280
Telephone: (21) 393-1130
Fax: (21) 393-1139
Email: secretaria@cilisboa.org
Website: www.cilisboa.org

Jewish Club & Centre

Rua Rosa Araujo 10
Telephone: (21) 385-8604

EMBASSY

Embassy of Israel

Rua Antonio Enes 16-4 1020-025
Telephone: (21) 355-3640
Fax: (21) 355-3658
Email: israemb@mail.telepac.pt

JEWISH TOURS

Jewish Heritage Tours

Avenida 5 de Outubro, 321 1649-015
Telephone: (21) 791-9954
Fax: (21) 791-9959
Email: fit.lisboa@space.pt
Website: www.jewishheritage.pt

Tours to explore Jewish ancestral roots in Portugal and to meet the descendants of the *Conversos*, the 'secret' Jews.

KOSHER FOODS

Mrs R. Assor

Rua Rodrigo da Fonseca 38.1'D
Telephone: (21) 386-0396
Fax: (21) 385-6336
Email: iassor@mail.telepac.pt

Kosher meals and delicatessen are obtainable if prior notice is given. For kosher meals, contact the communal offices.

SYNAGOGUES

Ashkenazi

Ohel Jacob,

Rua Elias Garcia 110
Telephone: (21) 7971-033

OPORTO

SYNAGOGUES

Mekor Haim

Rua Guerra Junqueiro 340

TOMAR

TOURIST SITES

Sephardi Museum

Between Rua Direita dos A ougues and Rua dos Moinhos

There is an interesting Sephardi museum in the old synagogue

PUERTO RICO

The Jewish community in Puerto Rico is just over 100 years old, with the first Jews arriving from Cuba in 1898 after the beginning of American rule. During the Second World War, many Jewish American servicemen went to the island, along with refugees from Nazism. The Jewish Community Centre dates from the early war years. After the war the community grew with an influx of Cuban and American Jews.

The Capital,San Juan, has the largest Jewish population, and there are two synagogues. There is also a Hebrew school,held in the Community Centre. The first Chief Justice of Puerto Rico was Jewish.

GMT -4 hours
Country calling code: (+1 787)
Total population: 3,771,000
Jewish population: 2,500
Emergency telephone: (Police–343-2020)
(Fire–343-2330)
Electricity voltage: 120

ISLA VERDE

SYNAGOGUES

Orthodox

Chabad of Puerto Rico

18 Rosa Street 00979
Telephone: (787) 253-0894
Fax: (787) 791-3187
Email: Rabbi@chabadpuertorico.com
Website: www.chabadpuertorico.com

Notes: Kosher takeout available, for menu please call (787)-723-0894

Postal Address: PMB 122 5900 Isla Verde Ave L-2

SAN JUAN-SANTURCE
SYNAGOGUES
Shaare Zedeck
903 Ponce de Leon Av., Santurce 00907
Telephone: (787) 724-4157
Fax: (787) 722-4157
Services: Monday 7.00 am, Thursday 7.00 am, Kabalat Shabbat Friday 6.30 pm, Shabbat 9.00 am, Sunday 9.00 am

Reform
Temple Beth Shalom
San Jorge Av. & Loiza St., 00907
Email: ctbs@att.net.
Website: www.uahc.org/congs/ot/ot023

REUNION
SYNAGOGUES
Communaute Juive de la Reunion
8 rue de l'Est, 97400
Telephone: 23-78-83
High Holy Day services and communal seder held here.

ROMANIA
Romanian Jewry began at the time the Romans gave the country its name and language. In the fifteenth century community life had begun to be organised, and settlement had spread to the town of Iasi and some Moldavian towns. Jews were welcomed from Poland and other east European countries, despite the opposition of the Church. Over the years the community grew in size with further immigration, but emigration became the dominant factor after 1878, when the Treaty of Berlin, which demanded equal rights for Jews, was not implemented in Romania. Following Romania's acquisition of the large area of Transylvania from Hungary after 1918, the Jewish population increased once more. The Jews were finally emancipated, but harsh discriminatory decrees were passed in 1937, and Romania's alliance with Nazi Germany during the war led to 385,000 of the 800,000 Romanian Jews being killed in the Holocaust.

It is ironic that Romanian Jewry was able to function relatively normally under the harsh Ceausescu regime. He was the only Warsaw Pact leader not to sever relations with Israel in 1967, and he allowed Jewish practices to continue, even permitting the then Chief Rabbi, Dr Moses Rosen, to have a seat in the parliament. This freedom also tolerated emigration to Israel, which was seen by Ceausescu as being advantageous to Romania. Post-1989 the community still has its central body, the Federation of Jewish Communities, and there are kosher cafeterias in several cities. The community is ageing, but many synagogues are still functioning, and there are also Jewish newspapers and a Yiddish theatre.The Choral Synagogue in Bucharest is of particular interest to visitors.

GMT +2 hours
Country calling code: **(+40)**
Total population: **22,520,000**
Jewish population: **12,000**
Emergency telephone: **(Police–995) (Fire–981) (Ambulance–961)**
Electricity voltage: **220**

ARAD
COMMUNITY ORGANISATIONS
Community Offices
10 Tribunal Dobra Street
Telephone: (257) 281-310

RESTAURANTS
Ritual
22, 7 Episcopei Street
Telephone: (257) 280-731

SYNAGOGUES
Muzeul Judetean
Piata George Enescu 1
Telephone: (257) 280-114

Neologa
10 Tribunal Dobra Street

Orthodox
Arad Synagogue
12 Cozia Street

BACAU
COMMUNITY ORGANISATIONS
Community Offices
11 Alexandru cel Bun Street
Telephone: (234) 134-714

RESTAURANTS
Kosher Restaurant
11 Alexandru cel Bun Street

SYNAGOGUES
Avram A. Rosen Synagogue
31 V. Alecsandri Street

Cerealistilor
29 Stefan cel Mare Street

BOTOSANI
COMMUNITY ORGANISATIONS
Community Offices
220 Calea Nationala
Telephone: (231) 0315-14659

MIKVAOT
Botosani Mikvaot
67 7 Aprilie Street

RESTAURANTS
Kosher Restaurant
69 7 Aprilie Street
Telephone: (231) 0315-15917

SYNAGOGUES
Botosani Synagogue
1a Marchian Street

Mare
18 Muzicantilor Street

Yiddish
10 Gh. Dimitrov Street

BRASOV
COMMUNITY ORGANISATIONS
Community Offices
27 Poarta Schei Street 500020
Telephone: (268) 143-532
Mobile Phone: 0040744327105
Central organisation: Federation of Jewish Communities

RESTAURANTS
Kosher Restaurant
27 Poarta Schei Street
Telephone: (268) 144-440

SYNAGOGUES
Brasov Synagogue
27 Poarta Schei Street

BUCHAREST
COMMUNITY ORGANISATIONS
Federation of Jewish Communities of Romania
Str. Sf. Vineri 9-11, Sector 3 030202
Telephone: (21) 313-2538
Fax: (21) 312-0869
Email: asivan@pcnet.ro
Website: www.romanianjewish.org /
www.jewish.ro

Kosher supervision on 9 restaurants in the main Jewish communities of Romania; (Arad, Bacau, Brasov, Bucharest, Cluj, Galati, Ilasi, Orade, Timisoara

EMBASSY
Embassy of Israel
1 Dimitrie Cantemir Bd.
Telephone: (21) 613-2634/5/6

MIKVAOT
Bucharest Mikvaot
5 Negustori Street

MUSEUMS
The History Museum of the Romanian Jews
3 Mamoulari Street
Telephone: (21) 3110870
Fax: (21) 3151045
Hours: Sunday to Thursday 9.00am to 1.00pm

RELIGIOUS ORGANISATIONS
Chief Rabbi of Romania
Strada St. Vineri 9 020481
Telephone: (21) 312-2196
Fax: (21) 312-0869
Mobile Phone: 740540542
Email: sapirjlm@netvision.net.il

RESTAURANTS
Jewish Community
18 Popa Soare Street
Telephone: (21) 322-4067
Fax: (21) 322-4067
Email: fcerdas@com.pcnet.ro
This restaurant is operated by the Jewish Community

SYNAGOGUES
Choral Temple
Strada Sf. Vineri 9, Sector 3
Telephone: (21) 313-1782
Fax: (21) 312-0869
Email: ccmailb@dial.kappa.ro

Credinta
48 Vasile Toneanu Street

Sephardi
Great Synagogue
9-11 Vasile Adamache Street
Telephone: (21) 615-0846

THEATRE
Jewish State Theatre
15 Juliu Barash Str., Sector 3 74212
Telephone: (21) 323-4530
Fax: (21) 323-2746
Email: tes@dnt.ro
Website: www.dnt.ro/users/tes

999

999999999999999999999

CLUJ NAPOCA
COMMUNITY ORGANISATIONS
Community Offices
25 Tipografiei Street
Telephone: (264) 11667

MIKVAOT
Cluj Napoca Mikvaot
16 David Fransisc Street

RESTAURANTS
Kosher Restaurant
5-7 Paris Street
Telephone: (264) 11026

SYNAGOGUES
Beth Hamidrash Ohel Moshe
16 David Fransisc Street

Sas Hevra
13 Croitorilor Street

Templul Deportatilor
21 Horea Street

CONSTANTA
COMMUNITY ORGANISATIONS
Jewish Community Office and Cultural Club
3 Sarmisagetuza Street
Telephone: (241) 611598

SYNAGOGUES
Constanta Synagogue
3 Sarmisagetuza Street

Great Temple Synagogue
2 C.A. Rosetti Street

DOROHOI
COMMUNITY ORGANISATIONS
Community Office
95 Spiru Haret Street
Telephone: (31) 611797

SYNAGOGUES
Great Synagogue
4 Piata Unirii Street

GALATI
COMMUNITY ORGANISATIONS
Community Office
9 Dornei Street
Telephone: (236) 413662

RESTAURANTS
Kosher Restaurant
9 Dornei Street
Telephone: (236) 413662

SYNAGOGUES
Meseriailor
11 Dornei Street

IASI (JASSY)
COMMUNITY ORGANISATIONS
Community Office
15 Elena Doamna Street
Telephone: (232) 114414

MIKVAOT
Iasi Mikvaot
15 Elena Doamna Street

RESTAURANTS
Kosher Restaurant
15 Elena Doamna Street
Telephone: (232) 117883

SYNAGOGUES
Schor
5 Sf. Constantin Street

ORADEA
COMMUNITY ORGANISATIONS
Community Office
4 Mihai Viteazu Street
Telephone: (259) 134843

MIKVAOT
Oradea Mikvaot
5 Mihai Viteazu Street

RESTAURANTS
Kosher Restaurant
5 Mihai Viteazu Street
Telephone: (259) 131383

SYNAGOGUES
Oradea Synagogue
4 Mihai Viteazu Street

PIATRA NEAMT
COMMUNITY ORGANISATIONS
Community Office
7 Petru Rares Street
Telephone: (33) 623815

SYNAGOGUES
Leipziger
12 Meteorului Street

Old Baal Shem Tov
7 Meteorului Street
Old historical monument

RADAUTI

COMMUNITY ORGANISATIONS
Community Office
11 Aleea Primaverii, Block 14, Apt.1
Telephone: (30) 461333

SYNAGOGUES
Radauti Synagogue
2, 1 Mai Street

Vijnitzer
49 Libertatii street

SATU MARE

Satu Mare is the Romanian name for the town
of Szatmar, where the famous Hassidic sect
originated. It is in the north west of Romania,
very near the border with Hungary. Before
World War One the town itself used to be in
Hungary.

COMMUNITY ORGANISATIONS
Comunitatea Evreilor
4/a Decebal Street 440006
Telephone: (61) 713703
Fax: (61) 713703
Email: cesm@rdslink.ro

SYNAGOGUES
Share Tora Sinagogue
4/a Decebal Street 440006
Telephone: (61) 713703
Fax: (61) 713703
Email: cesm@rdslink.ro

SFANTU GHEORGHE

TRAVEL AGENTS
International Tourism and Trade
Jozef Bem Str. 2, SF . Gheorghe , PO Box 152 520023
Telephone: (267) 316-375
Fax: (267) 351-551
Mobile Phone: 744 343 201
Email: it&t@honoris.ro
Website: www.loveromania.com
Central organisation: National Association of Tourism
Agencies (NATA)

SIGHET

COMMUNITY ORGANISATIONS
Community Office
8 Basarabia Street

SYNAGOGUES
Sighet Synagogue
8 Basarabia Street

SUCEAVA

Community Office
8 Armeneasca Street
Telephone: (30) 213084

TIMISOARA

Tourist Information
5 Gh. Lazar Street
Telephone: (56) 132813

MIKVAOT
Timisoara Mikvaot
55 Resita Street

RESTAURANTS
Kosher Restaurant
10 Marasesti Street
Telephone: (56) 136924

SYNAGOGUES
Cetate
6 Marasesti Street

Fabric
2 Splaiul Coloniei

Iosefin
55 Resita Street

TIRGU MURES

COMMUNITY ORGANISATIONS
Community Office
10 Brailei Street
Telephone: (65) 115001

SYNAGOGUES
Tirgu Mures Synagogue
21 Aurel Filimon Street

TUSHNAD

Kosher
Olt Hotel
c/o Interom Tours
Telephone: (972) 3924-6425
Fax: (972) 3579-1720

VATRA DORNEI

COMMUNITY ORGANISATIONS
Community Office
54 M Eminescu Street
Telephone: (30) 371957

SYNAGOGUES
Vijnitzer
14 Luceafarul Street

RUSSIAN FEDERATION

In early Russian history Jews were not
allowed to settle, and the few who did
were later expelled by various Czars. After
1772, however, Russia acquired a large
area of Poland, where a significant number
of Jews.lived There were still restrictions

against the Jews, but eventually they were allowed to settle in the 'Pale of Settlement', an area in the west of the Russian Empire. Between 1881 and 1914 2,000,000 Jews emigrated from the Empire, escaping from anti-semitism.

Jews were only allowed into Russia itself in the mid-nineteenth century, and by 1890 there were 35,000 Jews in Moscow. Most were expelled the following year. The community grew after the Second World War, drawing Jewish immigration from Belarus and Ukraine to cities such as Moscow and Leningrad. Birobidzhan was a failed experiment to give the Jews their own 'Autonomous District', and those who moved there (in the far east, near China) soon moved away. Under communism both religious practices and emigration were restricted, but since 1991 there has been a revival in Jewish learning. There are synagogues functioning in many cities, and there are now 100 Jewish schools. The major threat is still from anti-semitic right-wing groups, who are unfortunately increasing their activity.

GMT +2 to +12 hours
Country calling code: **(+7)**
Total population: **146,100.000**
Jewish population: **300,000**
Emergency telephone: **(Police–02) (Fire–01) (Ambulance–03)**
Electricity voltage: **220**

ASTRAKHAN
Astrakhan Synagogue
30 Babushkin Street

BIROBIDJAN
Birobidjan, the size of Belgium, was created in 1934 as a Jewish homeland in the wilds of Siberia. It was not a success and was effectively terminated in the 1940s. There has, however, now been a resurgence of interest in what was known as the 'Jewish Autonomous District'.

Birobidjan Synagogue
9 Chapaev Street, Khabarovsk Krai

BRYANSK
SYNAGOGUES
Bryansk Synagogue
Narodov Vostoka Street 82 Lermontov Street

Lubavitch
Synagogue of Bryansk
27a Uritskovo Street 241000
Telephone: (832) 445-515

DERBENT
SYNAGOGUES
Derbent Synagogue
94 Tagi-Zade street

Lubavitch
Jewish Community of Derbent
23 Kandelaky Street 368600
Telephone: (8724) 021-731

EKATERINBURG
Ekaterinburg Synagogue
18/2 Kirov Street

IRKUTSK
Irkutsk Synagogue
17 Karl Liebknecht Street

KAZAN
The capital of Tatarstan, an autonomous Russian republic, has 10,000 Jews', an Ort school and its own Jewish newspaper.

SYNAGOGUES
Lubavitch
Synagogue of Kazan
15 Profsouznaya Street 420111
Telephone: (8432) 329-743

KOSTRAMA
Synagogue of Kostrama
16a Sennoi Peroulok 156026
Telephone: (942) 514-388

KRASNOYARSK
Synagogue of Krasnoyarsk
65 Surikova Street 660049
Telephone: (3912) 223-615
Fax: (3912) 440-137
Email: jckras@hotmail.com

KURSK
Kursk Synagogue
3 Bolshevitskaya Street

MAKHACHKALA
Makhachkala Synagogue
111 Yermoshkin Street

MOSCOW

Around 200,000 Jews now live in Moscow, and since the collapse of the USSR in 1991 the community has experienced a revival. The Choral Synagogue on Arkhipova Street, which was built in 1891 and was used during the Soviet regime, is again the focus of Jewish religious life. The Lubavitch movement has its own centre, and there has been an upsurge of interest in Jewish education.

CONTACT INFORMATION
Chief Rabbi of Moscow
Rabbi Pinchas Goldschmidt
Telephone: (95) 923-4788, 924-2424

EMBASSY
Embassy of Israel
Bolshaya Ordinka 56
Telephone: (95) 230-6777
Fax: (95) 238-1346

KOSHER FOODS
Kosher Food
Spassoglinishevsky per., 10

LIBRARIES
Central Library
A Jewish literature reading hall opened in 2002. The hall holds the state Library's Jewish Literature collection.

RESTAURANTS
Kosher Food
The Restaurant on Nikitskaya
Nikitskaya Str., 47
Telephone: (95) 291-4045

Meat
King David Club
Bolshoi Spasoglinishchevsky per. (Arkhipova St.) 6, door code 77
Telephone: (95) 925-4601
Fax: (95) 924-4243
Email: ail@ail.msk.ru
Supervision: Rabbi Pinchas Goldschmidt, Chief Rabbi of Moscow

This kosher food centre serves as a glatt kosher restaurant and a mini hotel. Catering services are available, as are lunchboxes.

Na Monmartre
Vetoshny per., 9
Telephone: (95) 745-5230
Fax: (95) 745-5239
Supervision: Rabbi Berl Lazar

On the 5th floor of a modern shopping centre.(the Frech Gallery Mall) near Redsquare.

SYNAGOGUES
Lubavitch
Chabad Lubavitch
4 Novousushevsky Peroulok 103055
Telephone: (95) 218-0001
Fax: (95) 219-9707
Email: lazar@glasnet.ru

Chabad Lubavitch Synagogue
6 Balshaya Bronya Street 103104
Telephone: (95) 202-4530
Fax: (95) 291-6483
Known as the Polyakov synagogue after the railway and banking family

Darkei Shalom Synagogue
1 Novovladikinsky Peroulok 103055
Telephone: (95) 903-0782
Fax: (95) 903-2218

SYNAGOGUES
Orthodox
Moscow Choral Synagogue
Bolshoi Spasoglinishchevsky per. (Arkhipova St) 10
Telephone: (95) 924-2424

NALCHIK
Nalchik Synagogue
73 Rabochaya Street, cnr. Osetinskaya

NIZHNY NOVGOROD
Lubavitch
Nizhny Novgorod Synagogue
5a Gruzinskaya Street 603000
Telephone: (8312) 336-345
Fax: (8312) 303-759

NOVOSIBIRSK
SYNAGOGUES
Novosibirsk Synagogue
23 Luchezarnaya Street

Lubavitch
Synagogue of Novosibirsk
14 Kominististheskaya
Telephone: (3832) 210-698

PENZA
Penza Synagogue
15 Krasnaya Street

PERM
Perm Synagogue
Pushkin Street

ROSTOV-NA-DONU
Lubavitch
Synagogue of Rostov-na-Donu
18 Gazetny Peroulok 344007

Telephone: (8632) 624-759
Fax: (8632) 624-119

SACHKHERE
Sachkhere Synagogue
145 Sovetskaya Street 105 Tsereteli Street

SAMARA
Samara Synagogue
3 Chapaev Street

SYNAGOGUES
Lubavitch
The Samara Jewish Community Centre
84B Chapaevskaya St 443099
Telephone: (8462) 334-064
Fax: (8462) 320-242
Email: samara@fjc.ru

The community center has a school, kindergarten, library, women's Mikveh, and a kosher lemihadrin kitchen

SARATOV
SYNAGOGUES
Saratov Synagogue
Posadskov Street

Saratov Synagogue
2 Kirpichnaya Street

Lubavitch
Synagogue of Saratov
208 Posadskovo Street 410005
Telephone: (8452) 249-592

ST PETERSBURG
With 100,000 Jews, St Petersburg is witnessing a similar Jewish revival to Moscow. There are opportunities to pray, learn and eat kosher. This was not the case (in general) before 1991 in the USSR. Americans and Israelis are the main motivators behind the revival, but St Petersburg Jewry is also eager to learn about religion, now that there is the freedom to do so.

MIKVAOT
St Petersburg Mikvaot
2 Lermontovsky Prospekt
Telephone: (812) 114-4428
Fax: (812) 113-6209
Email: synagog@peterlink.ru

RESTAURANTS
Meat
Shalom
8 Koli Tomchaka Street
Telephone: (812) 327-5475

SYNAGOGUES
The Grand Choral Synagogue of St. Petersburg
2 Lermontovsky Prospekt 190121
Telephone: (812) 337-2478
Fax: (812) 320-1329
Email: tourismsynagogue@mail.ru

The Synagogue is open daily 8.30 am to 8.00 pm. The daily services are held at the Small Synagogue at 9.00 am. Shabbat services at 10.00 am at the Grand Choral Synagogue. Mikvah is open on request, please call 812 713-6209. Tourism department open daily 11.00am to 7.00 pm except Saturdays and Sundays. Guided tours of the Synagogue and Jewish Museum, cantor concerts, the Jewish city excursions.

TOURS
Zekher Avoteinu Jewish Tourist and Genealogical Agency
Nastavnikov Av., 26-1-318 195298
Telephone: (812) 945-0874
Fax: (812) 560 - 5828
Email: zekhera@hotmail.com
Website: www.zekhera.hypermart.net
Can be contacted in the USA telephone: 001-718-236-6037

Zekher Avoteinu

- General and Jewish sightseeing in Russia and Scandinavia
- Participation in cultural and social life of local communities
- Shabbat hospitality

www.zekhera.hypermart.net

e-mail: zekhera@hotmail.com

Pr. Nastavnikov, 26-1-318, St. Petersburg, Russia, 195298.
Tel: +7-812-945 0874
Fax: +7-812-560 5828

6801 19th Avenue #4c, Brooklyn, NY 11204, USA.
Tel./Fax +1-718-236 6037

TSHELYABINSK
Lubavitch
Synagogue of Tshelyabinsk
PO Box 16187 454091
Telephone: (3512) 633-618, 632-468, 634-971;633-419
Fax: (3512) 632-468
Email: chabadural@mail.ru

TULA
Tula Synagogue
15 Veresaevskaya Street

VLADIKAVKAZ
Vladikavkaz Synagogue
Revolutsiya Street

VOLGOGRAD
Chabad of Volgograd
Novorosiyskaya 43 400087
Telephone: (8442) 378-308
Email: volgograd@fjc.ru

YEKATRINBURG
Lubavitch
Yekatrinburg Synagogue
118/93 Shekmana Street 620144
Telephone: (3432) 236-440
Fax: (3432) 293-054

SINGAPORE

As Singapore developed into an important south-east Asian trading centre in the mid-nineteenth century, some Jewish traders from India and Iraq set up a community there in 1841. A synagogue was built in 1878, and another in 1904. By the time of the Japanese occupation in the Second World War the community had grown to 5,000, and included some eastern European Jews. The Japanese imprisoned the community and took their property. After the war emigration to Australia and the USA reduced numbers, but in recent years Israelis who work in the country and other Jews have moved in. Ninety per cent of the community are Sephardi.

David Marshall, who was a POW in Japan, returned to Singapore and in 1955 became Chief Minister.

One of the two synagogues is used regularly, and there is a mikvahh and a

newsletter. The Sir Manasseh Meyer Community Centre is the hub of Jewish life. The Jewish community today is small and mainly composed of professionals.

Country calling code: (+65)
Total population: **3,737,00**
Jewish population: **300**
Emergency telephone: (Police–999) (Fire–999) (Ambulance–999)
Electricity voltage: **220/240**

COMMUNITY ORGANISATIONS
Jewish Welfare Board
Robinson Road, PO Box 474

CONTACT INFORMATION
Rabbi Abergel
Telephone: 737-9112
Email: mordehai@singnet.com.sg
Contact for more detailed information on the community and availability of kosher products

EMBASSY
Embassy of Israel
58 Dalvey Road S-1025
Telephone: 235-0966
Fax: 733-7008

SYNAGOGUES
Orthodox
Chesed-El
2 Oxley Rise S-0923
Telephone: 732-8832
Services Monday only, Shacharit and Mincha/Maari.

Maghain Aboth Synagogue
24/26 Waterloo Street 187950
Telephone: 337-2189
Fax: 336-2127
Email: jewishwb@singnet.com.sg
Daily and Sabbat services are held, except for Monday when services are held at Chesed-El Synagogue. Because Singapore has equatorial times, Mincha/ Maariv commences at 6.45 pm throughout the year. Shacharit: weekdays, 7.30 am, Friday night Shabbat meal served after evening service. Shabbat 9.00 am. Every Shabbat lunch is served for the community. Breakfast is currently served every morning after services. Mikvah is available for use. For details please contact 737-9112 Rabbi Mordechai Abergel. There are kosher meat, cheeses wine, and other grocery items on sale at the synagogue.

SLOVAKIA

Slovakia has passed through the control of various countries over the centuries, finally gaining independence after the peaceful splitting of Czechoslovakia in 1992. Before 1918 the region was part of Hungary, and many in southern Slovakia, near the Hungarian border still speak Hungarian.

In 1939 the Jewish population in the Slovak area of Czechoslovakia numbered 150,000, but the Hungarians occupied the south of the country and assisted the Germans in deporting Jews to Auschwitz and other camps. Many survivors emigrated after the war, but some remained and are now redis-covering their Jewish heritage. Since inde-pendence, B'nai B'rith and Maccabi have been established, but anti-semitism has re-emerged. There are kosher restaurants in Bratislava and Kosice, and Jewish educa-tion is available once more.

GMT +1 hours
Country calling code: (**+421**)
Total population: **5,383,000**
Jewish population: **5,000**
Emergency telephone: (**Police–158**) (**Fire–150**) (**Ambulance–155**)
Electricity voltage: **220**

BRATISLAVA
Known in German as Pressburg, Bratislava was a key centre of Judaism when Slovakia was under Hungarian rule before the First World War. Bratislava was especially famous for the number of Jewish scholars living there, including the Chatam Sofer. The preserved underground tomb of the Chatam Sofer and other rabbis is now a place of pilgramage.

BED AND BREAKFAST
Chez David
Zamocka 13 81101
Telephone: (2) 544-13824, 544-16943
Fax: (2) 544-12642
Email: recepcia@chezdavid.sk
Website: www.chezdavid.sk
Supervision: Rabbi Baruch Myers

COMMUNITY ORGANISATIONS
Central Union of Jewish Religious Communities in the Slovak Republic
Kozia ul. 21 81447
Telephone: (2) 544-12167, 544-18357
Fax: (2) 544-11106
Email: uzzo@netax.sk

MIKVAOT
Bratislava Mikvaot
Zamocka 13 81101
Telephone: (2) 544-17829
Fax: (2) 544-17814
Email: chabad@mail.eurotel.sk

MUSEUMS
The Museum of Jewish Culture
Zidovska Street 81101
Telephone: (2) 593-49142/3/4
Fax: (2) 593-49145
Email: mzk@shm.sk
Website: www.slovak-jewish-heritage.org
Contact: Prof. Dr. Pavol Mest'an Dr. Sc.

Underground Mausoleum
Contains the graves of eighteen famous rabbis, including the Chatam Sofer. The key is available from the community office.

RESTAURANTS
Meat
Chez David
Zamocka 13 81101
Telephone: (2) 544-13824; 544-16943
Fax: (2) 544-12642
Email: recepcia@chezdavid.sk
Website: www.chezdavid.sk

SYNAGOGUES
Bratislava Synagogue
Heydukova 11-13
Services held Monday, Thursday and Saturday

GALANTA
MIKVAOT
Galanta Synagogue
Partizanska 907

SYNAGOGUES
Galanta Synagogue
Partizanska 907
Daily services held

KOSICE
RESTAURANTS
Meat
Community Centre
Zvonarska Ul 5, Kaschau 4001
Telephone: (55) 622-1047

SYNAGOGUES
Beth Hamidrash
Zvonarska Ul 5, Kaschau
Daily services held

Kosice Synagogue
Puskinova Ul 3, Kaschau

PIESTANY
CEMETERIES
Old Cemetery
Janosikova Ul 606

SYNAGOGUES
Piestany Synagogue
Hviezdoslavova 59
Shabbat and festival services held

TRNAVA
MONUMENT
Monument of Deportees
Halenarska Ul 32
In the courtyard of the former synagogue

SYNAGOGUES
Synagogue
Kapitulska Ul 7

SLOVENIA

Maribor was the centre for medieval Jewish life in what is now Slovenia. Expulsion followed after the Austrian occupation in the late Middle Ages, but in 1867 the Jews in the Austrian empire were emancipated and some returned to Slovenia. The community was never large. During the Second World War the members of the small Jewish community either escaped to Italy, fought with the Yugoslav partisans, or were deported.

There is a Jewish Community of Slovenia, connected to the Croatian community. There is one synagogue in Maribor that is classed as a historic monument and dates from the Middle Ages. There are also some sites from medieval times such as the cemeteries in the capital Ljubljana and Murska Sobota.

GMT +1 hours
Country calling code: (+386)
Total population: **1,987,000**
Jewish population: **Under 100**
Emergency telephone: (Police–93) (Fire–92)
(Ambulance–94)
Electricity voltage: 220

LJUBLJANA
COMMUNITY ORGANISATIONS
Jewish Community of Slovenia
Trzaska 2 1000
Telephone: (61) 2521-836
Fax: (61) 2521-836
Email: jss@siol.net
Website: www.jewishcommunity.si

SOUTH AFRICA

Although some believe that Jews were present in the country at around the time of the first European settlement in the area in the seventeenth century the community only really began in the nineteenth century, when religious freedom was granted. In 1836 the explorer Nathaniel Isaacs published 'Travels and Adventures in Eastern Africa', an important contemporary account of Zulu life and customs.

The year 1841 saw the first Hebrew Congregation in Cape Town, and the discovery of diamonds in the Transvaal later in the century prompted a wave of Jewish immigration.

The main immigration of Jews into South Africa occurred at the end of the nineteenth century, when many thousands left Eastern Europe, the majority from Lithuania (40,000 had arrived by 1910). Although the country did not officially accept refugees from the Nazis, about 8,000 Jews managed to enter the country after their escape from Europe.

Today the community is affluent and has good relations with the government. There is a South African Board of Deputies, and many international Jewish associations are present in the country. There are kosher hotels and restaurants, and Jewish museums. Kosher wine is produced at the Zaandwijk Winery.

GMT +2 hours
Country calling code: (+27)
Total population: **43,336,00**
Jewish population: **80,000**
Emergency telephone: (Police–1011) (Fire–1022)
(Ambulance–10222)
Electricity voltage: 220/250

Eastern Cape

EAST LONDON
Reform
Synagogue
Belgravia Crescent

PORT ELIZABETH

MUSEUMS
Jewish Pioneers' Memorial Museum
Raleigh Street cnr Edward Street
Telephone: (41) 373-5197
Fax: (41) 374-3612
Open between 10.00 am and noon every Sunday. The museum has a ramp for disabled access. It is also a National Monument . For further information visitors may phone Dr Sam Abrahams (41) 583-3671.

SYNAGOGUES
Orthodox
Port Elizabeth Hebrew Congregation
Abraham Levy Centre, Barris Walk, Glendinningvale 6001
Telephone: (41) 373-1332
Fax: (41) 374-3612
Email: peheb@xsinet.co.za

Progressive
Temple Israel
Upper Dickens Street
Telephone: (41) 373-6642

Free State

BLOEMFONTEIN
RELIGIOUS ORGANISATIONS
United Hebrew Institutions
Community Centre, 1 Dickie Clark Street, PO Box 1152
Telephone: (51) 436-2207
Fax: (51) 436-6447
Mornings

SYNAGOGUES
Bloemfontein Synagogue
1 Dickie Clark Street, Dan Pienaar, PO Box 9300
Telephone: (51) 436-2207
Fax: (51) 436-6447
Mikvah also available.

Gauteng

BRAKPAN
RELIGIOUS ORGANISATIONS
Brakpan Synagogue
cnr. Victoria Avenue and Cavendish
Telephone: (53) 832-5652
For further information phone Mr Waner, tel: (011) 740-0903

JOHANNESBURG
The largest city in South Africa also has the largest Jewish community. About 70% of the country's Jews live there (a community of some 55,000) and the headquarters of many of South African Jewry's institutions are housed there. There are more than fifty synagogues in the city.

BAKERIES
Brooklyn Bagel
Shop 7, Lyndhurst Discount Centre, cnr Modderfontein & Pretoria Rds, Lyndhurst
Telephone: (11) 882-2474
Fax: (11) 882-8565
Supervision: Johannesburg Beth Din

Friends Bakery
53 Ridge Road, Glenhazel
Telephone: (11) 440-5094
Fax: (11) 440-5096
Supervision: Johannesburg Beth Din

Shirley's
114 William Road, Norwood
Telephone: (11) 728-0974
Fax: (11) 728-2807
Supervision: Johannesburg Beth Din

Shula's
173 Oxford Road, Rosebank
Telephone: (11) 880-6989
Fax: (11) 880-6605
Supervision: Johannesburg Beth Din

BED AND BREAKFAST
Kosher Bed and Breakfast
124 Third Avenue, Fairmount
Telephone: (11) 485-5006
Fax: (11) 485-5518
Supervision: Johannesburg Beth Din

BOOKSELLERS
Chadbad House books
Fairmount Shopping Centre, George Street, Fairmount
Telephone: (11) 485-1957
Kollel Bookshop
Pick 'N' Pay Shopping Centre, 54 Sixth Ave., Gardens
Telephone: (11) 728-1822
Fax: (11) 728-1813

BUTCHERS
Bolbrand Poultry Shoppe
74-76 George Avenue, Sandringham 2192
Telephone: (11) 640-4080
Supervision: Johannesburg Beth Din

Gallo Manor Kosher Butchery
Morning Glen Shopping Centre, cnr. Braides & Kelvin Sts, Gallo Manor
Telephone: (11) 802-3539
Fax: (11) 802-6546
Supervision: Johannesburg Beth Din

Gardens Kosher
cnr. Grant & 6th Avenue, Norwood 2052
Telephone: (11) 483-3357
Fax: (11) 728-1562
Supervision: Johannesburg Beth Din

Maxi Discount Kosher Butcher
74 George Avenue, Sandringham 2192
Telephone: (11) 485-1485, 485-1486
Fax: (11) 485-2991
Supervision: Johannesburg Beth Din

Nussbaums
434 Louis Botha Avenue, cnr. Main St., Rouxville
Telephone: (11) 485-2303
Fax: (11) 640-4663
Email: nussbaums@telkomsa.net
Supervision: Johannesburg Beth Din

Rishon Balfour
Checker Balfour Park, cnr. Louis Botha & Athol Sts,
Highlands North
Telephone: (11) 786-9626
Fax: (11) 885-1996
Supervision: Johannesburg Beth Din

Saveways Spar
Fairmount Shopping Centre, cnr Sandler and
Livingstone St, Fairmount
Telephone: (11) 640-6592
Fax: (11) 640-3057
Supervision: Johannesburg Beth Din

Trevors
Bramley Gardens Shopping Centre
Telephone: (11) 885-3663
Fax: (11) 887-9502
Supervision: Johannesburg Beth Din

DELICATESSEN AND BAKERIES

Fegel's Kosher Delicatessan
Bramley Gardens Shopping Centre, Shop 1, 280
Corlett Drive
Telephone: (11) 887-9505/6
Fax: (11) 887-9507
Supervision: Johannesburg Beth Din
Hours: Friday, 7.30 am to 4.30 pm; Sunday, 8.00 am to 1.00
pm; Monday to Thursday, 10.00 am to 5.00 pm

Feigel's Kosher Delicatessan
Shop 3, Queens Place, Kingswood Road, Glenhazel
2192
Telephone: (11) 887-1364
Supervision: Johannesburg Beth Din

Kosher King
74 George Avenue, Sandringham
Telephone: (11) 640 6234
Supervision: Johannesburg Beth Din
Hours: Monday to Thursday, 8.30 am to 5.00 pm; Friday,
8.00 am to 3.00 pm; Sunday, 9.00 am to 1 pm

Pick 'N' Pay
cnr. Grant Avenue & 6th Street, Norwood
Telephone: (11) 483-3357
Fax: (11) 728-1562
Supervision: Johannesburg Beth Din

Pie Works and Deli
Shop 35 Greenhill Road, Emmarentia 2195
Telephone: (11) 486-1502
Fax: (11) 486-0580
Email: feigfam@mweb.co.za
Supervision: Johannesburg Beth Din
Hours: weekdays, 8.00 am to 5.30 pm; Friday to 4.00 pm;
Sunday 9.00 am to 2.00 pm

Saveways Spar Supermarket
Fairmount Shopping Centre, cnr. Livingstone St. &
Sandler Avenue Fairmount 2192
Telephone: (11) 640-3056
Fax: (11) 640-3057
Supervision: Johannesburg Beth Din
Hours: Monday to Thursday, 8.00 am to 6.00 pm; Sunday
and public holidays, 8.00 am to 12.00 pm

Shoshana's Bakery
Stan Tech House, cnr. Cross Road and Queens
Square, Glenhazel
Telephone: (11) 85-1039
Supervision: Johannesburg Beth Din

The Pie Works
74 George Avenue, Sea Point, Sandringham 2192
Telephone: (11) 485-2447
Supervision: Johannesburg Beth Din
Hours: weekdays, 8.00 am to 5.00 pm; Friday, to 4.00 pm;
Sunday to 2.00 pm

LIBRARIES

Kollel Library
5 Water Lane, Orchards 2198
Telephone: (11) 728-1308
Fax: (11) 728-8597

MEDIA

Newspapers

The S.A. Jewish Report
Suite 175, Postnet X10039, Randburg 2125
Telephone: (11) 866-0162
Fax: (11) 886-4202
Email: carro@global.co.za

Periodicals

Jewish Affairs
2 Elray Street, Raedene
Telephone: (11) 645-2500
Fax: (11) 645-2559
Email: sajbod@iafrica.com
Quarterly journal of the South African Jewish Board of
Deputies

Jewish Heritage
PO Box 3 7179 Birnham Park 2015
Telephone: (11) 880-1830

Jewish Tradition
PO Box 46559, Orange Grove 2119
Telephone: (11) 485-4865
Fax: (11) 640-7528
Email: isaacrez@yebo.co.za

Publication of the Union of Orthodox Synagogues of South Africa

South African Jewish Observer
PO Box 29189, Sandringham 2131
Telephone: (11) 440-2206
Fax: (11) 786-8155
Email: mizrachi@netactive.co.za
A publication of the Mizrachi Organisation of South Africa

MIKVAOT
Adase Yashurun Mikvah
34 Fortesque Road, Yeoville
Telephone: (11) 648-6300
By appointment only phone Mrs Levy (11) 648-6751

Glenhazel Mikvah (Be'er Rachel)
65 Nicholson Avenue, Glenkay
Telephone: (11) 485-1555
Email: naodawn@global.co.za

Sandton Mikvah
211 Rivonia Road, Morningside
Telephone: (11) 883-4210

RELIGIOUS ORGANISATIONS
The Southern African Union for Progressive Judaism
357 Louis Botha Avenue, Highlands North
Telephone: (11) 640-6614

Union of Orthodox Synagogues of South Africa
58 Oaklands Road, Orchards 2192
Telephone: (11) 485-4865
Fax: (11) 640-7528
Email: jhb@uos.co.za
The office of the Chief Rabbi as well as the Beth Din are located at the same address and phone number

RESTAURANT/COFFEE SHOP
Milchik/Parev
Kosher Kafe
Shop 174, Balfour Park Shopping centre, cnr. Athol Road, Highlands North
Telephone: (11) 440-8822
Fax: (11) 466-1876
Supervision: Johannesburg Beth Din

RESTAURANTS
Dairy
Shula's
173 Oxford Road, Rosebank 2196
Telephone: (11) 880-6969
Fax: (11) 880-6605
Supervision: Johannesburg Beth Din
Pareve and milk restaurant. Hours: Sunday to Thursday, 7.00 am to 11.00 pm; Friday, to 4.00pm; Motzei Shabbat to 1.00 am.

Meat
D.J's Take Away
Balfour Park Shopping Centre, Shop No. 232, Balfour Park 2090
Telephone: (11) 440-1792
Supervision: Johannesburg Beth Din

Marc Chagall's
Upper Level, Balfour Park Shopping Centre, cnr. Athol Road, Highlands North
Telephone: (11) 786-0593
Supervision: Johannesburg Beth Din

On The Square
Shop No. 7, Shell Court, cnr. Craddock Avenue & Baker Street, Rosebank 2196
Telephone: (11) 880-4153; 447-4891
Supervision: Johannesburg Beth Din
Hours: Sunday to Thursday 10.00 am to 3.00 pm; 6.00 pm to 10.00 pm; Motzei Shabbat, 1 hour after Shabbat to 12.00 am

The Junction Grill
4 Dunnottar Street, Sydenham
Telephone: (11) 485-2585
Fax: (11) 485-3707
Supervision: Johannesburg Beth Din

SYNAGOGUES
There are more than fifty synagogues in Johannesburg. Please contact the appropriate Religious Organisation for details

TOURS
African Kosher Safaris
PO Box 51380, Raedene 2124
Telephone: (11) 485-4635
Email: yoni@aksafaris.com
Website: www.aksafaris.com
Kosher tours, safaris and youth camps in Southern Africa for all budgets and interest groups run by Rabbi Yoni Isaacson. Victoria Falls, Cape Town, Garden Route, St Lucia Wetlands, Kruger, Blyde River Canyon etc.

African Safaris Experience
26 Kings Road, Bedfordview
Telephone: (11) 832-5652
Email: ase@cgs.co.za
Website: www.asesouthafrica.co.za

Celafrica Tours
PO Box 357, Highlands North, 2037
Telephone: (11) 887-5262
Fax: (11) 885-3097
Mobile Phone: 82 320 5525
Email: celeste@celafrica.com
Website: www.celafrica.com
The company specialises in kosher tours to southern Africa, for people needing kosher food and Shabbat arrangements

KRUGERSDORP

SYNAGOGUES
Krugersdorp Synagogue
1 Cilliers Street, Monument
Telephone: (11) 954-1367
Fax: (11) 953-4905

PRETORIA

EMBASSY
Embassy of Israel
3rd Floor, Dashing Centre, 339 Hilda Street, Hatfield
Telephone: (12) 342-2693

KASHRUT INFORMATION
Pretoria Council of BOD
Telephone: (12) 344-2372
Fax: (12) 344-2059

KOSHER FOODS
Pick 'N' Pay
Brooklyn Square Mall, Middle Street, Muckleneuk
Telephone: (12) 346-8680
Kosher prepacked food under the Johannesburg Beth Din

Spar
Groenkloof Plaza, George Stonar Drive, Groenkloof
Telephone: (12) 346-5555
Kosher food prepacked under the Johannesburg Beth Din

MUSEUMS
Sammy Marks Museum
PO Box 4197, Old Brokhorstpruit 1
Telephone: (12) 802-1150
Fax: (12) 802-1292
Email: smarks@nfi.co.za
Website: www.afsef.com/sammymarks
Hours of opening: Tuesday to Sunday, 10.00 am to 4.00 pm

RESTAURANTS
JAFFA Old Age Home
42 Mackie Street, Baileys Muckleneuk 181
Telephone: (12) 346-2006
Fax: (12) 346-2008
Email: jaffa@smartnet.co.za
Website: www.jaffa.org.za
Hotel as well, prior booking necessary. Kosher catering, resident mashgiach. Kosher meals, both meat and dairy, available on request.

SYNAGOGUES
Orthodox
Adath Israel Centre
246 Schroder Stresst, Groenkloof
Telephone: (12) 460-7991
Fax: (12) 480-5911
Email: phc@netactive.co.za
Website: www.phc-org.za

Progressive
Temple Menorah
315 Bronkhorst Street, New Muckleneuk, PO Box 1497
Telephone: (12) 467-296

SPRINGS
Springs Synagogue
40 Charterland Avenue, Selcourt
Telephone: (11) 818-2572

KwaZulu-Natal

DURBAN

BED AND BREAKFAST
Beit Ya'akov
75 Windmill Road, PO Box 47314, Greyville 4023
Telephone: (31) 202-7275
Fax: (31) 202-7302
Email: koby@global.co.za
Run by family who are shomer mitzvot

BUTCHERS
Pick 'N' Pay
Musgrave Centre, Berea 4001
Telephone: (31) 201-4208
Bakery as well

COMMUNITY ORGANISATIONS
Council of KwaZulu-Natal Jewry
44 Old Fort Road, Durban 4001
Telephone: (31) 337-2581
Fax: (31) 337-9600
Email: cknj@djc.co.za
Mailing address: PO Box 10797, Marine Parade 4056

Durban Jewish Club
44 Old Fort Road, Durban 4001
Telephone: (31) 335-4450
Fax: (31) 337-9600
Email: cknj@djc.co.za
Mailing address: PO Box 10797, Marine Parade 4056

RESTAURANTS
Café Shalom
Durban Hebrew Congregation, cnr. Essenwood & Silverton Roads
Telephone: (31) 201-5177
Fax: (31) 202-8925

Dairy
Great Synagogue
Cnr. Silverton & Essenwood Roads, PO Box 50044, Musgrave Road 4062
Telephone: (31) 302-1205
Fax: (31) 209-2925
Email: studycentre1@freemail.absa.co.za

SYNAGOGUES
Orthodox
Durban United Hebrew Congregation The Great Synagogue
Cnr. Essenwood & Silverton Roads , PO Box 50044,
Musgrave Road 4062
Telephone: (31) 201-5177
Fax: (31) 202-8925
Email: shul@duhc.org.za

The Vryheid Memorial Shul
Cnr. Old Fort & Plasyfair Rds.
Telephone: (31) 201-5177
Fax: (31) 202-8925
Email: shul@duhc.org.za

Progressive
Durban Progressive Jewish Congregation
369 Ridge Road
Telephone: (31) 208-6105
Fax: (31) 209-2429
Email: dpjc@sbsa.com

UMHLANGA
CONTACT INFORMATION
Chabad of Umhlanga
PO Box 474 4320
Telephone: (31) 561-2487
Fax: (31) 561-5845
Website: www.chabadonline.com/kwazulu-natal
Open all hours. Regular minyanim especially Shabbat and
Yomim Tovim. Ladies' mikvah twenty minutes away. Kosher
hospitality. For kosher tours in Southern Africa contact
Slomo.

Northern Cape
KIMBERLEY
Orthodox
Griqualand West Hebrew Congregation
20 Synagogue Street 8301
Telephone: (53) 832-5652
Fax: (53) 832-3632
Email: ahorwitz@lantic.net

Western Cape
CAPE TOWN
BAKERIES
Checkers
Gallaria Centre, Regent Road, Sea Point
Telephone: (21) 439-6159
Supervision: Cape Beth Din

BOOKSELLERS
Chabad Centre
20 S. Johns Road, Sea Point 8001
Telephone: (21) 434-3740
Email: reception@chabad.co.za
Supervision: Rabbi Mendel Popack

BUTCHERS
Claremont Kosher Butchers and Deli
150 Main Road, Corner Oliver, Sea Point, Claremont
7800
Telephone: (21) 439-6909
Fax: (21) 439-6920
Email: adlercaz@hixnet.co.za
Supervision: Cape Beth Din
Can deliver to your door.

Pick 'N' Pay
Constantia Village
Telephone: (21) 794-5960
Supervision: Cape Beth Din.
Prepacked with Beth Din Hechser sign only

Pick 'N' Pay
Main Road, Claremont
Telephone: (21) 683-2724
Supervision: Cape Beth Din
Prepacked with Beth Din hecher sign only

Pick 'N' Pay
Adelphi Centre, Main Road, Sea Point
Telephone: (21) 434-8987
Supervision: Cape Beth Din

COMMUNITY ORGANISATIONS
Astra Centre incorporating Jewish Sheltered Employment
20 Breda Street, Gardens 8001
Telephone: (21) 465-4200
Fax: (21) 465-4231
Email: jsec@africa.com
Website: www.jsec.org.za

Cape Town Jewish Community Centre
87 Hatfield Street, Gardens 8001
Telephone: (21) 464-6700
Fax: (21) 461-5805
Email: sajbd2@ctjc.co.za

DELICATESSEN
Goldies Nosh Bar
64 Regent Road, Sea Point 8001
Telephone: (21) 434-1116
Fax: (21) 438-3851
Supervision: Cape Beth Din
Sit -down deli and take-away. Meat and pareve. Hours:
Sunday to Thursday, 7.00am to 8.00 pm; Friday, to 5.00 pm.

GROCERIES
Pick 'N' Pay
Centre Point Milnerton
Telephone: (21) 552-2057
Supervision: Cape Beth Din
Prepacked with Beth Din Hechser only

Spar
Regent Road, Sea Point
Telephone: (21) 439-0913
Supervision: Cape Beth Din
Prepacked with Beth Din Hechser only

HOTELS
Kosher
The Belmont Shareblock
3 Holmfirth Road, Sea Point 8005
Telephone: (21) 439-1155
Fax: (21) 434-9451
Supervision: Cape Beth
Breakfast and lunch only

LIBRARIES
Jacob Gitlin Library
Albow Centre, 88 Hatfield Street 8001
Telephone: (21) 462-5088
Fax: (21) 465-8671
Email: gitlib@netactive.co.za

MIKVAOT
Chabad Centre
20 S. Johns Road, Sea Point 8005
Telephone: (21) 434-3740
Fax: (21) 434-2821
Email: reception@chabad.co.za
Website: www.chabad.co.za
Supervision: Rabbi Mendel Popack

Mikvah Aaron
31 Arthur's Road, Sea Point 8005
Telephone: (21) 434-3148
Website: www.uos.co.za
Central organisation: Union of Orthodox Synagogues

MUSEUMS
Cape Town Holocaust Centre
88 Hatfield Street, Gardens 8001
Telephone: (21) 462-5553
Fax: (21) 462-5554
Email: admin@ctholocaust.co.za
Website: www.museums.org.za/holocaust
Open Sunday to Thursday 10.00 am to 5.00pm Friday 10.00 am to 1.00 pm

South African Jewish Museum
88 Hatfield Street, Gardens 8001
Telephone: (21) 465-1546
Fax: (21) 465-0284
Email: info@sajewishmuseum.co.za
Website: www.sajewishmuseum.co.za
Open Sunday to Thursday 10.00 am to 5.00 pm; Fridays, 10.00 am to 2.00 pm. Museum shop and café. Closed Saturdays, open Public Holidays

RESTAURANTS
Dairy
Café Riteve
88 Hatfield Street, Gardens
Telephone: (21) 465-1594
Fax: (21) 465-5980
Supervision: Cape Beth Din

Meat
Aron's Place Restaurant & Grill
19/33 Regent Road, Sea Point
Telephone: (21) 439-7610
Fax: (21) 439-7599
Email: avronsplace@netactive.co.za
Supervision: Cape Beth Din
Delivery within 5km radius

Goldies Bakery & Deli
66 Regent Road, Sea Point
Telephone: (21) 439-0628
Supervision: Cape Beth Din

Kaplan Student Canteen
University of Cape Town
Telephone: (21) 650-2688
Fax: (21) 650-3064
Supervision: Cape Beth Din
Lunches, take-away and orders. Meat and pareve. Open Monday to Friday. Closed December/January for varsity holidays and during summer vacation.

Sylvlah's Restaurant
11 Regent Road, Sea Point
Telephone: (21) 433-2303

SYNAGOGUES
Chabad Centre
20 S. Johns Road, Sea Point 8001
Telephone: (21) 434-3740
Email: reception@chabad.co.za
Supervision: Rabbi Mendel Popack

Orthodox
Beit Midrash Morasha
31 Arthur's Road, Sea Point 8005
Telephone: (21) 434-8680
Fax: (21) 434-0314
Email: morasha@cybersmart.co.za

Camps Bay
Chilworth Road, Camps Bay
Telephone: (21) 438-8082
Fax: (21) 438-8082
Email: cbhc@netactive.co.za

Cape Town Hebrew Congregation
84 Hatfield Street, Gardens
Telephone: (21) 465-1405
Fax: (21) 461-7659
Email: cthc@isoft.co.za
Website: www.gardensshul.org

Cape Town Synagogue
Camp Road, Muizenberg
Telephone: (21) 785-5611
Fax: (21) 785-5611

Claremont Hebrew Congregation
Grove Avenue (at Morris Rd.), PO Box 23035, Claremont 7735
Telephone: (21) 671-9006
Fax: (21) 683-3011

Email: info@claremontshul.co.za
Website: www.claremontshul.co.za

Constantia Hebrew Congregation
93 Old Kendal Road, Constantia 7806
Telephone: (21) 713-1818
Fax: (21) 715-3110
Email: constantiashul@herzlia.com
Website: www.shul.org.za

Green & Sea Point Hebrew Congregation
10 Marais Road, Sea Point
Telephone: (21) 439-7543
Fax: (21) 434-3760
Email: gspheb@mweb.co.za

Milnerton
29 Fitpatrick Road, Cambridge Estate 7441
Telephone: (21) 551-0442
Fax: (21) 552-4285

Sephardi Hebrew Congregation
Weizmann Hall, 65 Regent Road, Sea Point
Telephone: (21) 439-1962
Fax: (21) 439-9620
Email: sephardicape@xsinet.co.za

Wynberg Hebrew Congregation
1 Mortimer Road, Wynberg 7806
Telephone: (21) 797-5029
Fax: (21) 797-5029

Reform
Temple Israel
Upper Portswood Road, Green Point
Telephone: (21) 434-9721
Fax: (21) 434-2400
Email: templect@africa.com

TOURS
Lion of Africa
PO Box 64189, Highlands North 2037
Telephone: (21) 640 1608
Fax: (21) 640 1608
Email: lion2@roary.com
Website: www.roary.com

OUDTSHOORN
SYNAGOGUES
United Hebrew Institutions
291 Buitenkant Street
Telephone: (44) 272-3068
Fax: (44) 272-3068
There is a Jewish section in the C.P. Nel Museum

PAARL
Paarl Synagogue
Herzlia School
Telephone: 872-4087
For further information phone Mr Kaufman (083) 325-6603

SPAIN

Spain has an ancient connection with the Jews, and the term 'Sephardi' originates from the Hebrew word for Spain. Beginning in Roman times the Jews have suffered the usual cycle of acceptance and persecution, with a 'golden age' under the Islamic Moorish occupation which began in 711. Great Jewish figures arose from the Spanish community, such as Ibn Ezra and the Ramban. However, the situation changed when the Christians gained the upper hand, and blood libels began. In 1492, almost 100 years after a particularly violent period of persecution, the Jews were expelled from Spain. Many thousands were baptised but practised Judaism in secret (the *Conversos*), and many were caught and burnt at the stake.

Jewish life began again in the nineteenth century. The Inquisition ended in 1834 and by 1868 Spain had promulgated religious tolerance. Synagogues could be built after 1909, and Spain accepted many thousands of Jewish refugees before and during the Second World War. Angel Sanz-Briz alone helped to save thousands of Hungarian Jews by issuing 'letters of protection' and entry visas.

There has been a recent immigration from North Africa, and the community today has a central body and synagogues in several towns (including Torremolinos and Malaga). Rambam's synagogue in Cordoba can be visited, and there are several other old synagogues throughout the country.

GMT +1 hours
Country calling code: (+34)
Total population: **39,270,000**
Jewish population: **14,000**
Emergency telephone: (**Police–092 or 091**)
(**Fire–080**) (**Ambulance–092**)
Electricity voltage: **220**

ALICANTE
COMMUNITY ORGANISATIONS
Communidad Israelita
Apdo. 189, Playa de San Juan 3540
Telephone: (96) 515-1572

SYNAGOGUES
Alicante Synagogue
Vila Carlota, 15 Urb Montivoli, Villajoyosa

SYNAGOGUES
Reform
Synagogue
Belgravia Crescent

BARCELONA

The ancient community of the city lived in the
area of the Calle (from the Hebrew Kahall) and
the cemetery was in Montjuic (Mountain of the
Jews). Most of the original tombstones are now
in the Provincial Archaeological Museum.

BUTCHERS
Carniceria
Porvenir 24
Telephone: (93) 200-3375
Supervision: Barcelona Rabanut

COMMUNITY ORGANISATIONS
Communidad Israelita de Barcelona
Avenir 24 08021
Telephone: (93) 200-6148
Fax: (93) 200-6148

Community Centre
Porvenir 24 8071
Telephone: (93) 200-6148 or 8513
Kosher meals available on request

KOSHER FOODS
Kosher Food Service
Telephone: (93) 439-9934
Email: kosherservice@chabadbarcelona.org
Supervision: Rabbi Libersohn
Mrs Libersohn 607 922 805

MIKVAOT
Barcelona Mikvaot
Povenir 24 8071
Telephone: (93) 200-6148; 8513

RESTAURANTS
Vegetarian
Self Naturista
Carrer de Santa Anna 11-17 08002
Telephone: (93) 318-2684
Fax: (93) 412-5413

SYNAGOGUES
Orthodox
Communidad Israelita de Barcelona
Porvenir 24 8021
Telephone: (93) 200-8513
The first synagogue to be built in Spain since the Inquisition

SYNAGOGUES
Progressive
Communitat Jueva ATID de Catalunya
Castanyer 27, Bajos, Izquierda 8022
Telephone: (93) 417-3704
Fax: (93) 417-3704
Email: atid@arquired.es
Website: www.atid.freeservers.com

TOURS
Urban Cultours Project
Telephone: (93) 417-1191
Fax: (93) 417-1191
Website: www.urbancultours.com
Walk of the Calle (Jewish Quarter) by a Jewish American
architect. Visits to other places of Jewish interest in
Catalonia can also be arranged

TRAVEL AGENCIES
Jewish Travel Agency
Viajes Morava, Consejo de Ciento 380
Telephone: (93) 246-0300

BENIDORM
KASHRUT INFORMATION
Benidorm Kashrut Information
Telephone: (96) 522-9360

BURGOS
During the 13th century Burgos was the largest
Jewish community in North Castie. The Juderia
was in the area of the Calle Fernan Gonzalez.

**There are no other specific locations of
interest to travellers.**

CORDOBA
This is an ancient synagogue (declared as a
monument). Near by, a statue of Maimonides
has been erected in the Plazuela de
Maimonides. The entrance to the ancient
Juderia is near the Almodovar Gate.

TOURIST SITES
Ancient Synagogue
Calle de los Judios 20
This is an ancient synagogue built in 1315 and one of only
three pre-expulsion ones remaining. It was declared a
national monument in 1985. Nearby, a statue of
Maimonides has been erected in the Plaza de Tiberiades
(named to perpetuate the connection between his birthplce
and where he is buried).

EL ESCORIAL
LIBRARIES
San Lorenzon Monastry
The library of the San Lorenzo Monastry contains a
magnificent collection of medieval Hebrew Bibles and
illuminated manuscripts. On the walls of the Patio of Kings,
in the Palace of Philip II, are sculpted effigies of six Kings of
Judah.

ESTELLA
The Jewish community here was one of the most important in the kingdom of Navarre. The Santa Maria de Jus Castillo Church was once a synagogue.

There are no other specific locations of interest to travellers.

GIRONA
ORGANISATIONS
Patronat Municipal Calle De Girona
8 Carrer de la Forca 17004
Telephone: 972 21 67 61
Fax: 972 21 46 18
Email: callgirona@ajgirona.org
Website: www.ajgirona.org/call
Built where there was once a 15th century synagogue, in the heart of the Jewish neighbourhood. It comprises the Museum of the History of Jews and Nahmanides Institute for Jewish Studies. Open May to October: Monday to Saturday 10.00 am to 8.00 pm, Sunday and Bank Holidays 10.00 am to 3.00 pm; November to April: Monday to Saturday 10.00 am to 6.00 pm, Sundays and Bank Holidays 10.00 am to 3.00pm.

GRANADA
Originally the Jewish community was one of the most important in spain. It is believed that the 'lion fountain', in the courtyard of the Alhambra, was a gift from the Jews of the city and is based upon a fountain in King Solomon's palace.

There are no other specific locations of interest to travellers.

HERVAS
This village in the Gredos Mountains, 150 miles west of Madrid has a well-preserved Juderia, which has been declared a national monument. It's main street has been renamed Calle de la Amistad Judeo Cristiana.

There are no other specific locations of interest to travellers.

MADRID
About 3,500 Jews live in Madrid. A new synagogue was completed in 1968, and there is a community centre providing kosher food. The Prado has a number of paintings of Jewish interest.
BUTCHERS
Elias Shoshanna
35 Calle Viriato
Telephone: (91) 446-7847
Fax: (91) 593-0668
Supervision: Harav Ben Dahan, Rabbi of the community.

COMMUNITY ORGANISATIONS
Community Centre
Calle Balmes 3
Telephone: (91) 591-3131
Fax: (91) 594-1517
Email: cjmsecretaria@terra.es

EMBASSY
Embassy of Israel
Calle Velasquez 150, 7th floor 28002
Telephone: (91) 411-1357

GIFT SHOP
Sefarad Handicrafts
Gran Via 54
Telephone: (91) 548-2577, 547-6142
Fax: (91) 548-2577
Email: sefaradgalleries@bravored.com
Jewish religious articles

MIKVAOT
Madrid Mikvaot
Calle Balmes 3
Telephone: (91) 591-3131

MUSEUMS
Museo Arqueologico
Calle de Serrano 13
Permanent exhibition of casts of Hebrew inscriptions from medieval buildings

RESTAURANTS
La Escudilla
Santisima Trinidad 16
Telephone: (91) 445-7380

RESTAURANTS
Kosher Meat & Sephardi Cuisine
Naomi Grill
Pensamiento, 25 28020
Telephone: (91) 5716923
Email: naomikasher@terra.es
Supervision: Rabanut of the Madrid Jewish Community
Take-away and group reservations closed on Friday night until Saturday night

RESTAURANTS
Meat
Community Centre
Calle Balmes 3 28010
Telephone: (91) 591-3131
Fax: (91) 594-1517
Email: secretaria@comjudiamadrid.org
Website: comjudiamadrid.org
For groups only

SYNAGOGUES

Conservative
Congregation Bet El
5 Calle Boix y Moer, 5
Telephone: (91) 662-3241
Email: sinagoga@bet-el.org
Website: www.bet-el.org

Orthodox
Madrid Synagogue
Calle Balmes 3
Telephone: (91) 591-3131
Fax: (91) 594-1517
Email: cjmsecretaria@terra.es
The capital's first synagogue since the expulsion of Jews in 1492 was opened in December 1968. The building also houses the Community Centre, as well as mikvah, library, classrooms, an assembly hall and the office of the community.

TOURS
Alex Benarroch
Telephone: (91) 607 716 642
Fax: (91) 416-4246
Email: koteltravel@hotmail.com
Website:
www.puertademadrid.com/rentacellphone
Jewish heritage tours in Spain and Morocco. Discover Sefarad and Moroccan roots of well known Rabbis. Tours, hotels, kosher food delivered to your hotel, cell phone rental and all travel arrangements. Please contact Alex Benarroch.

MALAGA
BUTCHERS
Carmiceria Kosher
Calle Somera 14 29001
Telephone: (95) 260-4201

MIKVAOT
Malaga Mikvaot
Calle Somera 12 29001

SYNAGOGUES
Malaga Synagogue
Alameda Principal, 47 20B 29001
Telephone: (95) 260-4094

TOURIST SITES
Statue
There is a statue of the eleventh-century Hebrew poet Shlomo Ibn-Gabirol, a native of Malaga, in the gardens outside the Alcazaba Castle, in the heart of the city.

MARBELLA
COMMUNITY ORGANISATIONS
Community Centre
Paseo Maritima

GROCERIES
Hipercor
El Corte Ingles, Section No 16, Puerto Banus
Mrs Jacqueline Ohayon
Telephone: (952) 826-649
Kosher poultry and wine

MEDIA
Periodicals
Edificio Marbella 2000
Paseo Maritima
Focus
PO Box 145 29600
Community journal

SYNAGOGUES
Orthodox
Beth El Marbella Jewish Community
Urbanizacion El Real, KM 184, Jazmines Str. 21
Telephone: (952) 859-395
Fax: (952) 765-783
Email: cimarbella@yahoo.es
Website: www.marbellajewishcommunity.com
About two miles from the town centre to the east. Services: Friday (winter) 7.00 pm, (summer) 8.30 pm; Shabbat morning & fesivals 10.00 am. Mikveh, catering for all occasions. Kosher food available on request, rooms and apartments for rent.

SALAMANCA
RESTAURANTS
Vegetarian
El Trigal
Calle Libreros 20

SARAGOSSA
This city was once a very important Jewish centre. A mikvahh has been discovered in the basement of a modern building at 126-132 Calle del oso.

There are no other specific locations of interest to travellers.

SEGOVIA
The Alcazar contains the 16th Century 'Tower of the Jews'. Calle de la Juderia Vieja and Calle de la Juderia Nueva are the sites of the medieval Jewish quarters, where the former synagogue now houses the Corpus Christi Convent.

There are no other specific locations of interest to travellers.

SEVILLE
The first mention of a Jewish community in Seville was in the 4th century. In 1391 riots broke out and many synagogues were converted into churches. The most important of these and well worth visiting is the Church of

Santa Maria la Blanca.
The Archives of the Indies holds an extensive collection of documents relating to both north and south Americas and include the account books of Luis de Santagel, a *Converso*, who financed Columbus and assisted Jews to leave the country in 1492.

MUSEUMS
Casa de Sefarad – Casa de la Memoria
Calle Judi'os (Esquina calle Averroes) 41004
Telephone: (95) 7203-605
Fax: (95) 4560-670
Email: memorias@teleline.es;
casadesefarad@gmail.com
Website: www.csadesefarad.com

A small museum which contains items from local pre-expulsion Jewish homes and also an exhibition on the Sephardic tradition. There is also an area dedicated to Sephardic (Ladino) music.

SYNAGOGUES
Communidad Israelita de Sevilla
Calle Bustos Tavera 8 41003
Telephone: (95) 427-5517

TARRAGONA
The Cathedral, Calle de Escribanias Viejas has a seventh-century stone inscribed in Latin and Hebrew in its cloister. Some very old coins are preserved in the Provincial Archaeological

Museum. The gate to the medieval Juderia still stands at the entrance to Calle de Talavera.

There are no other specific locations of interest to travellers.

TOLEDO

Though it now has no established community, Toledo is the historical centre of Spanish Judaism. Well worth a visit are two ancient former synagogues. One is the El Transito (in Calle de Samuel Levi), founded by Samuel Levi, the treasurer of King Pedro I, in the 14th century. It has been turned by the Spanish Government into a museum of Sephardi culture. The other, now the Church of Santa Maria la Blanca, is the oldest Jewish monument in Toledo, built in the 13th century. It stands in a quiet garden in what was once the heart of the Juderia, not far from the edge of the Tagus River. Also of interest is the house of Samuel Levi, in which the famous painter, El Greco lived. The house is now a museum of his works.

Plaza de la Juderia, half-way between El Transito and Santa Maria la Blanca, was part of the city's two ancient Jewish quarters, where many houses and streets are still much as they were 500 years ago.

JUDAICA

Casa de Jacob
Calle del Angel 15 45002
Telephone: (925) 216-454
Fax: (925) 216-454
Email: liberia-judaica@casadejacob.com
Website: www.casadejacob.com
We also stock some canned kosher food and wines

TORREMOLINOS

BAKERIES

Panaderia
c/Casablanca, 27 (Local 9B) 29620
Telephone: (95) 374-975
Website: www.perso.wanadoo.es/k
Close to synagogue

HOTELS

N.CH Hotel
5, Plaza Gamba Alegre 29620
Telephone: (95) 237-3780
Fax: (95) 238-2724
Email: nch@n-chhotel.com
Website: www.n-chhotel.com

SYNAGOGUES

Beth Minzi
Calle Skal la Roca 13 29620
Telephone: (95) 383-952
Fax: (95) 237-0444

Sephardi and Ashkenazi services are held on Sabbath morning at 9.30 am and Friday evening services are held at 6.30 pm in winter and 8.30 pm in summer

Rabbi Shaul Khalili
Av. Palma de Mallorca, Castillo S. Luis 29620
Telephone: (95) 237-7414
Fax: (95) 205-4114
Mobile Phone: 627723324
Email: sykhalili@telefonica.net
Website: www.jewish-torremolinas.com

TUDELA

The remains of the Juderia are near the cathedral. There is a memorial stone to the great Jewish traveller, Benjamin of tudela author of Book of Travels (1172/3)

There are no other specific locations of interest to travellers.

VALENCIA

RESTAURANTS

Vegetarian
Buffet Chino Veg
Conde Altea 46
Telephone: (96) 334-7061

La Lluna
San Ramon 23
Telephone: (96) 392-2146

SYNAGOGUES

Valencia Synagogue
Calle Asturias 7-4i
Telephone: (96) 334-3416
Services: Friday evening & festivals

SYNAGOGUES

Conservative
Masorti
Masorti La Javura
Calle Uruguay 59, pta 13 46007
Telephone: (96) 380-2129
Email: atoscano@arrakis.es
Website: www.uscj.org/world/valencia
Tours of medieval Jewish quarter. The synagogue is a room in a private home. Kabalat Shabbat every Friday evening at 8pm. All festivals are celebrated. Rosh Hashanah and Yom Kippur are held in the hotel Astoria Palace (Valencia).

SYNAGOGUES

Orthodox Sephardi
Communidad Israelita de Valencia
Calle Ingeniero Joaquin Benlloch, 29, 1st Floor, Apart #2 46006
Telephone: (96) 334-6848
Fax: (96) 335-27981
Email: civ@ctv.es
Supervision: Madrid Chief Rabbi Mr Moshe Bendahan

Opening hours: Every Friday, 8.30 pm, Jewish Holy Days:
morning 9.00 am, evening 8.30 pm

VITORIA
The monument on the Campo de Judimendi
commemorates the ancient Jewish cemetery
which, following the edict of expulsion in 1492
the town council undertook to take care of, and
never to build over it.

**There are no other specific locations of
interest to travellers.**

Spanish Islands

BALEARIC ISLANDS

Majorca
Majorca's Jewish population today numbers
about 300, although fewer than 100 are
registered with the community. Founded in
1971, it was the first jewish community in Spain
to be officially recognised since 1435. The
Jewish cemetery is at Santa Eugenia, some 12
miles from Palma.

Palma Cathedral contains some interesting
Jewish relics, including a candelabrum with
365 lights, which was originally in a synagogue.
In the Tesoroi room are two unique silver
maces, over 6 feet long, converted from Torah
'rimonimi' brought from Sicily in 1493. The
Santa Clara Church stands on the site of
another pre-Inquisition synagogue. The
Montezion Church was, in the 14th century, the
Great Synagogue. In Calle San Miguel is the
Church of San Miguel, which also stands on the
site of a former synagogue. It is not far from the
Calle de la Plateria, once a part of the Palma
Ghetto.

PALMA
COMMUNITY ORGANISATIONS
Communidad Israelita de Mallorca
Apartado Correos 389
Telephone: (971) 283-799

SYNAGOGUES
Orthodox
**Communidad Israelita de Mallorca (Jewish
Community of Mallorca)**
Palma de Mallorca 7014
Telephone: (971) 283-799
Email: r_ajkatz@hotmail.com
Website:
www.fortunecity.com/victorian/coldwater/252
This synagogue was dedicated to the community in June
1987. Services are held on Fridays and Holy Days. A
communal seder is also held. THe community invites all
congregants and guest to kiddush following the services.

CANARY ISLANDS

Gran Canaria
LAS PALMAS
SYNAGOGUES
Las Palmas Synagogue
Ap. Correos 2142 35080
Telephone: (928) 823-1976

Las Palmas Synagogue
Ap. Correos 2142 35080
Telephone: (928) 823-1976

Tenerife
COMMUNITY ORGANISATIONS
Commundad Israelite de Tenerife
Telephone: (922) 247-296; 247-246

KASHRUT INFORMATION
Tenerife Kashrut Information
General Mola 4, Santa Cruz, Holdings 38006
Telephone: (922) 274-157
Welcomes all Jewish visitors

Overseas Territories
Ceuta is on page 47
Melilla is on page 149

SRI LANKA

Islamic and Samaritan legend relates that
Adam came to the island after his expulsion from Eden and that Noah's Ark came
to rest there. Solid evidence for Jewish settlement was recorded about 1.000 years
ago by Muslim travellers. There was a
small Jewish community when the Dutch
took the island as a colony. This attracted
Jews from southern India to the island
because of the possibility of trade.

There was a plan put forward when the
island came under British rule for mass
Jewish immigration. The Chief Justice Sir
Alexander Johnston appeared to consider
the idea a serious one, but the British government did not act on it. A coffee estate
was founded in 1841 near Kandy by
European Jews.

There is no communal organization on the
island. The Sri Lankans appear supportive
of Israel, despite the government's official

pro-Arab stance. Diplomatic relations with Israel were resumed in May 2000.

GMT +5 1/2 hours
Country calling code: **(+94)**
Total population: **18,552,000**
Jewish population: **Under 100**
Emergency telephone: **(Police – 43 3333) (Fire – 42 2222) (Ambulance – 42 2222)**
Electricity voltage: **230/240**

SURINAME

Suriname's Jewish community is very old. The first Jews settled here in the seventeenth century, escaping from persecution in Brazil. Later Jews came from Britain,after the country passed into British hands. Suriname welcomed more Jewish refugees from the Caribbean and the country became a Dutch colony in 1668, bringing Sephardi Jews from Amsterdam. Eventually, half the white population in the country was Jewish, and there was a 'Jodensavanne' (Jewish savannah), where the Jews owned large sugar plantations. They called the plantations by Hebrew names and built a synagogue in 1685. The community began to decline in the nineteenth century. Recently, many have emigrated to Israel.

Today there are two synagogues in Paramaribo, the capital. The Ashkenazi synagogue, like the one in Curaçao, has a sandy floor which is symbolic of the 40 years in the desert, and was also said to have muffled the footsteps of the *Conversos* as they carried out their Judaism in secret.

GMT -3 hours
Country calling code: **(+597)**
Total population: **437,000**
Jewish population: **200**
Electricity voltage: **110/220**

PARAMARIBO

KASHRUT INFORMATION
Paramaribo Kashrut Information
Commewijnestr. 21
Telephone: 400-236
Fax: 471-154

ORGANISATIONS
Suriname Jewish Community
Keizerstraat 82-84
Telephone: 400-236, 473-896
Fax: 102-380, 471-154

SYNAGOGUES
Sedek Ve Shalom
Herenstr. 20
The entire contents of this eighteenth century synagogue are currently on 'long term loan' to the Israel Museum in Jerusalem. The building is now being used as an internet café.

SYNAGOGUES
Ashkenazi
Neveh Shalom
Keizerstr. 82

TOURIST SITES
Joden Savanah
Sights to see include the Joden Savanah (Jewish Savanah) one of the oldest Jewish settlements in the Americas

SWEDEN

Sweden was under the influence of the Lutheran church until the late eighteenth century, and was opposed to Jewish settlement. Aaron Isaac from Mecklenburg in Germany, a seal engraver, was the first Jew admitted into the country in 1774. The emancipation of Jews in Sweden was a slow process; Jews had limited rights, as they were designated a 'foreign colony'. After a gradual lifting of restrictions in the nineteenth century Jews were fully emancipated in 1870, although the right to hold ministerial office was closed to them until 1951.

The emancipation heralded the growth of the community, and many eastern European Jews found refuge in Sweden at the beginning of the twentieth century. The initial refusal to accept Jews fleeing the Nazis changed to sympathy as evidence for the Holocaust mounted, and in 1942 many Jews and other refugees were allowed into the country, followed, in 1943, by almost all of Danish Jewry. Sweden also accepted Hungarian, Czechoslovakian and Polish Jews after the war.

There is an Official Council of Jewish Communities in Sweden, and many international Jewish groups are represented. There are three synagogues in Stockholm, including the imposing Great Synagogue built in 1870. There are synagogues in other large towns. Although shechita is forbidden, kosher food is imported, and there are some kosher shops.

GMT +1 hours
Country calling code: **(+46)**
Total population: **8,847,000**
Jewish population: **16,000**
Emergency telephone: **(Police–112) (Fire–112)**
(Ambulance–112)
Electricity voltage: **220**

BORAS
COMMUNITY ORGANISATIONS
Jewish Community of Boras & Synagogue
Jewish Organisation of Boras & Synagogue
Varbergsvagen 21, Box 46 50305
Telephone: (33) 124-892
Email: s.rytz@vertextrading.se

GOTHENBURG
The Jewish Community of Gothenburg
Ostra Larmgatan 12 S-411 07
Telephone: (31) 177254
Fax: (31) 7119360
Email: kansli@judiskforsamlingen.se

GROCERIES
Dr. Allards
Gata 4
Telephone: (31) 741-1545

SYNAGOGUES
Conservative
The Jewish Community of Gothenburg
Ostra Larmgatan 12 411 07
Telephone: (31) 177-245
Fax: (31) 711-9360
Email: kansli@judiskforsamlingen.se

Orthodox
Beith Tefilah
Storgatan 5
Telephone: (31) 7117872
Email: info@ben-menachem
Website: www.welcome.to/minyan
Supervision: Chabad
Mikvah on the premises

MALMO
COMMUNITY ORGANISATIONS
Jewish Community Centre
Kamrergatan 11, Box 4198 20313
Telephone: (40) 611-6460, 8860; 976-043 (Rabbi)
Fax: (40) 234-469
Email: rabeli@alfa.telenordia.se

MIKVAOT
Malmo Mikvaot
Kamrergatan 11
Telephone: (40) 118-860

SYNAGOGUES
Orthodox
Malmo Orthodox Synagogue
Foreningsgatan
The Moorish style building celebrated its centenary during 2003

STOCKHOLM
Stockholm has a number of Jewish facilities. In addition, the Raoul Wallenberg Park is worth a visit.

COMMUNITY ORGANISATIONS
Jewish Community Centre
Judaica House, Nybrogatan 19, PO Box 5053 10242
Telephone: (8) 5878-5800
Fax: (8) 5878-5870
Email: info@jf-stockholm.org
Website: www.jf-stockholm.org

Jewish Community of Stockholm
Wahrendensdorffsgatan 3, PO Box 7427 103 91
Telephone: (8) 5878-5800
Fax: (8) 5878-5858
Email: info@jf-stockholm.org
Website: www.jf-stockholm.org
Open Monday to Thursday 9am to 5pm, Friday 9am to 4pm
(closed for lunch noon to 1pm)

EMBASSY
Embassy of Israel
Torstenssongatan 4, PO Box 14006 104 40
Telephone: (8) 663-1465
Fax: (8) 662-5301
Email: israel.embassy.swipnet.se

GIFT SHOP
Menorah: Community Centre Shop
Judaica House, Nybrogatan 19, PO Box 5053 102 42
Telephone: (8) 663-6580

GROCERIES
Kosherian Blecher &Co
Nybrogatan 19, PO Box 5053 102 42
Telephone: (8) 663-6580
Fax: (8) 663-6580
Mobile Phone: 46 70 7928316
Email: Denny.sthlm@hotmail.com
Supervision: Orthodox Rabbi Stockholm
Kosher groceries. Also offers cooked meals such as burgers, sausages, meat sandwiches etc., delivery to groups, hotels

KASHRUT INFORMATION
Rabbi Meir Horden
Jewish Community House, Wahrendorffsgatan 3b,
PO Box 7472 103 91
Telephone: (8) 587-858-00
Fax: (8) 587-858-58
Email: meir.horden@jf-stockholm.org
Website: www.jf-stockholm.org/centret/judendom/kosher
Rabbi Meir Horden supervises kashrut in Stockholm. Look at www.jf-stockholm.org/kosher for the latest updated information.

LIBRARIES
The Jewish Library
Wahrendorffsgatan 3, PO Box 7427 103 91
Telephone: (8) 587-858-34
Fax: (8) 587-858-58
Email: judiska.biblioteket@jf-stockholm.org
Website: www.jf-stockholm.org/biblioteket
The Raoul Wallenberg Room is also on the premises, named after the Swedish diplomat who saved scores of thousands of Hungarian Jews from the Nazis, was arrested by the Russians in Budapest in 1945, and disappeared. Open to the public, it holds 25,000 books on Judaism, Jewish history, particularly Swedish-Jewish history, and other Judaica. Sweden's largest collection of books in Yiddish.

MEDIA
Periodicals
Judisk Kronika
PO Box 5053 102 42
Telephone: (8) 660-3872
Fax: (8) 660-3892
Email: judisk.kronika@swipnet.se

Menorah
PO Box 5053 102 42, 102 42
Telephone: (8) 667-6770
Fax: (8) 663-7676
Email: redaktion@menorah-sweden.com
Website: www.menorah-sweden.com

MIKVAOT
Community Centre
Judaica House, Nybrogatan 19 102 42
Telephone: (8) 5878-5867
Fax: (8) 5878-5870
Email: info@jf-stockholm.org
Website: www.jf-stockholm.org
The Mikva is located in the Judaica House.

MONUMENT
The Holocaust Monument
Wahrendorffsgatan 3
The monument was opened in 1998 by King Carl Gustaf of Sweden, and records over 8,500 Holocaust victims who are relatives of Jews residing in Sweden

MUSEUMS
Jewish Museum
Halsingegatan 2
Telephone: (8) 318-404
Fax: (8) 318-404
Email: info@judiska-museet.a.se
Website: www.judiska-museet.a.se
Arranges exhibitions about the history of Swedish Jewry and is open every day, except Saturday, between noon and 4.00 pm

RESTAURANTS
Community Centre
Nybrogatan 19 102 42
Telephone: (8) 663-6580
Email: info@jf-stockholm.org
Supervision: Rabbi Meir Horden

Kosher lunches at the Community Centre are available during the summer. Dinners can also be arranged at the Community Centre for groups. Contact Mr Ika Tankus, Tel: (8) 647-4475.

Lao Wai
Luntmakargatan 74
Telephone: (8) 673-7800
Supervision: Rabbi Meir Horden

Mino's Caf
Tegnergatan 36
Telephone: (8) 307-742
Jewish North African Cuisine. All meat is said to be kosher but there is no kosher licence.

SYNAGOGUES
Masorti
Great Synagogue
Wahrendorffsgatan 3, PO Box 7427 103 91
Telephone: (8) 5878 -5800
Fax: (8) 587 -85858
Email: info@jf-stockholm.org
Website: www.jf-stockholm.org
Erected in 1876; Services: Monday and Thursday mornings, Friday evenings and Saturday morning. Open for tourists during Summer.

Orthodox
Adat Jeshurun
Riddargatan 5, PO Box 5053 102 42
Telephone: (8) 679-2900
Fax: (8) 663-6580
Daily services: weekdays 7.45 am, shabbat 9.00 am, Sunday 8.30 am. The interior originally comes from a synagogue in Hamburg which survived Kristallnacht in Germany.

Adat Jisrael
St. Paulsgatan 13 11846
Telephone: (8) 679-2900
Situated in an 18th century building it was renovated some 20 years ago. Daily Services: weekdays 7.30 am, Shabbat 9.00 am, Sunday 8.15 am

UPPSALA

ORGANISATIONS
Jewish Students Club
Dalgatan 15
Telephone: (8) 125-453

SWITZERLAND

Swiss Jewry originated in medieval times and their history followed the standard course of medieval European Jewry: working as money-lenders and pedlars, attacked by the local population who accused them of causing the Black Death, then resettling a few years afterwards, only to be subsequently expelled.

By the late eighteenth century, when the Helvetic Confederation was formed, there were three small communities. Freedom of movement was allowed, and full emancipation was granted in 1866. Theodor Herzl held the first World Zionist Conference in Basle in 1897.

Although Switzerland accepted some refugees from Nazism many were refused, and most of the new refugee Jewish population emigrated soon after the war. The community today has a central body and is made up of various factions, from ultra-Orthodox to Reform. The major towns have synagogues and kosher meat is imported. There are several hotels with kosher facilities. Over half of the community live in the German-speaking area, the French-speaking area has the second largest number, and a small population is found in the southern Italian-speaking area.

Switzerland elected its first Jewish (and first female) president, Ruth Dreifuss.

In 2001 it was reported that evidence had been found of an early Jewish presence in the country a ring bearing images of a menorah and a ram's horn dating from 200CE.

GMT +1 hours
Country calling code: (+41)
Total population: 7,085,000
Jewish population: 18,000
Emergency telephone: (Police–117) (Fire–118) (Ambulance–144)

Electricity voltage: 220

AROSA

Levin's Hotel Metropol 7050
Telephone: (81) 378-8181
Fax: (81) 378-8161
Email: hotel@levinarosa.com
Website: www.levinarosa.com
Mikva on premises, own kosher bakery

BADEN

KOSHER FOODS
Atrium Hotel Blume
Kurplatz 4 5400
Telephone: (56) 222-5569; 200-0200
Fax: (56) 222-4298; 200-0250
Email: info@blume-baden.ch
Website: www.blume-baden.ch
Prepacked kosher meals on request.

SYNAGOGUES
Israelitische Kultusgemeinde Baden
Parkstrasse 17 5400
Telephone: (56) 221-5128
Fax: (56) 222-9447
Email: ikgb@dplanet.ch
Friday nights: Winter 6.30 pm; Summer 7.30 pm Shabbat and Festivals: mornings 8.45 am

BASLE

The Jewish community dates back to the beginning of the 12th century. This lasted for some two hundred years until the Jews had to flee from persecution. They returned in the 16th century and Basle became a centre for jewish printing.
Basle is of course famous for the first Zionist Conference of 1897. A plaque on the wall of the Concert Hall commemorates this event.

BAKERIES
Bakery Schmutz
Austrasse 53
Telephone: (61) 272-4765

BOOKSELLERS
Victor Goldschmidt
Mostackerstrasse 17 4051
Telephone: (61) 261-6191
Fax: (61) 261-6123
Email: vgb@econophone.ch

BUTCHERS
Juedische Genossenschafts-Metzgerei
Friedrichstrasse 26 4055
Telephone: (61) 301-3493
Fax: (61) 301-6882
Supervision: Both Basel Rabbinates
Also sells groceries and wine. Open 7.30 am to 12.00 noon, 3.00 pm to 6.00 pm. Closed Friday afternoon.

HOTELS
Hotel Euler
Centralbahnplatz 14 4002
Telephone: (61) 275-8000
Fax: (61) 275-8050
Offers kosher meals on request, has a synagogue on the premises

MIKVAOT
Basle Mikvaot
Eulerstr. 10 4051
Telephone: (61) 301-6831
Thannerstrasse 60
Telephone: (61) 301-2220

MUSEUMS
Jewish Museum of Switzerland
Kornhausgasse 8 4051
Telephone: (61) 261-9514
Email: museum-judaistik@unibas.ch
Hours: Monday to Wednesday, 2.00 pm to 5.00 pm; Sunday, 11.00 am to 5.00 pm. Free entrance.

RESTAURANTS
Holbein Cafe
Leimenstrasse 67 4051
Telephone: (61) 270-6810
Fax: (61) 270-6800
Email: info@holbeinhof.ch
Supervision: Basle Rabbinate IGB
Serves both meat and dairy

Restaurant Topas
Leimenstrasse 67 4051
Telephone: (61) 206-9500
Fax: (61) 206-9501
Email: info@restaurant-topas.ch
Website: www.restaurant-topas.ch
Supervision: Local rabbinical authority
Hours: 11.30 am to 2.00 pm Sunday to Friday,. 6.30 pm to 9.00 pm Sunday to Thursday, Friday night, Shabbat lunch and holidays by reservation before 2.00 pm preceding day

Vegetarian Kosher
Falafel & Pitahaus
Oberwilerstrasse 46 4102
Telephone: (61) 423-7575
Fax: (61) 423-7575
Email: info@fatafel-und-pitahaus.ch
Website: www.falafel-und-pitahaus.ch

SYNAGOGUES
Israelitische Religionsgesellschaft
Ahornstrasse 14
Telephone: (61) 301-4898
Rabbi, tel: (61) 302-1434

Orthodox
Israelitische Gemeinde Basel
Leimenstrasse 24 4003
Telephone: (61) 279-9850
Fax: (61) 279-9851
Email: igb@igb.ch

BERN
EMBASSY
Embassy of Israel
Alpenstrasse 32 3006
Telephone: (31) 356-3500
Fax: (31) 356-3556
Email: info@emb.israel.ch

SYNAGOGUES
Conservative Traditional
Synagogue & Community Center
Kapellenstrasse 2
Telephone: (31) 381-4992
Fax: (31) 382-3861
Email: info@jgb.ch
Website: www.jgb.ch
Rabbi Dr Michael Leipziger, tel: (31) 381-7303

BIEL/BIENNE
Biel/Bienne Synagogue
Ruschlistrasse 3
Telephone: (32) 377-3619
Fax: (32) 377-3619

BREMGARTEN/AARGAU
CONTACT INFORMATION
Israelitische Cultusgemeinde
Werner Meyer-Moses, Ringstrasse, 37 5620
Telephone: (56) 633-6626
Fax: (56) 633-6626

ENDINGEN
J. Bloch
Buckstr. 2 5304
Telephone: (56) 242-1546
Visits to the old synagogue and cemetery can be arranged

FRIBOURG
Fribourg Synagogue
9 Avenue de Rome
Telephone: (26) 322-1670

GENEVA

Originally Jews were not allowed to settle in Geneva itself but only the surrounding district. They had come from France in 1182. In 1490 however they were expelled.

After Geneva's annexation by France, at the end of the 18th century, Jews were allowed back in. They were not allowed civic rights until 1841.

BAKERIES
Mon Petit Boulanger Chen'
Rue des Eaux Vives 72
Telephone: (22) 736-7078
Fax: (22) 736-1730
Ask for kosher bread

BUTCHERS
Boucherie Kosher
Biton 21, rue de Montchoisi
Telephone: (22) 736-3168

EMBASSY
Permanet Mission of Israel to the United Nations
9 Chemin Bonvent, Cointrin 1216

MIKVAOT
Geneva Mikvaot
Telephone: (22) 346-9732
Fax: (22) 736-9632

RESTAURANTS
Meat
Le Jardin Rose
10 rue St-Leger
Telephone: (22) 317-8910
Fax: (22) 317-8990
Only open for lunch but arrangements can be made so that lunches and dinners can be delivered to any hotel downtown

R. Liebermann
Av. Jules Crosnier 4 1206
Telephone: (22) 346-0892
Fax: (22) 346-0830
Supervision: Machsike Hadas

SYNAGOGUES
Orthodox
Beth Habad
12 rue du Lac
Telephone: (22) 736-3682

The Geneva Synagogue (Ashkenazi)
Place de la Synagogue

Sephardi
Hekhal Haness
54 ter route de Malagnou
Telephone: (22) 736-9632

TOURIST SITES
Cathedrale St-Pierre
Place du Bourg-Four S 21204
Telephone: (22) 311-7575
Fax: (22) 310-0225
There is an interesting stained glass window depicting Moses in the Chapelle des Macchabees

LA-CHAUX-DE-FONDS
La-Chaux-De-Fonds Synagogue
Rue de Parc 63 2300
Telephone: (39) 231-794
Jews first came to the town from Alsace in 1777. The synagogue was built in 1896.

LAUSANNE
COMMUNITY ORGANISATIONS
Communaute Israelite de Lausanne
3 Avenue Geogette 1001
Telephone: (21) 341-7240
Fax: (21) 341-7241
Email: secretariat.cil@vtx.ch
Website: www.cisrl.ch

GROCERIES
Kolbo Shalom
7 Avenue Juste-Olivier
Telephone: (21) 312-1265

MIKVAOT
Lausanne Mikvaot
1 Avenue Juste-Olivier
Telephone: (21) 617-5818

RESTAURANTS
Community Centre
3 Avenue Geogette 1003
Telephone: (21) 341-7242
Serves lunches only, from 12.00 pm to 2.00 pm

SYNAGOGUES
Orthodox
Lausanne Orthodox Synagogue
1 Avenue Juste-Olivier
Telephone: (21) 320-9911

LENGNAU
Tourist Information
Telephone: (56) 241-1203
For visits to the old synagogue and cemetery

LUCERNE

BUTCHERS
Judische Metzgerei
Bruchstrasse 26
Telephone: (41) 240-2560

MIKVAOT
Lucerne Mikvaot
Bruchstrasse 51
Telephone: (41) 320-4750

SYNAGOGUES
Lucerne Synagogue
Bruchstrasse 51
Telephone: (41) 240-6400

LUGANO

GROCERIES
Koschere Lebensmittel erhaltlich bei
Frutor SA via Bagutti 4
Telephone: (91) 922-8522, 922-8590
Fax: (91) 923-9824
Email: nnova.frutor@bluewin.ch

HOTELS
Hotel Dan
Via Fontana 1 6902
Telephone: (91) 985-7030
Fax: (91) 985-7031
Email: danlugano@yahoo.com
Website: www.pibt.de/l/dan.htm
Supervision: Rabbinate Lugano's Jewish Community

MIKVAOT
Lugano Mikvaot
Via Maderno 11
Telephone: (91) 923-8952

SYNAGOGUES
Lugano Synagogue
Via Maderno 11
Telephone: (91) 923-5698

NEUKIRCH-EGNACH

CENTRAL ORGANISATIONS
Vegetarian Society
Schweizerische Vereinigung fur Vegetarismus
Bahnhofstr 52 9315
Telephone: (71) 477-3377
Fax: (71) 477-3378
Email: svv@vegetarimus.ch
Website: www.vegetarimus.ch
Can supply information on those who wish to eat
vegetarian in Switzerland

ST GALLEN
St Gallen Synagogue
Frongartenstrasse 18
Telephone: (71) 223-5923

ST MORITZ
Bermann's Hotel Edelweiss 7500
Telephone: (81) 836-5555
Fax: (81) 833-5556
Email: edelweiss@econophone.ch
Supervision: Rabbi Rabbinowitz, Lugano

VEVEY

RESTAURANTS
Les Bergers du Leman
Telephone: 923-5355
Fax: 922-5923

WINTERTHUR
Winterthur Synagogue
Rosenstrasse 5
Telephone: (52) 232-8136

YVERDON

CONTACT INFORMATION
Dr Maurice Ellkan
1400 Cheseaux-noreaz
Telephone: (24) 425-1851

ZUG
Restaurant Glashof
Baarerstr. 41 6301
Telephone: (42) 221-248
Prepared kosher meals are available

ZURICH
Jews first arrived in Zurich in 1273. Over the next
200 years Jews were repeatedly expelled and
allowed to return. There are five stained glass
Chagall windows in the Fraumunster Church
(located at Munsterhof Square) of which four are
on themes from the Hebrew Bible.

BAKERIES
Bäckerei Bollag
Waffenplazstrasse 5, (near Bahnhof Enge) 8002
Telephone: (1044) 202-3045
Fax: (1044) 291-4684
Email: baeckerei@freesurf.ch

BOOKSELLERS
Morascha
Seestrasse 11 8002
Telephone: (1044) 201-1120
Fax: (1044) 201-3120
Email: morascha@bluemail.ch
Website: www.morascha.com

BUTCHERS
Zukom
8 Aemtlerstrasse
Telephone: (1044) 451-8384
Fax: (1044) 451-8386
Supervision: Judische Gemeinde Aguda Achim and
Israelitsche Religionsgellschaft

GROCERIES
Jelmoli Department Store
Bahnhofstrasse
Has a kosher section
Pick 'N' Pay
Lavaterstrasse
Has a kosher section

MEDIA
Periodicals
Israelitsches Wochenblatt/Revue Juive
Telephone: (1044) 206-4222
Fax: (1044) 206-4220
Email: redotion@revue-juive.ch

Jewish City Guide of Switzerland
Spectrum Press International, Im Tannegg 1,
Friesenbergstrasse 221 8055
Telephone: (1044) 462-6411, 462-6412
Fax: (1044) 462-6462
Email: info@jewishguide.ch
Website: www.jewishguide.ch
Published quarterly in English and German, a guide to
Jewish communities throughout Switzerland

Tachles Irevve Juive
Rudigerstr 10, Postfach 8027
Telephone: (1044) 206-4200
Fax: (1044) 206-4210
Email: redaktion@tachles.ch
Weekly magazine

MIKVAOT
Zurich Mikvaot
Freigutstrasse 37
Telephone: (1044) 201-7306
Appointment by phone between 9.00 am and 11.00 am.

RESTAURANTS
Restaurant Schalom
G. van Dijk, Lavaterstrasse 33-37 8002
Telephone: (1044) 283-2233
Fax: (1044) 283-2234
Email: catering.schalom@bleuwin.ch
Supervision: Rabbi Rothchild

Dairy
Fein & Schein
Schontalstrasse 14, corner/Ecke Hallwylstrasse
Telephone: (1044) 241-3040
Fax: (1044) 241-2112
Supervision: Rabbi Daniel Levy

Rimon Take Away
Zelgstr. 1 8003
Telephone: (1044) 960-2323

Meat
Club Savjon
G. van Dijk-Neufeld, Lavaterstr. 33
Telephone: (1044) 201-1476
Fax: (1044) 201-1496
Email: catering.schalom@bluewin.ch
Supervision: Rabbi Rothchild

SYNAGOGUES
Israel Religionsgesellschaft
Freigutstrasse 37 8002
Telephone: (1044) 201 6746

Israelitische Cultusgemeinde Zurich
Lavaterstrasse 33 8002
Telephone: (1044) 283-2222
Fax: (1044) 2893-2223
Email: info@icz.org

Judische Gemeinde Agudas Achim
Erikastrasse 8 8003
Telephone: (1044) 463-8033
Fax: (1044) 463-8045

Zurich Synagogue
Freigutstrasse 37
Telephone: (1044) 201-4998

Orthodox
Minjan Machsikei Hadass
Anwandstrasse 60
Telephone: (1044) 241-3759
Fax: (1044) 241-2668
Rabbi Schmerier: (1) 242-9046

Schalom
Restaurant
AirCatering
CateringService

G. van Dijk-Neufeld
Lavaterstrasse 33-37
8002 Zürich

Telefon +41 (0)1 283 22 33
Fax +41 (0)1 283 22 34
E-mail: catering.schalom@bluewin.ch

club
Savyon

The kosher meeting place in Zurich with ambience for business
lunches and receptions. Under supervision of Rabbi Rothschild.
We offer Friday take away from 11.30 am until 14.00 pm. The
Club and Restaurant are closed Friday and Saturday.

Minjan Wollishofen
Etzelstrasse 6 8038
Telephone: (1044) 286-5010
Fax: (1044) 286-5018
Email: minjan.wollishofen@schweiz.ch
Contact: Dr. Sigmund Pugatsch

TAHITI

The first known Jew in Tahiti was
Alexander Salmon, who arrived in 1841
and later married the Queen's sister. No
community developed however until the
1960s when refugees came from Algeria.

SYNAGOGUES
Tahiti Synagogue
121196 Temple Dorette Assael, Rue Morenhouy,
Papette
Telephone: (689) 437-156
Fax: (689) 410-392
Email: Acispo@mail.pf

TAIWAN

The US Army brought the first Jews to
Taiwan in the 1950s. In the 1970s some
Jewish businessmen began to work on the
island. Most are Americans, although there
are some Israelis and other nationalities.
Services are held on Shabbat in a hotel,
and there is a Jewish community centre.

GMT +98 hours
Country calling code: (+886)
Total population: 21,854,000
Jewish population: Under 100
Emergency telephone: (Police–110) (Fire–119)
(Ambulance–119)
Electricity voltage: 110

TAIPEI
COMMUNITY ORGANISATIONS
Taiwan Jewish Community Centre
37 Lane 315, Shihpai Road, Shihlin
Telephone: (2) 396-0159
Fax: (2) 396-4022
Email: thejc@yahoo.com
Services are held on most Friday evenings at 7.30 pm.
Visitors should check in advance. All Holy Days and major
festivals are celebrated.

SYNAGOGUES
Orthodox
Ritz Landis Hotel
41 Min Chuan East Road
Telephone: (2) 597-1234

Fax: (2) 596-9223
Email: ritz@theritz-taipei.com
Shabbat and festival service are held here, also, when
minyan is available, weekday Services.

TAJIKISTAN

A former Soviet Republic, Tajikistan has a
small Jewish population. After the fall of the
Soviet Union many Jews emigrated to Israel.
The community is a mix of 40% Bokharan
and 60% Soviet Jews who migrated to
Tajikistan during World War II. Bokharan
Jews are believed to be descendants of
Persian Jewish exiles. Dushanbe, the capital,
and Shakhrisabz have synagogues.
Dushanbe also has a library.

GMT +5 hours
Country calling code: (+7)
Total population: 5,513,000
Jewish population: 1,500
Electricity voltage: 220

DUSHANBE
SYNAGOGUES
Ashkenazi
Proletarsky Street

Bokharan
Nazyina Khikmeta Street 26

SHAKHRISABZ
Shakhrisabz Synagogue
23 Bainal Minal Street

THAILAND

1890 saw the first confirmed presence of
Jews in Thailand, but Thai Jewry really
began with Jews escaping Russia and
eastern Europe in the 1920s and 30s
although most of them emigrated after 1945.

The present community arrived in the post-
war period of the 1950s and 60s. They
came from Syria, Lebanon, Europe and
America. Some Israelis also came. Another
relatively large influx came in 1979 as Jews
left Iran after the fall of the Shah.

Bangkok has Ashkenazi, Sephardi and
Lubavitch synagogues. The community
centre is in the Ashkenazi synagogue. The
Lubavitch synagogue offers several
communual activities, including Seders at

Passover, which have a large attendance.

GMT +7 hours
Country calling code: **(+66)**
Total population: **60,206,000**
Jewish population: **250**
Electricity voltage: **220**

BANGKOK

COMMUNITY ORGANISATIONS
Jewish Community of Thailand
Beth Elisheva Building, 121 Soi Sai Nam Thip 2,
Sukhumvit Soi 22
Telephone: (2) 663-0244
Fax: (2) 663-0245
Email: ykantor@ksc15.th.com
Website: www.jewishthailand.com
Friday night and Shabbat services with Kiddush and
Shabbat meal. Holiday sevices. call to confirm.

EMBASSY
Embassy of Israel
'Ocean Tower II' 25th floor, 75 Sukhumvit Soi 19,
Asoke Road 10110
Telephone: (2) 204-9200
Fax: (2) 204-9255
Email: consul.bkk@israelfm.org

KASHRUT INFORMATION
Bankok Kashrut Information
Telephone: (2) 318-1577, 234-0606, 237-1697

MIKVAOT
Jewish Community of Thailand
Beth Elisheva Building, 121 Soi Sai, Nam Thip 2,
Sukhumvit Soi 22 10110
Telephone: (2) 663-0244
Fax: (2) 663-0245
Mobile Phone: 661083707618
Email: rabbi@jewishthailand.com
Website: www.jewishthailand.com

RESTAURANTS
Ohr Menachem – Chabad House
96 Ram Buttri Rd., Kaosarn Road, Banglampoo
Telephone: (2) 282-6388
Fax: (2) 629-1153
Supervision: Rabbi Y. Kantor
Open 12.00 noon to 9.00 pm daily. Bakery and store. Tel:
(2) 629-2944/5.

SYNAGOGUES
Orthodox
Beth Elisheva
121 Soi Sai, Nam Thip 2, Sukhumvit Soi 22
Telephone: (2) 663-0244
Fax: (2) 663-0245
Email: rabbi@jewishthasiland.com
Friday night service at candle lighting time followed by
Shabbat meal. Shabbat services 10.00 am with Kiddush
and Shabbat meal. Call to confirm.

Even Chen
Chao Phya Office Tower, 4th floor, Soi
Charoenkrung, 42/1 New Road (Silom Road area)
Telephone: (2) 630-6120
Fax: (2) 237-3225
Email: rabbi@jewishthailand.com

Ohr Menchachem – Chabad House
96 Ram Buttri Rd., Kaosarn Road, Banglampoo
Telephone: (2) 282-6388
Fax: (2) 629-1153
Email: rabbi@chabadthailand.com
Website: www.chabadthailand.com
Daily services: Friday evenings at sundown with Shabbat
meal, attracts young Jewish travellers

CHIANG MAI
Chiang Mai Synagogue
189/15 Chang-Clan Road 50000
Telephone: 53279015
Email: cm@chabadthailand.com
Website: ww.chabadthailand.co.il
Restaurant, please contact for reservation

KOH SAMUI
Koh Samui synagogue
162/3 Chawang Beach, Moo- 2T Bophut
Email: ks@chabadthailand.com
Restaurant, please contact for reservation

TUNISIA

There is written proof of Jewish
settlement in Carthage in 200CE, when
the region was under Roman control. The
community was successful and left in
peace. Under the Byzantine Empire
conditions for the Jews worsened, but
after the Islamic conquest the 'Golden
Age' of Tunisian Jewry occurred. There
was prosperity and many centres of
learning were established. This did not
continue into the Middle Ages, as
successive Arab and Spanish invasions
led to discrimination. Emancipation came
from the French, but the community
suffered under the Nazi-influenced Vichy
government. After the war many
emigrated to Israel or to France and the
community is currently shrinking.

There are several synagogues in the
country, together with kindergartens and
schools. Tunisia is not as extreme in its
attitude towards Israel as some Arab
states, and there has been communication

between the two countries at a high level. An Israeli Interest Bureau in Tunis acts as an unofficial embassy. The Bardo Museum in Tunis has an exhibition of Jewish ritual objects.

GMT +1 hours
Country calling code: (+216)
Total population: 9,215,000
Jewish population: 1,500
Electricity voltage: 220

JERBA

There are Jews in two villages on this small island.There is also a magnificent old synagogue in Hara Kebira, on al Ghariba, in the Hara al-Saghira in the centre of the island.

Each year traditional Lag B'Omei celebrations are held. Following the terrorist attack in 2001 attendance dropped. Jewish silversmiths are prominent in Hournt souk on rue Bizerte.

The community in Jerba is possibly the oldest continuous one outside Israel. There are two small Jewish towns; Hara Saghira and Hara Kebira. Most of the Jews live in Hara Kebira.

TUNIS
COMMUNITY ORGANISATIONS
Community Offices
15 rue de Cap Vert
Telephone: (1) 282-496, 287-153

KASHRUT INFORMATION
Communautee Juive de Tunisie
15 Rue de Cap Vert 1002
Telephone: (1) 832 469 , 831 503
Fax: (1) 832 364
Email: cit@cjt.org.tn

SYNAGOGUES
Grande
43 Av. de la Liberte

Lubavich Yeshiva
73 rue de Palestine
Telephone: (1) 791-429

TURKEY

There have been Jews in Turkey since at least the 4th century BCE, making Turkey one of the earliest Jewish communities. The 15th and 16th centuries were periods of major prosperity for Turkish Jews.

After their expulsion from Spain in 1492, at a time when Jews were not tolerated in most Western European Christian countries, the then Ottoman (Turkish) Empire was

their principal refuge. The Sultan was reported to have said of the Spanish King: 'By expelling the Jews, he has impoverished his country and enriched mine'.

During World War II Turkey was neutral and accepted those Jews able to enter it.

GMT +2 hours
Country calling code: (+90)
Total population: 63,745,00
Jewish population: 20,000
Emergency telephone: (Police–155) (Fire–110) (Ambulance–11)
Electricity voltage: 220

ANKARA
EMBASSY
Embassy of Israel
Mahatma Gandhi Sok 85, Gaziosmanpasa
Telephone: (312) 446-3605
Fax: (312) 446-8071

BALAT
A coastal town about 20 miles west of Istanbul which has a 500 year old synagogue. Now closed the keys are with the mosque next door.

ISTANBUL
In the 12th century Benjamin Tudela said of the city 'There is no city like her except Baghdad'. At that time it was one of the most important Jewish centres in the world.

Since 1949 the Jewish community has had autonomy in its own affairs.

COMMUNITY ORGANISATIONS
The Jewish Community of Turkey
Tunel Yemenici No 23 Sokak 34430
Telephone: (212) 293-8794
Fax: (212) 244-1980
Email: info@muservicemaati.com
Secretary General: Lina Filiba

EMBASSY
Consul General of Israel
Valikonag Caddesi No 73
Telephone: (212) 255-1040
Fax: (212) 255-1048
Email: isrcon@comnet.com.tr

MUSEUMS
Zulfari Museum
Telephone: (212) 274-2607
Fax: (212) 274-2607
Contains material on Jewish members of the Ottoman Parliament, physicians at the Imperial Court, diplomats, academics, police officers and civil servants. Contact Mr H Ojalvo (212) 275-3944 for further information.

RELIGIOUS ORGANISATIONS
Chief Rabbinate
Yemenici Sokak 23, Beyoglu, Tunel 80050
Telephone: (212) 293-8794/5
Fax: (212) 244-1980

RESTAURANTS
Levi Restaurant
Tustempasamah Kalcin Sok, Cavustasa Han (2nd floor)
Telephone: (212) 512-1196

Meat
Carne Restaurant
Muallim Naci Cad. 17, Ortakoy
Telephone: (212) 260-8424

SYNAGOGUES
Askenazi Synagogue
Yusekkaldinm Sok No 37, Galata
Telephone: (212) 252-2157
Fax: (212) 244-2975
Email: eskenazivakli@superonline.com

Beth Israel
Efe Sok No 4, Sisli
Telephone: (212) 240-6599
Every day

Caddesbostan Synagogue
Tasmektep Sok, Gaoztepe
Telephone: (212) 356-5922
Every day

Etz Ahayim Synagogue
Muallim Naci Cad No 40 & 41, Ortakoy
Telephone: (212) 260-1896
Every day

Hemdat Israel synagogue
Izettin Sok No 65, Kadikoy
Telephone: (212) 336-5293
Every day

Hesed Leavraam Synagogue
Pancur Sok No 15, Buyukada
Telephone: (212) 382-5788
June to September including High Holy days

Italian Synagogue
Sair Ziya Pasa Yokusu No 27, Karakoy, Galata
Telephone: (212) 293-7784

Neve Shalom Buyuk Hendek Sok
No 61, Galata
Telephone: (212) 293-7566
Saturdays only

IZMIR
COMMUNITY ORGANISATIONS
Jewish Community Council
Azizler Sokak 920/44, Guzelyurt
Telephone: (232) 421-1290
Fax: (232) 463-5225
Email: isakalaluf@superonline.com.tr

SYNAGOGUES
Beth Israel
265 Mithatpasa Street, Karatas, Kanamursil District
Shaar Ashamayan
1390 Sokak 4/2, Bikur Holim

UKRAINE

The Ukraine has had a long and complicated history, with areas of the present country being under the rule of various other countries from Austria to Romania. The history of the Jews who live in modern Ukraine is long and tragic. From settlement in Kiev in the 10th century, before the concept of Ukrainian national identity, the Jewish community grew and was joined by Jews from central Europe. The Chmielnicki massacre of 1648, in which up to 100,000 were killed, was the worst event to befall the Jews before the Holocaust, and much destruction occurred in the west of the country.

Throughout the 19th century the Ukraine was mainly under Russian domination. After 1918 the Ukraine attempted to become independent, and many Jews were killed in the fighting. The Ukraine absorbed some of south-eastern Poland in 1939 and, after the German invasion of the Soviet Union, the Jewish community suffered terrible losses in the Holocaust.

The community today remains fairly large, and is slowly emerging from atheist Soviet rule. Most Jews live in towns, and Kiev is a major centre. There are now Jewish schools, and kosher food can be obtained. There are many interesting places to visit. Graves of famous Hassidic masters and the monument to the Babi Yar massacre (near Kiev) are popular trips. There are memorials erected all over the country to events which happened during the Holocaust.

GMT +2 hours
Country calling code: (+380)
Total population: 58,800,000
Jewish population: 180,000
Emergency telephone: (Police–02) (Fire–01) (Ambulance–03)
Electricity voltage: 220

BERDICHEV

MIKVAOT
Berdichev Mikvaot
4 Dzherzhinskaya Street
Telephone: (4143) 23938; 20222

SYNAGOGUES
Berdichev Synagogue
4 Dzherzhinskaya Street
Telephone: (4143) 23938; 20222
Kosher kichen on premises

BEREGOVO
Beregovo Synagogue
17 Sverdlov Street

BERSHAD
Bershad Synagogue
25 Narodnaya Street

CHERNIGOV
Chernigov Synagogue
34 Kommunisticheskaya Street

CHERNOVTSY
Chernovtsy Synagogue
24 Lukyana Kobylitsa Street
Telephone: 54878

CHMELNITSY
Chmelnitsy Synagogue
58 Komminnestnaya Street

DNEPROPETROVSK
Synagogue of Dnepropetrovsk
7 Kotsubinskovo St. 320030
Telephone: (56) 342-120
Fax: (56) 342-137
Email: dnepr@jewcom.dp.ua
Website: www.jew.dp.ua

DONETSK
Synagogue of Donetsk
Oktiabrskaya Str. 36 83086
Telephone: (62) 345-0052
Fax: (62) 335-7725
Email: office@jewish-com.dn.ua

IVANO-FRANKIVSK
Synagogue of Ivano-Frankivsk
Strachenya 7 284000
Telephone: (34) 222-3029
Fax: (34) 325-367
Rabbi Rolesnik (223-4894) will assist those doing
historical or genealogical research in Western Ukraine
(Galicia)

KHARKOV
Kharkov Synagogue
48 Kryatkovskaya Street
Website: www.kharkovejewish.com

Orthodox Union Jewish Community of Kharkov
Sumskaya 45
Telephone: (577) 140-301
Fax: (577) 140-515
Mobile Phone: 380675700899

Synagogue of Kharkov
12 Pushkinskaya Street 310057
Telephone: (577) 126-526
Fax: (577) 452-140
Email: chabad@kharkov.com

KHERSON
Synagogue of Kherson
27 Gorkovo Street 325025
Telephone: (552) 223-334
Fax: (552) 325-367

KIEV
Kiev's position at the crossroads of Western
Europe and central Asia attracted Jewish settlers
as early as the 8th century. The usual unfortunate
cycle of persecution and resettlement then began.
In 1911 Kiev was the location of a modern blood
libel case 'the Beilis affair'.

CENTRAL ORGANISATIONS
Vaad
6 Kurskaya Street
Telephone: (44) 276-1214

EMBASSY
Embassy of Israel
Lesi Ukrainki 34, GPE-S 252195

SYNAGOGUES
The Central Synagogue
13 Shota Rustavely
Telephone: (44) 225-0246
Originally built in 1897 the synagogue was, under Soviet
rule, converted into a puppet theatre. Today it is both a
puppet theatre and a synagogue.

SYNAGOGUES
Orthodox
Galitzky Shul
97a Zhilanska Street
Telephone: (44) 494-7-1737

Podil Synagogue
29 Shcekovytska Street
Telephone: (44) 463-7087
Fax: (44) 463-7088
Email: kievrabbi@yahoo.com

Reform
Reform Congregation
7 Nemanskaya Street
Telephone: (44) 296-3961
Fax: (44) 295-9604

TOURIST SITES
Babi Yar Monument
Melnikova Street
The monument, in the form of a menorah was erected in 1991, fifty years after the two days on which 33,371 Jews were murdered by the Nazis

Sholom Aleichem Statue
Near Basseynye Street
Shalom Aleichem (Shalom Rabinovitz) was born in 1859 in Pereyaslav, near Kiev

KORSTEN
Korsten Synagogue
8 Shchoksa Street

KREMENCHUG
Kremenchug Synagogue
50 Sverdlov Street

LVIV
Situated on the edge of shifting imperial boundaries, this city has been under Austrian, Polish and Soviet control. It has had as many names as its number of rulers. Now called Lviv in Ukrainian, there are 6,000 Jews in the city, once a major Jewish centre in Galicia. A couple of synagogues are still functioning, and a number of monuments have been erected commemorating the Holocaust. Many Jews on 'Heritage tours' use the town as a base to explore the region, and guides (generally Yiddish-speaking) are available.

TOURIST INFORMATION
Beis A'aron V'Yisroel
4 Brativ Michnovskich Street 79018
Telephone: (322) 333-535
Email: bald@link.lviv.ua
Restaurant order to be placed in advance. Tourist information.

NIKOLAYEV
Synagogue of Nikolayev
13 Karl Libknechta street 327001
Telephone: (512) 358-310
Fax: (512) 353-072

ODESSA
SYNAGOGUES
Chabad
21 Osipovo St.
Telephone: (482) 728-0770
Fax: (482) 496-301

Email: secretary@shomrei.farlep.net
School Chabad: 13 Vodoprovodnaya St, Orphanage
Chabad: 2 Yevreiskaya St 65011

Great Choral Synagogue
25 Evreyskaya Street
Telephone: (482) 243-694
Fax: (482) 347-850
Email: orphans@te.net.ue
Website: www.tikvaodessa.org

SIMFEROPOL
JEWISH CENTRE
Chabad
Mironova 24, Crimea 95001
Telephone: (52) 510-773
Fax: (52) 510-773
Email: chabadcrimea@cris.crimea.ua

SYNAGOGUES
Orthodox
Krasna Znamyonaya 78
Telephone: (52) 510-773
Fax: (52) 510-773
Also has a mikvah, information on kosher matters is available from main office

SLAVUTA
SYNAGOGUES
Kuzovskaya Street 2
Telephone: (447) 925-452
The first edition of Tanya was printed here by the Shapira family, whose tombs are in the cemetery

UMAN
Each year followers of the Breslau Chassidic sect visit the grave of founding Rabbi Lachman of Breslau for Rosh Hashana.

ZAPAROZHE
Synagogue of Zaparozhe
22 Turgeneva Street 330063
Telephone: (612) 642-961

ZHITOMIR
Synagogue of Zhitomire
7 Malaya, Berdishevskaya St. 262001
Telephone: (412) 226-608
Fax: (412) 373-428

Jewish Day Schools & Dormitories
Kevarim Tours of Ukraine
Synagogue
7 Malaya Berdichevskaya Street, 57 Chekhova Street 10014
Telephone: (412) 226-608
Fax: (412) 227-734
Email: office@chabad.zt.ua
Reb Ze'ev Wolf, disciple of Dov Baer, is buried in the Smolanka cemetery. The synagogue makes kevarim tours all over the Ukraine.

UNITED KINGDOM

There were probably individual Jews in England in Roman and (though less likely) in Anglo-Saxon times, but the historical records of any organised settlement start after the Normal Conquest of 1066. Jewish immigrants arrived early in the reign of William the Conqueror and important settlements came to be established in London (at a site still known as Old Jewry), Lincoln and many other centres. In 1190 massacres of Jews occured in many cities, most notably in York. This medieval settlement was ended by Edward I's expulsion of the Jews in 1290, after which date, with rare and temporary exceptions, only converts to Christianity or secret adherents of Judaism could live in the country.

After the expulsion of the Jews from Spain in 1492, a secret *Converso* community became established in London, but the present Anglo-Jewish community dates in practice from the period of the Commonwealth. In 1650 Menasseh ben Israel, of Amsterdam, began to champion the cause of Jewish readmission to England, and in 1655 he led a mission to London for this purpose. A conference was convened at Whitehall and a petition was presented to Oliver Cromwell. Though no formal decision was then recorded, in 1656 the Spanish and Portuguese Congregation in London was organised. It was followed towards the end of the seventeenth century by the establishment of an Ashkenazi community, which increased rapidly inside London as well as throwing out offshoots to a number of provincial centres and seaports. The London community, however, has always comprised the largest section of Anglo-Jewry.

Although Jews in Britain had achieved a virtual economic and social emancipation by the early nineteenth century, they had not yet gained 'political emancipation'. Minor Jewish disabilities were progressively removed and Jews were admitted to municipal rights and began to win distinction in the professions.

During the 19th century British Jews diversified from those callings which had hitherto been regarded as characteristic of the Jews.

There has always been a steady stream of immigration into Britain from Jewish communities in Europe, originally from the Iberian Peninsula and northern Italy, later from western and central Europe. The community was radically transformed by the large influx of refugees which occured between 1881 and 1914, the result of the intensified persecution of Jews in the Russian Empire. The Jewish population rose from about 25,000 in the middle of the nineteenth century to nearly 350,000 by 1914. It also became far more dispersed geographically.

From 1933 a new emigration of Jews commenced, this time from Nazi persecution, and again many settled in this country. Since the end of the Second World War and notably since 1956, smaller numbers of refugees have come from Iran, Arab countries and eastern Europe.

Counties are currently being restructured into Counties and Unitary Authorities. The new designations are not yet in common use and for this year the 'old' County names and areas have been retained.

Country calling code: **(44)**
Emergency telephone: **(Police–999)** **(Fire–999)** **(Ambulance–999)**
Electricity voltage: **240**

Avon

BRISTOL

Bristol was one of the principal Jewish centres of medieval England. Even after the Expulsion from England in 1290 there were occasional Jewish residents or visitors. A community of *Conversos* lived here during the Tudor period. The next Jewish settlement in Bristol was around 1754 and its original synagogue opened in 1786. The present building dates from 1871 and incorporates fittings from the earlier building.

DELICATESSEN
British Hebrew Congregation
Telephone: (0117) 970-6938
Open alternate Sundays at 10.00 am.

ORGANISATIONS
Hillel House
45 Oakfield Road, Clifton BS8 2BA
Telephone: (0117) 946-6589

RESTAURANTS
Vegetarian
Millwards Vegetarian Restaurant
40 Alfred Place, Kingsdown BS2 8HD
Telephone: (0117) 924-6026

SYNAGOGUES
Bristol Hebrew Congregation
9 Park Row BS1 5LP
Telephone: (0117) 927-3334
Email: simon770@aol.com
Services: Friday night at 183 Bishop Road BS7. Summer
7.45 pm, Winter 7.00 pm. Saturday at synagogue 9.45 am.

Progressive
Bristol & West Progressive Jewish Congregation
43-47 Bannerman Road, Easton BS5 0RR
Telephone: (0117) 954-1937
Email: bwpjc@bwpjc.org

Bedfordshire

LUTON
Synagogue
PO Box 215 LU1 1HW
Telephone: (01582) 25032
Friday night and Sabbath morning services. Office open
9.30 am to 12.30 pm on Sundays.

Berkshire

MAIDENHEAD
Reform
Synagogue
Grenfell Lodge, Ray Park Road Maidenhead,
SL6 8QX
Telephone: (01628) 637-012
Fax: (01628) 625-536
Email: mheadsyn@aol.com
Services: Friday 8.30 pm; sunday 10.30 am.

READING
SYNAGOGUES
Orthodox
Reading Synagogue
Goldsmid Road RG1 7YB
Telephone: (0118) 957-1018
Email: secretary@rhc.org.uk
Website: www.rhc.org.uk

Progressive
Thames Valley Progressive Jewish Community
6 Church Street
Telephone: (0118) 781-971

Buckinghamshire
MILTON KEYNES
BUTCHERS
Gilbert's Kosher Foods
Kestral House, Mount Avenue MK1 1LJ
Telephone: (01908) 646-787
Fax: (01908) 646-788
Supervision: London Board of Shechita

SYNAGOGUES
Reform
Milton Keynes and District Reform Synagogue
Telephone: (01908) 560-714
Email: mkdrsoffice.org.uk
Website: www.mkdrs.org.uk

Cambridgeshire
CAMBRIDGE
COMMUNITY ORGANISATIONS
Cambridge University Jewish Society
33 Thompson's Lane CB5 8AQ
Telephone: 354-783
Email: soc-cujs@lists.cam.ac.uk
Website: www.cam.ac.uk/societies/cujs

Chabad House
15 Grange Road CB3 9as
Telephone: 354 603
Email: info@cuchabad.org
Website: www.cuchabad.org
Supervision: Rabbi Reuven and Rochel Leigh

The Cambridge University CULanu Centre
33 Bridge Street CB2 1UW
Telephone: 366-338
Fax: 366-338
Email: dansilverstein@hotmail.com
The CULanu Centre organises, with the Cambridge
University Jewish Society a programme of education
events, debates and socials. There are regular Friday night
meals.

GROCERIES
Student Canteen
3 Thompson's Lane
Telephone: (01223) 352-145
There is a kosher canteen during term time serving lunch
most weekdays and Friday night and Shabbat meals

KOSHER FOODS
Derby Stores
Derby Street
Telephone: (01223) 354-391
Stocks arange of kosher food and wine; fresh bread
products each Thursday lunchtime. Can purchase goods to
order.

SYNAGOGUES
Orthodox
Cambridge Synagogue
Syn/Student Centre, 3 Thompson's Lane CB5 8AQ
Telephone: (01223) 354-783 or 368-346 answer
phone
Email: ctjcorguk@aol.com
Website: www.ctjc.org.uk
Daily morning and evening service during term time. Friday
evening and Saturday morning during vacations, other
services by arrangement.

Reform
Beth Shalom Reform Synagogue
PO Box 756 CBS5 9WB
Email: info@beth-shalom.org.uk
Website: www.beth-shalom.org.uk

Cornwall
TRURO
Kehillat Kernow
Owl Cottage, 11 Mill Road, Penponds TR14 0QH
Telephone: (01209) 719-672
Website: www.kehillatkernow.com

Cumbria
GRASMERE
HOTELS
Vegetarian
Lancrigg Vegetarian Country House Hotel
Easedale LA22 9QN
Telephone: (01539) 435-317

Devon
EXETER
In pre-Expulsion times, Exeter was an
important Jewish centre. Jews were first
mentioned in 1181, After the resettlement a
community was again established in 1728.

SYNAGOGUES
Hebrew Congregation
Synagogue Place, Mary Arches Street EX4 3BA
Telephone: (01392) 251-529
Email: welcome@exetersynagogue.org.uk
The synagogue was built in 1763, and is a Grade II* listed
building with beautiful interior. The historic cemetery in
Magdalen Road dates from 1757.

PLYMOUTH
The congregation was founded in 1752 and a
synagogue erected ten years later. This is now
the oldest Ashkenazi synagogue building in
England still used for its original purpose. It is a
scheduled historical monument. In 1815
Plymouth was one of the most important
provincial centres of Anglo-Jewry.

LIBRARIES
Holcenberg Collection
Plymouth Central Library, Drake Circus PL4 8AL
Telephone: (01752) 305-907/8
Fax: (01752) 305-905
Email: ref@plymouthl.gov.uk
Website: www.plymouthlibraries.info
A Jewish collection of fiction and non-fiction books, mainly
lending copies.

RESTAURANTS
Vegetarian
Plymouth Arts Centre Vegetarian Restaurant
38 Looe Street PL4 0EB
Telephone: (01752) 202-616
Fax: (01752) 206-118
Email: arts@plymouthac.org.uk
Website: www.plymouthac.org.uk
Hours: lunch, Monday to Saturday, 12.00 noon to 2.00 pm;
dinner, Tuesday to Saturday, 5.00 pm to 8.30 pm. Light
refreshments served from 10.00 am.

SYNAGOGUES
Orthodox
Plymouth Hebrew Congregation
Catherine Street PL1 2AD
Telephone: (01752) 263162
Mobile Phone: 07811406878
Email: tony-aggiss@hotmail.com
Website: www.plymouthsynagogue.com
Services: Friday, 6.00 pm; Saturday, 9.30 am. The
congregation offers use of minister's flat as holiday
accommodation in return for conducting Orthodox Friday
evening and Saturday morning services.

TORQUAY
Torquay Synagogue
Old Town Hall, Abbey Road TQ1 1BB
Telephone: (01803) 607-197
Covering also Brixham and Paignton. Services first Sabbath
of every month and festivals, 10.30 am.

TOTNES
Reform
Totnes Reform Jewish Group
1 Maudlin Cottages Maudlin Road, TQN 5TG
Telephone: (01803) 867-461

Dorset
BOURNEMOUTH
The Bournemouth Hebrew Congregation was
established in 1905, when the Jewish population
numbered fewer than 20 families. Today, the
town's permanent Jewish residents number
3,500 out of a total population of some 15,000.
During the holiday season, however, there are
many more Jews in Bournemouth, for it is an
extremely popular resort, with kosher hotels,
guest houses and other holiday accommodation.

COMMUNITY ORGANISATIONS
Bournemouth Jewish Representative Council
2 Imperial Court, Ravine Rd,Canford Cliffs, Poole
BH13 7HX
Telephone: (01202) 701-011

DELICATESSEN
Jacob's Larder Deli (Kosher)
224 Holdenhurst Road BH8 8AX
Telephone: (01202) 291-918
Fax: (01202) 291-918
Website: www.kosherbournemouth.co.uk
Supervision: BHC

The Deli
7 Holdenhurst Road BH8 8EH
Telephone: (01202) 292-800
Email: thedeli@virgin.net

HOTELS
The Acacia Gardens Hotel
12 Manor Road, East Cliff BH1 3HU
Telephone: (01202) 553127
Email: AcaciaGardens@hotmail.co.uk
Supervision: Manchester Beth Din

HOTELS
Kosher
New Ambassador Hotel
Meyrick Road, East Cliff BH1 3DP
Telephone: (01202) 555-453
Fax: (01202) 311-077
Email: sales@newamb.com
Website: www.newamb.com
Supervision: London Beth Din
112 rooms, all with bathroom en suite.

Normandie Hotel
Manor Road, East Cliff BH1 3HL
Telephone: (01202) 552-246, Reservation Phone
No. 291-770
Fax: (01202) 291-178
Email: normandiehotel@aol.com
Supervision: Kedassia

MIKVAOT
Bournemouth Hebrew Congregation
Synagogue Chambers, Wootton Gardens BH1 1PW
Telephone: (01202) 557-443

RESTAURANTS
Falafel Restaurant (Kosher)
218 Holdenhurst Road, BH8 8AX
Telephone: (01202) 552-277
Website: www.kosherbournemouth.co.uk

The Arbory at The Acacia Gardens Hotel
12 Manor Road, East Cliff BH1 3HU
Telephone: (01202) 553127
Email: AcaciaGardens@hotmail.co.uk

SYNAGOGUES
Orthodox
Synagogue
Synagogue Chambers, Wootton Gardens BH1 1PW
Telephone: (01202) 557-433
Fax: (01202) 557-578
Email: bhc.1@virgin.net

Reform
Bournemouth Reform Synagogue
53 Christchurch Road BH1 3PN
Email: synagogue@btinternet.com

Essex
BARKING & BECONTREE
SYNAGOGUES
Orthodox
Synagogue
200 Becontree Ave., Dagenham, RM8 2TR
Telephone: (020) 8590-2737

BARKINGSIDE
BUTCHERS
La Boucherie
145 High Street IG6 2AJ
Telephone: (020) 9215 (5 lines)
Fax: (020) 8551-9977
Email: orders@laboucherie.co.uk
Supervision: With the Sanction of the Rabbinic Authority of the London Board for Shechita

CHIGWELL
Orthodox
Chigwell Synagogue
Limes Avenue, Limes Farm Estate IG7 5NT
Telephone: (020) 8500-2451
Email: chshul@btinternet.com

COLCHESTER
Independent
**Colchester and District Jewish Community
Synagogue**
Fennings Chase, Priory Street CO1 2QG
Telephone: (01206) 545-992
Email: tanenb@essex.ac.uk
Services every Friday at 8.00 pm, on the High Holydays and
most festivals.

HARLOW
Reform
Harlow Jewish Community
Harberts Road CM20 4DT
Telephone: (01279) 432-503

ILFORD
GROCERIES
Brownstein's
Cranbrook Road, Gants Hill
Telephone: (020) 8550-3900
Email: deli@brownsteins.co.uk
Website: www.brownsteins.co.uk
Supervision: London Beth Din

MIKVAOT
Ilford Mikvah Federation of Synagogues
463 Cranbrook Road, Ilford IG
Telephone: (020) 8554-8532
Correspondence to 367 Cranbrook Road, Ilford.

SYNAGOGUES
Orthodox
Clayhall
Sinclair House, Woodford Bridge Road, Ilford
IG4 5QR
Email: clayhallsynagogue.co.uk
Ilford
22 Beehive Lane, Ilford IG1 3RT
Telephone: (020) 8554-5969

Newbury Park
23 Wessex Close, Ilford IG3 8SU
Telephone: (020) 8597-0958

LOUGHTON
Orthodox
Loughton Synagogue
Borders Lane IG10 1TE
Telephone: (020) 8508-0303
Email: loughtonsynagogue@lineone.net
Friday evening, 7.00 pm; Saturday morning 9.00 am.

REDBRIDGE
BAKERIES
Golan Bakery
388 Cranbrook Road, Ilford
Telephone: (020) 8554-8202
Supervision: London Beth Din

BUTCHERS
N. Goldberg
12 Claybury Broadway, Redbridge IG
Telephone: (020) 8551-2828
Supervision: London Board for Shechita

ROMFORD
Romford Synagogue
25 Eastern Road, RM1
Telephone: (01708) 741-690

SOUTHEND-ON-SEA
Jews began settling in the area in the late 19th
century, mainly from the East End of London.
The first temporary synagogue was built in
1906. The Jewish population is 4,500.

BOOKSELLERS
Dorothy Young
21 Colchester Road SS2 6HW
Telephone: (01702) 331-218
Email: dorothy@dorothyyoung.co.uk
Website: www.dorothyyoung.co.uk
Religious articles, Israeli giftware, etc., also stocked. Jewish
software ordered. Call for appointment.

SYNAGOGUES
**Southend and Westcliff Hebrew
Congregation**
Finchley Road SS0 8AD
Telephone: (01702) 344-900
Fax: (01702) 391-131
Email: swhc@btclick.com
Website: www.swhc.org.uk

Southend Reform Synagogue
851 London Road, Westcliff SS0
Telephone: (01702) 711116 (evenings only)

Gloucestershire
CHELTENHAM
The congregation was established in 1824 and
the present synagogue opened in 1839. However,
after two generations, the congregation declined
and the synagogue was closed in 1903. At the
outbreak of the Second World War, the
synagogue was re-opened following the influx of
Jewish newcomers to the town.

RESTAURANTS
Vegetarian
The Orange Tree
317 High Street GL50 3HW
Telephone: (01452) 234-232
Fax: (01452) 234-232
Email: shaipateluk@yahoo.co.uk
Strictly vegan & vegetarian cuisine. Fully licensed with selection of organic wines & beers.

SYNAGOGUES
Orthodox
Synagogue
Bramble Cottage, Dog Lane, Crickley Hill GL3 4ug
Telephone: (01452) 862399

Traditional
Cheltenham Hebrew Congregation
St James Square GL50 3PU
Telephone: (01452) 578-893
Fax: (01452) 578-893
Services every Friday at 7.00 pm and High Holy Days, Festivals etc. as advised

Hampshire
ALDERSHOT
CONTACT INFORMATION
Jewish Committee for H.M. Forces
25 Enford Street W1H 2DD
Telephone: (01252) 724-7778
Fax: (01252) 706-1710
Email: jmcouncil@btinternet.com
Website: www.jmcouncil.org
Inquiries to Senior Jewish Chaplain

PORTSMOUTH & SOUTHSEA
The Portsmouth community was founded in 1746. Its first synagogue was in Oyster Row, but the congregation moved to a building in White's Row which it continued to occupy for almost two centuries. A new building was erected in 1936. The cemetery is in a street which was once known as Jews' Lane.
Southampton

SYNAGOGUES
Synagogue Chambers
The Thicket, Southsea
Telephone: (023) 9282-1494

SOUTHAMPTON
LIBRARIES
Hartley Library
University of Southampton SO17 1BJ
Telephone: (023) 592721
Fax: (023) 593007
Email: archives@soton.ac.uk
Houses both the Parkes Library and the Anglo-Jewish Archives

SYNAGOGUES
Synagogue
Moordaunt Road, The Inner avenue SO2 0GP
Services Saturday morning 10.00 am

Hertfordshire
BARNET
Orthodox
Synagogue
Eversleigh Rd. EN5 1NE
Telephone: (020) 8449-0145
Email: administrator@barnetsynagogue.org.uk

BOREHAMWOOD
Borehamwood & Elstree
Croxdale Road WD6
Telephone: (020) 8386-5227
Email: admin@bwoodshul.demon.co.uk

BUSHEY
BUTCHERS
J.D. Glass & Co
100 High Road, Bushey Heath, Bushey WD2 3JE
Telephone: (020) 8420-4443
Supervision: London Board for Shechita

SYNAGOGUES
Orthodox
Bushey and District
177 Sparrows Herne WD23 1AJ
Telephone: (020) 8950-7340
Fax: (020) 8421-8267
Email: administrator@busheyus.org

COCKFOSTERS
GROCERIES
The World of Kosher
Telephone: (020) 8441-3621

EAST BARNET
BUTCHERS
La Boucherie
4 Cat Hill EN4 8JB
Telephone: (020) 8441-9251 (5 lines)
Fax: (020) 8441-1848
Email: orders@laboucherie.co.uk
Supervision: With the Sanction of the Rabbinic Authority of the London Board for Shechita

HEMEL HEMPSTEAD
SYNAGOGUES
Morton House
Midland Road HD1 1RP
Telephone: (01923) 232-007

RADLETT

SYNAGOGUES

Orthodox

Synagogue
22 Watling St. WD7 7PN
Telephone: (01923) 856-878
Email: radlettus.@hotmail.com

Reform
Radlett and Bushey Reform Syngogue
118 Watling Street, WD7 7AA
Telephone: (01923) 856-110
Fax: (01923) 854-444
Website: www.rbrs.org.uk

SAWBRIDGEWORTH

BANQUETING SUITE
Manor of Groves
High Wych CM21 0JU
Telephone: (0870) 410 8833
Fax: (0870) 417 8833
Email: events@manorofgroves.co.uk
Website: www.manorofgroves.com

SHENLEY

Orthodox
Shenley Synagogue
PO Box 205
Telephone: (01923) 857-786
Website: www.shenleyunited.org

ST ALBANS

SYNAGOGUES

Masorti
St Albans Masorti Synagogue
PO Box 23 AL1 4PH
Telephone: (01727) 860-642
Email: info@e-sams.org
Website: www.e-sams.org

Orthodox
St Albans United Synagogue
Oswald Road AL1 3AQ
Telephone: (01727) 854-872

WATFORD

Synagogue
16 Nascot Road WD17 3RE
Telephone: (01923) 222-755
Fax: (01923) 222-755
Email: wadshul@btopenworld.com

Covers also Abbots, Langley, Carpenters Park, Croxley
Garden, Garston, Kings Langley and Rickmansworth.

WELWYN GARDEN CITY

Synagogue
Barn Close, Handside Lane AL8 6St
Telephone: (01438) 715-686
Email: doraprag@aol.com
gunter.tuch@ntlworld.com

Humberside

HULL

In Hull, as in other English port towns, a Jewish community was formed earlier than in inland areas. The exact date is unknown, but it is thought to be the early 1700s. There were enough Jews in Hull to buy a former Roman Catholic chapel, damaged in the Gordon Riots of 1780, and turn it into a synagogue. Hull was then the principal port of entry from northern Europe, and most Jewish immigrants came through it. Both the Old Hebrew Synagogue in Osborne Street and the Central Synagogue in Cogan Street were destroyed in air raids during the Second World War.

MUSEUMS
Hull Synagogue Museum
Linneaus Street HU3 2PD
Telephone: (01482) 217-153
Fax: (01482) 216-565
Email: info@jcsc.info, jcsc@exobus.org

SYNAGOGUE
Orthodox
Hull Hebrew Congregation
30 Pryme Street, Anlaby HU10 6SH
Telephone: (01482) 653-242; 653-398

Reform
Neve Shalom Reform Synagogue
Great Gutter Lane, West Willerby HU10 7JT
Telephone: (01482) 658-312
Fax: (01482) 835-864
Email: ian@isa.karoo.co.uk
Website:
www.beehive.thisishull.co.uk/hullreformsynagogue

Kent

CANTERBURY

TOURIST SITES
The Old Synagogue
King Street CT1 2ES
Telephone: (01227) 595-544
Fax: (01227) 595-589

The Old Synagogue, an Egyptian-style building of 1847, stands in King Street and is now used by the Kings School for recitals.

MARGATE
Synagogue
Godwin Road, Cliftonville CT9 2HA
Telephone: (01843) 223-219

RAMSGATE
SYNAGOGUES
Montefiore Endowment
Hereson Road

Montefiore Mausoleum Synagogue
33 Luto Avenue, Broadstairss
Telephone: (01843) 862-507

Reform
Thanet and District Reform Synagogue
293a Margate Road, CT12 6TE
Telephone: (01843) 851-164

ROCHESTER
Magnus Memorial Synagogue
366 High Street ME1 1DJ
Telephone: (01634) 847-665
Grade II, listed building known as The Chatham Memorial Synagogue.

Lancashire
BLACKPOOL
DELICATESSEN
The Deli
6 Station Road, Lytham St Annes
Telephone: (01253) 735-861

SYNAGOGUES
Orthodox
United Hebrew Congregation
Synagogue Chambers, Leamington Road FY1 4HD
Telephone: (01253) 28164

Reform
Reform Jewish Congregation
40 Raikes Parade FY1 4EX
Telephone: (01253) 623-687

CHEADLE
BUTCHERS
Hymark Kosher Meat Ltd
39 Wilmslow Road
Telephone: (0161) 428-3400
Supervision: Manchester Beth Din
Meat department only.

DELICATESSEN
Hyman's Delicatessen
41 Wilmstow Road
Telephone: (0161) 491-1100
Fax: (0161) 491-1100
Supervision: Manchester Beth Din

SYNAGOGUES
Yeshurun Hebrew Congregation
Coniston Road, Gatley-Cheadle, Cheshire SK8 4AP
Telephone: (0161) 428-8242
Fax: (0161) 491-5265
Email: yeshurun@btinternet.com
Website: www.yeshurun.co.uk

HALE BARNS
BUTCHERS
Hymark of Hale
The Square, Hale Barns, Cheshire
Telephone: (0161) 980-2836
Supervision: Manchester Beth Din

MIKVAOT
Naomi Grenberg South Manchester Mikvah
Hale Synagogue, Shay Lane, Hale Barns
Telephone: (0161) 904-8296
Use is by appointment only.

SYNAGOGUES
Orthodox
Hale and District Hebrew Congregation
Shay Lane, Hale Barns, Cheshire WA15 8PA
Telephone: (0161) 980-8846
Fax: (0161) 980-1802

LANCASTER
BED AND BREAKFAST
Lancaster University Jewish Society
Interfaith Chaplaincy Centre , University of Lancaster, Bailrigg Lane LA1 4YW
Telephone: (01524) 594-075
Jewish rooms and kosher kitchen. Contact Rev Malcolm Wiseman.

LIVERPOOL
There is evidence of an organised community before 1750, believed to have been composed of Sephardi Jews and to have had some connection with the West Indies and with Dublin, although some authorities believe they were mainly German Jews. The largely Ashkenazi community, who arrived later, were to some degree intending emigrants for the USA and the West Indies who changed their minds and stayed in Liverpool. By 1807 the community had a building in Seel Street, the parent of today's synagogue in Princes Road, one of the handsomest in the country.

BOOKSELLERS
Liverpool Jewish Book & Gift Centre
Harold House, Dunbabin Road L15 6XL
Telephone: (0151) 475-5671
Fax: (0151) 475-2212
Full range of Jewish books, artefacts and gifts. Sundays 11.00 am to 1.00 pm.

COMMUNITY ORGANISATIONS
Merseyside Jewish Representative Council
433 Smithdown Road L15 3JL
Telephone: (0151) 733-2292
Fax: (0151) 734-0212
Email: mjrcshifrin@hotmail.com
Website: www.merseyside-jewish-
community.org.uk, www.liverpooljewish.com

KASHRUT INFORMATION
Liverpool Kashrut Commission (inc. Liverpool Shechita Board)
c/o Shifrin House, 433 Smithdown Road L15 6XL
Telephone: (0151) 733-2292
Fax: (0151) 734-0212

MEDIA
Newspapers
Jewish Telegraph
Harold House, Dunbabin Road L15 6XL
Telephone: (0151) 475-6666
Fax: (0151) 475-2222
Email: liverpool@jewishtelegraph.com
Website: www.jewishtelegraph.com

MIKVA
Childwall Hebrew Congregation
Dunbabin Road L15 6XL
Telephone: (0151) 722-2079
Fax: (0151) 722-2079

RESTAURANTS
JLGB Centre
Telephone: (0151) 475-5825; 475-5671
Open Sunday, Tuesday, Thursday 6.30 pm to 11.00 pm.
Licensed bar. Out-of-town visitors welcome. Also take-away service.

Kosher
The Liverpool Jewish Youth and Community Centre
Harold House, Dunbabin Road , Childwall L15 6XL
Telephone: (0151) 475-5671; 5825
Fax: (0151) 475-2212
Email: info@liverpooljewish.com
Website: www.liverpooljewish.com
Supervision: Liverpool Kashrut Commission
Also does take-away

Vegetarian
Munchies Eating House
Myrtle Parade
Telephone: (0151) 709-7896

SYNAGOGUES
Orthodox
Allerton Hebrew Congregation
cnr. Mather & Booker Avenues, Allerton L18 9TB
Telephone: (0151) 427-6848

Childwall Hebrew Congregation
Dunbabin Road, L15 6XL
Telephone: (0151) 722-2079
Fax: (0151) 722-2079

Greenbank Drive Hebrew Congregatrion
Green bank Drive L17 1AN
Telephone: (0151) 733-1417
Fax: (0151) 733-3862

Liverpool Old Hebrew Congregation
Synagogue Chambers, Princes Road L8 1TG
Telephone: (0151) 709-3431
Fax: (0151) 709-3431
Email: lohc1@aol.com
Website: www.exobus.org
Grade II Listed Building. Guided talks available during the week daily. Pre-booking essential. Other times by special arrangement.

Progressive
Liverpool Progressive Synagogue
28 Curch Road North L15 6TF
Telephone: (0151) 733-5871

MANCHESTER
The Manchester Jewish community is the second largest in the United Kingdom, numbering about 35,000. There was no organised community until 1780. The present Great Synagogue claims to be the direct descendant of this earliest community. The leaders of Manchester Jewry in those early days came from the neighbouring relatively important Jewish community of Liverpool. In 1871 a small Sephardi group from North Africa and the Levant drew together and formed a congregation, which extended to fill two handsome synagogues. One has now been turned into a Jewish museum.

BAKERIES
State Fayre Bakeries
Unit 1, Empire Street M3
Telephone: (0161) 832-2911
Supervision: Manchester Beth Din

BREAD & CONFECTIONERY
Delicatessen
State Fayre
77 Middleton Road M8
Telephone: (0161) 740-3435
Supervision: Manchester Beth Din

BUTCHERS
Lloyd Grosberg (J. Kreger)
102 Barlow Road M20
Telephone: (0161) 445-4983
Supervision: Manchester Beth Din

Grocery
J.A. Hyman (Titanic) Ltd
123/9 Waterloo Road M8
Telephone: (0161) 792-1888
Email: info@titanics.co.uk
Website: www.titanics.co.uk
Supervision: Manchester Beth Din
Suppliers of meat and poultry, cooked meats and
delicatessen products.

KASHRUT INFORMATION
Manchester Beth Din
MJCC, Bury Old Road, Manchester, M7 4QY
Telephone: (0161) 740-9711
Fax: (0161) 721-4249
Contact them to ensure an establishment is still certified.

LIBRARIES
Central Library
St Peter's Square M2 5PD
Telephone: (0161) 234-1983; 1984
Email: socsi@libraries.manchester.gov.uk
Collection of Jewish reference and loan books, including
books on Hebrew. Contact the Social Sciences Library.

MUSEUMS
Manchester Jewish Museum
190 Cheetham Hill Road M8 8LW
Telephone: (0161) 834-9879; 832-7553
Fax: (0161) 834-9801
Email: info@manchesterjewishmuseum.com
Website: www.manchesterjewishmuseum.com
Exhibitions, Heritage trails, Demonstrations and Talks.
Details of events available on request. Educational visits for
school and adult groups must be booked in advance. Open
Monday to Thursday, 10.30 am to 4.00 pm, Sundays 10.30
am to 5.00 pm. Admission charge. Contact Don Rainger.

RESTAURANTS
Antonio's Restaurant
JCLC, Corner Bury Old Road & Park Road
Telephone: (0161) 795-8911
Fax: (0161) 795-8911
Supervision: Manchester Beth Din
Open Monday to Thursday 5.00 pm to 11.00 pm. Winter
11/2 hours after Shabbat until 2.00 pm.

SYNAGOGUES
Orthodox
Cheetham Hebrew Congregation
Jewish Cultural Centre, Bury Old Road M7 4QY
Telephone: (0161) 740-7788

Heaton Park Hebrew Congregation
Ashdown, Middleton Road M8 6JX
Telephone: (0161) 740-4766

United Synagogue
Meade Hill Road M8 4LR
Telephone: (0161) 7409586

Reform
Cheshire Reform Congregation Menorah Synagogue
Altrincham Road M22 4RZ
Telephone: (0161) 428-7746
Fax: (0161) 428-0937
Email: office@menorah.org

Manchester Reform Synagogue
Jackson's Row M2 5NH
Telephone: (0161) 834-0415
Fax: (0161) 834-0415

TRAVEL AGENTS
ITS: Israel Travel Service
427/430 Royal Exchange, Old Bank street M2 7EP
Telephone: (0161) 839-1111
Fax: (0161) 839-0000
Email: all@itstravel.co.uk
Website: www.itstravel.co.uk
Freephone 0800-0181-839

PRESTWICH
BOOKSELLERS
B. Horwitz
20 King Edwards Buildings, Bury Old Road M7 4QJ
Telephone: (0161) 740-5897
Open 9.30 am to 5.30 pm Monday to Friday; 10.00 am to
1.00 pm Sunday; 9.00 am to 2.00 pm Fridays during winter.

B. Horwitz Judaica World
2 Kings Road M25 0LE
Telephone: (0161) 773-4956
Fax: (0161) 773-4956
Email: horbroom@aol.com

BUTCHERS
Kosher Foods
49 Bury New Road M25
Telephone: (0161) 773-1308
Supervision: Manchester Beth Din
Sells groceries as well

Kosher Supreme
61 Bury Old Road M25
Telephone: (0161) 773-2020
Supervision: Manchester Beth Din

Vidal's Kosher Meats
75 Wndsor Road M25
Telephone: (0161) 740-3365
Supervision: Manchester Beth Din

DELICATESSEN
Deli King
Kings Road M25 8LQ
Telephone: (0161) 798-7370
Fax: (0161) 798-5654
Supervision: Manchester Beth Din

Haber's
8 Kings Road M25 0LE
Telephone: (0161) 773-2046
Fax: (0161) 773-9101
Supervision: Manchester Beth Din

MEDIA
Newspapers
Jewish Telegraph
Telegraph House, 11 Park Hill, Bury Old Road
M25 0HH
Telephone: (0797) 694-5210
Fax: (0161) 740-5555
ISDN: (0161) 720-8120
Email: manchester@jewishtelegraph.com
Website: www.jewishtelegraph.com

MIKVAOT
Manchester & District Mikva (Machzikei Hadass)
Sedgley Park Road, Prestwich M25
Telephone: (0161) 773-1537; 795-2223

RESTAURANTS
Asher's
5 Kings Road, Prestwich
Telephone: (0161) 773-1414
Supervision: Manchester Beth Din

Meat
J.S. Kosher Restaurant
7 Kings Road, Prestwich M25 0LE
Telephone: (0161) 798-7776
Supervision: Manchester Beth Din
Glatt Kosher.

SYNAGOGUES
Orthodox
Higher Prestwich
445 Bury Old Road, Prestwich M25 1QP
Telephone: (0161) 773-4800

Holy Law South Broughton Congregation
Bury Old Road, Prestwich M25 0EX
Telephone: (0161) 792-6349; 721-4705
Fax: (0161) 720-6623
Email: office@holylaw.org.uk

Prestwich Hebrew Congregation
Bury New Road, Prestwich M25 9WN
Telephone: (0161) 773-1978
Fax: (0161) 773-7015

Sedgley Park (Shomrei Hadass)
Park View Road, Prestwich M25 5FA
Telephone: (0161) 773-4828; 740-1969
Email: laurencemiller@hotmail.com

SALE
Sale & District Hebrew Congregation
14 Hesketh Road, Sale M33 5Aa
Telephone: (0161) 973-2172

SOUTHPORT
COMMUNITY ORGANISATIONS
Southport Jewish Representative Council
Telephone: (01704) 540-704
Fax: (01704) 540-704

SYNAGOGUES
Orthodox
Southport Hebrew Congregation
Arnside Road PR9 0QX
Telephone: (01704) 532-964
Fax: (01704) 532-964
Mikvah on premises

Reform
New (Reform) Synagogue
Portland Street PR8 1LR
Telephone: (01704) 535-950
Email: snewsyn@aol.com

WHITEFIELD
BUTCHERS
Park Lane Kosher Meats
142 Park Lane, Whitefield M45 7PX
Telephone: (0161) 766-5091
Supervision: Manchester Beth Din
Hours: Sunday 8.30 am to 1.00 pm; Monday & Friday 8.00
am to 1.00 pm; Tuesday, Wednesday & Thursday 8.00 am to
6.00 pm

DELICATESSEN
Cottage Deli
83 Park Lane , Whitefield M
Telephone: (0161) 766-6216
Supervision: Manchester Beth Din

MIKVAOT
Whitefield Mikvah
Park Lane, Whitefield M45 7PB
Telephone: (0161) 796-1054
Fax: (0161) 767-9453
Ansaphone. Evenings only: 773-7830. Use is by
appointment only.

SYNAGOGUES
Orthodox
Hillock Hebrew Congregation
Beverley Close, Ribble Drive, Whitefield M45 8LB
Telephone: (0161) 959-5663
Mailing adddress is 13 Mersey Close, whiefield,
Manchester, M45 8LB.

Whitefield Hebrew Congregation
Park Lane, Whitefield M45 7PB
Telephone: (0161) 766-3732
Fax: (0161) 767-9453
Email: mail@whitefieldshul.co.uk

Reform
Sha'arei Shalom North Manchester Reform Synagogue
Elms Street , Whitefield M45 8GQ
Telephone: (0161) 796-6736
Fax: (0161) 796-6736

SALFORD
BAKERIES
Brackman's
45 Leicester Road Salford M7
Telephone: (0161) 792-1652
Supervision: Manchester Beth Din

BOOKSELLERS
Hasefer Book Store
18 Merrybower Road, Salford M7
Telephone: (0161) 740-3013
Fax: (0161) 721-4649

J. Goldberg
11 Parkside Avenue, Salford M7 0HB
Telephone: (0161) 740-0732

Jewish Book Centre
25 Ashbourne Grove, Salford M7 4DB
Telephone: (0161) 792-1253
Fax: (0161) 661-5505
Hours: Sunday to Thursday, 9.00 am to 9.00 pm; Friday, 9.00 am to 1.00 pm.

BUTCHERS
Halberstadt Ltd
55 Leicester Road, Salford M7 4AS
Telephone: (0161) 792-1109
Supervision: Manchester Beth Din
Open full day Tuesday, Wednesday and Thursday. Open half day Sunday, Monday and Friday. Only Glatt Beth Yosef Meat-Mehadrin Poultry. Electric doors/disabled ramp.

GROCERIES
Halperns Kosher Food Store
57-59 Leicester Road, Salford M7 4DA
Telephone: (0161) 792-1752 Office 792-2992
Fax: (0161) 708-8881
Email: halperns.kosherfood@virgin.net
Supervision: Manchester Beth Din

HOTELS
Fulda's Hotel
144 Old Bury Road, Salford M7 4QY
Telephone: (0161) 740-4551
Fax: (0161) 795-5920
Website: www.here.at/fuldas.com
Supervision: Manchester Beth Din

Four-star hotel open all year. Glatt kosher. Within easy access of motorways, and uniquely placed in the heart of the Manchester Jewish community in Broughton Park. Within easy walking distance of numerous synagogues and shopping facilities.

MIKVAOT
Manchester Communal Mikvah
Broome Holme, Tetlow Lane, Salford M7 0BU
Telephone: (0161) 792-3970
During opening hours only. For appointments for Friday night and Yom Tov evenings: 740-4071; 740-5199. For tevilat kelim, 795-2272.

RESTAURANTS
Dairy
Brackman's Bakery & Coffee Shop
45 Leicester Road,
Telephone: (0161) 792-1652
Supervision: Manchester Beth Din

SYNAGOGUES
Orthodox
Ohel Torah
132 Leicester Road, Salford M7 0EA
Telephone: (0161) 740-2568
Fax: (0161) 745-8876

Adass Yeshurun
Cheltenham Crescent, Salford M7 0FE
Telephone: (0161) 792-1233

Adath Yisroel Nusach Ari
Upper Park Road, Salford M7 0HL
Telephone: (0161) 740-3905

Central & Manchester (incorporating Hightown Central and Beth Jacob)
Leicester Road, Salford M7 4GP
Telephone: (0161) 740-4830

Congregation of Spanish and Portuguese
18 Moor Lane, Kersal, Salford M7 4WX
Telephone: (0161) 795-1212 Office and Home 773-8984
Fax: (0161) 792-7406
Email: ahodari@antonyhodari.co.uk
Website: www.18moorlane.freeserve.co.uk

Higher Crumpsall & Higher Broughton
Bury Old Road, Salford M7 4PX
Telephone: (0161) 740-1210

Kahal Chassidim Lubavitch
62 Singleton Road, Salford M7 4LU
Telephone: (0161) 740-3632
Fax: (0161) 720-9514
Website: www.lubavitch.co.uk

Machzikei Hadass
17 Northumberland Street, Salford M7 0FE
Telephone: (0161) 792-1313

Manchester Great & New Synagogue
Stenecourt, Holden Road, Salford M7 4LN
Telephone: (0161) 792-8399
Fax: (0161) 792-1991

North Salford
2 Vine Street, Salford M7 0NX
Telephone: (0161) 792-3278

TRAVEL AGENTS
Goodmos Tours (Man) Ltd.
23 Leicester Road, Salford M7 0AS
Telephone: (0161) 792-7333
Fax: (0161) 792-7336
Email: goodmos836@aol.com

ST ANNES ON SEA
Synagogue
Orchard Road FY8 1PJ
Telephone: 721-831
Services 7.30 am and 8.00 pm

Leicestershire
LEICESTER
There has been a Jewish presence here since the Middle Ages, but the first record of a 'JewsÕ Synagogue' dates from 1861 in the Leicester Directory. In 2001 the Leicester City Council finally renounced a ban on Jews living in the city which was originally imposed in 1731.

LIBRARIES
Jewish Library and Bookshop
Community Hall, Highfield Street LE2 0NQ
Telephone: (0116) 212-8920

MIKVAOT
Leicester Mikvaot
Synagogue Building, PO Box 6836 LE2 1WZ
Telephone: (0116) 270-6672
Fax: (0116) 270-8796
Email: stanley.lidiker@btopenworld.com

RESTAURANTS
Vegetarian
The Good Earth
19 Free Lane LE1 1JX
Telephone: (0116) 262-6260

SYNAGOGUES
Leicester Progressive Jewish Congregation
24 Avenue Road LE2 3EA
Telephone: (0116) 271-5584
Fax: (0116) 271-7571
Email: jeffrey@kaufmans.co.uk
Website: www.thisisleicestershire.co.uk
Central organisation: Liberal Judaism

Orthodox
Synagogue
Highfield Street LE2 1WZ
Telephone: (0116) 254-0477
Mikvah on premises. Mailing address: PO Box 6836, Leicester, LE2 1WZ.

GRIMSBY
Sir Moses Montefiore Synagogue
Heneage Road DN32 9DZ
Telephone: (01472) 824463
Fax: (01472) 824463
Email: leo-solomon@tiscali.co.uk
Services every Friday, 7.00 pm and all major festivals

KILLINGHOLME
COMMUNITY ORGANISATIONS
Lincolnshire Jewish Community
3 West End Road, Ulceby
Telephone: (01469) 588-951

LINCOLN
Lincoln was one of the centres of medieval Jewry. One of England's oldest stone houses in the city is known as Aaron the Jew's House. The site of Old synagogue is remembered now at Jews' Court. In the cathedral is a recent token of ecclesiastical apology for the 13th-century incident of the 'blood libel', retold in Chaucer. Jews returned to the area in the 19th century. The current community is of very recent date.

TOURIST SITES
Aaron the Jew's House
47 Steep Hill
Believed to be the home of Aaron of Lincoln (c1123-1186) the most prominent Anglo-Jewish financier of the time. A Grade I listed building.

Jew's Court
2 Steep Hill
Telephone: (01522) 521337
Fax: (01522) 521337
Website: www.lincolnshirepast.org.uk
Site of the pre-expulsion synagogue. A Grade I listed building

LONDON
Jews came to London with the Normans following their conquest of England in 1066. A Jewish area in London is first mentioned in 1128; known as 'the Jewish quarter', it was situated around Old Jewry, a street in the City of London close to the Bank of England. Nearby to the west is the church of St Lawrence of Jewry and about one mile to the east is Jewry Street. The community expanded and until 1177 had the only Jewish cemetery in the country. Although there is now no evidence of early Jewish life, the remains of a

mikveh were found in 2001 in Milk Street, close to Old Jewry. It is one of the earliest pieces of physical evidence of Jews in Europe and is the only identifiable structure that has survived from that Jewish community. It will be dismantled and moved to the Bevis Marks synagogue.

The community flourished as arrivals, including a number of scholars, came into the country. In 1194 it contributed a large sum towards the levy raised to ransom Richard I.

In due course, anti-Jewish feeling developed and Jews were expelled from the whole country in 1290. At that time the population was estimated to be around 500.

Until the resettlement the only Jews in London, apart from the converts to Christianity who lived in the Domus Conversorum, a home established for that purpose in New Street, now Chancery Lane, were rare occasional visitors. After the expulsion from Spain in 1492, however, services were held in the city in secret by groups of crypto-Jews.

In December 1656, with resettlement, the estimated 20 families then living in the country established a synagogue in Creechurch Lane (a plaque now commemorates this just under one mile east of the original settlement), and in the following year a cemetery was acquired.

Following the accession of William of Orange the number of Spanish and Portuguese Jews arriving from Holland increased. Included among these were merchants and brokers. As a result, in 1697 'Jew Brokers' were allowed to trade on the Royal Exchange. In due course, Ashkenazi settlers arrived, establishing their own community in 1690.

During the 19th century both communities expanded. In 1835 David Salomons (1797–1873) was elected a sheriff of the city. In 1847 he became the first Jewish alderman and in 1855 the first Jewish lord mayor of the City of London. In 1851 he had been elected a member of parliament but was unable to take his seat as he refused to take the oath of allegiance 'on the true faith of a Christian'. After the oath was amended in 1858, he sat as a member from 1859 until his death. The first Jew to take his seat, however, was Lionel de Rothschild, some months earlier in 1858.

From the 1880s until controls on immigration were established by the 1905 Aliens Act, around 100,000, generally poor, Jews arrived from Russia, Poland and other eastern European countries both to avoid pogroms and as 'economic migrants'.

A Reform community was established in 1840. Jews College (now London School of Jewish Studies) was established in 1855 and the Board of Guardians for the Relief of the Jewish Poor in 1859.

Jewish London is split into a number of areas. Central, the East End and the city, the traditional home of immigrants into England; North London, which contains Stamford Hill, the most Orthodox area; and the North-West where the majority of London Jews now live. The remaining parts of London, the South and the East, have communities but offer little interest to a visitor.

Central London

The Hebrew section of the British Library, situated in Euston, has a large collection of interest to all Jewish visitors to the city. There is a Holocaust Memorial Garden in Hyde Park in the centre of London.

The East End and the City

There is little remaining of Jewish life apart from the historical Jewish sites. Of particular interest is Bevis Marks Synagogue, which was built in 1701 and is almost a duplicate of the Spanish and Portuguese Great Synagogue in Amsterdam. It is the oldest synagogue in the country (some of the oak benches come from the original synagogue in Creechurch Lane). It is still almost exactly the same now as it was 300 years ago, and is still lit by candles. Also worth a visit is the Spitalfields Heritage Centre, devoted to the history of immigration into the country. It is on the site of Princelet Street synagogue, originally a Huguenot family house.

North London

Stamford Hill is the centre of London Jewish hassidic life. It is full of shteibels and small Jewish shops. also in Stamford Hill is the Jewish Military Museum. Nearby in Camden Town is the Ben Uri Art Gallery and the Jewish Museum dealing with Jews in Britain and throughout the world. The Jewish Museum further north in Finchley covers the social history of London Jewry itself. It is in the grounds of the Sternberg Centre for Judaism, which also includes Leo Baeck College.

North-West

Apart from two restaurants in the West End of London, this is the place to go if one wishes to eat kosher. The area around Golders Green and Edgware abounds in restaurants of varying cuisine and quality. There is also an abundance of many Jewish shops of many kinds.

South London

Visitors to London should endeavour to go to the Holocaust Exhibition at the Imperial War Museum in Lambeth. In addition to the exhibition itself, the Imperial War Museum has much of interest.

Currently, around three-quarters of the approximate 300,000 Jews living in Britain live in London.

BAKERIES

Carmelli Bakeries Ltd
126-128 Golders Green Road, GoldersGreen NW11
Telephone: (020) 8455-2074
Fax: (020) 8455-2789
Email: orders@carmelli.co.uk
Website: www.carmelli.co.uk
Supervision: London Beth Din, Kedassia

Créme de la Créme
5 Temple Fortune Parade, Bridge Lane NW11 1QN
Telephone: (020) 8458-9090
Supervision: Kedassia

Daniel's Bagel Bakery
12-13 Hallswelle Parade, Finchley Road, Golders
Green NW11 0DL
Telephone: (020) 8455-5826
Fax: (020) 8455-5826
Supervision: London Beth Din

David Bagel Bakery
38 Vivian Avenue, Hendon NW4 3XP
Telephone: (020) 8203-9995
Supervision: London Beth Din, Kedassia

Dinos Bakeries
11 Edgwarebury Lane, Edgware HA8 8LH
Telephone: (020) 8958-1554
Fax: (020) 8958-2554
106 Brent Street, Hendon NW4 2HH
Telephone: (020) 8203-6623
Supervision: London Beth Din, Kedassia

Hendon Bagel Bakery
55-57 Church Road, Hendon NW4
Telephone: (020) 8203-6919
Fax: (020) 8203-8843
Supervision: Kedassia

Hendon Bagel Bakery
55-57 Church Road, Hendon NW4
Supervision: The Federation of Synagogues Kashrus

J. Grodzinski & Daughters
9 Northways Parade NW3 5EN
Telephone: (020) 7722-4944
Email: info@grodzinski.co.uk
Website: www.grodzinski.co.uk
Supervision: London Beth Din, Kedassia

M & D Grodzinski
223 Golders Green Road, Golders Green NW11 9ES
Telephone: (020) 8458-3654
Fax: (020) 8905-5382
Supervision: London Beth Din, Kedassia

Mr Baker
119-121 Brent Street, Hendon NW4 2DX
Telephone: (020) 8202-6845
Supervision: The Federation of Synagogues Kashrus

Parkway Patisserie Ltd.
30a North End Road, Golders Green NW11
Telephone: (020) 8455-5026

326-328 Regents Park Road , Finchley N3
Telephone: (020) 8346-0344
Supervision: London Beth Din, Kedassia

The Cake Company
2 Sentinel Square, Hendon NW4 2EL
Telephone: (020) 8202-2327
Fax: (020) 8202-8058
Email: cakes@thecakecompany.co.uk
Website: www.thecakecompany.co.uk
Supervision: London Beth Din, Kedassia

Woodberry Down Bakery
47 Brent Street, Hendon NW4
Telephone: (020) 8202-9962
Supervision: London Beth Din, Kedassia

BED AND BREAKFAST

Harold Godfrey Hillel House
25 Louisa Street, Stepney E1 4NF
Telephone: (020) 7790-9557
Summer accommodation in London. Twenty-three rooms,
self-catering separate meat and milk kitchens. Very close to
Stepney Green tube station with easy access to all London
attractions. Please contact the warden at the above
address for more information or to book a room.

Orthodox

Kacenberg's Guest House
1 Alba Gardens, Near Alba Court , Golders Green
NW11 9NS
Telephone: (020) 8455-3780
Fax: (020) 8381-4250
Shabbat meals available

BOOKSELLERS

Boreham Wood Judaica
11 Croxdale Road, Borehamwood WD6 4QD
Telephone: (020) 8381-5559

Carmel Gifts
62 Edgware Way, Middx.
Telephone: (020) 8958-7632
Fax: (020) 8958-6226
Email: info@carmelgifts.co.uk
Website: www.carmelgifts.co.uk

Hebrew Book and Gift Centre
24 Amhurst Parade, Amhurst Park N16 5AA
Telephone: (020) 8802-0609
Fax: (020) 8802-0609
Website: www.hebrewbooks.co.uk

J. Aisenthal
11 ashbourne Parade, Finchley Road , Temple
Fortune NW11 0AD
Telephone: (020) 8455-0501
Email: infor@aisenthal.co.uk
Website: www.aisenthal.co.uk

Jerusalem the Golden
146a Golders Green Road, Golders Green
NW11 8HE
Telephone: (020) 8455-4960
Fax: (020) 8203-7808

Joseph's Bookstore & Cafe Also
1255-1257 Finchley Road, Temple Fortune
NW11 0AD
Telephone: (020) 8731 7575 cafe Also 8455 6890
Fax: (020) 8731 6699
Email: info@josephsbookstore.com
Website: www.josephsbookstore.com
Cafe Also strictly fish and vegetarian
Regular programme of cultural events including The Society
of Jewish Study, Cafe Scientifique, Jazz and Klezmer

Menorah Book and Gift Centre
16 Russel Parade, Golders Road NW11 9NN
Telephone: (020) 8458-8289
Fax: (020) 8731-8403

Steimatzky Hasifria
46 Golders Green Road NW11 8LL
Telephone: (020) 8458-9774
Fax: (020) 8458-3449
Email: info@steimatzkyuk.co.uk
Website: www.steimatzkyuk.co.uk

Torah Treasures
4 Sentinel Square, Brent Street, Hendon NW4 2EL
Telephone: (020) 8202-3134
Fax: (020) 8202-3161
Email: torahtreasures@btinternet.com
Seforim, Judica and gifts.

BUTCHERS

A. Perlmutter & Son
1-2 Onslow Parade, Hampden Square, Southgate
N14 5JN
Telephone: (020) 8361-5441/2
Fax: (020) 8361-5442
Supervision: London Board of Shechita

Frohwein's
1095 Finchley Road, Temple Fortune NW11
Telephone: (020) 8455-9848
Supervision: Kedassia
Deli and cooked food available for weekends and Shabbat.

Golders Green Kosher
132 Golders Green Road, Golders Green
NW11 8HB
Telephone: (020) 8381-4450
Fax: (020) 8731-6450

Greenspans
9-11 Lyttelton Road N2 0DW
Telephone: (020) 8455-9921
Fax: (020) 8455-3484
Supervision: London Board of Shechita

Jack Schlagman
112 Regents Park Road, Finchley N3
Telephone: (020) 8346-3598
Supervision: London Board of Shechita

La Boucherie
4 Cat Hill, East Barnet EN4 8JB
Telephone: (020) 8449-9215
Fax: (020) 8441-1848
Supervision: London Board of Shechita

La Boucherie Express
The Broadway, Stanmore
Email: orders@laboucherie.co.uk
Supervision: With the Sanction of the Rabbinic Authority of
the London Board for Shechita

Louis Mann
23 Edgwarebury Lane, Edgware HA8
Telephone: (020) 8958-3789
Supervision: London Board of Shechita

M. Lipowicz
9 Royal Parade, Ealing W5
Telephone: (020) 8997-1722
Fax: (020) 8997-0048
Supervision: London Board of Shechita

Mehadrin Meats
25 Belfast Road, Stamford Hill N16
Telephone: (020) 8806-0000
Fax: (020) 8880-0500
19 Russell Parade, Golders Green NW11 9NN
Telephone: (020) 8455-9992
Fax: (020) 8455-3777; 8599-0984
Supervision: Kedassia

Menachem's
15 Russell Parade, Golders Green Road , Golders Green NW11
Telephone: (020) 8201-8629
Fax: (020) 8201-8629
Supervision: London Board of Shechita

R. Wolff
84 Edgware Way, Edgware HA8 8JS
Telephone: (020) 8958-8454
Supervision: London Board of Shechita

COMMUNITY ORGANISATIONS
Board of Deputies of British Jews
6 Bloomsbury Square WC1A 2LP
Telephone: (020) 7534-5400
Fax: (020) 7534-0010
Email: info@bod.org.uk
Website: www.bod.org.uk

The Sephardi Centre
2 Ashworth Road W9 1JY
Telephone: (020) 7266-3682
Fax: (020) 7289-5957
Email: sephardicentre @spsyn.org.uk

CONTACT INFORMATION
Jewish Community Information (JCI)
6 Bloomsbury Square WC1A 2LP
Telephone: (020) 7543-5421
Fax: (020) 7543-0100
Email: jci@bod.org.uk
Website: www.bod.org.uk
The basic information service for all aspects of the Jewish Community in Britain. Available Monday to Friday throughout the year, 10.00 am to 4.30 pm (1.30 pm on Fridays) excluding Public and Jewish Holidays.

Jewish Memorial Council (Jewish Committee for H.M. Forces)
25-26 Enford Street, W1H 1DW
Telephone: (020) 7724-7778
Fax: (020) 7706-1710
Email: jmcouncil@btinternet.com

The International Jewish Vegetarianism Society
Bet Teva, 855 Finchley Road NW11 8LX
Telephone: (020) 8455-0692
Fax: (020) 8455-1465
Email: ijvs@yahoo.com
The International Jewish Vegetarian Society was formed 35 years ago to promote vegetarianism from a Jewish perspective.

DELICATESSEN
Kosher Deki at SainsburyÕs O2 Centre
Finchley Road NW3 6LU
Telephone: (020) 7433-1493 ext: 258

Munch Box
41 Greville Street EC1
Telephone: (020) 7242-5487
Supervision: London Beth Din

Parkview
56 The Market Place, Hampstead Garden Suburb NW11 6JP
Telephone: (020) 8458-1878

EMBASSY
Consul General of Israel
15a Old Court Place, Kensington W8 4QB
Telephone: (020) 7957-9500
Fax: (020) 7957-9577
Website: www.israel-embassy.org.uk/london
Nearest tube station: High Street Kensington. Consular office hours: Monday to Thursday, 10.00 am to 1.00 pm; Friday, 10.00 am to 12.00 pm. Postal address: Consulate Section, Embassy of Israel, 2 Palace Green, London W8 4Q8

Embassy of Israel
2 Palace Green, Kensington W8 4QB
Telephone: (020) 7957-9500
Fax: (020) 7957-9555
Email: info-assist@london.mfa.gov.il
Website: www.london.mfa.gov.il

FISH MONGERS
Leveyuson
47a Brent Street, Hendon NW4
Telephone: (020) 8202-7834
Supervision: London Beth Din

Sam Stoller
28 Temple Fortune Parade, Finchley Road, Golders Green NW11 0QS
Telephone: (020) 8455-1957; 8458-1429
Fax: (020) 8445-1957
Supervision: Sephardi Kashrut Authority

GROCERIES
B Kosher
91 Bell Lane, Hendon NW4 2as
Telephone: (020) 82020-1711
Fax: (020) 8202-1599
Opposite Vincent Court

Carmel Fruit Shop
40 Vivian Avenue, Hendon NW4
Telephone: (020) 8202-9587
Fresh fruit and vegetables as well as a good supply of kosher products,cakes and biscuits.

Kosher Kingdom
7 Russell Parade, Golders Green Road NW11 9NN
Telephone: (020) 8455-1429
Fax: (020) 8201-8924
Email: koshking@aol.com
Supervision: London Beth Din

Kosher Net
293 Hale Lane, Edgware HA8 7AX
Telephone: (020) 8281-1656
Supervision: London Beth Din

Kosher Paradise
10 Ashbourne Parade, Finchley Road, Temple
Fortune NW11 0AD
Telephone: (020) 8455-2454
Fax: (020) 8731-6919

Pelter Stores
82 Edgware Way, Edgware HA8
Telephone: (020) 8958-6910
Supervision: Beth Din of the Federation of Synagogues.

Pelters
82 Edgware Way, Edgware
Telephone: (020) 8958-6910

Steve's Kosher Delicatessen
5 Canons Corner, Stanmore, Middx HA8 8Ae
Telephone: (020) 8958-9446
Fax: (020) 8905-4700
Email: stephen@mrbutler.net

Website: www.mrbutler.net
Supervision: London Beth Din
Freshly cooked deli food and take-away. Made on premises.

Yarden
123 Golders Green Road, Golders Green NW11
Telephone: (020) 8458-0979
Free delivery on orders over £25. Hours: Sunday,
Wednesday, Thursday, 8.00 am to 10.00 pm; Monday,
Tuesday, 8.00 am to 9.00 pm; Friday, 8.00 am.

GROCERIES
Paperware disposables
Maxine's
20 Russell Parade, Golders Green Road , Golders
Green NW11 9NN
Telephone: (020) 8458-3102
Fax: (020) 8455-3632
Kedassia Deli. Deliveries

GUEST HOUSE
Sharon Guest House
7 Woodlands Close, Golders Green
Telephone: (020) 8458-8531
Email: jlazenga@gmail.com slazenga@gmail.com
Supervision: Although not officially supervised it is said to
be Shomer Shabbat Dati.

HOTELS

Central Hotel
35 Hoop Lane, Golders Green NW11 8BS
Telephone: (020) 8458-5636
Fax: (020) 8455-4792
Private bathrooms and parking

Croft Court Hotel
44 Ravenscroft Avenue, Golders Green N11 8AY
Telephone: (020) 8458-3331
Fax: (020) 8455-9175
Email: enquiries@croftcourthotel.co.uk
Website: www.croftcourthotel.co.uk
Supervision: Kedassia

King Solomon Palace Hotel
155-159 Golders Green Road NW11 9BX
Telephone: (020) 8201-9000
Fax: (020) 8201-9853

Kosher
Kadimah Hotel
146 Clapton Common, Stamford Hill E5 9AG
Telephone: (020) 8800-5960
Fax: (020) 8800-6237
Website: www.kadimahotel.co.uk
Supervision: Kedassia

KASHRUT INFORMATION

Federation of Synagogues Kashrus Board-KF
65 Watford Way, London NW4 3AQ
Telephone: (020) 8202-2263
Fax: (020) 8203-0610
Email: info@kfkosher.org
Website: www.kfkosher.org

Joint Kashrus Committee-Kedassia (Union of Orthodox Hebrew Congregation)
140 Stamford Hill, Stamford Hill N16 6QT
Telephone: (020) 8800-6833
Fax: (020) 8809-7092

London Beth Din
735 High Road, Finchley N12 0US
Telephone: (020) 8343-6255 (Kashrut hotline: 8343-6333)
Fax: (020) 8343-6254
Email: info@kosher.org.uk
Website: www.kosher.org.uk
Publishes 'The Really Jewish Food Guide', which contains a list of all the establishments it certifies, as well as guidance for the shopper in buying general consumer products.

National Council of Shechita Boards
Elscot House, Arcadia Avenue, Finchley N3 2JU
Telephone: (020) 8349-9160
Fax: (020) 8346-2209
Email: shechita@tiscali.co.uk

Sephardi Kashrut Authority
2 Ashworth Road, Maida Vale W9 1JY
Telephone: (020) 7289-2573
Fax: (020) 7289-7663
Email: dvsteinhof@onetel.com
Website: www.sephardikashrut.com

KOSHER FOODS
Kosher Corner
42 St George's Rd, Wimbledon SW19 4ED
Telephone: (020) 8944-1581
Email: Lubwdon@aol.com

LIBRARIES
British Library, Asia, Pacific and Africa Collections - Hebrew Section
96 Euston Road NW1 2DB
Telephone: (020) 7412-7646
Fax: (020) 7412-7641/7870
Email: ilana.tahan@bl.uk
Website: www.bl.uk/cllections/hebrew.html
The Hebrew section contains over 70,000 printed books, 3,000 manscripts and some 10,000 Genizah fragments. Orriental reading room open to holders of readers' passes: Monday 10.00 am to 5.00 pm; Tuesday to Saturday 9.30 am to 5.00 pm. Hebrew manscripts on permanent display in the treasures gallery of the library. The Golden Haggadah is included in th e electronic 'Turning the Pages' programme.

Institute of Contemporary History and Wiener Library
4 Devonshire Street W1W 5BH
Telephone: (020) 7636-7247
Fax: (020) 7436-6428
Email: info@weinerlibrary.co.uk
Website: www.weinerlibrary.co.uk
The world's oldest institution dedicated to the documentation of Nazi Germany and the Holocaust. The collection includes 60,000 books and pamphlets, periodicals, documents, videos and photographs as well as extensive press cuttings from 1933 onwards. Other subjects include 20th century Jewish history, anti-semitism, refugees, minorities, fascism, citizenship, etc.

The Jewish Studies Library
University College London Library , Gower Street WC1E 6BT
Telephone: (020) 7679-2598
Fax: (020) 7679-7373
Email: library@ucl.ac.uk
Website: www.ucl.ac.uk/library/
In addition to materials purchased for the CollegeÕs Department of Hebrew Studies, it tncorporates the Mocatta Library, Altmann Library, William Margulies Yiddish Library and the Library of the Jewish Historical Society of England. Applications to use or view the collections should be made in advance in writing to the Librarian.

MEDIA
Directory
Jewish Year Book
Vallentine Mitchell, Premier House, Suite 314, 112-114 Station Road Edgware Middlesex HA 7BJ,
Telephone: (020) 8952 9526
Fax: (020) 8952-
Email: jyb@vmbooks.com
Website: www.vmbooks.com
Annual directory of all information relating to the British Jewish Community

Internet
Brijnet
11 The Lindens, Prospect Hill, Waltham Forest E17 3EJ
Telephone: (020) 8520-3531
Email: info@brijnet.org
Website: www.brijnet.org

Listings
The Diary
32 Bell Lane NW4 2AD
Telephone: (020) 8922-5437
Fax: (020) 8922-8709

Newspapers
Essex Jewish News
Suite 314, Premier House 112-114 Station Road, Edgware, Middlesex HA8 7BJ
Telephone: (020) 8952-9526
Fax: (020) 8952-9242
Email: info@vmbooks.com
Quarterly publication serving East London and Essex

Hamodia
149 Kyverdale Road N16 6PS
Telephone: (020) 8806-7577
Fax: (020) 8806-1222
Email: Post@Hamodia.demon.co.uk

Jewish Chronicle
25 Furnival Street EC4A 1JT
Telephone: (020) 7415-1500
Fax: (020) 7405-9040
Email: editorial@thejc.com
Website: www.thejc.com

Established 1841, worlds oldest and most influential Jewish newspaper weekly publication.

Jewish News
Unit 611 Highate Studios, 53-79 Highate Road, Kentish Town NW5 1TL
Telephone: (020) 7692-6929
Fax: (020) 7692-6689
Email: info@totallyjewish.com
Website: www.totallyjewish.com

MIKVAOT
Adath Yisroel Synagogue Mkikvah
40a Queen Elizabeth's Walk, Stamford Hill N16 0HH
Telephone: (020) 8802-2554

Craven Walk Mikvah
72 Lingwood Road, Stamford Hill N16
Telephone: (020) 8800-8555
Evening telephone number: (020) 8809-6279

Edgware & District Communal Mikvah
Edgware United Synagogue Grounds, 22 Warwick Avenue Drive, Edgware HA8
Telephone: (020) 8958-3233
Fax: (020) 8958-4004
Email: estrin@clara.co.uk

North West London Communal Mikvah
10a Shirehall Lane, Hendon NW4
Telephone: (020) 8202-1427
Evenings: (020) 8202-8517/5706

Satmar Mikkvah
62 Filey Avenue, Stamford Hill N16
Telephone: (020) 8806-3961

South London Mikvah
42 St Georges Road, Wimbledon SW19 4ED
Telephone: (020) 8944-7149
Fax: (020) 8944-7563
Email: lubwdon@aol.com

Stamford Hill & District Mikvah
Margaret Road, Stamford Hill N16
Telephone: (020) 8806-3880
Other telephone numbers: (020) 8809-4064 or (020) 8800-5119.

The New Central London Mikvah

21 Andover Place NW6 5ED
Telephone: (020) 7372-7237
By appointment only.

The Sternberg Centre for Judaism

80 East End Road, Finchley N3 2SY
Telephone: (020) 8349-2568
Fax: (020) 8349-5699
Email: sylvia.morris@reformjudaism.org.uk
Website: www.refsyn.org.uk
By prior appointment

Union of Orthodox Hebrew Congregations

140 Stamford Hill, Stamford Hill N16 6QT
Telephone: (020) 8802-6226
Fax: (020) 8809-7097

MUSEUMS

Ben Uri Gallery, The London Jewish Museum of Art

108a Boundary Road, St Johns Wood NW8 0RH
Telephone: (020) 7604-3991
Fax: (020) 7604-3992
Email: info@benuri.org.uk
Website: www.benuri.org.uk
Supervision: David Glasser

Ben Uri Gallery, the London Jewish Museum of Art, is Britain's oldest Jewish Cultural Organisation. Our missions are to inform the widest public in Britain and abroad of the life, work and contrbution of British and European artists of Jewish descent and their contemporaries.Major exhibitions include: Sir Solomon J Solomon RA (1990), Abram Games (1991), Claude Rogers (1992), Bernard Cohen (1994), Bernard Meninsky (2001) ,Ludwig and Else Meidner (2002), Mark Gertler (2002), The Tortoise and the Hare: William Roberts & Jacob Kramer (2003), Rediscovering Wolmark (2004), Abram Games (2005), Chagall and his circle (2005), Joash Woodrow (2005). Open Monday to Thursday 10.00 amm to 5.30 pm, Sunday 12.00 am to 4.00 pm Friday (summer) 10.00 am to 5.30 pm, Friday (winter) 10.00 am to 3.00 pmm. Closed Jewish Holy days.

Jewish Military Museum and Memorial Room

AJEX House, East Bank, Stamford Hill N16 5RT
Telephone: (020) 8800-2844
Fax: (020) 8800-1117
Email: ajexuk@talk21.com
Website: www.ajex.org.uk

Memorabilia, artefacts, medals, letters, documents, pictures and uniforms all illustrating British Jewry's contribution to the Armed Forces of the Crown from the Crimea to the present day. By appointment, Sunday to Thursday, 11.00 am to 4.00 pm.

Museum of Immigration

19 Princelet Street E1

A museum devoted to the history of immigration into Great Britain. Included in the site is Princelet Street Synagogue, a 1870 synagogue built onto a Grade II* listed Georgian town house.

The Holocaust Exhibition

Imerial War Museum, Lambeth Road SE1 6HZ
Telephone: (020) 7416-5439
Fax: (020) 7416-5457
Email: groups@iwm.org.uk or to book advance tickets boxoffice@iwm.org.uk
Website: www.iwm.org.uk
Central organisation: Imperial War Museum

The Exhibition covers two floors and uses original artefacts, film, documents and photographs to tell the story of the Nazis' genocidal programme. Rare and important historical material, some lent by former concentration and extermination camp inmates. Opening hours: 10.00 am to 6.00 pm.

The Jewish Museum

The Sternberg Centre, 80 East End Road, Finchley N3 2SY
Telephone: (020) 8349-1143
Fax: (020) 8343-2162
Email: enquiries@jewishmuseum.org.uk
Website: www.jewishmuseum.org.uk

Permanent exhibitions trace history of London Jewry with reconstructions of a tailoring and furniture workshop. Holocaust education is also a major feature of the Museum's work and the Museum's displays include a moving exhibition on London-born Holocaust survivor,

Leon Greenman. Open Monday to Thursday: 10.30 am to 5.00 pm, and Sunday 10.30 am to 4.30 pm. Closed Jewish festivals and Public Holidays and 25 December to 5 January.

The Jewish Museum
Raymond Burton House, 129-131 Albert Street, Camden Town NW1 7NB
Telephone: (020) 7284-1997
Fax: (020) 7267-9008
Email: admin@jmus.org.uk
Website: www.jewishmuseum.org.uk

The Museum's attractive premises include a History Gallery, Ceremonial Art Gallery and a Temporary Exhibitions gallery offering a varied programme of changing exhibitions. The Museum has been awarded Designated status by the Museums and Galleries Commission in recognition of its outstanding collections of Jewish Ceremonial Art, which are amongst the finest in the world. Open Monday to Thursday 10.00 am to 4.00 pm, and Sunday 10.00 am to 5.00 pm. Last Admission to the Gallery half an hour before closing. Closed Jewish Festivals and 25, 26 December and 1 January, and Bank Holidays. Group visits by prior arrangement. Admission charge.

RELIGIOUS ORGANISATIONS
Assembly of Masorti Synagogues
1097 Finchley Road, Golders Green NW11 0PU
Telephone: (020) 8201-8772
Fax: (020) 8201-8917
Email: office@masorti.org.uk
Website: www.masorti.org.uk

Liberal Judaism
The Montagu Centre, 21 Maple Street W1T 4BE
Telephone: (020) 7580-1663
Fax: (020) 7631-9838
Email: montagu@liberaljudaism.org
Website: www.liberaljudaism.org

Reform Synagogue
The Sternberg Centre for Judaism, 80 East End Road, Finchley N3 2SY
Telephone: (020) 8349-5640
Fax: (020) 8343-5699
Email: admin@reformjudaism.org.uk
Website: www.reformjudaism.org.uk

Spanish & Portugese Jews' Congregation
2 Ashworth Road, Maida Vale W9 1JY
Telephone: (020) 7789-2573
Fax: (020) 7289-2709
Email: howardmiller@spsyn.org.uk
Website: www.sandp.org.uk

Union of Orthodox Hebrew Congregations
140 Stamford Hil l N16 6QT
Telephone: (020) 8802-6226
Fax: (020) 8809-7902

United Synagogue
Adler House, 735 High Road, Finchley N12 0US
Telephone: (020) 8343-8989
Fax: (020) 8343-6262
Website: www.unitedsynagogue.org.uk

RESTAURANTS
Bevis Marks The Restaurant
Bevis Marks EC3
Telephone: (020) 7283-2220
Fax: (020) 7283-2221
Email: enquiries@BevisMarksTheRestaurant.com

Dairy
Art 2 Heart
109a Golders Green, London NW11
Telephone: (020) 8201-9991
Supervision: London Beth Din

Bon Baggeute
122 Golders Green Road, NW11 8HB
Telephone: (020) 8209-0232
Supervision: London Beth Din

Café Dan
14 Halleswelle Parade, Finchley Road NW11 8HB
Telephone: (020) 8455-3731
Supervision: London Beth Din

Café on the Green
122 Golders Green Road, Finchley Road NW11 8HB
Telephone: (020) 8209-0232
Supervision: London Beth Din
Chalav Yisrael. Open Motzei Shabbat in winter.

-- MENAHEL --
The synagogue membership system
www.brianplen.com
Tel: +44(0)208 349 9640 Fax: +44(0)208 346 5020 email: office@brianplen.com

Isola Bella Café

63 Brent Street, Hendon NW4 2EA
Telephone: (020) 8203-2000
Website: www.isolabellacafe.com
Supervision: London Beth Din of the Federation of
Synagogues, Sephardi Kashrut Authority.

Isola Bella Café

63 Brent Street, Hendon NW4 3EA

Milk n' Honey

124 Golders Green Road, Golders Green
NW11 8HB
Telephone: (020) 8455-0664
Supervision: Kedassia

Vegetarian/dairy restaurant/coffee shop/air-conditioned.
Menus in English and Hebrew. Also take-away available.

Orli Café

96 Brent Street, Hendon NW4 2HH
Telephone: (020) 8203-7555
108 Regents Park Road, Finchley N3 3JG
Telephone: (020) 8371-9222
295 Hale Lane, Edgware HA8 7AX
Telephone: (020) 8958-1555
Supervision: Kedassia

Pita

98 Golders Green Road NW11 8HB
Telephone: (020) 8381-4080
Supervision: The Federation of Synagogues Kashrus

Slice

8 Princes Parade NW11 9PS
Telephone: (020) 8458-9483
Supervision: The Federation of Synagogues Kashrus

Taboon

17 Russell Parade, Golders Green Road NW11 9NN
Telephone: (020) 8455-7451
Supervision: Sephardi Kashrut Authority, Kedassia.

Tasti Pizza

252 Golders Green Road, Golders Green NW11
Telephone: (020) 8209-0023
Supervision: London Beth Din, Kedassia

Tasty Pizza

23 Amhurst Parade, Amhurst Park, Stamford Hill
N16 5AA
Telephone: (020) 8802-0018
Supervision: London Beth Din, Kedassia

Meat

'86'

86 Brent Street, Hendon NW4
Telephone: (020) 8202-5575
Supervision: The Federation of Synagogues Kashrus

Amors Takeaway

8 Russell Parade, golders Green NW11
Telephone: (020) 8458-4221
Supervision: Kedassia
Serves meat and fish

Dizengoff Kosher Restaurant Limited

118 & 122 Golders Green Road, London NW11 8SP
Tel: 020 8458 7003 020 8209 0232 Fax: 020 8457 7543
www.dizengoffkosherrestaurant.co.uk   www.kosherfriedchicken.co.uk

BRINGING A WORLD OF FOOD TO YOU

Whatever your culinary tastes we can cater for you at one of our restaurants
Fine Dining ∗ Casual Dining ∗ Take Away

Middle Eastern Cuisine
Far Eastern Cuisine
American Style Cuisine

Open Sun-Thu 11:30-23:30
Fri 11:30-15:00
Motsei Shabbat until 2:00am

Under Supervision of Sephardi Kashrut Authority

Aviv
87 High Street, Edgware
Telephone: (020) 8952-2484
Fax: (020) 8952-0200
Email: info@avivrestaurant.com
Website: www.avivrestaurant.com
Supervision: Beth Din of the Federation of Synagogues

Bloom's
130 Golders Green Road, London NW11 8HP
Telephone: (020) 8455 1338
Fax: (020) 8455 3033
Email: bloomsrestaurant@btclick.com
Supervision: London Beth Din

Dizengoff Kosher Fried Chicken (DKFC)
122 Golders Green Road, Golders Green
NW11 8HB
Telephone: (020) 8209-0232
Fax: (020) 8457-7543
Email: dizengoff@btopenworld.com
Website: www.Dizengoffkosherfriedchicken.co.uk
Supervision: Sephardi Kashrut Authority

Hours: Sunday to Thursday, 11.00 am to midnight; Friday to
4.00 pm; Saturday night one hour after shabbat until 4.00
am

Dizengoff Kosher Restaurant
118 Golders Green Road, Golders Green
NW11 8HB
Telephone: (020) 8458-7003
Fax: (020) 8457-7543
Email: dizengoff@btconnect.com
Website: www.Dizengoffkosherrestaurant.co.uk
Supervision: Sephardi

Israeli style grill

Folman's Restaurant
134 Brent Street NW4
Telephone: (020) 8202-5592
Supervision: London Beth Din

Kaifeng
51 Church Road, Hendon NW4 4DU
Telephone: (020) 8203-7888
Fax: (020) 8203-8263
Website: www.kaifeng.co.uk

Supervision: London Beth Din

Chinese Restaurant with take-away and delivery service.
Free delivery with minimum order of £30. Hours: Sunday to
Thursday, 12.30 pm to 2.30 pm, 5.30 pm to 10.30 pm; open
Saturday evening, September to April.

Kinneret
313 Hale Lane HA8 7AX
Telephone: (020) 8958-4955
Supervision: Beth Din of the Federation of Synagogues.

Lemonade
87 Brent St. NW4
Telephone: (020) 8201-5222
Supervision: Sephardi Kashrut Authority

Marcus's
5 Hallswelle Parade, Finchley Road, Golders Green
NW11 0DL
Telephone: (020) 8458-4670
Website: www.marcuss.co.uk
Supervision: London Beth Din

Penashe Glatt BBQ Grill
60 Edgware Way (Mowbray Parade), Edgware
HA8 8JS
Telephone: (020) 8958-6008
Website: www.penashe.co.uk

Reubens
79 Baker Street W1M 1AJ
Telephone: (020) 7486-0035
Fax: (020) 7486-7079
Supervision: Sephardi Kashrut Authority

Open daily except for Shabbat; open Friday until two hours
before sundown.

Sami's Restaurant
157 Brent Street, Hendon NW4 4DJ
Telephone: (020) 8203-8088
Fax: (020) 8203-1040
Supervision: Beth Din of the Federation of Synagogues

Glatt kosher Middle Eastern cuisine

Six 13 Restaurant
19 wigmore Street W1H 9LA
Telephone: (020) 7629-6133
Fax: (020) 7629-6135
Email: inquiries@six13.com
Website: www.six13.com
Supervision: London Beth Din
Opening times: Monday to Thursday Lunch 12.00 to 2.30 pm, Dinner 5.00 pm to 10.30 pm. Weekdays for exclusive hire.

Solly's
148a Golders Green Road, Golders Green NW11
Telephone: (020) 8455-0004
Supervision: London Beth Din

Solly's Exclusive
146-150 Golders Green Road, Golders Green NW11
Telephone: (020) 8455-2121
Supervision: London Beth Din

The White House Restaurant
10 Bell Lane, Hendon NW4
Telephone: (020) 8203-2427
Website: www.whitehouserestaurant.co.uk
Supervision: London Beth Din of the Federation of Synagogues, Sephardi Kashrut Authority

New York Deli & Restaurant
Zvika
8 Great Chapel Street, Off Oxford Street
Telephone: (020) 7434-2733
Fax: (020) 7287-0954
Supervision: Sephardi Beth Din
Opening Times: Mon to Thurs 11.00 am to 11.00 pm, Fri 11.00 am to 3.00 pm, Sun 11.00 am to 11.00 pm

Snack Bar
Sue Harris Student Centre
B'nai BÕrith-Hillel Foundation, 1-2 Endsleigh Street WC1H 0DS
Telephone: (020) 7388-0801
Fax: (020) 7380 6599
Email: info@ujshillel.co.uk
Website: www.ujshillel.co.uk
Supervision: London Beth Din
Hours: Monday to Thursday. Please phone for details of summer months opening. Re-opens for students and all other visitors mid-September.

SELF-CATERING
Yamor
Golders Green
Telephone: (020) 7968-387499
Fax: (020) 8455-4231
Website: www.yamor.com

TRAVEL AGENTS

LestAir Services
80 Highfield Ave., Golders Green NW11 9TT
Telephone: (020) 8455-9654
Fax: (020) 455-9654
Email: family.schleimer@ukgateway.net
Promoting Jewish Heritage Tours to the Czech Republic, Poland, Hungary, Byelorus, Latvia and Lithuania and can be contacted for detailed information and guidance

Longwood Travel
3 Bourne Court, Southend Road, Woodford Green IG8 8HD
Telephone: (020) 8551-4466
Fax: (020) 8551-5588

Mozes Travel
Dunstan House, 14a St Cross Street EC1N 8XA
Telephone: (020) 7430-2230
Fax: (020) 7405-5049

Peltours
11-19 Ballards Lane, Finchley N3 1UX
Telephone: (020) 8346-9144
Fax: (020) 8343-0579
Email: sales@peltours.com

Peltours AMG Travel
70 Edgware Way, Edgware HA8 8JS
Telephone: (020) 8958-3188
Fax: (020) 8958-8898

Sabra Travel Ltd.
9 Edgwarebury Lane, Edware HA8 8LH
Telephone: (020) 8958-3244/7

Travelink Group Ltd.
50 Vivian Avenue NW4 3XH
Telephone: (020) 8931-8000
Fax: (020) 8931-8877
Email: info@travelinkuk.com
Website: www.travelinkuk.com

West End Travel
Barratt House, 341 Oxford Street W1R 2LE
Telephone: (020) 7629-6299
Fax: (020) 7499-0865
Email: admin@westendtravel.co.uk

Pesach, Shavuot, Sukkot
Kosher Hotels & Cruises Worldwide
Telephone: (020) 8203-4482
Email: info@kosherhotels.co.uk
Website: www.kosherhotels.co.uk

Middlesex

STAINES

Orthodox
Staines & District Synagogue
Westbrook Road, South Street TW18 4PR
Telephone: (017) 8425-4604
Fax: (017) 8425-4604

Norfolk

NORWICH

Norwich is the site of the first recorded 'blood libel' in Europe when in 1144, William of Norwich was found murdered. At that time Jews were connected with the woollen and worsted trades for which the city was at that time famous. Resettlement took place in the early 18th century and the present community was established in 1813.

SYNAGOGUES

Norwich Synagogue
3a Earlham Road NR2 3RA
Telephone: (01603) 503434

Progressive Jewish Community of East Anglia
c/o Frimette Carr NR2 3RA
Telephone: (01603) 714162

Northampton

NORTHAMPTON

Northampton Synagogue
Overstone Road BB1 3JW
Telephone: (01604) 33345
Services on Friday night.

Nottinghamshire

NEWARK

HOLOCAUST MEMORIAL CENTRE

Beth Shalom
Laxton, Newark, Notts NG22 0PA
Telephone: (01623) 836627
Fax: (01623) 836647

Beth Shalom Holocaust Memorial Centre was conceived as a place where some of the implications of the Holocaust can be faced. It is an education centre where Jews and non-Jews work together to forge a united front against the perils of anti-Semitism and racism in society today.

NOTTINGHAM

Jews settled in Nottingham as early as medieval times, and centres of learning and worship are known to have existed in that period. The earliest known record of an established community dates from 1822 when a grant of land for burial purposes was made by the Corporation.

The synagogue in Shakespeare Street (originally a Methodist Church) is a Grade II listed building.

RESTAURANTS

Vegetarian
Maxine's Salad Table
56 Upper Parliament Street NG1 2AG
Telephone: (0115) 947-3622

SYNAGOGUES

Liberal
Nottingham Progressive Jewish Congregation
Lloyd Street, Sherwood NG5 4BP
Telephone: (0115) 962-4761
Email: npjc@liberaljudaism.org
Website: www.npjc.org.uk

Orthodox
Synagogue
Shakespeare Stret NG1 4FQ
Telephone: (0115) 947-2004

Oxfordshire

OXFORD

There was an important medieval community, and the present one dates back to 1842. The Oxford Synagogue and Jewish Centre, opened in 1974, serves both the city and the university. It is available for all forms of Jewish worship.

COMMUNITY ORGANISATIONS

L'Chaim Society
Albion House, Little Gate OX
Telephone: (01865) 794-462

SYNAGOGUES

The Synagogue and Jewish Centre
21 Richmond Road OX1 2JL
Telephone: (01865) 553-042
Email: information@oxford-synagogue.org.uk
Regular Orthodox Masorti and Progressive Services. Wide range of communal activities. A kosher meals service operates during term-time. Phone or email for information.

Staffordshire

STOKE ON TRENT

Synagogue
Birch Terrace, Hanley ST1 3JN
Telephone: (01782) 616-417

Surrey

GUILDFORD

MUSEUMS

Guildford Museum
Castle Arch GU1 3SX
Telephone: (01483) 444-750
Fax: (01483) 532-391
Email: museum@guildford.gov.uk
Website: www.guildfordmuseum.co.uk

SYNAGOGUES

Orthodox
Guildford & District Synagogue
York Road GU1 4DR
Telephone: (01483) 576-470
Website:
www.geocities.com/guildfordjewishcommunity
Correspondence: Irene Black 11Grasmere Close, Merrow, Guildford GU1 2TG

TOURIST SITES
Medieval Synagogue
Enquiries about the discovery of a medieval synagogue in the town may be addressed to the Guildford Museum

WEYBRIDGE

Reform
North West Surrey Synagogue
Hovath Close, Rosslyn Park Oaklands Drive KT13 9QZ
Telephone: (01932) 855-400
Fax: (01932) 855-400

Sussex East

BRIGHTON AND HOVE
The first known Jewish resident of Brighton lived here in 1767. The earliest synagogue was founded in Jew Street in 1789. Henry Solomon, vice-president of the congregation, was the first Chief Constable of the town. His brother-in-law, Levi Emanuel Cohen, founded the Brighton Guardian, and was twice elected president of the Newspaper Society of Great Britain. The town's Jewish population today is about 8,000.

COMMUNITY ORGANISATIONS
Lubavitch Chabad House
15 Upper Drive BN3 6GR
Telephone: (01273) 321-919
Fax: (01273) 821-518

DELICATESSEN
Cantor's of Hove
20 Richardson Road, Hove BN3 5BB
Telephone: (01273) 723-669

MEDIA
Newspapers
Sussex Jewish News
PO Box 2178 BN3 3SZ
Telephone: (01273) 330-550
Fax: (01273) 726-342
Email: doris@sjnews.fsnet.co.uk /
doris@sussexjewishnews.com`
Website: www.jewishsussex.com
Monthly magazine covering the Jewish community in Sussex (and more) Publication date: 1st of every month. Deadline date: 12th of month preceding publication. Subscription: £15 per annum.

MIKVAOT
Brighton and Hove Mikvaot
Prine Regent Swimming Pool Complex, Church Street BN1 1YA
Telephone: (01273) 321-919

ORGANISATIONS
Hillel House
18 Harrington Road BN1 6RE
Telephone: (01273) 503-450
Closed during summer vacation. Friday evening meals available.

RELIGIOUS ORGANISATIONS
Brighton and Hove Joint Kashrus Committee
c/o B.H.H.C., 31 New Church Road, Hove BN3 4AD
Telephone: (01273) 888-855
Fax: (01273) 888-810

RESTAURANTS
Vegetarian
Food for Friends
17-18 Price Albert Street, The Lanes
Telephone: (01273) 202-310
Fax: (01273) 774-171
Email: simon@foodies.freeserve.co.uk
Website: www.foodforfriends.com

Wai Kika Moo Kau Limited
42 Meeting House Lane
Telephone: (01273) 323-824

SYNAGOGUES

Orthodox

Brighton & Hove Hebrew Congregation
Middle Street Synagogue, 66 Middle Street
Bn1 1AL
Telephone: (01273) 888-855
Fax: (01273) 888-810
The synagogue, which was built in 1874 when Brighton was very fashionable, has an elaborate Victorian interior. It is a Grade II listed building.

Hove Hebrew Congregation
79 Holland Road, Hove BN3 1JN
Telephone: (01273) 732-035

West Hove Synagogue
31 Curch Road, Hove BN3 4AD
Telephone: (01273) 888-855
Fax: (01273) 888-810
Email: bhhc@breathemail.net

Progressive Synagogue
6 Landsdown Road BN3 1FF
Telephone: (01273) 737-223
Hours: 9.30 am to 1.00 pm

Reform

Palmeira Avenue BN3 3Ge
Telephone: (01273) 735-343
Fax: (01273) 734-537
Email: office@bh-rs.org
Website: www.bh-rs.org

EASTBOURNE

SYNAGOGUES

Orthodox

Eastbourne Hebrew Congregation
22 Susans Road BN21 3TJ
Telephone: (01323) 640441

Tyne and Weir

GATESHEAD

A community with many schools, yeshivot and other training institutions.

BAKERIES

Stenhouse
215 Coatsworth Road NE8 1SR
Telephone: (0191) 477-2001
Fax: (0191) 478 4778
Mobile Phone: 07778148902
Supervision: Gateshead Kashrus Authority

BOOKSELLERS

J. Lehmann
28-30 Grasmere Street NE8 1TS
Telephone: (0191) 477-3523
Fax: (0191) 430-0555
Email: info@lehmanns.co.uk
Also has wholesale and mail order, Unit E, Rolling Mill Road, NE32 3DP. Tel: (0191) 430-0333

BUTCHERS

K.L. Kosher Butcher
83 Rodsley Avenue NE8
Telephone: (0191) 477-3109
Kosher

MIKVAOT

Gateshead Mikvaot
180 Bewick Road NE8 1UF
Telephone: (0191) 477-3552

SYNAGOGUES

Gateshead Synagogue
138 Whitehall Road NE8 1TP
Telephone: (0191) 477-3012
180 Berwick Road NE8 1UF
Telephone: (0191) 477-0111

NEWCASTLE UPON TYNE

The community was established before 1831, when a cemetery was acquired. Jews have lived in Newcastle since 1775. There are about 1,200 Jews in the city today.

KASHRUT INFORMATION

Kashrus Committee
Lionel Jacobson House, Graham Park Road, Gosforth NE3 4BH
Telephone: (0191) 284-0959
Fax: (0191) 284-0959

MEDIA

Newspapers
The North-East Jewish Recorder
24 Adeline Gardens NE3 4JQ
Telephone: (0191) 285-1253
Fax: (0191) 242-1316
Email: clivando@hotmail.com
Website: www.northeastjewish.org.uk

MIKVAOT

Newcastle Upon Tyne Mikvaot
Graham Park Road NE3 4BH
Telephone: (0191) 284-0959

RELIGIOUS ORGANISATIONS

Representative Council of North-East Jewry
Telephone: (0191) 215-6253
Fax: (0191) 215-6080

RESTAURANTS

Vegetarian
The Supernatural
2 Princess Square NE1 8ER
Telephone: (0191) 261-2730

SYNAGOGUES
Orthodox
United Hebrew Congregation
Graham Park Road NE3 4BH
Telephone: (0191) 284-0959
Mikva on premises

Reform
Newcastle Reform Synagogue
The Croft, off Kenton Road NE3 4RF
Telephone: (0191) 284-8621

SUNDERLAND
MIKVAOT
Sunderland Mikvaot
11 The Oaks East, Ryhope Road SR2 8EX
Telephone: (191) 565-0224

SYNAGOGUES
Orthodox
Sunderland Hebrew Congregation
Ryhope Road SR2 7EQ
Telephone: (191) 565-8093
This building has been given Grade II listed status.

West Midlands
BIRMINGHAM
This Jewish community is one of the oldest outside London, dating from at least 1730. Birmingham was a centre from which Jewish pedlars covered the surrounding country week by week, returning home for Shabbat.

The first synagogue of which there is any record was in The Froggery in 1780. There was a Jewish cemetery in the same neighbourhood in 1730. The synagogue of 1780 was extended in 1791, 1809 and 1827. A new and larger synagogue, popularly known as 'Singers Hill', opened in 1856. Today's Jewish population stands at about 2,300.

BOOKSELLERS
Lubavitch Bookshop
95 Willow Road B12 9QF
Telephone: (0121) 440-6673
Fax: (0121) 446-4199

DELICATESSEN
Gee's Butchers Ltd
75 Pershore Road B5 7NX
Telephone: (0121) 440-2160
Fax: (0121) 440-2421
Kosher butcher, baker and deli

INFORMATION AND RESOURCE CENTRE
Israel Information Centre for the Midlands
Singers Hill, Ellis Street B1 1 HL
Telephone: (0121) 643-2688
Fax: (0121) 643-2688

Email: rjacob@iicmids.u-net.com
Hours of opening: 10.00 am to 4.00 pm Monday , Tuesday, Thursday or by appointment.

KASHRUT INFORMATION
Shechita Board
Singers Hill, Ellis Street B1 1HL
Telephone: (0121) 643-0884

MIKVAOT
Birmingham Central Synagogue
133 Pershore Road B5 7PA
Telephone: (0121) 440-4044
Fax: (0121) 440-5405

SYNAGOGUES
Liberal
Progressive Synagogue
4 Sheepcote Street B16 8AA
Telephone: (0121) 643-5640
Fax: (0121) 633-8372
Email: bps@uips.org
Website: www.bps-pro-syn.co.uk

Orthodox
Birmingham Hebrew Congregation
Singers Hill, Ellis Street B1 1HL
Telephone: (0121) 643-0884
Fax: (0121) 643-5950

Central Synagogue
133 Pershore Road, Edgbaston B5 7PA
Telephone: (0121) 440-4044
Fax: (0121) 440-5405

COVENTRY
Coventry Hebrew Congregation
Barras Lane CV1 3BW
Telephone: (024) 7622-0168
The Jewish presence in Coventry dates back to 1775, if not earlier.

SYNAGOGUES
Reform
Coventry Jewish Reform Community
24 Nightingale Lane, Canley Gardens CV5 6AY
Telephone: (024) 7667-2027

SOLIHULL
Orthodox
Solihull & District Hebrew Congregation
3 Monastery Drive B91 1DW
Telephone: (0121) 706-5199
Fax: (0121) 706-8736
Email: shul@solihullshul.org
Website: www.solihullshul.org
Services: Friday evening 6.30 pm winter, 8.00 pm summer, Saturday 9.45 am, Sunday 9 am

Yorkshire North
HARROGATE
Harrogate Hebrew Congregation
St Mary's Walk
Telephone: (01423) 871-713
Fax: (01423) 879-143
Email: philip.morris@ukgateway.net
Services: Saturday 9.30 am. First Friday evening in month
Winter 6.00 pm / Summer 7.00 pm.

YORK
TOURS
Yorkwalk
3 Fairway, Clifton YO30 5QA
Telephone: (01904) 622-303
Fax: (01904) 656-244
Email: admin@yorkwalk.fsnet.co.uk
Website: www.yorkwalk.co.uk
Offer a walk called The Jewish Heritage walk

Yorkshire South
SHEFFIELD
SYNAGOGUES
Orthodox
Sheffield Jewish Congregation and Centre
Kingfield Synagogue, Brincliffe Crescent S11 8UX
Telephone: (0114) 255-2296
There is a mikveh in the building. There is also a kosher
restaurant and butcher on Thursday only.

Reform
Sheffield & District Reform Jewish
Congregation
PO Box 675 S11 8TE
Mobile Phone: 0771 920 9259 (answerphone)
Email: sdrjc@dsl.pipex.com
Website: www.shef-ref.co.uk
Service alternate Friday evenings and Saturday mornings,
and High Holy Days.

Yorkshire West
BRADFORD
The Jewish community, although only about
140 years old, has exercised much influence on
the city's staple industry: wool. Jews of German
descent developed the export trade of wool
yarns and fabrics.

SYNAGOGUES
Orthodox
Bradford Hebrew Congregation
Springhurst Road, Shipley BD18 3DN
Telephone: (01274) 581189
Fax: (01274) 374101
Services 10 am monthly on Shabbat Mevorachim, High
Holy Days & certain festivals.

Reform
Bradford Synagogue
7A Bowland Street, Manningham Lane BD1 3BW
Telephone: (01274) 728-925 / 01274 544420
Service Saturday 11.00 am; Festivals, 6.00 pm and 11.00 am.
Grade II listed building, built in 1873 in the Moorish style.

LEEDS
The Leeds Jewish community is the second
largest in the provinces, and numbers about
12,000. The community dates only from the
1820s, although a few Jews are known to have
lived there in the previous half-century. The
first synagogue was built in 1860.
The population which peaked at around 20,000
in the 1920s, and was possibly the city which
had largest population of Jews in the country, is
now less than 8,000.

BAKERIES
Chalutz Bakery
378 Harrogate Road LS17 6PY
Telephone: (0113) 269-1350
Supervision: Leeds Beth Din
Hours: Monday to Thursday , 8.00 am to 6.00 pm; Friday to
one hour before Shabbat; Saturday, from one hour after
Shabbat to 2.00 pm Sunday.

BUTCHERS
Fisher's Deli
391 Harrogate Road LS17 6DJ
Telephone: (0113) 268-6944
Supervision: Leeds Beth Din Butcher and deli

Gourmet Foods
Sandhill Parade, 584 Harrogate Road LS17 8DP
Telephone: (0113) 268-2726
Supervision: Leeds Beth Din Butcher and deli

COMMUNITY ORGANISATIONS
Leeds Jewish Representative Council
c/o Shadwell Lane Synagogue LS17
Telephone: (0113) 269-7520
Fax: (0113) 237-0851
Publishes Year Book

DELICATESSEN
The Kosherie
410 Harrogate Road LS17 6PY
Telephone: (0113) 268-2943
Fax: (0113) 269-6979
Supervision: Leeds Beth Din

LIBRARIES
Jewish Library
Porton Collection; Leeds Central Library. , Municipal
Buildings LS1 3AB
Telephone: (0113) 247-8282
Fax: (0113) 395-1833
Email: businessandresearch@leedslearning.net
Website: www.leeds.gov.uk

MEDIA

Newspapers
Jewish Telegraph
1 Shaftsbury Avenue LS8 1DR
Telephone: (0113) 295-6000
Fax: (0113) 295-6006
Email: leeds@jewishtelegraph.com
Website: www.jewishtelegraph.com

MIKVAOT
Makor Jewish and Israel Centre
411 Harrogate Road LS17 7BY
Telephone: (0113) 268-0899

RELIGIOUS ORGANISATIONS
Orthodox
Beth Din
Etz Chaim Synagogue, 411 Harrogate Road
LS17 6BY
Telephone: (0113) 266-2214
Fax: (0113) 237-1183
Information about kosher food and accommodation may
be obtained here

RESTAURANTS
Hansa's Gujarati Restaurant
72 North Street LS2 7PN
Telephone: (0113) 244-4408
Website: www.hanasrestaurant.co.uk
Indian vegetarian restaurant

SYNAGOGUES
Orthodox
Beth Hamidrash Hagadol
399 Street Lane LS17 6HQ
Telephone: (0113) 269-2181
Fax: (0113) 237-0113
Email: office@bhhs.freeserve.co.uk

Chassidishe
c/o Donisthorpe Hall, Shadwell Lane LS17 6AW

Etz Chaim
411 Harrogate Road LS17 7By
Telephone: (0113) 266-2214
Fax: (0113) 237-1183
Email: admin@etzchaim.co.uk
Website: www.etzchaim.co.uk

Queenshill Synagogue
Marjorie and Arnold Ziff Community Centre, 311
Stonegate Road LS17 6AZ
Telephone: (0113) 268-7364
Email: sabrah2936@aol.com
Mailing address: 49 Queenshill Drive, Moortown, LS17 5BG.

Shadwell Lane Synagogue (United Hebrew Congregation)
151 Shadwell Lane LS17 8DW
Telephone: (0113) 269-6141
Email: minyan@uhcleeds.fsnet.co.uk
Website: www.uhcleeds.com

Shomrei Hadass
368 Harrogate Road LS17 6QB
Telephone: (0113) 268-1461

Reform
Sinai Synagogue
Roman Avenue, off Street Lane LS8 2AN
Telephone: (0113) 266-5256
Fax: (0113) 266-1539
Email: synagogue@sinaileeds.freeserve.co.uk

CHANNEL ISLANDS

ALDERNEY
Corblets Road

There is a memorial to the victims of the Nazis during their
occupation of the Channel Islands during the Second World
War. It bears plaques in English, French, Hebrew and
Russian..

JERSEY

ST BRELADE
CONTACT INFORMATION
16 La Rocquaise, La Route des Genets, St Brelade
JE3 8HY
Telephone: (01534) 742-819
Fax: (01534) 747-554
Email: mgmort@jerseymail.co.uk
Honorary secretary of the Jersey Jewish Congregation.

SYNAGOGUES
Jersey Jewish Congregation
La Petite Route des Mielles, St Brelade JE3 8FY
Telephone: (01534) 865-333
Fax: (01534) 861-431
Shabbat morning service: 10.30 am; Holy days, 7.00 pm
and 10.00 am

ISLE OF MAN

DOUGLAS
SYNAGOGUES
Hebrew Congregation
Telephone: (01624) 24214
There are more than 70 Jews on the island

SCOTLAND

FIFE

DUNDEE
SYNAGOGUES
Dundee Synagogue
St Mary Place DD1 5RB
Telephone: (01382) 223-557

DUNOON
Argyll & Bute Jewish Community
Telephone: (01369) 705-118

ST ANDREWS
CONTACT INFORMATION
Jewish Student's Society
c/o Students' Union, University of St Andrews
KY16 9UY

GRAMPIAN
ABERDEEN
RESTAURANTS
Vegetarian
Lemon Tree Café
5 West North Street AB24 5AT
Telephone: (01224) 621-610
Fax: (01224) 630-888
Email: bar@lemontree.org
12 noon to 4.00 pm Tuesday to Sunday

SYNAGOGUES
Aberdeen Synagogue
74 Dee Street AB11 6DS
Telephone: (01224) 582-135

LOTHIAN
EDINBURGH
The Town Council and Burgess Roll minutes of
1691 and 1717 record applications by Jews for
permission to live and trade in Edinburgh.

KASHRUT INFORMATION
Rabbi D Sedley
Telephone: (0131) 667-9360

RESTAURANTS
Vegetarian
Black Bo's
Blackfriars Street EH
Telephone: (0131) 557-6136

Henderson's
94 Hanover Street EH2 1DR
Telephone: (0131) 225-2131
Fax: (0131) 220-3542
Email: mail@hendersonsofedinburgh.co.uk
Website: www.hendersonsofedinburgh.co.uk
Hours: 8.00 am to 10.30pm, closed on Sundays. Adjoining
Bistro is also vegetarian (open on Sunday).

Kalpna Restaurant
2/3 St Patrick Sq. EH8 9EZ
Telephone: (0131) 667-9890
Fax: (0131) 443-8782
Email: kalpnarestaurant@yahoo
Website: www.kalpna.co.uk
Hours: Lunch 11.00 am–2.00 pm, dinner 5.30 pm–11.00 pm

SYNAGOGUES
Orthodox
Edinburgh Synagogue
4 Salisbury Road EH16 5AB
Telephone: (0131) 667-3144
Fax: (0131) 01324-613-750
Email: ray.taylor@lineone.net

STRATHCLYDE
GLASGOW
The Glasgow Jewish community dates from 1823.
The oldest synagogue building is the Garnethill
Synagogue, now the home of the Scottish Jewish
Archives opened in 1879. The community grew
rapidly from 1891 with many Jews settling in the
Gorbals. Recently the community has spread
southwards and is now mainly situated in the
Giffnock and Newton Mearns areas.

BOOKSELLERS
J & E Levingstone
47/55 Sinclair Drive G42 9PT
Telephone: (0141) 649-2962
Fax: (0141) 649-2962
Religious requisities also stocked

Well of Wisdom
Giffnock Synagogue G46
Telephone: (0141) 577-8260
Fax: (0141) 620-0823

COMMUNITY ORGANISATIONS
Jewish Community Centre
222 Fenwick Road G46 6UE
Telephone: (0141) 577-8200
Fax: (0141) 577-8202
Email: glasgow@j-scot.org
Website: www.j-scot.org/glasgow

DELICATESSEN
Hello Deli
200 Fenwick Road G46
Telephone: (0141) 638-8267
Fax: (0141) 621-2290

Marlenes Kosher Deli
2 Burnfield Road G46 7QB
Telephone: (0141) 638-4383

Michael Morrison and Son
52 Sinclair Drive G42 9PY
Telephone: (0141) 632-0998
Fax: (0141) 632-6091
Email: kosher@talk21.com
Not under official supervision. Stockist of many glatt kosher
items. Will deliver to hotels.

GUEST HOUSE
Bed and Breakfast
Mrs A. Malcolm, 26 St Clair Avenue G46 7QE
Telephone: (0141) 638-3924
Kosher, but not supervised, 2 twin bedded rooms

MEDIA

Newspapers
Jewish Telegraph
May Terrace, Giffnock G46 6DL
Telephone: (0141) 621-4422
Fax: (0141) 621-4333
Email: glasgow@jewishtelegraph.com
Website: www.jewishtelegraph.com

MIKVAOT

Giffnock & Newlands Synagogue
Maryville Avenue G46 7NE
Telephone: (0141) 577-8269
Fax: (0141) 577-8252

SYNAGOGUES

Orthodox
Garnethill
129 Hill Street G3 6UB
Telephone: (0141) 332-4151
Shabbat services 10.00 am, Yomtov services 9.45 am

Giffnock & Newlands Hebrew Congregation
Maryville Avenue G46 7NE
Telephone: (0141) 577-8250
Fax: (0141) 577-8252
Email: rabbimrubin@talk21.com

Langside
125 Niddrie Road G42 8QA
Telephone: (0141) 423-4062

Netherlee & Clarkston
Clarkston Road at Randolph Drive G44
Telephone: (0141) 637-8206; 639-7194
Fax: (0141) 616-0743

Newton Mearns
14 Larchfield Court G77 5Bh
Telephone: (0141) 639-4000
Fax: (0141) 639-4000
Email: office@nmhc.org.uk

Reform
Glasgow New Synagogue Or Chadash
147 Ayr Road, Newton Mearns G77 6RE
Telephone: (0141) 639-4083
Fax: (0141) 639-4083
Email: shu@gns.org.uk
Website: www.gns.org.uk
Central organisation: RSGB

WALES

CARDIFF

MIKVAOT
Cardiff Mikvaot
Wales Empire Pool Building, Wood Street CF1 1PP
Telephone: (029) 2038-2296

RESTAURANTS

Vegetarian
Munchies Wholefood Co-op
60 Crwys Road, Cathays CF2 4NN
Telephone: (029) 2039-9677

SELF-CATERING
Student Accomodation
Hillel House CF2 5NR
Telephone: (029) 2022-8845
Self catering for students

SYNAGOGUES

Orthodox
Cardiff United Synagogue
Cyncoed Gardens, Cyncoed CF23 5SL
Telephone: (029) 2047-3728
Fax: (029) 2047-3728
Email: C.U.S@btopenworld.co.uk
Website: www.cardiffunited.org.uk

Reform
Cardiff New Synagogue
Moira Terrace CF24 0EJ
Telephone: (029) 2049-1689
Email: info@ardiffnewsyn.org
Website: www.cardiffnewsyn.org

LLANDUDNO

HOTELS

Vegetarian
Plas Madoc Vegetarian Guesthouse
60 Church Walks LL30 2HL
Telephone: (01492) 876-514
Email: plasmadoc@vegetarianguesthouse.com
Website: www.vegetarianguesthouse.com

SYNAGOGUES
Llandudno Synagogue
28 Church Walks LL30 2HL
Telephone: (01492) 572-549

SWANSEA

RESTAURANTS
Vegetarian
Chris's Kitchen
The Market SA1 3PE
Telephone: (01792) 643-455
Hours: 8.30 am to 5.30 pm Monday to Saturday

SYNAGOGUES
Ffynone
17 Ffynone Drive SA1 6DB
Telephone: (01792) 473-333

NORTHERN IRELAND ON PAGE 163

UNITED STATES OF AMERICA

The first Jews came to what is now the United States of America in 1654. The ship had come from the West Indies and included 23 Jews from Brazil, attempting to escape the arrival of the Inquisition following Portugal's recapture of Brazil from the Dutch earlier that year. It is believed they thought they were travelling to Amsterdam in the Netherlands, rather than to New Amsterdam (as New York was then called). Within ten years, however, the community was moribund. The surrender of New Amsterdam to the British in 1664 brought substantial changes to the Jewish settlement as some restrictions to both civil and religious rights were lifted. In a few colonies they were even granted the right to vote.

Following the English takeover communities were established along the eastern coast, and by 1700 there were between 200 and 300 Jews in the country. At the time of the Revolution there were between 1,500 and 2,000 Jews and they served both in the Militia (which was compulsory) and as officers and soldiers. In the decades immediately before the Civil War, the Jewish population rose from 15,000 to 150,000 as a result of emigration, mainly from German areas. During that war Jews served on both sides with their respective communities.

Immigration was at its peak between 1880 and 1925 (when free emigration ended) and during this period the Jewish population grew from 280,000 to 4,500,000. Unfortunately, during the 1930s, only a small number of the Jewish refugees trying to escape from Germany were able to enter the USA. America's numerical position in world Jewry has declined, with its population being in 1948 as much as ten times the population of Israel, to its current approaching parity. The largest concentration by far has always been in New York.

Each of the main religious groups has its own association of synagogues and rabbis and, unlike many other countries, there is no central religious organisation. There is therefore no central supervision of kashrut.

Instead there are many hashgachot issued by both individual local communal organisations and rabbis, as well as by companies who issue such certificates on a commercial basis. Travellers may always check with a local rabbi to ascertain the appropriate supervisory body in a relevant location.

Travellers should also be aware that, following a decision in the Brooklyn (New York) District Court in July 2000, discussions are under way in several other jurisdictions to prepare for the eventuality that New York's kosher laws may be rendered unconstitutional on appeal.

Country calling code: **(1)**
Total population: **274,520,000**
Jewish population: **5,700,000**
Emergency telephone: **(Police–911) (Fire–911) (Ambulance–911)**
Electricity voltage: **110/220**

Alabama

BIRMINGHAM

COMMUNITY ORGANISATIONS
Birmingham Jewish Federation
3966 Montclair Road 35213
Telephone: (205) 803-0416
Fax: (205) 803-1526

CONTACT INFORMATION
Rabbi Avraham Shmidman
3225 Montevallo Road 35223
Telephone: (205) 879-1664
Fax: (205) 879-5774
Email: kicongreg@aol.com

DELICATESSEN
Browdy's
2607 Cahaba Road 35223
Telephone: (205) 879-6411

MIKVAOT
Knesseth Israel
3225 Montevallo Rd., 35213
Telephone: (205) 879-1464

SYNAGOGUES

Conservative
Beth-El
2179 Highland Avenue 35205
Telephone: (205) 933-2740
Fax: (205) 933-2747

MOBILE

SYNAGOGUES

Reform
Spring Hill Avenue Temple
1769 Spring Hill Avenue 36607
Telephone: (334) 478-0415

MONTGOMERY

COMMUNITY ORGANISATIONS
Jewish Federation
PO Box 20058 36120
Telephone: (334) 277-5820
Fax: (334) 277-8383

SYNAGOGUES

Conservative
Agudath Israel
3525 Cloverdale Road 36111
Telephone: (334) 281-7394

Orthodox
Etz Ahayem (Sephardi)
725 Augusta Road 36111
Telephone: (334) 281-9819

Reform
Beth Or
2246 Narrow Lane 36106

Alaska

ANCHORAGE

GROCERIES
Carr's Market
Diamond Boulevard and Seward Hwy
Telephone: (907) 341-1020

SYNAGOGUES

Orthodox
Congregation Shomrei Ohr
1210 E. 26th 99508
Telephone: (907) 279-1200
Fax: (907) 279-7890
Email: lubavitchofak@gci.net

Reform
Beth Sholom
7525 E. Northern Lights Blvd 99504
Telephone: (907) 338-1836
Fax: (907) 337-4013
Email: sholom@alaska.net

JUNEAU
Juneau Jewish Community
Telephone: (907) 463-4333

Arizona

PHOENIX

COMMUNITY ORGANISATIONS
Jewish Federation of Greater Phoenix
32 W. Coolidge, Suite 200 85013
Telephone: (602) 274-1800

Orthodox Rabbinical Council of Greater Phoenix
515 E. Bethany Home Road 85012
Telephone: (602) 277-8858
Fax: (602) 274-0713
Email: Bethjoseph515@hotmail.com
Supervision: Rabbi David Rebibo

KASHRUT INFORMATION
Rabbi David Rebibo
Phoenix Vaad Hakashruth, 515 E. Bethany Home
Rd. 85012
Telephone: (602) 277-8858
Fax: (602) 274-0713
Email: bethjoseph515@hotmail.com
Website: www.phoenixbethjoseph.org and click on vaad

MEDIA

Newspapers
Jewish News of Greater Phoenix
162 E. Northern Ave., Suite 106 85020
Telephone: (602) 870-9470
Fax: (602) 870-0426
Email: editor@jewishaz.com
Website: www.jewishaz.com

Shalom Arizona
32 W. Coolidge, Suite 200 85013
Telephone: (602) 274-1800

RESTAURANTS
King Solomon's Pizza
4810 N. 7th Street
Telephone: (602) 870-8655

Meat
Segal's Kosher Foods
4818 N. 7th Street
Telephone: (602) 285-1515
Fax: (602) 277-5760
Email: segalkosh@aol.com
Supervision: Vaad Hakashrut of Phoenix

SYNAGOGUES

Conservative
Beth El Congregation
1118 W. Glendale 85021
Telephone: (602) 944-3359
Fax: (602) 944-3565
Website: www.bethelphoenix.com

Temple Beth Sholom
3400 N. Dobson Road, Chandler 85224
Telephone: (602) 897-3636
Fax: (602) 897-3633
Email: office@templebethsholomaz.org
Website: www.templebethsholomaz.org

Orthodox
Congregation Beth Joseph
515 E. Bethany Home Road 85012
Telephone: (602) 277-8858
Fax: (602) 274-0713
Email: bethjoseph514@hotmail.com
Website: www.phoenixbethjoseph.org
Supervision: Rabbi David Rebibo

Congregation Beth Shaarei Tzedek
7608 N. 18th Avenue 85021
Telephone: (602) 944-1133

Young Israel of Phoenix
745 E. Maryland Avenue, Ste. 120 85014
Telephone: (602) 265-8888
Fax: (602) 265-8867
Email: cnsil5@home.com

Reform
Temple Beth Ami
4545 N. 36th Street, No. 211 85018
Telephone: (602) 956-0805

Temple Chai
4545 East Marilyn Rd 85032
Telephone: (602) 971-1234

SCOTTSDALE
MUSEUMS
Sylvia Plotkin Judaica Museum
10460 N. 56th St. 85253
Telephone: (480) 951-0323
Fax: (480) 951-7150
Email: museum@templebethisrael.org
Website: www.spjm.org

SYNAGOGUES
Conservative
Beth Emeth of Scottsdale
5406 E. Virginia Avenue 85254
Telephone: (480) 947-4604

Har Zion
5929 E. Lincoln Drive 85253
Telephone: (480) 991-0720

SYNAGOGUES
Orthodox
Chabad of Scottsdale
10215 North Scottsdale Road 85253
Telephone: (480) 998-1410
Website: www.chabadofscottsdale.org

SYNAGOGUES
Reform
Temple Kol Ami
15030 N. 64th Street 85254
Telephone: (480) 951-9660
Fax: (480) 951-5231
Email: templekolami@aol.com

Temple Solel
6805 E. MacDonald Drive 85253
Telephone: (480) 991-7414
Fax: (480) 451-0829
Email: mleano@templesolel.org
Website: www.templesolel.org

SIERRA VISTA
Temple Kol Hamidbar
Po Box 908 85636
Telephone: (520) 458-8637 (ans. phone only)
Email: tkh85636@hotmail.com
Website: www.uahcweb.org/congs/az/tkh/

SUN CITY
Beth Shalom of Sun City
12202 101st Avenue 85351
Telephone: 977-3240
Fax: 977-3214
Email: tbsaz@goodnet.com

SUN CITY WEST
SYNAGOGUES
Conservative
Beth Emeth Congregation of the Sun Cities & West Valley of Phoenix
13702 West Meeker Blvd. 85375
Telephone: (623) 584-7210
Fax: (623) 975-2976
Email: info@bethemethaz.org
Website: www.bethemethaz.org

TEMPE
COMMUNITY ORGANISATIONS
Tri-City Jewish Community Center
1965 E. Hermosa Drive 85282
Telephone: (602) 897-0588

SYNAGOGUES
Orthodox
Chabad-Lubavitch Center
23 W. 9th Street 85281
Telephone: (602) 966-5163

Reform
Temple Emanuel
5801 Rural Road 85283
Telephone: (602) 838-1414

TUCSON

BAKERIES
Nadine's Pastry Shoppe
4553 Broadway Blvd.
Telephone: (520) 326-0735

BUTCHERS
Feig's Kosher Market & Deli
5071 E. 5th Street 85711
Telephone: (520) 325-2255
Fax: (520) 325-2978
Supervision: Rabbi R.Eisen

COMMUNITY ORGANISATIONS
Jewish Federation of Southern Arizona
3822 E. River Rd. 85718
Telephone: (520) 577-9393
Fax: (520) 577-0734
Email: stumellan@jon.cjfny.org

SYNAGOGUES
Conservative
Congregation Bet Shalom
3881 E. River Road 85718
Telephone: (520) 577-1171
Fax: (520) 577-8903
Email: cbs3881@juno.com
Supervision: Rabbi Leo M Abrami

Orthodox
Congregation Chofetz Chayim
5150 E. 5th Street 85711
Telephone: (520) 747-7780
Fax: (520) 745-6325
Email: ewbecker@flash.net

Young Israel of Tucson
2443 E. 4th Strret 85710
Telephone: (520) 326-8362

Arkansas

EL DORADO
SYNAGOGUES
Reform
Beth Israel
1130 E. Main Street

HELENA
Temple Beth-El
406 Perry Street 72342
Telephone: (501) 338-6654

HOT SPRINGS
SYNAGOGUES
House of Israel
300 Quapaw Avenue 71901
Telephone: (501) 623-5821
Email: houseofi@hotsprings.net

LITTLE ROCK
COMMUNITY ORGANISATIONS
Jewish Federation of Arkansas
425 N. University Ave. 72205
Telephone: (501) 663-3571
Fax: (501) 663-7286
Email: jfair@aristotle.net

SYNAGOGUES
Orthodox
Congregation Agudath Achim
7901 W. 5th St. 72205
Telephone: (501) 225-1683
Fax: (501) 225-3177
Email: rav613@hotmail.com
Mikvah open to the Jewish community and visitors. To use mikvah call Synagogue office, Home Hospitality call Rabbi Applebaum at Synagogue office.

Reform
B'nai Israel
3700 Rodney Parham Rd., 72212
Telephone: (501) 225-9700
Fax: (501) 225-6058
Email: elevy@snider.net

California
As the general population of California continues to increase, the Jewish community is growing as well. Places of worship abound, from Eureka in the north to San Diego in the south, but the major part of the community lives in the Los Angeles metropolitan area.

ALAMEDA
Temple Israel
3183 McCartney Road 94502
Telephone: (510) 522-9355
Fax: (510) 522-9356
Email: tialameda@prodigy.net

SYNAGOGUES
Conservative
Temple Beth Emet
1770 W. Cerritos Avenue 92804
Telephone: (714) 772-4720
Fax: (714) 772-4710
Email: the-anaheim@adelphia.net

ARCADIA
Congregation Shaarei Torah
550 S. 2nd Avenue 91006
Telephone: (818) 445-0810

BAKERSFIELD
B'nai Jacob
600 17th Street 93301
Telephone: (661) 325-8017

SYNAGOGUES
Reform
Temple Beth El
2906 Loma Linda Drive 93305
Telephone: (661) 322-7607
Fax: (661) 322-7807
Email: kernjew@aol.com
Website: www.templebethel_ca.homestead.com

BERKELEY
MIKVAOT
Mikvah Taharas Israel
2520 Warring St., 94704-3111
Telephone: (510) 848-7221
Fax: (510) 217-3596
Email: vaad@flash.net

MUSEUMS
Judah L. Magnus Museum
2911 Russell St. 94705
Telephone: (510) 549-6950
Fax: (510) 849-3673
Email: info@magnesmuseum.org
Website: www.judahmagnesmuseum.org

RESTAURANTS
Dairy
Noah's Bagels
1883 Solano Avenue
Telephone: (510) 525-4447
Supervision: The Vaad Kakashrus of Northern California.

SYNAGOGUES
Conservative
Netivot Shalom
1841 Berkeley Way 94708
Telephone: (510) 549-9447
Fax: (510) 549-9448
Email: administrator@netivotshom.org
Website: www.netivotshalom.org

Egalitarian
Berkeley Hillel Foundation
2736 Bancroft ay 94704
Telephone: (510) 845-7793
Fax: (510) 845-7753

Jewish Renewal
Aquarian Minyan
c/o Goldfarb, 2020 Essex 94703

Kehilla
PO Box 3063 94703

Orthodox
Chabad House
2643 College Avenue 94704
Telephone: (510) 540-5824

Congregation Beth Israel
1630 Bancroft Way 94703
Telephone: (510) 843-5246
Fax: (510) 843-5058
Email: office@beth-israel.berkeley.ca.us
Website: www.beth-israel.berkeley.ca.us

Reform
Congregation Beth El
2301 Vine Street 94708
Telephone: (510) 848-3988
Fax: (510) 848-9434
Email: frontoffice@bethelberkeley.org
Website: www.bethelberkeley.org

BEVERLY HILLS
SYNAGOGUES
Orthodox
Beth Jacob
9030 Olympic Boulevard 90211
Telephone: (310) 278-1911
Fax: (310) 278-9186

Young Israel of Beverly Hills
8701 Pico Blvd, (Between Robertson & La Cienega) 90035
Telephone: (310) 275-3020
Fax: (310) 275-3031
Email: rabbispan@yahoo.com

Young Israsel of North Beverly Hills
9350 Civic Center Drive, North Beverly Hills 90210
Telephone: (310) 203-0170
Fax: (310) 276 - 0734

Orthodox Sephardi
Magen David
322 N. Foothill 90210

BONITA
SYNAGOGUES
Orthodox
Beth Eliyahu Torah Center
5012 Central Avenue 91902
Telephone: (619) 472-2144
Fax: (619) 472-0718

BURBANK
SYNAGOGUES
Conservative
Temple Emanu-El
1302 N. Glenoaks Boulevard, burbank 91504
Telephone: (818) 845-1734
Website: BTEE.ORG

BURLINGAME
SYNAGOGUES
Reform
Peninsula Temple Sholom
1655 Sebastian Drive 94010
Telephone: (415) 697-2266
Fax: (415) 697-2544

CARMEL
Congregation Beth Israel
5716 Carmel Valley Road 93923
Telephone: (831) 624-2015
Fax: (831) 624-4786
Email: shalomcbi@aol.com

CASTRO VALLEY
Shir Ami
4529 Malabar Avenue 94546
Telephone: (415) 537-1787

CHULA VISTA
SYNAGOGUES
Conservative
Temple Beth Sholom
208 Madrona Street 91910
Telephone: (619) 420-6040
Email: dglick@cox.net
Website: www.uscj.org/pacsw/chulavista
Services Friday 7.30pm, Saturday 9.30am and holidays.
Visitors welcome.

COSTA MESA
GIFT SHOP
The Golden Dreidle
1835 Newport Blvd. #A111 92627
Telephone: (714) 645-3878
Fax: (714) 646-5081

DALY CITY
SYNAGOGUES
Conservative
B'nai Israel
1575 Annie Street 94015
Telephone: (415) 756-5430

DAVIS
SYNAGOGUES
Reform
Davis Jewish Fellowship
1821 Oak Avenue 95616
Telephone: (916) 758-0842

DOWNEY
Temple Ner Tamid
10629 Lakewood Boulevard 90241
Telephone: (310) 861-9276

ENCINITAS
Temple Solel
552 S. Camino Real 92024
Telephone: (760) 436-0654
Fax: (760) 436-2748
Email: info@templesolel.net

ENCINO
SYNAGOGUES
Conservative
Valley Beth Shalom
15739 Ventura Blvd, 91316
Telephone: (818) 788-6000

Orthodox
Chabad House
4917 Hayvenhurst, 91346

Reform
Shir Chadash
17000 Ventura Blvd,

EUREKA
Temple Beth El
Hodgson & T Streets, PO Box 442 95502
Telephone: (707) 444-2846
Fax: (707) 444-2846

FRESNO
COMMUNITY ORGANISATIONS
Jewish Federation Office
1340 W. Heerndon, Suite 103 93711

SYNAGOGUES
Conservative
Beth Jacob
406 W. Shields Avenue 93704
Telephone: (209) 222-0664

Reform
Temple Beth Israel
6622 N. Maroa Avenue 93704
Telephone: (209) 432-3600

GARDENA
SYNAGOGUES
Conservative
Southwest Temple Beth Torah
14725 S. Gramercy Place 90249
Telephone: (310) 327-8734

GRANADA HILLS
COMMUNITY ORGANISATIONS
North Valley Center
16601 Rinaldi Street, Granada Hills 91344

HOLLYWOOD

KASHRUT INFORMATION
Kosher Information Bureau
15365 Magnolia Blvd, Sherman Oaks 91403
Telephone: (818) 762-3197 & 262-5351
Fax: (818) 766-8537
Email: eeidlitz@kosherquest.org
Website: www.kosherquest.org

IRVINE

COMMUNITY ORGANISATIONS
Jewish Federation of Orange County
1 Federation Way, Suite 210 92603
Telephone: (949) 435-3484
Fax: (949) 435-3485
Email: info@jfoc.org
Website: www.jewishorangecounty.org

LA JOLLA

SYNAGOGUES

Conservative
Congregation Beth El
8660 Gilman Drive, 92037
Telephone: (619) 452-1734
Fax: (619) 452-5578
Email: congregationbethel.com

Orthodox
Congregation Adat Yeshurun
8625 La Jolla scenic Dr. 92037
Telephone: (619) 535-1196
Fax: (619) 535-0037
Email: adatyeshurun.org
Website: www.adatyeshurun.org

LA MESA

MEDIA

Newspapers
San Diego Jewish Times
4731 Palm Avenue, La Mesa 91941
Telephone: (619) 463-5515
Fax: (619) 463-1309
Email: jewishtimes@earthlink.net

LAFAYETTE

SYNAGOGUES

Reform
Temple Isaiah
3800 Mt. Diablo Blvd 94549
Telephone: (925) 283-8575
Fax: (925) 283-8355
Email: temple-isaiah@temple-isaiah.org
Website: www.temple-isaiah.org

LAGUNA HILLS

DELICATESSEN
The Kosher Bite
23595 Moulton Parkway 92653
Telephone: (949) 770-1818
Fax: (949) 770-5321
Website: www.kosherbite.com
Supervision: Rabinical Council of Orange County

LAKEWOOD

SYNAGOGUES

Conservative
Temple Beth Zion Sinai
6440 Del Amo Blvd. 90713
Telephone: (310) 429-0715
Fax: (310) 429-0715
Email: tbzs@jps.net

LONG BEACH

BAKERIES
Fairfax Kosher Market & Bakery
11196-98 Los Alamitos Blvd. 90720
Telephone: (562) 828-4492

COMMUNITY ORGANISATIONS
Jewish Federation of Greater Long Beach & W, Orange County
3801 E. Willow St. 90815
Telephone: (562) 426-7601

MEDIA

Newspapers
Jewish Community Chronicle
3801 E. Willow St. 90815-1791

MIKVAOT
Long Beach Mikvaot
3847 Atlantic Avenue 90807

SYNAGOGUES

Orthodox
Congregation Lubavitch
3981 Atlantic Avenue 90807
Telephone: (562) 596-1681

Young Israel of Long Beach
PO Box 7041 90807-0041
Telephone: (562) 527-3163

Reform
Temple Beth David
6100 Hefley Street, Westminster 92683
Telephone: (562) 892-6623
Fax: (562) 897-5306
Email: tbdavid@aol.com
Website: www.templebethdavid.org

Temple Israel
338 E. 3rd Street 90812

LOS ANGELES

Los Angeles is America's, and the world's, second largest Jewish metropolis, with a Jewish population of around 600,000. Fairfax Avenue and Beverly Blvd together form the crossroads of traditional Jewish life, while a growing Orthodox enclave centers around Pico and Robertson Blvds.

Important note: Area telephone codes have recently been split to 310 and 213 for central Los Angeles. We have endeavoured in all cases to correct our information, but cannot guarantee the accuracy of those who did not send in updates.

BAKERIES
Noah's New York Bagels
1737 Santa Rita Road #400, Pleasanton 94566
Telephone: (213) 485-1921
Email: noah@noahs.com
Supervision: California Rabbinical Council

Schwartz Bakery
441 N. Fairfax Av. 90036
Telephone: (213) 653-1683
Fax: (213) 653-6142
8616 W. Pico Blvd
Telephone: (213) 854-0592
Fax: (213) 653-6142
Supervision: RCC

COMMUNITY ORGANISATIONS
Board of Rabbis of Southern California
6505 Wilshire Blvd., Suite 430 90048
Telephone: (213) 761-8600
Fax: (213) 761-8603

Jewish Federation of Greater Los Angeles
6505 Wilshire Blvd. 90048
Telephone: (213) 761-8000
Fax: (213) 761-8123
Website: www.jewishla.org

West Side Jewish Community Center
5870 W. Olympic Blvd. 90036
Telephone: (323) 938-2531
Fax: (323) 954-9175
Email: info@westsidejcc.org
Website: www.westsidejcc.org

DELICATESSEN
Pico Kosher Deli
8826 W. Pico Blvd 90035
Telephone: (213) 273-9381
Fax: (213) 273-8476
Supervision: RCC

EMBASSY
Consul General of Israel
Suite 1700, 6380 Wilshire Blvd 90048
Telephone: (213) 852-5523
Fax: (213) 852-5555
Email: israinfo@primenet.com

Website: www.israelemb.org/la

GROCERIES
Kosher food to go
PS Kosher Food Services
9760 W. Pico Blvd. , MOT cafeteria 90035
Telephone: (213) 553-8804
Fax: (213) 553-8989
Mobile Phone: 001 310 717 2102
Email: psfood@juno.com
Website: www.pskosherfood.com
Supervision: RCC
Services for travellers. Glatt, Cholse Yisrael

HOSPITAL
Cedars Sinai Hospital
8700 Beverly Blvd
Telephone: (213) 855-4797
Supervision: RCC

KASHRUT INFORMATION
Rabbi Bukspan
6407 Orange Street 90048
Telephone: (213) 653-5083

MEDIA
Newspapers
Heritage Southwest Jewish Press
20201 Sherman Way, Ste., 204, Winetka 91306

Jewish Journal
Weekly publication, coming out on Fridays

MIKVAOT
Museum of Tolerance (Beit Hashoah)
9786 West Pico Boulevard 90035
Telephone: (310) 553-8403
Fax: (310) 553-4521
Email: information@wiesenthal.net
Website: www.wiesenthal.com/library

MUSEUMS
Museum of Tolerance
9786 West Pico Blvd 90035
Telephone: (310) 800-900-9036
Fax: (310) 553-4521
Website: www.museumoftolerance.com

ORGANISATIONS
Jewish Social Action Organisation
Simon Wiesenthal Center, 1399 South Roxbury Dr. 90035
Telephone: (310) 553-9036
Fax: (310) 553-4521
Email: information@wiesenthal.com
Website: www.wiesenthal.com

RESTAURANTS
Dairy
Fish Grill
7226 Beverley Blvd
Telephone: (213) 937-7162

Fish Place Restaurant
9340 W. Pico Blvd
Telephone: (213) 858-8737
Supervision: Kehila kosher

Milk & Honey
8837 W. Pico Blvd
Telephone: (213) 858-8850

Nagila Pizza Restaurant
9411 W. Pico Blvd.
Telephone: (213) 788-0111

Pizza Delight
435 N. Fairfax Avenue
Telephone: (213) 655-7800

Pizza World
368 S. Fairfax Ave.
Telephone: (213) 653-2896

Meat
Chick 'N Chow
9301 W. Pico Blvd.
Telephone: (213) 274-5595

Cohen Restaurant
316 E. Pico Blvd. 90015
Telephone: (213) 742-8888
Fax: (213) 742-0066
Supervision: RCC

Encino Grill & Wok
16340 Ventura Blvd.
Telephone: (213) 905-8622

Glatt Hut
9303 W. Pico Blvd.
Telephone: (213) 246-1900

Jeff's Gourmet Sausage Factory
8930 W. Pico Blvd.
Telephone: (310) 858-8590
Fax: (310) 858-8138
Email: links@jeffsgourmet.com
Website: www.jeffsgourmet.com

Kabob & Chinese Food
11330 Santa Monica
Telephone: (213) 914-3040

La Gondola Ristorante Italiano
6405 Wilshire Blvd.
Telephone: (213) 852-1915

Magic Carpet
8566 W. Pico Blvd 90035
Telephone: (310)-652-8507
Fax: (310)-652-3568
Supervision: Kehillah of Los Angeles

Mr Pickles Deli
13354 Washington Blvd.
Telephone: (213) 822-7777

Nathan's Famous
9216 W. Pico Blvd.
Telephone: (213) 273-0303

Simon's La Glatt
446 N. Fairfax Avenue
Telephone: (213) 658-7730

Pizzerias
Pizza Delight
435 N. Fairgfax avenue 90036
Telephone: (213) 655-7800
Fax: (213) 655-1142
Suprvision: Kehillah of Los Angeles.

Shalom Pizza
8715 W. Pico Blvd.
Telephone: (213) 271-2255
Email: shalompizza@la.com
Supervision: RCC

SYNAGOGUES
Conservative
Adat Shalom
3030 Westwood Blvd
Telephone: (213) 475-4985

Sinai Temple
10400 Wilshire Blvd 90024
Telephone: (213) 474-1518
Fax: (213) 474-6801

Temple Beth Am
1039 S. La Cienega Blvd 90035
Telephone: (213) 652-7353
Fax: (213) 652-2384
Email: betham@tbala.org
Website: www.tbala.org

Orthodox
Chabad House
741 Gayley Avenue, West Los Angeles 90025

Etz Jacob Congregation
7659 Beverley Blvd
Telephone: (213) 938-2619
Fax: (213) 930-2373
Email: office@etzjacob.org

Los Angeles Orthodox Synagogue
9317 West Pico Blvd, Century City 90035
Telephone: (310) 273-6954
Fax: (310) 273-7103
Email: shuloffice@yicc.org
Website: www.yicc.org

Ohel David
7967 Beverley Blvd

Young Israel of Hancock Park
225 South La Brea
Telephone: (213) 931-4030
Fax: (213) 935-3819

Young Israel of Los Angeles
660 N. Spaulding Avenue 90036
Telephone: (213) 655-0300
Fax: (213) 655-0322

Orthodox Sephardi
Kahal Joseph
1005 Santa Monica Blvd 90025
Telephone: (213) 474-0559

Temple Tifereth Israel
10500 Wilshire Blvd 90024
Telephone: (213) 475-7311
Fax: (213) 470-9238

Reconstructionist
Kehillat Israel
16019 Sunset Blvd. Pacific Palisades 90272
Telephone: (213) 459-2328
Fax: (213) 573-2098
Email: kihome@aol.com

Reform
Leo Baeck Temple
1300 N. Sepulveda Blvd 90049
Telephone: (213) 476-2861

Stephen S. Wise Temple
15500 Stephen S. Wise Drive, Bel Air 90024
Telephone: (213) 476-8561
Fax: (213) 476-3587

Temple Akiba
5249 S. Sepulveda Blvd. Culver City 90230
Telephone: (213) 398-5783
Fax: (213) 398-1637
Website: www.temakiba

Temple Isaiah
10345 W. Pico Blvd. 90064

University Synagogue
11960 Sunset Blvd 90049
Telephone: (213) 472-1255
Fax: (213) 476-3237

Wilshire Blvd Temple
3663 Wilshire Blvd 90010
Telephone: (213) 388-2401
Fax: (213) 388-2595

NORTH HOLLYWOOD
KASHRUT INFORMATION
The Kashrus Information Bureau
12753 Chandler Blvd., N. Hollywood 91607
Telephone: (818) 762-3197; 262-5351
Fax: (818) 766-8537
Email: eeidlitz@kosherquest.org
Website: www.kosherquest.org
The Kosher Information Bureau is a worldwide kashrus

information only organization. It produces a weekly
fax/email update, quarterly magazine and has a book titled
'Is It Kosher'. At the website you can find travel information
for western U.S. Kol Tuv.

MIKVAOT
Teichman Mikvah Society
12800 Chandler Blvd., N. Hollywood
Telephone: (818) 506-0996

RESTAURANTS
Meat
Flora Falafel
12450 Burbank Blvd., North Hollywood
Telephone: (818) 766-6567
Supervision: RCC

Golan
13075 Victory Blvd.
Telephone: (818) 763-5375

SYNAGOGUES
Orthodox
Shaarey Zedek
12800 Chandler Blvd., N. Hollywood 91607
Telephone: (818) 763-0560
Fax: (818) 763-8215

NORTHRIDGE
SYNAGOGUES
Conservative
Temple Ramat Zion
17655 Devonshire Avenue, Northridge
Telephone: (818) 360-1881

SYNAGOGUES
Orthodox
Young Israel of Northridge
17511 Devonshire Street 91325
Telephone: (818) 368-2221
Fax: (818) 360-5754
Email: rabbi@yion.org
Website: www.yion.org
Supervision: Rabbi Aharon Simkin
Central organisation: National Council of Young Israel
Only daily Minyan in San Fernando Valley morning and
evening

Reform
Temple Ahavat Shalom
11261 Chimineas Avenue, Northridge

OAKLAND
COMMUNITY ORGANISATIONS
Berkeley/Richmond JCC
1414 Walnut St., Berkeley 94709
Telephone: (510) 848-0237
Fax: (510) 848-0170
Email: info@brjcc.ofrg
Website: www.brjcc.org

Jewish Community Federation of the Greater Eastern Bay
300 Grand Ave 94610
Website: www.jfed.org

DELICATESSEN
Holy Land Restaurant
677 Rand Avenue 94610
Telephone: (510) 272-0535

MIKVAOT
Beth Jacob Synagogue
3778 Park Blvd 94610
Telephone: (510) 482-1147
Fax: (510) 482-2374
Email: bjc-office@eb.jfed.org

SYNAGOGUES
Conservative
Beth Abraham
327 MacArthur Blvd. 94610
Telephone: (510) 832-0936

Beth Sholom
642 Dolores, San Leandro 94577

Independent
B'nai Israel of Rossmoor
c/o Fred Rau, 2601 Ptarmigasn #3 , Walnut Greek 94595

Beth Chaim
PO Box 23632, Pleasant Hill 94577

Orthodox
Beth Jacob Synagogue
3778 Park Blvd 94610
Telephone: (510) 482-1147
Fax: (510) 482-2374
Email: bjc-office@eb.jfed.org

Reform
Beth Emek
PO Box 722, Livermore 94550

Beth Hillel
801 Park Central, Richmond 94803

Temple Beth Torah
42000 Paseo Padre Pkwy. Fremont 94538
Telephone: (510) 656-7141
Website: www.bethtorah-fremont.org

Temple Sinai
2808 Summit 94609
Telephone: (510) 451-3263
Fax: (510) 465-0603
Email: templeoffice@oaklandsinai.org

ONTARIO
SYNAGOGUES
Conservative
Temple Sholom
963 West 6th St 91762
Telephone: (909) 983-9661
Rabbi Gil Alchadeff

TRAVEL
Ontario Travel Bureau
Laurie Neuman van Esschoten Your Kosher Travel Specialists , 1044 West 4th Street 91762
Telephone: (909) 984-2761 or (800) 893-5617
Fax: (909) 984-2764
Email: laurie@ontariotravelbureau.com
Website: www.thewanderingjew.net

PALM SPRINGS
SYNAGOGUES
Conservative
Temple Isaiah
322 W. Alejo Road 92262
Telephone: (760) 325-2281
Fax: (760) 325-3235

Orthodox
Chabad of Palm Springs
425 Avenue, Ortega
Telephone: (760) 325-0774

Desert Synagogue
1068 N. Palm Canyon Drive
Telephone: (760) 327-4848
Fax: (760) 322-5238
Email: theshul@earthlink.net
Website: www.desertshul.org

PALO ALTO
COMMUNITY ORGANISATIONS
Albert L. Schultz Community Center
655 Arastradero Road 94306
Telephone: (650) 439-9400

GROCERIES
Garden Fresh
1245 W. El Camino Road, Mount View 94040
Telephone: (650) 961-7795

SYNAGOGUES
Orthodox
Chadbad of Greater South Bay
3070 Louis Road 94303
Telephone: (650) 424-9800
Fax: (650) 493-3425
Email: chabad@jewish.org

Palo Alto Orthodox Minyan
260 Sheridan Avenue 94306
Telephone: (650) 948-7498

PASADENA
SYNAGOGUES
Conservative
Pasadena Jewish Temple and Center
1434 North Altadena Drive 91107
Telephone: (626) 798-1161

POMONA
SYNAGOGUES
Reform
Temple Beth Israel
3033 North Towne Ave. Pomona CA
Telephone: (909) 626-1277

POWAY
SYNAGOGUES
Orthodox
Chadad of Poway
16934 Chabad Way 92064
Telephone: (858) 451-0455
Fax: (858) 637-0299
Email: chabad-poway@cox.net
Website: www.chabad.poway.com

Reform
Temple Adat Shalom
15905 Pomerado Road, 92064
Telephone: (858) 451-1200
Fax: (858) 451-2409

RAMONA
Etz Chaim
PO Box 1138, Ramona 92065
Telephone: (760) 789-7393

RANCHO CUCAMONGA
SYNAGOGUES
Chadbad of the Inland Empire (Lubavitch)
8710 Baker 91730
Telephone: (909) 949-4553
Rabbi Sholom Harlig

SACRAMENTO
COMMUNITY ORGANISATIONS
Jewish Federation of Sacramento
2351 Wyda Way 95825
Telephone: (916) 486 0906
Fax: (916) 486-0816
Email: jfed@juno.com
Website: www.jewishsac.org

MIKVAOT
Sacramento Mikvaot
1024 Morse Ave 95864
Telephone: (916) 481-1158

RESTAURANTS
Meat
Bob's Butcher Block
6436 Fair Oaks Blvd., Carmichael Oaks Shopping Ctr.
Telephone: (916) 482-6884

SYNAGOGUES
Conservative
Mosaic Law
2300 Sierra Blvd. 95825
Telephone: (916) 488-1122
Fax: (916) 488-1165
Website: www.mosaiclaw.org

Orthodox
Kenesset Israel Torah Center
1165Morse Avenue 95864
Telephone: (916) 481-1159
Fax: (916) 489-6918
Email: itc1159@earthlink.net
Website: www.kitcsacramento.org

Reform
B'nai Israel
3600 Riverside Blvd. 95818
Telephone: (916) 446-4861

Beth Shalom
4746 El Camino Avenue 09608
Telephone: (916) 485-4478
Fax: (916) 485-0776
Email: office@cbshalom.org
Website: www.cbshalom.org

SAN BERNARDINO
Emanu El
3512 N. E. Street 92405
Telephone: (909) 886-4818
Fax: (909) 883-5892
Email: cee@emanuelsb.org

SAN CARLOS
CONTACT INFORMATION
Jewish Travel Network
PO Box 283 94070
Telephone: (650) 368-0880
Fax: (650) 599-9066
Email: info@jewishtravelnetwork.com
Website: www.jewishtravelnetwork.com/

SAN DIEGO
BAKERIES
Sheila's Café & Bakery
4577 Claremont Drive 92117
Telephone: (619) 270-0251
Fax: (619) 274-5797
Email: sheilassandiego@hotmail.com
Website: www.sheilascafe.com

COMMUNITY ORGANISATIONS
United Jewish Federation of San Diego County
4950 Murphy Canyon Road, San Diego 92123
Telephone: (858) 571-3444
Fax: (858) 571-0701
Email: otutreach@ujfsd.org
Website: www.jewishinsandiego.org

MEDIA
Newspapers
San Diego Jewish Press Heritage
PO Box 19363
Telephone: (619) 265-0808
Fax: (619) 265-0850
Email: sdheritag@cox.net
San Diego Jewish Times
4731 Palm Avenue, La Mesa 91941
Telephone: (619) 463-5515
Fax: (619) 463-1309
Email: jewishtimes@earthlink.net

RESTAURANTS
Dairy
Aarons Glatt Kosher Market
4488 Convoy Street 92111
Telephone: (619) 636-7979
Fax: (619) 636-7980
Website: www.kosherfooddelivery.com
Sababa, Kosher Restaurant
7520 El Cajon Blvd. 92115
Telephone: (619) 337-1880
Fax: (619) 523-9963
Shmoozers Vegetarian & Pizzeria
6366 El Cajon Blvd. 92115
Telephone: (619) 583-1636
Fax: (619) 683-1635
Email: shmoozers1@aol.com
Supervision: Vaad HaRabbanim of San Diego
Dairy Market
Lang's Premium Kosher
6165 El Cajon Blvd 92115
Telephone: (619) 287-7306; 800-60-LANGS
Fax: (619) 582-1545
Website: www.kosherbread.com
Supervision: Vaad of San Diego
Meat
Sheila's Café & Bakery
4577 Clairemont Dr. 92117
Telephone: (619) 270-0251
Fax: (619) 274-5797
Email: sheilassandiego@hotmail.com
Website: www.sheilascafe.com

SYNAGOGUES
Conservative
Congregation Beth Am
5050 Black Mtn. Road 92130
Telephone: (619) 481-8454
Fax: (619) 481-6068
Email: betham@betham.com
Ner Tamid
16770 West Bernardo Drive, Suite A 92127
Telephone: (619) 592-9141
Fax: (619) 592-4889
Email: nertamid@altavista.com
Tifereth Israel Synagogue
6660 Cowles Mountain Blvd. 92119
Telephone: (619) 697-6001
Fax: (619) 697-1102
Website: www.tiferethisrael.com
Orthodox
Beth Jacob Synagogue
4855 College Avenue 92115
Telephone: (619) 287-9890
Fax: (619) 287-0578
Chabad
6115 Montezuma Road 92115
Telephone: (619) 265-0519
Fax: (619) 265-0346
Email: chabadhousesd@aol.com
Chabad of La Jolla
3813 Governor Drive, Suite N 92122
Telephone: (619) 455-1670
Fax: (619) 451-1443
Ohr Shalom
1260 Morena Blvd, Suite 100 92100
Telephone: (619) 275-9299
Fax: (619) 275-2078
Young Israel Congregation of San Diego
7291 Navajo Road 92119
Telephone: (619) 589-1447
Reconstructionist
Congregation Dor Hadash
4858 Ronson Court, Suite A 92111
Telephone: (619) 268-3674
Fax: (619) 794-4087
Reform
Congregation Beth Israel of San Diego
9001 Towne Centre Drive 92122
Telephone: (619) 535-1111
Fax: (619) 535-1130
Email: bmiller@cbisd.org
Website: www.cbisd.org
Temple Emanu-El
6299 Capri Drive 92120
Telephone: (619) 286-2555
Fax: (619) 286-3176

SAN FERNANDO VALLEY
BAKERIES
Continental Kosher Bakery
12419 Burbank Blvd.
Telephone: (818) 762-5005

RESTAURANTS
Apropo Falafel
6800 Reseda Blvd.
Telephone: (818) 881-6608

Hadar Restaurant and Catering
12514 Burbank Blvd 91607
Telephone: (818) 762-1155
Supervision: RCC

Meat
Sportsman Lodge
Sherman Oaks
Telephone: (818) 984-0202

Pizzerias
La Pizza
12515 Burbank Blvd.
Telephone: (818) 760-8198

SYNAGOGUES
Conservative
Beth Meir Congregation
11725 Moorpark, Studio City 91604
Telephone: (818) 769-0515
Fax: (818) 769-7127
Email: congbethmeier@sbcglobal.net
Website: www.congregationbethmeier.org

Temple B'nai Hayim
4302 Van Nuys Blvd., Sherman Oaks
Telephone: (818) 788-4664

SAN FRANCISCO
BAKERIES
Noahs Bagels
3519 California Street, Willow Glen
Telephone: (415) 387-3874

COMMUNITY ORGANISATIONS
Jewish Com. Fed. of San Francisco, the Peninsula, Marin & Sonoma Counties
121 Steuart St. 94105
Telephone: (415) 777-0411
Fax: (415) 495-6635
Email: jewishnfo@sfjcf.org   info@sfjcf.org
Website: www.jewishfed.org
Notes: Central organisation for fundraising, planning, outreach and leadership development.

EMBASSY
Consul General of Israel
Suite 2100, 456 Mongomery Street 94104

GROCERIES
Jacob's Kosher Meats
2435 Noriega street 94122
Telephone: (415) 564-7482

Kosher Meats Israel & Cohen Kosher Meats
5621 Geary Blvd. 94121
Telephone: (415) 752-3064

Kosher Nutrition Kitchen
Montefiore Senior Center, 3200 California Av
Supervision: Orthodox Rabbinical Council

Tel Aviv Strictly Kosher Meats
2495 Irving Street 94122
Telephone: (415) 661-7588
Fax: (415) 661-8258
Supervision: Orthodox Rabbinical Council

LIBRARIES
Holocaust Library & Research Center
601 14th Avenue 94118
Telephone: (415) 751-6040

MIKVAOT
Mikva
3355 Sacramento Street 94118
Telephone: (415) 921-4070

MUSEUMS
The Magnes Museum
121 Steuart St. 94105
Telephone: (415) 591-8800
Fax: (415) 591-8815
Email: info@magnesmuseum.org
Website: www.magnesmuseum.org

RESTAURANTS
Meat
Sabra
419 Grant Avenue, Chinatown
Telephone: (415) 982-3656
Fax: (415) 982-3650
Supervision: Vaad Hakashrus of Northern California

This is It
430 Geary Street 94210
Telephone: (415) 749-0201

SYNAGOGUES
Conservative
Beth Israel-Judea
625 Brotherhood Way 94132
Telephone: (415) 586-8833

Beth Sholom
1301 Clement Street 94118
Telephone: (415) 221-8736
Fax: (415) 221-3944
Email: enichol@bethsholomsf.org
Website: www.bethsholomsf.org

B'nai Emunah
3595 Taraval Street 94116
Telephone: (415) 664-7373
Fax: (415) 664-4209
Email: emuna@jps.net
Website: www.bnaiemunahsf.org

Ner Tamid
1250 Quintara street 94116
Telephone: (415) 661-3383

Orthodox
Adath Israel
1851 Noriega Street 94122
Telephone: (415) 564-5565

Anshey Sfard
1500 Clement Street 94118
Telephone: (415) 752-4979

Chevra Tehilim
751 25th Avenue 94121
Telephone: (415) 752-2866

Kenesseth Israel
873 Sutter Street 94109
Telephone: (415) 771-3420

Torat Emeth
768 27th Avenue 94121
Telephone: (415) 386-1830

Young Israel of San Francisco
1806 A Noriega Street 94122
Telephone: (415) 387-1774

Reform
Emanu-El
Arguello Blvd. & Lake Street 94118
Telephone: (415) 751-2535
Fax: (415) 751-2511
Email: mail@emanuelsf.org

Sha'ar Zahav
290 Dolores Street 94103
Telephone: (415) 861-6932
Fax: (415) 841-6081
Email: office@shaarzahav.org

Sherith Israel
2266 California Street 94115
Telephone: (415) 346-1720
Fax: (415) 673-9439
Email: ed@sherithisrael.org

Sephardi
Magain David
351 4th Avenue 94118
Telephone: (415) 752-9095

TOURIST INFORMATION
Jewish Community Information & Referral
121 Steuart St. 94105
Telephone: (415) 777-4545
Fax: (415) 495-4897
Email: info@jewishnfo.org

Website: www.jewishnfo.org
Central organisation: Jewish Community Federation

SAN JOSE
BOOKSELLERS
Alef Bet Judaica
14103-0 Winchester blvd. Los Gatos 95032
Telephone: (408) 370-1818
Fax: (408) 725-8269
Email: nurit@best.com

COMMUNITY ORGANISATIONS
Jewish Federation of Greater San Jose
14855 Oka Road, Los Gatos 95030
Telephone: (408) 358-3033
Fax: (408) 356-0733

MIKVAOT
Mikvah Society of San Jose
1670 Phantom Avenue 95125
Telephone: (408) 371-9548 for appointments; 264-3138 for info
Fax: (408) 264-3139
Email: bergman.d@sbcglobal.net

SYNAGOGUES
Conservative
Congregation Beth David
19700 Prospect Road, Saratoga 95070
Telephone: (408) 257-3333
Fax: (408) 257-3338
Email: admin@beth-david.org
Website: www.beth-david.org

Congregation Emeth
PO Box 1430, Gilroy 95021
Telephone: (408) 847-4111

Congregation Sinai
1532 Willowbrae Avenue 95125-4450
Telephone: (408) 264-8542
Fax: (408) 264-4316
Email: sinai_sj@juno.com

Orthodox
Ahavas Torah
1537-A Meridian Avenue 95125
Telephone: (408) 266-2342
Fax: (408) 264-3139
Email: ahavastorahsj@aol.com
Website: www.ahava.org

Almaden Valley Torah Center
1422 Helmond Lane 95118
Telephone: (408) 445-1770
Fax: (408) 267-9812
Email: rabbi770@sbcglobal.net
Website: www.rabbi770.com

Am Echad Community
1504 Meridian Avenue 95125
Telephone: (408) 267-2591
Email: info@amechad.org
Website: www.amechad.org

Reform
Congregation Shir Hadash
20 Cherry Blossom Lane 95032
Telephone: (408) 358-1751
Fax: (408) 358-1753
Website: www.shirhadash.org

Temple Beth Sholom
2270 Canoas Garden Avenue 95125
Telephone: (408) 978-5566

Temple Emanu-El
1010 University Avenue 95126
Telephone: (408) 292-0939

SAN RAFAEL
Rodef Sholom
170 N. San Pedro Rd. 94903
Telephone: (415) 479-3441

SANTA BARBARA
SYNAGOGUES

Orthodox
Chabad of Santa Barbara
6047 Stow Canyon Road, Goleta 93117
Telephone: (805) 683-1544
Fax: (805) 683-1545
Email: rabbi@sbchabad.org
Website: www.sbchabad.org

Young Israel of Santa Barbara
1826 Cliff Drive 93109
Telephone: (805) 966-4565

SYNAGOGUES
Reform
Congregation B'nai B'rith
1000 San Antonio Creek Road 93111
Telephone: (805) 964-7869
Fax: (805) 683-6473

SANTA MONICA
SYNAGOGUES
Orthodox
Chabad House
1428 17th Street 90404

Young Israel of Santa Monica
21 Hampton Avenue
Telephone: (310) 399-8514

Reform
Beth Shir Sholom
1827 California Avenue 90403
Telephone: (310) 453-3361
Fax: (310) 453-6827

Website: www.bethshirsholom.com

SANTA ROSA
SYNAGOGUES
Conservative
Beth Ami
4676 Mayette Avenue 95405
Telephone: (707) 545-4334

SYNAGOGUES
Reform
Congregation Shomrei Torah
1717 Yulupa Avenue 95405
Telephone: (707) 578-5519
Fax: (707) 578-3967
Email: shomrei@pacbell.net

SHERMAN OAKS
RESTAURANTS
Dairy
Fish Grill
13628 Ventura Blvd.
Telephone: (818) 788-9896

STOCKTON
Stockton is one of the oldest communities west of the Mississippi River, founded in the days of the California Gold Rush. Temple Israel was founded as Congregation Ryhim Ahoovim in 1850 and erected its first building in 1855.

SYNAGOGUES
Reform
Temple Israel
5105 N. El Dorado St. 95207
Telephone: (209) 477-9306

SUNNYVALE
SYNAGOGUES
Bar Yohai Sefardic Minyan
1030 Astoria Drive 94087
Website: www.baryohai.org

TARZANA
BAKERIES
Unique Pastry Bakery and Café
18385 Ventura Blvd. 91356
Telephone: (818) 757-3100
Fax: (818) 757-3144

BOOKSELLERS
Steimatzky
19566 Ventura Blvd. 91356
Telephone: (818) 708-2347
Fax: (818) 708-2319
Email: stmla@earthlink.net

SYNAGOGUES
Reform
Temple Judea
5429 Lindley Avenue,

THOUSAND OAKS
SYNAGOGUES
Conservative
Temple Etz Chaim
1080 E. Janss Rd. 91360
Telephone: (805) 497-6891
Fax: (805) 497-0086

TIBURON
Congregation Kol Shafar
215 Blackfield Dr. 94920
Telephone: (415) 388-1818

TUSTIN
Congregation B'nai Israel
655 S. 'B' St 92680
Telephone: (714) 259-0655

VALLEJO
SYNAGOGUES
Unaffiliated
Congregtion B'nai Israel
1256 Nebraska St. 94590
Telephone: (707) 642-6526

VALLEY VILLAGE
SYNAGOGUES
Conservative
Adat Ari El
12020 Burbank Blvd., 91607-2198
Telephone: (816) 766-9426

VAN NUYS
COMMUNITY ORGANISATIONS
Valley Cities Center
13164 Burbank Blvd., Van Nuys 91401

VENICE
SYNAGOGUES
Orthodox
Pacific Jewish Center
Shul on the Beach 505 Ocean Front Walk, Venice
Beach 90291
Telephone: (310) 392-8749
Fax: (310) 392-4557
Email: office@pjcenter.com
Website: www.pjcenter.com

VENTURA
COMMUNITY ORGANISATIONS
Jewish Community Centre
259 Callens Road 93004
Telephone: (805) 647-4181

SYNAGOGUES
Reform
Temple Beth Torah
7620 Foothill Road 93004
Telephone: (805) 647-4181

WALNUT CREEK
COMMUNITY ORGANISATIONS
Contra Costa JCC
2071 Tice Valley Blvd. 94595
Telephone: (925) 937-0765

SYNAGOGUES
Conservative
Congregation B'nai Synagogue
74 Eckley Lane 94596
Telephone: (925) 934-9446
Fax: (925) 934-9450
Email: office@bshalom.org
Website: www.bshalom.org

Contra Costa Jewish Community Center
2071 Tice Valley blvd 94595

Orthodox
Chabad of Contra Costa
1671 Newell Ave. 94595
Telephone: (925) 837-4101
Email: info@chabadcoco.com
Website: www.chabadcoco.com

Reform
Congregation B'nai Tikvah
25 hillcroft Way 94595
Telephone: (925) 933-5397

WEST HILLS
COMMUNITY ORGANISATIONS
West Valley Center
22622 Vanowen Street, West Hills 91307

SYNAGOGUES
Conservative
Shomrei Torah Synagogue
7353 Valley Circle, West Hills 91304
Telephone: (818) 346-0811
Fax: (818) 346-3956
Email: shomrei@sbglobal.net
Website: www.shomreitorahsynagogue.org

WHITTIER
Beth Shalom Synagogues Center
14564 E. Hawes Street 90604
Telephone: (310) 914-8744

Colorado
BOULDER
COMMUNITY ORGANISATIONS
Boulder JCC
3800 Kalmia Avenue 80301
Telephone: (303) 998-1900
Fax: (303) 998-1965
Email: linda@boulderjcc.org
Website: www.bjcf.org

ORGANISATIONS
Lubavitch of Boulder County
4900 Sioux Drive 80303
Telephone: (303) 494-1638
Fax: (303) 938-8350
Email: lubavbldr@cs.com
Website: www.lubavitchofbouldeer.org

SYNAGOGUES
Hillel Foundation
2795 colorado Avenue, University of Colorado
Telephone: (303) 442-6571

Conservative
Congregation Bonai Shalom
1527 Cherryvale Rd., 80303
Telephone: (303) 442-6605
Fax: (303) 442-7545
Email: bonaishalom@aol.com
Website: www.bonaishalom.org

Orthodox
Chabad Lubavitch of Boulder
4900 Sioux Drive 80303
Telephone: (303) 494-1638
Email: lubavbldr@cs.com
Website: Lubavitchofboulder.org

Reform
Congregation Har Hashem
3950 Baseline Road 80303
Telephone: (303) 499-7077

Jewish Renewal Community of Boulder
5001 Pennsylvania 80303
Telephone: (303) 271-3541

COLORADO SPRINGS
SYNAGOGUES
Conservative & Reform
Temple Shalom
1523 E. Monument street 80909
Telephone: (719) 634-5311
Fax: (719) 447-9385
Email: Tshalom@qwest.net
Website: www.templeshalom.com

DENVER
BAKERIES
The Bagel Store
942 South Monaco 80224
Telephone: (303) 388-2648
Supervision: Vaad Hakashrus of Denver

COMMUNITY ORGANISATIONS
Allied Jewish Federation of Colorado
300 S. Dahlia Street 80246
Telephone: (303) 316-6491
Fax: (303) 322-8328
Email: mgardenswartz@ajfcolorado.org
Website: jewishcolorado.org

Jewish Family & Children's Service
1355 S. Colorado Blvd 80222
Telephone: (303) 759-4890
Fax: (303) 759-5998
Email: jfs@jewishfamilyservice.org
Website: www.jewishfamilyservice.org

GROCERIES
Auerbach's
4810 Newport St.
Telephone: (303) 289-4521

Cub Foods
1985 Sheridan Blvd., Edgewater
Telephone: (303) 232-8972

King Soopers
890 S. Monaco Parway
Telephone: (303) 333-1535
6470 East Hampden Avenue
Telephone: (303) 758-1210

Safeway
7150 Leetsdale Drive (& Quebec)
Telephone: (303) 377-6939
640 E. Yale (& Monaco)
Telephone: (303) 691-8870

KASHRUT INFORMATION
Scoll K Vaad Hakashrus of Denver
1350 Vrain 80204
Telephone: (303) 595-9349
Fax: (303) 629-5159

MEDIA
Newspapers
Intermountain Jewish News
1275 Sherman Avenue, Suite 214 80203
Telephone: (303) 861-2234
Fax: (303) 832-6942
Email: email@ijn.com

MIKVAOT
Mikvah of Denver
1404 Quitman 80204
Telephone: (303) 893-5315
Fax: (303) 825-5810

RELIGIOUS ORGANISATIONS
Synagogue Council of Greater Denver
Po Box 102732 80250
Telephone: (303) 759-8484

RESTAURANTS
Meat
Jeff's Diner
731 Quebec Street 80220
Telephone: (303) 333-4637

RESTAURANTS
Pizzeria
Pete's Kosher Pizza
5606 E. Cedar Avenue 80204
Telephone: (303) 255-5777

SYNAGOGUES
Conservative
Beth Shalom
2280 East Noble Place, Littleton 80121
Telephone: (303) 794-6643

Hebrew Educational Alliance (HEA)
3600 South Ivanhoe St. 80237
Telephone: (303) 758-9400
Fax: (303) 758-9500
Email: info@headenver.org

Rodef Shalom
450 S. Kearney 80224
Telephone: (303) 399-0035
Fax: (303) 399-7623
Email: mainoffice@rodef-shalom.org
Website: www.rodef-shalom.org

Orthodox
Aish/Ahavas Yisroel; a Center for Jewish Learning
9550 E. Belleview Ave., Greenwood Village 80111
Telephone: (303) 220-7200
Fax: (303) 290-9191
Email: ymeyer@aish.com

Bais Medrash Kehillas Yaakov
295 S. Locust Street 80222
Telephone: (303) 377-1200
Fax: (303) 355-6010
Email: tai@jewishpeople.com

Congregation Zera Abraham
1560 Winona Court 80204
Telephone: (303) 825-7517

Reform
Beth Shalom
2280 E. Noble Place 80121
Telephone: (303) 794-6643

Temple Micah
2600 Leyden street 80207
Telephone: (303) 388-4239
Fax: (303) 377-4816
Email: office@micahdenver.org
Website: www.micahdenver.org

Temple Sinai
3509 South Glencoe street 80237
Telephone: (303) 759-1827
Fax: (303) 759-2519
Email: mail@sinaidenver.org
Website: www.sinaidenver.org

Traditional
B.M.H.-BJ Congregation
560 S. Monaco Pkwy. 80224
Telephone: (303) 388-4203
Fax: (303) 388-4210

EVERGREEN
SYNAGOGUES
Reconstructionist
Congregation Beth Evergreen
PO Box 415 80439
Telephone: (303) 670-4294
Fax: (303) 670-6930
Email: shalom@bethevergreen.org
Website: www.bethevergreen.org
Congregation Beth Evergreen offers inclusive, warm welcoming services and programmes in an intimate atmosphere. We are committed to fostering community by offering opportunities for meaningful worship, the pursuit of spirituality and lifelong Jewish education.

PUEBLO
SYNAGOGUES
Conservative
United Hebrew Congregation
106 W. 15th street 81003
Telephone: (719) 544-9897; 583-8303

Reform
Temple Emanuel
1325 Grand Avenue 81003
Telephone: (719) 544-6448
Email: mikeaa@coloradobluesky.org

Connecticut
BRIDGEPORT
COMMUNITY ORGANISATIONS
Jewish Center for Community Services of Eastern Fairfield County
4200 Park Avenue 06604
Telephone: (203) 372-6567
Fax: (203) 374-0770
Email: info@jccs.org

MEDIA
Radio
WVOF Radio
c/o Fairfield University, Fairfield 06430
Telephone: (203) 254-4111

MIKVAOT
Mikveh Israel
1326 Stratfield Road, Fairfield 06432

RELIGIOUS ORGANISATIONS
Va'ad of Fairfield County
1571 Stratfield Road, Fairfield 06432
Telephone: (203) 372-6529
Fax: (203) 373-0467
Email: rbaun64732@aol.com

RESTAURANTS
Cafe Shalom
c/o Abel, Community Center
Telephone: (203) 372-6567

SYNAGOGUES
Conservative
B'nai Torah
5700 Main St., Trumbull 06611

Rodeph Sholom
2385 Park Avenue 06604
Telephone: (203) 334-0159
Fax: (203) 334-1411
Email: cong.rodeph.sholom@snet.net
Website: www.rodephsholom.com

Orthodox
Agudas Achim
85 Arlington Street 06606

Bikur Cholim
Park & Capitol Avenue 06604
Telephone: (203) 336-3383
Email: jbm@ou.org
Website: www.ou.org

Reconstructionist
Congregation Shirei Shalom
Po Box 372, Monroe 06468

Reform
Temple B'nai Israel
2710 Park Avenue 06604
Telephone: (203) 336-1858
Fax: (203) 367-7889
Email: welcome@congregationbnaiisrael.org

DANBURY
COMMUNITY ORGANISATIONS
Jewish Federation
69 Kenosia Avenue 06810
Telephone: (203) 792-6353
Fax: (203) 748-5099

Email: info@thejf.org
Website: www.thejf.org

SYNAGOGUES
Conservative
Congregation B'nai Israel
193 Clapboard Ridge Road 06811
Telephone: (203) 792-6161
Fax: (203) 792-8315
Email: cbi193clab@juno.com

Orthodox
Chabad
9 Golden Heights Road 06811
Telephone: (203) 790-4700
Email: lgurkov@juno.com

Reform
United Jewish Center
141 Deer Hill Avenue 06810
Telephone: (203) 748-3335

FAIRFIELD
BAKERIES
Carvel Ice Cream Bakery
1838 Black Rock Turnpike
Telephone: (203) 384-2253
Supervision: Vaad Hakashrus of Fairfield County

SYNAGOGUES
Conservative
Congregation Beth El
1200 Fairfield Woods Rd., Fairfield 06825
Telephone: (203) 374-5544
Fax: (203) 374-4962
Email: congbethel@aol.com
Website: www.uscj.org/ctvalley/fairfield

Orthodox
Congregation Ahavath Achim
1571 Stratfield Road, Fairfield 06825
Telephone: (203) 372-6529
Fax: (203) 373-0647

HARTFORD
COMMUNITY ORGANISATIONS
Jewish Federation of Hartford
333 Bloomfield Avenue 06117
Telephone: (860) 232-4483

KASHRUT INFORMATION
Kashrut Commission
162 Brewster Road 06117
Telephone: (860) 563-4017

MEDIA
Guide
All Things Jewish
333 Bloomfield Avenue 06117
Telephone: (860) 232-4483

MIKVAOT
Mikva
61 Main Street 06119

SYNAGOGUES
Conservative
Beth El
2626 Albany Avenue, West Hartford 06117

Beth Tefilah
465 Oak St., East Hartford 06118

Congregation B'nai Sholom
26 Church St. Newington 06111-4401
Telephone: (860) 667-0826
Fax: (860) 667-0827
Email: president@cbsnewington.com
Website: www.cbsnewington.org

Emanuel synagogue
160 Mohegan Dr., West Hartford 06117
Telephone: (860) 236-1275
Fax: (860) 231-8890
Email: emansyn@emanuelsynagogue.org

Orthodox
Agudas Achim
1244 N. Main St., West Hartford 06117

Beth David Synagogue
20 Dover Road, West Hartford 06117
Telephone: (860) 236-1241
Fax: (860) 232-8272
Email: rabbi@bethdavidwh.org

Teferes Israel
27 Brown St., Bloomfield 06002

United Synagogue of Greater Hartford
840 N. Main S., West Hartford 06117

Reform
Temple Sinai
41 W. Hartford Road, Newington 06011

MANCHESTER
SYNAGOGUES
Conservative
Temple Beth Sholom
400 Middle Turnpike E. 06040
Telephone: (603) 643-9563
Fax: (603) 643-9565
Email: riplavin@prodigy.net
Website: www.uscj.org/ctvalley/manchestertbs

MERIDEN
SYNAGOGUES
Conservative
B'nai Abraham
127 E. Main St., 06450
Telephone: (203) 235-2581

MIDDLETOWN
SYNAGOGUES
Conservative
Adath Israel
48 Church St., 06457
Telephone: (860) 346-4709

NEW BRITAIN
SYNAGOGUES
Conservative
B'nai Israel Conservative Synagogue
265 W. Main St., 06051
Telephone: (860) 224-0479

Orthodox
Tephereth Israel
76 Winter Street 06051

NEW HAVEN
COMMUNITY ORGANISATIONS
Jewish Federation of Greater New Haven
360 Amity Road, Woodbridge Ct. 06525
Telephone: (203) 387-2424

CONTACT INFORMATION
Young Israel House at Yale University
c/o Joseph Slifka center, 80 Wall Street 06510
Telephone: (203) 432-1134
Fax: (203) 776-4212
Email: rabbiisaac@cs.com
Website: www.yale.edu/hillel/org/yihy.html

DELICATESSEN
The Westville
1460 Whalley Avenue 06515
Telephone: (203) 397-0839
Fax: (203) 387-4129
Email: pweinb@aol.com

Zackey's
1304 Whalley Avenue 06515
Telephone: (203) 387-2454

GROCERIES
Westville Kosher Meat Market
95 Amity Road 06525
Telephone: (203) 389-1723

LIBRARIES
Center Cafe & Jewish Library
360 Amity Road 06525
Telephone: (203) 387-2424

MIKVAOT
New Haven Mikvah Society
86 Hubinger Street 06511
Telephone: (203) 387-2184

RESTAURANTS
Dairy
Claire's Gourmet Vegetarian Restaurant & Caterer
1000 Chapel Street 06510
Telephone: (203) 562-3888
Supervision: Young Israel of New Haven

SYNAGOGUES
Conservative
Beth-El Keser Israel
85 Harrison Street 06515
Telephone: (203) 389-2108

Orthodox
Beth Hamedrosh Westville
74 West Prospect Street 06515
Telephone: (203) 389-9513

Congregation Bikur Cholim Sheveth Achim
112 Marvel Road 06515
Telephone: (203) 387-4699

Yeshiva of New Haven
765 Elm Street, New Haven 06511
Telephone: (203) 777-2200
Fax: (203) 777-7198
Email: info@yeshivanewhaven.org
Website: www.yeshivanewhaven.org

NEW LONDON
COMMUNITY ORGANISATIONS
Jewish Federation of Eastern Connecticut
28 Channing Street 06320
Telephone: (860) 442-8062
Fax: (860) 443-4175
Email: jfischer@jfec.com
Website: www.jfec.com

NORWICH
SYNAGOGUES
Orthodox
Brothers of Joseph
Broad & Washington Avs., 06360
Telephone: (203) 887-3777

STAMFORD
COMMUNITY ORGANISATIONS
United Jewish Federation of Greater Stamford, New Canaan and Darien
1035 Newfield Avenue, Suite 200 06905-2591
Telephone: (203) 321-1373
Fax: (203) 322-3277
Email: office@ujf.org
Website: www.ujf.org

DELICATESSEN
Delicate-Essen at the JCC
1035 Newfield Avenue 06902
Telephone: (203) 322-0944
Fax: (203) 322-5160
Email: bhert2b111@aol.com
Supervision: Vaad Hakashrus of Fairfield County.

SYNAGOGUES
Orthodox
Young Israel of Stamford
69 Oak Lawn Avenue 06905
Telephone: (203) 348-3955

WATERBURY
COMMUNITY ORGANISATIONS
Jewish Communities of Western CT, Inc.
73 Main Street, South Woodbury 06798
Telephone: (203) 263-5121
Fax: (203) 263-5143
Email: jfedwtby@aol.com

WEST HARTFORD
BOOKSELLERS
The Judaica Store
31 Crossroads Plaza 06117
Telephone: (860) 236-9956
Fax: (860) 236-9956

SYNAGOGUES
Orthodox
Young Israel of West Hartford
2240 Albany Avenue 06117
Telephone: (860) 233-3084
Fax: (860) 232-5850
Email: westhartfordrav@aol.com
Website: www.youngisraelwh.org

Reform
Congregation Beth Israel
701 Farmington Avenue 06119
Telephone: (860) 233-8215
Fax: (860) 523-0223
Email: bethisrael@cbict.org
Website: www.cbict.org

WESTPORT
SYNAGOGUES
Orthodox
Synagogue Westport
215 Post Road West 06880
Telephone: (203) 226-6901

WOODBRIDGE

LIBRARIES

Department of Jewish Education Library
360 Amity Road 06525
Telephone: (203) 387-2424 ext. 330
Fax: (203) 387-1818
Email: library@jewishnewhaven.org
Judaic Library open to the public. Collection includes books
and A/V materials (VHS, CD, Audio-cassette) for all ages.

Delaware

DOVER

SYNAGOGUES

Conservative
Congregation Beth Sholom of Dover
PO Box 223 19903
Telephone: (302) 734-5578

NEWARK

SYNAGOGUES

Reconstructionist
Temple Beth El
101 Possum Park Rd 19711
Telephone: (302) 366-833

WILMINGTON

COMMUNITY ORGANISATIONS

Jewish Community Center
101 Garden of Eden Road 19803
Telephone: (910) 478-5660
Fax: (910) 478-6068
Email: jccinfo@jccdelaware.org

SYNAGOGUES

Conservative
Beth Shalom
18th St. and Baynard Blvd 19802

Orthodox
Adas Kodesh Shel Emeth
Washington Blvd & Torah Drive 19802
Telephone: (302) 762-2705
Fax: (302) 762-3236
Email: www.akse.org

Reform
Beth Emeth
300 W. Lea Blvd. 19802
Telephone: 764-2393
Fax: 764-2395

District of Columbia

WASHINGTON

CONTACT INFORMATION

Eruv in Georgetown
Telephone: (202) 338-ERUV

DELICATESSEN

Hunan Deli
H Street
Telephone: (202) 833-1018

Posins Bakery & Deli
5756 Georgia Avenue
Telephone: (202) 726-4424

EMBASSY

Embassy of Israel
3514 International Drive 20008
Telephone: (202) 364-5500
Fax: (202) 364-5423

MEDIA

Newspapers
The Jewish Week
1910 'K' Street 20006

MUSEUMS

**B'nai B'rith Klutznick National Jewish
Museum**
1640 Rhode Island Av. 20036
Telephone: (202) 857-6583
Fax: (202) 857-1099
Email: eberman@bnaibrith.org
Website: www.BBInet.org

**Jewish Historical Society of Greater
Washington**
701 3rd street N.W. 20001
Telephone: (202) 789-0900
Fax: (202) 789-0485
Email: info@jhsgw.org
Website: www.jhsgw.org
Notes: Also the lillian & Albert Small Jewish Museum.
Hours: Sunday to Thursday Open by Appointment.

Lillian & Albert Small Museum
701 3rd Street N.W. 20001
Telephone: (202) 789-0900
Fax: (202) 789-0485
Email: info@jhsgw.org

**National Museum of American Jewish
Military History**
1811 R. Street N.W 20009
Telephone: (202) 265-6280
Fax: (202) 462-3192
Email: mnmajmh@nmajmh.org
Website: www.nmajmh.org

Smithsonian Institute
The National History Building, 10th & Constitution
Avs. N.W. 20001

The National Portrait Gallery
F Street between 7th & 8th Sts.

United States Holocaust Memorial Museum
100 Raoul Wallenberg Place. S.W. 290024-2150
Telephone: (202) 488-0400, group tours phone:
(202) 488-0455
Fax: (202) 488-2606
Email: group_visit@ushmm.org
Website: www.ushmm.org
Notes: Hours: 10.00 am to 5.30 pm. The Museum is
accessible to people with disabilities. The permanent
exhibition recommended for visitors eleven years and older,
presents a comprehensive history of the Holocaust through
artefacts, photographs, films and eyewitness testimonies.
There are other changing special exhibitions and a special
exhibition designed for children and families.

RESTAURANTS
Jewish Community Centre
16th Street at Q
Supervision: Va'ad Hakashrut of Washington

TOURIST SITE
John F. Kennedy Center
2700 'F' Street

Florida

BOCA RATON

COMMUNITY ORGANISATIONS
**Jewish Federation of South Palm Beach
County**
9901 Donna Klein Blvd. 33428-1788
Telephone: (561) 852-3100

JUDAICA
Holyland Judaica
Del Mar Shopping Village, 7080 Beracasa Way
Telephone: (561) 367-8277

MIKVAOT
Boca Raton Synagogue
7900 Montoya Circle 33433
Telephone: (561) 394-5854

RESTAURANTS
Dairy
Campus Café
Cultural Arts Building, 9801 Donna Klein Blvd.
33428-1788
Telephone: (561) 852-3200 ext. 4103
Fax: (561) 852-3282
Supervision: Jewish Federation of South Palm Beach County

Eilat Café
6853 SW 18th Street, Wharfside Shopping Center
33428-1788
Telephone: (561) 368-6880

Jon's Place
22191 Powerline Road (outhwest corner Palmetto
& Powerline
Telephone: (561) 338-0008

My Favourite Café
3369 Sheridan Street
Telephone: (561) 965-0111

Meat
Café Haifa
2901 N. Federal Highway 33431
Telephone: (561) 955-8500

City Grill
Delmar Shopping Village, 7158 N. Beracasa Way
33434
Telephone: (561) 417-8936

Jerusalem
8255 International Drive
Telephone: (561) 248-9494
Website: www.jerusalemglatt.com
Supervision: Rabbi Konig

Jerusalem Grill
19635 US Highway 411, Boca Plaza Greens 33428
Telephone: (561) 470-1120

Sagi's Falafel Armon
22767 State Road 7 33428
Telephone: (561) 477-0633

SYNAGOGUES

Conservative
Beth Ami Congregation
1401 N.W. 4th Avenue 33432
Telephone: (561) 347-0031
Fax: (561) 393-5326
Email: bethamicong@aol.com

Orthodox
Boca Raton Synagogue
7900 Montoya Circle 33433
Telephone: (561) 394-5732
Fax: (561) 394-0180
Website: www.brsweb.org

Young Israel of Boca Raton
7200 Palmetto Circle Blvd 33433
Telephone: (561) 391-3235
Fax: (561) 391-5509
Email: yiboca@bellsouth.net

Reform
Congregation B'nai Israel
2200 Yamato Road 33431
Telephone: (561) 241-8118
Fax: (561) 241-8118

CLEARWATER
COMMUNITY ORGANISATIONS
Jewish Federation of Pinellas county
13191 Starkey Road, Suite 8, Largo 33773-1438
Telephone: (727) 530-3223
Fax: (727) 531-0221
Email: jewishfed@tbi.net
Website: www.jfedpinellas.org

SYNAGOGUES
Conservative
Beth Shalom
1325 S. Belcher Road 33764
Telephone: (727) 531-1418
Fax: (727) 531-0798

Reform
B'nai Israel
1685 S. Belcher Road 34624
Telephone: (727) 531-5829

Temple Ahavat Shalom
1575 Curlew Road, Palm Harbor 34683
Telephone: (727) 785-8811
Fax: (727) 785-8822
Email: rabgar@tampabay.rr.com

DAYTONA BEACH
COMMUNITY ORGANISATIONS
Jewish Federation of Volusia & Flagler
Counties
470 Andalusin Ave., Ormond Beach 32174
Telephone: (904) 672-0294
Fax: (904) 673-1316

SYNAGOGUES
Conservative
Temple Israel
1400 S. Peninsula Drive 32118
Telephone: (904) 252-3097

SYNAGOGUES
Reform
Temple Beth El
579 N. Nova Road, Ormond Beach 32174
Telephone: (904) 677-2484

DEERFIELD BEACH
SYNAGOGUES
Orthodox
Young Israel of Deerfield Beach
202 Century Blvd. 33442
Telephone: (954) 571-3904
Fax: (954) 571-5234
Email: YIDB@BellSouth.net

DELRAY BEACH
GROCERIES
Meat Market
Oriole Kosher Market, 7345 West Atlantic Ave.
33446

SYNAGOGUES
Conservative
Temple Anshei Shalom of West Delray
Oriole Jewish Center, 7099 W Atlantic Avenue
33446
Telephone: (561) 495-1300

Temple Emeth
5780 W. Atlantic Avenue 33446
Fax: (561) 498-3536

Orthodox
Anshei Emuna
16189 Carter Road 33445
Telephone: (561) 499-9229

Reform
Temple Sinai of Palm Beach County
2475 W. Atlantic Avenue 33445
Telephone: (561) 276-6161
Fax: (561) 276-3485
Email: sinai2475@att.net
Website: www.TempleSinaiPBC.org

FORT LAUDERDALE
DELICATESSEN
East Side Kosher Restaurant & Deli
6846 W. Atlantic Blvd., Margate 33063

KOSHER FOOD
Meat
Galt Kosher Market
3515 Galt Ocean Drive 33308
Telephone: (954) 563-2026

RESTAURANTS
Amore' Ristorante
8067 West Oakland Park Blvd., Sunrise
Telephone: (954) 749-6888
Supervision: Glatt kosher

SYNAGOGUES
Orthodox
Temple Ohel B'nai Raphael
4351 West Oakland Park Blvd. 33313
Telephone: (954) 733-7684

SYNAGOGUES
Sephardi
B'nai Sephardim
3670 Stirling Rd., Ft Lauderdale

FORT MEYERS
SYNAGOGUES
Reform
Temple Beth El
16225 Winkler Road Ext 33908
Telephone: (941) 433-0018

FORT PIERCE
Temple Beth-El Israel
4600 Oleander Drive 34982
Telephone: (407) 461-7428

HALLANDALE
RESTAURANTS
Dairy
Fressers at Tierra Mar
1960 S. Ocean Dr.
Telephone: (305) 889-0075

Meat
Kosher World
514-41st St.
Telephone: (305) 532-2210

Pita Loca South Beach Israeli Restaurant
601 Collins Ave., Suite #5
Telephone: (305) 673-3388
Fax: (305) 673-6051
Website: www.pitaloca.8m.com

HOLLYWOOD & VICINITY
COMMUNITY ORGANISATIONS
Jewish Federation of South Broward
2719 Hollywood Blvd. 33020
Telephone: (954) 921-8810

JUDAICA
Holyland Judaica
5650 Stirling Road, Hollywood 33021
Telephone: (954) 964-4288
Fax: (954) 964-0189
Email: holylandjudaica@aol.com

KOSHER FOOD
Ilana's Cookies
5650 Stirling Road, Hollywood
Telephone: (954) 963-6130

MIKVAOT
Mikveh/Young Israel of Hollywood-Ft Lauderdale
3291 Stirling Road, Fort Lauderdale x 33312
Telephone: (954) 963-3952
Fax: (954) 962-5566

RESTAURANTS
Dairy
Sara's
3944 N. 6th Avenue 33021
Telephone: (954) 986-1770
Fax: (954) 986-2602

Meat
Pita King
5650 Stirling Road 33021
Telephone: (954) 985-8028

Pizzerias
Jerusalem Pizza
5650 Stirling Road 33021
Telephone: (954) 964-6811
Fax: (954) 964-2911

SYNAGOGUES
Conservative
B'nai Aviv
1410 Indian Trace, Weston 33326

Century Pines Jewish Center
13400 S.W. 10 St., Pembroke Pines 33027
Telephone: (954) 431-3300

Hallandale Jewish Center
416 N.E. Eigth Av., Hallandale 33009
Telephone: (954) 454-9100

Temple Beth Ahm Israel
9730 Stirling Rd. 33024
Telephone: (954) 431-5100

Temple Judea of Carriage Hills
6734 Stirling Rd. 33021
Telephone: (954) 987-0026

Orthodox
Chabad of Southwest Broward
11251 Taft St., Pembroke Pines

Congregation Ahavat Shalom
315 Madison St., PO Box 220918 33022-0918
Telephone: (954) 922-4544
Fax: (954) 922-4523

Congregation Levi Yitzchok-Lubavitch
1295 E. Hallandale Beach Blvd.33009
Telephone: (954) 458-1877
Fax: (954) 458-1651
Email: chai@dialisdn.com

Young Israel of Hollywood/Ft Lauderdale
3291 Stirling Road, Ft Lauderdale 33312
Telephone: (954) 966-7877
Fax: (954) 9625566
Email: yih@bellsouth.net

Young Israel of Pembroke Pines
13400 S.W. 10 St., Pembroke Pines

Reform
Temple Beth El
1351 S. 14 Av, Hollywood 33020
Telephone: (954) 920-8225

Temple Beth Emet
4807 South Flamingo Road, Cooper City, Pembroke Pines
Telephone: (954) 680-1882
Email: bethemet@aol.com

Temple Solel
5100 Sheridan St., Hollywood 33021
Telephone: (954) 989-0205

JACKSONVILLE
COMMUNITY ORGANISATIONS
Jacksonville Jewish Federation
8505 San Jose Blvd. 32217
Telephone: (904) 448-5000

MIKVAOT
Etz Chaim
10167 San Jose Blvd. 32257
Telephone: (904) 262-3565

ORGANISATIONS
Community Kosher Nutrition Program
5846 Mt Carmel Terrace 32216
Telephone: (904) 737-9075
Website: www.jfcsjax.org
Central organisation: Jewish Family and Community Services
Lunch program for Mt. Carmel Gardens residents. Additional in-house programs 'Kosher Kart' program supplying meals to homebound patrons. Kosher catering for community events or personal needs.

SYNAGOGUES
Orthodox
Eitz Chaim Synagogue
10167 San Jose Boulevard 32217
Telephone: (904) 262-3565

KENDALL
Young Israel of Kendall
7880 SW 112th Street Miami, Fl 33156
Telephone: (305) 232-6833
Fax: (305) 232-6418
Email: yikendall@aol.com

KEY WEST
SYNAGOGUES
Conservative
B'nai Zion
750 United Street 33040-3251
Telephone: (305) 294-3437

LAKELAND
Temple Emanuel
600 Lake Hollingsworth Drive 33803
Telephone: (813) 682-8616

MELBOURNE
GROCERIES
Brevard Kosher Zone
416N Harbor City Blvd., 1/4 mile south of Eau Gallie
Telephone: (321) 752-8000
Fax: (321) 752-8000
Email: bkz1@mindspring.com

MIAMI / MIAMI BEACH
BOOKSELLERS
Jerusalem Judaica
459 41st Street 33140
Telephone: (305) 535-8888

EMBASSY
Consul General of Israel
Suite 1800, 100N Biscayne Blvd 33132

GROCERIES
Kosher world-Fine Food Market
514 W. 41st Street 33140
Telephone: (305) 532-2210
Fax: (305) 532-8816

HOTELS
Saxony Hotel
3201 Collins Avenue, Miami Beach 33140
Telephone: (305) 538-6811
Fax: (305) 672-3721
Supervision: National Kashruth

MEDIA
Directory
Jewish Life in Dade County
4200 Biscayne Blvd. 33137
Telephone: (305) 576-4000
Fax: (305) 573-8115
Website: www.jewishmiami.org

Radio
Shalom South Florida (WAXY 790 AM)

MIKVAOT
B'nai Israel & Greater Miami Youth Synagogue Mikveh
16260 S. W. 288th Street, Naranja 33033
Telephone: (305) 264-6488

Congregation and Mikvah Adas Dej
225 37th Street 33140
Telephone: (305) 674-8204

Daughters of Israel
2530 Pinetree Drive 33140
Telephone: (305) 672-3500

Mikveh Blima of North Dade, Inc.
1054 N.E. Miami Gardens Drive 33179
Telephone: (305) 949-9650

Rabbi Meisel's Mikveh
Washington Av. & 2nd Street 33139
Telephone: (305) 673-4641

Shul of Bal Harbour Mikvah
9540 collins Avenue, Surfside 331545
Telephone: (305) 868-1411
Email: info@theshul.org

MUSEUMS
Jewish Museum of Florida
301 Washington Avenue, Miami Beach 33139-6965
Telephone: (305) 672-5044
Fax: (305) 672-5933
Email: mzerivitz@aol.com
Website: www.jewishmuseum.com

RELIGIOUS ORGANISATIONS
Young Israel Southern Regional Office
173575 NE 7th Avenue 33162
Telephone: (305) 770-3993
Fax: (305) 770-3993
Email: ncyi.south@youngisrael.org

RESTAURANTS
Pita Loca Glatt Kosher
601 Collins Ave., Suite 5, (on 6th Street between
Collins Ave & Ocean Dr., in South Beach) 33139
Telephone: (305) 673-3388

Dairy
Bagel Time
3915 Alton Road 33140
Telephone: (305) 538-0300
Supervision: Star-K

Gitty's Hungarian Kitchen
6565 Collins Avenue, Sherry Frontenac Hotel 33141
Telephone: (305) 865-4893

Milky Way
530 41st Street
Telephone: (305) 534-4144

Meat
Europa Grill
5445 Collins Avenue
Telephone: (305) 993-3924

Jerusalem Peking
4299 Collins Avenue, Miami Beach
Telephone: (305) 522-2263

Mexico Bravo
16850 Collins Avenue, Sunny Isles Beach
Telephone: (305) 945-1999
Fax: (305) 949-5560
Supervision: Star-K

Original Pita Hut
530 41st Street
Telephone: (305) 534-4144

Shalom Tokyo Steak House
5101 Collins Avenue, Miami Beach
Telephone: (305) 866-6039

Pizzerias
Shemtov's Pizza
514 41st Street 33140
Telephone: (305) 538-2123
Fax: (305) 534-4213
Supervision: Star-K

SYNAGOGUES
Orthodox
The Shul of Bal Harbor, Bay Harbor & Surfside
9540 Collins Avenue 33154
Telephone: (305) 868-1411
Email: info@theshul.org

Young Israel of Miami Beach
4221 Pine Tree Drive 33140
Telephone: (305) 538-9462

NORTH MIAMI / NORTH MIAMI BEACH
RESTAURANTS
Mexico Bravo
16850 Collins Aveue, Sunny Isles Beach
Telephone: (305) 945-1999

Dairy
The Noshery
Saxony Hotel, 3201 Collins Ave. 33140
Telephone: (305) 538-6811
Yummy Miami
18090 Collins Ave.
Telephone: (305) 466-1010

Meat
China Kikar Tel Aviv
5005 Collins Av. 33140
Telephone: (305) 866-3316

Giuliani's Café
3439 NE 163rd Street North Miami Beach
Telephone: (305) 940-8141

Kosher World
514 41st
Telephone: (305) 532-2263

Shalom Haifa
18533 W. Dixie Hwy., Avenue
Telephone: (305) 936-1800
Fax: (305) 936-1811

Subrific
1688 NE Street
Telephone: (305) 946-7811

Tai Treat
2176 123rd Street
Telephone: (305) 892-1118

Wing Wan II
1640 N.E. 164 Street 33162
Telephone: (305) 945-3585

Pizzerias
Jerusalem Pizza
761 N.E. 167 Street 33162
Telephone: (305) 653-6662

Sarah's Kosher Pizza
2214 N.E. 123rd Street 33181
Telephone: (305) 891-3312

Sarah's Kosher Pizza
1127 N.E. 163 Street 33162
Telephone: (305) 948-7777

SYNAGOGUES
Orthodox
Young Israel of Greater Miami
990 N.E. 171st Street, North Miami Beach 33162

Young Israel of Sky Lake
1850 N.E. 183rd Street, North Miami Beach 33179
Telephone: (305) 945-8712/8715

Young Israel of Sunny Isles
17395 North Bay Road, North Miami Beach 33160
Telephone: (305) 935-9095

ORLANDO
COMMUNITY ORGANISATIONS
Jewish Federation of Greater Orlando
851 N. Maitland Avenue, Maitland 32751
Telephone: (407) 645-5933
Fax: (407) 645-1172
Email: postmaster@orlandojewishfed.org

DELICATESSEN
Market Place Deli, Hyatt Orlando
6375 W. Bronson Highway
Telephone: (407) 396-1234

GROCERIES
Amira's Catering and Speciality
1351 E. Altamonte, Altamonte Springs
Telephone: (407) 767-7577

HOTELS
Quality Inn Kosher Hotel
4944 W. 192 Orlando-Kissimmee 34746
Telephone: (407) 787-3400
Fax: (407) 397-1116
Website: www.kosherinflorida.com

MIKVAOT
Mikvah Yisrael
8 Lake Howell Road 32751
Telephone: (407) 644-2362

RESTAURANTS
The Lower East Side Restaurant
8548 Palm Parkway 32836
Telephone: (407) 465-0565
Fax: (407) 238-6427
Supervision: Florida Kosher Services

SYNAGOGUES
Conservative
Congregation Beth Shalom
13th & Center Streets, Leesburg 32748
Telephone: (407) 742-0238

Congregation Ohev Shalom
5015 Goddard Avenue 32804
Telephone: (407) 298-4650

Congregation Shalom (Williamsburg)
11821 Soccer Lane, c/o Sydney Ansell 32821-7952

Congregation Shalom Aleichem
PO Box 424211, Kissimmee 34742-4211

Southwest Orlando Jewish Congregation
11200 S. Apopka- Vineland Road 32836
Website: www.sojc-orlando.org

Temple Israel
4917 Eli Street 32804
Telephone: (407) 647-3055

Orthodox
Congregation Ahavas Yisrael/Chabad
708 Lake Howell Road, Maitland 32751
Telephone: (407) 644-2500
Fax: (407) 644-7763
Email: rabbidubov@aol.com

Reform
Congregation of Liberal Judaism
928 Malone Drive 32810
Telephone: (407) 645-6444

PALM BEACH
SYNAGOGUES

Conservative
Temple Emanu-el
190 N. County Road 33480
Telephone: (561) 832-0804

Orthodox
Palm Beach Synagogue
120 N. County Road, PO Box 1028 33480
Telephone: (561) 838-9002
Fax: (561) 838-5356
Email: pbsynagogue@bellsouth.net
Website: www.pbos.org

PALM CITY
SYNAGOGUES

Conservative
Treasure Coast Jewish Center Congregation Beth Abraham
3998 S.W. Leighton Farms Avenue 34990
Telephone: (407) 287-8833

PALM COAST
Temple Beth Shalom
40 Wellington Drive, POB 350557 32135-0557
Telephone: (904) 445-3006

PEMBROKE PINES
SYNAGOGUES

Orthodox
Young Israel of Pembroke Pines
13400 SW. 10th Street 33027
Telephone: (954) 433-8666

PENSACOLA
SYNAGOGUES

Conservative
B'nai Israel
1829 N. 9th Avenue, PO Box 9002 32513
Telephone: (850) 433-7311
Fax: (850) 435-9597

Reform
Temple Beth El
800 N. Palafox Street 32501
Telephone: (850) 438-3321
Fax: (850) 434-7575

ROCKLEDGE
COMMUNITY ORGANISATIONS
Jewish Federation of Brevard
108A Barton Avenue
Telephone: (321) 636-1824
Fax: (321) 636-0614
Email: jfbrevard@aol.com

SARASOTA
Sarasota-Manatee Jewish Federation
580 S. McIntosh Road 34232-1959
Telephone: (941) 371-4546
Fax: (941) 378-2947
Email: smjf@jon.cjfny.org

SYNAGOGUES

Conservative
Temple Beth Shalom
1050 South Tuttle Avenue 34237
Telephone: (941) 955-8121

ST AUGUSTINE
SYNAGOGUES

Orthodox
The First Congregation Sons of Israel
161 Cordova Street 43084

ST PETERSBURG
DELICATESSEN
Jo-El's Delicatessen & Marketplace
2619 23rd Ave N 33713
Telephone: (727) 321-3847
Fax: (727) 327-0682
Email: catercat@Tampabay.rr.com

GROCERIES
Jo-El's Specialty Foods
2619 23rd Avenue N. 33713
Telephone: (727) 321-3847
Fax: (727) 327-0682
All Kosher products

SYNAGOGUES

Conservative
Beth Shalom
1844 54th Street S. 33707
Telephone: (727) 3380

Congregation B'nai Israel of St. Petersburg
300 58th Street North 33710
Telephone: (727) 381-4900
Fax: (727) 344-1307
Email: rabbissec@cbistpete.org
Website: www.cbistpete.org

Reform
Beth-El
400 Pasadena Avenue S. 33707
Telephone: (727) 347-6136

TALLAHASSEE
SYNAGOGUES
Conservative
Congregation Shomrei Torah
4858 Kerry Forest Parkway 32309
Telephone: (850) 893-9674
Email: administrator@shomreitorahonline.org
Website: www.shomreitorahonline.org

TAMARAC
SYNAGOGUES
Orthodox
Young Israel of Taramac
8565 W. McNab Road 33321
Telephone: (954) 726-3586

TAMPA
COMMUNITY ORGANISATIONS
Tampa Jewish Federation
13009 Community Campus Drive 33625-4000
Telephone: (813) 264-9000
Fax: (813) 265-8450
Email: info@jewishtampa.com
Website: www.jewishtampa.com

MIKVAOT
Bais Tefilah
14908 Pennington Road 33624
Telephone: (813) 963-2317

SYNAGOGUES
Conservative
Congregation Rodeph Sholom
2713 Bayshore Blvd. 33629
Telephone: (813) 837-1911
Fax: (813) 832-4168
Email: rsholom@tampabay.rr.com
Website: www.rsholom.org

Kol Ami
3919 Moran Road 33618
Telephone: (813) 962-6338

Temple David
2001 Swann Avenue 33606
Telephone: (813) 254-1771

Orthodox
Hebrew Academy
14908 Pennington Road 33624
Telephone: (813) 963-0706

Young Israel of Tampa
3721 W. Tacon Street 33629
Telephone: (813) 832-3018

Reform
Schaarai Zedek
3303 Swann Avenue 33609
Telephone: (813) 876-2377

Temple Shalom
4630 Pine Ridge Road 34119
Telephone: (813) 455-3030
Fax: (813) 455-4361
Website: www.naplestemple.org

VERNO BEACH
Temple Beth Shalom
365 43rd Avenue 32968
Telephone: (772) 569-4700
Fax: (772) 569-4701
Email: tbsoff@aol.com

WEST PALM BEACH
COMMUNITY ORGANISATIONS
Jewish Federation of Palm Beach County
4601 Community Drive 33417
Telephone: (561) 478-0700
Fax: (561) 478-9696

Georgia
ATHENS
SYNAGOGUES
Reform
Congregation Children of Israel
Dudley Drive 30606
Telephone: (404) 549-4192

ATLANTA
COMMUNITY ORGANISATIONS
Jewish Federation
1753 Peachtree Road, NE 30309
Telephone: (404) 873-1661
Fax: (404) 874-7043

EMBASSY
Consul General of Israel
Suite 440, 1100 Spring Street, NW 30309-2823

HOTELS
Bed & Breakfast Atlanta
1608 Briarcliff Road, Suite 5 30306
Telephone: (404) 875-0525
Fax: (404) 875-8198
Website: www.bedandbreakfast.com

KASHRUT INFORMATION
Atlanta Kashrut Commission
1855 La Vista Road, N.E. 30329
Telephone: (404) 634-4063
Fax: (404) 634-4254
Email: akc613@usa.com

RESTAURANTS
Dairy
Broadway Café
2168 Briarcliff Road 30329
Telephone: (404) 329-0888
Fax: (404) 329-9888
Supervision: Atlanta Kasrut Commission

Wall Street Pizza
2470 Briarcliff Road 30329
Telephone: (404) 633-2111
Supervision: Atlanta Kasrut Commission

Glatt Koher Chinese
Chai Peking
2205 La Vista Road, N.E. (inside Kroger) 30329
Telephone: (404) 327-7810
Fax: (404) 327-7811
Website: www.chaipeking.com
Supervision: Atlanta Kasrut Commission

Meat
Quality Kosher
Off Broadway, 2166 Briarcliff Road 30329
Telephone: (404) 633-9288
Fax: (404) 636-8675
Email: broadwaycafe@jfga.org
Supervision: Atlanta Kasrut Commission

SYNAGOGUES
Conservative
Ahavath Achim
600 Peachtree Battle Avenue
Telephone: (404) 355-5222

Orthodox
Anshi S'Fard
1324 North Highland Avenue, N.E. 30306
Telephone: (404) 874-4513
Email: greggbrenner@aol.com

Congregation Beth Jacob
1855 La Vista Road NE 30329
Telephone: (404) 633-0551
Fax: (404) 320-7912
Email: admin@bethjacobatlanta.org
Website: www.bethjacobatlanta.org
Beth Jacob's mission is to follow and teach Orthodox Judaism in an environment of acceptance, warmth and mutual respect so that all Jews can grow and practise at their own pace.

Young Israel of Toco Hills
2074 La Vista Road, Toco Hills 30329
Telephone: (404) 315-1417
Fax: (404) 315-1417
Email: info@yith.org
Website: www.yith.org

Reform
Temple Sinai
5645 Dupree Drive, N.W. 30327
Telephone: (404) 252-3073

The Temple
1589 Peachtree Road
Telephone: (404) 873-1731

Sephardi
Ner Hamizrach
1858 La Vista Road, N.E. 30329
Telephone: (404) 315-9020

AUGUSTA
BAKERIES
Sunshine Bakery
1209 Broad Street 30902

DELICATESSEN
Parti-Pal
Daniel Village 30904

Strauss
965 Broad Street 30902

SYNAGOGUES
Orthodox
Adas Yeshuron
935 Johns Road, Walton Way 30904
Telephone: (404) 733-9491

COLUMBUS
SYNAGOGUES
Conservative
Shearith Israel
2550 Wynnton Road 31906
Telephone: (614) 323-1443

SYNAGOGUES
Reform
Temple Israel
1617 Wildwood Avenue 31906
Telephone: (614) 323-1617

DECATUR
RESTAURANTS
Meat
Twelve Oaks Barbecue
1451 Scot Blvd.
Telephone: (404) 377-0120

TOURS OF JEWISH INTEREST
Kosher Expeditions
2932 Westbury Drive, Suite 100
Telephone: (404) 441-2545
Fax: (404) 234-5170
Email: dl@kosherexpeditions.com
Website: www.kosherexpeditions.com

MACON
SYNAGOGUES
Conservative
Sha'arey Israel
611 First Street 31201
Telephone: (478) 745-4571
Fax: (478) 745-5892
Website: www.csimacon.org

Reform
Beth Israel
892 Cherry street 31201
Telephone: (478) 745-6727

SAVANNAH
COMMUNITY ORGANISATIONS
Savannah Jewish Federation
511 Abercorn Street 31405
Telephone: (912) 355-8111
Fax: (912) 355-8116
Email: sharon@savj.org

CONTACT INFORMATION
Rabbi Avigdor Slatus
5444 Abercorn Street 31405
Telephone: (912) 354-7721
Fax: (912) 354-9923
Email: bbjsynagogue@bellsouth.net
Website: www.bbjsynagogue

GUEST APARTMENTS
Buckingham South
5450 Abercorn Street 31405
Telephone: (912) 355-5550
Fax: (912) 353-9393
Email: information@buckinghamsouth.com
Supervision: Rabbi Avigdor Slatus

SYNAGOGUES
Conservative
Agudath Achim
9 Lee Blvd. 31405
Telephone: (912) 352-4737
Fax: (912) 352-3477
Email: agudatha@aol.com
Website: agudath-achim.com

Orthodox
B'nai B'rith Jacob
5444 Abercorn Street 31405
Telephone: (912) 354-7721
Fax: (912) 354-9923

Reform
Mickve Israel
Bull & Gordon Sts. 31401
Telephone: (912) 233-1547

Hawaii

KONA
SYNAGOGUES
Reform
Kona Beth Shalom Kailua-Kona
Telephone: (808) 322-4192 or 322-6004

MAUI
ReformCongregation Gan Eden
PO Box 555 Kihei Road 96753
Telephone: (808) 879-9221
Fax: (808) 874-8570

OAHU
GROCERIES
Marzal's Kosherland
555 North king Street ~13 96817
Telephone: (808) 848-1700
Supervision: Chabad of Hawaii will deliver Shabbat Meals to your hotel room on Fridays. Can deliver meals and small groceries on other days.

Down to Earth
King's Street, Near University Avenue

Foodland Supermarket Beretania
1460 S Beretania Street

SYNAGOGUES
ConservativeCongrgation Sof Ma'arav
2500 Pali Highway 96817
Telephone: (808) 595-3678

OahuReformTemple Emanu-El
2550 Pali Highway 96817
Telephone: (808) 595-7521

WAIKIKI
SYNAGOGUES
Orthodox
Chabad
Hawaiian Monarch Hotel, Nieu Street

Illinois

CHAMPAIGN-URBANA
COMMUNITY ORGANISATIONS
Champaign-Urbana Jewish Federation
503 E. John St. 61820
Telephone: (217) 367-9872
Fax: (217) 344-1540
Email: cujf@shalomcu.org
Website: www.shalomcu.org

SYNAGOGUES
Reform
Sinai Temple
3104 Wndsor Road 61821
Telephone: (217) 352-8140

CHICAGO
BOOKSELLERS
Chicago Hebrew Book Store
2942 W. Devon 60659
Telephone: (312) 973-6636
Fax: (312) 973-6465

Rosenblum's World of Judaica, Inc.
2906 W. Devon Ave. 60659
Telephone: (312) 262-1700
Fax: (312) 262-1930
Email: avi@alljudaica.com
Website: www.alljudaica.com

The Bariff Shop for Judaica
Spertus Institute of Jewish Studies, 618 S. Michigan
Avenue 60605
Telephone: (312) 322-1768 Toll Free 888-322-1740
Fax: (312) 922-6406
Email: bariff_shop@spertus.edu
Website: www.bariff.org

DELICATESSEN
Romanian Kosher Sausage
7200 N. Clark 60625
Telephone: (312) 761-4141
Supervision: Orthodox Union

EMBASSY
Consul General of Israel
Suite 1308, 111 East Wacker Drive 60601

MIKVAOT
Bnei Ruven
6350, N. Whipple 60659
Telephone: (312) 743-4282

MUSEUMS
Spertus Museum
Spertus Institute of Jewish Studies , 618 S. Michigan
Avenue 60605
Telephone: (312) 322-1747
Fax: (312) 922-3934
Email: musm@spertus.edu
Website: www.spertus.edu

RESTAURANTS
Dairy
Jerusalem Kosher Restaurant
3014 W. Devon 60659
Telephone: (312) 262-0515
Supervision: OK

Meat
Great Chicago Food & Beverage Co.
3149 W. Devon 60659
Telephone: (312) 465-9030
Fax: (312) 465-9011
Email: gcfbken@aol.com
Supervision: Chicago Rabbinical Council

Mi Tsu Yun Kosher Chinese Restaurant
3010 W. Devon 60659
Telephone: (312) 262-4630
Fax: (312) 262-4835
Supervision: Chicago Rabbinical Council

Shallots
2324 N. Clark St. 60614
Telephone: (312) 755-5205
Website: www.shallots-chicago.com

SYNAGOGUES
Conservative
Anshe Emet Synagogue
3751 North Broadway 60613-4104
Telephone: (312) 281-1423
Fax: (312) 281-2813
Website: www.ansheemet.org

Orthodox
K.I.N.S. of West Rogers Park
2800 W. North Shore Avenue 60645
Telephone: (312) 761-4000
Fax: (312) 761-4959
Email: congkins@cs.com

Lake Shore Drive Synagogue
70 E. Elm Street 60611
Telephone: (312) 337-6811

Loop Synagogue
16 S. Clark Street 60603

Young Israel of Chicago
4931 North Kimball Street 60625
Telephone: (312) 338-6380

Young Israel of West Rogers Park
2706 West Touhy Avenue 60645
Telephone: (312) 743-9400

HIGHLAND PARK
DELICATESSEN
Now We're Cooking Grill
710 Central 60035
Telephone: (847) 432-7310
Fax: (847) 432-8352
Supervision: Chicago Kashrut Association Inc.

SYNAGOGUES
Orthodox
North Surburban Synagogue Beth El
1175 Sheridan Road 60035
Telephone: (847) 432-8900

NORTHBROOK
Young Israel of Northbrook
3545 Walters Road 60062
Telephone: (847) 480-9462
Fax: (847) 205-1967

PEORIA
Agudas Achim
5614 North University Street 61614
Telephone: (309) 692-4849
Fax: (309) 692-7255

SYNAGOGUES
Reform
Anshai Emeth
5614 North University Street 61614
Telephone: (309) 691-3323
Email: rariel@aol.com

ROCK ISLAND
COMMUNITY ORGANISATIONS
Jewish Federation of the Quad Cities
209 18th Street 61201
Telephone: (309) 793-1300
Fax: (309) 793-1345

ROCKFORD
Jewish Federation of Greater Rockford
1500 Parkview Avenue 61107
Telephone: (815) 399-5497
Fax: (815) 399-9835
Email: rockfordfederation@juno.com

SYNAGOGUES
Conservative
Ohave Sholom
3730 Guildford Road 61107
Telephone: (815) 226-4900

Reform
Temple Beth El
1203 Comanche Drive 61107
Telephone: (815) 398-5020

SKOKIE
BAKERIES
Chaim's Kosher Bakery
4964 Dempster Street 60077
Telephone: (847) 675-1005
Fax: (847) 675-0028
Website: www.chaimkosher.com

JUDAICA
Hamakor Gallery Ltd.
4150 Dempster Street 60076
Telephone: (847) 677-4150
Fax: (847) 677-4160
Email: gallery@jewishsource.com
Website: www.jewishsource.com

MEDIA
Newspapers
Chicago Jewish Star
PO Box 268 60076
Telephone: (847) 674-7827
Fax: (847) 674-0014
Email: chicago-jewish-star@mcimail.com

RESTAURANTS
Dairy
Bagel Country
9306 Skokie Blvd. Il 60077
Telephone: (847) 673-3030
Fax: (847) 673-4040
Email: bcskokie@aol.com
Supervision: Chicago Rabbinical Counci

Da'Nali's
4032 W. Oakton 60076
Telephone: (847) 677-2782
Supervision: Chicago Rabbinical Council

Meat
Bugsy's Charhouse
3355 W. Dempster 60076
Telephone: (847) 679-4030
Fax: (847) 835-3354
Email: gcfbken@aol.com
Supervision: Chicago Rabbinical Council

Hy Life
4120 W. Dempster, Skokie 60076
Telephone: (847) 674-2021
Supervision: Chicago Rabbinical Council

Ken's Diner
3353 W. Dempster 60076
Telephone: (847) 679-4030
Fax: (847) 835-3354; 3835- Deli
Email: gcfbken@aol.com
Supervision: Chicago Rabbinical Council

Vegetarian
Mysore Woodlands
2548 Devon Avenue 60659
Telephone: (847) 338-8160
Fax: (847) 338-8162
Supervision: CKA

SYNAGOGUES
Orthodox
Young Israel of Skokie
3740 W. Dempster 60076
Telephone: (847) 329-0990

SPRINGFIELD
SYNAGOGUES
Conservative
Temple Israel
1140 West Governor Street 62704
Telephone: (413) 546-2841
Fax: (413) 726-9857
Email: templeisrael@springnet1.com

Indiana
BLOOMINGTON
SYNAGOGUES
Orthodox
Chabad House
516 E. 17th Street 47408
Telephone: (8112) 332-6784

Reform
Congregation Beth Shalom
3750 E. Third 47401
Telephone: (8112) 334-2440

EAST CHICAGO
SYNAGOGUES
Orthodox
B'nai Israel
3517 Hemlock Street 46312

EVANSVILLE
SYNAGOGUES
Conservative
Temple Adath B'nai Israel
3600 E. Washington Avenue 47715
Telephone: (812) 477-1577
Fax: (812) 477-1577
Email: tabi@evansville.net

Reform
Temple
Washington Avenue Temple, 100 Washinton Avenue
47714

FORT WAYNE
SYNAGOGUES
Conservative
B'nai Jacob
7227 Bittersweet Moors Drive 46814
Telephone: (219) 672-8459
Fax: (219) 672-8928

Reform
Congregation Achduth Vesholom
5200 Old Mill Road 46807
Telephone: (219) 260-744-4245
Fax: (219) 260-744-4246
Email: office@TempleCAV.org
Website: www.templecav.org

GARY
Temple Israel
601 N. Montgomery Street 46403
Telephone: (219) 938-5232

HAMMOND
SYNAGOGUES
Temple Beth-El
6947 Hohman Avenue 46324
Telephone: (219) 932-3754

Conservative
Beth Israel
7105 Hohman Avenue 46324
Telephone: (219) 931-1312

HIGHLAND
COMMUNITY ORGANISATIONS
Jewish Federation of North West Indiana
2939 Jewett Street, Highland 48322-3005
Telephone: (219) 661-0840
Fax: (219) 661-4204
Email: info@holocaustcenter.org
Website: www.holocaustcenter.org

INDIANAPOLIS
Jewish Federation of Greater Indianapolis
6705 Hoover Road 70002-4826
Telephone: (317) 888-2209

SYNAGOGUES
Conservative
Congregation Shaarey Tefilla
5879 Central Avenue 46220-2509
Telephone: (317) 253-4591
Fax: (317) 253-8529
Email: shaareytefilla@ameritech.net
Website: www.shaareytefilla.org
Shabbat services are held on the first Friday evening of
each month and monthly Friday Night Live or Saturday
Morning Awake, family orientated services led by our
elementary school aged children.

Conservative/Reconstructionist
Beth-El Zedek
600 W. 70th Street 46260
Telephone: (317) 253-3441
Fax: (317) 259-6849
Email: bez613@bez613.org
Website: www.bez613.org

Orthodox
B'nai Torah
6510 Hoover Road 46260
Telephone: (317) 253-5253
Fax: (317) 253-5459
Email: scrandall@iquest.net

Etz Chaim Sephardic Congregation
826 West 64th Street 46260
Telephone: (317) 251-6220

Reform
Indianapolis Hebrew Congregation
6501 N. Meridian Street 46260
Telephone: (317) 255-6647

LAFAYETTE
Temple Sholom
603 Lee Avenue, PO Box 53711 70505
Telephone: (317) 234-3760

SYNAGOGUES
Orthodox
Sons of Abraham
661 N. 7th Street 47901
Telephone: (317) 742-2113
Email: retrovir@bragg.bio.purdue.edu

MICHIGAN CITY
SYNAGOGUES
Reform
Sinai Temple
2800 S. Franklin Street 46360
Telephone: (219) 874-4477

MUNCIE
Temple Beth El
525 W. Jackson Street, cnr. Council Street 47305
Telephone: (765) 288-4662
Email: simon@purde.edu Edward Simon (President)
info@soalafayette.org (General inquiry)
Website: www.soalafayette.org

SOUTH BEND
COMMUNITY ORGANISATIONS
Jewish Federation of St. Joseph Valley
3202 Shalom Way 46615
Telephone: (574) 233-1164
Fax: (574) 288-4103
Email: dbarton@jfedsjv.org
Website: www.jfedsjv.org

CONTACT INFORMATION
Rabbi Y. Gettinger
Hebrew Orthodox Congregation, 3207 S. High
Street 71301

KASHRUT INFORMATION
Hebrew Orthodox Congregation
3207 S. High Street 46614
Telephone: (574) 291-4239
Fax: (574) 291-9490
Rabbi Yisrael Gettinger

SYNAGOGUES
Conservative
Sinai
1102 E. Laselle Street 46617
Telephone: (574) 234-8584
Fax: (574) 234-6856
Email: sinai@michiana.org
Website: www.uscj.org/midwest/southbend

Orthodox
Hebrew Orthodox Congregation
3207 S. High Street 46614
Telephone: (574) 291-4239
Fax: (574) 291-9490

Reform
Beth El
305 W. Madison Street 46601
Telephone: (574) 234-4402

TERRE HAUTE
DELICATESSEN
Kosher Meats & Sandwiches
410 W. Western Avenue 71301
Telephone: (812) 445-9367
Fax: (812) 445-9369

VALPARAISO
SYNAGOGUES
Conservative
Temple Israel
Po Box 2051 46383

WEST LAFAYETTE
SYNAGOGUES
Reform
Synagogue West Lafayette
620 Cumberland Street 47906
Telephone: (765) 463-3455
Fax: (765) 463-4650
Email: temple@iquest.net

WHITING
SYNAGOGUES
Orthodox
B'nai Judah
116th Street & Davis Avenue 46394
Telephone: (219) 659-0797

Iowa

CEDAR RAPIDS
SYNAGOGUES
Reform
Temple Judah
3221 Lindsay Lane S.E. 52403
Telephone: (319) 362-1261

DAVENPORT
Temple Emanuel
12th Street & Mississippi Avenue 52803

DES MOINES
COMMUNITY ORGANISATIONS
Jewish Federation of Greater Des Moines
910 Polk Blvd. 50312
Telephone: (515) 277-6321
Fax: (515) 277-4069
Email: jcrc@dmjfed.org
Website: www.dmjfed.org

DELICATESSEN
The Nosh
800 First Street 70898
Telephone: (515) 291-5895

SYNAGOGUES
Conservative
Tifereth Israel
924 Polk Blvd. 50312
Telephone: (515) 255-1137

Orthodox
Beth El Jacob
954 Cummins Parkway 50312
Telephone: (515) 274-1551
Fax: (515) 274-1552
Website: www.cyberconnect.com/bej

Reform
Temple B'nai Jeshurun
5101 Grand Avenue 50312
Telephone: (515) 274-4679
Fax: (515) 274-2072
Email: arptbj@aol.com
Website: www.templebnaijeshurun.org

DUBUQUE
Beth El
475 W. Locust Street 52001
Telephone: (563) 583-3483

FORT DODGE
SYNAGOGUES
Conservative
Fort Dodge Conservative Synagogue
501 N. 12th Street 50501
Telephone: (515) 572-8925

IOWA CITY
SYNAGOGUES
Conservative & Reform
Agudas Achim Congregation
602 E. Washington Street 52240
Telephone: (319) 337-3813
Fax: (319) 337-6764
Email: agudasachim@aol.com
Website: www.agudasachimic.org

POSTVILLE
SYNAGOGUES
Orthodox
Synagogue Postville
440 South Lawlor Street
Telephone: (319) 863-3013

SIOUX CITY
SYNAGOGUES
Conservative
Congregation Beth Shalom
815 38th Street 51104
Telephone: (712) 255-1990
Fax: (712) 258-0619
Email: drosen4005@aol.com

SYNAGOGUES
Orthodox
United Orthodox
Nebraska & 14th Street 51105
Telephone: (712) 255-4455

Kansas

LAWRENCE
SYNAGOGUES
Lawrence Jewish Community Center
917 Highland Drive 66046
Telephone: (785) 841-7636
Email: ljcc@sunflower.com
Website: www.ljcc.info

OVERLAND PARK
BUTCHERS
Jacobsons Strictly Kosher Foods
5200 West 95th Street 70115
Telephone: (913) 897-8246

MEDIA
Newspapers
Kansas City Jewish Chronicle
7373 W 107th Street 66212
Telephone: (913) 648-4620
Email: chronicle@sunpublications.com
Website: www.kcjc.com

SYNAGOGUES
Conservative
Beth Shalom\z
14200 Lamar 66223

Orthodox
Congregation Beth Israel Abraham & Voliner
9900 Antioch 66212
Telephone: (913) 341-2444
Fax: (913) 341-2467

Kehilath Israel Synagogue
10501 Conser 66212
Telephone: (913) 642-1880
Fax: (913) 642-7332

Reform
Congregation Beth Torah
6100 W. 127th Street 66209
Telephone: (913) 498-2212
Fax: (913) 498-1071

PRAIRE VILLAGE
SYNAGOGUES
Conservative
Ohev Sholom
5311 W. 75th Street 66208
Telephone: (913) 642-6460
Fax: (913) 385-9962
Email: rabbiscott@sbcglobal.net

TOPEKA
COMMUNITY ORGANISATIONS
Topeka Lawrence Jewish Federation
4200 Munson Street 70002
Telephone: (785) 828-2125
Fax: (785) 828-2827

SYNAGOGUES
Reform
Beth Sholom
4200 SW. Munson Avenue 66604-1818
Telephone: (785) 272-6040

WICHITA
GROCERIES
Dillon's
21st Street & Rock Road 70002
Telephone: (316) 828-2125
Fax: (316) 828-2827
Email: jewishnews@jewishnola.com

Dillon's
13th Street & Woodlawn Street 70002
Telephone: (316) 888-2010
Fax: (316) 888-2014
Website: www.koshercajun.com

Foodbarn
Woodlawn & Central Sts. 68154
Telephone: (316) 334-8200

The Bread Lady
20205 Rock Road, Suite 80 67208

SYNAGOGUES
Reform
Congregation Emanu-El
7011 E. Central Street 67206
Telephone: (316) 685-5148

Traditional
Hebrew Congregation
1850 N. Woodlawn 67208
Telephone: (316) 685-1339

Kentucky
LEXINGTON
COMMUNITY ORGANISATIONS
Central Kentucky Jewish Federation
340 Romany Road 67208

SYNAGOGUES
Conservative
Lexington Havurah
685 Shasta Circle 40503
Telephone: (859) 223-1299

Ohavay Zion
2048 Edgewater Ct. 40502
Telephone: (859) 266-8050
Fax: (859) 268-3357
Email: ozslex@gte.net
Website: www.ozs.org

Reform
Adath Israel
124 N. Ashland Avenue 40502
Telephone: (859) 269-2979
Fax: (859) 269-7347

LOUISVILLE
COMMUNITY ORGANISATIONS
Jewish Community Federation
3630 Dutchmans Lane 40205
Telephone: (502) 451-8840
Fax: (502) 458-0702
Email: jfed@iglou.com
Website: www.jewishlouisville.org
Notes: We publish an annual 'Guide to Jewish Louisville' that is available free upon request. It includes detailed information about all aspects of our Jewish community. We also publish a bi-weekly newspaper, 'Community'.

SYNAGOGUES
Conservative
Adath Jeshurun
2401 Woodbourne Avenue 40205
Telephone: (502) 458-5359
Fax: (502) 451-5634
Email: webmaster@adathjeshurun.com
Website: www.adathjeshurun.com

Knesseth Israel
2531 Taylorsville Road 40205
Telephone: (502) 459-2780

Orthodox
Anshei Sfard
3700 Dutchman's Lane 40205
Telephone: (502) 451-3122

Reform
Temple Shalom
4615 Lowe Road 40220
Telephone: (502) 458-4739
Fax: (502) 451-9750
Email: rsmiles@pipeline.com
Central organisation: Union for Reform Judaism

The Temple
5101 Brownsboro Road 40241
Telephone: (502) 423-1818
Fax: (502) 423-1835
Email: gronkin@thetempleaibs.org
Website: www.uahcweb.org/ky/thetemple

PADUCAH
Temple Israel
330 Joe Clifton Drive, PO Box 1141 42001
Telephone: 442-4104

Louisiana

ALEXANDRIA
CONTACT INFORMATION
Jewish Welfare Federation
Telephone: (318) 445-4785

GROCERIES
Dr & Mrs B Kaplan
100 Park Place 66211
Telephone: (318) 327-8100
Fax: (318) 327-8110
Website: www.jewishkc.org

LIBRARIES
Meyer Kaplan Memorial Library (Judiaca)
c/o B'nai Israel, 1908 Vance Street 66604

SYNAGOGUES
Conservative
B'nai Israel
1907 Vance Street 71301
Telephone: (318) 445-9367; 619-9177
Mailing Address: c/o Meyer Kaplan, 211 Fourth Street
~30119 Alexandria, Louisianna, 71301

Reform
Gemiluth Chassodim
2021 Turner Street 71301
Telephone: (318) 445-3655

BATON ROUGE
COMMUNITY ORGANISATIONS
Jewish Federation of Greater Baton Rouge
PO Box 80827 66207
Telephone: (504) 648-3880

SYNAGOGUES
Reform
B'nai Israel
3354 Kleinert Avenue 70806
Telephone: (504) 343-0111

Beth Shalom
9111 Jefferson Highway 70809
Telephone: (504) 924-6773

NEW ORLEANS
COMMUNITY ORGANISATIONS
Jewish Federation of Greater New Orleans
3500 N. Causeway Blvd., Suite 1240, Metairie
66204

DELICATESSEN
Kosher Cajun Deli & Grocery
3519 Severn St., Metairie 63146
Telephone: (504) 569-2770

GROCERIES
Casablanca
3030 Seven Avenue, Metairie 63146
Telephone: (504) 569-2770
Fax: (504) 569-2774

Touro Infirmary
1401 Foucher Street 63146

GUEST HOUSE
Guest House
2405 St. Charles Avenue
Telephone: (504) 581-5858
Fax: (504) 891-5626
Email: paulag@sunshinebrokers.com

MEDIA
Newspapers
The Jewish News
Goldring-Woldenberg Jewish Community Campus,
Harry & Jeanette Weinberg Building, 3747 West
Esplanade Avenue, Metairie 70002
Telephone: (504) 780-5614
Fax: (504) 780-5601
Email: jfedstl@neworleansjewishnews.com

MIKVAOT
Beth Israel
7000 Canal Blvd. 64114

Chabad House
7037 Freret St. 70118
Telephone: (504) 866-5164
Website: www.chabadneworleans.com

RESTAURANTS
Meat
Casablanca
3030 Severn Avenue, Metairie
Telephone: (504) 888-2209
Fax: (504) 888-5605
Website: www.kosherneworleans.com
Supervision: Lubavitch Shechita & Chabad

Creole Kosher Kitchen
115 Chartres Street
Telephone: (504) 529-4120
Supervision: Beth Israel Congregation

SYNAGOGUES
Orthodox
Anshe Sfard
2230 Carondelet Street 70130
Telephone: (504) 522-4714

Chabad House
7037 Freret Street
Telephone: (504) 866-5164
Website: www.chabadneworleans.com

SHREVEPORT
SYNAGOGUES
Conservative
Agudath Achim
9401 Village Green Drive 71115
Telephone: (318) 797-6401
Fax: (318) 797-6402

Reform
B'nai Zion
245 Southfield Road 71105
Telephone: (318) 861-2122

Maine
AUBURN
COMMUNITY ORGANISATIONS
Lewiston-Auburn Jewish Federation
74 Bradman Street 04210
Telephone: (207) 786-4201
Fax: (207) 786-4202
Email: temple6359@aol.com

SYNAGOGUES
Conservative
Congregation Beth Abraham
Main Street & Laurel Avenue 04210
Telephone: (207) 783-1302

Temple Shalom
74 Bradman Street 04210
Telephone: (207) 786-4201
Fax: (207) 786-4202
Email: temple6359@aol.com

AUGUSTA
SYNAGOGUES
Reform
Temple Beth El
PO Box 871, Woodlawn Street 04330
Telephone: (404) 622-7450

BANGOR
RESTAURANTS
Bagel Central
33 Central Street 04401
Telephone: (207) 947-1654
Supervision: Beth Abraham Rabbi Fred Neble

SYNAGOGUES
Conservative
Congregation Beth Israel
144 York Street 04401
Telephone: (207) 945-3433
Fax: (207) 945-3840

Orthodox
Beth Abraham
145 York Street 04401
Telephone: (207) 942-8093
Email: rabbi@jewishbangor.com
Website: www.jewishbangor.com

OLD ORCHARD BEACH
KASHRUT INFORMATION
Eber Weinstein
187 E. Grand Avenue 04064
Telephone: (207) 934-7522

PORTLAND
BUTCHERS
Penny Wise Super Market
182 Ocean Avenue 55812
Telephone: (503) 724-8857

COMMUNITY ORGANISATIONS
Jewish Fed. Com. Council of Southern Maine
57 Ashmont Street 55907
Telephone: (503) 288-7500
Fax: (503) 286-9329
Email: rabbigreen@charter.net

MIKVAOT
Shaarey Tphiloh
76 Noyes Street 55416
Telephone: (503) 381-3410
Fax: (503) 381-3401
Email: jschachtman@jccminneapolis.org

SYNAGOGUES
Conservative
Temple Beth El
400 Deering Avenue 04103
Telephone: (503) 774-2649
Fax: (503) 774-7518
Email: office@templebethel.maine.org

Orthodox
Shaarey Tphiloh
76 Noyes Street 04103
Telephone: (503) 773-0693

ROCKLAND
SYNAGOGUES
Conservative
Adas Yoshuron
Willow Street
Telephone: (207) 594-4523

Maryland
Bethesda, Bowie, Chevy Chase, Gaithersburg,
Greenbelt, Hyattsville, Kensington, Laurel,
Lexington Park, Olney, Potomac, Rockville,
Silver Spring & Wheaton and Temple Hills are
all part of Greater Washington, DC.

ANNAPOLIS
Congregation Kol Ami
1909 Hidden Meadow Lane 21401
Telephone: (410) 266-6006
Email: kolami2@toadmail.toad.net

SYNAGOGUES
Orthodox
Congregation Knesseth Israel
1125 Spa Road, Annapolis, Maryland 21403
Telephone: (410) 263-3924

Reform
Temple Beth Shalom
1461 Baltimore-Annapolis Blvd 21012

BALTIMORE
BAKERIES
Alder's Bakery
1860D Reisterstown Road
Telephone: (410) 653-1119

Dunkin Donuts
1508 Reisterstown Road 21208
Telephone: (410) 653-8182
Supervision: Rabbi Salfer

Dunkin Donuts
7000 Reisterstown Road 21215
Telephone: (410) 764-6846
Supervision: Rabbi Salfer

Goldman's Kosher Bakery
6848 Reisterstown Road, Fallstaff Shopping Center
21215
Telephone: (410) 358-9625
Fax: (410) 358-5859
Email: goldman's.bakery@verizon.net
Supervision: Star-K of Baltimore
All products are Pareve, Pas Yisroel and Yoshon. Packaged
dairy products are available and are Star-K, Cholov Yisroel.

Pariser's Kosher Bakery
6711 Reisterstown Road 48104
Telephone: (410) 995-3276
Fax: (410) 996-2479
Email: chabad@jewmich.com

Schmell & Azman Kosher Bakery
1351 Lamberton Drive 48075
Telephone: (410) 559-5005/06
Fax: (410) 559-5202

Schmell-Azman
7006 Reisterstown Road 21215
Telephone: (410) 484-7373
Supervision: Star K

BUTCHERS
Shlomo Meat & Fish Market
4135 Amos Ave., (Menlo Industrial Park) 21215
Telephone: (410) 358-9633

Wasserman & Lemberger
7006-D Reisterstown Road 20208
Telephone: (410) 486-4191

COMMUNITY ORGANISATIONS
**Associated Jewish Community Federation of
Baltimore**
101 W. Mount Royal Avenue 55416
Telephone: (410) 926-3829
Fax: (410) 920-2184
Email: office@kenessethisrael.org
Website: www.jirs.info

Jewish Information and Referral Service
5750 Park Heights Avenue 48075
Telephone: (410) 466-4636
Fax: (410) 664-0551
Email: cordetroit@hotmail.com
Website: www.jirs.info

DELICATESSEN
Knish Shop
508 Reisterstown Road 21208
Telephone: (410) 484-5850

Liebes Kosher Deli Carry Out
607 Reisterstown Road 211208
Telephone: (410) 653-1977
Glatt Kosher, Sunday to Wednesday 8.30 am to 6.00 pm.

GROCERIES
Seven Mile Market
4000 Seven Mile Lane 21208
Telephone: (410) 653-2000; 2002
Email: sevenMilemarket@covad.net
Supervision: Star K

Shlomo Meat & Fish
506 Reisterstown Road 48237

Wasserman & Lemberger
706-D Reisterstown Road 48237
Telephone: (410) 443-2425

KASHRUT INFORMATION
Star-K Kosher Certification
122 Slade Avenue, Suite 300 48075
Telephone: (410) 443-2425
Email: star-k@star-k.org
Website: www.star-k.org

MIKVAOT
Mikva of Baltimore Inc.
3207 Clarks Lane 50312
Telephone: (410) 277-6321

MUSEUMS
The Jewish Museum of Maryland
15 Lloyd Street 55116

RESTAURANTS
Café Shalom
2401 West Belvedere Avenue 21215
Telephone: (410) 601-5000 ext 3971
Fax: (410) 601-6312
Supervision: Star-K

Goldberg's Bagels
708 Reisterstown Road
Telephone: (410) 415-7001
Supervision: Star-K
Supervision:

Krispy Kremes
10021 Reisterstown road (nr. Painters Mill Rd.)
Telephone: (410) 356-2655
Supervision: Star-K

Mama Leah's Pizza
1852 Reisterstown Road
Telephone: (410) 653-7600
Supervision: Star-K.

Dairy
Caramel's Pizza & Ice Cream
700 Reisterstown Road
Telephone: (410) 486-2365
Supervision: Star-K.

Milk and Honey Bistro
Commercecentre, 1777 Reisterstown Road
Telephone: (410) 484-3544
Supervision: Star-K.

Meat
David Chu's China Bistro
7105 Reisterstown Road 21215
Telephone: (410) 602-5008
Fax: (410) 602-3570
Supervision: Star-K.

Kosher Bite
6309 Reisterstown Road 48502
Telephone: (410) 767-5922
Fax: (410) 767-9024
Email: fjf@tm.net

Royal Restaurant
7006 Reisterstown Road 21208
Telephone: (410) 661-1000
Fax: (410) 661-3680

Szechuan Dynasty
1860C Reisterstown Road
Telephone: (410) 602-1817

The Brasserie
Pomona Square Shopping Center, 1700
Reisterstown Road 50265

Pizzeria
Tov Pizza
6313 Reisterstown Road
Telephone: (410) 358-5238
Website: www.tovpizza.com
Supervision: KOF-K

TOURS OF JEWISH INTEREST
Holocaust Memorial
Gay & Lombard Sts. 51105
Telephone: (410) 258-0618

BETHESDA
COMMUNITY ORGANISATIONS
United Jewish Appeal Federation of Greater Washington
7900 Wisconsin Avenue 48034

BOWIE
SYNAGOGUES
Conservative
Nevey Shalom
12218 Torah Lane 20715
Telephone: (301) 262-9020
Fax: (301) 262-9015
Email: neveyshalom@maxinter.net

SYNAGOGUES
Reform
Bowie Reform Synagogue
2901 Mitchelville Road 20716
Telephone: (301) 249-2424

CHEVY CHASE
SYNAGOGUES
Conservative
Ohr Kodesh
8402 Freyman Drive 20815
Telephone: (301) 589-3880
Fax: (301) 495-4801
Email: okcjmm@erols.com

Reform
Temple Shalom
8401 Grubb Road 20815
Telephone: (301) 587-2273

CUMBERLAND
SYNAGOGUES
Conservative
Beth Jacob
1 Columbia street 21502
Telephone: (301) 777-3717

Reform
B'Er Chayim
107 Union Street 21502
Telephone: (301) 722-5688
Website: www.berchayim.org

GAITHERSBURG
SYNAGOGUES
Conservative
Kehilat Shalom
9915 Apple Ridge Road 20886
Telephone: (301) 869-7699
Fax: (301) 977-7870
Email: mail@kehilatshalom.org
Website: www.kehilatshalom.org

GREEN BELT
Mishkan Torah
Westway and Ridge Road 20770
Telephone: (301) 474-4223

HAGERSTOWN
SYNAGOGUES
Reform
B'nai Abraham
53 E. Baltimore Street 21740
Telephone: (301) 733-5039

HYATTSVILLE
SYNAGOGUES
Conservative
Beth Torah Congregation
6700 Adelphi Road 20782
Telephone: (301) 927-5525
Email: bethtorah@starpower.net
Website: www.bethtorah.ws

KEMP MILL
SYNAGOGUES
Kemp Mill Synagogue
11910 Kemp Mill Road
Telephone: (301) 593-0966

KENSINGTON
SYNAGOGUES
Reform
Temple Emanuel
10101 Connecticut Avenue 20895
Telephone: (301) 942-2000
Fax: (301) 942-9488

LAUREL
SYNAGOGUES
Reconstructionist
Oseh Shalom
8604 Briarwood Drive 20708
Telephone: (301) 498-5151

LEXINGTON PARK
SYNAGOGUES
Conservative
Beth Israel Congregation
PO box 1683, 21780 Bunker Hill Drive 20653
Telephone: (301) 862-2021
Email: bethisraelsyna@geocities.com
Website: www.geocities.com/bethisraelsyna

OLNEY
B'nai Shalom
18401 Burtfield Drive 20832
Telephone: (301) 774-0879

POCOMOKE
Temple Israel
3rd Street 21851

POTOMAC
Har Shalom
11510 Falls Road 20854
Telephone: (301) 299-7087
Email: shalom@harshalom.org
Website: www.harshalom.org

SYNAGOGUES
Orthodox
Beth Sholom Congregation and Talmud Torah
11825 Seven Locks Road 20854
Telephone: (301) 279-7010
Fax: (301) 279-5815
Website: www.bethsholom.org

Young Israel Ezras Israel of Potomac
11618 Seven Locks Road 20854
Telephone: (301) 299-2827
Website: www.yieip.org

ROCKVILLE
GROCERIES
Katz Supermarket
4860 Boiling Brook Parkway
Telephone: (301) 468-0400

RESTAURANTS
Dairy
Siena's
Nicholson Road
Telephone: (301) 770-7474

Meat
Royal Dragon
4840 Boiling Brook Parkway
Telephone: (301) 468-1922

Meat and Dairy
Kat'z Kafe
4860 Boiling Brook Parkway 46614
Telephone: (301) 291-4239
Fax: (301) 291-9490

SYNAGOGUES
Conservative
B'nai Israel
6301 Montrose Road 20852
Telephone: (301) 881-6550
Fax: (301) 881-6221

Tikvat Israel
2200 Baltimore Road 20851
Telephone: (301) 762-7338
Fax: (301) 424-4399

Orthodox
Magen David Sephardic Congregation
11215 Woodglen Drive, 20852
Telephone: (301) 770-6818
Fax: (301) 881-0498

Reform
Temple Beth Ami
14330 Travilah Road 20850
Telephone: (301) 340-6818
Fax: (301) 738-0094
Email: cgs@bethami.org

SALISBURY
SYNAGOGUES
Conservative
Beth Israel
600 Camden Ave 21801
Telephone: (410) 742-2564
Fax: (410) 742-2697
Email: bethisrael1231@cs.com
Website: www.bethisraelsalisbury.org

SILVER SPRING
BAKERIES
Kosher Pastry Oven
2521 Ennalls Avenue
Telephone: (301) 946-0159

Schmell and Azman
Kemp Mill Shopping Center, Arcola Avenue
Telephone: (301) 593-4785

The Wooden Shoe Pastry Shop
11301 Georgia Avenue 20902
Telephone: (301) 942-9330

Virtuoso
11230a Lockwood avenue 50901
Telephone: (301) 593-6034

BOOKSELLERS
Lisbon's Hebrew Books & Gifts
2305 University Blvd. West, Wheaton 46260
Telephone: (301) 726-5450
Fax: (301) 205-0307
Email: hnadler@jewishinindy.org

The Jewish Bookstore
11252 Georgia Avenue 40502
Telephone: (301) 268-0672
Fax: (301) 268-0775
Email: ckjf@jewishlexington.org

GROCERIES
Shalom
2309 University Blvd. 21215
Telephone: (301) 764-1448
Fax: (301) 578-0018

Shaul & Hershel Meat Market
Telephone: (301) 949-8477

MIKVAOT
Mikva
8901 Georgia Avenue 46322
Telephone: (301) 972-2251
Fax: (301) 972-4779

RESTAURANTS
Dairy
Ben Yehuda Pizza
Kemp Mill Shopping Center, off Arcola Avenue

The Nut House
11419 Georgia Avenue 40205
Telephone: (301) 451-8840
Fax: (301) 458-0702
Email: jfed@iglou.com

Meat
Max's
2309 university Blvd.
Telephone: (301) 949-6297

SYNAGOGUES
Conservative
Har Tzeon-Agudath Achim
1840 University Blvd. W 20902

Shaare Tefila Congregation
11120 Lockwood Drive 20901
Telephone: (301) 593-3410
Fax: (301) 593-3860
Email: mgreen@shaaretefila.org
Website: www.shaaretefila.org

Orthodox
Silver Spring Jewish Center
1401 Arcola Avenue 46614
Telephone: (301) 291-4239
Fax: (301) 291-9490

South-East Hebrew Congregation
10900 Lockwood Drive 20902

Woodside Synagogue Ahavas Torah
9001 Georgia avenue 20910
Telephone: (301) 587-8252; 565-5005
Email: information@wsat.org
Website: www.wsat.org
Supervision: Members of the OU and Capitol K
North Eastern intersection of Georgia Avenue and Noyes Drive, in historic Silver Spring, Maryland, very close to Washington D.C. Our shul is only two blocks from the subway, several hotels, Mikvah and downtown Silver Spring. Rav of the shul is Rabbi Yitzchok Breitowitz.

Young Israel of White Oak
PO Box 10613, Hite Oak 20914
Telephone: (301) 369-1531

Young Israel Shomrai Emunah of Greater Washington
1132 Arcola Avenue 20902
Telephone: (301) 593-4465
Fax: (301) 593-2330
Email: yise@erols.com

TEMPLE HILLS
SYNAGOGUES
Conservative
Shaare Tikva
5405 Old Temple Hills Road 20748
Telephone: (301) 894-4303

Massachusetts
ACTON
SYNAGOGUES
Independent
Beth Elohim
10 Hennessy Drive 07120
Telephone: (978) 263-8610

AMHERST
Jewish Community
742 Main Street 21215
Telephone: (413) 358-6349
Supervision: Star-K.

ANDOVER
SYNAGOGUES
Reform
Temple Emanuel
7 Haggett's Pond Road 01810
Telephone: (978) 470-1356
Fax: (978) 470-1783
Email: info@templeemanuel.net
Website: www.templeemanuel.net

ATHOL
SYNAGOGUES
Conservative
Temple Israel
107 Walnut Street 01331
Telephone: (978) 249-9481

ATTLEBORO
SYNAGOGUES
Reconstructionist
Agudas Achim Congregation
901 N. Main Street 02703
Telephone: (508) 222-2243
Email: agudasachim@netzero.net
Website: www.shamash.org/jrf/agudasma

AYER
SYNAGOGUES
Independent
Congregation Anshey Sholom
Cambridge Street 01432
Telephone: (508) 772-0896

BELMONT
SYNAGOGUES
Reform
Beth El Temple Center
2 Concord Avenue 02478
Telephone: (617) 484-6668
Fax: (617) 484-6020
Website: www.uahc.org/ma/betc

BEVERLY
SYNAGOGUES
Conservative
B'nai Abraham
200 E. Lothrop Street 01915
Telephone: (978) 927-3211
Fax: (978) 922-5281
Email: TBA200East@cs.com

BOSTON
Office of the Chaplain, City of Boston
15 School Street
Telephone: (617) 227-8200
Fax: (617) 227-8420
Email: rebbe@rebbe
Website: www.rebbe.org
Supervision: Grand Rabbi Y. A. Korff (Zvhil-Mezbuz Rebbe)

EMBASSY
Consul General of Israel
1020 Statler Office Blvd 02116

KASHRUT INFORMATION
Synagogue Council of Massachusetts
1320 Centre Street, Newton Centre 21215
Telephone: (617) 358-9625
Fax: (617) 358-5859
Email: mcohn@comcast.net

The Kashruth Commission
177 Tremont Street 02111
Telephone: (617) 764-1700

MEDIA
The Jewish Advocate
15 School Street 02108
Telephone: (617) 367-9100
Fax: (617) 367-9310
Email: thejewishadvocate@thejewishadvocate.com
Website: www.thejewishadvocate.com
Supervision: Star-K.

Guide
Jewish Guide to Boston and New England
15 School Street 02108
Telephone: (617) 367-9100
Fax: (617) 367-9310
Email: thejewishadvocate@thejewishadvocate.com

Newspapers
Boston Jewish Times
15 School Street 02108
Telephone: (617) 484-3544
Supervision: Star-K.

RELIGIOUS ORGANISATIONS
Rabbinical Council of New England
177 Tremont Street 02111
Telephone: (617) 426-2139
Email: rabbi@kvh613.org

RESTAURANTS
Dairy
Kosher Restaurant
50 Milk Street 21208
Telephone: (617) 486-4191

SYNAGOGUES
Orthodox
Chabad House
491 Commonwealth Avenue 02215
Telephone: (617) 424-1190
Fax: (617) 266-5997
Email: chabad@peoplepc.com

The Boston Synagogue (at Charles River Park)
55 Martha Road 02114
Telephone: (617) 523-0453
Fax: (617) 723-2863

Zvhil-Mezbuz Beis Medrash (Zvhil-Mezbuz Rebbe)
15 School Street 02108
Telephone: (617) 227-8200
Fax: (617) 227-8420
Email: rebbe@rebbe.org
Website: www.rebbe.org
Supervision: Grand Rabbi Y. A. Korff (Zvhil-Mezbuz Rebbe)

Reform
Temple Israel
Longwood Ave. & Plymouth Street 02215
Telephone: (617) 566-3960
Fax: (617) 731-3711
Website: www.tisrael.org

BRAINTREE
SYNAGOGUES
Conservative
Temple Bnai Shalom
41 Storrs Avenue 02184
Telephone: (781) 843-3687

BRIGHTON
MIKVAOT
Daughters of Israel
101 Washington Street, Brighton 02135
Telephone: (617) 466-4636
Fax: (617) 664-0551
Email: jirs@org
Website: www.jifrs.info

SYNAGOGUES
Conservative
Temple B'nai Moshe
1845 Commonwealth Avenue, Brighton 02135
Telephone: (617) 254-3620
Fax: (617) 254-3620
Email: templebnaimoshe.org

Orthodox
Chai Odom
77 Englewoood Av. 02135
Telephone: (617) 734-5359
Website: www.chaiodom.org

Congregation Kadimah-Toras Moshe
113 Washington Street, Brighton 02135
Telephone: (617) 254-1333

Lubavitch Shul of Brighton
239 Chestnut Hill Avenue, Brighton 02135
Telephone: (617) 782-8340

Talner Congregation Beth David
64 Corey Road 02135
Telephone: (617) 232-2349

BROCKTON
SYNAGOGUES

Conservative
Temple
479 Torres Street 02401
Telephone: (508) 583-5810

Orthodox
Agudas Achim
144 Belmont Avenue 02301
Telephone: (508) 583-0717

BROOKLINE
BAKERIES
Catering by Andrew
402 Harvard Street 02446
Telephone: (617) 731-6585
Fax: (617) 232-3788
Email: cbandrew@aol.com
Supervision: Vaad Harabonim of Massachusetts

Kupel's
421 Harvard Street
Telephone: (617) 566-9528

GROCERIES
Beacon Kosher
1706 Beacon Street
Telephone: (617) 734-5300

JUDAICA
Israel Book Shop, Inc.
410 Harvard Street
Telephone: (617) 566-7113
Fax: (617) 566-0006
Email: info@israelbookshop.com
Website: www.israelbookshop.com

RESTAURANTS
Dairy
Café Eilat
420 Harvard Street 02446
Telephone: (617) 277-7770

Meat
Rami's
324 Harvard Street 02446
Telephone: (617) 738-3577

Rubin's Kosher Deli and Restaurant
500 Harvard Street, Brookline 02146
Telephone: (617) 731-8787

Ruth's Kitchen
401 Harvard street 02446
Telephone: (617) 484-4110
Fax: (617) 653-9294
Email: star-k@star-k.org

Taam China
423 Harvard Street
Telephone: (617) 264-7274

SYNAGOGUES

Conservative
Kehillath Israel
384 Harvard Street 2146
Telephone: (617) 277-9155

Shalom Hunan
92 Harvard Street 02445-46
Telephone: (617) 731-9778
Fax: (617) 731-9760

Orthodox
Beth Pinchas (Bostoner Rebbe)
1710 Beacon Street 02146
Telephone: (617) 734-5100
Fax: (617) 739-0163
Email: rofeh@world.std.com

Congregation Lubavitch
100 Woodcliff Road 02467
Telephone: (617) 469-5000
Fax: (617) 469-0089
Email: lubavitch@juno.com
Website: www.congregationlubavitch.org

Young Israel Brookline
62 Green Street 02446
Telephone: (617) 734-0276
Fax: (617) 734-7195
Email: office@yibrookline.org
Website: www.yibrookline.org

Reform
Ohabei Shalom
1187 Beacon Street 2446
Telephone: (617) 277-6610
Email: dberman@ohabei.org
Website: www.ohabei.org

Temple Sinai
50 Sewall Ave., Coolidge Corner 02146
Telephone: (617) 277-5888

Sephardi
Sephardic Congregation of New England -
Beth Abraham
18 Williston Road 02445
Telephone: (617) 308-0602
Fax: (617) 527-5436
Website: www.bethabraham.net

BURLINGTON
SYNAGOGUES
Reform
Temple Shalom Emeth
14-16 Lexington Street 01803
Telephone: (718) 272-2351

CAMBRIDGE
KASHRUT INFORMATION
Harvard Hillel
Harvard University, 52 Mt. Auburn Street 21202
Telephone: (617) 732-6400
Fax: (617) 732-6451
Email: info@jewishmuseummd.org
Website: www.jewishmuseummd.org

RESTAURANTS
Kosher Restaurant
52 Mt Auburn Street 02138
Telephone: (617) 495-4695
Fax: (617) 864-1637
Email: linda@hillel.harvard.edu
Website: www.hillel.harvard.edu

Meat
M.I.T. Hillel Amherst Street Deli
40 Massachusetts Avenue 02139
Telephone: (617) 253-2982
Fax: (617) 253-3260
Email: hillel@mit.edu
Website: web.mit.edu/dining/locations/kosher.html
Supervision: Vaad Harabonim of Massachusetts.

SYNAGOGUES
Conservative
Temple Beth Shalom of Cambridge
8 Tremont Street 02139
Telephone: (617) 864-6388
Fax: (617) 864-0507
Email: office@tremonstreetshul.org
Website: www.tremonstreetshul.org

Orthodox
Chabad
38 Banks Street 02138
Telephone: (617) 547-6124
Email: info@chabadharvard.org

Harvard Hillel Synagogue
52 Mt.Auburn Street 01238
Telephone: (617) 495-4695
Fax: (617) 864-1637
Email: lind@hillel.harvard.edu
Website: www.hillel.harvard.edu

CANTON
SYNAGOGUES
Conservative
Beth Abraham
1301 Washington Street 02021
Telephone: (781) 828-5250

Reform
Temple Beth David of the South Shore
1060 Randolph Street 02021
Telephone: (781) 828-2275
Fax: (781) 821-3997
Email: info@templebethdavid.com
Website: www.templebethdavid.com

CAPE COD
SYNAGOGUES
Orthodox
Beth Israel
Cnr. of Onset Avenue & Locust Street, PO Box 24,
Onset 02558
Telephone: (508) 295-9185
Email: capeshul@att.net
Website: www.home.att.net/capeshul

CHELMSFORD
SYNAGOGUES
Reform
Congregation Shalom
Richardson Road 01824
Telephone: (978) 251-8090

CLINTON
SYNAGOGUES
Independent
Shaarei Zedek
Water Street 01510
Telephone: (978) 365-3320

EAST FALMOUTH
SYNAGOGUES
Reform
Falmouth Jewish Congregation
7 Hatchville Road 02536
Telephone: (508) 540-0602
Fax: (508) 540-8094
Website: www.falmouthjewish.org

EASTON
SYNAGOGUES
Traditional
Temple Chayai Shalom
238 Depot Street 02334
Telephone: (508) 238-6385

EVERETT
Tifereth Israel
34 Malden Street 02149
Telephone: (617) 387-0200

FALL RIVER
COMMUNITY ORGANISATIONS
Fall River Jewish Community Council
Room 377, 56 N. Main St. 21201
Telephone: (508) 727-4828

SYNAGOGUES
Conservative
Beth El
385 High Street 02720
Telephone: (508) 674-9761
Orthodox
Adas Israel
1647 Robeson Street 02720
Telephone: (508) 674-9761
Fax: (508) 678-3195

FRAMINGHAM
RESTAURANTS
Meat
Rami's of Framington
341 Cochituate Rd. 01701
Telephone: (508) 370-3577

SYNAGOGUES
Conservative
Temple Beth Sholom
50 Pamela Road 01701
Telephone: (508) 877-2540
Fax: (508) 877-8278
Website: www.beth-sholom.org

Orthodox
Chabad House
74 Joseph Road 01701
Telephone: (508) 877-5313
Fax: (508) 877-5313

Reform
Beth Am
300 Pleasant street 01701
Telephone: (508) 872-8300
Fax: (508) 872-9773
Email: tempbetham@aol.com

Temple Beth Am
100 Pleasant street 01701
Telephone: (508) 872-8300
Fax: (508) 872-9773
Email: shalom@templebetham.org
Website: www.templebetham.org

GLOUCESTER
SYNAGOGUES
Conservative
Ahavat Achim
86 Middle Street 01930
Telephone: (978) 281-0739
Fax: (978) 281-0739

GREENFIELD
Temple Israel
27 Pierce Street 01301
Telephone: (413) 773-5884

HAVERHILL
SYNAGOGUES
Orthodox
Anshe Sholom
427 Main Street 01830
Telephone: (508) 372-2276

Reform
Temple Emanu-El
514 Main Street 01830
Telephone: (508) 373-3861

HINGHAM
Congregation Sha'aray Shalom
1112 Main Street, Hingham, MA 02043
Telephone: (781) 749-8103
Fax: (781) 740-1480
Email: cssadm@aol.com
Website: http://www.shaaray.org

HOLBROOK
SYNAGOGUES
Conservative
Temple Beth Shalom
95 Plymouth Street 02343
Telephone: (617) 767-4922

HOLLISTON
Temple Beth Torah
2162 Washington Street 01746
Telephone: (508) 429-6268
Fax: (508) 429-7729
Email: tbt@bethtorah.org

HOLYOKE
Sons of Zion
378 Maple Street 01040
Telephone: (413) 534-3369

SYNAGOGUES
Orthodox
Rodphey Sholom
12800 Northampton Street 01040
Telephone: (413) 534-5262

HULL
SYNAGOGUES
Conservative
Temple Beth Sholom
600 Nantasket Avenue 02045
Telephone: (617) 925-0091
Fax: (617) 925-9053

Temple Israel of Nantasket
9 Hadassah Way 02045
Telephone: (617) 925-0289

HYANNIS
SYNAGOGUES
Reform
Cape Cod Synagogue
145 Winter Street 02601
Telephone: (508) 775-2988

HYDE PARK
SYNAGOGUES
Conservative
Temple Adas Hadrath Israel
28 Arlington Street 02136
Telephone: (617) 364-2661

LAWRENCE
COMMUNITY ORGANISATIONS
Jewish Community Council of Greater Lawrence
580 Haverhill Street 20910
Telephone: (913) 565-3737

SYNAGOGUES
Orthodox
Anshai Sholom
411 Hampshire Street 01843
Telephone: (913) 683-4544

LEOMINSTER
SYNAGOGUES
Conservative
Congregation Agudat Achim
268 Washington Street 01453
Telephone: (508) 534-6121

LEXINGTON
Temple Emunah
9 Piper Road 02421
Telephone: (781) 861-0300
Fax: (781) 861-7141
Email: rholmes@emunahlex.org
Website: www.templeemunah.org
Supervision: Rabbi David G. Lerner
Conservative, egalitarian.

SYNAGOGUES
Orthodox
Chabad Center
9 Burlington Street 02173
Telephone: (859) 863-8656

Reform
Temple Isaiah
55 Lincoln Street 02173
Telephone: (859) 862-7160

LONGMEADOW
MIKVAOT
Mikveh Association
1104 Converse, Long. MA 2558
Telephone: (413) 295-9820

SYNAGOGUES
Conservative
B'nai Jacob
2 Eunice Drive 01106
Telephone: (413) 567-0058

Orthodox
Beth Israel
1280 Williams St. 01106
Telephone: (413) 567-3210

Lubavitcher Yeshiva Synagogue
1148 Converse St 01106
Telephone: (413) 567-8665

LOWELL
MIKVAOT
Lowell Mikvaot
48 Academy Drive
Telephone: (978) 933-1800
Fax: (978) 933-7466
Email: slisbon@idsonline.com

SYNAGOGUES
Conservative
Temple Beth El
105 Princeton Blvd. 01851
Telephone: (978) 453-7744

Orthodox
Montefiore Synagogue
460 Westford Street 20902
Telephone: (978) 649-4425
Fax: (978) 649-1274

Reform
Temple Emanuel of Merrimack Valley
101 W. Forest Street 01851
Telephone: (978) 454-1372
Email: info@temv.org
Website: www.temv.org

LYNN
SYNAGOGUES

Orthodox
Ahabat Sholom
151 Ocean Street, Lynn, MA 01902
Telephone: (617) 593-9255
Fax: (617) 593-9255
Email: ahabat@juno.com
Website: www.ahabatsholom.org

Anshai Sfard
150 South Common Street 01905
Telephone: (617) 599-7131

MALDEN
SYNAGOGUES

Conservative
Ezrath Israel
245 Bryant Street 02148
Telephone: (781) 322-7205

Orthodox
Congregation Beth Israel
10 Dexter Street 02148
Telephone: (781) 322-5686
Fax: (781) 3226678
Email: congbi@aol.com

Young Israel of Malden
45 Holyoke Street 02148
Telephone: (781) 961-9817

Reform
Tifereth Israel
539 Salem Street 02148
Telephone: (781) 322-2794

Traditional
Agudas Achim
160 Harvard Street 02148
Telephone: (781) 322-9380

MARBLEHEAD
SYNAGOGUES

Conservative/Masorti
Temple Sinai
1 Community Road 01945

Telephone: (617) 631-2763
Fax: (617) 631-2244
Email: Tmpsinai@gis.net

Orthodox
Orthodox Congregation of the North Shore
4 Community Road 01945
Telephone: (617) 598-1810

Reform
Temple Emanu-El
393 Atlantic Avenue 01945
Telephone: (617) 631-9300

MARLBORO
SYNAGOGUES

Conservative
Temple Emanuel
150 Berlin Road 01752
Telephone: (508) 485-7565

MEDFORD
Temple Shalom
475 Winthrop Street 02155
Telephone: (781) 396-3262

MELROSE
SYNAGOGUES

Reform
Temple Beth Shalom
21 E. Foster Street 02176
Telephone: (617) 665-4520

MILFORD
SYNAGOGUES

Conservative
Temple Beth Shalom
55 Pine Street 01757
Telephone: (508) 473-1590
Website: www.templebethshalom.com

MILLIS
Ael Chunon
334 Village Street 02054
Telephone: (508) 376-5984
Fax: (508) 533-3802
Email: TNULB@medione.net

MILTON
Temple Shalom
180 Blue Hill Avenue 02186
Telephone: (617) 698-3394
Fax: (617) 696-9265
Email: office@templeshalomonline.org
Website: www.templeshalomonline.org

SYNAGOGUES
Orthodox
B'nai Jacob
100 Blue Hill Parkway 02187
Telephone: (617) 698-0698
Supervision: Rabbi Nathan Korff.

NATICK
SYNAGOGUES
Conservative
Temple Israel
145 Hartford Street   01760
Telephone: (508) 650-3521
Fax: (508) 655-3440
Website: www.tiofnatick.org

NEEDHAM
Temple Aliyah
1664 Central Avenue 02492
Telephone: (781) 444-8522
Fax: (781) 449-7066
Website: www.templealiyah.com

SYNAGOGUES
Reform
Temple Beth Shalom
670 Highland Avenue 02494
Telephone: (781) 444-0077
Fax: (781) 449-3274
Email: tbshalom@ix.netcom.com
Website: www.templebethshalom.info

NEW BEDFORD
COMMUNITY ORGANISATIONS
Jewish Federation of Greater New Bedford
467 Hawthorn Street, N. Dartmouth 20902
Telephone: (508) 942-5900

SYNAGOGUES
Conservative
Tifereth Israel
145 Brownell Avenue 02740
Telephone: (508) 997-3171
Fax: (508) 997-3173

Orthodox
Ahavath Achim
385 County Street 02740
Telephone: (508) 994-1760
Fax: (508) 994-81286
Email: rabbibarry@aol.com
Website: www.members.aol.com/rabbibarry

NEWBURYPORT
SYNAGOGUES
Conservative
Congregation Ahavas Achim
Washington & Olive Streets 09150
Telephone: (508) 462-2461

NEWTON
COMMUNITY ORGANISATIONS
Jewish Community Center of Greater Boston
333 Nahanton Street 20902
Telephone: (617) 946-1041

RESTAURANTS
Rosenfeld Bagels
1280 Centre Street, Newton Center 02459
Telephone: (617) 527-8080

SYNAGOGUES
Orthodox
Beth El Ateret Israel
561 Ward Street 02459
Telephone: (617) 244-7233

Congregation B'nai Jacob (Zvhil-Mezbuz Rebbe)
955 Beacon Street
Telephone: (617) 227-8200
Fax: (617) 227-8420
Email: rebbe@rebbe.org
Website: www.rebbe.org
Supervision: Grand Rabbi Y. A. Korff (Zvhil-Mezbuz Rebbe)

Shaarei Tefila
35 Morseland Avenue 02459
Telephone: (617) 527-7637

NORTH ADAMS
SYNAGOGUES
Reform
Congregation Beth Israel
53 Lois Street, North Adams, MA 01247
Telephone: (413) 663-5830
Fax: (413) 663-5830
Email: cbi@bcn.net
Website: www.cbiweb.org

NORTHAMPTON
SYNAGOGUES
Conservative
B'nai Israel
253 Prospect Road 01060
Telephone: (413) 584-3593

NORWOOD
Temple Shaare Tefilah
556 Nichols Street 02062
Telephone: (781) 762-8670
Fax: (781) 762-8670
Website: www.uscj.org/neweng/norwood

ONSET
HOTELS
Bridge View Hotel
12 S. Water Street 20814
Telephone: (508) 652-6480

PEABODY
SYNAGOGUES

Conservative
Temple Ner Tamid
368 Lowell Street 001960
Telephone: (508) 532-1293
Fax: (508) 532-0101
Email: audrey368@aol.com
Website: www.templenertamid.org

Independent
Congregation Tifereth Israel
Pierpont Street 01960
Telephone: (508) 531-8135

Reform
Beth Shalom
489 Lowell Street 01960
Telephone: (508) 535-2100
Fax: (508) 536-3115

Traditional
Congregation Sons of Israel
Park & Spring Streets 01960
Telephone: (508) 531-7576

PITTSFIELD
COMMUNITY ORGANISATIONS
Jewish Federation of the Berkshires
196 South Street 01201
Telephone: (413) 442-4360
Fax: (413) 443-6070
Website: www.jewishberkshires.org

PLYMOUTH
SYNAGOGUES

Reform
Congregation Beth Jacob
Synagogue on Pleasant Street, Community Center on Court Street, PO Box 3284 02361
Telephone: (508) 746-1575
Email: cbethjacob@juno.com

QUINCY
SYNAGOGUES

Conservative
Temple Beth El
1001 Hancock Street 02169
Telephone: (617) 479-4309

Orthodox
Beth Israel
33 Grafton Street, PO Box 690388 02269-0388
Telephone: (617) 472-6796

RANDOLPH
BOOKSELLERS
Davidson's Hebrew Book Store
1106 Main Street 4130

SYNAGOGUES

Orthodox
Young Israel - Kehillath Jacob of Mattapan & Randolph
374 N. Main Street, PO Box 880 02368
Telephone: (781) 986-6461
Email: youngisrael@juno.com

REVERE
DELICATESSEN
Myer's Kosher Kitchen
168 Shirley Avenue 4103
Telephone: (617) 773-7254

SYNAGOGUES
Independent
Temple B'nai Israel
1 Wave Avenue 02151
Telephone: (617) 284-8388

Orthodox
Ahavas Achim Anshei Sfard
89 Walnut Way 02151
Telephone: (617) 289-1026

Tifereth Israel
43 Nahant Avenue 02151
Telephone: (617) 284-9255

SALEM
SYNAGOGUES

Conservative
Temple Shalom
287 Lafayette Street 01970
Telephone: (508) 741-4880
Fax: (508) 741-4882
Email: www.templeshalomsalem.org

SHARON
HOTELS
Sharon Woods Inn
80 Brook Road 02067
Telephone: (781) 784-9401
Fax: (781) 784-5162
Email: kctova@yahoo.com

MIKVAOT
Chevrat Nashim
9 Dunbar Street 4103
Telephone: (781) 773-0693

RELIGIOUS ORGANISATIONS
Eruv Society
Telephone: (781) 997-7471

SYNAGOGUES
Conservative
Adath Sharon
18 Harding Street 02067
Telephone: (781) 784-2517

Temple Israel
125 Pond Street 02067
Telephone: (781) 784-3986
Fax: (781) 784-0719

Orthodox
Chabad Center
101 Worcester Road 02067
Telephone: (781) 784-8167

Young Israel of Sharon
100 Ames Street 02067
Telephone: (781) 784-6112
Fax: (781) 784-7758
Website: www.yisharon.org

Reform
Temple Sinai
25 Canton Street 02067
Telephone: (781) 784-6081
Fax: (781) 784-2616
Email: office@temple-sinai.com

SOMERVILLE
SYNAGOGUES
Independent
B'nai B'rith of Somerville
201 Central Street 02145
Telephone: (617) 625-0333
Email: tbb@templebnaibrith.org
Website: www.templebnaibrith.org

SPRINGFIELD
COMMUNITY ORGANISATIONS
Jewish Community Center
1160 Dickinson Street 02607
Email: blev@springfieldjcc.org
Website: www.springfieldjcc.org

GROCERIES
Waldbaum's Food Mart
355 Belmont Avenue 2368
Telephone: (413) 961-4929

RESTAURANTS
Vi's Coffee Shoppe
Jewish Community Center, 1160 Dickinson Street
01108
Telephone: (413) 739-4715
Fax: (413) 739-4747
Email: agoldsmith@springfieldjcc.org

SYNAGOGUES
Orthodox
Congregation Kodimoh
124 Sumner Avenue, Springfield 01108
Telephone: (413) 781-0171
Fax: (413) 737-8002
Email: kodimohÕTheSpa.com

Kesser Israel
19 Oakland Street 01108
Telephone: (413) 732-8492

Reform
Temple Sinai
1100 Dickinson Street 01108
Telephone: (413) 736-3619

STOUGHTON
BAKERIES
Ruth's Bake Shop
987 Central Street 02072
Telephone: (781) 344-8993
Supervision: Vaad Harabonim of Massachusetts

SYNAGOGUES
Conservative
Adhavath Torah Congregation
1179 Central Street 02072
Telephone: (781) 344-8733
Fax: (781) 344-4315

SUDBURY
SYNAGOGUES
Independent
Congregation B'nai Torah
225 Boston Post Road (Rt. 20), PO Box 273,
Sudbury MA 01776
Telephone: (978) 443-2082

Reform
Congregation Beth El
105 Hudson Road 01776
Telephone: (978) 443-9622
Fax: (978) 443-9629
Email: secretary@bethelsudbury.org
Website: www.bethelsudbury.org

SWAMPSCOTT
SYNAGOGUES
Conservative
Beth El
55 Atlantic Avenue 01907
Telephone: (617) 599-8005
Fax: (617) 599-1860

Temple Israel
837 Humphrey Street 01907
Telephone: (617) 595-6635
Fax: (617) 595-0033
Website: www.templeisraelswampscott.org

VINEYARD HAVEN
SYNAGOGUES
Reform
Martha's Vineyard Hebrew Center
Center Street 02568
Telephone: (508) 693-0745

WAKEFIELD
SYNAGOGUES
Conservative
Temple Emanuel
120 Chestnut Street 01880
Telephone: (781) 245-1886
Website: www.geocities.com/temple_emanuel

WALTHAM
SYNAGOGUES
American Jewish Historical Society (Brandies University Campus)
2 Thornton Road 02154
Telephone: (617) 891-8110
Fax: (617) 899-9208

Conservative
Beth Israel
25 Harvard Street 02154
Telephone: (617) 894-5146

WAYLAND
SYNAGOGUES
Reform
Temple shir Tikva
141 Boston Post Road 01778
Telephone: (508) 358-5312

WELLESLEY HILLS
Beth Elohim
10 Bethel Road 02181
Telephone: (617) 235-8419

WEST ROXBURY
SYNAGOGUES
Reconstructionist
Hillel B'nai Torah
120 Corey St., W. Roxbury 02132
Telephone: (617) 323-0486
Fax: (617) 327-8338
Email: office@templehbt.org
Website: www.templehbt.org
Supervision: www.templehbt.org
Central organisation: Reconstructionist (JRF)

WESTBOROUGH
SYNAGOGUES
Reform
Congregation B'nai Shalom
117 E. Main street, PO Box 1019 01581-6019
Telephone: (508) 366-7191

WESTWOOD
Beth David
40 Pond Street 02090
Telephone: (617) 769-5270

WINCHESTER
Temple Shir Tikvah
PO Box 373 01890
Telephone: (617) 792-1188

WINTHROP
SYNAGOGUES
Conservative
Tifereth Israel
93 Veterans Road 02152
Telephone: (617) 846-1390

Orthodox
Tifereth Abraham
283 Shirley Street 02152
Telephone: (617) 846-5063

WORCESTER
COMMUNITY ORGANISATIONS
Jewish Community Centre of Worcester
633 Salisbury Street
Telephone: (508) 756-7109

Jewish Federation
633 Salisbury Street 2159
Telephone: (508) 558-6522

CONTACT INFORMATION
Agudath Israel of America Hachnosas Orchim Committee
69 S. Flagg Street 01602
Telephone: (508) 754-3681
Mrs Reuven Fischer

Rabbi Hershel Fogelman
22 Newton Avenue 2138
Telephone: (508) 495-4696
Fax: (508) 864-1637
Email: linda@hillel.harvard.edu

MIKVAOT
Mikva
Huntley Street 2151

SYNAGOGUES
Conservative
Beth Israel
15 Jamesbury drive
Telephone: (508) 756-6204
Website: www.bethisraelworc.org

Orthodox
Young Israel of Worcester
889 Pleasant Street 01602
Telephone: (508) 754-3681

Reform
Temple Emanuel
280 May Street
Telephone: (508) 755-1257
Website: www.temple-emanuel.org

Temple Sinai
661 Salisbury Street
Telephone: (508) 755-2519

Michigan
ANN ARBOR
COMMUNITY ORGANISATIONS
Jewish Federation of Washtenaw County
2939 Birch Hollow drive 2135
Telephone: (734) 6770100
Fax: (734) 677-0109
Email: info@jewishannarbor.org
Website: www.jewishannarbor.org

MIKVAOT
Chabad House
715 Hill 48104
Telephone: (734) 995-3276

SYNAGOGUES
Orthodox
Ann Arbor Orthodox Minyan
1429 Hill Street 48104
Telephone: (734) 994-5822

BENTON HARBOR
SYNAGOGUES
Conservative
Temple B'nai Shalom
2050 Broadway 49022
Telephone: (212) 925-8021

BLOOMFIELD HILLS
COMMUNITY ORGANISATIONS
Jewish Federation of Metr. Detroit
Telegraph Road, PO Box 2030 48303-2030
Telephone: (248) 642-4260
Website: www.thisisfederation.org

DETROIT
GROCERIES
One Stop Kosher
Greenfield Road, North of Ten Mile Road
Telephone: (313) 569-5000

KASHRUT INFORMATION
Council of Orthodox Rabbis of Greater Detroit
16947 W. Ten Mile Road, Southfield 1602
Telephone: (313) 755-1257

MEDIA
Newspapers
Jewish News
Franklin Road, Southfield 1970
Telephone: (313) 745-4222
Fax: (313) 741-7507
Email: mail@jfns.org

MIKVAOT
Mikvah Israel
15116 W. Ten Mile Road, Oak Park 48237
Telephone: (313) 967-5402
Fax: (313) 967-5403

ORGANISATIONS
Machon L'torah (The Jewish Network of Michigan)
W. Ten Mile Road 1851
Telephone: (313) 459-9400

RELIGIOUS ORGANISATIONS
Council of Orthodox Rabbis of Detroit (Vaad Harabonim)
16947 W. Ten Mile Road, Southfield 2108
Telephone: (313) 367-9100
Fax: (313) 367-9310
Email: thejewishadvocate@thejewishadvocate.com

Jewish Community Center of Metr. Detroit
6600 W. Maple Road, W. Bloomfield 2111
Telephone: (313) 426-2139
Fax: (313) 426-6268

RESTAURANTS
Dairy
Jerusalem Pizza
26025 Greenfield, Southfield 48034
Telephone: (313) 552-0088
Fax: (313) 552-0087

Meat
Unique Kosher
25270 Greenfield, Southfield
Telephone: (313) 967-1161

EAST LANSING
SYNAGOGUES
Conservative & Reform
Shaarey Zedek
1924 Coolidge Road 48823

FLINT
COMMUNITY ORGANISATIONS
Flint Jewish Federation
619 Wallenberg Street 1201
Telephone: (810) 442-4360

SYNAGOGUES
Conservative
Congregation Beth Israel
5240 Calkins Road 48532
Telephone: (810) 732-6310
Fax: (810) 732-6314
Email: cbiflint@tir.com
Website: www.uscj.org/michigan/flint/

Orthodox
Chabad House
5385 Calkins 48532
Telephone: (810) 230-0770

Reform
Temple Beth El
501 S. Ballenger Highway 48532
Telephone: (810) 232-3138

GRAND RAPIDS
SYNAGOGUES
Conservative
Congregation Ahavas Israel
2727 Michigan Street N.E. 49506
Telephone: (616) 949-2840
Fax: (616) 949-6929
Email: office@ahavasisrael.org
Website: www.ahavasisraelgr.org

Orthodox
Chabad House of Western Michigan
2615 Michigan Street N.E. 49506
Telephone: (616) 957-0770
Email: RABBIYYW@CHABADWM.COM
Website: WWW.CHABADWM.COM

Reform
Temple Emanuel
1715 E. Fulton Street 49503
Telephone: (616) 459-5976

JACKSON
Temple Beth Israel
801 W. Michigan Avenue 49202
Telephone: (517) 784-3862

KALAMAZOO
SYNAGOGUES
Conservative
Congregation of Moses
2501 Stadium Drive 49008
Telephone: (616) 342-5463

LANSING
SYNAGOGUES
Reconstructionist
Kehillat Israel
2014 Forest Road 48910-3711
Telephone: (517) 882-0049
Fax: (517) 882-9270
Email: kilori@msu.edu
Website: www.kehillatisrael.net
Supervision: Rabbi Michael Zimmerman

SAGINAW
SYNAGOGUES
Conservative
Temple B'nai Israel
1424 S. Washington Avenue 48601
Telephone: (517) 753-5230

Reform
Congregation Beth El
100 S. Washington Avenue 48607
Telephone: (517) 754-5171

SOUTH HAVEN
SYNAGOGUES
Orthodox
First Hebrew Congregation
249 Broadway 49090
Telephone: (616) 637-1603

SOUTHFIELD
Young Israel of Southfield
27705 Lahser Road 48034
Telephone: (248) 358-0154
Fax: (248) 358-0154
Email: rabg@aol.com

WEST BLOOMFIELD
MUSEUMS
Holocaust Memorial Center
28123 Orchard Lake Road, Framington Hills, MI
48334-3738
Telephone: (248) 553-2400
Fax: (248) 553-2433

Email: info@holocaustcenter,org
Website: www.holocaustcenter.org
Notes: First free-standing holocaust museum in America.
Consists of three-part museum: Museum of European
Jewish Heritage Holocaust Museum.

SYNAGOGUES
Orthodox
Young Israel of West Bloomfield
6111 West Maple Road, Suite 408 48322
Telephone: (248) 661-4182

Minnesota

DULUTH
COMMUNITY ORGANISATIONS
Jewish Federation & Com. Council
1602 E. 2nd Street 1108
Telephone: (218) 737-4313

SYNAGOGUES
Conservative & Reform
Temple Israel
1602 E. 2nd Street 55812
Telephone: (218) 724-88

Orthodox
Adas Israel
302 E. Third Street 55802
Telephone: (218) 722-6459

MINNEAPOLIS
COMMUNITY ORGANISATIONS
Sabes Jewish Community Center
4330 Cedar Lake Rd. S. 1108
Telephone: (612) 739-4715
Fax: (612) 739-4747

GROCERIES
Fishman's Kosher Market
4100 Minnetonka Blvd. St Louis Park 55416
Telephone: (612) 926-5611

MIKVAOT
Knesseth Israel
4330 W. 28th Street. St Louis Park 1108
Telephone: (612) 732-3866

RESTAURANTS
Dairy
Calypso Coffee Co.
3238 W. Lake St. 55416

SYNAGOGUES
Orthodox
Congregation Bais Yisroel
4221 Sunset Blvd. 55416
Telephone: (612) 924-0654
Fax: (612) 926-2936
Email: BaisLine@mninter.net
Website: www.baisyisroel.org

ROCHESTER
HOME HOSPITALITY
Lubavitch Bais Chaya Moussia Hospitality Center
730 2nd Street S.W. 1106
Telephone: (716) 567-1607

SYNAGOGUES
Reform
B'nai Israel Synagogue
621 SW 2nd Street 55902
Telephone: (716) 288-5825
Email: bnaisrael@aol.com

ST LOUIS PARK
SYNAGOGUES
Orthodox
Knesseth Israel Congregation
4330 W. 28th Street , 55416
Telephone: (952) 920-2183
Fax: (952) 920-2184
Mobile Phone: 952 2509376
Email: rabbi@kenessethisrael.org
Website: www.kenessethisrael.org

ST PAUL
GROCERIES
L'Chaim
655 Snelling Avenue 1002
Telephone: (612) 256-0160
Fax: (612) 256-1588
Email: JCA.info@verizon.net
Website: www.j-c-a.org

RESTAURANTS
Dairy
Old City Cafe
1571 Grand Avenue
Telephone: (612) 291-6240

Mississippi

GREENVILLE
SYNAGOGUES
Reform
Hebrew Union Congregation
504 Main Street 38701
Telephone: (662) 332-4153

GREENWOOD
SYNAGOGUES
Orthodox
Ahavath Rayim
Market & George Streets, PO Box 1235 38935-1235
Telephone: (662) 453-7537

JACKSON
SYNAGOGUES
Reform
Congregation Beth Israel
5315 Old Canton Road 39211
Telephone: (517) 956-6215
Email: bic5315@mindspring.com

NATCHEZ
B'nai Israel
Washigton & S. Commerce Streets, PO Box 2081
39120

TUPELO
SYNAGOGUES
Conservative
Tupelo Synagogue
Marshall & Hamlin Streets 38801
Telephone: (601) 842-9169

Missouri

JEFFERSON CITY
SYNAGOGUES
Reform
Temple Beth El
238 East High Street 65101
Telephone: (573) 635-8727

KANSAS CITY
RESTAURANTS
Sensations
1148 W. 103 Street
Telephone: (816) 424-0191

SYNAGOGUES
Conservative
Congregation Beth Shalom
9400 Wornall Road 64114
Telephone: (816) 361-2990
Fax: (816) 361-4495

Reform
The New Reform Temple
7100 Main 64114
Telephone: (816) 523-7809
Fax: (816) 523-2454
Email: nrt7100@aol.com

ST JOSEPH
SYNAGOGUES
Conservative
Temple B'nai Sholem
615 S. 10th Street 64501
Telephone: (816) 279-2378
Fax: (816) 361-4495

ST LOUIS
BAKERIES
Schnuck's Nancy Ann Bakery
Olive & Mason
Telephone: (314) 569-0727
Fax: (314) 569-1723

BUTCHERS
Diamant's Kosher Meat Market
618 North & South Road
Telephone: (314) 712-9624

Simon Kohn's Kosher Meat & Deli
10405 Old Olive Street, St Louis, MO 63141
Telephone: (314) 569-0727
Website: http://www.kohnskosher.com

Sol's Kosher Meat Mart
8627 Olive Street
Telephone: (314) 721-9624

COMMUNITY ORGANISATIONS
Jewish Federation of St Louis
12 Millstone Campus Drive, St Louis, Missouri
63146
Telephone: (314) 432-0020
Fax: (314) 432-1277
Email: jfedstl@jfedstl.org
Website: www.jewishinstlouis.org
Supervision: Orthodox Rabbinic Council of Greater Boston.
Founded in 1901, Jewish Federation is the central fundraising and planning organisation for the 60,000 member St Louis Jewish Community. The Federation supports 48 local, national and international human and social service organisations.

LIBRARIES
The Brodsky Jewish Community Library
12 Millstone Campus Drive
Telephone: (314) 734-9810
Email: brodsky-library@jfedstl.org
Website: www.brodskylibrary.org

MIKVAOT
Mikva
4 Millstone Campus
Telephone: (314) 569-2770 ext.14
Fax: (314) 569-2774

MUSEUMS
Holocaust Museum and Learning Center
12 Milestone Campus Drive
Telephone: (314) 432-0020
Fax: (314) 432-1277
Email: jcavender@jfedstl.com
Website: www.hmlc.org

RELIGIOUS ORGANISATIONS
The Vaad Hoeir (United Orthodox Jewish community of St Louis)
4 Millstone Campus
Telephone: (314) 970-2008
Fax: (314) 569-2774
Email: avieovkosher.org
Website: www.oukosher.org

RESTAURANTS
Meat
Diamant's
618 North & South Rd.
Telephone: (314) 291-6050

Simon Kohn's
10405 Old Oolive Street, St Louis , MO 63141
Telephone: (314) 560-0727
Website: http://www.kohnskosher.com

SYNAGOGUES
Young Israel of St Louis
8101 Delmar Blvd 63130
Telephone: (314) 727 1880
Fax: (314) 727-2177
Email: yi-stlAjuno.com

Montana
BILLINGS
SYNAGOGUES
Reform
Congregation Beth Aaron
1148 N. Broadway 59101
Telephone: (406) 248-6412

GREAT FALLS
Aitz Chaim
PO Box 59406-6192, 1015 1st Avenue North, Suite 304 59401
Telephone: (406) 468-2073 and 216-5071
Fax: (406) 761-3601
Email: aaron@weissman.com aitzchaim@national-general.com
Website: http://urj.org/mt/aitzchaim/

MISSOULA
SYNAGOGUES
Har Shalom
PO Box 7581 59807
Telephone: (406) 549-9595

Email: toba@bigsky.net
Website: www.har-shalom.org

Nebraska
LINCOLN
SYNAGOGUES
Conservative
Congregation Tifereth Israel
3219 Sheridan Blvd. 68502
Telephone: (402) 423-8569
Fax: (402) 423-0178

Reform
South Street Temple B'nai Jeshurum
20th & South Streets 68502
Telephone: (402) 423-8004

OMAHA
COMMUNITY ORGANISATIONS
Jewish Federation of Omaha
333 S. 132nd Street
Telephone: (402) 993-9977

MIKVAOT
Com. Mikva
323 S. 132nd Street
Telephone: (402) 334-8200
Fax: (402) 334-1330
Email: jkatzman@jewishomaha.org
Website: www.jewishomaha.org
Central organisation: Jewish Federation of Omaha

SYNAGOGUES
Conservative
Beth El Synagogue
14506 California Street 68154
Telephone: (402) 492-8550
Fax: (402) 492-8520
Email: exec@bethel-omaha.org
Website: www.bethel-omaha.org

Orthodox
Beth Israel
1502 N. 52nd Street 68104
Telephone: (402) 556-6288

Beth Israel Synagogue
12604 Pacific Street, Omaha, NE 68104
Telephone: (402) 556-6288
Email: bethisrael@novia.net

Reform
Temple Israel
7023 Cass Street 68132
Telephone: (402) 556-6536

Nevada
LAS VEGAS
DELICATESSEN
Casba Glatt Kosher
2845 Las Vegas Blvd.
Telephone: (702) 791-3344

Rafi's Place
6135 West Sahara 89102
Telephone: (702) 253-0033

Sara's Place
4972 S. Maryland

MIKVAOT
1260 S. Arville
Telephone: (702) 259-0770 ext 8

RESTAURANTS
Meat
Haifa Restaurant
855 E. Twain
Telephone: (702) 791-1956
Fax: (702) 791-2966

Las Vegas Kosher Deli
3317 L.V. Blvd S.
Telephone: (702) 892-9080

Shalom Hunan
4850 W. Flamingo Road
Telephone: (702) 871-3262
Fax: (702) 871-3083
Email: yosstheboss@earthlink.net
Supervision: Chabad of southern Nevada

SYNAGOGUES
Conservative
Temple Emanu-El
4925 South Torrey Pines Drive 89118
Telephone: (702) 254-3270

Orthodox
Chabad of Southern Nevada
1261 S. Arville
Telephone: (702) 877-4700
Email: chabadlv@aol.com
Website: www.chabadlv.org

Congregation Or-Bamidbar
2991 Emerson Av.
Telephone: (702) 369-1175

Young Israel of Las Vegas
9590 West Sahara 89117
Telephone: (702) 360-8909
Fax: (702) 360-9627; Wyne Family 360-8908
Email: ywyne@aish.com
Website: www.aish.combranches/las_vegas

Reform
Adat Ari El
4675 W Flamingo Road #2 89103
Telephone: (702) 221-1230
Fax: (702) 221-1385
Email: info@adatariel.com
Affiliated with Union Reform Judaism

Congregation Ner Tamid
2761 Emerson Av.
Telephone: (702) 733-6292
Fax: (702) 733-8553
Email: info@lvnertamid.org
Website: www.lvnertamid.org

Temple Beth Am
9001 Hillpointe Road
Telephone: (702) 254-5110
Fax: (702) 254-0997

Temple Bett Emet
St. Andrew Lutheran Church , 8901 Del Webb Blvd.,
Sun City
Telephone: (702) 243-5781

Traditional
Chabad of Summerlin
2620 Regatta Dr. Suite 117
Telephone: (702) 259-0770
Fax: (702) 242-4318

RENO
SYNAGOGUES
Reform
Temple Sinai
3405 Gulling Road 89503
Telephone: (775) 747-5508
Fax: (775) 747-1911
Email: temple.sinai@pyramid.net
Website: www.templesinai-reno.com

New Hampshire
BETHLEHEM
HOTELS
Arlington Hotel
Telephone: (603) 869-3353

MIKVAOT
Machzikei Hadas
Lewis Hill Road 03574
Telephone: (603) 869-3336

SYNAGOGUES
Conservative
Bethlehem Hebrew Congregation
Strawberry Hill 03574
Telephone: (603) 869-5465

Orthodox
Machzikei Hadas
Lewis Hill Road 03574
Telephone: (603) 869-3336

CONCORD
SYNAGOGUES
Reform
Temple Beth Jacob
67 Broadway 03301
Telephone: (603) 228-8581
Email: tbjconcord@aol.com

MANCHESTER
COMMUNITY ORGANISATIONS
Jewish Federation of Greater Manchester
698 Beech Street 03104
Telephone: (603) 627-7679
Fax: (603) 627-7963

MEDIA
Newspapers
The Reporter
698 Beech Street 03104
Telephone: (603) 627-7679
Fax: (603) 627-7963

SYNAGOGUES
Orthodox
Lubavitch
7 Camelot Drive 03104
Telephone: (603) 647-0204

Reform
Adath Yeshurun
152 Prospect Street 03104
Telephone: (603) 669-5650

PORTSMOUTH
SYNAGOGUES
Conservative
Temple Israel
200 State Street 03801
Telephone: (603) 436-5301

New Jersey
ABERDEEN
SYNAGOGUES
Orthodox
Bet Tefilah
479 Lloyd Road 07747
Telephone: (732) 583-6262

ATLANTIC CITY
RESTAURANTS
Meat
Jerusalem
6410 Ventnor Ave, Ventnor 08406
Telephone: (609) 822-2266
Supervision: Rabbi Abraham Spacirer

SYNAGOGUES
Conservative
Beth El
500 N. Jerome Ave, Margate 08406
Fax: (609) 823-1810

Beth Judah
700 N Swarthmore Avenue, Ventor 08406
Telephone: (609) 822-7116
Fax: (609) 822-4654
Email: congbethjudah@aol.com

Chelsea Hebrew Congregation
4001 Atlantic Av 08401
Telephone: (609) 345-0825

Community Synagogue
Maryland & Pacific Avs 08401
Telephone: (609) 345-3282

Orthodox
Rodef Shalom
3833 Atlantic Av 08401
Telephone: (609) 345-4580

Reform
Beth Israel
2501 Shore Rd, Northfield 08225
Telephone: (609) 641-3600

Temple Emeth Synagogue
8501 Ventnor Av, Margate 08402
Telephone: (609) 822-4343

BAYONNE
COMMUNITY ORGANISATIONS
Jewish Community Centre
1050 Kennedy Blv 07002
Telephone: (201) 436-6900

SYNAGOGUES
Conservative
Temple Emanuel
735 Kennedy Blvd 07002
Telephone: (201) 436-4499

Orthodox
Ohab Sholom
1016-1022 Ave. C 07002

Ohav Zedek
912 Ave. C 07002
Telephone: (201) 437-1488

Uptown Synagogue
49th St. & Ave. C 07002

Reform
Temple Beth Am
111 Ave. B 07002
Telephone: (201) 858-9052

BELMAR
SYNAGOGUES

Orthodox
Sons of Israel Congregation
PO Box 298 07719
Telephone: (973) 681-3200

BERGENFIELD
BUTCHERS
Glatt World
89 Newbridge Road
Telephone: (201) 439-9675
Fax: (201) 439-0342
Supervision: RCBC

DELICATESSEN
Foster Village Kosher Delicatessen & Catering
469 S. Washington Avenue 07621
Telephone: (201) 384-7100
Fax: (201) 384-0303
Supervision: Quality Kashrut Supervisory Service

SYNAGOGUES
Conservative
Congregation Beth Israel of Northern Valley
169 N. Washington Avenue 07621
Telephone: (201) 384-3911
Fax: (201) 384-3738
Email: cbitemple@juno.com
Website: www.uscj.org/njersey/bergenfield

BRADLEY BEACH
SYNAGOGUES
Orthodox
Congregation Agudath Achim
301 McCabe Avenue 07720
Telephone: (973) 774-2495

BRIDGETON
SYNAGOGUES
Conservative
Congregation Beth Abraham
330 Fayette Street 08302

BURLINGTON
B'nai Israel
212 High Street
Telephone: (201) 858-9052

CHERRY HILL
BUTCHERS
Cherry Hill Kosher Market
907 W. Marlton Pike 08002
Telephone: (856) 428-6663
Fax: (856) 216-0752

DELICATESSEN
Leo's Deli
J.C.C. 1301 Springdale Road
Telephone: (856) 424-4444 Ext 158
Supervision: Tri-County Vaad

MIKVAOT
Sons of Israel
720 Cooper Landing Road 08002
Telephone: (856) 667-3515
Email: Tasha.flecha@verizon.net
Website: www.sonsisrael.net

RESTAURANTS
Meat
Maxim's Restaurant
404 Route 70
Telephone: (856) 428-5045

SYNAGOGUES
Conservative
Beth El
2901 W. Chapel Avenue 08002
Telephone: (856) 667-1300

Beth Shalom
1901 Kresson Road 08003
Telephone: (856) 751-6663

Congregation Beth Tikva
115 Evesboro-Medford Road, Marlton,

Orthodox
Congregation Sons of Israel
720 Cooper Landing Road 08002
Telephone: (856) 667-9700
Fax: (856) 667-9765
Email: Tasha.flecha@verizon.net

Reform
Congregation M'kor Shalom
850 Evesham Road
Telephone: (856) 424-4220
Fax: (856) 424-2890

Temple Emmanuel
1101 Springdale Road

CINNAMINSON

SYNAGOGUES

Conservative

Temple Sinai

2101 New Albany Road 08077
Telephone: (609) 829-0658
Fax: (609) 829-0310
Email: tsoffice@snip.net
Website: www.uscj.org/njersey/cinnaminson

CLARK

Temple Beth O'r

111 Valley Road 07066
Telephone: (732) 381-8403
Fax: (732) 381-8403

CLIFTON

COMMUNITY ORGANISATIONS

Jewish Federation of Greater Clifton-Passaic

199 Scoles Avenue 07012
Telephone: (973) 777-7031
Fax: (973) 777-6701
Email: planned.giving@verizon.net

MEDIA

Newspaper

Jewish Community News

199 Scoles Avenue 07012

RESTAURANTS

Jerusalem II Pizza

224 Brook Avenue 07055
Telephone: (973) 778-0960

SYNAGOGUES

Conservative

Clifton Jewish Center

18 Delaware Street 07011
Telephone: (973) 772-3131

Reform

Beth Shalom

733 Passaic 07012
Telephone: (973) 773-0355

COLONIA

SYNAGOGUES

Conservative

Ohev Shalom

220 Temple Way 07067
Telephone: (908) 388-7222

CRANBURY

Jewish Congregation of Concordia

c/o Club House 08512
Telephone: (609) 655-8136

CRANFORD

CONTACT INFORMATION

Rabbi Hoffberg

Telephone: (201) 276-9231

SYNAGOGUES

Conservative

Temple Beth El Mekor Chayim

338 Walnut Avenue 07016
Telephone: (201) 276-9231
Fax: (201) 276-6570
Website: www.uscj.org/njersey,cranfotb

DEAL

RESTAURANTS

Pizzerias

Jerusalem II Pizza

106 Norwood Avenue 07723
Telephone: (732) 531-7936

SYNAGOGUES

Orthodox

Ohel Yaacob Congregation

6 Ocean Avenue, PO Box 225 07723
Telephone: (732) 531-0217/531-2405

Synagogue

128 Norwood Avenue 07723
Telephone: (732) 531-3200

EAST BRUNSWICK

BUTCHERS

East Brunswick Kosher Meats

1020 State Highway 18 08816
Telephone: (908) 257-0007

SYNAGOGUES

Conservative

East Brunswick Jewish Center

511 Ryders Lane 08816
Telephone: (908) 257-7070

Reform

Temple B'nai Shalom

Fern & Old Stage Road, PO Box 957 08816
Telephone: (908) 732-251-4300

EDISON

COMMUNITY ORGANISATIONS

Jewish Community Center of Middlesex County

1775 Oak Tree Road 8820
Telephone: (732) 494-3232
Fax: (732) 548-2850

SYNAGOGUES
Conservative
Beth El
91 Jefferson Blvd 08817
Telephone: (732) 985-7272

ELIZABETH
RESTAURANTS
Dairy
Dunkin' Donuts
186 Elmora Avenue 07202

Meat
New Kosher Special
163 Elmora Avenue 07202
Telephone: (908) 353-1818

Pizzerias
Jerusalem Restaurant
150 Elmora Avenue 07202
Telephone: (908) 289-4810

SYNAGOGUES
Orthodox
Adath Israel
1391 North Avenue 07208
Telephone: (908) 355-4850
Fax: (908) 289-5245
Website: www.theJEC.org

Bais Yitzchak
153 Bellevue Street 07202
Telephone: (908) 354-4789

ELMWOOD PARK
COMMUNITY ORGANISATIONS
Elmwood Park Jewish Center
100 Gilbert Avenue
Telephone: (201) 797-7320/797-9749

ENGLEWOOD
GROCERIES
Kosher By the Case & Less
255 Van Norstrand Avenue 07631
Telephone: (201) 568-2281
Fax: (201) 568-5681
Supervision: RCBC

MIKVAOT
Mikva
89 Huguenot Avenue
Telephone: (201) 567-1143

RESTAURANTS
Meat
Sol & Sol
34 E Palisade Avenue 07631
Telephone: (201) 541-6880
Fax: (201) 541-6883
Supervision: Kashrut Committee of Bergen County

SYNAGOGUES
Conservative
Temple Emanu-el
147 Tenafly Road 07631
Telephone: (201) 567-1300
Fax: (201) 569-7580

Orthodox
Ahavath Torah
240 Broad Avenue, NJ 07631
Telephone: (201) 568-1315
Fax: (201) 568-2991
Email: egorlyn@ahavathtorah.org
Website: www.ahavathtorah.org

Shomrei Emunah
89 Huguenot Avenue 07631
Telephone: (201) 567-9420

FAIR LAWN
BAKERIES
New Royal Bakery
19-09 Fair Lawn Avenue 07410
Telephone: (201) 796-6565
Fax: (201) 796-8501
Supervision: RCBC

BUTCHERS
Food Showcase
24-28 Fair Lawn Avenue 07410
Telephone: (201) 475-0077
Fax: (201) 794-6728
Superviosion: RCBC

RESTAURANTS
Dairy
J.C. Pizza of Fairlawn
14-20 Plaza Road 07410
Telephone: (201) 703-0801
Supervision: RCBC

SYNAGOGUES
Orthodox
Bris Arushon
22-24 Fairlawn Avenue 07410
Telephone: (201) 791-7200

FORT LEE
BUTCHERS
Blue Ribbon Self-Service Kosher Meat Market
1363 Inwood Terrace 07024
Telephone: (201) 224-3220
Fax: (201) 224-7281
Email: koshercomida@msn.com

DELICATESSEN
Al's Kosher Deli
209 Main Street 07024
Telephone: (201) 461-3044
Fax: (201) 461-7188
Supervision: Quality Kashrut Supervisory Service

SYNAGOGUES
Conservative
Jewish Community Center of Fort Lee
1449 Anderson Avenue 07024
Telephone: (201) 947-1735
Fax: (201) 947-1530
Email: aschafer@jcc.org

Orthodox
Young Israel of Fort Lee
1610 Parker Avenue 07024
Telephone: (201) 592-1518
Fax: (201) 592-8414

FREEHOLD
RESTAURANTS
Fred and Murry's
Pond Road Shopping Center, Route 9 07728
Telephone: (732) 462-3343
Website: www.fredandmurrys.com

SYNAGOGUES
Orthodox
Agudath Achim/Freehold Jewish Center
Broad & Stokes Streets 07728
Telephone: (732) 462-0254
Fax: (732) 462-0217

HACKENSACK
COMMUNITY ORGANISATIONS
Jewish Federation of Community Services of Bergen County
170 State Street 07601

SYNAGOGUES
Conservative
Temple Beth El
280 Summit Avenue 07601
Telephone: (201) 342-2045

HADDONFIELD
BUTCHERS
Sarah's Kosher Kitchen
63 Ellis Road

HASBROUCK
SYNAGOGUES
Reform
Temple Beth Elohim
Bourlevard & Charlton Aves
Telephone: (201) 393-7707

HIGHLAND PARK
GROCERIES
Berkley Bakery
405 Raritan Avenue 08904
Telephone: (732) 220-1919

Kosher Catch
239 Raritan Avenue
Telephone: (732) 572-9052

MIKVAOT
Park Mikva
112 S. 1st Avenue 08904
Telephone: (732) 249-2411

SYNAGOGUES
Conservative
Highland Park Conservative Temple & Center
201 S. 3rd Avenue 08904
Telephone: (732) 545-6482
Fax: (732) 246-3100

Orthodox
Congregation Ahavas Achim
216 S. 1st Avenue
Telephone: (732) 247-0532
Fax: (732) 247-6739
Email: info@ahavasachim.org
Website: www.ahavasachim.org
Supervision: Rabbi Steven Miodownik

Congregation Etz Ahaim (Sephardi)
230 Denison Street NJ 08904
Telephone: (732) 247-3839
Fax: (732) 545-3191
Email: etzahaim@earthlink.net
Website: www.home.earthlink.net/~etzahaim

HILLSIDE
SYNAGOGUES
Conservative
Shomrei Torah Ohel Yosef Yitzchok
910 Salem Avenue 07205
Telephone: (908) 289-0770

Orthodox
Congregation Sinai Torath Chaim
1531 Maple Avenue 0705
Telephone: (908) 923-9500

JAMESBURG
SYNAGOGUES
Rossmoor Jewish Congregation Meeting Room
Telephone: (609) 655-0439

JERSEY CITY
SYNAGOGUES
Orthodox
Congregation Mount Sinai
128 Sherman Avenue 07307
Telephone: (201) 659-4267
Fax: (201) 659-4267
Email: congmtsinai@netzero.net
Website: www.mtsinai.net

LAKEWOOD
BAKERIES
Gelbsteins Bakery
415 Clifton Avenue 08701
Telephone: (732) 363-3636
Supervision: Orthodox

Lakewood Heimishe Bakeshop
225-2nd Street 08701
Telephone: (732) 905-9057
Supervision: Orthodox

BOOKSELLERS
Torah Treasures
254-2nd Street 08701
Telephone: (732) 901-1911
Fax: (732) 905-6482

BUTCHERS
Shloimy's Kosher World
23 E. County Line Road 08701
Telephone: (732) 363-3066

COMMUNITY ORGANISATIONS
Jewish Federation of Ocean County
301 Madison Avenue 08701
Telephone: (732) 363-0530
Fax: (732) 363-2097
Email: ocjf@optonline.net
Website: www.jewishoceancounty.org

KASHRUT INFORMATION
KCC - Cashrus Council of Lakewood
Telephone: (732) 901-1888

MIKVAOT
Congregation Mikvah Tahara
1101 Madison Avenue 08701
Telephone: (732) 370-1666

RESTAURANTS
Dairy
Bagel Nosh
380 Clifton Avenue 08701
Telephone: (732) 363-1115
Fax: (732) 363-5745
Meat

R & S Kosher Restaurant and Deli
416 Clifton Avenue 08701
Telephone: (732) 363-6688
Supervision: Kashrus supervision: Lakewood Satmar Dayan

Yum Mee Glatt
116 Clifton Avenue 08701
Telephone: (732) 886-9688

Euro Cut/LaBriute Meals
520 James Street, Unit 1C 08701
Telephone: (732) 905-1555
Fax: (732) 905-5636
Email: info@labruitemeals.com
Website: www.labruitemeals.com

Pizzeria
Pizza Plus
241 4th Street 08701
Telephone: (732) 367-0711
Supervision: Orthodox

SYNAGOGUES
Orthodox
Kol Shimson
323 Squamkum Road 08701
Telephone: (732) 901-6680

Lakewood Yeshiva
617 Private Way (Sixth Street) 08701
Telephone: (732) 367-1060

Sons of Israel
Madison Avenue & 6th Street 08701
Telephone: (732) 364-2800

THEATRE
Conservative
Ahavat Shalom
1075 Forest Avenue 08701
Telephone: (732) 363-5190
Fax: (732) 363-5225
Email: ahavat_shalom_nj@netzero.com
Website: www.uscj.org/njersey/lakewood

LAWRENCEVILLE
SYNAGOGUES
Orthodox
Young Israel of Lawrenceville
2556 Princeton Pike 08648
Telephone: (609) 883-8833
Website: www.yiol.com

LINDEN
SYNAGOGUES
Conservative
Mekor Chayim Suburban Jewish Center
Deerfield Road & Academy Terrace 07036
Telephone: (908) 925-2283

Orthodox
Congrgation Anshe Chesed
100 Orchard Terrace at St George Ave. 07036
Telephone: (908) 486-8616

LIVINGSTON
RESTAURANTS
Dairy
Jerusalem Restaurant
99-101 West Mt Pleasant Avenue 07039
Telephone: (973) 533-1424
Fax: (973) 533-9275
Supervision: Vaad Hakashrus of the Council of Orthodox
Rabbis Metrowest

Meat
Moshavi
515 S. Livingston Avenue 07039
Telephone: (973) 740-8777
Supervision: Vaad Hakashrus of the Council of Orthodox
Rabbis Metrowest

SYNAGOGUES
Conservative
Temple Beth Shalom
193 E. Mt Pleasant Avenue 07039
Telephone: (973) 992-3600

Independent
Temple B'Nai Abraham
300 East Northfield Road 07039
Telephone: (973) 994-2290
Fax: (973) 994-1838
Email: tbainfo@tbanj.org
Website: www.tbanj.org

Orthodox
Etz Chaim Synagogue
1 Lafayette Drive 07039
Telephone: (973) 597-1655

Synagogue of the Suburban Torah Center
85 W Mount Pleasant Avenue 07039
Telephone: (973) 994-2620/994-0122
Fax: (973) 535-3898
Email: admin@suburbantorah.org
Website: www.suburbantorah.org

SYNAGOGUES
Reform
Temple Emanu-el of West Essex
264 W. Northfield Road 07039
Telephone: (973) 992-5560

MAHWAH
Temple Beth Haverim
280 Remjo Valley Road
Telephone: (201) 512-1983

MAPLEWOOD
BOOKSELLERS
Skybook
1923 Springfield Avenue 07040
Telephone: (973) 763-4244/4245
Fax: (973) 763-1412

METUCHEN
SYNAGOGUES
Conservative
Neve Shalom
250 Grove Avenue 08840
Telephone: (732) 548-2238
Fax: (732) 548-2238
Email: neve.shalom@verizon.net
Website: www.neveshalom.net

MORRIS PLAINS
DELICATESSEN
Jonathan's Deli Restaurant
2900 Route 10 West 07950
Telephone: (973) 539-6010
Fax: (973) 539-6011

MORRISTOWN
KASHRUT INFORMATION
Rabbinical College of America
226 Sussex Avenue 07960
Telephone: (973) 267-9404
Fax: (973) 267-5208
Email: rca226@aol.com

MIKVAOT
Mikvah Bais Chana, Sarah Esther Rosenhaus
Mikvah Institute
93 Lake Road 07960
Telephone: (973) 292-3932

SYNAGOGUES
Conservative
Morristown Jewish Center
177 Speedwell Avenue 07960
Telephone: (973) 538-9292

Orthodox
Congregation Ahavath Yisrael
9 Cutler Street 07960
Telephone: (973) 267-4184
Fax: (973) 898-1711
Email: sofernj@aol.com

Congregation Levi Yitzchok
226 Sussex Avenue 07960
Telephone: (973) 984-6326

NEW BRUNSWICK
SYNAGOGUES
Conservative
Congrgation B'nai Tikvah
1001 Finnegans Lane 08902
Telephone: (732) 297-0696
Fax: (732) 297-2673
Email: office@bnaitikvah.org
Website: www.bnaitikvah.org

Orthodox
Chabad House Friends of Lubavitch
8 Sicard Street 08901
Telephone: (732) 828-9191

Congregation Poile Zedek
145 Neilson Street 08901
Telephone: (732) 545-6123
Email: admin@poilzedek.org
Website: www.poilezedek.org

Reform
Anshe Emeth Memorial Temple
222 Livingston Avenue 08901
Telephone: (732) 545-6484
Fax: (732) 745-7448
Email: temple@aemt.net
Website: www.aemt.net

OLD BRIDGE
SYNAGOGUES
Conservative
Ohav Shalom
3018 Bordertown Avenue 08859
Telephone: (201) 727-4334

PARAMUS
BUTCHERS
Harold's Self-Service Kosher Meat
67-A E. Ridgewood Avenue
Telephone: (201) 262-0030

COMMUNITY ORGANISATIONS
Jewish Center of Paramus
304 Midland Avenue
Telephone: (201) 262-7691

SYNAGOGUES
Conservative
Jewish Community Center of Paramus
E-304 Midland Avenue 07652
Telephone: (201) 262-7691
Fax: (201) 262-6516
Email: jccparam@mail.idt.net
Website: www.uscj.org/njersey/paramus

PARSIPANNY
DELICATESSEN
Arlington Kosher Deli, Restaurant & Caterers
Arlington Shopping Center, 744 Route 46W 07054
Telephone: (973) 335-9400

PASSAIC
B&Y Kosher Korner Inc.
200 Main Avenue 07055
Telephone: (973) 777-1120

SUPERMARKET
Kosher Konnection
200 Main Avenue 07055
Telephone: (973) 777-1120
Fax: (973) 777-4991

SYNAGOGUES
Orthodox
Young Israel of Passaic-Clifton
200 Brook Avenue
Telephone: (973) 778-7117

PATERSON
SYNAGOGUES
Conservative
Temple Emanuel
151 E. 33rd Street 07514
Telephone: (973) 684-5565

PERTH AMBOY
Beth Mordechai
224 High Street 08861
Telephone: (732) 442-2431

SYNAGOGUES
Orthodox
Shaarey Teflioh
15 Market Street 08861
Telephone: (732) 826-2977

PLAINFIELD
United Orthodox Synagogue
526 W. 7th Street 07063
Telephone: (908) 755-0043

SYNAGOGUES
Reform
Temple Sholom
815 W. 7th Street 07063
Telephone: (908) 756-6447

PRINCETON
SYNAGOGUES
Conservative
The Jewish Center of Princeton
435 Nassau Street 08540
Telephone: (609) 921-0100
Fax: (609) 921-7531
Email: info@the jewishcenter.org
Website: www.thejewishcenter.org

RAHWAY
Temple Beth Torah
1389 Bryant Street 07065
Telephone: (609) 576-8432

RANDOLPH
SYNAGOGUES
Orthodox
Mount Freedom Jewish Center
1209 Sussex Turnoike 07970
Telephone: (781) 895-2100

RIDGEWOOD
SYNAGOGUES
Conservative
Temple Israel
475 Grove Street
Telephone: (201) 444-9320

RIVER EDGE
SYNAGOGUES
Reform
Temple Sholom
385 Howland Avenue 07661
Telephone: (201) 489-2463
Fax: (201) 489-0775
Website: www.uahcweb.org/nj/tsholomre/

ROSELLE
MEDIA
Guide
Shalom Book
843 St Georges Avenue 07203
Telephone: (908) 298-8200
Fax: (908) 298-8220

RUMSON
SYNAGOGUES
Conservative
Congregation B'nai Israel
Hance & Ridge Roads 07760
Telephone: (908) 842-1800

SCOTCH PLAINS
COMMUNITY ORGANISATIONS
Jewish Federation of Central New Jersey
1391 Martine Avenue
Telephone: (908) 889-5335/351-5060

SYNAGOGUES
Conservative
Congregation Beth Israel
1920 Cliffwood Street 07076
Telephone: (908) 889-1830
Fax: (908) 889-5523

SHORT HILLS
SYNAGOGUES
Reform
B'Nai Jeshurun
1025 South Orange Avenue 07078
Telephone: (973) 379-1555
Fax: (973) 379-4345
Email: info@tbj.org
Website: www.tbj.org

SOMERSET
SYNAGOGUES
Conservative
Temple Beth El
1945 Amwell Road 08873
Telephone: (873-2325) 873-2325

SOUTH ORANGE
GROCERIES
Zayda's Super Value Meat Market & Deli
309 Irvington Avenue 07079
Telephone: (973) 762-1812

SYNAGOGUES
Conservative
Oheb Shalom Congregation
170 Scotland Road 07079
Telephone: (973) 762-7067

Reform
Temple Sharey Tefilo-Israel
432 Scotland Road 07079
Telephone: (973) 763-4116

SOUTH RIVER
COMMUNITY ORGANISATIONS
Jewish Federation of Greater Middlesex County
230 Old Bridge Turnpike 08882
Telephone: (732) 432-7711
Fax: (732) 432-0292
Email: info@jf-gmc.org
Website: www.jfgmc.org

SYNAGOGUES
Traditional
Congregation Anshe Emeth of South River
88 Main Street 08882
Telephone: (732) 257-4190
Fax: (732) 254-8819
Website: www.members.home.net/ebweiss

SPOTSWOOD
SYNAGOGUES
Reform
Monroe Township Jewish Center
11 Cornell Avenue 08884
Telephone: (201) 251-1119

TEANECK
BAKERIES
Butterflake Bake Shop
448 Cedar Lane 07666
Telephone: (201) 836-3516
Fax: (201) 836-3056
Supervision: RCBC

Gruenebaum Bakeries
477B Cedar Lane 07666
Telephone: (201) 839-3128

Korn's Bakery
1378 Quenn Anne Road 07666
Telephone: (201) 833-0114

Sammy's New York Bagels
1443 Queen Anne Road 07666
Telephone: (201) 837-0515
Fax: (201) 837-9733
Supervision: Kof-K

BOOKSELLERS
Zoldan's Judaica Center
406 Cedar Lane 07666
Telephone: (201) 907-0034

BUTCHERS
Glatt Express
1400 Queen Anne Road 07666
Telephone: (201) 837-8110
Fax: (201) 837-0084
Supervision: RCBC

DELICATESSEN
Kosher
Chinese
Chopstix
172 West Engleford Avenue 07666
Telephone: (201) 833-0200
Fax: (201) 833-8326
Supervision: RCBC

JUDAICA
Books
Judaica House
478 Cedar Lane 07666
Telephone: (201) 801-9001
Fax: (201) 801-9004
Email: judaica.house@verizon.net

MIKVAOT
Mikveh
1726 Windsor Road 07666
Telephone: (201) 837-8220

RESTAURANTS
Dairy
Jerusalem Pizza
496 Cedar Lane 07666
Telephone: (201) 836-2120
Fax: (201) 836-2261
Supervision: RCBC

Plaza Pizza & Restaurant
1431 Queen Anne Road 07666
Telephone: (201) 837-9500
Fax: (201) 836-2261
Supervision: RCBC

Shelly's
482 Cedar Lane
Telephone: (201) 692-0001
Fax: (201) 692-1890
Email: shellys@noahsark.net
Supervision: RCBC

Meat
Hunan Teaneck
515 Cedar Lane 07666
Telephone: (201) 692-0099
Fax: (201) 692-1907
Supervision: RCBC

Noah's Ark
493 Cedar Lane 07666
Telephone: (201) 692-1200
Fax: (201) 692-

SYNAGOGUES
Conservative
Congrtation Beth Shalom
354 Maitland Avenue 07666
Telephone: (201) 833-2620
Fax: (201) 833-2620
Email: bsteaneck@aol.com
Website: www.uscj.org/njersey/teaneckcbs

Jewish Center of Teaneck
70 Sterling Place 07666
Telephone: (201) 833-0515
Fax: (201) 833-0511
Email: execdir@aol.com
Website: www.jewishcenterofteaneck.org

Also with alternative;Orthodox Mechitza service, Shira
Hadasha service, Family service

Orthodox
Congregation Beth Aaron
950 Queen Anne Road 07666
Telephone: (201) 836-6210
Fax: (201) 836-0005
Email: mail@bethaaron.org
Website: www.bethaaron.org

Congregation Bnai Yeshurun
641 W. Englewood Avenue 07666
Telephone: (201) 836-8916
Fax: (201) 836-1888
Email: bnaiyeshurun@aol.com
Website: www.bnaiyeshurun.org

Rinat Yisrael
389 W. Englewood Avenue 07666
Telephone: (201) 837-2795
Email: office@rinat.org

Roemer Synagogue
Whittier School, W. Englewood Avenue 07666

Reform
Congregation Beth Am
1148 Converse Street 01106
Telephone: (201) 413-567-8665
Fax: (201) 410-567-2233
Email: rabbink@comcast.net
Website: www.lya.org

Temple Emeth
1666 Windsor Rd 07666
Telephone: (201) 833-1322
Fax: (201) 833-4831
Email: temple@emeth.org
Website: www.emeth.org

TENAFLY
Temple Sinai of Bergen County
1 Engle Street 07670
Telephone: (201) 568-3035
Fax: (201) 568-6095
Email: temsinai@idt.net
Website: www.uahc.org/congs.nj/nj009

TRENTON
COMMUNITY ORGANISATIONS
Jewish Federation of Mercer & Bucks Counties
999 Lower Ferry Road 08628
Telephone: (609) 883-5000

UNION
SYNAGOGUES
Conservative
Beth Shalom
2046 Vauxhall Road 07083
Telephone: (908) 686-6773

Temple Israel
2372 Morris Avenue 07083
Telephone: (908) 686-2120

VAUXHALL
RESTAURANTS
Meat
Mosaica
2933 Vauxhall Road
Telephone: 206-9911

VINELAND
COMMUNITY ORGANISATIONS
Jewish Federation of Cumberland County
1063 East Landis Avenue, Suite B 08360-3785
Telephone: (856) 696-4445
Fax: (856) 696-3428
Email: jfedcc@aol.com

SYNAGOGUES
Conservative
Beth Israel
1015 E. Park Avenue 08630
Telephone: (856) 691-0852

SYNAGOGUES
Orthodox
Ahavas Achim
618 Plum Street 08360
Telephone: (856) 691-2218

Synagogue
321 Grape Street 08360
Telephone: (856) 692-4232
Fax: (856) 691-4985

WARREN
SYNAGOGUES
Reform
Temple Har Shalom
104 Mount Horeb Road 07059-5529
Telephone: (732) 356-8777
Fax: (732) 356-0580

WASHINGTON TOWNSHIP
Temple Beth Or
56 Ridgewood Rd
Telephone: (201) 664-7422

WAYNE
COMMUNITY ORGANISATIONS
Jewish Federation of New Jersey
1 Pike Drive 07470
Telephone: (973) 595-0555

SYNAGOGUES
Conservative
Shomrei Torah
30 Hinchman Avenue 07470
Telephone: (973) 694-6274

Reform
Temple Beth Tikvah
950 Preakness Avenue 07470
Telephone: (973) 595-6565
Fax: (973) 595-8192

WEST CALDWELL
DELICATESSEN
David's Deco-Tessen
555 Passaic Avenue 07006
Telephone: (973) 808-3354
Fax: (973) 808-5806
Email: davidsdecotessen@aol.com
Supervision: Rabbi Herman Savitz (Conservative)

WEST NEW YORK
SYNAGOGUES
Orthodox
Congregation Shaare Zedek
5308 Palisade Avenue 07093
Telephone: (201) 867-6859

WEST ORANGE
GROCERIES
Gourmet Galaxy
659 Eagle Rock Avenue 07052
Telephone: (973) 736-0060
Supervision: Vaad Hakashrus of the Council of Orthodox
Rabbis Metrowest

JUDAICA
Lubavitch Center of Essex County
456 Pleasant Valley Way 07052
Telephone: (973) 731-0770
Fax: (973) 731-6821

RESTAURANTS
Meat
Eden Wok
478 Pleasant Valley Way 07052
Telephone: (973) 243-0115
Fax: (973) 243-1332
Supervision: Vaad Hakashrus of the Council of Orthodox
Rabbis Metrowest

Pleasantdale Kosher Meat
470 Pleasant Valley Way 07052
Telephone: (973) 731-3216

SYNAGOGUES
Conservative
B'Nai Shalom
300 Pleasant Valley Way 07052
Telephone: (973) 731-0160
Fax: (973) 731-1160
Email: bnai@aol.com

Orthodox
Congregation Ahawas Achim B'nai Jacob and David
700 Pleasant Valley Way 07052
Telephone: (973) 736-1407
Fax: (973) 736-8006
Email: shul.aabjdmail@verizon.com

WESTFIELD
SYNAGOGUES
Reform
Temple Emanu-El
756 E. Broad Street 07090
Telephone: (908) 232-6770
Fax: (908) 233-3959
Email: cshane@tewnj.org
Website: www.westfieldnj.com/temple

WHIPPANY
COMMUNITY ORGANISATIONS
United Jewish Federation of Metrowest
901 Route 10 07981
Telephone: (973) 884-4800
Fax: (973) 884-7361

MEDIA
Newspaper
The New Jersey Jewish News
901 Route 10 07981
Telephone: (973) 887-8500
Fax: (973) 887-4152
Email: njjewnews@aol.com

WILLINGBORO
SYNAGOGUES
Reform
Adath Emanu-El
299 John F. Kennedy Way 08046
Telephone: (609) 871-1736

WOODBRIDGE
SYNAGOGUES
Conservative
Adath Israel
424 Amboy Avenue 07095
Telephone: (203) 634-9601
Fax: (203) 634-1593
Email: lina1330@bellatlantic.net

WYCKOFF
SYNAGOGUES
Reform
Temple Beth Rishon
585 Russell Ave
Telephone: (201) 891-4466
Fax: (201) 891-0508
Email: bethrish@bellatlantic.net

New Mexico
ALBUQUERQUE
COMMUNITY ORGANISATIONS
Jewish Federation of Greater Albuquerque
5520 Wyoming Blvd N.E 87109
Telephone: (505) 821-3214
Fax: (505) 821-3351
Email: reception@jewishnewmexico.org
Website: www.jewishnewmexico.org

KASHRUT INFORMATION
JFGA
Telephone: (505) 821-3214

MEDIA
Newspaper
The Link
5520 Wyoming Blvd 87109
Telephone: (505) 821-3214
Fax: (505) 821-3351

SYNAGOGUES
Conservative
Congregation B'nai Israel
4401 Indian School Road 87110
Telephone: (505) 266-0155
Fax: (505) 268-6136
Website: www.bnaiisrael-nm.org

SYNAGOGUES
Orthodox
Chabad of New Mexico
4000 San Pedro 87110
Telephone: (505) 880-1181

LAS CRUCES
SYNAGOGUES
Reform
Temple Beth El
702 Parker Road, at Melendres 88004
Telephone: (505) 524-3380
Fax: (505) 521-3737
Email: rabbikane@cs.nmsu.edu
Website: www.uahc.org/nm/nm002/

LOS ALAMOS
SYNAGOGUES
Conservative
Los Alamos Jewish Center
2400 Canyon Road 87544
Telephone: (505) 662-2440

RIO RANCHO
SYNAGOGUES
Reform
Rio Rancho Jewish Center
2009 Grande Blvd 87124
Telephone: (505) 892-8511

SANTA FE
SYNAGOGUES
Orthodox
Chabad Jewish Center
242 West S. Mateo (corner Galisteo)
Telephone: (505) 983-2000
Fax: (505) 983-2055
Email: ChabadSantaFe@aol.com
Website: www.chabadsf.com

Pardes Yisroel
1307 Don Diego Avenue 87505
Telephone: (505) 986-1603
Email: shammes@pardes-yisroel.org
Website: www.pardes-yisroel.org/py/

Reform
Congregation Beit Tikvah
PO Box 2112 87504
Telephone: (505) 820-2991
Fax: (505) 820-2991
Email: rap1818@aol.com
Website: www.beittikva.org

Temple Beth Shalom
205 E. Barcelona Road 87505
Telephone: (505) 982-1376
Fax: (505) 983-7446
Email: nfo@sftbs.org
Website: www.sftbs.org

New York State
New York City encompasses so much territory and so much activity that it can sometimes be easy to forget that there is also a whole state named New York. The Empire State stretches from New York City in the south to the Canadian border at Quebec and Ontario provinces in the north; from the New England border with Connecticut, Massachusetts and Vermont in the east to Pennsylvania and the Great Lakes of Erie and Ontario in the southwest and west.

Within this 50,000 square mile expanse lie metropolis, suburb, small town, large city, village, vast state parks and preserves, seashores, islands, high mountains and rolling foothills, and abundant natural wilderness.

To New York City residents, anything outside the five boroughs (Manhattan, Queens, Brooklyn, the Bronx, and Staten Island) is either upstate or Long Island. But within those areas are numerous large and thriving Jewish communities. The cities of Buffalo, Rochester, Binghamton, Syracuse, and Schenectady, the suburban counties of Westchester and Rockland, and the Long Island counties of Nassau and Suffolk count hundreds of thousands of Jews among their residents.

Jewish settlement began in New York in early September 1654 when twenty-three Sephardic and Ashkenazi Jews disembarked at the harbour of New Amsterdam from the French ship St Catherine. They had escaped the Spanish Inquisition in Recife, Brazil to settle in the Dutch colony. Though Governor Peter Stuyvesant forbade their admission to his jurisdiction, the travellers' protests to his bosses at the Dutch West India Company were accepted and the Jews were allowed to settle. Ten years later, in 1664, four British men-of-war appropriated New Amsterdam in the name of King Charles II of England, who, in turn, made a gift of it to his brother, James, Duke of York. Hence the name, New York.

Jewish immigration was sparse for the next 150 years, but it increased dramatically, especially in New York City between 1880 and 1924, as more than two million Jews made their way to 'der goldene medinah' (the golden door) from eastern and central Europe.

From that original group of twenty-three Jews in 1654, some made their way up the Hudson River as far as Albany (now the state capital). Two of them, Asser Levy and Jacob de Lucena, became Hudson River traders and also dealt in real estate in the Albany and Kingston areas. South of Albany, in nearby Newburgh, Jewish merchants established a trading post in 1777, but no Jewish community existed there until 1848.

New York's first Jewish community outside of New York City was the town of Sholom in the Catskill mountains in Ulster county. Founded by twelve families, it no longer exists. The oldest existing community is Congregation Beth El, founded in 1838 in Albany and later merged with Congregation Beth Emeth.

Westchester (just north of New York City) county's present Jewish population of close to 150,000 dates from 1860.

Rockland

Southeast of the Catskills, in Rockland county just north of New York City, are a number of communities with large Hasidic and Orthodox populations. New Square, a corruption of the name Skvir, was founded by the Skvirer Hasidim and is incorporated as a separate village within the town of Ramapo. With such an administrative and legal designation, New Square has its own zoning rules, its own village council, its own mayor, etc., and is run on strictly orthodox precepts. Monroe, Monsey and Spring Valley have very large Orthodox and Hasidic communities. Though observant Jews are predominant, these communities are also home to non-Jews and less-observant Jews. There are a number of villages in the area which have been incorporated with the express purpose of keeping Orthodox and Hasidim out, through regulations such as zoning to prevent synagogues from being built too close to residences and through the prohibition of having a synagogue in one's house.

ALBANY

GROCERIES
Price Chopper Market
1892 Central Avenue 12205
Telephone: (518) 456-2970
Supervision: Vaad Hakashruth
Full service kosher department.

JEWISH STUDENT CENTRE
Shabbos House
State University of New York, 316 Fuller Road
Telephone: (518) 438-4227
Email: shabbos@albany.net
Website: www.shabboshouse.com
Is also a synagogue.

MIKVAOT
Mikva
340 Whitehall Road
Telephone: (518) 437-1303

SYNAGOGUES
Conservative
Ohav Shalom
New Krumkill Rd 12208
Telephone: (518) 489-4706

Temple Israel
600 New Scotland Ave 12208
Telephone: (518) 438-7858
Fax: (518) 482-5762
Email: timain@templeisraelalbany.org
Website: www.templeisraelalbany.org

Orthodox
Beth Abraham-Jacob
380 Whitehall Road 12208
Telephone: (518) 489-5819/5179
Fax: (518) 489-5179
Email: mbomzer@aol.com

Chabad-Lubvitch Center of the Capital District
122 Main Avenue 12208
Telephone: (518) 482-5281
Fax: (518) 482-3684
Email: albanychabad@knick.net
Website: www.chabadonline.com/albany

Shomray Torah
463 New Scotland Avenue 12208
Telephone: (518) 438-8981

Reform
B'nai Sholom
420 Whitehall Rd 12208
Telephone: (518) 482-5283

Beth Emeth
100 Academy Rd 12208
Telephone: (518) 436-9761
At this 160-year-old congregation, Rabbi Isaac Mayer Wise, founder of American Reform Judaism, served when he first arrived in the United States.

Daughters of Sarah Senior Community
180 Washington Avenue Extension 12203
Telephone: (518) 456-7831
Fax: (518) 456-1563
Email: info@daughtersofsarah.org
Website: www.daughtersofsarah.org
Traditional service, Saturday 9:15 am. Reform service, Friday 3 pm. Traveller's advisory and kosher facility.

AMSTERDAM
SYNAGOGUES
Conservative
Congregation of Sons of Israel
355 Guy Park Avenue 12010
Telephone: (518) 842-8691

BEACON
Hebrew Alliance
55 Fishkill Avenue 12508
Telephone: (845) 831-2012

BINGHAMTON
MIKVAOT
Beth David Synagogue
39 Riverside Drive 13905
Telephone: (607) 722-1793
Fax: (607) 722-7121
Email: bethdavidrabbi@aol.com

SYNAGOGUES
Community Center
500 Clubhouse Road 13903
Telephone: (607) 724-2417
Fax: (607) 824-2311
Email: JCC13850@AOL.com

Conservative
Temple Israel
Deerfield Place, Vestal 13850
Telephone: (607) 723-7461

Reform
Temple Concord
9 Riverside Drive 13905
Telephone: (607) 723-7355

BUFFALO
COMMUNITY ORGANISATIONS
Jewish Federation of Greater Buffalo
787 Delaware Avenue 14209
Telephone: (716) 886-7750
Fax: (716) 886-1367

DELICATESSEN
Tops Kosher Deli
Cnr of North Bailey and Maple Road
Telephone: (716) 615-0076

GROCERIES
Grocers
Corner of North Bailey and Maple Road
Telephone: (716) 515-0075

MEDIA
Guide
Shalom Buffalo
787 Delaware Ave. 14209
Telephone: (716) 886-7750
Fax: (716) 886-1367

Newspaper
Buffalo Jewish Review
15 Mohawk Street 14203
Telephone: (716) 54-2192

MIKVAOT
Mikva
1248 Kenmore Avenue 14216
Telephone: (716) 632-1531

MUSEUMS
Benjamin & Dr. Edgar R. Cofeld Judaic Museum
700 Sweet Home Rd. 14226
Telephone: (716) 836-6565
Fax: (716) 831-1126
Email: TBZ@TBZ.org
A collection of more than a thousand Judaic artifacts dating from the tenth century to the present. There are unique Ben Shahn stained glass windows in the building.

SYNAGOGUES

Conservative
Hillel of Buffalo
Campus Center for Jewish Life, 520 Lee Entrance,
The Commons/Suite #204, Amherst 14228
Telephone: (716) 716) 639-8361
Fax: (716) 639-7817

Shaarey Zedek
621 Getzville Rd 14226
Telephone: (716) 838-3232

Temple Beth El of Greater Buffalo
2368 Eggert Road, Tonawanda 14150
Telephone: (716) 836-3762
Fax: (716) 836-3764
Email: templebethel@juno.com
Website: http://bethelbuffalo.uscjhost.net

Orthodox
B'nai Shalom
1675 N. Forest Rd 14221
Telephone: (716) 689-8203

Beth Abraham
1073 Elmwood Avenue 14222
Telephone: (716) 874-4786

Chabad House
3292 Main St., & N. Forest Rd 14214 &14068
Telephone: (716) 688-1642

Saranac Synagogue
85 Saranac Avenue 14216
Telephone: (716) 876-1284
Fax: (716) 833-7178
Daily Minyan.

Young Israel of Greater Buffalo
105 Maple Rd, Williamsville 14221
Telephone: (716) 634-0212

Reconstructionist
Temple Sinai
50 Alberta Dr., Amherst 14226
Telephone: (716) 834-0708
Fax: (716) 838-2597
Email: templesinai@juno.com

Reform
Beth Am
4660 Sheridan Drive 14221
Telephone: (716) 633-8877
Fax: (716) 633-8952
Email: rabbif@aol.com

Congregation Havurah
6320 Main St. 14221
Telephone: (716) 874-3517

Temple Beth Zion
805 Delaware Avenue 14209
Telephone: (716) 886-7150
Fax: (716) 831-1126
Email: tbz@tbz.org
Website: www.tbz.org

Traditional
Kehilat Shalom
700 Sweet Home Rd 14226
Telephone: (716) 885-6650

CATSKILLS

ELLENVILLE
MIKVAOT
Congregation Ezrath Israel
Rabbi Herman Eisner Square 12428
Telephone: (845) 647-4450/72
Fax: (845) 647-4472
Email: ezrathisrael@cs.com
Mikvah - call for hours.

FLEISCHMANNS
HOTELS
Kosher
Oppenheimer's Regis
PO Box 700, Fleischmanns 12430
Telephone: (845) 254-5080
Fax: (845) 254-4399
Email: kurtopp@aol.com
Supervision: Rabbinate of Kõhal Adas Jeshurun, NYC
Open from Pesach to Succos. Off-season: Fax 1-732-367-5417.

LOCH SHELDRAKE
RESTAURANTS
Meat
Kikar Tel Aviv
Vacation Village
Telephone: (845) 434-0600

SYNAGOGUES
Orthodox
Young Israel of Vacation Village
PO Box 650 12759
Telephone: (845) 436-8359

MONTICELLO
HOTELS
Kutsher's Country Club
Kutshers Road 12701
Telephone: (845) 794-6000
Fax: (845) 794-0157
Email: kutshers@warwick.net
Daily services.

MIKVAOT
Mikva
16 North Street 12701
Telephone: (845) 794-6757
Summer: opens at sunset for two hours. Winter: by
appointment only.

SYNAGOGUES
Orthodox
Landfield Avenue Synagogue
18 Landfield Avenue 12701
Telephone: (845) 794-8470
Fax: (845) 794-8478
Daily services.

SYNAGOGUES
Reform
Temple Sholom
Port Jervis & Dillon Roads 12701
Telephone: (845) 794-8731
Daily services.

SHARON SPRINGS
HOTELS
Yarkony's Adler Spa Hotel
PO Box 328 13459
Telephone: (845) 284-2285 or 1 800 448-4314
Fax: (845) 284-2215
Supervision: OU

WOODRIDGE
The Lake House Hotel
Telephone: (845) 434-7800
Glatt kosher. Chalav Yisrael products only. Open Pesach to
Succot.

CLIFTON PARK
SYNAGOGUES
Conservative
Beth Shalom
Clifton Park, Center Road 12065
Telephone: (716) 371-0608

DELMAR
SYNAGOGUES
Orthodox
Chabad House of Delmar
109 Elsmere Avenue 12054
Telephone: (518) 439-8280
Fax: (518) 439-3226
Email: DelmarChabadSimon@juno.com

Reconstructionist
**Reconstructionist Havurah of the Capital
District**
98 Meadowland Street 12054
Telephone: (518) 439-5870

ELMIRA
SYNAGOGUES
Orthodox
Shomray Hadath
Cobbles Park 14905
Telephone: (607) 732-7410

SYNAGOGUES
Reform
B'nai Israel
Water & Guinnip Streets 14905
Telephone: (607) 734-7735

GENEVA
Temple Beth El
755 South Main Street 14456
Telephone: (315) 789-9710
Email: rosenfield@hws.edu
Website: http://www.templebethelgenevany.org

GLEN FALLS
SYNAGOGUES
Conservative
Shaaray Tefila
68 Bay Street 12801
Telephone: (518) 792-4945
Fax: (518) 792-5966
Email: Shaarayt@localnet.com

Reform
Temple Beth El
3 Marion Avenue 12801
Telephone: (518) 792-4364

GLOVERSVILLE
SYNAGOGUES
Community Center
28 E. Fulton Street 12078

Conservative
Knesseth Israel
34 E. Fulton Street 12078
Telephone: (518) 725-0649

HUDSON
Anshe Emeth
240 Jolsen Blvd 12534
Telephone: (518) 828-9040

ITHACA
Temple Beth El
402 N. Tioga Street 14850
Telephone: (607) 273-5775
Fax: (607) 273-5804
Email: rabbi@tbeithaca.org
Website: www.tbeithaca.org

SYNAGOGUES
Orthodox
Young Israel of Cornell
106 West Avenue 14850
Telephone: (607) 272-5810

LAKE PLACID
SYNAGOGUES
Lake Placid Synagogue
30 Saranac Avenue, Post Office Box 521 12946
Telephone: (518) Answering machine: 523-3876
Email: learlan@adelphia.net
Website: www.lakeplacidsynagogue.org

SYNAGOGUES
Traditionalist
Lake Placid Synagogue
30 Saranac Avenue, PO Box 521 12946-0521
Telephone: (518) 523-3876
Fax: (518) 891-2629

LONG ISLAND

Nassau County

BALDWIN
LONG ISLAND
RESTAURANTS
Ben's Kosher Delicatessen
933 Atlantic Avenue
Telephone: (516) 868-2072
Fax: (516) 868-2062
Email: info@bensdeli.net
Website: www.bensdeli.net
Supervision: Supervised

CEDARHURST
BAKERIES
Zomick's Bake Shop
444 Central Avenue,
Telephone: (516) 569-5520
Supervision: Vaad HaKashrus of the Five Towns

BOOKSELLERS
Judaica Plus
530 Central Avenue
Telephone: (516) 295-4343

RESTAURANTS
Dairy
Ruthie's Kosher Dessert and Dairy Café
560A Central Avenue
Telephone: (516) 569-1818
Email:
Supervision: Vaad HaKashrus of the Five Towns

RESTAURANTS
Meat
Burger Express
140 Washington Ave
Telephone: (516) 295-2040
Supervision: Supervised

K Roasters
72 Columbia Avenue
Telephone: (516) 791-5100
Vaad HaKashrus of the Five Towns

K.D.'s El Passo BBQ
546 Central Avenue
Telephone: (516) 569-2920
Supervision: Supervised

King David Delicatessen
550 Central Avenue 11516
Telephone: (516) 569-2920
Vaad HaKashrus of the Five Towns

Wok Tov
594 Central Avenue
Telephone: (516) 295-3843
Fax: (516) 295-3865
Vaad HaKashrus of the Five Towns

GREAT NECK
BUTCHERS
Great Neck Glatt
501 Middle Neck Road 11023
Telephone: (516) 773-6328
Fax: (516) 773-4694
Email: Supervision: Vaad Harabonim of Queens

MEDIA
Newspapers
Long Island Jewish Week
98 Cutter Mill Road 11020
Telephone: (516) 773-3679

Long Island Jewish World
115 Middle Neck Road 11021
Telephone: (516) 829-4000

MIKVAOT
Mikvaot
26 Old Mill Road 11023
Telephone: (516) 487-2726

RESTAURANTS
Dairy
Kings Kosher Pizza
605 Middle Neck Road 11023
Telephone: (516) 482-0400
Fax: (516) 482-0405
Supervision: Star K

RESTAURANTS
Meat
Bistro Grill
132 Middle Neck Road
Telephone: (516) 829-4428
Fax: (516) 829-3320

Chattanooga
37 Cuttermill Road
Telephone: (516) 487-4455

Colbeh
75 N. Station Plaza
Telephone: (516) 466-8181
Supervision: Kof-K

Danny's
624 Middle Neck Road
Telephone: (516) 487-6666

Hunan
507 Middle Neck Road
Telephone: (516) 482-7912
Supervision: Vaad Rab. of Queens

Soprano's
113 Middle Neck Road
Telephone: (516) 482-0000
Fax: (516) 482-0560

GREENVALE
Ben's Kosher Delicatessen
140 Wheatley Plaza
Telephone: (516) 621-3340
Fax: (516) 621-2178
Email: info@bensdeli.net
Website: www.bensdeli.net
Supervision: Supervised

JERICHO
DELICATESSEN
Delicatessen
437 No. Broadway
Telephone: (516) 939-2367
Fax: (516) 939-2294
Email: info@bensdeli.net
Website: www.bensdeli.net
Supervision: Supervised

LAWRENCE
BAKERIES
Tasty Heimish Bakery
343 Central Avenue,
Telephone: (508) 569-5551/5552

RESTAURANTS
Dairy
Dairy Review
143 Washington Avenue
Telephone: (508) 295-7417
Supervision: Vaad HaKashrus of the Five Towns

Primavera
Telephone: (508) 374-5504
Fax: (508) 374-5589
Supervision: Supervised

Meat
Burger Express
140 Washington Avenue
Telephone: (508) 374-1714
Supervision: Vaad HaKashrus of the Five Towns

Cho-Sen Island
367 Central Avenue
Telephone: (508) 374-1199
Fax: (508) 374-1459
Supervision: Vaad HaKashrus of the Five Towns

Traditions
302 Central Avenue
Telephone: (508) 295-3630

LONG BEACH
MIKVAOT
Mikva
Sharf Manor, 274 W. Broadway 11561
Telephone: (310) 431-7758

SYNAGOGUES
Conservative
Beth Shalom of Long Beach and Lido
700 E. Park Ave 11561
Telephone: (310) 432-7464

Orthodox
Temple Beth El
570 W. Walnut Street 11561
Telephone: (310) 432-1678

SYOSSET
COMMUNITY ORGANISATIONS
Conference of Jewish Organisations of Nassau County
North Shore Atrium, 6900 Jericho Turnpike 11791
Telephone: (516) 364-4477
Fax: (516) 921-5092

WEST HEMPSTEAD
MIKVAOT
Mikva
775 Hempstead Avenue 11552
Telephone: (516) 489-9358

RESTAURANTS
Meat
Wing Wan
248 Hempstead Avenue
Telephone: (516) 482-7912

WOODBURY

RESTAURANTS
Ben's Kosher Delicatessen
7971 Jericho Turnpike
Telephone: (516) 496-4236
Fax: (516) 496-4354
Email: info@bensdeli.net
Website: www.bensdeli.net
Supervision: Supervised

WOODMERE

KASHRUT INFORMATION
Vaad HaKashrus of the Five Towns
859 Peninsula Blvd., Woodmere 11598
Telephone: (516) 569-4536
Fax: (516) 295 4212

SYNAGOGUES
Orthodox
Young Israel of North Woodmere
634 Hungry Harbor Road, 11581
Telephone: (516) 791-5099
Email: info@yinw.org

Suffolk County

COMMACK

COMMUNITY ORGANISATIONS
Suffolk Council of Jewish Organizations
74 Hauppauge Road 11725
Telephone: (631) 462-5826
Email: suffolkCOJO@att.net
Website: www.lijewishlinks.org
Publishes 'Suffolk Jewish Directory'.

RESTAURANTS
Meat
Pastrami 'N Friends
110a Commack Road 11725
Telephone: (631) 499-9537

SYNAGOGUES
Orthodox
Young Israel of Commack
40 Kings Park Road 11725
Telephone: (631) 543-1441
Fax: (631) 543-1482
Email: rwizman@optonline.net

DIX HILLS

TOURIST INFORMATION
Jewish Genealogy Society of Long Island
37 Westcliff Drive 11746-5627
Telephone: (631) 549-9532
Email: jgsli@suffolk.lib.ny.us
Website: www.jewishgen.org/jgsli
Offers assistance to Jewish travellers on their New York or US roots.

MONROE

SYNAGOGUES
Reform
Temple Beth-El
Monroe Temple of Liberal Judaism, 314 N. Main St. 10950
Telephone: (845) 783-2626
Website: www.monroetemplebeth-el.org

WESTHAMPTON BEACH

RESTAURANTS
Beach Bakery Café
112 Main Street 11978
Telephone: (631) 288-6552
Supervision: Rabbi Ariel Konstantyn

SYNAGOGUES
Orthodox
Hampton Synagogue
154 Sunset Avenue 11978
Telephone: (631) 288-0534

NEWBURGH

KASHRUT INFORMATION
Agudas Israel
290 North Street 12550
Telephone: (845) 562-5604
Fax: (845) 562-5622
Email: agudasisrael@aol.com

MUSEUMS
Gomez Mill House
Millhouse Road, Marlboro 12542
Telephone: (845) 236-3126
Fax: (845) 236-3365 and 236-3126
Email: gomezmillhouse@juno.com
Website: www.gomez.org
Oldest Jewish residence now maintained as a museum.

NEW YORK CITY
Nowhere in the United States is there a city richer in Jewish heritage than New York. From the city's beginnings as a Dutch trading post in the 17th century up to the present day, Jews have flocked to New York, made it their home, and left an indelible mark on the city's heritage, language, culture, physical structure, and day-to-day life. There are more Jews in the New York metropolitan area than in any other city in the world, and more than in any country except Israel. So, without a great deal of effort, just being in this largest urban Jewish community in history affords you the opportunity to be a tourist without concern about the ease of observing kashrut and Shabbat.

New York City is the largest Jewish community in the world outside Israel. The estimated Jewish population of New York City proper is just over one million. Another million or so live in the immediate suburbs, which include not only New York, but also New Jersey and Connecticut. Roughly one-third of American Jews live in and around New York City and virtually every national Jewish organization has its headquarters here.

New York City neighbourhoods with large Jewish populations are the upper west and upper east sides of Manhattan (modern Orthodox and secular Jewish), Borough Park, Williamsburg (Orthodox and Hasidic) and Brighton Beach (Russian) in Brooklyn, Forest Hills (Israelis and Russians), Kew Gardens, Kew Garden Hills (Orthodox) in Queens, Riverdale in the Bronx, and Staten Island.

In this largest urban Jewish community in history, the Jewish traveller is overwhelmed with choices of where to eat, where to find a minyan, what to see of Jewish interest and so on. And the variety of kosher restaurants makes choosing a pleasure: Chinese, Moroccan, Italian (both meat and dairy), traditional European, Indian, Japanese and seafood.

Though Jews from numerous countries of origin live together throughout New York's Jewish communities, many groups tend to congregate in their own neighbourhoods or sections of neighbourhoods.

Ever since the fateful year of 1654 Jews have been coming to New York City. Sometimes a few, sometimes more, and sometimes by the boatload, as was the case between 1880 and 1924 when some two million Jews entered the United States. And though one might argue cause and effect, New York City is still the commercial, intellectual and financial center of the country.

Synagogues

Hundreds if not thousands of synagogues, chavurot and shtiblech lie within the city, representing the myriad expressions of Judaism: Orthodox, Hasidic, Conservative, Reform and Reconstructionist.

Complete lists of synagogues in all five boroughs can be obtained from the various umbrella organizations listed in the beginning of the section on the USA.

The 1,300-seat, Moorish-style Central Synagogue (Reform) at 652 Lexington Avenue in Manhattan reopened its doors in October 2001, three years after a devastating fire. It is the city's oldest synagogue on an original site and is an official New York City landmark; the oldest Ashkenazi congregation, founded in 1825, is B'nai Jeshrun (Conservative) at 270

West 89th Street; Shearith Israel, the Spanish and Portuguese synagogue on Central Park West at 70th Street, is one of the oldest congregations in the United States and originated with those 23 refugees from the Spanish Inquisition in Brazil in 1654. The present building still has religious items from the earliest days of the congregation and its small chapel is representative of the American colonial period; Temple Emanu-El (Reform) at Fifth Avenue and 65th Street is not only the city's largest, but the world's largest synagogue. The congregation was founded in 1848 and the building, built in 1929, can seat over 2,000 people; the Fifth Avenue synagogue at 5 East 62nd Street was, until early 1967, presided over by the then Rabbi Dr Immanuel Jakobovits, who later became the Chief Rabbi of Great Britain and the Commonwealth; the Park East synagogue at 163 East 67th Street, on the very fashionable Upper East Side, was founded in 1890 and is a historic landmark. Kehilath Jeshrun (Orthodox), 125 East 85th Street, is a popular option if you are on the Upper East Side. On the Upper West Side, Lincoln Square Synagogue (Orthodox), 200 Amsterdam Avenue at 69th Street, and Ohab Zedek (Orthodox), 118 West 95th Street, are both very popular options.

Visitors may be interested in a late 9 am minyan on the Upper West Side at 303 W.91st East between West End Avenue and Riversdale Drive.

Libraries, Museums, and Institutes of Learning

New York's newest educational research center and one of the country's most important resources for Jewish scholarship opened in October 2000 and is located at 15 West 16th Street. The centre is a partnership of five major institutions of Jewish scholarship: American Jewish Historical Society, American Sephardi Federation, Leo Baeck Institute, Yeshiva University Museum and YIVO Institute for Jewish Research. The combined collections and the professional staff of these five institutions create an opportunity for an unparalleled comprehensive study of modern Jewish history.

The Jewish Museum (Fifth Avenue and 92nd Street, 212-423-3200) has been in existence since 1904. Under the auspices of the Conservative Jewish Theological Seminary, the museum has permanent and changing exhibits and programmes and an excellent collection of Jewish ritual and ceremonial objects.

The library at the Jewish Theological Seminary (3080 Broadway at 122nd Street, 212-678-8000) houses one of the greatest collections of Judaica and Hebraica in the world. Its holdings include a rare manuscript by Maimonides (the Rambam).

Other libraries with large Judaica collections are at Yeshiva University (212-960-5400), the Judaica Collection at the New York Public Library (212-340-0849), New York University (212-998-1212), Columbia University (212-854-1754), the House of Living Judaism at Temple Emanu-El (212-744-1400) and the Leo Baeck Institute (212-744-6400). Inquire at each one individually as to availability of the collections.

One of New York's living museums is the Eldridge Street Synagogue (14 Eldridge Street, 212-219-0888). At over 100 years old, the Eldridge Street synagogue is a ghost of its former splendour. But, in its heyday at the turn of the century, it was among the busiest synagogues on the Lower East Side, and the first built for that purpose by New York's eastern European Jews. An official New York City landmark, and listed on the National Register of Historic Places, the synagogue is an ongoing restoration project. The synagogue functions as a museum and has a whole host of programmes.

In the same neighbourhood and sociologically related is the Lower East Side Tenement Museum (97 Orchard Street, 212-431-0233). Contrary to popular opinion, the word tenement does not mean slum housing, but a particular building design devised to house the masses of immigrants who came to New York in the latter part of the 19th century. Tenements are five- or six-storey walk-up buildings distinguished by narrow entry halls and a central air shaft. Each floor contained four apartments. Toilet facilities, located in the hallway, were shared by all the residents. Baths were taken at numerous local public bath houses. The museum, located in a restored tenement built in 1863, shows visitors what tenement life was like via a model apartment. In addition, actors in period dress present 90-minute shows in a small theatre. This is how the vast majority of Jews lived when they first came to New York City.

Ellis Island National Monument (212-269-5755) was once the point of entry for Jews and other immigrants. Some five million Jews came to the United States between 1850 and 1948 and most were processed through immigration at Castle Garden (the present ferry ticket office) or, after 1890, Ellis Island.

Neighbourhoods and areas of historical interest

Manhattan

The Lower East Side has physically changed very little in over a century. Cramped tenements and crowded, dirty streets have always characterised the area. But for the absence of vendors calling out 'I cash clothes'

one can get a pretty good idea of what life looked like for Jews newly arrived in New York City from eastern European countries, although it is difficult to imagine the strangeness of a new language or being away from home for the first time.

Although the Lower East Side is not as Jewish as it once was and many Jewish shops have closed, it is appropriate that historical jaunts in New York begin in its tangle of streets and alleys. For the ancestors of some 80 per cent of American Jews, this was the first piece of America they saw. Now other immigrant groups call the Lower East Side home. Settlement houses such as the Henry Street Settlement and the Educational Alliance on East Broadway once served the Jewish immigrant population in their need to learn English and become Americanised. Still in existence, they provide services to current residents, Jewish and non-Jewish alike.

Many Jews still do business in the neighbourhood and the area is full of historic buildings, Jewish shops, foodstores and stores selling all manner of ritual items (kipot, taliltot, tefilin, siddurim, etc.). Look along Essex, Orchard, Grand, Rivington, Hester and Canal streets.

One of the best guidebooks for this area (as well as the rest of New York City) is the 'AIA [American Institute of Architects] Guide to New York City' by Elliot Willensky and Norval White. An organization called Big Onion Walking Tours gives Lower East Side tours and they are worth a telephone call (212-439-1090).

You may notice that a number of churches on the Lower East Side used to be synagogues. They were re-consecrated as churches when the Jewish community dwindled. But in many cases you still can tell which were synagogues. Look for things like Stars of David on building cornerstones, darkened mezuzah shaped areas on doorposts, and shadows of Stars of David on building facades. They are quite evident if you look.

Synagogues of note in the area are the Bialystoker synagogue (7 Wilet Street); Beth Midrash HaGadol (60 Norfolk Street); First Roumanian American Congregation (89 Rivington Street); and the Eldridge Street Synagogue (14 Eldridge Street).

The only kosher winery in Manhattan is Schapiro's kosher Winery (126 Rivington Street, 674-4404), founded in 1899. Call for tour information.

Along Second Avenue below 14th Street you can still see the remnants of the scores of Yiddish theatres that once lined the street. Note particularly the movie theatre on Second

Avenue at 12th Street, currently the City Cinemas Village East. In the upper level auditorium you can get an idea of what the place looked like when stars like Molly Picon and Boris Tomeshevsky held forth on the stage.

Forty-seventh Street between Fifth Avenue and Avenue of the Americas is the diamond centre. Some 75 per cent of all the diamonds which enter the United States pass through here. As this is overwhelmingly a Jewish and Hasidic business, the street is bustling with diamond dealers concluding deals in the open market atmosphere that is pervasive. Most deals are made with a handshake. There are a number of kosher restaurants up and down the block and on the mezzanines of office buildings.

Historical Cemeteries
Manhattan

Shearith Israel Cemeteries
Vestiges of early Jewish settlement in New York can be gleaned from the remnants of the community's first cemeteries. The following three are owned by New York's oldest congregation, Shearith Israel, the Spanish Portuguese Synagogue.

First: Shearith Israel Graveyard: 55 St. James Place (between Oliver and James St), the first Jewish cemetery in New Amsterdam, was consecrated in 1656 and was located near the present Chatham Square. Its remains were moved to this location. It contains the remains of Sephardic Jews who emigrated from Brazil.

Second: Cemetery of the Spanish and Portuguese Synagogue (1805–1829): 72–76 West 11th Street, just east of Sixth Avenue on the south side of the street.

Third: Cemetery of the Spanish and Portuguese Synagogue (1829–1851): 98–110 West 21st Street, just west of Sixth Avenue on the south side of the street.

Brooklyn
Green-Wood Cemetery (Fifth Avenue and Fort Hamilton Parkway, Brooklyn) contains the graves of many prominent Jewish figures.

Queens
Fourth Cemetery of the Spanish and Portuguese Synagogue: Cypress Hills Street and Cypress Avenue, Queens. The beautiful chapel and gate were built in 1885.

Arts and Entertainment
As American entertainment is largely a secular Jewish enterprise, one need not look very far for Jewish references in plays and musicals. However, there are some dedicated Jewish theatrical companies and venues: the Jewish Repertory Company (212-831-2000); the

American Jewish Theater (212-633-1588); the YM & YWHA (212-427-6000) has several outstanding lecture series, some with specific Jewish themes. For other events of Jewish interest consult one of the weekly listings magazines such as Time Out New York or New York Magazine, or the Sunday Arts & Leisure section of the New York Times. Jewish newspapers with events listings are Jewish Week, Forward and Jewish Press, all available at most newsstands.

Jewish Neighbourhoods of Interest outside Manhattan

Brooklyn
Williamsburg was for many years the centre of Hasidic life in New York City. But in the last decade many rebbes and their followers have moved to the suburbs, particularly Rockland county. However, a trip to Williamsburg is still worthwhile.

Boro Park is almost completely Orthodox and is a world apart from the rest of the city.

Crown Heights is populated by Hasidim of many sects, but particularly the Lubavitch, whose world headquarters is at 770 Eastern Parkway. The neighbourhood is not totally Jewish and there are often clashes (sometimes violent) between the Caribbean residents and Jewish residents.

New Jersey
Many towns in northern and central New Jersey are less than 40 minutes travel time by either car or public transport from Manhattan, and as such are part of metropolitan New York. They are: Bayonne, Clifton, Elizabeth, Englewood, Fairlawn, Hackensack, Hoboken, Jersey City, Newark, Passaic, Teaneck, Union and West New York.

Restaurants
By law in New York State, the selling of non-kosher food as kosher is a punishable fraud. Administered by the kosher Law Enforcement Section of the New York State Department of Agriculture, heavy penalties are imposed on violators. An Orthodox rabbi oversees the operation. Businesses selling kosher food must display proper signage, indicating under whose hashgacha they operate, and establishments which sell both kosher and non-kosher food must display that as well, with a sign in block letters no smaller than four inches high.

In July 2000 a Federal Judge ruled that this law violated the First Amendment. In September 2002 there was a further stay of this ruling pending appeal.

'The Kosher Directory', issued by the Union of Orthodox Jewish Congregations, lists foods and services which bear the symbol. It is available for a charge by calling 212-563-4000. Other reliable kashruth insignias also exist.

Note that kosher packaged foods, including bread, meat, fish, cake, biscuits and virtually anything you can think of, are widely available in supermarkets throughout the New York metropolitan area. Many foodstores, especially on the Upper West Side of Manhattan and in Jewish neighbourhoods in Brooklyn and Queens, sell fresh kosher prepared meals as well.

BRONX
RESTAURANTS
Second Helping
3532 Johnson Avenue 10463
Telephone: (718) 548-1818
Supervision: Vaad Harabonim of Riverdale
Take-out food only; Glatt kosher.

Yeshiva University: Bronx Center
Eastchester Rd & Morris Park Avenue 10461
Telephone: (718) 430-2131

Yeshiva University: Bronx Center
Eastchester Rd & Morris Park Avenue 10461
Telephone: (718) 430-2131

RESTAURANTS
Dairy
Main Event
3708 Riverdale Avenue, Riverdale 10463
Telephone: (718) 601-6246
Fax: (718) 601-0008
Email: maineventc@aol.com
Supervision: Rabbi Jonathan Rosenblatt, Riverdale Jewish Center

RESTAURANTS
Meat
Riverdelight
3534 Johnson Avenue, Riverdale 10463
Telephone: (718) 543-4270
Fax: (718) 543-7545
Supervision: Vaad Harabonim of Riverdale
Glatt kosher. Grill, deli and Middle-Eastern cuisine. Take-out and catering.

BROOKLYN
HOTELS
Avenue Plaza Hotel
4624 13th Avenue 11219
Telephone: (718) 552-3200
Fax: (718) 552-3276
Email: info@theavenueplaza.com
Website: www.theavenueplaza.com

Midwood Suites
1078 East 15 S
Telephone: (718) 253-9535
Fax: (718) 253-3269
Email: shalom@midwoodsuites.com

Scharf's Ateret of Midwood
1410 East 10th Street 11230
Telephone: (718) 998-5400
Fax: (718) 645-8600
Email: ateretavoth@aol.com
Daily Minyon. Under strict Hashgocha. Cholov Yisroel/Glatt Kosher

The Crown Palace Hotel
570-600 Crown Street
Telephone: (718) 604-1777
Glatt kosher.

LIBRARIES
Levi Yitzhak Library
305 Kingston Avenue 11213

MUSEUMS
The Chasidic Art Institute
375 Kingston Avenue

Jewish Children's Museum
792 Eastern Parkway
Brooklyn, NY 11213
Telephone: (718) 467-0600
Fax: (718) 467-1300
Email: info@cm.museum
Website: www.jcm.museum

RESTAURANTS
Dairy
Broadway's J-2 N.Y.C. Pizza
926 3rd Ave.
Telephone: (718) 768-7437

Bella Luna
557 Kings Highway
Telephone: (718) 376-2999

Chapp-u-Ccino
4815 12th Avenue
Telephone: (718) 633-4377
Supervision: Rabbi Amrom Roth

Fontana Bella
2086 Coney Island Avenue
Telephone: (718) 627-3904
Supervision: Rabbi Gornish

Gio Caffe
448 Avenue P
Telephone: (718) 375-5437

Milk N Honey
5013 - 10 Ave.
Telephone: (718) 871-4319
Fax: (718) 871-4297
Supervision: Rabbi Friedlander

Sunflower Café
1223 Kings Highway, cor. E. 13th St.
Telephone: (718) 336-1340
Supervision: Rabbi Gornish

Tea For Two Café
547 Kings Highway
Telephone: (718) 998-0020
Supervision: Rabbi Gornish

Wendy's Plate
434 Avenue U
Telephone: (718) 376-3125
Fax: (718) 871-4297
Supervision: Rabbi Friedlander

Meat
1st Jerusalem Steak House
533 Kings Highway
Telephone: (718) 336-5115

47th St. Kosher Restaurant
274 47th Street , (off 3rd Ave.)
Telephone: (718) 492-2000
Fax: (718) 492-4199

A-Kosher Delight
4600 13th Ave.
Telephone: (718) 435-8500
Fax: (718) 435-1669

Bamboo Garden
904 Kings Highway
Telephone: (718) 375-8501
Supervision: Rabbi Yisroel P. Gornish

Cancun
448 Avenue P.
Telephone: (718) 375-4916
Supervision: Vaad Harabonim of Flatbush

Chap-A-Nosh Plus
1424 Elm Avenue
Telephone: (718) 627-0072
Fax: (718) 645-6336
Supervision: Rabbi G. Reisman

China Glatt
4413 13th Ave
Telephone: (718) 438-2576

Dougies
4310 18th Ave, Bet. McDonald Ave. & E. 2nd St, Off
Ocean Parkway
Telephone: (718) 686-8080
Supervision: Udvar Kashruth of America

Essex on Coney
1359 Coney Island Ave
Telephone: (718) 253-1002
Supervision: Vaad Harabonim of Flatbush

Fuji Hana
512 Av. U
Telephone: (718) 336-3888

Supervision: Vaad Harabonim of Flatbush

Glatt-a-la-Carte
5502 18th Ave.
Telephone: (718) 621-3697
Supervision: R'Yechiel Babad

Jerusalem Steak House II
1316 Ave. M
Telephone: (718) 376-0680

Kaosan
1387 Coney Island Ave.
Telephone: (718) 252-6969

Kineret Steak House
521 Kings Highway, Bet. E. 2nd - E. 3rd Sts
Telephone: (718) 336-8888
Supervision: Kehilah Kashruth

McFleishig's
5508 16th Avenue
Telephone: (718) 435-2779
Supervision: Rabbi Babad, Tartikover

Olympic Pita
1419 Coney Island Avenue, Bet. J & K
Telephone: (718) 258-6222
Fax: (718) 258-3106
Supervision: Kehilah Kashrus

Shang-Chai
2189 Flatbush Ave.
Telephone: (718) 377-6100

Tokyo of Brooklyn
2954 Ave. U., off Nostrand Ave.
Telephone: (718) 891-6221
Supervision: Kehilah Kashrus

Yunkee
1424 Elm Ave, (cor. E. 15th/St & Ave. M)
Telephone: (718) 627-0072
Fax: (718) 645-6336
Supervision: Rabbi G. Reisman

SYNAGOGUES
Orthodox
Lubavitch Movement
770 Eastern Parkway 11213
Telephone: (718) 774-4000
Fax: (212) 774-2718
Email: info@lubavitch.com
Website: : www.lubavitch.com

Lubavitch Movement
770 Eastern Parkway,
Telephone: (718) 774 4000
Fax: (718) 774 2718

MANHATTAN
BAKERIES
H & H Bagels
2239 Broadway at 80th Street 10024
Telephone: (212) 595-8000
Fax: (212) 799-6765
Supervision: Kof-K

H & H Bagels
639 West 46th Street
Telephone: (212) 765-7200
Fax: (212) 765-7391
Email: shipping-hhbagels@nyc.rr.com
Website: www.hhbagels.com
Supervision: Star K

BOOKSELLERS
J. Levine Judaica
5 West 30th Street
Telephone: (212) 695-6888
Fax: (212) 643-1044
Email: sales@levinejudaica.com
Website: LevineJudaica.Com

EMBASSY
Consul General of Israel
800 Second Avenue 10017
Telephone: (718) 499-5400
Fax: (212)499-5555

JUDAICA
Eichler's of Manhattan
62 West 45th St.
Telephone: 1-877-EICHLERS
Website: www.EICHLERS.com

LIBRARIES
Butler Library of Colombia University
Broadway at 116th Street 10027
Has some 6,000 Hebrew books and pamphlets, plus 1,000 manuscripts and a Hebrew psalter printed at Cambridge University in 1685 and used by Samuel Johnson at the graduation of the first candidates for bachelor's degrees.

The Jewish Division of the New York Public Library
Fifth Avenue at 42nd Street 10018
Telephone: (718) 930-0601
Fax: (212) 642-0141
Has 125,000 volumes of Judaica and Hebraica, along with extensive microfilm and bound files of Jewish publications, one of the finest collections in existence.

MUSEUMS
Center for Jewish History
15 West 16th Street 10011
Telephone: (212) 294-8301
Fax: (212) 294-8302
Email: cjh@cjh.org
Website: www.cjh.org
The Center has brought together the following five institutes to create the largest single repository for Jewish history in

the Diaspora: American Jewish Historical Society, American Sephardi Federation, Leo Baeck Institute, Yeshiva University Museum and YIVO Institute for Jewish Research. It has over 500,000 volumes and over 100 million documents. A wide variety of exhibitions illustrate the diversity of Jewish art, history and culture. Tours are available and there is a kosher dairy cafe open Monday to Thursday 9.15 am to 4.30 pm and Sunday 11.00 am to 4.30 pm.

Jewish Theological Seminary of America
3080 Broadway at 122nd Street 10027
Telephone: (212) 678-8975
Fax: (212) 678-8891
Email: shmintz@jtsa.edu
The Library of the Jewish Theological Seminary is one of the world's premier research libraries of Judaica and Hebraica. More than a thousand years of written history are to be found within the library's 375,000 rare books, 40,000 Genizah fragments and thousands of rare documents and prints. The remarkable treasures represent scholarship in the areas of Bible, liturgy, rabbinics, kabbala, philosophy and history. Throughout the year, exhibitions featuring selected pieces from the collection, showcase the library's treasures. Sundays, 10am to 5pm; Monday through Thursday, 9am to 6pm; Fridays, 9am to 2pm; closed Saturday.

Lower East Side Tenement Museum
90 Orchard Street 10002
Telephone: (212) 431-0233
Fax: (212) 431-0402
Website: www.tenement.org
Housed in a 1863 structure, the Museum presents and interprets the variety of immigrant experience on Manhattan's Lower East side, 'A gateway to America'.

The House of Living Judaism
5th Avenue and 65th Street
Frequently shows paintings and ritual objects. Twelve marble pillars symbolise the Twelve Tribes.

The Jewish Museum
1109 Fifth Avenue 10128
Telephone: (212) 423-3200
This is one of the outstanding museums in the city and a must not just for Jewish visitors but for all interested in art. The permanent display consists of one of the finest collection of Jewish ritual and ceremonial art in the world, along with notable paintings and sculptures.

The Museum of Jewish Heritage—A Living Memorial to the Holocaust
36 Battery Place 10280
Telephone: (212) 437 4340
Fax: (212) 437 4341
Email: scohen@mjhnyc.org
Website: mjhnyc.org
A living memorial to the Holocaust.

Theological Seminary of America
Fifth Avenue & 92nd Street 10028
An outstanding museum, with permanent displays of Jewish ritual and ceremonial art, along with notable paintings and sculptures.

ORGANISATIONS
UJA-Federation Resource Line
130 E. 59th Street 10022
Telephone: (212) 753-2288
Fax: (212) 888-7538
Email: resourceline@ujafedny.org
Website: www.ujafedny.org

RESTAURANTS
Dairy
Ben's Kosher Delicatessen
209 West 38th Street
Telephone: (212) 398-2367
Fax: (212) 398-3354
Email: info@bensdeli.net
Website: www.bensdeli.net
Supervision: Supervised
Hours: 11am to 9.30 pm.

Yeshiva University: Main Center
500 W. 185th Street 10033-3201
Telephone: (212) 960-5248
Fax: (212) 960-0070

American Cafe
160 Broadway
Telephone: (212) 732-1426

Bagels & Co.
1428 York Ave., cnr. E. 76th St.
Telephone: (212) 717-0505
Supervision: New York Kosher

Broadway's Jerusalem 2
1375 Broadway, at 38th Street 10018
Telephone: (212) 398-1475
Fax: (212) 398-6797
Email: n.y.pies@.com
Supervision: OU
Chalav Yisrael, Prs Yisruel. Home of the N.Y. Flying Pizza Pies. Visit the 'Jewish Wall of Fame', 7.00 am to 12.00 pm. Saturday nights to 2.00 am.

Café 18
8 East 18th Street, Bet. 5th and Broadway
Telephone: (212) 620-4182

Cafe Roma Pizzeria
175 W. 90th Street
Telephone: (212) 875-8972

Diamond Dairy Kosher Lunchonette
4 W. 47th Street 10036
Telephone: (212) 719-2694
On the gallery overlooking the diamond & jewelry exchange. Hours: Monday to Thursday, 7:30 am to 5 pm; Friday, to 2 pm.

EEE's Bakery & Café
105 East 34th Street

Gusto va Mare
237 E. 53rd St.
Telephone: (212) 583-9300
Supervision: Organised Kashrut

JT Café
226 W. 72 St.
Telephone: (212) 724-2424

Mom's Bagels of NY
240 West 35th Street 10001
Telephone: (212) 494-0440
Fax: (212) 494-0402
Email: info@momsbagelsnyc.com
Supervision: Kof-K
Chulov Yisruel

My Most Favorite Dessert
120 West 45th Street
Telephone: (212) 997-5130
Fax: (212) 997 5046
Supervision: OU
Chalav Yisrael.

Provi, Provi
228 W, 72nd St., Bet. B'way and West End Ave.
Telephone: (212) 875-9020
Supervision: Organised Kashrut

Va Bene
1589 Second Avenue 10028
Telephone: (212) 517-4448
Fax: (212) 517-2258
Supervision: OU
Chalav Yisrael Italian restaurant.

Vegetable Garden
48 East 41st St., (Bet. Mad & Park)
Telephone: (212) 883-7668

Indian Vegetarian
Saffron
81 Lexington Avenue 10016
Telephone: (212) 696-5130
Fax: (212) 696-5146

Kosher Vegetarian
Great American Health Bar
35 W. 57th Street
Telephone: (212) 355-5177
Website: www.57thstreetkosher.com

Meat
A-Kosher Delight
1359 Broadway
Telephone: (212) 563-3366
Fax: (212) 268-9352

Abigael's Grill and Caterers
9 East 37th Street 10016
Telephone: (212) 725-0130
Fax: (212) 725-3577
Supervision: Kof-K
Glatt kosher.

Abigael's on Broadway
1407 Broadway, at 39th Street 10018
Telephone: (212) 575-1407
Fax: (212) 869-0666

Supervision: Kof-K
Glatt kosher. Lunch Monday-Friday 12pm-3pm. Dinner Sun-Thursday 5pm-10pm.
Open Saturday nights October - April.

Cafe Classico
35 West 57th Street
Telephone: (212) 355-5411
Website: www.57thstreetkosher.com
Glatt kosher.

Colbeh
43 West 39 St, (Mid Town)
Telephone: (212) 354-8181

Deli Kasbah
2553 Amsterdam Avenue
Telephone: (212) 568-4600

Domani Ristorante
1590 First Ave., Bet. 82nd-83rd St.
Telephone: (212) 717-7575/7557
Supervision: Organised Kashrut

Dougies
222 West 72nd
Telephone: (212) 724-2222
Fax: (212) 724-3421
Website: www.Dougiesbbq.com

Eden Wok
127 W. 72 Street 10023
Telephone: (212) 787-8700
Fax: (212) 787-9801
Supervision: OU

Essex on Coney Downtown
17 Trinity Place
Telephone: (718) 809-3000

Estihana
221 W. 79 St.
Telephone: (212) 501-0393
Fax: (212) 501-0458
Website: www.estihana.com
Japanese cuisine, glatt kosher

Glatt Dynasty
1049 Second Avenue, East 55th & East 56th Street
10022
Telephone: (212) 888-9119
Fax: (212) 888-9163
Supervision: Kof-K
Glatt kosher.

Haikara
1016 2nd Avenue 10022
Telephone: (212) 355-7000
Supervision: OU

Hapisgah Steakhouse
147-25 Union Turnpike, Kew Gardens Hills
Telephone: (212) 380-4449

Il Patrizio
206 East 63rd St., Bet. 2nd and 3rd Aves
Telephone: (212) 980-4007

Supervision: OU

Jasmine

11 East 30 Street, between Madison and 5th
Avenues
Telephone: (212) 251-8884

Supervision: Vaad I'Kashrut Badatz Sepharadic

Glatt kosher Persian and Middle Eastern cuisine. Open
Sunday to Friday, for lunch and dinner.

Jewish Theological Seminary Dining Hall

3080 Broadway at 122nd Street 10027
Telephone: (212) 678-8822

Open September through to July (closed August) for
breakfast and lunch: 7.30am to 10.00am; 11.00am to
2.00pm. Strictly kosher, Shomer Shabbat.

Kasbah Restaurant

251 W. 85th Street
Telephone: (212) 496-1500
Fax: (212) 496-2273

Supervision: Circle K

Hours: Sunday to Thursday, 12 pm to 11 pm. American and
Mediterranean food.

Kosher Delight

1359 Broadway (37th Street)
Telephone: (212) 563-3366

Kosher Deluxe

10 W. 46th St, (Off 5th Avenue)
Telephone: (212) 869-6699

Le Marais

150 W. 46th Street 10036
Telephone: (718) 869-0900
Fax: (718) 869-1016
Email: lemaraisat46@hotmail.com
Website: www.lemarais.net

Supervision: OU

Glatt kosher. Hours: Sunday to Thursday, 12 pm to 12 am;
Friday, to 3 pm; Saturday, October to May, one hour after
sundown to 1 am.

Le Marais 2

15 John St
Telephone: (212) 285-8585
Fax: (212) 791-3280

Supervision: Organised Kashrut

Levana

141 West 69th Street 10023
Telephone: (212) 877-8457
Fax: (212) 595-7522
Email: info@levana.com
Website: www.levana.com

Supervision: Orthodox Union

Glatt kosher.

Mendy's

Rockfeller Center, 30 Rockfeller Plaza
Telephone: (212) 262-9600

Mendy's West

208 West 70th Street 10023
Telephone: (212) 877-6787

Supervision: OU

Mr Broadway

1372 Broadway, (Bet. 37 & 38 St)
Telephone: (212) 921-2152

Penguin

258 W. 15th St., Bet. 7-8 Ave.
Telephone: (212) 255-3601

Supervision: Vaad Hakashrus

Pita Express

1470 2nd Avenue (77th Street)
Telephone: (212) 249-1300

Glatt kosher.

Prime Grill

60 East 49th St.
Telephone: (212) 692-9292
Fax: (212) 883-8752

Second Avenue Delicatessen-Restaurant

156 2nd Avenue, cnr. 10th Street
Telephone: (212) 677-0606
Fax: (212) 477-5327
Email: 2ndavedeli@quicklink.com

Hours - Sunday-Thursday 7.30am-12.00am. Friday &
Saturday 7.30am-3.00am.

Shallots

550 Madison Avenue 10022
Telephone: (212) 833-7800
Email: shallotsny.com

In the Sony Plaza Atrium. Between 55th and 56th Sts

Tevere '84'

155 E. 84 St.

The Box Tree

250 East 49th Street
Telephone: (212) 758-8320

Tuscan Grill

228 West 72nd Street, (Bet. Bway & West End)
Telephone: (212) 875-9020

Village Crown Italian

94 Third Avenue   (212) 777-8816
Fax: (212) 388-9639
Email: info@villagecrown.com
Website: www.villagecrown.com

Supervision: Kof-K: Cholev Israel

11.30am to 11.00pm Sunday through Thursday, 11.30am to
2.00pm Friday. One hour after Shabbat until 12.00am
Saturday (September thru June)

Village Crown Moroccan

96 Third Avenue 10003
Telephone: (212) 647-2061
Fax: (212) 388-9639
Email: info@villagecrown.com
Website: www.villagecrown.com

Supervision: Kof-K

We also provide Shabbat meal delivery

Wolf & Lamb Steakhouse
10 E. 48th St., Nr Rockerfeller Ctr., Between 5th & Madison 10017
Telephone: (212) 317-1950
Fax: (212) 317-0159
Supervision: Organised Kashrut

Organic
Caravan of Dreams
405 East 6th Street, Bet. 1st Ave. & Ave. A
Telephone: (212) 254-1613
Email: angel@caravanofdreams.net
Supervision: Orthodox Rabbinical

Vegetarian
Maharani Restaurant
156 W. 29 St, (Bet. 6 & 7 Ave.)
Telephone: (212) 868-0707/2211

Quintessence
566 Amsterdam Ave.
Telephone: (212) 501-9700 or (646)-654-1823

SYNAGOGUES
Conservative
B'nai Jeshrun
270 West 89th Street, NY 10010
Telephone: (212) 787 7600

Park Avenue Synagogue
50 East 87th Street, NY 10128
Telephone: (212) 369 2600
Fax: (212) 410 7879

United Synagogue of America
155 Fifth Avenue, NY 10010
Telephone: (212) 533 7800
World Council of Synagogues can be found at the same location.

Orthodox
Agudat Israel World Organization
84 William Street, NY 10038
Telephone: (212) 797 9600
Fax: (212) 269 2843

Fifth Avenue Synagogue
5 East 62nd Street, NY, 10021
Telephone: (212) 838 2122
Fax: (212) 319 6119
Email: info@5as.org
Website: www.5as.org

Kehilath Jeshurun
125 East 85th Street, NY 10028
Telephone: (212) 427 1000

Lincoln Square
220 Amsterdam Avenue at 69th Street, NY, 10023
Telephone: (212) 874 6100

National Council of Young Israel National Office
3 West 16th Street, NY 10011
Telephone: (212) 929 1525
Fax: (212) 727 9526
Email: nyci

Ohab Zedeck
118 West 95th Street, NY 10025
Telephone: (212) 749 5150

Park East
163 East 67th Street, NY 10021
Telephone: (212) 737 6900
Fax: (212) 570 648

Union of Orthodox Jewish Congregations of America
333 Seventh Avenue, NY 10001
Telephone: (212) 563 4000
Fax: (212) 613 8333

Union of Orthodox Jewish Congregations of America
11 Broadway 10004
Telephone: (212) 563-4000
Fax: (212) 564-9058
Email: info@ou.org
Website: www.ou.org

Progressive
World Union for Progressive Judaism
838 Fifth Avenue, NY 10021
Telephone: (212) 650 4090
Fax: (212) 650 4090
Email: 5448032

Reform
Central Synagogue
652 Lexington Avenue, NY, 10022
Telephone: (212) 838 5122

Temple Emanuel-El
1 East 65th Street, NY, 10023
Telephone: (212) 744 1400

Union of America Hebrew Congregations
838 Fifth Avenue, NY 10021
Telephone: (212) 650 4085
Fax: (212) 650 4169

Sephardi
Shearith Israel
2 West 70th Street, NY, 10023

Union of Sephardi Congregations
8 West 70th Street, NY 10023
Telephone: (212) 873 0300

THEATRE
Jewish Repertory Theatre
c/o Midtown YMHA, 344 E. 14th Street
Telephone: (212) 505-2667; 674-7200

QUEENS

BUTCHERS

Herskowitz Glatt Meat Market
164-08 69th Avenue, Hillcrest 11365
Telephone: (718) 591-0750
Fax: (718) 591-0750
Supervision: Vaad Harabonim of Queens

DELICATESSEN

Berso Foods
64-20 108th Street, Forest Hills 11375
Telephone: (718) 275-9793
Supervision: Vaad Harabonim of Queens
Take-out only.

Meal Mart
72-10 Main Street, Flushing 11367
Telephone: (718) 261-3300
Fax: (718) 261-3435
Supervision: Vaad Harabonim of Queens
Catering and take out.

RESTAURANTS

Ben's Best Deli Restaurant
96-40 Queens Blvd, Rego Park, Rego Park 11374
Telephone: (718) 897-1700
Fax: (718) 997-6503
Email: bensbest@worldnet.att.net
Website: www.benbest.com

Dairy
Habustan Mediterranean Cuisine
188-202 Union Turnpike, Jamaica Estate

Kosher Corner Dairy
73-01 Main Street, Kew Gardens Hills
Telephone: (718) 263-1177

Zen Pavillion
251-15 Northern Blvd, Little Neck
Telephone: (718) 281-1500

Meat
Burger Nosh
69-48 Main Street, Kew Gardens Hills
Telephone: (718) 520-1933

Cho-Sen Garden
64-43 108th Street, Forest Hills 11375
Telephone: (718) 275-1300
Supervision: Vaad Harabonim of Queens
Chinese food.

Colbeh
68-34 Main Street, Flushing
Telephone: (718) 268-8181
Supervision: Kof-K

Da Mikelle II
102-39 Queens Blvd, Forest Hills
Telephone: (718) 997-6166

Dougie's
73-27 Main Street, Kew Gardens Hills
Telephone: (718) 793-4600
Fax: (718) 793-9003
Supervision: Vaad Harabonim of Queens

Glatt Kosher International Restaurant
JFK Airport, Terminal 4, 3rd floor, Forest Hills
Telephone: (718) 751-4787
Email: erwin7@nyc.rr.com
Supervision: Vaad Harabonim of Queens

Glatt Wok Express
190-11 Union Turnpike, Jamaica 11366
Telephone: (718) 740-1675
Supervision: Vaad Harabonim of Queens
Chinese food. Take-away service available.

Hapisgah Steakhouse
147-25 Union Turnpike, Kew Gardens Hills
Telephone: (718) 380-4449

La France
111-08 Queens Blvd
Telephone: (718) 520-6488

Pita House
98-102 Queens Blvd, Bet. 66-67th Ave., Flushing
Telephone: (718) 897-4829
Supervision: Rabbi David Katz

RESTAURANTS

Vegetarian
Budda Bodai
42-96 Main Street, Flushing
Telephone: (718) 939-1188
Supervision: Rabbi Mayer Steinberg

STATEN ISLAND

KASHRUT INFORMATION

Directory
Organised Kashrus Laboratories
PO Box 218, Brooklyn
Telephone: (718) 851-6428
Including the Circle K trademark.

NIAGARA FALLS

COMMUNITY ORGANISATIONS
Jewish Federation of Niagara Falls
c/o of Beth Israel
Telephone: (716) 284-4575

SYNAGOGUES

Conservative
Beth Israel
College & Madison Avenues 14305
Telephone: (716) 285-9894

Reform
Beth El
720 Ashland Avenue 14301
Telephone: (716) 282-2717
Call for time of services.

POUGHKEEPSIE
COMMUNITY ORGANISATIONS
Jewish Community Center of Dutchess County
110 Grand Avenue 12603
Telephone: (845) 471-0430

SYNAGOGUES
Conservative
Temple Beth El
118 Grand Avenue 12603
Telephone: (845) 454-0570
Fax: (845) 454-7257
Website: www.uscj.org/empire/poughktb

Orthodox
Shomre Israel
18 Park Avenue 12603

Reform
Vassar Temple
140 Hooker Avenue 12601
Telephone: (845) 454-2570

ROCHESTER
BAKERIES
Brighton Donuts
Monroe Avenue
Telephone: (716) 271-6940

COMMUNITY ORGANISATIONS
Jewish Community Federation
441 East Avenue 14607
Telephone: (716) 461-0490
Fax: (716) 461-0912
Website: www.jewishrochester.org

DELICATESSEN
Brownstein's Deli and Bakery
1862 Monroe Avenue 14618

Fox's Kosher Restaurant and Deli
3450 Winton Place 14623

MEDIA
Newspaper
Jewish Ledger
2525 Brighton-Henrietta Town Line R 14623

RESTAURANTS
Meat
Jewish Home of Rochester Cafeteria
2021 S. Winton Road 14618

SYNAGOGUES
Conservative
Temple Beth Hamedrash-Beth Israel
1369 East Avenue 14610
Telephone: (716) 244-2060

Orthodox
Congregation Beth Sholom
1161 Monroe Avenue 14620
Telephone: (716) 473-1625

Rockland County

HAVERSTRAW
SYNAGOGUES
Orthodox
Congregation Sons of Jacob
37 Clove Avenue 10927
Telephone: (845) 429-4644

MONSEY
BAKERIES
Bubba's Bagels
Wesley Hills Plaza, Wesley Hills 10952
Telephone: (845) 362-1019
Fax: (845) 362-0549
Supervision: Va'ad Harabonim of Greater Monsey

DELICATESSEN
Sammy's Bagels
421 Route 59 10952
Telephone: (845) 356-3030

HOME HOSPITALITY
Mendel & Margalit Zuber
32 Blauvelt Road, 10952
Telephone: (845) 425-6213
The Zuber's write "Anyone wishing to spend a Shabbat or Yom Tov with us is more than welcome. We are Lubavitch Chasidim, glatt kosher."

RESTAURANTS
Mehadrin Restaurant
82 Route 59 10952

Dairy
Al di La
455 Route 306, Wesley Hills 10952
Telephone: (845) 354-2672
Supervision: Va'ad Harabonim of Greater Monsey
Italian/Dairy. Cholov Yisrael.

Chai Pizza
94 Route 59 10952
Telephone: (845) 356-2135

Jerusalem Pizza & Restaurant
190 Route 59 10952
Telephone: (845) 426-1500

Kol Tov Pizza
118 Rte 59

Meat
Glat Wok
106 Rte 59
Telephone: (845) 426-3600

Kyo Sushi and Steak
419 Rte 59
Telephone: (845) 371-5855

SYNAGOGUES
Orthodox
Young Israel of Monsey and Wesley Hills Inc
58 Parker Blvd 10952
Telephone: (845) 362-1838

NEW CITY
DELICATESSEN
Steve's Deli-Bake
179 South Main Street 10956
Telephone: (845) 634-8749

GROCERIES
M&S Kosher Meats
191a South Main Street 10956
Telephone: (845) 638-9494

SYNAGOGUES
Conservative
New City Jewish Center
47 Old Schoolhouse Road 10956
Telephone: (845) 634-3619
Fax: (845) 634-3481
Email: ncjc@j51.com
Website: www.uscj.org/metny/newcity/index.html

Reform
Temple Beth Sholom
228 New Hempstead Road 10956
Telephone: (845) 638-0770
Fax: (845) 638-1696
Website: www.templebethsholom.info

ORANGEBURG
SYNAGOGUES
Conservative
Orangetown Jewish Center
8 Independence Avenue 10962
Telephone: (845) 359-5920

SPRING VALLEY
DELICATESSEN
GPG Deli
Main Street 10977

RESTAURANTS
Eli's Bagel Shop
58 N. Myrtle Avenue 10977
Telephone: (845) 425-6166
Hours: Sunday - Thursday 6.30am-5.00pm. Friday 6.30am-2.00pm. Open Motzei Shabbos from after Succos until Pesach. Catering and Platters for all occasions. Under the Hashgocha of Rabbi B. Gruber/Yoshen.

RESTAURANTS
Dairy
Sheli's Café and Pizza
126 Maple Avenue 10977
Telephone: (845) 426-0105
Fax: (845) 362-5004
Email: shely@ucs.net
Supervision: Rabbi Breslaver

SYNAGOGUES
Orthodox
Young Israel of Spring Valley
23 Union Road
Telephone: (845) 356-3363

SUFFERN
Bais Torah
89 West Carlton Road 10901
Telephone: (845) 352-1343
Fax: (845) 352-0841
Email: yhaber@ou.org

SARATOGA SPRINGS
SYNAGOGUES
Conservative
Shaare Tefilah
84 Weibel Avenue 12866
Telephone: (518) 584-2370

Orthodox
Chabad-Lubavitch Center of the Capital District
122 S. Main Avenue 12208
Telephone: (518) 482-5781
Fax: (518) 482-6330
Email: Rabbirubin@saratogachabad.com
Website: www.Saratogachabad.com
See website for Upstate Tourist Kosher, Minyan and Mikva services,. Daily Minyan in Lake George in August

Congregation Mikveh Israel
26 Lafayette Street 12866
Telephone: (518) 584-6338
Services in July & August. Kosher food available

Orthodox Minyan
510 1/2 Broadway 12866
Telephone: (518) 437-1738

SCHENECTADY
Agudat Achim
2117 Union Street 12309
Telephone: (518) 393-9211

SYNAGOGUES
Orthodox
Beth Israel
2195 Eastern Parkway 12309
Telephone: (518) 377-3700

SYNAGOGUES
Reform
Gates of Heaven
852 Ashmore Avenue 12309
Telephone: (518) 374-8173

SYRACUSE
SYNAGOGUES
Orthodox
Young Israel Shaarei Torah of Syracuse
4313 E. Genesee Street 13214
Telephone: (315) 446-6194
Fax: (315) 446-7936

TROY
MIKVAOT
Troy Chabad Center
2306 15th Street 12180
Telephone: (518) 274-5572

SYNAGOGUES
Conservative
Temple Beth El
411 Hoosick Street 12180
Telephone: (518) 272-6113

Reform
Congregation Berith Shalom
167 3rd Street 12180
Telephone: (518) 272-8872
Fax: (518) 272-8984

UTICA
COMMUNITY ORGANISATIONS
Jewish Community Federation of the Mohawk Valley
2310 Oneida Street, 13501
Telephone: (315) 733-2343
Fax: (315) 733-2346
Email: jcci@borg.com
The Federation supports the Jewish Community Center.

SYNAGOGUES
Conservative
Temple Beth El
1607 Genesee Street 13501
Telephone: (315) 724-4751

Orthodox
Congregation Zvi Jacob
112 Memorial Parkway 13501
Telephone: (315) 724-8357

Reform
Temple Emanu-El
2710 Genesee Street 13502
Telephone: (315) 724-4177

VESTAL
COMMUNITY ORGANISATIONS
Jewish Federation of Broome County
500 Clubhouse Road 13850
Telephone: (607) 724-2332
Fax: (607) 724-2311
Email: earlejfbc@stny.rr.com

MEDIA
Newspaper
The Reporter
500 Clubhouse Road 13850
Telephone: (607) 724-2360
Fax: (607) 724-2311
Email: reporter@aol.com

Westchester County

HARRISON
Young Israel of Harrison
207 Union Avenue 10528
Telephone: (914) 777-1236

MOUNT VERNON
Brothers of Israel
116 Crary Avenue 10550
Telephone: (914) 667-1302
Fax: (914) 667-0278

Fleetwood
11 East Broad Street 10552
Telephone: (914) 664-5581
Fax: (914) 699-6954
Email: rabbi@fleetwoodsynagogue.org
Website: www.fleetwoodsynagogue.org

NEW ROCHELLE
RESTAURANTS
Eden Wok
1327 North Avenue 10804
Telephone: (914) 637-9363
Fax: (914) 637-9371
Supervision: Vaad of Westchester

SYNAGOGUES
Conservative
Bethel
Northfield Road

Reform
Temple Israel
1000 Pine Brook Blvd 10804

Orthodox
Cong. Anshe Sholom
50 North Avenue 10805
Telephone: (914) 632-9220
Fax: (914) 632-8182
Email: asnewroch@aol.com

Young Israel of New Rochelle
1228 North Avenue 10804
Telephone: (914) 777-1236
Contact Rabbi on 835-5581

PEEKSKILL
SYNAGOGUES
Conservative
First Hebrew Congregation
1821 E. Main Street 10566
Telephone: (914) 739-0500
Fax: (914) 739-0684

PORT CHESTER
RESTAURANTS
Vegetarian
Green Symphony
427 Boston Post Road 10573
Telephone: (914) 937-6537

RESTAURANTS
Vegetarian Kosher
Vegetarian Kosher
427 Boston Post Road
Telephone: (914) 937-6537

SYNAGOGUES
Conservative
Kneses Tifereth Israel
575 King Street 10573
Telephone: (914) 939-1004
Fax: (914) 939-1086

SCARSDALE
SYNAGOGUES
Conservative
Young Israel of Scarsdale
1313 Weaver Street 10583
Telephone: (914) 636-8686
Fax: (914) 636-1209
Email: yisecy@yahoo.com

Orthodox Sephardi
Magen David Sephardic Congregation
1225 Weaver Street, P O B 129H 10583
Telephone: (914) 633-3728
Fax: (914) 636-0608
Email: mitchser@aol.com

WHITE PLAINS
SYNAGOGUES
Conservative
Temple Israel Center
280 Old Mamaroneck Road, at Miles Avenue 10605
Telephone: (914) 948-2800
Fax: (914) 948-4755

Orthodox
Hebrew Institute of White Plains
20 Greenridge Avenue 10605
Telephone: (914) 948-3095
Fax: (914) 949-4676
Email: office@hiwp.org

Young Israel of White Plains
135 Old Mamaroneck Road, 10605
Telephone: (914) 683-YIWP
Email: yiwp.org
Website: www.yiwp.org

Reconstructionist
Bet Am Shalom
295 Soundview Avenue 10606
Telephone: (914) 946-8851

Reform
Jewish Community Center
252 Soundview Avenue 10606
Telephone: (914) 949-4717

YONKERS
SYNAGOGUES
Conservative
Agudas Achim
21 Hudson Street 10701

Orthodox
Lincoln Park Jewish Center
323 Central Park Avenue 10704
Telephone: (914) 965-7119
Website: www.lpjc.org

Reform
Temple Emanu-El
306 Rumsey Road 10705
Telephone: (914) 963-0575

WEST POINT
SYNAGOGUES
United States Military Academy Jewish Chapel
Building 750 10096
Telephone: (845) 938-2766
Fax: (845) 446-7706
With a local community of over 200 the Chapel was designed by the firm responsible for the United Nations building and the Lincoln Center

North Carolina

ASHEVILLE
SYNAGOGUES

Conservative
Congregation Beth Israel
229 Murdock Avenue 28804
Telephone: (704) 252-8431
Fax: (704) 252-3882
Email: bethisrael@buncombe.main.nc.us

Reform
Beth Ha-Tephila
43 N. Liberty Street 28801
Telephone: (704) 253-4911
Email: tephila@worldnet.att.net

CHARLOTTE
COMMUNITY ORGANISATIONS
Jewish Federation
5007 Providence Road 28226
Telephone: (704) 366-5007

DELICATESSEN
The Kosher Mart & Delicatessen
Amity Gardens Shopping Center, 3840 E.
Independence Blvd 28205
Telephone: (704) 563-8288
Fax: (704) 532-9111
Email: koshermartusa@mindspring.com
Website: www.koshermartusa.com

LIBRARIES
Speizman Jewish Library
5007 Providence Road 28226

MEDIA
Newspaper
Charlotte Jewish News
Telephone: (704) 366-5007

MIKVAOT
Chabad House
6619 Sardis Road 28270
Telephone: (704) 366-3984
Fax: (704) 362-1423

SYNAGOGUES

Conservative
Temple Israel
4901 Providence Road
Telephone: (704) 362-2796
Fax: (704) 362-1098
Email: templeisraelnc.org

Orthodox
Chabad House
6619 Sardis Road 28270
Telephone: (704) 366-3984
Fax: (704) 362-1423
Email: sardis@earthlink.net

Reform
Temple Beth El
5101 Providence Road 28207
Telephone: (704) 366-1948

DURHAM
COMMUNITY ORGANISATIONS
Durham-Chapel Hill Jewish Federation and Community Council
205 Mt. Bolus Road, Chapel Hill 27514
Telephone: (919) 967-6916

KASHRUT INFORMATION
Dr Ed Halpern
c/o Duke University Medical centre

SYNAGOGUES

Conservative
Beth El
1004 Watts Street 27701
Telephone: (919) 682-1238

Reform
Judea Reform Congregation
1955 Cornwallis Road 27705
Telephone: (919) 489-7062
Fax: (919) 489-0611
Email: infobox@judeareform.org

FAYETTEVILLE
SYNAGOGUES

Conservative
Beth Israel Congregation
2204 Morganton Road 28303
Telephone: (910) 484-6462

GREENSBORO
COMMUNITY ORGANISATIONS
Greensboro Jewish Federation
5509 C West Friendly Avenue 27410-4211
Telephone: (336) 852-5433
Fax: (336) 852-4346
Email: mfcgsonc@jon.cjfny.org

SYNAGOGUES

Conservative
Beth David
804 Winview Drive 27410
Telephone: (336) 294-0007
Fax: (336) 294-7011
Email: info@bethdavidsynagogue.org
Website: www.bethdavidsynagogue.org

HENDERSONVILLE
Agudas Israel Congregation
328 N. King Street, PO Box 668 28793

RALEIGH
GROCERIES
Eshel Kosher Market
5540 Atlantic Springs Road
Telephone: (919) 872-7757

MIKVAOT
Congregation of Sha'arei Israel
7400 Falls of the Neuse Road 27615
Telephone: (919) 847-8986

SYNAGOGUES
Conservative
Beth Meyer
504 Newton Road 27615
Telephone: (919) 848-1420

Orthodox
Congregation of Sha'arei Israel - Lubavitch
7400 Falls of the Neuse Road 27615
Telephone: (919) 847-8986
Fax: (919) 847-3142

SYNAGOGUES
Reform
Temple Beth Or
5315 Creedmoor Road 27612
Telephone: (919) 781-4895
Fax: (919) 781-4697
Email: tempbethor@aol.com
Website: www.templebethor-raleigh.org

WILMINGTON
SYNAGOGUES
Conservative
B'nai Israel
2601 Chestnut Street 28405
Telephone: (302) 762-1117

Reform
Temple Emanuel
201 Oakwood Drive 27103
Telephone: (302) 722-6640

Temple of Israel
1 South 4th Street 28401
Telephone: (302) 762-0000

North Dakota
BISMARK
Bismark Hebrew Congregation
703 North Fifth Street 58103
Telephone: (701) 258-3572

FARGO
Temple Beth El
809 11th Avenue S 58103
Telephone: (701) 232-0441

Ohio
AKRON
COMMUNITY ORGANISATIONS
Jewish Community Board of Akron
750 White Pond Drive 44320
Telephone: (330) 869-2424
Fax: (330) 867-8498
Email: www.jewishakron.org

MIKVAOT
Mikva
Telephone: (330) 867-6798

SYNAGOGUES
Conservative
Beth El
464 S. Hawkins Avenue 44320
Telephone: (330) 864-2105

Orthodox
Anshe Sfard Synagogue
646 N.Revere Road 44333
Telephone: (330) 867-7292
Fax: (330) 867-7719

Reform
Temple Israel
133 Merriman Road 44303
Telephone: (330) 762-8617
Fax: (330) 762-8619
Email: rabbi@neo.rr.com
Website: www.templeisraelakron.org

BEACHWOOD
SYNAGOGUES
Orthodox
Young Israel of Greater Cleveland
2463 South Green Road, 44122
Telephone: (216) 382-5740
Fax: (216) 382-8722
Email: office@yigc.org
Website: www.yigc.org

CANTON
COMMUNITY ORGANISATIONS
Jewish Community Federation
2631 Harvard Avenue 44709
Telephone: (781) 452-6444

SYNAGOGUES

Conservative
Shaaray Torah
423 30th Street N.W 44709
Telephone: (781) 492-0310

Orthodox
Agudas Achim
2508 Market Street N. 44704
Telephone: (781) 456-8781

Reform
Temple Israel
333 25th Street N.W 44709
Telephone: (781) 455-5197

CINCINNATI

BAKERIES
Just Desserts
6964 Plainfield Road 45236
Telephone: (513) 793-6627

COMMUNITY ORGANISATIONS
Jewish Community Center of Cincinnati
7420 Montgomery Road 45236
Telephone: (513) 761-7500
Fax: (513) 761-0084
Email: info@jcc-cinci.com
Website: www.jcc-cinci.com

Jewish Federation
1811 Losantiville, Suite 320 45237
Telephone: (513) 351-3800

DELICATESSEN
Bilkers
7648 Reading Road 45237

LIBRARIES
**The Hebrew Union College-Jewish Institute
of Religion**
3101 Clifton Avenue 45220
Telephone: (513) 221-1875
Fax: (513) 221-0519
Email: klau@cn.huc.edu

LIBRARIES
Graduate School
**The Hebrew Union College-Jewish Institute
of Religion**
3101 Clifton Avenue 45220
Telephone: (513) 221-3274
Fax: (513) 221-0519
Email: klau@huc.edu

MEDIA
Newspaper
American Israelite
906 Main Street 45202

MIKVAOT
Kehelath B'nai Israel
1546 Beaverton Avenue 45237
Telephone: (513) 761-5260

RESTAURANTS
Dairy
Dunkin' Donuts
9385 Colerain Avenue 45231
Telephone: (513) 385-0930

Marx Hot Bagels
9701 Kenwood Road, Blue Ash 45242
Telephone: (513) 891-5542
Fax: (513) 891-1063

Meat
Pilder's Deli
4070 East Galbraith Road 45236
Telephone: (513) 792-9961
Fax: (513) 792-9605

SYNAGOGUES

Conservative
**Northern Hills Synagogue - Congregation
B'nai Avraham**
5714 Fields Ertel Road 45249
Telephone: (513) 931-6038
Fax: (513) 530-2002
Email: berniceu@fuse.net
Website: www.nhs-cba.org

Orthodox
Downtown Synagogue
Bartlett Building, 36 E. Fourth, 7th Floor 45202
Telephone: (513) 241-3576

Golf Manor Synagogue
6442 Stover Avenue 45237
Telephone: (513) 531-6654

Sephardic Beth Shalom
Manss Avenue, PO Box 37431 45222
Telephone: (513) 793-6936

Reform
Isaac M. Wise Temple
8329 Ridge Road 45236
Telephone: (513) 793-2556

CLEVELAND

BAKERIES
Breadsmith
9708 Kenwood Road, Blue Ash 45242
Telephone: (216) 791-8817

BUTCHERS
Tibor's Glatt Meat Market
2185 S. Green Road, S. Euclid 44121
Telephone: (216) 381-7615
Fax: (216) 381-5215

COMMUNITY ORGANISATIONS
Jewish Community Federation of Cleveland
1750 Euclid Avenue 44115
Telephone: (216) 566-9200
Fax: (216) 861-1230
Email: info@jcfcleve.org
Website: www.jewishcleveland.org

DELICATESSEN
Unger's Kosher Market and Bakery
1831 S. Taylor Road, Cleveland Heights 44118
Telephone: (216) 321-7176
Fax: (216) 321-0777

MEDIA
Newspaper
Cleveland Jewish News
23880 Commerce Park, Suite 1 44122
Telephone: (216) 454 8300
Fax: (216) 454 8200
Website: www.clevelandjewishnews.com

MIKVAOT
Charlotte Goldberg Community Mikvah of the Park Synagogue
3300 Mayfield Road, Cleveland Heights 44118
Telephone: (216) 371-2244 ext 198
Fax: (216) 321-0639

K'hal Yereim Synagogue
1771 S. Taylor Road, Cleveland Heights 44118
Telephone: (216) 321-5855

Mikva
Cleveland Heights
Telephone: (216) 387-1040

MUSEUMS
Park Synagogue
3300 Mayfield Road 44118

RESTAURANTS
Dairy
Issi's Place
14431 Cedar Road, , South Euclid 44121
Telephone: (216) 291-9600

Meat
Abba's Market and Grille
13937 Cedar Road, S. Euclid 44121
Telephone: (216) 321-5660
Fax: (216) 321-4135

Contempo Cuisine
13898 Cedar Road, University Heights 44118
Telephone: (216) 397-3520
Fax: (216) 397-3523

Empire Kosher Kitchen
2234 Warrensville Center Road, University Heights
Telephone: (216) 691-0006

Ruchama's Singapore
2172 Warrensville Center Road, University Heights 44118
Telephone: (216) 321-1100
Fax: (216) 321-1485

SYNAGOGUES
Orthodox
Congregation Shomre Shabbos
1801 S. Taylor Road, Cleveland Heights 44118
Telephone: (216) 371-0033

K'hai Yereim
1771 S. Taylor Road, Cleveland Heights 44118
Telephone: (216) 321-6855

COLUMBUS
RESTAURANTS
Dairy
Sammy's New York Bagels
40 N. James Road 43213
Telephone: (614) 246-0426
Fax: (614) 246-0427
Email: sammysbagel@msn.com
Website: www.sammysbagels.net
Supervision: Vaad Ho-ir of Columbus

SYNAGOGUES
Orthodox
Agudas Achim Synagogue
2767 E. Broad Street 43209
Telephone: (614) 237-2747

Congregation Ahavas Sholom
2568 E. Broad Street 43209
Telephone: (614) 252-4815
Fax: (614) 252-1316
Email: ahavas@beol.net
Website: www.ahavas-sholom.org

DAYTON
BAKERIES
Rinaldo's Bakery
910 West Fairview Avenue 45406
Telephone: (937) 274-1311
Supervision: Rabbi Hillel Fox, Beth Jacob Congregation.

COMMUNITY ORGANISATIONS
Jewish Federation of Greater Dayton
4501 Denlinger Road 45426
Telephone: (937) 854-4150

HOME HOSPITALITY
Shomrei Emunah
1706 Salem Avenue 45406
Telephone: (937) 274-6941
Fax: (937) 274-7511
Email: shomrei@earthlink.net

MEDIA
Newspaper
Dayton Jewish Observer
4501 Denlinger Road 45426
Telephone: (937) 854-4150
Fax: (937) 854-2850
Email: dayjobs@aol.com

The Dayton Jewish Advocate
Telephone: (937) 854-4150 ext. 118

MIKVAOT
Mikva
556 Kenwood Avenue 45406
Telephone: (937) 275-1436

SYNAGOGUES
Orthodox
Beth Jacob Congregation
7020 North Main Street 45415
Telephone: (937) 274-2149
Fax: (937) 274-9556
Email: bethjacob1@aol.com
Website: www.bethjacobcong.org
Supervision: Rabbi Hillel Fox, Beth Jacob Congregation

LORAIN
SYNAGOGUES
Conservative
Agudath B'nai Israel
1715 Meister Road 44053
Telephone: (216) 282-3307

TOLEDO
B'nai Israel
2727 Kenwood Blvd. 43606
Telephone: (419) 531-1677

SYNAGOGUES
Orthodox
Congregation Etz Chayim
3852 Woodley Road 43606
Telephone: (419) 473-2401

Reform
The Temple-Congregation Shomer Emunium
6453 Sylvania Avenue 43560
Telephone: (419) 883-3341

YOUNGSTOWN
COMMUNITY ORGANISATIONS
Youngstown Area Jewish Federation
505 Gypsy Lane 44501
Telephone: (330) 746-3251

MIKVAOT
Children of Israel
3970 1/2 Logan Way 44505
Telephone: (330) 759-2167

SYNAGOGUES
Conservative
Beth Israel Temple Center
2138 E. Market Street, Warren 44483-6104
Telephone: (330) 395-3877
Fax: (330) 394-5918
Email: bethisrael1@juno.com

Ohev Tzedek-Shaarei Torah
5245 Glenwood Avenue 44512
Telephone: (330) 758-2321
Fax: (330) 758-2322
Email: ot20@juno.com

Temple El Emeth
3970 Logan Way 44505
Telephone: (330) 759-1429

SYNAGOGUES
Reform
Rodef Sholom
Elm Street & Woodbine Avenue 44505
Telephone: (330) 744-5001

Oklahoma

OKLAHOMA CITY
BAKERIES
Ingrid's Kitchen
2309 N.W. 36th Street 73112

KASHRUT INFORMATION
Chabad House
6401 Lenox Avenue, 73116
Telephone: (405) 810-1770
Fax: (405) 810-1772

SYNAGOGUES
Conservative
Emanuel Synagogue
900 N.W. 47th Street 73106
Telephone: (405) 528-2113

Reform
Temple B'nai Israel
4901 N. Pennsylvania Avenue 73112
Telephone: (405) 848-0965

TULSA
COMMUNITY ORGANISATIONS
Jewish Federation of Tulsa
2021 E. 71st Street 74136
Telephone: (918) 495-1100
Fax: (918) 495-1220
Email: federation@jewishtulsa.org

KASHRUT INFORMATION
Chabad House
6622 S. Utica Avenue 74136
Telephone: (918) 492-4499; 493-7006
Fax: (918) 492-4499

MEDIA
Newspaper
Tulsa Jewish Review
2021 E. 71st Street 74136
Telephone: (918) 495-1100

MIKVAOT
Congregation B'nai Emunah
1719 S. Owasso 74120
Telephone: (918) 583-7121
Fax: (918) 747-9696
Email: thenicepeople@tulsagogue.com
Website: www.tulsagogue.com

Mikva Shoshana - Chabad
6622 So. Utica Avenue 74136
Telephone: (918) 493-7006

MUSEUMS
The Sherwin Miller Museum of Jewish Art
2021 East 71st Street 74136
Telephone: (918) 492-1818
Fax: (918) 492-1888
Email: info@jewishmuseum.net
Website: www.jewishmuseum.net

SYNAGOGUES
Conservative
Congregation B'nai Emunah
1719 S. Owasso 74120
Telephone: (918) 583-7121
Fax: (918) 747-9696
Email: thesynagogue@bnaiemunah.com

Orthodox
Chabad House
6622 S Utica Avenue 74136
Telephone: (918) 492-4499; 493-7006
Fax: (918) 492-4499

Reform
Temple Israel
2004 E. 22nd Place 74114
Telephone: (918) 747-1309
Fax: (918) 747-3564
Email: templeis@ionet.net

Oregon

ASHLAND
Temple Emek Shalom-Rogue Valley Jewish Community
1081 East Main St
Telephone: (541) 488-2909
Fax: (541) 488-2814
Email: TEShalom@emekshalom.org
Website: www.emekshalom.org

EUGENE
SYNAGOGUES
Conservative
Temple Beth Israel
42 W. 25th Avenue 97405
Telephone: (541) 485-7218

PORTLAND
COMMUNITY ORGANISATIONS
Jewish Federation of Portland
6680 S.W. Capitol Highway 97219
Telephone: (503) 245-6219
Fax: (503) 245-6603
Email: federation@jewishportland.org
Website: www.jewishportland.org

GROCERIES
Albertson's
5415 SW Beaverton Hillsdale Highway 97221
Telephone: (503) 246-1713

MIKVAOT
Ritualarium
1425 S.W. Harrison Street 97219
Telephone: (503) 224-3409

MUSEUMS
Oregon Jewish Museum
310 NW Davis Street 97209
Telephone: (503) 226-3600
Fax: (503) 226-1800
Email: Email: museum@ojm.org
Website: www.ojm.org

RESTAURANTS
Mittleman Jewish Community Center (Kosher restaurant)
6651 S.W. Capitol Highway 97219
Telephone: (503) 244-0111

SYNAGOGUES
Conservative
Congregation Neveh Shalom
2900 SW Peaceful Lane 97239
Telephone: (503) 246-8831
Fax: (503) 246-7553
Email: rothstein@nevehshalom.org
Website: www.nevehshalom.org

Orthodox
Ahavath Achim
3225 S.W. Barbur Blvd 97201
Telephone: (503) 775-5895

Kesser Israel
136 S.W. Meade Street 97201
Telephone: (503) 222-1239

Shaare Torah
920 N.W. 25th Avenue 97210
Telephone: (503) 226-6131
Fax: (503) 226-0241
Email: nfo@shaarietorah.org
Website: www.shaarietorah.org

Reform
Temple Beth Israel
1972 NW Flanders 97209
Telephone: (503) 222-1069

SALEM
SYNAGOGUES

Reconstructionist
Beth Shalom
1795 Broadway NE 97303
Telephone: (508) 362-5004

Temple Beth Shalom
1795 Broadway, NE 97303
Telephone: (508) 362-5004

Pennsylvania

ALLENTOWN
COMMUNITY ORGANISATIONS
Jewish Federation of Le High Valley
702 22nd Street 18104
Telephone: (610) 821-5500
Fax: (610) 821 8946
Email: www.jewishlehighvalley.org
Kosher food available

MIKVAOT
Mikva
1834 Whitehall Street 18104
Telephone: (610) 776-7948

RESTAURANTS

Meat
Glatt Kosher Community Center
702 N. 22nd Stree 18104
Telephone: (610) 435-3571

SYNAGOGUES

Conservative
Temple Beth El
1702 Hamilton Street 18104
Telephone: (610) 435-3521

Orthodox
Congregation Agudas Achim
625 North Second Street 18102
Telephone: (610) 432-4414

Congregation Sons of Israel
2715 Tilghman Stree 18104
Telephone: (610) 433-6089
Fax: (610) 433-6080
Email: rabbi@att.net
Website: www.sonsofisrael.net

Reform
Congregation Keneseth Israel
2227 Chew Street 18104
Telephone: (610) 435-9074
Email: congki@enter.net

BALA CYNWYD
BOOKSELLERS
Rosenberg Hebrew Book Store
144 Montgomery Avenue 19004
Telephone: (610) 667-9299
Fax: (610) 667-4810

BENSALEM
MIKVAOT
Bucks County Mikveh
2454 Bristol Road 19020
Telephone: (215) 891-5565

SYNAGOGUES
kehillas B'nai Shalom
2446 Bristol Road 19020
Telephone: (215) 750-0604
Supervision: Rabbi Moshe Travitsky - Orthodox

BETHLEHEM
SYNAGOGUES

Conservative
Congregation Brith Sholom
Macada & Jacksonville Roads 18017
Telephone: (603) 866-8009

Orthodox
Agudath Achim
1555 Linwood Street 18017
Telephone: (603) 866-8891

EASTON
SYNAGOGUES

Conservative
B'nai Abraham
16th & Bushkill Streets
Telephone: (508) 258-5343

Reform
Temple Covenant of Peace
1451 Northampton Street 18042
Telephone: (508) 253-2031
Fax: (508) 253-7973
Email: tcp@ fast.net

ELKINS PARK

MUSEUMS

Temple Judea Museum of Kenesseth Israel
8339 Old York Road 19027
Telephone: (215) 887-2027; 887-8700
Fax: (215) 887-1070
Email: tjmuseum@aol.com

SYNAGOGUES

Orthodox

Young Israel of Elkins Park
7715 Montgomery Avenue 19027
Telephone: (215) 635-3152
Email: host@yiep.org
Website: www.yiep.org

TOURIST INFORMATION

Beth Sholom
8231 Old York Park 19027
Telephone: (215) 887-1342
Fax: (215) 887-6605
Website: www.bethssholomcongregation.org

ERIE

SYNAGOGUES

Conservative
Brith Sholom Jewish Center
3207 State Street 16508
Telephone: (814) 454-2431
Fax: (814) 452-0790

Reform
Temple Anshe Hesed
930 Liberty Street 16502
Telephone: (814) 454-2426
Fax: (814) 454-2427
Email: anshhsd@velocity.net

HARRISBURG

COMMUNITY ORGANISATIONS

United Jewish Community of Greater Harrisburg
100 Vaughn Street 17110
Telephone: (717) 236-9555

GROCERIES

Bakeries Giant Food Store and Weis Market
Linglestown Road

Quality Kosher
7th Division Street 17110

KOSHER FOOD

Norman Gras Catering
3000 Green Street 17110-1234
Telephone: (717) 234-2196
Fax: (717) 234-3943
Email: normangras@aol.com

SYNAGOGUES

Conservative
Beth El
2637 N. Front Street 17110
Telephone: (717) 232-0556
Fax: (717) 232-6240

Chisuk Emuna
5th & Division Streets 17110
Telephone: (717) 232-4851
Fax: (717) 232-7950
Email: muroff@juno.com

Orthodox
Kesher Israel
2945 N. Front Street 17110
Telephone: (717) 238-0763

Reform
Ohev Sholom
2345 N. Front Street 17110
Telephone: (717) 233-6459
Fax: (717) 236-7844

HAZELTON

SYNAGOGUES

Conservative
Agudas Israel
77 N. Pine Street 18201
Telephone: (717) 455-2851

Reform
Beth Israel
98 N. Church Street 18201
Telephone: (717) 455-3971

HERSHEY

SNACK BAR

Meat
Central PA's Kosher Mart
Hershey Park
Telephone: (717) 392-1503

JOHNSTOWN

COMMUNITY ORGANISATIONS

United Jewish Federation of Johnstown
700 Indiana Street 15905
Telephone: (814) 536-0647

SYNAGOGUES

Conservative
Beth Sholom Congregation
700 Indiana Street 15905
Telephone: (814) 536-0647

LANCASTER
COMMUNITY ORGANISATIONS
Jewish Federation
2120 Oregon Pike 17601
Telephone: (717) 597-7354

SYNAGOGUES
Conservative
Beth El
1836 Rohrerstown Road 17601
Telephone: (717) 581-7891
Fax: (717) 581-7870
Email: templebethel@dejazzd.com

Orthodox
Degel Israel
1120 Columbia Avenue 17603
Telephone: (717) 397-0183
Fax: (717) 509-6188
Email: ourkehilla@mail.com
Website: : www.ourkehilla

Reform
Temple Shaarei Shomayim
N. Duke & James Streets 17602
Telephone: (717) 397-5575

MCKEESPORT
SYNAGOGUES
Conservative
Tree of Life-Sfard
Cypress Avenue 15131
Telephone: (412) 673-0938

Orthodox
Gemilas Chesed
1400 Summit Street, White Oak 15131
Telephone: (412) 678-9859

Reform
B'nai Israel
536 Shaw Avenue 15132
Telephone: (412) 678-6181
Fax: (412) 678-6908
Email: tbi536@juno.com or tbi536@aol.com

PHILADELPHIA
BAKERIES
Arthur's Bakery
Academy Plaza, Red Lion and Academy Roads
19114
Telephone: (215) 637-9146
Supervision: Rabbinical Assembly

Best Cake Bakery
7594 Haverford Avenue 19151
Telephone: (215) 878-1127
Email: rugalach@aol.com
Supervision: Orthodox Vaad of Philadelphia

Buy the Dozen
219 Haverford Avenue, Narberth 19072
Telephone: (215) 610-667-9440
Supervision: Orthodox Vaad of Philadelphia

Dante's Bakery
Richboro Centre, Bustleton and Second Street Pikes,
Richboro 18954
Telephone: (215) 357-9599
Supervision: Rabbinical Assembly

Hesh's Eclair Bake Shoppe
7721 Castor Avenue 19152
Telephone: (215) 742-8575
Supervision: Vaad Hakashruth

Hutchinson's Classic Bakery
13023 Bustleton Pike 19116
Telephone: (215) 676-8612
Supervision: Rabbinical Assembly

Kaplan's New Model Bakery
901 North 3rd Street 19123
Telephone: (215) 627-5288
Supervision: Rabbi Solomon Isaacson

Lipkin and Sons Bakery
8013 Castor Avenue 19152
Telephone: (215) 342-3005
Supervision: Rabbi Abraham Novitsky

Michael's
6635 Castor Avenue 19149
Telephone: (215) 745-1423
Supervision: Rabbi Dov Brisman

Moish's Addison Bakery
10865 Bustleton Avenue 19116
Telephone: (215) 469-8054
Supervision: Rabbinical Assembly

Rilling's Bakery
2990 Southampton Road 19154
Telephone: (215) 698-6171
Supervision: Rabbinical Assembly

Viking Bakery
39 Cricket Avenue, Ardmore 19003
Telephone: (215) 642-9227
Supervision: Rabbi Joshua Toledano

Weiss Bakery
6635 Castor Avenue 19149
Telephone: (215) 722-4506
Supervision: Rabbi Dov Brisman

Zach's Bakery
6419 Rising Sun Avenue 19111
Telephone: (215) 722-1688
Supervision: Rabbinical Assembly

BOOKSELLERS

Gratz College
Old York Road and Melrose Avenue, Melrose Park
19027
Telephone: (215) 635-7300
Fax: (215) 635-7320
Email: Email: gratzinfo@aol.com

Jerusalem Israeli Gift Shop
7818 Castor Avenue 19152
Telephone: (215) 342-1452

Rosenberg Hebrew Book Store
409 Old York Road, Jenkintown 19046
Telephone: (215) 884-1728; 800-301-8608
Fax: (215) 884-6648

BUTCHERS

Aries Kosher Meats
6530 Castor Avenue 19149
Telephone: (215) 533-3222
Supervision: Vaad Hakashruth

Best Value Kosher Meat Center
8564 Bustleton Avenue 19152
Telephone: (215) 342-1902
Fax: (215) 342-5775
Supervision: Rabbi Dov Brisman

Bustleton Kosher Meat Market
6834 Bustlton Avenue 19149
Telephone: (215) 332-0100
Supervision: Rabbi Shalom Novoseller

Glendale Meats
7730 Bustleton Avenue 19152
Telephone: (215) 725-4100
Supervision: Vaad Hakashruth

Main Line Kosher Meats
75621 Haverford Avenue 19151
Telephone: (215) 877-3222
Supervision: Vaad Hakashruth

Simons Kosher Meats and Poultry
6926 Bustleton Avenue 19149
Telephone: (215) 624-5695
Supervision: Vaad Hakashruth

Wallace's Krewstown Kosher Meat Market
8919 Krewstown Road 19115
Telephone: (215) 464-7800
Supervision: Vaad Hakashruth

CONTACT INFORMATION

Jewish Information and Referral Service
2100 Arch Street, 7th Floor 19103
Telephone: (215) 832-0821
Fax: (215) 832-0833
Email: lyouman@philafederation.org

EMBASSY

Consul General of Israel
230 South 15th Street 19102
Telephone: (215) 546-5556
Fax: (215) 545-3986
Email: info.ph@israelfm.org
Website: www.israelemb.org/pa

GROCERIES

Best Value Kosher Meat Center
8564 Bustleton Avenue 19152
Telephone: (215) 342-1902
Supervision: Rabbi Dov Brisman

GROCERIES

Milk and Honey
7618 Castor Avenue 19152
Telephone: (215) 342-3224
Supervision: Vaad Hakashruth

HISTORIC SITE

Congregation Beth T'fillah of Overbrook Park
7630 Woodbine Avenue 19151
Telephone: (215) 477-2415
Fax: (215) 477-2417

Mikveh Israel Cemetery
8th and Spruce Streets 19107
Telephone: (215) 922-5446

The Frank Synagogue
Albert Einstein Medical Center, Old York and Tabor
Roads 19141
Telephone: (215) 456-7890

JUDAICA

Bala Judaica and Jewelry Center
222 Bala Avenue, Bala Cynwyd 19004
Telephone: (215) 610-664-1303
Fax: (215) 610-664-4319
Email: jewishwedding@erols.com

KASHRUT INFORMATION

Board of Rabbis of Greater Philadelphia
2100 Arch Street - 3rd Floor 19103
Telephone: (215) 832-0675
Fax: (215) 832-0689
Email: info@brdavphila.com

Ko Kosher Service
5871 Drexel Road 19131
Telephone: (215) 696-0408
Fax: (215) 696-9249
Email: ko_kosher_service@msm.com
Website: www.ko-kosher-service.org

Orthodox Vaad of Philadelphia
7505 Brookhaven Road 19151
Telephone: (215) 658-1967
Fax: (215) 473-6220

Rabbinical Assembly
United Synagogue of Conservative, Judaism, 1510
Chestnut Street 19102

Telephone: (215) 563-8814

Rabbinical Council of Greater Philadelphia
44 North 4th Street 19106
Telephone: (215) 922-5446
Fax: (215) 922-1550

Vaad Hakashruth and Beth Din of Philadelphia
1147 Gilham Street 19111
Telephone: (215) 725-5181
Fax: (215) 725-5182

LIBRARIES

Annenberg Research Institute
420 Walnut Street 19106
Telephone: (215) 238-1290

Mordecai M Kaplan
1299 Church Road, Wyncote 19095
Telephone: (215) 576-0800 ext 232
Fax: (215) 576-8163
Email: kaplan library@rrc.edu
Website: www.rrc.edu
Central organisation: Reconstructionist Rabbinical College

Philadelphia Jewish Archives Center
Balch Institute for Ethnic Studies, 18 South 7th Street 19106
Telephone: (215) 925-8090

Talmudical Yeshivah Library
6063 Dexel Road 19131
Telephone: (215) 477-1000
Fax: (215) 477-5065

Temple University
Paley Library, 13th Street and Berks Mall 19122
Telephone: (215) 787-8231

The Free Library of Philadelphia
Central Library, Logan Square 19103
Telephone: (215) 686-5392
Fax: (215) 563-3628
Website: www.library.phila.gov

Tuttleman Library
Gratz College, Mandell Education Campus, 7605 Old York Road, Melrose Park 19027
Telephone: (215) 635-7300 ext. 169
Fax: (215) 635-7320
Email: libraryinfo@gratz.edu

University of Pennsylvania
Van Pelt Library, 3420 Walnut Street 19104
Telephone: (215) 898-7556

MEDIA

Newspapers

Jewish Exponent
Jewish Publishing Group, 2100 Arch Street 19103
Telephone: (215) 832-0700
Fax: (215) 832-0786
Email: dalpher@jewishexponent.com

Jewish Post
P.O.Box 442, Yardley 19067
Telephone: (215) 321-3443

Jewish Times
Jewish Publishing Group, 103A Tomlinson Road, Huntingdon Valley 19006
Telephone: (215) 938-1177

Mir
P.O. Box 6162 19115
Telephone: (215) 934-5512

Periodicals

Inside Magazine
Jewish Publishing Group, 2100 Arch Street 19103
Telephone: (215) 893-5797
Fax: (215) 546-3957
Email: rleiter@jewishexponent.com

Jewish Quarterly Review
420 Walnut Street 19106
Telephone: (215) 238-1290
Email: jqroffice@sas.upenn.edu

Shofar Magazine
P.O. Box 51591 19115
Telephone: (215) 676-8304

Radio

Meridian
Telephone: (215) 962-8000

Radio & TV

Barry Reisman Show
Telephone: (215) 365-5600

Bucks County Jewish Life
Telephone: (215) 949-1490

Comcast Cablevision of Philadelphia
4400 Wayne Avenue 19140
Telephone: (215) 673-6600

Pulse
WSSJ, Camden
Telephone: (215) 365-5600

MEMORIAL

Monument to the Six Million Jewish Martyrs
16th Street and the Benjamin Franklin Parkway 19103

MIKVAOT

Mikveh Association of Philadelphia (Ardmore)
Torah Academy, Wynnewood and Argyle Roads, Ardmore 19003
Telephone: (215) 642-8679

Mikveh association of Philadelphia (Northern)
7525 Loretto Avenue, Philadelphia 19111
Telephone: (215) 745-3334

MUSEUMS

Balch Institute for Ethnic Studies
18 South 7th Street 19106
Telephone: (215) 925-8090

Borowsky Gallery
Jewish Community Centers of Greater, Philadelphia,
401 South Broad Street 19147
Telephone: (215) 545-4400
Email: www.gershmany.org

Fred Wolf Jr Gallery
Jewish Community Centers of Greater, Philadelphia,
10100 Jamison Avenue 19116
Telephone: (215) 698-7300

Holocaust Awareness Museum
Gratz College, Mandell Education Campus, 7601
Old York Road, Melrose Park 19027
Telephone: (215) 635-6480

National Museum of American Jewish History
55 North 5th Street, Independence Mall East
19106-2197
Telephone: (215) 923-3811
Fax: (215) 923-0763
Email: nmajh@nmajh.org
Website: www.nmajh.org

Rosenbach Museum & Library
2010 Delancey Place 19103
Telephone: (215) 732-1600
Fax: (215) 545-7529
Email: info@rosenbach.org

RESTAURANTS

Dairy

Cherry Street Chinese Vegetarian
1010 Cherry Street 19107
Telephone: (215) 923-3663
Supervision: Rabbinical Assembly

Pizzerias

Holyland Pizza
8010 Castor Avenue
Telephone: (215) 725-7444

Shalom Pizza
7598a Haverford Avenue
Telephone: (215) 878-1500
Email: shalom2u@rcn.com

SYNAGOGUES

Center City Eruv Corporation
44 North 4th Street 19106
Telephone: (215) 922-5446
Fax: (215) 922-1550
Email: info@mikvehisrael.org
Website: www.mikvehisrael.org

Philadelphia Congregation Rodeph Shalom
615 North Broad Street 19123
Telephone: (215) 627-6747

Conservative

Congregation Beth El
21 Penn Valley Road, Fallsington, Levittown 19054
Telephone: (215) 945-9500

Ohev Shalom
2 Chester Road, Wallingford 19086
Telephone: (215) 874-1465
Email: www.uscj.org/delvlly/wallingford

Tiferet Bet Israel
1920 Skippack Pike, Blue Bell 19422
Telephone: (215) 275-8797

Orthodox

Young Israel of Oxford Circle
6427 Large Street 19149
Telephone: (215) 743-2848

Young Israel of the Main Line
273 Montgomery Ave, Bala-Gynwyd 19004
Telephone: (215) 610-667-3255
Email: audveag@evols.com

Orthodox Sephardi

Congregation Mikveh Israel
44 North Fourth Street 19106
Telephone: (215) 922-5446
Fax: (215) 922-1550
Email: info@mikvehisrael.org
Website: www.mikvehisrael.org

Reform

Congregation Rodeph
615 North Broad Street
Telephone: (215) 627-6747

Temple Shalom
Edgley Road, off Mill Creek Pkwy., Levittown
19057
Telephone: (215) 945-4154

THEATRE

Theatre Ariel/Habima Ariel
PO Box 0334, Merion Station 19066
Telephone: (215) 567-0670

TOURS OF JEWISH INTEREST

American Jewish Committee Historic Tour
117 South Seventeenth Street, Suite 1010
Telephone: (215) 665-2300
Fax: (215) 665-8737

PITTSBURGH

BAKERIES

Pastries Unlimited
2119 Murray Avenue 15217
Telephone: (412) 521-6323

BOOKSELLERS

Pinskers Judaica Center
2028 Murray Avenue 15217
Telephone: (412) 421-3033;

1- 800-JUDAISM (1-800-583-2476)
Fax: (412) 421-6103
Email: info@judaism.com
Website: www.judaism.com

COMMUNITY ORGANISATIONS

United Jewish Federation of Greater Pittsburgh
234 McKee Place 15213
Telephone: (412) 681-8000
Fax: (412) 681-3980
Email: enaveh@ujf.net
Website: www.ujf.net

GROCERIES

Brauner's Emporium
2023 Murray Avenue 15217

MEDIA

Newspaper
Pittsburgh Jewish Chronicle
5600 Baum Blvd 15206
Telephone: (412) 687-1000
Fax: (412) 687-5119
Email: news@pittchron.com
Website: www.pittchron.com

MIKVAOT

Mikva
2326 Shady Avenue 15217
Telephone: (412) 422-8010

MUSEUMS

Holocaust Center of the United Jewish Federation of Greater Pittsburgh
5738 Darlington Road 15217
Telephone: (412) 421-1500
Fax: (412) 422-1996
Email: lhurwitz@ujf.net
Website: www.ujfhc.net

RESTAURANTS

Meat
Greenberg's Kosher Poultry
2223 Murray Avenue 15217

Platters Restaurant
2020 Murray Avenue 15217
Telephone: (412) 422-3370

Prime Kosher
1916 Murray Avenue 15217
Telephone: (412) 421-1015

SYNAGOGUES

Conservative
Ahavath Achim
500 Chestnut St., Carnegie 15106
Telephone: (412) 279-1566

Beth El of South Hills
1900 Cochran Rd 15220
Telephone: (412) 561-1168

Beth Shalom
Beacon & Shady Avs 15217
Telephone: (412) 421-2288
Fax: (412) 421-5923
Email: www.bethshalom-pgh-org

New Light
1700 Beechwood Blvd. 15217
Telephone: (412) 421-1017

Parkway Jewish Center
300 Princeton Dr. 15235
Telephone: (412) 823-4338
Fax: (412) 823-4338
Website: www.parkwayjewishcenter.com

Tree of Life
Wilkins & Shady Avs 15217
Telephone: (412) 521-6788
Fax: (412) 521-7846
Email: tolpon@aol.com

Orthodox
B'nai Emunoh Congregation
4315 Murray Av. 15217
Telephone: (412) 521-1477
Fax: (412) 521-1762
Email: drmaimon@netzero.net

Beth Hamedrash Hagodol - Beth Jacob Congregation
1230 Colwell St. 15219
Telephone: (412) 471-4443
Fax: (412) 281-1965

Bohnei Yisroel
6401 Forbes Av. 15217
Telephone: (412) 521-6047

Kether Torah
5706 Bartlett St. 15217
Telephone: (412) 521-9992

Poale Zedeck
6318 Phillips Avenue 15217
Telephone: (412) 421-9786
Fax: (412) 421-3383
Email: mil313@aol.com
Website: www.pzonline.com

Shaare Tefillah
5741 Bartlett St. 15217
Telephone: (412) 521-9911

Shaare Torah
2319 Murray Av. 15217
Telephone: (412) 421-8855

Torath Chaim
728 North Negley Av. 15206
Telephone: (412) 362-7736
Email: joeberger1@juno.com
Contact Person is Joe Berger (412 521-4060)

Young Israel of Greater Pittsburgh
5831 Bartlett Street 15217-1636
Telephone: (412) 421-7224

Reconstructionist
Dor Hadash
6328 Forbes Av. 15217
Telephone: (412) 422-5158
Email: dh15217@verizon.net

Reform
Rodef Shalom
4905 5th Av. 15213
Telephone: (412) 621-6566
Fax: (412) 621-5475
Email: herzog@rodefshalom.org

Temple David
4415 Northern Pike, Monroeville 15146

Temple Emanuel of South Hills
1250 Bower Hill Rd. 15243
Telephone: (412) 279-2600
Fax: (412) 279-7628

Temple Sinai
5505 Forbes Av. 15217
Telephone: (412) 421-9715

Traditional
Young Peoples Synagogue
6404 Forbes Av. 15217
Telephone: (412) 521-1440
Website: www.youngpeoples.org
Traditional service, all volunteer synagogue, separate
seating.

POTTSTOWN
SYNAGOGUES
Conservative
Congregation Mercy & Truth
575 N. Keim Street 19464
Telephone: (610) 326-1717

Kesher Zion
Eckert & Perkiomen Streets 19602
Telephone: (610) 374-1763

Orthodox
Shomrei Habrith
2320 Hampden Blvd. 19604
Telephone: (610) 921-0881
Fax: (610) 685-3866
Email: lipsker@aol.com
Website: www.l-chaim.org
Supervision: Rabbi Yosef Lipsker

SYNAGOGUES
Reform
Reform Congregation Oheb Sholom
555 Warwick Drive, Wyomissing 19610
Telephone: (610) 375-6034
Fax: (610) 375-6036
Email: office@ohebsholom.org
Website: www.ohebsholom.org

READING
COMMUNITY ORGANISATIONS
Jewish Federation
1700 City Line St 19604
Telephone: (610) 921-2766
Fax: (610) 921-2766
Email: sramati@epix.net

SCRANTON
BUTCHERS
Blatt's Butcher Block
420 Prescott Avenue 18510
Telephone: (570) 342-3886
Fax: (570) 342-9711
Supervision: Rabbi Fine and Rabbi Herman of Scranton
Rabbinate

COMMUNITY ORGANISATIONS
**Jewish Federation of Northeastern
Pennsylvania**
601 Jefferson Avenue 18510
Telephone: (570) 961-2300
Fax: (570) 346-6147
Email: jfednepa@epix.net

MUSEUMS
Houdini Museum Tour and Magic Show
1433 N. Main 18508
Telephone: (570) 342-5555
Email: magicusa@microserve.net
Website: www.houdini.org

SYNAGOGUES
Conservative
Temple Israel
Gibson Street & Monroe Avenue 18510
Telephone: (570) 342-0350
Fax: (570) 342-7250
Email: tiscran@epix.net

Orthodox
Beth Shalom
Clay Avenue at Vine Street 18510
Telephone: (570) 346-0502
Fax: (570) 346-8800
Email: bethshalom2@aol.com

Congregation Machzikeh Hadas
600 Monroe Avenue 18510
Telephone: (570) 342-6271
Email: info@ohavzedek.org
Website: www.ohavzedek.org

Ohev Zedek
1432 Mulberry Street 18510
Telephone: (570) 343-2717

Reform
Temple Hesed
Lake Scranton 18505
Telephone: (570) 344-7201

SHARON
Temple Beth Israel
840 Highland Road 16146
Telephone: (781) 346-4754
Fax: (781) 981-4424

WILKES-BARRE
COMMUNITY ORGANISATIONS
Jewish Federation of Greater Wilkes-Barre & Community Center
60 S. River Street
Telephone: (570) 822-4146
Fax: (570) 824-5966

SYNAGOGUES
Conservative
Temple Israel
236 S. River Street 18702
Telephone: (570) 824-8927

Orthodox
Ohav Zedek
242 S. Franklin Street 18701
Telephone: (570) 825-6619
Fax: (570) 825-6634
Email: info@ohavzedek.org

Reform
B'nai B'rith
408 Wyoming Street, Kingston 18704

WILLIAMSPORT
SYNAGOGUES
Conservative
Ohev Sholom
Cherry & Belmont Streets 17701
Telephone: (717) 322-4209

Reform
Beth Ha-Sholom
425 Center Street 17701
Telephone: (717) 323-7751

Rhode Island
BARRINGTON
Temple Habonim
165 New Meadow Road 02806
Telephone: (401) 245-6536

CRANSTON
SYNAGOGUES
Conservative
Temple Torat Yisrael
330 Park Avenue 02905
Telephone: 785-1800

Reform
Temple Sinai
30 Hagan Avenue 02920
Telephone: 942-8350

MIDDLETOWN
SYNAGOGUES
Conservative
Temple Shalom
223 Valley Road 02842
Telephone: (860) 846-9002
Fax: (860) 682-2417

NARRAGANSETT
Congregation Beth David
Kingstown Road 02882
Telephone: (401) 846-9002

NEWPORT
HOTELS
Admiral Weaver Inn
28 Weaver Avenue 02840
Telephone: (401) 849-0051
Email: olgat@gis.net
Website: www.kosherbedandbreakfast.com

TOURS OF JEWISH INTEREST
Touro Synagogue
85 Touro Street 02840
Telephone: (401) 847-4794
Fax: (401) 847-8121

PROVIDENCE
COMMUNITY ORGANISATIONS
Jewish Federation of Rhode Island
130 Sessions Street 02906
Telephone: (401) 421-4111

Rhode Island Jewish Historical Association
Telephone: (401) 863-2805

KASHRUT INFORMATION
Brown University-RISD Hillel
80 Brown Street 02906
Telephone: (401) 863-2805
Fax: (401) 863-1591
Email: spf@brown.edu

Vaad Hakashrut
Telephone: (401) 621-9393
Fax: (401) 331-9393
Email: bethshalom1@juno.com

MEDIA
Periodical
L'Chaim
130 Sessions Street 02906
Telephone: (401) 421-4111

MIKVAOT
Mikva
401 Elmgrove Avenue 02906
Telephone: (401) 751-0025

MUSEUMS
Rhode Island Holocaust Memorial Museum
401 Elmgrove Avenue 02906
Telephone: (401) 861-8800

SYNAGOGUES
Conservative
Temple Emanu-El
99 Taft Avenue 02906
Telephone: (401) 331-1616

Orthodox
Beth Sholom
275 Camp Avenue 02906
Telephone: (401) 621-9393
Fax: (401) 331-9393
Email: bethsholom1@hotmail.com
Congregation Sons of Jacob
24 Douglas Avenue 02908
Telephone: (401) 274-5260
Mishkon Tfiloh
203 Summit Avenue 02906
Telephone: (401) 521-1616
Shaare Zedek
688 Broad Street 02907
Telephone: (401) 751-4936

Reform
Beth El
70 Orchard Avenue 02906
Telephone: (401) 331-6070

WARWICK
SYNAGOGUES
Conservative
Temple Am David
40 Gardiner Street 02888
Telephone: (401) 463-7944

WESTERLY
SYNAGOGUES
Orthodox
Congregation Shaare Zedek
Union Street 02891
Telephone: (401) 596-4621

WOONSOCKET
SYNAGOGUES
Conservative
Congregation B'nai Israel
224 Prospect Street 02895
Telephone: (401) 762-3651

Fax: (401) 767-5243
Email: cbi_synagogue@juno.com
Website: www.shalom-cbi.org

South Carolina

CHARLESTON
BAKERIES
Ashley Bakery
1662 Savannah Highway 29407
Telephone: (843) 763-4125
Cookie Bouquet
280 W. Coleman Road
Telephone: (843) 881-0110

COMMUNITY ORGANISATIONS
Jewish Federation and Community Center
1645 Raoul Wallenberg Blvd, PO Box 31298 29416
Telephone: (843) 571-6565
Fax: (843) 556-6206

DELICATESSEN
Nathan's Deli
1836 Ashley River Road 29407
Telephone: (843) 556-3354

SYNAGOGUES
Orthodox
Brith Sholom Beth Israel
182 Rutledge Avenue
Telephone: (843) 577-6599
Fax: (843) 577-6699
Email: sholomsc@aol.com
Website: www.bs-bi.com

Reform
Beth Elohim
90 Hasell Street 29401
Telephone: (843) 723-1090
Fax: (843) 723-0537
Email: office@kkbe.org
Website: www.kkbe.org
Notes: Dating from 1749, it is the birthplace of Reform
Judaism in the United states, the second oldest synagogue
building in the country, and the oldest suriviving Reform
Synagogue in the world. It has been designated as a
national historic landmark

COLUMBIA
COMMUNITY ORGANISATIONS
Columbia Jewish Federation
4540 Trenholm Road, Cola 29206
Telephone: (803) 787-2023

DELICATESSEN
Groucho's
Five Points 29205

SYNAGOGUES

Conservative
Beth Shalom
5827 North Trenholm Road 29206
Telephone: (803) 782-2500
Fax: (803) 782-5420
Email: bethshalom@bellsouth.net
Website:
www.midnet.sc.edu/beth_shalom/index.htm

Reform
Tree of Life
6719 Trenholm Road 29206
Telephone: (803) 787-2182
Fax: (803) 787-0309
Email: tolcong@bellsouth.net
Website: www.jewishcolumbia.com

GEORGETOWN

CEMETERIES
Old Cemetery

MYRTLE BEACH

RESTAURANTS
Jerusalem Kosher Restaurant
1007 Withers Drive
Telephone: (803) 946-6650

SYNAGOGUES

Conservative
Temple Emanuel
406 65th Ave N 29577
Telephone: (803) 449-5552

Orthodox
Beth El
401 Highway 17 N., 56th Avenue 29577
Telephone: (803) 449-3140

Chabad Lubavitch
2803 N. Oak Street
Telephone: (803) 448-0035
Fax: (803) 626-6403

South Dakota

ABERDEEN

SYNAGOGUES

Conservative
Congregation B'nai Isaac
202 North Kline Street 57401
Telephone: (732) 225-7360
Email: beapre@iw.net

RAPID CITY

SYNAGOGUES
Reform
Synagogue of the Hills

417 N. 40th Street 57702
Telephone: (605) 348-0805
Email: bhshul@rapidnet.com

Tennessee

CHATTANOOGA

COMMUNITY ORGANISATIONS
Jewish Community Federation
5326 Lynnland Terrace 47311
Telephone: (423) 894-1317
Fax: (423) 894-1319

SYNAGOGUES

Conservative
B'nai Zion
114 McBrien Road 37411
Telephone: (423) 894-8900

Orthodox
Beth Sholom
20 Pisgah Avenue 37411
Telephone: (423) 894-0801

Reform
Mizpah Congregation
923 McCallie Avenue 37403
Telephone: (423) 237-9771
Fax: (423) 267-9773
Email: mizpah@mizpahcongregation.org

Siskin Museum of Religious Artifacts
1 Siskin Plaza 37403
Telephone: (423) 267-9771
Fax: (423) 634-1717

MEMPHIS

COMMUNITY ORGANISATIONS
Jewish Federation and Community Center
6560 Poplar Avenue 38138
Telephone: (901) 767-7100

DELICATESSEN
Kroger Kosher Deli
540 S. Mendenhall
Telephone: (901) 683-8846

Schnuck's Kosher Deli
799 Truse Parkway
Telephone: (901) 682-2989

KASHRUT INFORMATION
Vaad Hakehilloth of Memphis
Memphis Orthodox Jewish Community Council, PO
Box 41133 38104
Telephone: (901) 767-2263
Fax: (901) 761-3788

MIKVAOT
Anshei Sphard
120 E. Yates Rd.
Telephone: (901) 682-6302

Baron Hirsch Congregation
400 South Yates Road 38120
Telephone: (901) 683-7485
Fax: (901) 683-7499
Email: Email: general@baronhirsch.org
Website: www.baronhirsch.org

SYNAGOGUES
Orthodox
Anshei Sephard-Beth El Emeth
120 E.Yates Road N. 38117
Telephone: (901) 682-1611

Baron Hirsch Congregation
369 Winter Oak
Telephone: (901) 683-7485

Kesser Torah
531 S. Yates
Telephone: (901) 761-6060

Reform
Temple Israel
1376 E. Massey Road
Telephone: (901) 761-3130

NASHVILLE
COMMUNITY ORGANISATIONS
Jewish Federation of Nashville and Middle Tennessee
801 Percy Warner Blvd. 37205
Telephone: (615) 356-3242
Fax: (615) 352-0056

MIKVAOT
Sherith Israel
3600 West End Avenue 37205
Telephone: (615) 292-6614
Fax: (615) 463-8260
Email: SylvL@AOL.com

RESTAURANTS
Vegetarian
Grins
Schulman Centre, Corner of 25th Av. S. and
Vanderbilt Place
Supervision: Sherith Israel

SYNAGOGUES
Conservative
West End Synagogue
3814 West End Avenue 37205
Telephone: (615) 269-4592
Fax: (615) 269-4695
Email: office@westendsyn.org or
exec@westendsyn.org

Reform
The Temple
5015 Harding Road 37205
Telephone: (615) 352-7620
Fax: (615) 352-9365

OAK RIDGE
SYNAGOGUES
Conservative
Jewish Congregation of Oak Ridge
101 W. Madison Lane 37830
Telephone: (423) 482-3581

Texas

AMARILLO
SYNAGOGUES
Reform
Temple B'nai Israel
4316 Albert Street 79106
Telephone: (806) 352-7191

ARLINGTON
MEDIA
Newspaper
Texas Jewish Post
3120 South Freeway , 7920 Beltline Rd., #680
Dallas., 75254, Ft. Worth 76110
Telephone: (817) 458 7283
Fax: (817) 458 7299
Email: news@texasjewishpost.com
Website: texasjewishpost.com

SYNAGOGUES
Reform
Congregation Beth Shalom
1210 Thannisch Drive 76011
Telephone: (817) 860 5448
Email: bethshalom.org

AUSTIN
COMMUNITY ORGANISATIONS
Jewish Federation and Community Center of Austin
7300 Hart Lane 78731
Telephone: (512) 331 1144
Fax: (512) 331 7059

SYNAGOGUES
Conservative
Agudas Achim
4300 Bull Creek Road 78731
Telephone: (512) 459 3287

Congregation Beth El
8902 Mesa Drive 78759
Telephone: (512) 346-1776
Fax: (512) 233-004
Email: difriedman@aol.com

Reform
Temple Beth Israel
3901 Shoal Creek Blvd. 78756
Telephone: (512) 454-6806

BAYTOWN
SYNAGOGUES
Unaffiliated
K'nesseth Israel
100 W. Sterling, PO Box 702 77522
Telephone: (281) 424-8765

BEAUMONT
SYNAGOGUES
Reform
Temple Emanuel
1120 Broadway 7740
Telephone: (409) 832-6131

CORPUS CHRISTI
SYNAGOGUES
Conservative
B'nai Israel
3434 Fort Worth Street 78411
Telephone: (361) 855-7308
Fax: (361) 855-7309
Email: CGDK@aol.com

Reform
Temple Beth El
4402 Saratoga Street 78413
Telephone: (361) 857-8181

DALLAS
COMMUNITY ORGANISATIONS
Jewish Federation of Greater Dallas
7800 Northaven Road 75230
Telephone: (214) 369-3313
Fax: (214) 369-8943
Email: contact@jfgd.org
Website: www.jewishdallas.org

HOTELS
The Westin Galleria, Dallas
13340 Dallas Parkway
Telephone: (214) 934-9494
Fax: (214) 851-2869
Email: galas@westin.com

MIKVAOT
Mikvah Association
5640 McShan 75230
Telephone: (214) 776-0037

RELIGIOUS ORGANISATIONS
Dallas Area Torah Association (Kollel)
5840 Forest Lane 75230
Telephone: (214) 987-3282
Fax: (214) 987-1764
Email: data@datanet.org
Website: www.datanet.org

SITE
Zaide Reuven's Esrog Farm
Telephone: (214) 931-5596
Fax: (214) 931-5476
Email: zrsesrog@aol.com
Website: www.members.aol.com/arsesrog

SYNAGOGUES
Orthodox
Chabad of Dallas
7008 Forest Lane 75230
Telephone: (214) 361-8600
Fax: (214) 361-8680
Email: shull@airmail.net
Website: www.chabadcenters.com/dallas

Ohr HaTorah
12800 Preston Road
Telephone: (214) 404-8980

Shaare Tefilla
6131 Churchill Way, off Preston Road 75230
Telephone: (214) 661-0127
Fax: (214) 661-0150
Email: shaaretefilla@juno.com

Reform
Temple Emanu-El
8500 Hillcrest Road 75230
Telephone: (214) 706-0000
Fax: (214) 706-0025
Website: www.tedallas.org

Sephardi
Magen David Congregation
7314 Campbell Road 75248
Telephone: (214) 386-7166

EL PASO
COMMUNITY ORGANISATIONS
Chabad House
6515 Westwind 79912
Telephone: (915) 584-8218
Website: www.chabadelpaso.com

MUSEUMS
El Paso Holocaust Museum and Study Center
401 Wallenberg Drive 79912
Telephone: (915) 833-5656
Fax: (915) 833-9523
Email: epholo@flash.net
Website: www.flash.net/~epholo.com

SYNAGOGUES
Conservative
B'nai Zion
805 Cherry Hill Lane 79912
Telephone: (915) 833-2222

Reform
Sinai
4408 N. Stanton Street 79902
Telephone: (915) 532-5959

HOUSTON

BAKERIES
Kroger's
S. Post Oak 77096
Telephone: (713) 721-7691
Supervision: Houston Kashruth Association

New York Bagel Shop
9724 Hillcroft 77096
Telephone: (713) 723-5879
Supervision: Houston Kashruth Association

Three Brothers Bakery
4036 S. Braeswood 77025
Telephone: (713) 666-2551
Supervision: Houston Kashruth Association

BUTCHERS
Kroger's
S. Post Oak 77096
Telephone: (713) 721-7691
Supervision: Houston Kashruth Association

COMMUNITY ORGANISATIONS
Jewish Federation of Greater Houston
5603 S. Braeswood Blvd. 77096
Telephone: (713) 729-7000
Fax: (713) 721-6232
Website: www.houstonjewish.org

EMBASSY
Consul General of Israel
Suite 1500, 24 Greenway Plaza 77046

GROCERIES
Albertson's
S. Braeswood
Telephone: (713) 271-1180
Supervision: Houston Kashruth Association

JEWISH CENTER
TORCH - Torah & Outreach Resource Center of Houston
5821 Southwest Freeway, Suite 606 Houston 77057
Telephone: (713) 721-6400
Fax: (713) 721-6900
Email: ypolatsek@torchweb.com
Website: www.torchweb.com

KASHRUT INFORMATION
Houston Kashrut Association
9001 Greenwillow 77096
Telephone: (713) 723-3850
Fax: (713) 723-3852

MIKVAOT
Chabad Lubavitch Center
10900 Fondren Road 77096
Telephone: (713) 777-2000

United Orthodox Synagogues
4221 S. Braeswood Blvd. 77096
Telephone: (713) 723-3850

RESTAURANTS
Dairy
Saba's Mediterranean
9704 Fondren
Telephone: (713) 270-7222
Supervision: Houston Kashruth Association

Meat
Nosher's at the Jewish Community Centre
5601 S. Braeswood 77096
Telephone: (713) 729-3200
Supervision: Houston Kashruth Association

Vegetarian
Madras Pavilion
3910 Kirby Drive 77098
Telephone: (713) 521-2617
Supervision: Houston Kashruth Association

Wonderful Vegetarian Restaurant
7549 Westheimer 77063
Telephone: (713) 977-3137
Supervision: Houston Kashruth Association

SYNAGOGUES
Conservative
B'rith Shalom
4610 Bellaire Blvd. 77401
Telephone: (713) 667-9201

Beth Am
1431 Brittmore Rd. 77043
Telephone: (713) 461-7725
Fax: (713) 461-7773
Email: ebbe@earthlink.net
Website: www.bethamtx.org

Beth Yeshurun
4525 Beechnut St. 77096
Telephone: (713) 666-1881
Fax: (713) 666-7767
Email: arthur@bethyeshurun.org
Website: www.bethyeshurun.org

Congregation Shaar Hashalom
16020 El Camino Real 77062
Telephone: (713) 488-5861
Fax: (713) 488-3561
Email: stuartfederow@hotmail.com
Website: www.shaarshalom.org

Orthodox
Chabad Lubavitch of Houston
10900 Fondren Road 77096
Telephone: (713) 777-2000

Congregation Beth Rambam
11333 Braesridge Blvd. 77071
Telephone: (713) 723-3030
Fax: (713) 726-8737
Email: gez@flash.net
Website: www.flash.net/~bentzion/br.htm

United Orthodox Synogogues
9001 Greenwillow 77096
Telephone: (713) 723-3850
Website: www.uosh.org

Young Israel of Houston
7823 Ludinton Road 77071
Telephone: (713) 729-0719
Website: www.youngisraelofhouston.org

Reform
Beth Israel
5600 N. Braeswood Blvd. 77096
Telephone: (713) 771-6221
Fax: (713) 771-5705
Website: www.Beth-Israel.org

Congregation Emanu El
1500 Sunset Blvd. 77005
Telephone: (713) 529-5771
Fax: (713) 529-0703
Email: emanuelhouston.org
Website: www.emanuel.org

Congregation for Reform Judaism
801 Bering Dr. 77057
Telephone: (713) 782-4162
Fax: (713) 782-4167

Jewish Community North
5400 Fellowship Lane 77379
Telephone: (713) 376-0016
Fax: (713) 251-1033
Email: jcn@wt.net

LUBBOCK
GROCERIES
Albertson's
Telephone: (806) 794-6761

Lowe's Supermarket
82nd & Slide Rd

SYNAGOGUES
Reform
Congregation Shaareth Israel
6928 3rd Street 79424
Telephone: (806) 794-7517

SAN ANTONIO
COMMUNITY ORGANISATIONS
Jewish Federation
8434 Ahern Drive 78216
Telephone: (210) 341-8234

DELICATESSEN
Delicious Food
7460 Callaghan Road 78229
Telephone: (210) 366-1844

MUSEUMS
Holocaust Memorial
12500 N W Military Highway 78231

Telephone: (210) 302-6807
Fax: (210) 408-2332
Email: cohenm@jfstx.org

SYNAGOGUES
Conservative
Agudas Achim
1201 Donaldson Avenue 78228
Telephone: (210) 734-4216

Orthodox
Rodfei Sholom
3003 Sholom Drive 78230
Telephone: (210) 493 3558
Fax: (210) 492 0629
Email: rodfei@world-net.net
Website: www.ou.org

Reform
Beth El
Telephone: (210) 211 Belknap Place

WACO
SYNAGOGUES
Conservative
Agudath Jacob
4925 Hillcrest Drive 76710
Telephone: (254) 772-1451
Fax: (254) 772-2471
Email: Agudath@stonemedia.com
Website: www.agudath-jacob.org

Reform
Rodef Sholom
1717 N. New Road 76707
Telephone: (254) 754-3703
Fax: (254) 754-5538

Utah

SALT LAKE CITY
COMMUNITY ORGANISATIONS
United Jewish Federation of Utah
2416 East, 1700 South 84108
Telephone: (801) 581-0102
Fax: (801) 581-1334

DELICATESSEN
Kosher on the Go
1575 S. 1100 East
Telephone: (801) 463-1786

SYNAGOGUES
Orthodox
Chabad Lubavitch of Utah
1433 South 1100 East 84105
Telephone: (801) 467-7777
Fax: (801) 486-7526
Email: chabadutah@aol.com
Website: www.chabadutah.com

Reconstructionist
Chavurah B'yachad
Jubilee Center, 309 East 100 South 84111
Telephone: (801) 596-8996
Email: byachad@aol.com

Reform
Congregation Kol Ami
2425 E. Heritage Way 84109
Telephone: (801) 484-1501
Fax: (801) 484-1162
Email: clyon@conkolami.org
Website: www.conkolami.org

Vermont
BURLINGTON
SYNAGOGUES

Conservative
Ohavi Zedek
188 N. Prospect Street 05401
Telephone: (718) 802-864-0218
Fax: (718) 802-864-0219
Email: office@ohavizedek.com
Website: www.ohavizedek.com

Orthodox
Ahavath Gerim
cnr. Archibald & Hyde Streets 05401
Telephone: (718) 862-3001

Reform
Temple Sinai
500 Swift Street 05401
Telephone: (718) 862-5125

MONTPELIER
SYNAGOGUES
Congregation Beth Jacob
10 Harrison Avenue 05602
Telephone: (802) 229-9429

Virginia
ALEXANDRIA
SYNAGOGUES

Conservative
Agudas Achim
2908 Valley Drive 22302
Telephone: (318) 998-6460

Reform
Beth El Hebrew Congregation
3830 Seminary Road 22304
Telephone: (318) 370-9400
Fax: (318) 370-7730
Email: bethelhc@erols.com

ARLINGTON
SYNAGOGUES
Conservative
Congregation Etz Hayim
2920 Arlington Blvd. 22204
Telephone: (817) 703-979-4466
Fax: (817) 703-979-4468
Email: office@etzhayim.net
Website: www.arfax.org

CHARLOTTESVILLE
SYNAGOGUES
The Hillel Jewish Center
The University of Virginia, 1824 University Circle
22903
Telephone: (804) 295-4963

Reform
Congregation Beth Israel
301 E. Jefferson Street 22902
Telephone: (804) 295-6382
Fax: (804) 296-6491
Email: office@cbicville.org
Website: www.cbicville.org

DANVILLE
Temple Beth Sholom
Sutherlin Avenue
Telephone: (804) 792-3489

FAIRFAX
SYNAGOGUES
Conservative
Congregation Olam Tikvah
3800 Glenbrook Road 22031
Telephone: (703) 425-1880
Fax: (703) 425-0835

FALLS CHURCH
SYNAGOGUES
Reform
Temple Rodef Shalom
2100 Westmoreland Street 22043
Telephone: (703) 532-2217
Email: trsfcva@erols.com

HAMPTON
SYNAGOGUES
Conservative
Rodef Sholom
318 Whealton Road, Hampton 23666
Telephone: (757) 826-5894
Email: rabbirst@erols.com

Traditional
B'nai Israel
3116 Kecoughtan Road, Hampton 23661
Telephone: (757) 772-0100

NEWPORT NEWS
BAKERIES
Brenner's Warwick Bakery
240 31st Street 23607
Supervision: VaÔad Hakashrut

COMMUNITY ORGANISATIONS
United Jewish Community of the Virginia Peninsula
2700 Spring Road 23606
Telephone: (757) 930-1422

MIKVAOT
Adath Jeshurun
12646 Nettles Drive 23606
Telephone: (757) 930-0820
Email: adathjeshurun@juno.com

SYNAGOGUES
Reform
Temple Sinai
11620 Warwick Blvd. 23601
Telephone: (757) 596-8352

NORFOLK
COMMUNITY ORGANISATIONS
United Jewish Federation of Tidewater
5000 Corporate Woods Drive, Suite 200, Virginia Beach , Virginia Beach 23462
Telephone: (757) 965-6100
Fax: (757) 965-6102
Email: azelenka@ujft.org
Website: www.jewishVA.org

GROCERIES
Delicatessen and restaurant
The Kosher Place
738 W. 22nd Street 23517
Telephone: (757) 623-1770
Fax: (757) 965-4427
Email: info@kosherplacecafe.com
Website: www.kosherplacecafe.com
Supervision: Vaad Hakashrus of Tidewater

The Kosher Place is a combination grocery/butchers/deli and restaurant. Fleishig and Pareve entrees are available from a full deli menu as well as daily restaurant lunch and dinner specials. Catering and Shabbos meal packages are also featured.

HOTELS
Sheraton Norfolk Waterside Hotel
777 Waterside Drive 23510
Telephone: (757) 622-6664

KASHRUT INFORMATION
Vaad Hakashrus of Tidewater
PO Box 11082 23517
Telephone: (757) 627-7358
Fax: (757) 627-8544
Email: mostsky@hotmail.com
Website: www.vaadoftidewater.com

MIKVAOT
B'nai Israel Congregation
420 Spotswood Avenue 23517
Telephone: (757) 627-7358
Fax: (757) 627-8544
Email: office@bnaiisrael.org
Website: www.bnaiisrael.org

SYNAGOGUES
Conservative
Beth El
422 Shirley Avenue 23517
Telephone: (757) 625-7821
Fax: (757) 627-4905
Email: office@bethelnorfolk.com

Temple Israel
7255 Granby St. 23505
Telephone: (757) 489-4550

Orthodox
B'nai Israel
402 Spotswood Avenue 23517
Telephone: (757) 627-7358

Reform
Ohef Sholom
Stockley Gdns at Raleigh Avenue 23507
Telephone: (757) 625-4295

The Commodore Levy Chapel
Frazier Hall, Building C-7 (inside Gate 2), Norfolk US Navy Station
Telephone: (757) 444-7361
Fax: (757) 444-7362
Email: chaplain@nsn.cmar.navy.mil

RICHMOND
COMMUNITY ORGANISATIONS
Jewish Community Federation
5403 Monument Avenue 23226
Telephone: (804) 288-0045
Fax: (804) 282-7507
Website: www.jewishrichmond.org

HOTELS
The Farbreng-Inn Kosher Retreat Center
1800 SEE Virginia
23233
Telephone: (804) 740-2000/800-733-8474
Fax: (804) 750-1341
Email: info@chabadofva.org

MIKVAOT
Young Israel
4811 Patterson Avenue 23226
Telephone: (804) 353-3831
Fax: (804) 288-4381
Email: adere@juno.com

MUSEUMS
Beth Ahabah Museum & Archives
1109 W. Franklin Street 23220
Telephone: (804) 353 -2668
Fax: (804) 358-3451
Email: bama@bethahabah.org

SYNAGOGUES
Conservative
Or Atid
501 Parham Road 23229
Telephone: (804) 740-4747

Orthodox
Keneseth Beth Israel
6300 Patterson Avenue 23226
Telephone: (804) 288-7953
Fax: (804) 673-9558
Email: kbi6300@erols.com

Young Israel of Richmond
4811 Patterson Avenue 23226
Telephone: (804) 353-5831
Email: yosefb@juno.com

Reform
Or Ami
9400 N. Huguenot Road 23235
Telephone: (804) 272-0017

VIRGINIA BEACH
MEDIA
Newspapers
Southeastern Virginia Jewish News
5029 Corporate Woods Drive, Suite 225 23462
Telephone: (757) 671-1600
Fax: (757) 671-7613
Email: news@ujft.org
Website: www.jewishva.org

Periodical
Southeastern Virginia Jewish News &
RENEWAL Magazine
5041 Corporate Woods Drive #150 23462-4381
Telephone: (757) 671-1600
Fax: (757) 671-7613
Email: news@ujft.org
Website: www.jewishva.org

SYNAGOGUES
Conservative
Kempsville Conservative
952 Indian Lakes Blvd. 23464
Telephone: (757) 495-8510
Website: www.uscj.org/seabd/virginiabeach/

Temple Emanuel
25th Street 23451
Telephone: (757) 428-2591

Orthodox
Chabad Lubavitch
533 Gleneagle Drive 23462
Telephone: (757) 499-0507

Reform
Beth Chaverim
3820 Stoneshore Road 23452-7965
Telephone: (757) 463-3226
Fax: (757) 463-1134
Email: bethchaverim@ddaccess.com

Washington
ABERDEEN
SYNAGOGUES
Conservative
Temple Beth Israel
1219 Spur Street 98520
Telephone: (732) 533-3784

MERCER ISLAND
COMMUNITY ORGANISATIONS
Stroum Jewish Community Center of Greater Seattle
Mercer Island Facility, 3801 E. Mercer Way 98040
Telephone: (206) 232-7115
Fax: (206) 232-7119
Email: info@sjcc.org
Website: www.sjcc.org

MUSEUMS
Community Center
3801 E. Mercer Way 98040
Telephone: (206) 232-7115

OLYMPIA
SYNAGOGUES
Progressive
Temple Beth Hatfiloh
802 South Jefferson, SE 98057
Telephone: (206) 754-8519

SEATTLE

BAKERIES
Bagel Deli
340 15th Ave. E.
Telephone: (206) 322-2471

COMMUNITY ORGANISATIONS
Jewish Federation of Greater Seattle
2031 3rd Avenue 98121
Telephone: (206) 443-5400

Stroum Jewish Community Center of Greater Seattle
Northend Facility, 8606 35th Avenue NE 98115
Telephone: (206) 526-8073
Fax: (206) 526-9958
Email: NeReception@sjcc.org
Website: www.sjcc.org

Washington Association of Jewish Communities
2031 3rd Avenue 98121

JEWISH STUDENT CENTRE
Hillel, Foundation for Jewish Campus Life at the University of Washington
4745 17th Avenue N.E 98105
Telephone: (206) 527-1997
Fax: (206) 527-1999
Email: mail@hilleluw.org
Website: www.hilleluw.org

KASHRUT INFORMATION
Va'ad HaRabanim of Greater Seattle
5305 S. 52nd Avenue S, Suite 102 98118-2502
Telephone: (206) 760-0805
Fax: (206) 725-0347
Email: vaad@w-link.net
Website: www.seattlevaad.org

MEDIA
Periodical
The Jewish Transcript
2031 3rd Avenue 98121
Telephone: (206) 441-4553
Fax: (206) 441-2736
Email: jewishtran@aol.com

RESTAURANTS
Panini Grill
2118 NE 65 Street
Telephone: (206) 522-2730

Dairy
Leah's Deli
65 St. between 21st and 22nd
Telephone: (206) 524-3870

Vegetarian
Bamboo Garden
364 Roy Street, near Seattle Center 98109
Telephone: (206) 282-6616
Fax: (206) 284-2775
Email: bamboogarden@aol.com
Website: www.bamboogarden.net
Certified Kosher: Va'ad HaRabanim of Greater Seattle

Teapot Vegetarian House
125 E. 15th Avenue
Telephone: (206) 325-1010

SPOKANE
COMMUNITY ORGANISATIONS
Jewish Community Council
North 221 Wall, Suite 500 99201
Telephone: (509) 838-4261

SYNAGOGUES
Conservative
Temple Beth Shalom
1322, 30th Street 99203
Telephone: (509) 747-3304

West Virginia

CHARLESTON
SYNAGOGUES
Reform
Temple B'nai Israel
2312 Kanawha Boulevard 25311
Telephone: (843) 342-5852

Traditional
Congregation B'nai Jacob
1599 Virginia Street East 25311
Telephone: (843) 304-346-4722
Fax: (843) 304-344-4167
Email: wvrabbi@chater.net
Website: www.bnaijacob.com

HUNTINGTON
SUPERMARKET
Conservative & Reform
B'nai Sholom
949 10th Avenue 25701
Telephone: (304) 522-2980

Wisconsin

MADISON
COMMUNITY ORGANISATIONS
Madison Jewish Community Council
6434 Enterprise Lane 53179
Telephone: (608) 278-1808
Fax: (608) 278-7814
Email: mjcc@mjcc.net
Website: www.jewishmadison.org

SYNAGOGUES
Conservative
Beth Israel Center
1406 Mound Street 53711
Telephone: (608) 256-7763
Fax: (608) 256-9434
Email: office@bethisraelcenter.org
Website: www.bethisraelcenter.org

Orthodox
Chabad House
1722 Regent Street 53705
Telephone: (608) 231-3450
Fax: (608) 231-3790

Reform
Beth El
2702 Arbor Drive 53711
Telephone: (608) 238-3123

MILWAUKEE
COMMUNITY ORGANISATIONS
Coalition for Jewish Learning
6401 North Santa Monica Boulevard 53217
Telephone: (414) 962-8860
Fax: (414) 962-8852

MEDIA
Directory
Wisconsin Jewish Chronicle
1360 N. Prospect Avenue 53202
Telephone: (414) 390-5700
Fax: (414) 271-0487
Website: www.jewishchronicle.org

Newspaper
Wisconsin Jewish Chronicle
1360 N. Prospect Avenue 53202
Telephone: (414) 390-5888
Fax: (414) 271-0487
Email: milwaukeej@aol.com

RESTAURANTS
Meat
Kosher Meat Klub
4731 West Burleigh 53210
Telephone: (414) 449-5980
Fax: (414) 449-5985

SYNAGOGUES
Orthodox
Agudas Achim Chabad
2233 West Mequon Road, Mequon 53092
Telephone: (414) 242-2235
Fax: (414) 242-2268
Email: chabadmequon@aol.com
Website: www.chabadmequon.org

Beth Jehudah
3100 North 52nd Street 53216
Telephone: (414) 442-5730
Fax: (414) 442-6171
Email: bethjehudah@juno.com
Website: www.bethjehudah.org

Congregation Anshai Leibowitz
2415 West Mequon Road 53092
Telephone: (414) 512-1195
Fax: (414) 512-1695

SHEBOYGAN
SYNAGOGUES
Traditional
Temple Beth El
1007 North Avenue 53083
Telephone: (920) 452-5828
Email: bethelsheboygan@juno.com

Wyoming

CASPER
SYNAGOGUES
Reform
Casper Synagogue
4105 S. Poplar, PO Box 3534 82602
Telephone: (307) 237-2330

CHEYENNE
SYNAGOGUES
Conservative
Mount Sinai
2610 Pioneer Avenue 82001
Telephone: (307) 634-3052

LARAMIE
SYNAGOGUES
Reform
Laramie JCC
PO Box 202 82073
Telephone: (307) 760-9275
Email: www.uahc.org/wy/wy001

URUGUAY

After the *Conversos* in the sixteenth century, there was no known Jewish community in Uruguay until the late nineteenth century, when the country served as a stop-over on the way to Argentina. The Jewish population rose in the twentieth century with immigration from the Middle East and eastern Europe. A synagogue was opened by 1917. Despite restrictive immigration laws imposed against European Jews fleeing Nazism, 2,500 Jews managed to enter the country between 1939 and 1940. Further Jewish immigration followed from Hungary and the Middle East in the post-war period.

There are many Jewish organisations functioning in Uruguay, including Zionist and women's organisations. Kosher restaurants exist in Jewish institutions, and there are a number of synagogues.

GMT -3 hours
Country calling code: (+598)
Total population: 3,221,000
Jewish population: 25,000
Emergency telephone: (Police–999) (Fire–999)
(Ambulance–999)
Electricity voltage: 220

MONTEVIDEO
With approximately 10,000 families in the capital of Uruguay, Montevideo contains almost all of the country's Jewish community. There is a Museum of the Holocaust in Montevideo, and near the Teatro Solis opera house stands a Golda Meir monument. An Albert Einstein monument can be found in Rodo Park.

COMMUNITY ORGANISATIONS
Centro Lubavitch
Av. Brasil 2704, CP 111300
Telephone: (2) 709-3444, 708-5169
Fax: (2) 711-3696
Email: shemtov@chasque.apc.org

Comite Central Israelita Del Uruguay
Rio Negro 1308, P.5 11100
Telephone: (2) 901-6057 902-9195
Fax: (2) 900-6562
Email: cciu@cciu.org .uy
Website: www.cciu.org.uy

EMBASSY
Embassy of Israel
Bulevar Artigas 1585-89
Telephone: (2) 400-4164
Fax: (2) 409-5821
Email: info@montevideo.mfa.gov.il

GROCERIES
Mercadito Casher – Meat, Dairy, Vegetarian, Parve
Ellauri 696
Telephone: (2) 707-5360
Supervision: Local Rabbinate
Glatt/non-Glatt, Cholov Yisael. Opening times: Monday to Friday, 9.00 am to 1.00 pm and from 4.00 pm to 8.00 pm.

Yavne
Cavia 2800
Telephone: (2) 908-7869
Fax: (2) 707-0866
Email: yavne@adinet.com.uy

MEDIA
Newspapers
Semanario Hebreo
Soriano 875/201
Telephone: (2) 925-311
Spanish language weekly, editor also directs daily Yiddish radio programme

MIKVAOT
Beit Jabad
Auda, Brasil 2704
Telephone: (2) 709-3444
Email: jabad@chasque.net
Website: www.jabad.org.uy

MUSEUMS
Centro Recordatorio del Holocausto
Canelones 1084, P.3 11100
Telephone: (2) 622-7223
Fax: (2) 622-7223
Email: centroshoa@conectate.com.uy
First museum of the Shoah in South America

RESTAURANTS
Kasherisssimo
Camacua 623
Telephone: (2) 915-0128
Fax: (2) 208-1536
Supervision: Chief Rabbi Yosef Bitton
The restaurant is situated in the Hebraica Macabi building.

Dairy
Best Western Armon Suites
2885 21st September Rd

SYNAGOGUES

Comunidad Israelita Hungara
Durazno 972
Telephone: (2) 900-8456
Fax: (2) 900-8456

Social Isralite Adat Yeshurun
Alarcon 1396

Ashkenazi

Comunidad Israelita de Uruguay
Canelones 1084, Piso 1
Telephone: (2) 902-5750
Fax: (2) 902-5740
Email: kehila@adinet.com.uy

Conservative

Nueva Congregation Israelita
Wilson Ferreira Aldunate 1168
Telephone: (2) 902-6620
Fax: (2) 902-0589
Email: nci@adinet.com.uy

Orthodox

Vaad Ha'ir
Canelones 828
Telephone: (2) 900-6106
Fax: (2) 711-7736
Email: marebis@com.uy

Sephardi

Comunidad Israelita Sefardi
Buenos Aires 234, 21 de Setiembre 3111
Telephone: (2) 710-179

Templo Sefardi
de Pocitos L. Franzini 888

TOURIST SITES

Memorial to Golda Meir
Reconquista y Ciudadela
Email: cciu@adinet.com.uy

UZBEKISTAN

The ancient Jewish community in this central Asian republic is believed to have originated from Persian exiles in the fifth century. The Jews were subject to harsh treatment under the various rulers of the region, but still managed to become important traders in this area, which straddled the route between Europe and China and the Far East. In the late Middle Ages Jewish weavers and dyers were asked to help in the local cloth industry, and Bukhara became a key Jewish city after it became the capital of the country in the 1500s. Once the area had been incorporated into the Russian Empire in 1868, many Jews from the west of the Empire moved into Uzbekistan. A further influx occurred when Uzbekistan was used to shelter Jews during the Nazi invasion of the Soviet Union and many subsequently set up home there.

The original Bukharan Jews are generally more religious than the Ashkenazim who entered the area in the nineteenth and twentieth centuries. There are Jewish schools in the area, and although there is no central Jewish organisation, there are many Jewish bodies operating on separate levels for the Ashkenazim and the Bukharans.

GMT +5 hours
Country calling code: (+998)
Total population: 21,206,000
Jewish population: 15,000
Emergency telephone: (Police–03) (Fire–03)
(Ambulance–03)
Electricity voltage: 220

ANDIZHAN

Andizhan Synagogue
7 Sovetskaya Street

BUKHARA

Bukhara Synagogue
20 Tsentrainaya Street

KATTA-KURGAN

Katta-Kurgan Synagogue
1 Karl Marx Alley

KERMINE

Kermine Synagogue
36 Narimanov Street

KOKAND

Kokand Synagogue
Dekabristov Street, Fergan Oblast

MARGELAN

Margelan Synagogue
Turkilskaya Street, Fergan Oblast

NAVOY

Navoy Synagogue
36 Narimanov Street

SAMARKAND

3,000 Jews live in Samarkand. Many are Bukharan and live in the special mahala, the quarter designated for Jew.

SYNAGOGUES
Samarkand Synagogue
18 Esayva Street

Synagogue Gumbaz
2-i Llyazarov Proezd 1
Telephone: (66) 223-09-78, 235-78-62, 233-11-45
Fax: (66) 233-46-40

TASHKENT

COMMUNITY ORGANISATIONS
Jewish Community of Uzbekistan
2nd Kunaeva 15/17
Telephone: (71) 1525978
Fax: (71) 12064318
Email: jewish@bcc.com.uz
Website: www.jewish.uz

CONTACT INFORMATION
Lubavitch in Uzbekistan & Central Asia
30 Balakireva Street, Tashkent 700100
Telephone: (71) 253-8776
Fax: (71) 120-6431
Website: jewishhuz.com

EMBASSY
Embassy of Israel
16A Shakhrisabz Street, 5th Floor
Telephone: (71) 152-911
Fax: (71) 152-1378
Email: isremb@online.ru

SYNAGOGUES
Central Synagogue Beit Menachem
2- ya Kunaeva Str., 15/17 Uzbekistan 700015
Telephone: (71) 152-59-78, 256-51-14
Fax: (71) 120-64-31

Ashkenazi
Tashkent Ashkenazi Synagogue
77 Chempianov Street

Orthodox
Tashkent Orthodox Synagogue
9 Sagban Street, Tashkent, 700100

Sephardi
Kotel Levi Yitzchok
Shcolave 911, Tashkent 700100

Tashkent Sephardi Synagogue
3 Sagban Street
Telephone: (71) 40-0768

VENEZUELA

Settlement in Venezuela began in the early nineteenth century from the Caribbean. The Jews were granted freedom early (between 1819 and 1821), which encouraged more settlement. The community at that time was not religious. At the beginning of the twentieth century some Middle Eastern Jewish immigrants organised a central committee for the first time. The powerful influence of the Catholic Church meant few Jews were accepted as immigrants in the pre-war rush to escape Nazi Europe.

After the war however, the community began to expand, with arrivals from Hungary and the Middle East. The successful oil industry and the excellent Jewish education system attracted immigrants from other South American countries.

Today most Jews live in Caracas, the capital. Fifteen synagogues serve the country. The Lubavitch movement is present and maintains a yeshivah. Caracas has a Jewish bookshop and a weekly Jewish newspaper. Venezuela has an expanding Jewish community, in contrast to many of its South American neighbours. The oldest Jewish cemetery in South America, in Coro, with tombstones dating from 1832, is still in use today.

GMT -4 hours
Country calling code: (+58)
Total population: 22,777,000
Jewish population: 22,000
Emergency telephone: (Ambulance–545 4545)
(Doctor 02 483 7021)
Electricity voltage: 220

CARACAS
The first real Jewish settlement in the city dates from 1880, although there is mention of them being in the territory in the early 18th century. The present community is basically Sephardi.

BAKERIES
Le Notre
Avenida Andres Bello
Telephone: (2) 782-4488

Pasteleria Kasher
Avenida Los Proceres
Telephone: (2) 515-086

BOOKSELLERS
Liberia Cultural Maimonides
Av Altamira Edif. Carlitos PB, (near Av. Galapen),
San Bernardino
Telephone: (2) 551-6356
Fax: (2) 552-9127
Email: judaico@tecel.net.ve

COMMUNITY ORGANISATIONS
Chabad Lubavitch
9na. Trans. Altamira final de Ae Luis Roche Altamira
Telephone: (2) 264-0711
Fax: (2) 264-7011
Website: www.jabadve.com

Chabad Lubavitch
Avenue J Washington QTA Lore No. 8
Telephone: (2) 552-0044
Fax: (2) 552-2184
Email: www.jabadve.com

CONTACT INFORMATION
Chabad-Lubavitch Centre
Apartado 5454 1010A
Telephone: (2) 523-887

DELICATESSEN
La Belle Delicatesses
Av. Bogota, Edif Santa Maria, Local 2, Los Caobos
Telephone: (2) 781-7204
Fax: (2) 781-7182
Kosher delicatessen and mini-market, restaurant and take-away

EMBASSY
Embassy of Israel
Avenida Francisco de Miranda, Centro Empresarial
Miranda, 4 Piso Oficina 4-D, Apartado Postal Los
Ruices 70081
Telephone: (2) 239-4511, 239-4921
Fax: (2) 239-4320

GROCERIES
Mini Market
Avenida Los Caobos
Telephone: (2) 781-7204
Take-away

MEDIA
Newspapers
Nuevo Mundo Israelita
Av Marques del Toro 9, Los Caobos

MIKVAOT
Shomrei Shabbat Association Synagogue
Av Anauco, San Bernardino
Telephone: (2) 517-197

**Union Israelita de Caracas Synagogue &
Community Centre**
Av Marques del Toro 9, San Bernardino
Telephone: (2) 552-8222
Fax: (2) 552-7628
Email: rabino@brener@eldish.net

SYNAGOGUES
Ashkenazi
Great Synagogue of Caracas
Av Francisco Javier Ustariz, San Bernardino
Telephone: (2) 511-869

Shomrei Shabat Associacion Synagogue
Av Anauco, San Bernardino
Telephone: (2) 517-197

**Union Israelita de Caracas Synagogue &
Community Centre**
Av Marques del Toro 9, San Bernardino
Telephone: (2) 552-8222
Fax: (2) 552-7628
Email: rabino@brener@eldish.net
If notified in advance, they can arrange kosher lunches
there is also a meat snack bar open in the evening

Sephardi
Bet El
Av Cajigal, San Bernardino
Telephone: (2) 522-008

Keter Tora
Av Lopez Mendez, San Bernardino

Shaare Shalom
Av Bogota, quinta Julieta, Los Caobos
Telephone: (2) 782-6755
Email: isaac.sananes@hotmail.com

Tiferet Yisrael
Av Mariperez, Los Caobos
Telephone: (2) 781-1942

MARACAIBO
COMMUNITY ORGANISATIONS
Associación Israelita de Maracaibo
Calle 74 No 13-26
Telephone: (61) 70333

PORLAMAR
SYNAGOGUES
Or Meir
Calle Carnevali, Margarita Island
Telephone: (95) 634-433
Mikva on premises

VIRGIN ISLANDS (USA)

Jews first began to settle on the island in
1655, taking advantage of liberal Danish
rule. They were mainly traders in sugar

cane, rum and molasses, and by 1796 a synagogue had been founded. The Jewish population of 400 in 1850 made up half of the islands' white community. There have been three Jewish governors. One was Gabriel Milan, the first governor who was appointed by King Christian of Denmark.

The community began to shrink after the Panama Canal was opened in 1914, and by 1942 only 50 Jews remained. Since 1945, the community has expanded again, with families arriving from the US mainland.

GMT -4 hours
Country calling code: (1 340)
Total population: 115,000
Jewish population: 300

ST THOMAS
SYNAGOGUES
Hebrew Congregation of St Thomas
PO Box 266 St Thomas, VI 00804
Telephone: (340) 774-4312
Fax: (340) 774-3249
Email: hebrewcong@island.vi
Website: www.onepaper.com/synagogue
Located on 16A & B Crystal Gade, Charlotte Amalie. Open to visitors: Monday to Friday 9.00 am to 4.00 pm. Service schedule: Friday 6.30 pm Saturday 10.00 am.

YUGOSLAVIA

(Yugoslavia at present comprises Serbia and Montenegro.) The history of Serbian Jewry is both long and comparatively happy, with initial settlement occurring in Roman times. Afte the onset of Turkish domination in 1389, the community continued to thrive and also prospered under Austrian rule in the eighteenth century. The nineteenth century saw some measures being taken against the Jews after Serbia became independent, but these were quickly redressed in 1889, following the Treaty of Berlin.

After 1918, Serbia was united with Croatia, Slovenia and the other south Slavic states into one country, known as Yugoslavia. The community suffered heavily under Nazi domination. The Jews were active among the Yugoslav partisans and, after liberation, many who had hidden or fought with the partisans began to return to their homes. Before the break-up of Yugoslavia, the Jews were allowed contact with other communities, including Israel. Since the civil war, some Jews have remained in the country, and there is a synagogue and a Talmud Torah school in Belgrade.

GMT +1 hours
Country calling code: (+381)
Total population: 10,597,000
Jewish population: 2,500
Emergency telephone: (Police–92) (Fire–93) (Ambulance–94)
Electricity voltage: 220

BELGRADE
Some 2,000 Jews now live in the capital of Serbia, compared with hardly any during the latter stages of World War Two. There is an Ashkenazi synagogue which follows Sephardi tradition (or nusach), and there is a community centre, although kosher food is not available.

COMMUNITY ORGANISATIONS
Federation of Jewish Communities
7 Karlija Petra Street 71a/111 , PO Box 841 11001
Telephone: (11) 624-359, 621-837
Fax: (11) 626 674
Email: savezjev@infosky.net

MUSEUMS
Jewish Historical Museum
Kralja Petra Street 71a/1 11000
Telephone: (11) 2622-634
Fax: (11) 626-674
Email: muzej@eunet.yu
Website: www.jim-bg.org
Open daily from 10.00 am to 2.00 pm

SYNAGOGUES
Belgrade Synagogue
Birjuzova Street 19
Services are held Friday evenings and Jewish holidays

TOURIST SITES
Jewish Cemetery
There are monuments here to fallen fighters and martyrs of Fascism, and fallen Jewish soldiers in the Serbian army in the First World War. In 1990 a new monument to Jews killed in Serbia was erected by the Danube, in the pre-war Jewish quarter Dorcol.

SUBOTICA
Community Offices
Dimitrija Tucovica Street 13
Telephone: 28483

ZAMBIA

The Jewish community began in the early twentieth century, with cattle ranching being the main attraction for Jewish immigrants. The community grew, and the copper industry was developed largely by Jewish entrepreneurs. With refugees from Nazism and a post-war economic boom, the Jewish community in the mid-1950s totalled 1,200. The community declined after independence in 1964.

Today the Council for Zambian Jewry (founded in 1978) fulfils the role of the community's central body.

GMT +2 hours
Country calling code: (+260)
Total population: 9,715,000
Jewish population: Under 100
Emergency telephone: (Police–999) (Fire–999) (Ambulance–999)
Electricity voltage: 220

LUSAKA
COMMUNITY ORGANISATIONS
Council for Zambian Jewry
PO Box 30089 10101
Telephone: (1) 229-556
Fax: (1) 223-798
Email: galaun@zamnet.zm

SYNAGOGUES
Lusaka Hebrew Congregation
Chachacha Road, POB 30020 10101
Telephone: (1) 229-190
Fax: (1) 221-428
Mobile Phone: 95857565
Email: galaun@microlink.zm
Central organisation: African Jewish Congress

ZIMBABWE

Jews were among the earliest pioneers in Zimbabwe (formerly Rhodesia). The first white child born there (April 1894) was Jewish. The first synagogue in Zimbabwe was set up in 1894, in a tent in Bulawayo. In 1897 a Jew was elected as the first mayor of Bulawayo. The first Jews came from Europe (especially Lithuania), and they became involved in trade and managing hotels. They were joined in the 1920s and 1930s by Sephardis from Rhodes.

Some senior politicians in the country were Jewish, including one prime minister.

The 1970s saw the turbulent transition to Zimbabwe, and many Jews emigrated to escape the unrest. The community is now mainly Ashkenazi, with an important Sephardi component. Harare has both an Ashkenazi and a Sephardi synagogue; Bulawayo has a Ashkenazi synagogue. There are community centres and schools in both the towns, although the latter have many local, non-Jewish pupils.

GMT +2 hours
Country calling code: (+263)
Total population: 12,294,000
Jewish population: 900
Emergency telephone: (Police–999) (Fire–999) (Ambulance–999)
Electricity voltage: 220/240

BULAWAYO
SYNAGOGUES
Orthodox
Bulawayo Hebrew Congregation
PO Box 337, Sinai Centre, Corner Coghlan Avenue and Bailey Road
Telephone: (9) 78726, 259698
Fax: (9) 65535
Email: hms@netconnect.co.zw
Website: www.zjc.org.il
Supervision: Rabbi Nathan Asmoucha
Chevra Kadishah, Jewish Old Age Home and other charities

HARARE
COMMUNITY ORGANISATIONS
Zimbabwe Jewish Board of Deputies
PO BOX 1954
Telephone: (4) 702-507
Fax: (4) 702-506
Email: cazo@zol.co.zw
Hours of opening 8.30 am to 12.00 noon

SYNAGOGUES
Harare Hebrew Congregation
Milton Park Jewish Centre, Lezard Avenue, PO Box 342
Telephone: (4) 798-683
Fax: (4) 798-463

Sephardi Congregation
54 Josiah Chinamano Avenue, PO Box 1051
Telephone: (4) 722-899

Kosher Fish in Europe

CYPRUS

Antzouva(Anchovy)
Bacceliaos (Cod) Barbouni
(Pike) Cephalos (Perch)
Glossa (Sole) Lavraki (Bass)
Sardella (Pilchard) Scoumbri
(Mackerel) Tonos(Tuna)
Tsipoura (Bream)

CZECH REPUBLIC Ancovicka

(Anchovy) Belicka (Roach)
Kambala (Brill) Kapr(Carp)
Lin (Tench)
Losos (Salmon) Makrela
(Mackerel) Okoun (Perch)
Parmice (Mullet) Platejs (Dab)
Platyz (Plaice)
Plotice (Sole)
Prazama (Bream) Pstruh
(Trout) Sardinka (Sardine) Sled
(Herring)
Sprota (Sprat)
Stika (Pike)
Treska (Haddock) Tunak(Tuna)

DENMARK

Aborre (Perch)
Ansjos (Anchovy)
Bars (Bass)
Brasen (Bream) Brisling (Sprat)
Geode (Pike) Helleyflynder
     (Halibut)
Hvilling (Whiting)
Ising (Dab)
Karpe (Carp) Knurhane
(Gunard)
Kuller (Haddock) Kulmule
(Hake)
Laks (Salmon)
Lange (Ling)
Lubbe (Pollack) Makrel
(Mackerel) Multe (Mullet)
Orred (Trout) Rodspaette
(Plaice) Sardin (Sardine)
Sild (Herring)

Skalle (Roach) Skrubbe
(Flounder) Slethvarre (Brill)
Suder (Tench)
Torsk (Cod)
Tun fisk (Tuna) Tunge
(Sole)

FRANCE

Aiglefin (Haddock) Anchois
(Anchovy) Bar Commun (Bass)
Barbue (Brill)
Breme (Bream) Brochet (Pike)
Cabillaud (Cod)
Carpe (Carp)
Carrelet (Plaice) Daurade
(Bream) Epirlan (Smelt)
Flet (Flounder)
Fletan (Halibut) Gardon
(Roach) Grondin (Gunard)
Hareng (Herring)
Lieu Jaune (Pollack) Limande
(Dab)
Lingue (Ling) Maquereau
     (Mackerel)
Merlan (Whiting) Merlu
(Hake)
Mulet (Mullet) Perche
(Perch) Pilchard (Pilchard)
Plie (Plaice)
Sardine (Sardine) Saumon
(Salmon) Sole (Sole)
Sprat (Sprat) Tanche
(Tench) Thon (Tuna)
Truite (Trout)

GERMANY

Barsch (Perch)
Brasse (Bream) Flunder
(Flounder) Forelle (Trout)
Glattbutt (Brill)
Hecht (Pike)
Heilbutt (Halibut) Hering
(Herring) Kabeljau (Cod)
Knurrhahn (Gunard) Lachs
(Salmon)

Leng (Ling)
Makrele (Mackerel) Meerasche
(Mullet) Pilchard (Pilchard)
Plotze (Roach)
Pollack (Pollack) Sardelle
(Anchovy) Sardine (Sardine)
Scharbe (Dab) Schellfisch
(Haddock) Schlei (Tench)
Scholle (Plaice) Seebarsch
(Bass) Seehecht(Hake)
Seezunge (Sole) Sprotte (Sprat)
Thun (Tuna) Weissfisch (Carp)
Wittling (Whiting)

GREECE

Antjuga (Anchovy) Bakaliaros
(Cod) Chematida
(Flounder) Chromatida (Dab)
Gados (Haddock)
Giavros(Anchovy) Glinia
(Tench)
Glossa (Sole)
Glossaki (Plaice) Hippoglossa
(Halibut) Kaponi (Gunard)
Kephalos (Mullet) Kyprinos
(Carp) Lavraki (Bass)
Lestia (Bream) Papalina (Sprat)
Pentiki (Ling)
Perca chani(Perch) Pestropha
(Trout)
Pissi (Brill)
Regha (Herring) Romvos (Brill)
Sardella (Pilchard) Sardine
(Sardine) Scoumbri (Mackerel)
Solomos (Salmon) Tonnos
(Tuna)
Tourna (Pike)
Tsironi (Roach)

ITALY

Acciuga (Anchovy) Aringa
(Herring) Asinello (Haddock)
Brama (Bream)
Carpa (Carp)
Cefalo (Mullet) Halibut

(Halibut) Limanda (Dab)
Luccio (Pike) Maccerello
(Mackerel) Merlano (Whiting)
Merluzzo Bianco (Cod)
Merluzzo Giallo
(Pollack)
Molva (Ling) Nasello
(Hake)
Passera (Plaice) Passera
Pianuzza
(Flounder)
Pesce (Perch)
Pesce Capone
(Gunard)
Rombo Liscio (Brill) Salmone
(Salmon) Sardina (Sardine)
Sogliola (Sole)
Spigola (Bass)
Spratto (Sprat) Tinca (Tench)
Tonno (Tuna) Triotto (Roach)
Trota (Trout)

NETHERLANDS Aaldoe
(Mullet) Ansjovis (Anchovy)
Baars (Perch) Blankvoorn
(Roach) Bot (Flounder) Brasem
(Bream)
Forel (Trout)
Griet (Brill)
Harder (Mullet) Haring
(Herring)
Heek (Hake)
Helibot (Halibut) Kabeljauw
(Cod) Karper(Carp)
Leng (Ling)
Makree (Mackerel) Pelser
(Sardine)
Poon (Gunard)
Salm (Salmon)
Sardien (Sardine) Schar(Dab)
Schelvis (Haddock) Schol
(Plaice)
Snoek (Pike)
Sprot (Sprat)
Tong (Sole)
Tonijn (Tuna)
Wijting (Whiting) Witte koolvis
(Pollack) Zeebaars (Bass)

Zeelt (Tench)

PORTUGAL
Alabote (Halibut) Anchova
(Anchovy) Arenque (Herring)
Arinca (Haddock) Atum (Tuna)
Bacalhau (Cod) Badejo
(Pollack) Biqueirao (Anchovy)
Carpa (Carp)
Donzela (Ling) Espadilha
(Sprat) Linguado (Sole)
Lucio (Pike)
Perca (Perch)
Pescada (Hake) Petruca
(Flounder) Robalo (Bass)
Rodovalho (Brill) Ruivaca
(Roach)
Ruivo (Gunard) Salmao
(Salmon) Sarda (Mackerel)
Sardinha (Sardine) Sargo
(Bream)
Solha (Plaice)
Solhao (Dab)
Tainha (Mullet) Tenca(Tench)
Truta (Trout)

SPAIN
Abadejo (Pollack) Anchoa
(Anchovy)
Arenque (Herring) Atun (Tuna)
Bacalao (Cod) Bermejuela
(Roach) Boqueron (Anchovy)
Caballa (Mackerel) Carpa
(Carp)
Eglefino (Haddock) Espadin
(Sprat) Halibut (Halibut)
Lenguado (Sole) Limanda
(Dab)
Lisa (Mullet) Lubina (Bass)
Lucio (Pike) Maruca (Ling)
Merlan (Whiting) Merluza
(Hake) Perca (Perch)
Platija (Flounder) Remol
(Brill) Rubios (Gunard)
Salmon (Salmon) Sardina
(Sardine) Solla (Plaice)
Tenca (Tench) Trucha
(Trout)

TURKEY
Alabalik (Trout) Bakalyaro
(Whiting) Berlam (Hake)
Caca (Sprat)
Civisiz kalkan (Brill) Derepissi
(Flounder) Dil baligi (Sole)
Gelincik (Ling)
Hamsi (Anchovy) Kadife baligi
(Tench) Kefal (Mullet) Kirlangic
(Gunard) Kizilgoz (Roach)
Levrek (Bass)
Morina (Cod)
Palatika (Sprat)
Pisi baligi (Dab)
Ringa (Herring) Sardalya
(Sardine) Sardayalo (Pilchard)
Sazan (Carp)
Som baligi (Salmon) Tahta
baligi (Bream) Tatlisu levregi
(Perch) Ton baligi (Tuna)
Turna baligi (Pike) Uskumru
(Mackerel)

UNITED KINGDOM Anchovy
Barbel
Bass
Bloater
Bonito
Bream
Brill
Brisling
Buckling
Carp
Coalfish
Cod
Coley
Dab
Dace
Flounder
Fluke
Grayling
Gurnard
Haddock
Hake
Halibut
Herring
Hoki
John Dory

Keta Salmon Kipper
Ling
Mackerel
Megrim
Mock
Halibut
Mullet Grey
Mullet Red
Norway Haddock
Parrot Fish
Perch
Pike

Pilchard
Plaice
Pole
Pollack
Redfish
Roach
Saithe
Salmon
Sardine
Shad
Sild
Smelt

Snapper
Snoek
Sole Dover
Sole Lemon
Sprat
Tench
Tilapia
Trout
Tuna (Tunny) Whitebait
Whiting
Witch

Kosher Fish outside Europe

AUSTRALIA

Anchovy
Baramundi
Barracouta
Barracuda
Blue Eye
Blue Grenadier
Bream
Butterfly-fish
Cod
Coral Perch
Duckfish
Flathead
Flounder
Garfish
Groper
Gurnard
Haddock
Hake
Harpuka
Herring
Iewfish
John Dory
Lemon Sole
Mackerel
Morwong
Mullet
Murray Cod
Murray Perch
Orange Roughy
Perch

Pike
Pilchard
Red Emperor
Redfin
Salmon
Sardine
Sea Perch
Shad
Sild
Snapper
Tailor
Tasmanian
Trumpeter
Terakiji
Trevally
Trout Tuna:
    Albacore, Bluefin
    North bluefin
    South bluefin
    Skipjack (striped)
    Yellowtan
Whiting
Yellowtail

CANADA

Albacore
Anchovy
Bass
Boston Bluefish
Carp
Cisco

Cod
Flounder
Goldeye
Haddock
Hake
Halibut
Herring
Mackerel
Orange Roughy
Perch
Pickerel
Pike
Pollock
Pompano
Salmon
Sardine
Silverside
Smelt
Snapper
Sole
Sunfish
Tarpon
Trout
Tuna

CARIBBEAN

Bonito
Grouper
Kingsish
Mullet
Muttonfish

Pompano
Roballo
Smelt
Snapper Red/Yellow
Spanish Mackerel
Trout
Tuna

HONG KONG

Anchovy
Bigeyes
Carp
Crevalles
Croakers
Giant Perch
Grey Mullet
Grouper
Japanese Sea Perch
Leopard Coral Trout
Pampano
Pilchard
Red Sea Bream
Round Herring
Sardine
Scad
Whitefish

NEW ZEALAND

Hoki
John Dory
Kingfish

Mackerel
Mullet
Orange Roughy
Perch
Piper
Salmon
Smooth Black
Snapper
Sole
Southern Whiting
Terakihi
Trevally
Trout

SOUTH AFRICA
Albacore Tuna
Albacore
Butterfish
Carp
Euthynnus Tuna
Haddock
Herring
Kabeljou
Kingklip
Maas Banker
Mackerel

Pilchards
Salmon
Sardines
Seventy Four
Skipjack Tuna
Snoek
Sole
Steembras
Stock fish
Stump Nose
Tongol Tuna
Trout
Yellowfin Tuna

UNITED STATES OF AMERICA
Albacore
Alewife   Smelts
Amberjack
Anchovies
Angelfish
Barb
Barracouta
Barracuda
Bass
Bigeyes
Black Cod
Blackfish

Blueback
Bluefish
Bluegill
Bonito
Bream
Brill
Capelin
Carp
Cero
Char
Chub
Cisco
Coalfish
Cod
Crevalle
Dab
Flounders
Fluke
Gag
Grayling
Grouper
Haddock
Hake
Halibert
Herrings
John Dory
Kingfish
Mackeral
Mahi Mahi

Merluccio
MulletParrotfish
Perch
pike
Pilchard
Plaice
Pollock
Pomfrets
Red Snappers
Roach
Saithe
Salmon
Sardine
Shad
Sierra
Skipjack
Smelt
Snapper
Sole
Sprat
Tench
Tilapia
Trout
Tuna
Wahoo
Whitefish
Whiting
Yellowtail

Jewish Calendar

2006 (5766-5767)

Fast of Esther	Monday	March 13th
Purim	Tuesday	March 14th
First Day Pesach	Thursday	April 13th
Second Day Pesach	Friday	April 14th
Seventh Day Pesach	Wednesday	April 19th
Eighth Day Pesach (Yizkor)	Thursday	April 20th
Holocaust Memorial Day	Tuesday	April 25th
Israel Independence Day	Wednesday	May 3rd
Lag B'Omer	Tuesday	May 16th
First Day Shavout	Friday	June 2nd
Second Day Shavout (Yizkor)	Saturday	June 3rd
Fast of Tammuz	Thursday	July 13th
Fast of Av	Thursday	August 3rd
First Day Rosh Hashanah	Saturday	September 23rd
Second Day Rosh Hashanah	Sunday	September 24th
Fast of Gedaliah	Monday	September 25th
Yom Kippur (Yizkor)	Monday	October 2nd
First Day Succot	Saturday	October 7th
Second Day Succot	Sunday	October 8th
Shemini Atseret (Yizkor)	Saturday	October 14th
Simchat Torah	Sunday	October 15th
First Day Chanukah	Saturday	December 16th

2007 (5767-5768)

Fast of Esther	Thursday	March 1st
Purim	Sunday	March 4th
First Day Pesach	Tuesday	April 3rd
Second Day Pesach	Wednesday	April 4th
Seventh Day Pesach	Monday	April 9th
Eighth Day Pesach (Yizkor)	Tuesday	April 10th
Holocaust Memorial Day	Sunday	April 15th
Israel Independence Day	Tuesday	April 24th
Lag B'Omer	Sunday	May 6th
First Day Shavout	Wednesday	May 23rd
Second Day Shavout(Yizkor)	Thursday	May 24th
Fast of Tammuz	Tuesday	July 3rd
Fast of AV	Tuesday	July 24th
First Day Rosh Hashanah	Thursday	September 13th
Second Day Rosh Hashanah	Frisday	September 14th
Fast of Gedaliah	Sunday	September 16th
Yom Kippur (Yizkor)	Saturday	September 22nd
First Day Succot	Thursday	September 27th
Second Day Succot	Friday	September 28th
Shemini Atseret (Yizkor)	Thursday	October 4th
Simchat Torah	Friday	October 5th
First Day Chanucah	Wednesday	December 5th

Index

A

		Annapolis	288	Baden (Switzerland)	199
		Annecy	84	Baden-Baden	94
Aachen	93	Annemasse	84	Bagneux	78
Aberdeen (NJ)	309	Annweiler	94	Bagnolet	78
Aberdeen (Scotland)	245	Antibes-Juan-les-Pins	84	Bahamas	19
Aberdeen (SD)	360	Antony	78	Bahia Blanca	2
Aberdeen (WA)	367	Antwerp	22	Bakersfield	250
Acapulco	150	Arad (Israel)	118	Baku	18
Acton	292	Arad (Romania)	173	Bala Cynwyd	350
Addis Ababa	62	Arcachon	91	Balat	206
Adelaide	10	Arcadia	250	Balatonfured	107
Afula	117	Argentina	2	Baldwin	326
Agadir	153	Arica	47	Balearic Islands	195
Agen	91	Arlington (TX)	361	Ballarat	10
Aix-en-Provence	84	Arlington (VA)	365	Baltimore	288
Aix-les-Bains	84	Arlon	24	Bamberg	94
Akhalitsikhe	92	Armenia	6	Bangkok	205
Akko	117	Arnhem	160	Bangor	287
Akron	345	Arosa	199	Baranovichi	20
Alameda	250	Asheville	344	Baranquilla	50
Albania	1	Ashland	349	Barbados	19
Albany	322	Asmara	62	Barcelona	190
Albuquerque	321	Asnieres	78	Barking and Becontree	213
Alderney	244	Astana	144	Barkingside	213
Aldershot	216	Asti	134	Bar-le-Duc	63
Alexandria (Egypt)	60	Astrakhan	177	Barnet	216
Alexandria (LA)	286	Asuncion	166	Barrington	358
Alexandria (VA)	365	Athens (GA)	277	Basle	199
Algarve	171	Athens (Greece)	104	Baton Rouge	286
Algeria	1	Athis-Mons	78	Batumi	92
Algiers	1	Athol	292	Bayonne (France)	91
Alibag	110	Atlanta	277	Bayonne (NJ)	309
Alicante	189	Atlantic City	309	Bayreuth	94
Allentown	350	Attleboro	292	Baytown	362
Almaty	144	Auburn	287	Beachwood	345
Alsenz	94	Auckland	162	Beacon	323
Amarillo	361	Augusta (GA)	278	Beaumont	362
Amersfoort	157	Augusta (LO)	287	Beauvais	64
Amherst	292	Aulnay-Sous-Bois	78	Becontree	213
Amiens	63	Austin	361	Beersheba	118
Amsterdam (Netherlands)	157	Australia	6	Beijing	48
Amsterdam (NY)	323	Austria	14	Belarus	20
Anaheim	259	Avignon	85	Belem	29
Anchorage	248	Avihail	118	Belfast	163
Ancona	134	Ayer	292	Belfort	64
Andernach	94	Azerbaijan	18	Belgium	22
Andizhan	371			Belgrade	374
Andorra	1	**B**		Belleville	40
Andover	292			Belmar	310
Angers	68	Bacau	173	Belmont	292
Ankara	206	Bad Nauheim	94	Belmonte	171
Ann Arbor	303	Baden (Austria)	15	Belo Horizonte	28

Benfeld	64	Boulay	64	Cairo	60
Benidorm	190	Boulder	264	Calgary	35
Bensalem	350	Boulogne sur Seine	78	Cali	51
Benton Harbor	303	Boulogne-sur-Mer	64	Caluire- et- Cuire	85
Berdichev	208	Bournemouth	212	Cambridge (MA)	295
Beregovo	208	Bouxwiller	64	Cambridge (UK)	211
Bergenfield	310	Bouzonville	64	Campinas	31
Berkeley	251	Bowie	289	Campos	29
Berlin	94	Bradford	243	Canada	35
Bermuda	26	Bradley Beach	310	Canary Islands	195
Bern	200	Braintree(MA)	293	Canberra	6
Bershad	208	Brakpan	183	Cannes	85
Besancon	64	Brasilia	28	Canterbury	217
Bethesda	289	Brasov	174	Canton (MA)	295
Bethlehem (NH)	308	Bratislava	181	Canton (OH)	345
Bethlehem (PA)	350	Braunschweig	96	Cape Cod	295
Beverly	293	Brazil	28	Cape Town	187
Beverly Hills	251	Bremen	96	Caracas	372
Beziers	85	Bremgarten / Aargau	200	Cardiff	246
Biel/Bienne	200	Brest (Belarus)	20	Carmel	252
Bielsko-Biala	169	Brest (France)	68	Carpentras	86
Billings	307	Bridgeport	265	Casablanca	153
Binghamton	323	Bridgeton	310	Casale Monferrato	135
Birkirkara	149	Bridgetown	19	Casper	369
Birmingham (AL)	247	Brighton	293	Castro Valley	252
Birmingham (UK)	242	Brighton and Hove	240	Cavaillon	86
Birobidjan	177	Brisbane	9	Cedar Rapids	284
Bischeim-Schiltigheim	68	Bristol	210	Cedarhurst	326
Bishkek	145	Brno	55	Celle	96
Bismark	345	Brockton	294	Ceuta	47
Bitche	64	Bronx	332	Chalkis	105
Blackpool	218	Brookline	294	Chalon-sur-Saone	64
Blida	1	Brooklyn	332	Chalons-sur-Marne	64
Bloemfontein	183	Brussels	24	Chambery	64
Bloomfield Hills	303	Bryansk	177	Champaign-Urbana	279
Bloomington	282	Bucharest	174	Champigny	78
B'nei Berak	118	Budapest	108	Channel Islands	244
Bobigny	78	Buenos Aires	2	Charleroi	25
Bobruisk	20	Buffalo	323	Charleston (SC)	359
Boca Raton	270	Bukhara	371	Charleston (WV)	368
Bogota	50	Bulawayo	375	Charlotte	344
Bolivia	26	Bulgaria	34	Charlottesville	365
Bologna	134	Burbank	251	Chateauroux	69
Bologna (Spain)	190	Burgos	190	Chatham	40
Bondy	78	Burlingame	252	Chattanooga	360
Bonita	251	Burlington (MA)	295	Cheadle	218
Bonn	96	Burlington (NJ)	310	Chelles	78
Boras	196	Burlington (VT)	365	Chelmsford (MA)	295
Bordeaux	91	Bushey	216	Cheltenham	215
Borehamwood	216	Bussum	160	Chemnitz	97
Borisov	20			Chernigov	208
Boskovice	55	**C**		Chernovtsy	208
Bosnia-Hercegovina	27			Cherry Hill	310
Boston	293	Caen	68	Chevy Chase	290
Botosani	174	Caesarea	118	Cheyenne	369

Chiang Mai	205	Cranston	358	Dubuque	284
Chicago	280	Crete	105	Duluth	305
Chigwell	215	Creteil	79	Dundee	244
Chile	47	Croatia	52	Dunkirk	65
Chimkent	145	Cuba	53	Dunoon	245
China	48	Cuernavaca	150	Durban	186
Chisinau	152	Cumberland	290	Durham	344
Chmelnitsy	208	Cuneo	135	Dushanbe	204
Choisy-le-Roi	78	Curaçao	162	Dusseldorf	97
Christchurch	162	Curitiba	29		
Chula Vista	252	Cyprus	54	**E**	
Cincinnati	346	Czech Republic	55		
Cinnaminson	311			East Barnet	216
Clark	311	**D**		East Brunswick	311
Clearwater	271			East Chicago	282
Clermont-Ferrand	86	Dallas	362	East Falmouth	295
Cleveland	346	Daly City	252	East Lansing	304
Clichy-sur-Seine	78	Dan	118	East London (South Africa)	182
Clifton	311	Danbury	266	Eastbourne	241
Clifton Park	325	Danville	365	Easton (MA)	296
Clinton	295	Daugavpils	146	Easton (PA)	350
Cluj Napoca	175	Davenport	284	Ecuador	59
Coblenz (Koblenz)	97	Davis	252	Edinburgh	245
Cochabamba	26	Dayton	347	Edison	311
Cochin	110	Daytona Beach	271	Edmonton	35
Cockfosters	216	Dead Sea	118	Egypt	60
Colchester	215	Deal	311	Eilat	119
Cologne	97	Deauville	69	Eindhoven	160
Colmar	64	Decatur	278	Eisenstadt	15
Columbia (SC)	359	Deerfield Beach	271	Ekaterinburg	177
Colombia	50	Degania Alef	119	El Dorado	250
Colonia	310	Delft	160	El Escorial	190
Colorado Springs	264	Delmar	325	El Paso	362
Columbia	359	Delray Beach	271	El Salvador	60
Columbus (GA)	278	Denmark	57	Elbeuf	69
Columbus (CH)	347	Denver	264	Elizabeth	312
Commack	328	Derbent	177	Elkins park	350
Compiegne	65	Des Moines	284	Ellenville	324
Concord	309	Detroit	303	Elmira	325
Constanta	175	Dieuze	65	Elmwood Park	312
Copenhagen	57	Dijon	65	Emmendingen	97
Coquitlam	36	Dix Hills	328	Encinitas	252
Cordoba (Argentina)	5	Dnepropetrovsk	208	Encino	252
Cordoba (Spain)	190	Dominican Republic	59	Endingen	200
Corfu	105	Donetsk	208	Enghien	79
Cork	113	Dorohoi	175	Englewood	312
Corsica	92	Dortmund	97	Enschede	160
Corpus Christi	362	Douglas	244	Epernay	65
Costa Mesa	252	Dover	269	Epinal	65
Costa Rica	51	Downey	252	Erechim	30
Coventry	242	Dresden	97	Erfurt	98
Cracow	169	Druskininkai	147	Erie	350
Cranbury	311	Dublin	113	Ernakulam	110
Cranford	311	Dubrovnik	52	Esch-Sur-Alzette	148

Essaouira (formerly Mogador)
154
Essen 98
Essingen 98
Estella 191
Estonia 61
Ethiopia 61
Eugene 349
Eureka 252
Evansville 282
Everett 296
Evergreen 265
Evian 86
Exeter 212
Eze-Village 86

F

Fair Lawn 312
Fairfax 365
Fairfield 266
Fall River 296
Falls Church 365
Fargo 345
Faulquemont-Crehange 65
Fayetteville 344
Ferrara 135
Fez 154
Fiji 62
Finland 62
Fleischmanns 324
Flint 304
Florence 135
Fontainebleau 79
Fontenay aux Roses 79
Fontenay sous Bois 79
Forbach 65
Fort Dodge 284
Fort Lauderdale 271
Fort Lee 312
Fort Meyers 272
Fort Pierce 272
Fort Wayne 282
Framingham 296
France 63
Frankfurt 98
Fredericton 39
Freehold 313
Freeport 19
Freiburg 98
Frejus 86
Fresno 252
Fribourg 200
Friedberg 99

Furth 99

G

Gaithersburg 290
Galanta 181
Galati 175
Galilee 120
Gardena 252
Garges-les-Gonesse 79
Gary 282
Gateshead 241
Gelsenkirchen 99
Geneva (NY) 325
Geneva (Switzerland) 201
Genoa 136
Georgetown 360
Georgia 92
Germany 93
Ghent 25
Gibraltar 103
Girona 191
Glace Bay 39
Glasgow 245
Glens Falls 325
Gliwice 169
Gloucester (MA) 296
Gloversville 325
Golan Heights 120
Gold Coast 9
Gomel 20
Gori 92
Gorizia 136
Gorki 20
Gothenburg 196
Gran Canaria 195
Granada 191
Granada Hills 252
Grand Rapids 304
Grasmere 212
Graz 15
Great Falls 307
Great Neck 326
Greater Rio de Janeiro 29
Greece 104
Greenbelt 289
Greenfield 296
Greensboro 344
Greenvale 327
Greenville 305
Greenwood 306
Grenoble 86
Grimsby 223
Grodno 20

Groningen 160
Grosbliederstroff 65
Guadalajara 150
Guadeloupe 106
Guangzhou 48
Goangzhou 48
Guaruja 31
Guatemala 106
Guatemala City 107
Guildford 240
Gush Etzion 120

H

Haarlem 160
Hackensack 313
Haddonfield 313
Hadera 121
Hagen 99
Hagerstown 289
Hagondange 65
Haguenau 65
Haifa 121
Haiti 107
Hale Barns 218
Halifax 39
Hallandale 272
Halle 99
Hamburg 99
Hamilton (Bermuda) 26
Hamilton (Canada) 40
Hammond 282
Hampton 365
Hanita 122
Hanover 99
Haon 122
Harare 375
Harlow 215
Harrisburg 350
Harrison 342
Harrogate 243
Hartford 266
Hasbrouck Heights 313
Havana 54
Haverhill 296
Haverstraw 340
Hazelton 351
Hazorea 122
Heidelberg 99
Helena 250
Helsinki 62
Hemel Hempstead 216
Hendersonville 345
Herford 99

Hershey	351	Isle of Verde	172	Kibbutz Harduf	128
Hervas	191	Israel	114	Kibbutz Yotvata	128
Herzliya	122	Issy-Les-Moulineaux	79	Kiel	100
Highland	282	Istanbul	206	Kiev	208
Highland Park (IL)	280	Italy	134	Killingholme	223
Highland Park (NJ)	313	Ithaca	325	Kimberley	187
Hildesheim	99	Ivano-Frankivsk	208	Kingston (Canada)	40
Hillside	313	Izieu	87	Kingston (Jamaica)	143
Hingham	296	Izmir	207	Kippenheim	100
Hinterglemm	15			Kitchener	40
Hiroshima	143	**J**		Klaipeda	147
Hobart	10			Knokke	25
Hof	99	Jackson (MI)	304	Kobe	143
Holbrook	296	Jackson (MS)	306	Kobersdorf	16
Holesov	55	Jacksonville	273	Koh Samui	205
Holliston	296	Jaffa	123	Kokand	371
Hollywood (CA)	253	Jamaica	143	Kolkata	110
Hollywood & Vicinity (FL)	272	Jamesburg	313	Kona	279
Holyoke	296	Japan	143	Konstanz	100
Honduras	107	Jefferson City	306	Korazim	128
Hong Kong	48	Jerba	206	Korbin	21
Hornbaek	58	Jericho (NY)	327	Korsten	209
Hot Springs	250	Jersey	244	Kosice	181
Houston	363	Jersey City	314	Kostrama	177
Hudson Hull (MA)	297	Jerusalem	123	Krasnoyarsk	177
Hudson (NY)	325	Johannesburg	183	Krefeld	100
Hull (UK)	217	Johnstown	351	Kremenchug	209
Hungary	108	Juneau	248	Kreuzlingen	201
Huntington	368			Krugersdorp	186
Huntsville	247	**K**		Kuba	18
Hyannis	297			Kursk	177
Hyattsville	290	Kaifeng	50	Kutaisi	92
Hyde Park (MA)	297	Kaiserslautern	99	Kyrgyzstan	145
Hyeres	86	Kalamazoo	304		
		Kalinkovitch	21	**L**	
I		Kansas City	306		
		Karlsruhe	100	La Ciotat	87
Iasi (Jassy)	175	Kathmandu	156	La Courneuve	79
Ichenhausen	99	Katowice	169	La Garenne-Colombes	80
Ilford	215	Katta-Kurgan	371	La Jolla	253
India	110	Kaunas	147	La Mesa	253
Indianapolis	282	Kazakhstan	144	La Paz	26
Ingenheim	99	Kazan	177	La Rochelle	91
Ingwiller	65	Kelowna	36	La Serena	47
Innsbruck	15	Kemp Mill	290	La Seyne-sur-Mer	87
Insming	65	Kendall	273	La Varenne St-Hilaire	80
Ioannina	105	Kenitra	154	La-Chaux-de-Fonds	201
Iowa City	284	Kensington	290	Lafayette (CA)	253
Iquique	47	Kenya	145	Lafayette (IN)	283
Iran	112	Kermine	371	Laguna Hills	253
Irish Republic	112	Key West	273	Lake Placid	326
Irkutsk	177	Kfar Giladi	127	Lakeland	273
Irvine	253	Khamasa	110	Lakewood (CA)	253
Isfahan	112	Kharkov	208	Lakewood (NJ)	314
Isle of Man	244	Kherson	208	La Mesa	253

Lancaster (PA)	352	Llandudno	246	Manchester (NH)	309
Lancaster (UK)	218	Loch Sheldrake	324	Manchester (UK)	219
Landau	100	Lod	128	Manhattan	334
Lansing	304	Lodz	169	Manila	168
Laramie	369	Lohamei Hagetaot	128	Mantua	136
Larissa	105	London (Canada)	41	Maplewood	315
Larnaca	55	London (UK)	223	Maputo	155
Las Cruces	321	Long Beach (CA)	253	Maracaibo	373
Las Palmas	195	Long Beach (NY)	327	Marbella	192
Las Vegas	308	Longmeadow	297	Marblehead	298
Latvia	145	Lorain	348	Marburg an der Lahn	100
Launceston	10	Lorient	69	Margate	218
Laurel	290	Los Alamos	321	Margelan	371
Lausanne	201	Los Angeles	254	Marignane	88
Lawrence (KS)	284	Loughton	215	Marlboro	298
Lawrence (MA)	297	Louisville	285	Marrakech	154
Lawrence (NY)	327	Lowell	297	Marseilles	88
Lawrenceville	314	Lubbock	264	Martinique	149
Le Blanc Mesnil	80	Lubeck	100	Massy	80
Le Chesnay	80	Lublin	170	Maui	279
Le Havre	69	Lucerne	202	McKeesport	352
Le Kremlin-Bicetre	80	Lugano	202	Meaux	81
Le Mans	69	Luneville	65	Medellin	51
Le Perreux Nogent	80	Lusaka	375	Medford	298
Le Raincy	80	Luton	211	Meknes	154
Le Vesinet	80	Luxembourg	148	Melbourne (Australia)	10
Leeds	243	Luxembourg City	148	Melbourne (FL)	273
Leghorn	136	Lviv	209	Melilla	149
Legnica	169	Lynn	298	Melrose	298
Leicester	223	Lyon	87	Melun	81
Leiden	160			Memphis	360
Lengnau	201	**M**		Menton	89
Leominster	297			Merano	136
Les Lilas	80	Maagan	128	Mercer Island	367
Levallois Perret	80	Maastricht	160	Meriden	267
Lexington (KY)	285	Maayan Harod	128	Merlebach	65
Lexington (MA)	297	Macedonia	148	Metuchen	315
Lexington Park	290	Macon (France)	88	Metz	65
Liberec	55	Macon (GA)	279	Meudon-La-Foret	81
Libourne	91	Madison	369	Mexico	150
Liege	25	Madrid	191	Mexico City	150
Liepaja	146	Magdeburg	100	Miami/Miami Beach	273
Lille	65	Mahanayim	128	Michelstadt	100
Lima	167	Mahwah	315	Michigan City	283
Limoges	91	Maidenhead	211	Middletown (CT)	267
Lincoln (NE)	307	Mainz	100	Middletown (RI)	358
Lincoln (UK)	223	Maisons Alfort	80	Mikulov	56
Linden	314	Majorca	195	Milan	136
Linz	16	Makhachkala	177	Milford	298
Lisbon	172	Malaga	192	Millis	298
Lithuania	146	Malden	298	Milton	298
Little Rock	250	Malmo	197	Milton Keynes	211
Liverpool	218	Malta	149	Milwaukee	369
Livingston	315	Manaus	28	Minden	100
Ljubljana	182	Manchester (CT)	267	Minneapolis	305

Minsk	21	Natchez	306	Nottingham	239
Mississauga	41	Natick	299	Novosibirsk	178
Missoula	307	Navoy	371		
Mobile	248	Nazareth	129	**O**	
Modena	137	Needham	299		
Moghilev	21	Negev	129	Oahu	279
Mogi Das Cruzes	31	Nepal	156	Oak Ridge	361
Moldova	152	Netanya	129	Oakland	256
Monaco	152	Netherlands	156	Oakville	41
Monchengladbach	100	Neuilly	81	Obernai	66
Moncton	39	Neukirch-Egnach	202	Odenbach	101
Monroe	328	Neustadt	101	Odessa	209
Mons	26	New Bedford	299	Offenbach	101
Monsey	340	New Britain	267	Oklahoma City	348
Montauban	91	New Brunswick	316	Old Bridge	316
Montbeliard	66	New City	341	Old Orchard Beach	287
Monte Carlo	153	New Delhi	111	Olney	290
Monterrey	152	New Haven	267	Olomouc	56
Montevideo	370	New London	268	Olympia	367
Montgomery	248	New Orleans	286	Omaha	307
Monticello	324	New Rochelle	342	Onni	92
Montpelier	365	New Zealand	162	Onset	300
Montpellier (France)	89	Newark (DE)	269	Ontario (CA)	257
Montreal	45	Newark (UK)	239	Oporto	172
Montreuil	81	Newburgh	328	Oradea	175
Montrouge	81	Newburyport	299	Orangeburg	341
Morocco	153	Newcastle	6	Orlando	275
Morris Plains	315	Newcastle upon Tyne	241	Orleans	69
Morristown	315	Newport (RI)	358	Orsha	21
Moscow	178	Newport News	366	Oshawa	41
Moshav Shoresh	128	Newton	299	Osijek	53
Mount Vernon	342	Niagara Falls (Canada)	41	Osipovitshi	21
Mozambique	155	Niagara Falls (NY)	339	Oslo	164
Mozir	21	Nice	89	Osnabruck	101
Mulheim	100	Nicosia	55	Ostend	26
Mulhouse	66	Nikolayev	209	Oswiecim	170
Mumbai	111	Nimes	90	Ottawa	41
Muncie	283	Niteroi	30	Oudtshoorn	189
Munich	100	Nizhny Novgorod	178	Oujda	154
Myanmar	155	Noisy Le Sec	81	Overland Park	284
Myrtle Beach	360	Norfolk	366	Owen Sound	42
		North Adams	299	Oxford	239
N		North Bay	41		
		North Hollywood	256	**P**	
Nagasaki	144	North Miami / North Miami			
Nahariya	128	Beach	274	Paarl	189
Nairobi	145	Northampton (MA)	299	Paderborn	101
Nalchik	178	Northampton (UK)	239	Padua	138
Namibia	156	Northbrook	281	Paducah	286
Nancy	66	Northern Ireland	163	Palm Beach	276
Nantes	69	Northridge	256	Palm City	276
Naples	137	Norway	163	Palm Coast	276
Narragansett	358	Norwich (CT)	268	Palm Springs	257
Nashville	361	Norwich (UK)	239	Palma	195
Nassau	19	Norwood	299	Palo Alto	257

Panama	164	Porlamar	373	Rechitza	21
Panama City	165	Port au Prince	107	Recife	29
Panevezys	147	Port Chester	343	Redbridge	215
Pantin	81	Port Elizabeth	183	Regensburg	101
Paraguay	166	Portland (ME)	287	Regina	46
Paramaribo	196	Portland (OR)	349	Rehovot	130
Paramus	315	Porto Alegre	30	Reims	66
Paravur	111	Portsmouth (NH)	309	Rennes	69
Paris	69	Portsmouth &		Reno	308
Parma	138	Southsea (UK)	216	Reunion	173
Parsipanny	316	Portugal	171	Revere	300
Pasadena	258	Postville	284	Rezhitsa	146
Passaic	316	Poti	93	Rhodes	106
Passo Fundo	30	Potomac	290	Riccione	138
Paterson	316	Pottstown	357	Richmond (Canada)	36
Pau	91	Poughkeepsie	340	Richmond (VA)	366
Peabody	300	Poway	258	Richmond Hill	42
Peekskill	343	Prague	56	Ridgewood	317
Pelotas	30	Prairie Village	285	Riga	146
Pembroke Pines	276	Prestwich	220	Rijeka	53
Pensacola	276	Pretoria	186	Rio Rancho	321
Penza	178	Princeton	317	Ris-Orangis	82
Peoria	281	Providence	358	River Edge	317
Perigveux	91	Pueblo	265	Roanne	90
Perm	178	Puerto Rico	172	Rochester (MN)	305
Perpignan	90	Pune	112	Rochester (NY)	340
Perth	14			Rochester (UK)	218
Perth Amboy	316	**Q**		Rock Island	281
Peru	166			Rockford	281
Perugia	138	Qatzrin	130	Rockland	288
Petach Tikva	130	Quebec City	46	Rockledge	276
Peterborough	42	Queens	339	Rockville	291
Petropolis	30	Quincy	300	Roissy-En-Brie	82
Phalsbourg	66	Quito	60	Romania	173
Philadelphia	352			Rome	138
Philippines Republic	168	**R**		Romford	215
Phoenix	248			Rosario	5
Piatra Neamt	175	Ra'anana	130	Roselle	317
Piestany	181	Rabat	154	Rosh Hanikra	130
Pilsen	56	Radauti	176	Rosh Pina	130
Pinsk	21	Radlett	217	Rosny-Sous-Bois	82
Pisa	138	Rahway	317	Rostov-na-Donu	178
Pittsburgh	355	Raleigh	345	Rotterdam	161
Pittsfield	300	Ramat Gan	130	Rouen	69
Plainfield	316	Ramat Hanegev	130	Rousse	34
Plovdiv	34	Ramat Yohanan	130	Rumson	317
Plymouth (MA)	300	Ramona	258	Russian Federation	176
Plymouth (UK)	212	Ramsgate	218	Rzeszow	170
Pocomoke	290	Rancagua	47		
Poitiers	91	Rancho Cucamonga	258	**S**	
Poland	168	Randolph (MA)	300		
Polna	56	Randolph (NJ)	317	Saarbrucken	102
Polotosk	21	Rapid City	360	Sachkhere	179
Pomona	258	Reading (PA)	357	Sacramento	258
Ponta Delgada	172	Reading (UK)	211	Safed	131

Safi	155	Sarrebourg	67	Sorocaba	34
Saginaw	304	Sarreguemines	67	Sosua	59
Saint Germain	82	Sartrouville	83	South Africa	182
Saint John	39	Saskatoon	47	South Bend	283
Saint-Avold	66	Satu Mare	176	South Haven	304
Saint-Die	66	Savannah	279	South Orange	317
Saint-Etienne	90	Savigny sur Orge	83	South River	317
Saint-Fons	90	Sawbridgeworth	217	Southampton	216
Saint-Laurent-du-Var	90	Scarsdale	343	Southend-on-Sea	215
Saint-Leu-La-Foret	82	Schenectady	342	Southfield	304
Saint-Louis	66	Schwerin	102	Southport	222
Saint-Ouen-L'Aumõne	82	Scotch Plains	317	Spain	189
Saint-Quentin	67	Scotland	244	Speyer	102
Salamanca	193	Scottsdale	249	Spezia	141
Sale	221	Scranton	357	Split	53
Salem (MA)	300	Seattle	368	Spokane	368
Salem (OR)	350	Sedan-Charleville	67	Spotswood	318
Salford	221	Segovia	193	Spring Valley	341
Salisbury	291	Selestat	67	Springfield (IL)	282
Salt Lake City	364	Senigallia	140	Springfield (MA)	301
Salvador	28	Sens	67	Springs	186
Salzburg	16	Seville	193	Sri Lanka	195
Samara	179	Sevran	83	St Albans	217
Samarkand	372	Sf. Gheorghe	176	St Andrews	245
San Antonio	364	Shakhrisabz	204	St Annes On Sea	223
San Bernardino	258	Shanghai	50	St Augustine	276
San Carlos	258	Sharon (MA)	300	St Brelade	244
San Diego	258	Sharon (PA)	358	St Catharine's	42
San Fernando Valley	260	Sharon Springs	325	St Gallen	202
San Francisco	260	Sheboygan	369	St Joseph	306
San Jose (CA)	261	Sheffield	243	St Louis	306
San Jose (Costa Rica)	51	Shenley	217	St Louis Park	305
San Juan-Santurce	173	Sherman Oaks	262	St Moritz	202
San Pedro Sula	107	Shiauliai	147	St Paul	305
San Rafael	262	Short Hills	317	St Petersburg (FL)	276
San Salvador	61	Shreveport	287	St Petersburg (Russia)	179
Santa Barbara	262	Sicily	140	St Thomas	374
Santa Cruz	27	Siena	140	St. John's	39
Santa Fe	321	Sierra Vista	249	Staines	238
Santa Monica	262	Sighet	176	Stains	83
Santa Rosa	262	Silver Spring	291	Stamford	268
Santiago	47	Simferopol	209	Staten Island	399
Santo Andre	31	Singapore	180	Ste. Agathe des Monts	46
Santo Domingo	59	Sioux City	284	Stockholm	197
Santos	31	Skokie	281	Stockton	262
Sao Caetano do Sul	31	Skopje	149	Stoke On Trent	240
Sao Jose dos Campos	31	Slavuta	209	Stoughton	301
Sao Paulo	31	Slotsk	21	Strasbourg	67
Saragossa	193	Slovakia	180	Straubing	102
Sarajevo	27	Slovenia	182	Stuttgart	102
Sarasota	276	Sofia	34	Suceava	176
Saratoga Springs	341	Solihull	242	Sudbury (Canada)	42
Saratov	179	Somerset (NJ)	317	Sudbury (MA)	301
Sarcelles	82	Somerville	301	Suffern	341
Sardinia	140	Sopron	109	Sukhumi	93

Sun City	249	Thousand Oaks 263	United Kingdom 210

Sun City 249
Sun City West 249
Sunderland 242
Sunnyvale 262
Surami 93
Suriname 196
Surrey (Canada) 37
Suva 62
Swampscott 302
Swansea 246
Sweden 196
Switzerland 199
Sydney (Australia) 7
Sydney (Canada) 40
Syosset 327
Syracuse 342
Szczecin 170

T

Tahiti 204
Taipei 204
Taiwan 204
Tajikistan 204
Tallahassee 277
Tallinn 61
Tamarac 277
Tampa 277
Tangier 155
Tarragona 193
Tarzana 262
Tashkent 372
Ta-Xbiex 149
Tbilisi 93
Teaneck 318
Tegucigalpa 108
Tehran 112
Tel Aviv 131
Teleneshty 152
Tempe 249
Temple Hills 292
Temuco 48
Tenafly 319
Tenerife 195
Teplice 57
Terezin 57
Terre Haute 283
Tetuan 155
Thailand 204
Thane 112
The Hague 161
Thessaloniki 106
Thiais 83
Thionville 68
Thornhill 42

Thousand Oaks 263
Thunder Bay 43
Tiberias 133
Tiburon 263
Tijuana 152
Timisoara 176
Tirana 1
Tiaspol 152
Tirgu Mures 176
Tokyo 144
Toledo (OH) 348
Toledo (Spain) 194
Tomar 172
Topeka 285
Toronto 43
Torquay 212
Torremolinos 194
Totnes 212
Toul 68
Toulon 90
Toulouse 92
Tours 69
Trappes 83
Trenton 319
Trier 102
Trieste 141
Trikkala 106
Trnava 182
Trondheim 164
Troy 342
Troyes 68
Truro 212
Tshelyabinsk 180
Tshkinvali 93
Tskhakaya 93
Tucson 250
Tucuman 6
Tudela 194
Tula 180
Tulsa 348
Tunis 206
Tunisia 205
Tupelo 306
Turin 141
Turkey 206
Turku 63
Tushnad 176
Tustin 263

U

Ukraine 207
Uman 209
Umhlanga 187
Union 319

United Kingdom 210
United States of America 247
Uppsala 199
Urbino 141
Uruguay 370
Utica 342
Utrecht 161
Uzbekistan 371

V

Valdivia 48
Val-de-Marne 83
Valence 91
Valencia 194
Valenciennes 68
Vallejo 263
Valley Village 263
Valparaiso (IN) 283
Van Nuys 263
Vancouver 37
Vani 93
Vatra Dornei 176
Vauxhall 319
Veitshochheim 102
Venezuela 372
Venice (CA) 263
Venice (Italy) 141
Venissieux 91
Ventura 263
Vercelli 142
Verdun 68
Verno Beach 277
Verona 142
Versailles 83
Vestal 342
Vevey 202
Viareggio 142
Vichy 91
Victoria 38
Vienna 16
Villejuif 83
Villeneuve-la-Garenne 83
Villiers Sur Marne 83
Villiers-le-Bel-Gonesse 84
Vilnius 147
Vincennes 84
Vineland 319
Vineyard Haven 302
Virgin Islands (USA) 373
Virginia Beach 367
Vitebsk 22
Vitoria 195
Vitry-sur-Seine 84
Vittel 68

Vladikavkaz	180	West Orange	320	Woodridge	325
Volgograd	180	West Palm Beach	277	Woonsocket	359
Volos	106	West Point	343	Worcester	302
		West Roxbury	302	Worms	102
W		Westborough	302	Wrocklaw	171
		Westerly	359	Wuppertal	103
Waco	364	Westfield	320	Wurzburg	103
Waikiki	279	Westhampton Beach	328	Wyckoff	321
Wakefield	302	Westport	268		
Wales	246	Westwood	302	**Y**	
Walnut Creek	263	Weybridge	240		
Waltham	302	Whippany	320	Yangon (formerly Rangoon)	156
Warren	319	White Plains	343	Yarmouth (Canada)	40
Warsaw	170	Whitefield	222	Yekatrinburg	180
Warwick	359	Whiting	283	Yerevan	6
Washington	269	Whittier	264	Yerres	84
Washington Township	319	Wichita	285	Yonkers	343
Wasselonne	68	Wiesbaden	102	York	243
Waterbury	268	Wilkes-Barre	358	Youngstown	348
Waterloo	26	Williamsport	357	Yugoslavia	374
Watford	217	Willingboro	320	Yverdon	202
Wayland	302	Wilmington (DE)	269		
Wayne	319	Wilmington (OH)	345	**Z**	
Wellesley Hills	302	Winchester (MI)	302		
Wellington	163	Windhoek	156	Zagreb	53
Welwyn Garden City	217	Windsor (Canada)	45	Zambia	375
West Bloomfield	304	Winnipeg	38	Zaparozhe	209
West Caldwell	320	Winterthur	202	Zhitomir	209
West Hartford	268	Winthrop	302	Zichron Ya'achov	133
West Hempstead	327	Woodbridge (CT)	269	Zimbabwe	375
West Hills	263	Woodbridge (NJ)	320	Zug	202
West Lafayette	283	Woodbury	328	Zurich	202
West New York	320	Woodmere	328	Zwolle	161

Index to Advertisers

BOOKS AND GIFTS

Torah Treasures   226

BUTCHERS AND GROCERS

Kosher Kingdom   228

HOTELS AND GUEST HOUSES

Acacia Gardens Hotel
  (Bournemouth)   214
Central Hotel (London)   231
Croft Court Hotel (London)   229
Hotel Aida Opera (Paris)   71
Hotel Doria (Amsterdam)   158
Hotel Touring (Paris)   72
Hotel Villa Strand (Hornbaek)   58
King Solomon Palace   230
The Normandie Hotel
  (Bournemouth)   213

MISCELLANEOUS

Brian Plen Associates   233
Jewish Chronicle (London)
           Inside Back Cover
Kosher Prague   56
La Briute Meals
           Inside front cover

Ohel Menachem (Paris)   76
Spain Cellphone (Spain)   193
The Mincha Guide   239

MUSEUMS

Jewish Childrens Museum   333
The Jewish Museum (London)   232

RESTAURANTS

Blooms (London)   235
Dizengoff Kosher Restaurant Limited
  (London)   234
Kaifeng (London)   236
Le Chateaubriand (Paris)   75
Naomi Grill (Madrid)   192
Pita Loca (South Beach)   274
Schalom (Zurich)   203
Six13 (London)   237

TRAVEL

Amsterdam Tours   160
Zekher Avoteinu (St. Petersburg)   179
West End Travel   238

Please complete and return Jewish Travel Guide form to us by 1 September 2006

Please reserve the following advertising space in
Jewish Travel Guide 2007:

	Black and White	Colour	
☐ Full Page	£475	£750	181 x 115 mm
☐ Half Page	£245	£375	91 x 115 mm
☐ Quarter Page	£145	£225	45 x 115 mm

(UK advertisers please note that the above rates are subject to VAT)

Special positions by arrangement. Colour only available in either front or back colour section.

☐ **Please insert the attached copy (If setting is required a 10% setting charge will be made.)**

☐ **Copy will be forwarded from our Advertising Agents** *(see below)*

Contact Name:_____

Advertisers Name:_____

Address for invoicing:_____

_____

Tel: _____ Fax: _____

Signed: _____ Title: _____

VAT No: _____

Date:_____

Agency Name (if applicable):_____

Address:_____

_____

Tel:_____ Fax: _____

advertisements set by the publisher will only be included if they have been signed and approved by the advertiser.

To the Advertising Department
Jewish Travel Guide
Vallentine Mitchell Publishers
Suite 314, Premier House, 112-114 Station Road, Edgware, Middlesex HA8 7BJ
Tel. No.: +44(0)20 8952 9526   Fax: +44(0)20 8952 9242
Email: info@vmbooks.com   Website: www.vmbooks.com

Update for Jewish Travel Guide 2007

Readers are asked kindly to draw attention to any omissions or errors. If errors are discovered, it would be appreciated if you could give appropriate up-to-date information referring to the appropriate page, and send this form to the Editor at the address below.

We prefer you to email any changes to **jtg@vmbooks.com** or to fax them to **+44 (0)20 8952 9242**

With reference to the following entry:

Page:

Country:

Entry should read:

Email essential _____

Signed: _____ Date _____

Name (BLOCK CAPITALS) _____

Address: _____

_____

Telephone: _____

Fax: _____

The Editor
Jewish Travel Guide
Vallentine Mitchell Publishers
Suite 314, Premier House, 112-114 Station Road, Edgware, Middlesex HA8 7BJ
Tel. No.: +44(0)20 8952 9526   Fax: +44(0)20 8952 9242
Email: jtg@vmbooks.com   Website: www.vmbooks.com

Jewish Year Book 2006

The Jewish Year Book 2006 is a comprehensive directory of communal institutions and organisations, covering all aspects of British Jewish society and cultural and religious activities, together with details of their leading personalities. It offers an extensive guide to the primary organisations of the Jewish communities of the world and a substantial survey of Israel and its organisations having associations with British Jewry, including a list of Israel's overseas embassies and missions.

From the reviews

> '*In a Jewish world that at times seems mired in uncertainty and chaos, it is reassuring to greet the latest version of the enduring symbol of stability and durability that is* The Jewish Year Book ... *It presents a portrait of the current state of Jewish life in the British Isles, with fact-filled glimpses of Jewish communities world-wide. It is a trove of information, logically organized and clearly set forth.*'
>
> Jack E. Friedman, Jerusalem Post

Please send me____copies of the *Jewish Year Book 2006* at the price of £29.50 hardback

❏ I enclose a cheque for £ _____ made payable to **Vallentine Mitchell**

Postage and packing is free within the UK. Please add $4.95 and $1.50 for each subsequent book in North America. Rest of World: £2.50 first book, £1.50 each subsequent book. Airmail rates upon request. VAT registration No: GB 232 7273 75.

Please charge my   ❏ Visa   ❏ Mastercard   ❏ American Express

Card Number: _____   Issue No: _____

Expiry date: _____

Name: _____   Signature: _____

Address: _____

_____

_____

Tel: _____   Fax: _____

E-mail: _____

Recent publications from
Vallentine Mitchell

A Journal of Significant Thought and Opinion
Commentary Magazine 1945-1959
Nathan Abrams, University of Aberdeen

Launched in 1945, *Commentary* magazine became one of America's most celebrated periodicals. Under the editorship of Elliot E Cohen, it developed into the premier postwar journal of Jewish affairs attracting a readership far wider than its Jewish community origin. This book is the first detailed and critical study of *Commentary* magazine during its formative years. Abrams traces the development of the key issues that have occupied it: the construction of a new American Jewish identity, Judaism, the Holocaust, the State of Israel, and the Cold War. This account of the chief journal of Jewish thought, opinion, and culture in America will complete the picture of postwar American Jewish and general intellectual life.It is based upon a wide range of sources including archival and other material never before published in this context.

2006 244 pages 0 85303 663 2 cloth £45.00 / 0 85303 664 0 paper £19.50

Anglo-Jewish Poetry from Isaac Rosenberg to Elaine Feinestein
Peter Lawson, University of Joensuu
With a Foreword by **Anthony Rudolf**

This is the first book-length study to survey the phenomenon of twentieth-century Anglo-Jewish poetry. It proceeds by reading established Anglo-Jewish poets against the grain of conventional thinking about English verse. For example, rather than understanding Isaac Rosenberg and Siegfried Sassoon as simply First World War poets, it approaches them as minority Anglo-Jewish poets as well. A similar challenge to the notion of an undifferentiated English literature is made with respect to four other major writers: John Rodker (1894-1955), Jon Silkin (1930-97), Elaine Feinestein (1930-) and Karen Gershon (1923-93). All these poets share a peripheral relationship with English and Jewish culture, together with a common attachment to the diasporic narrative of exile and deferred return to a textually imagined homeland.

2005 256 pages 0 85303 616 0 cloth £45.00 / 0 85303 617 9 paper £19.50

Jews and the Olympic Games
Sport - A Springboard for Minorities
Paul Yogi Mayer
Introduction by **Sir Martin Gilbert**

Last century young Jews found they had a new opportunity to give expression to their physical talents and energy. How they and their successors grasped it is the theme of this engaging book. Even after the Holocaust, Jews were among the outstanding Olympians, with over 400 Jewish medallists from the first modern Games in Athens to the Sydney Millennium Games.
However, this is not merely a book of record and records, names and events. Yogi Mayer has drawn on his own memories as an athlete, coach, educator and sports journalist to create a compelling, illustrated eyewitness account. He has known many of the athletes who feature in the book and he describes their personalities, virtues, weaknesses and, in some cases, tragic fates.

2004 272 pages 0 85303 516 4 cloth £27.50 / 0 85303 451 6 paper £16.00

NOTES

NOTES

NOTES

NOTES